Japanese
the Manga
Way

マンガで学ぶ日本語文法

Japanese the Manga Way

An Illustrated Guide to Grammar & Structure

Wayne P. Lammers

Stone Bridge Press • Berkeley, California

Published by
Stone Bridge Press
P.O. Box 8208, Berkeley, CA 94707
Tel: 510-524-8732 • sbp@stonebridge.com • www.stonebridge.com

We want to hear from you! Updates? Corrections? Comments? Please send all correspondence regarding this book to sbp@stonebridge.com.

Contents

The Lessons

Appendixes

Tables and Sidebars

About This Book

Japanese has a reputation for being difficult, but the basic structure of the language is actually quite simple. This book sets out to prove the point by boiling all Japanese sentences down to three basic types, then, starting with the simplest single-word sentences of each type, gradually expanding to more complex expressions following a logical and systematic progression. The writing system (which is to be distinguished from the language itself) is admittedly a challenge, but even this has certain redeeming qualities, and it doesn't seem like nearly as big a hurdle if you're picking it up while you're having fun.

Whether you're learning the structure of the Japanese language or the intricacies of its writing system, making the process more fun is where *manga* come in. Even if you're one of those people whose eyes glaze over any time you hear the word "grammar," you'll find that having each new point illustrated with an example taken from a manga not only makes the learning process more entertaining, but establishes the point more clearly in your mind by rooting it in real-life circumstances and usage. With manga for illustrations and with each point explained in plain English, limiting linguistic jargon to an absolute minimum, *Japanese the Manga Way* aims to be the first grammar book you can actually read with enjoyment.

Manga, if you don't know, are Japanese comics and graphic novels, and they are now gaining ground with amazing speed in the United States and elsewhere; in Japan they have been a publishing phenomenon for over half a century, with roots that reach back deep into Japanese history as well as to early American comic strips. Japanese manga differ in many ways from American comics, including the nature of the artwork, which is almost always monochrome and crudely drawn by American standards, even as it makes use of highly sophisticated and innovative visual effects. But the most important aspect of manga for the language learner is that they are created for and read avidly by every segment of Japanese society—boys and girls as well as grown men and women, students and workers and homemakers as well as businessmen, professionals, and the movers and shakers; and they include not only the equivalent of American newspaper funnies (four-frame "gag" strips), Disneyesque children's fare, and adolescent superhero and science fiction fantasies, but socially realistic tales about ordinary people from every walk of life. Stories of the kind Americans are accustomed to finding only in prose fiction, with believable, well-motivated plots and characterizations, and serious social themes, are published as long-running manga series in weekly magazines and later compiled into books,

sometimes running to dozens of volumes. The tremendous variety of manga published means they literally offer something for everyone.

Almost any kind of manga can provide excellent study material for learners of Japanese, but realistic story manga are especially well-suited to the purpose because they depict Japanese life as it really is and model the kind of vocabulary and usage heard in the course of normal business and play. Most of the manga featured in this book fall into this category. The book also features quite a few four-frame gag strips; although their humorous twists can sometimes make their situations seem a little less "normal," and therefore more difficult, these in fact offer an opportunity for you to learn a little more about how the Japanese language works. If your taste runs to other genres of manga, don't despair. The grammar and structure of the language are the same in all manga, so what you learn in this book will apply to whatever kind of manga you want to read after you're done—as well as to however else you want to use the language.

If you're new to manga—or relatively so—and would like to know more about the whole phenomenon, an excellent place to start is Frederik L. Schodt's *Dreamland Japan: Writings on Modern Manga.*

Manga and language learning

When you're tackling a new language—whether in a formal class, with a private tutor, or on your own—you want to expose yourself to the language in as many ways as possible. For learning Japanese, manga are a perfect addition to whatever arsenal of text and audio-visual aids you may already be using. With this book, manga can even be a great place to start. To some extent, you want to take advantage of manga just because they're there: they are an important part of the culture and represent a major use of the language you are studying. But there are several more specific reasons why manga offer such perfect source material for learners of Japanese.

First and foremost, even though manga are a printed medium, most of the text is natural, conversational Japanese, not discursive prose. The language in the balloons models exactly the kind of language you want to learn to understand and speak, and it provides the perfect supplement to the dialogues and conversation drills found in language textbooks. Many language courses turn to prose texts, such as newspaper articles, essays, and fiction, when students are ready for additional material beyond textbook drills. But the transition can be awkward: even though the grammar doesn't change, the language is not used the same way in writing as in speaking; sentences grow longer and more convoluted. Manga, with their primarily conversational content, are a more logical next step for following up on textbook dialogues and broadening your exposure to the wide variations of conversational usage in real life.

Although prose fiction also contains dialogue, it uses narrative passages to set the stage and move the action forward. In manga, these purposes are served largely by the illustrations, allowing the action to move along much more quickly than when you're forced to tediously decipher passages of narrative. This in turn keeps the fun quotient much higher so you're inclined to read on—instead of losing steam because your progress is so slow. Of course, you may eventually want to gain full mastery of dense running prose as well—whether literary or nonliterary. But the illustrated and less densely packed format of manga makes them suitable as a supplement at a much earlier stage of study. As they always say, your mileage will vary, and the more advanced you are the greater the benefits you will reap. But with the help of this book, you should be able to start getting something out of manga from day one.

Not to detract from other valuable study tools, but manga have strengths that can help fill in for the weaknesses of other media. Textbook dialogues and drills are virtually indispensable for gaining spoken command of the language, but they are inevitably limited in variety and tend to emphasize polite language over what you're more likely to actually hear on the street. Divorced from much sense of context, they can be quite artificial, and over time the vocabulary tends to become outdated. With manga, the variety is effectively limitless. If you read current manga, you know you're getting current vocabulary, and you can even go back and plug that vocabulary into your textbook drills. The dialogues you see are arguably the most real conversational Japanese you'll find on the printed page—with starts and stops, contractions and omissions, exclamations and interjections, and all the other quirks of real-life conversations—not sentences created just for drill. Further, the format constantly reinforces the fact that every language act occurs in a very specific social context, with visual images providing many of the details of that context at a glance instead of requiring a lengthy verbal setting of the stage. If, in the absence of drills, you memorize a manga line you think you might want to use, you'll be doing it with a rock solid sense of the context in which the opportunity to use it might come up.

Any medium with a visual component, especially media that tell realistic stories, will naturally provide rich cultural information that drill-based textbooks cannot, some of it absorbed on a subliminal basis. Video materials such as films, TV programs, and anime offer audio as well, which is crucial in learning how the language actually sounds. But even though video has an important place in any language learner's toolbox, its constant forward motion can be a disadvantage, especially for relative beginners, who find everything spinning on by much too quickly. In manga, the action in each frame is frozen, and you can take all the time you need to absorb the images and dialogue—once again reinforcing their value at an earlier stage of study.

All print-based media for learning Japanese will sooner or later require that you come to terms with the Japanese writing system, which unlike the language itself, probably deserves the reputation for difficulty that it has (though you may recall that all those spelling tests you took in English were not exactly a picnic either). But once again, the lower-density text of manga is your friend: not only is it less intimidating when you don't have to face solid pages of nothing but text, but manga tend to use more of the easy-to-learn phonetic characters known as *kana* (you'll find more information about these in the Introduction) and fewer of the difficult ones known as *kanji* compared to discursive or literary prose. Whenever the fun quotient of manga keeps you reading just a little longer, you have that much more opportunity to pick up something new or reinforce what you've already learned—all while you're enjoying an entertaining story. Any task seems like a lot less work when you're having fun, and this goes for learning the Japanese script as well.

The origins of this book

In 1990, businessman and translator Vaughan Simmons launched a magazine called *Mangajin* that tapped into all of these benefits of manga for the language learner by reprinting a variety of four-frame strips and longer story episodes in a facing-page layout, with the manga on the left and a variety of helps on the right. He developed a four-line format that transcribed the text appearing in each balloon of the manga, spelled the full text out in roman letters (that is, the standard English alphabet), provided an initial word-for-word translation to show how the Japanese structure worked, and concluded with a polished translation that expressed what the sentence was really trying to say in fluid, natural English. Capping this off were bulleted notes offering further commentary on grammar, vocabulary, cultural background, and whatever else seemed to deserve comment.

Even for students who had already discovered the joys of manga, this format made things a whole lot easier—as well as more instructive. A certain amount of prior language learning was necessary if you wanted to fully understand the explanations, but for the most part, Simmons's system of helps took care of all the tedious dictionary and other reference work for the reader. Even if you had relatively limited language skills, you could follow the Japanese without being overwhelmed; if you were more advanced you could actually read at something close to a normal pace while picking up useful new tidbits along the way. And of course, no matter what your level, you could simply fall back on the provided translation any time you decided you'd had enough of a workout for one session but just had to find out how the story turned out.

Japanese the Manga Way has its roots in *Mangajin*. I was teaching Japanese at the University of Wisconsin–Madison when Simmons called to seek feedback on a prototype he had developed for the magazine. Upon launch of the magazine, I became one of several checkers for the drafts Simmons produced, and about a year later I took over most of the main manga translation and annotation work myself. I also began helping with another feature that had been part of the magazine from the start—a series called "Basic Japanese," which is the specific feature this book grew out of.

The notes to the manga featured in facing-page layouts had something of a chance quality, simply explaining whatever vocabulary or grammar point came up according to how it occurred in that specific context. The purpose of "Basic Japanese" was to allow more systematic treatment of a selected word or expression. Typically, some twelve to fifteen individual manga panels containing the chosen expression were brought together from as many different sources and folded into a single unified discussion that illustrated the full range of its uses. The series became an instant hit with readers because it focused on prominent and sometimes tricky expressions and gave an in-depth understanding of how and when they could be used. But even though each installment was indeed systematic and thorough in its treatment of the chosen topic, the selection of that topic remained quite random from one installment to the next. Especially once the series started being reprinted in separate volumes entitled *Mangajin's Basic Japanese Through Comics*, the idea of adapting its format to a more methodical and unified introduction to the language kept cropping up in various forms.

The result, after more twists and turns than I care to recall, is this book. When changing market conditions and falling ad revenues forced the magazine to go out of business at the end of 1997, it meant renegotiating from step one for permission to use the manga panels I'd chosen for my first draft, and new strictures and conditions forced me to replace between half and two-thirds of the examples I'd originally selected. The extensive revisions this prompted have without a doubt improved the book, but at the cost of years of delay as I worked on the text between my other projects as a commercial and literary translator. Still, the book's *raison d'être* remains unchanged: to provide a systematic introduction to basic Japanese grammar and structure using authentic examples from real manga.

Vaughan Simmons's original inspiration for launching a magazine featuring manga came as much from their cultural value as it did from their suitability as language texts. While living and working in Japan, he had seen that American and European companies could indeed succeed in the Japanese market if they first took the time to learn about the people who made up that market: the Japanese consumers. Although many books had been written about Japan and Japanese business practices since the nation's economy caught fire in the 1960s and turned the country into an international trade powerhouse, when it came to taking the true pulse of the people, they generally fell short. Simmons saw manga as a medium that reflected how the Japanese really lived and breathed, a window on their psyche, and he felt a magazine featuring manga as well as articles on other aspects of Japanese popular culture could help fill the information gap.

Manga are such an integral part of Japanese popular culture that even those who are already fluent in the language can benefit from a regular dose of the medium. Today, with a growing number of titles available in translation, it's possible to get a regular manga fix without knowing a word of Japanese. But the number of translated manga will always remain a small fraction of the full variety available in their native language, so whether you're interested in manga just for fun or for the cultural insights they offer, learning the language can still pay rich rewards.

If you're interested in finding out more about *Mangajin*, you can visit mangajin.com for a brief account of its rise and fall. You can also purchase individual copies or subscriptions to back issues of the magazine at the website (if you live in Japan, follow the link to the Japan site); as of this writing, substantial quantities remain of the bulk of the seventy issues published. Most of the illustrations used in this book were taken from titles featured in the magazine, so finding the right back issues will let you read more of those stories (see Appendix B); some of the illustrations were taken from the particular episodes that appeared in the magazine, and I'm grateful to Vaughan Simmons and *Mangajin* for permission to reuse or adapt portions of the translations and notes.

Who can benefit from this book?

No prior knowledge of Japanese is necessary to learn from this book. The Introduction provides a brief survey of the Japanese sound and writing systems, and after that the lessons in the first half of the book are organized on the model of the expansion drill sometimes used in language classes: Lesson 1 starts off by identifying the three basic sentence types and showing examples of the simplest sentences possible for each; the following lessons add new sentence parts one step at a time, gradually expanding the sentences into more complex constructions. Every grammar point and sentence example is explained in plain English, so you don't have to master a third language of linguistic jargon in order to learn Japanese. For basic terms like "noun" and "verb" and "adjective" that can't be avoided when describing language, clear definitions are provided when they first appear so you can be sure you understand what they refer to; a brief glossary is also provided in Appendix D for easy reference. Roughly the first half of the book, through Lesson 17, focuses on the basic building blocks of the language and how they fit together; the second half shows how verbs and adjectives are transformed to make the basic building blocks express a broad range of different senses.

If you're completely new to the language, this book will serve as a "from scratch" primer that is very comprehensive in terms of touching all the basic structural bases. This is not to say that the book covers all those bases exhaustively. To reach fluency, you will need to find additional help from publications, learning aids, and classes or other opportunities that offer extensive practice in actually speaking the language, not just reading and deciphering it. Manga are a wonderful learning tool for the spoken language because they provide endlessly varied examples of real colloquial Japanese rooted in real-life situations, but they don't actually teach you to converse—or even how to pronounce individual words properly. Even if your aim is only to learn to read—for example, you're a manga-in-translation fan who wants to read titles that haven't been translated—you will need additional helps to gain full command. Appendix A suggests some books and web-based resources you may find helpful to use alongside this book or after finishing it.

If you're already studying Japanese in a formal class or otherwise, this book can serve not only as an introduction to using manga to broaden your exposure to real Japanese, but as consolidation and review of what you've learned in class—and quite likely a little bit of preview, too. If you're one of those people who is struggling a little because you can't quite see how it all fits together, the way this book distills the grammar down to its bare essentials to reveal the simplicity of Japanese structure may be just the ticket for making everything finally fall into place. Similarly, if you tried to learn Japanese in the past but gave it up because you found it too overwhelming somehow, perhaps this book can give you the jump start you need to get back on track. Even if you're one of those who's sailing along without difficulty, you can benefit from the new light thrown on what you've learned, by both the focus on structure (especially if your course is organized more thematically or situationally) and the real manga approach that roots every example in real-life contexts.

If you've "completed" your study but you're looking for an enjoyable way to either keep up your language skills or revitalize them, the benefits of manga for language learners outlined above hold for you as well. In many cases, you may be able to simply pick up whatever manga suits your fancy and dive right in. But if it's been a while since you've had opportunities for regular practice or contact with the language, reading this book will provide you with the perfect refresher course for brushing things up, as well as a handbook for ongoing reference any time you feel yourself getting a little vague on some point or other.

Some notes about using this book

Each kind of reader mentioned above will probably use this book a little differently. But here are a few suggestions, and things to keep in mind:

- Most Japanese books and magazines, including manga, are opened and read from right to left. Text flows in vertical lines from top to bottom and right to left, and when the text is broken up in separate blocks, as in manga panels and balloons, the order of the blocks flows this same way. In this book, where manga extracts must mix with English text, the panels have been arranged to fit the convenience of the standard English left-to-right layout where possible. But the text and order of the balloons inside each panel remain in the traditional Japanese orientation and must be read starting at the top right. Panels or transcriptions have been numbered where there seems any possible uncertainty about the proper order.

- The standard four-line format for presenting the balloon text includes (a) a transcription of the text in Japanese script; (b) the same text romanized (i.e., spelled out in the familiar roman alphabet used for English); (c) a word-for-word translation of each part of the sentence; and (d) a polished English translation:

  (a) **Matsuda:** ハイ、 松田 です。
  (b)   *Hai, Matsuda desu.*
  (c)   yes/hello (name) is/am
  (d)   **"Hello, this is Matsuda."** (PL3)

  I have sometimes added a fifth line between (c) and (d) to help clarify how the individual parts of the sentence in (c) turn into the meaning shown in (d). The intermediate translation is intended to better reflect the original Japanese structure and the grammar point being made, since both of these can be obscured in the final translation.

- The modified Hepburn system of romanization is used for transcribing the Japanese in this book; details are provided in the Introduction. Published spellings are respected for author and publisher names. No hard and fast standards are available for hyphenating or dividing certain word forms and phrases when Japanese is romanized—hyphens are not used in Japanese script, and usually no spaces appear between words—so when you see a hyphenated word here, be prepared to see it either as a single melded word or as two (or more) separate words elsewhere.

- With the manga panels extracted from their original contexts, a book like this can only take partial advantage of one of the strengths of manga—the way they set the stage visually without the need for text narrative. Even when a single panel offers substantial visual cues, it's usually missing important information that was revealed in previous panels. To make up for this shortcoming, each panel in this book appears with a brief description of what's happening and any other necessary background information. Cross-references are provided, especially early on, to help you connect panels from the same story and to avoid having to repeat details already mentioned. Brief descriptions of each manga title as a whole are provided in Appendix B.

- The chapters are best read in sequence, especially in the first half of the book, since each lesson assumes the reader is familiar with the material covered in previous lessons. This is less important after about Lesson 21. By that point, all the basic structural elements and the most important verb and adjective transformations have been introduced, so you can probably follow the information in any given lesson with a minimum of difficulty even if something covered in another lesson is not explained.

- Even if you plan to use the book primarily as a reference handbook to dip into from the Index, I recommend that you read at least the first chapter, which sets the basic approach and defines some key terms. Better yet, give the full text a read-through so you get the benefit of the systematic sequential treatment once.

- The brief rundown of the sound and writing systems in the Introduction may contain more detail than you care to digest immediately, especially if you're entirely new to Japanese. It made best sense to present all this material here in a single place, but in fact, the only critical information before you get started is how to pronounce the vowels (*a, i, u, e, o*) and, to a lesser extent, the consonants (*k, s, t, n, h*, etc.—the Hepburn system of romanization is pretty intuitive for these). So once you've looked at those sections, go ahead and skip to Lesson 1 and get started on the fun if you want. You can come back for additional details when you're ready. Apart from the concise treatment here, this book offers only the random, pick-it-up-as-you-go approach to the Japanese writing system. For other books and resources that can help you with the task of mastering Japanese script, see Appendix A.

- Some readers may find it useful to read through the book quickly once, to get the lay of the land, before returning to the beginning to actively compile vocabulary lists, learn the Japanese script, memorize the model verbs and practice transforming them, and so forth. Even if you find yourself forgetting or only vaguely understanding something, the four-line format will always be there to help, along with cross-references and the Index if you need to find a previous explanation to refresh your memory. You'll probably pick up quite a bit of the vocabulary and script along the way without any special effort, and this may make your second pass that much easier.

- However you approach this book, it's probably worth spending some time memorizing the *hiragana* character set presented in the Introduction before you start or as you go through the first couple of lessons. It helps to practice writing the characters at the same time you work on recognizing them. There's no need to have the whole set nailed down for good before you proceed, but having focused on it intensively once will help you pick up more along the way—even if you're not trying to read everything in Japanese your first time through.

- When you do start trying to read everything in Japanese, be sure to always look at the actual manga balloon as well as its transcription. The transcription duplicates the characters, but it's laid out horizontally, some adjustments have been made in punctuation, and the words are spaced out for you. You instead want to get used to reading standard Japanese that's written vertically without spaces between the words; you also want to learn to take advantage of the small *hiragana* (not included in the transcription for space reasons) that are sometimes provided to help you read the more difficult kanji characters. For some of the more intricate and many-stroked kanji, however, you may find you have to rely on the transcription to make out their shapes clearly.

- There was no room in this book to offer practice drills or additional reading exercises, but a few suggestions for further reading are offered in Appendix A. You can partly compensate for the lack of drills by keeping categorized lists or flashcards of the words you want to learn and by trying them out in sentences modeled on subsequent examples that appear. Once you start learning how to make the different forms of a word—the easiest and in some ways most important transformation rules appear in Lesson 3, and the rest begin in Lesson 18—practice making each new form with every word of that kind you have on your list. Don't stop with just making the form, though; also try to think of specific contexts where you might use that form and try putting it in a sentence. The context given for the manga used to introduce the form should offer some help, but you'll find that in some cases the form doesn't make sense for a given word—in which case you can guess that it's probably not used.

- If you're not in a formal class and can't or don't want to join one, try to find a native speaker to check and correct your pronunciation and transformations and answer other questions that come up. You may be able to set up a language exchange with someone studying English at a nearby college or language school who could use the same kind of help in the opposite direction.

Acknowledgments

The debt *Japanese the Manga Way* owes to Vaughan Simmons and his pioneering efforts is incalculable. This book simply would not exist were it not for *Mangajin*, the magazine he created, and his continual fine tuning of the way it used manga to help students learn Japanese. The original conception for the book was born and fleshed out in discussions with him, and even after the project became my own he continued to offer suggestions and advice. I am deeply grateful to him.

For their help in arranging permissions for the manga illustrations, I would like to thank Andō Yuka and Suga Tomoko at Kōdansha, Honda Kenji and Nakano Masashi at Futabasha, and Tsujii Kiyoshi at Take Shobō. (Japanese names are given in Japanese order, surname first.) I am grateful to all of the individual artists listed on the copyright page for permission to use their work; special thanks go to Hirokane Kenshi, Oze Akira, Maekawa Tsukasa, Kobayashi Makoto, and Akizuki Risu, whose support at a crucial juncture saved the project from certain doom. I am also indebted to Moteki Hiromichi, Frederik L. Schodt, Ishimatsu Hisayuki, and Matsuzaki Kazuko for a variety of help in making the necessary contacts.

Thanks to Virginia Skord Waters and Chris Thompson for feedback on different early drafts when this book was still a *Mangajin* project; they may no longer recognize the book that has resulted but they did help shape it. Thanks to Harada Ako, Katabami Miyoko, and Frederik L. Schodt for responding to grammar and manga questions at various stages along the way. Thanks also to Ken Lunde of Adobe Systems for his generous help with software and fonts as changing technology repeatedly threatened to leave me behind during the many years this book was in the making.

My editor Elizabeth Floyd was my principal sounding board for final adjustments to the manuscript, and I'm grateful for the meticulous care with which she examined every element of the text. Her invaluable comments and queries resulted in numerous additions, clarifications, and corrections that should make things easier for learners to understand. Responsibility for any lingering errors or infelicities, of course, rests solely with me.

A special word of thanks goes to my publisher Peter Goodman for taking on the unusual demands and risks of this project after it was orphaned by the demise of *Mangajin*; and for having enough faith in the project to stick with it through repeated discouragements and delays over so many long years.

Finally, I would like to thank my wife Cheryl for her unstinting encouragement through all the twists and turns this project has taken, and especially for her patience during the final production phase when the seemingly endless details consumed so much more of my time for so much longer than either of us had ever imagined. I could never have done it without her understanding and support.

Wayne P. Lammers

Introduction

Pronunciation & Kana Guide

The language of manga may be ideal for people who want to learn spoken Japanese, since that's exactly what manga balloons contain. But there's one catch: manga are a printed medium, so you also have to learn to read Japanese script if you want to take advantage of what they have to offer. To let you begin learning Japanese from manga without first having to master Japanese script, the manga dialogue in this book is spelled out in the same alphabet you're used to using in English. That way, the complicated characters normally used to write Japanese don't have to get in the way of your learning the language, and you can decide for yourself how much effort you initially want to put into learning to read.

The alphabetic characters you read and write in English are called *romaji* in Japanese (lit. "Roman letters"), and in fact, enough language texts, dictionaries, handbooks, grammars, and other learning aids use romaji that it's even possible to become fluent in Japanese without ever

© Ueda Masashi. *Furiten-kun.* Take Shobō.

romaji transcription

Employee: 火事 だー!!
Kaji dā!!
fire is
"It's a fire!"
"Fire!"

learning the native script. But if you want to go beyond books that provide romaji transcriptions, putting time in on the Japanese writing system is an absolute must. So even if you don't make it a priority on your first pass through this book, be sure to hunker down and learn to read the Japanese script the next time around. The sooner you can read manga in the original, the sooner you can start learning from whatever kind of manga you enjoy the most.

You're likely to encounter several different romanization schemes as you study Japanese. This book uses what's called the "modified Hepburn" system. It's the system that comes closest to being intuitive for speakers of English.

Vowels

When reading romaji, you need to banish most of the vowel sounds you're used to using in English. The Japanese vowels are *a, i, u, e, o* (in that order), and they are always pronounced as follows, regardless of where or how they appear in a word.

     a   like the *a*'s in f*a*ther, or h*a* h*a* h*a*
     i   like the *i* in macaron*i*
     u   like the *u*'s in z*u*l*u*
     e   like the *e* in g*e*t, or *e*xtra
     o   like the *o*'s in s*o*l*o*

There are no *a*'s that sound like the *a* in "h*a*t" or "h*a*te"; *a* always sounds like the *a* in "f*a*ther." There are no *e*'s that sound like the *e* in "*e*ven," none that have the schwa sound (ə) shared with other vowels in English, and none that are silent at the end of words: *e* always sounds like the *e* in "g*e*t." You might notice that the *e* in "*e*ven" is almost the same sound as the *i* in "macaron*i*"; in English, the sound can be written with either vowel, depending on the word it is part of, but in romaji that sound is always written *i*, never *e*. The vowel *i* never sounds like the *i* in "*i*ce" or "p*i*ck."

The other vowels are just as consistent, and that means you need to be consistent, too. When you see the word *hate*, your English instincts will tell you to pronounce it as a single syllable (one unit or beat) with a long *a* and a silent *e*, rhyming with "bait," but if you're reading romaji you must pronounce the word as two distinct syllables with fully sounded vowels, *ha* + *te*, and the *a* must sound like the *a* in "father," the *e* like the *e* in "get." (In a few cases where Japanese words or names appear without italics in English sentences where they might be misread with a silent *e*, an accent mark is used to show that the *e* is not silent: "saké"; "Moé." But this is an English convention that's not used in romaji, so no accent marks are provided in the transcriptions here.)

The only significant variation that occurs in the pronunciation of vowels is how long the vowel is sounded: standard length or double length. In Hepburn romaji, the elongated vowels are written like this (the mark appearing over most of the vowels is called a "macron"):

> *ā*
> *ii*
> *ū*
> *ē* or *ei* (see page xxvi for the difference)
> *ō*

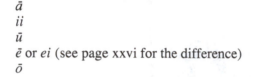

double-length vowels

Mother: まあ、　ふきのとう。
Mā,　*fukinotō.*
(interj.)　butterbur sprout
"Oh, my! Butterburs!"

春　　ねえ。
Haru　nē.
spring　(is-colloq.)
"It really is spring!"

When Japanese words and names are "romanized" for use in English, long vowels are often ignored and the macrons omitted. In this book, Japanese words appearing in the English translations or discussions are sometimes treated according to this English convention, but every effort has been made to accurately reflect the length of vowels in the romaji transcriptions. So, for example, you will see *Tōkyō* in the romaji transcription, but "Tokyo" in the translation. (The word "romaji" itself should strictly speaking be *rōmaji*, but the macron is customarily omitted when the word is used in English.)

Except as shown above for the long vowels *ii* and *ei*, if you see two or more vowels in a row (e.g., *kau, kuu, baai, ubaiau*), they belong to separate syllables and need to be pronounced as separate units (*ka-u, ku-u, ba-a-i, u-ba-i-a-u*). If the two vowels next to each other are the same, they will sound virtually the same as a long vowel, especially to the unpracticed ear; but if you listen very carefully to a native speaker saying the words, you'll often hear a slight catch in the middle to separate the syllables.

Sometimes *i* and *u* are not fully sounded between certain consonant combinations or at the end of words (e.g., the *i* in -*mashita* and the *u* in *desu*), but the degree varies from speaker to speaker and there are no fixed rules, so no effort has been made to indicate the difference in this book.

Consonants

The Japanese writing system uses what's called a "syllabary" instead of an alphabet to represent sounds. In a syllabary, each symbol represents a full syllable, not just part of one the way English letters usually do. A word like "syl-la-ble," which has three syllables, would be written with just three symbols instead of eight letters.

In the romaji syllabary, each vowel makes a full syllable by itself, but most of the syllables consist of a consonant (or sometimes two) followed by a vowel. In Hepburn romaji, you can for the most part sound the consonants exactly as you're used to doing in English, with the following conditions:

- *ch* is always like the *ch* in *ch*in, never like *ch*orus or *ch*arade; the latter two sounds would be spelled with *k* and *sh*, respectively. (Don't you wish spelling were so consistent in English?)

- *f* occurs only in the syllable *fu*, which you sound by shaping your lips as if to blow a speck of dust away, not by touching the upper teeth to the lower lip like you do for *f* in English. *Fu* should come out sounding almost like a very short "who."

- *r* is like a cross between English *r* and *l*, and it actually winds up sounding close to a *d*. You make the sound by lightly flicking the tip of your tongue against the ridge behind your upper teeth, slightly farther back than when saying *d*. If you pronounce the English name Eddie and make the *dd* sound very short and light, it comes out like the Japanese word *eri* ("collar").

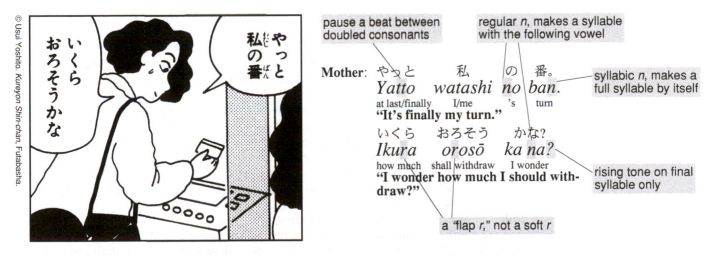

© Usui Yoshito, *Kureyon Shin-chan*, Futabasha.

pause a beat between doubled consonants

regular *n*, makes a syllable with the following vowel

syllabic *n*, makes a full syllable by itself

Mother: やっと　私　の　番。
Yatto　*watashi*　*no*　*ban*.
at last/finally　I/me　's　turn
"It's finally my turn."

いくら　おろそう　かな?
Ikura　*orosō*　*ka na?*
how much　shall withdraw　I wonder
"I wonder how much I should withdraw?"

a "flap *r*," not a soft *r*

rising tone on final syllable only

- *y* is always pronounced like the *y* in "year." It's never pronounced like the *y* in "my," nor can it stand in for a vowel like the *y* in "my": it's always a consonant, and always followed by a vowel, which must be pronounced together with it in a single unit (*ya yu yo*). If *y* is immediately preceded by another consonant, that consonant, too, must become part of the single unit (e.g., *kya kyu kyo*).

- *n* with a following vowel (*na, ni, nu, ne, no*) or *y* (*nya nyu nyo*) is pronounced just like English *n*. But *n* also occurs as a syllable by itself, and this "syllabic *n*" is a nasalized *n* halfway between *n* and *ng*. *N* is never part of the same syllable as the vowel before it, so any *n* not followed by a vowel or *y* is a syllable unto itself (but see following bullet point). If the next syllable begins with *m*, *b*, or *p*, the syllabic *n* actually sounds more like *m*, but you don't really need to worry about this rule because it will naturally sound like *m* in those combinations so long as you don't go out of your way trying to make it sound like *n*.

☛ If some of these points seem hard to grasp in the abstract, don't worry about them for now. Once you've taken a quick glance to see which consonants you might need to watch out for, just move on. You can come back later when you actually encounter those particular sounds in the manga examples.

- an **apostrophe** is inserted after a syllabic *n* when *n* is followed by an independent vowel or an independent syllable beginning with *y*—to show that the *n* is to be pronounced separately. For example, the word *kin'en* should be pronounced as four syllables, *ki-n-e-n*, and means "no smoking," while the apostropheless but otherwise identical *kinen* should be pronounced as three syllables, *ki-ne-n*, and means "commemoration"; *kin'yū* should be pronounced *ki-n-yū* and means "finance," while the apostropheless *kinyū* should be pronounced *ki-nyū* and means "fill out [a document/form]."

- **doubled consonants** are pronounced by pausing a beat after forming the first consonant, momentarily stopping the sound with your mouth in that position before saying the next syllable (i.e., the second of the doubled consonants plus its vowel). The first consonant is in effect a silent, single-consonant syllable, and it needs to take up the same amount of time as a syllable with a vowel. There's no exact equivalent in English, but the effect of *kk* in *sukkiri* ("clear") for example, is similar to the sound in the middle of "bookkeeper."

Stress and pitch

Japanese words are spoken with essentially even stress, without any particular syllable being spoken more strongly than any other. Slight changes of pitch do provide a kind of "pitch accent" within words, but they are usually not essential to the meaning. Beginners will do best to strive for a relatively flat stress and tone. But keep your ears tuned when listening to native speakers: in time you will be able to distinguish the words where pitch accent makes a difference and learn to say them properly yourself. Words can still be stressed for emphasis, just as in English.

Questions are indicated with rising intonation, but only on the last syllable of the sentence, unlike English where the rise typically occurs over the last several syllables.

Japanese script

To master the Japanese writing system you will need to learn three sets of symbols: *hiragana*, *katakana*, and *kanji*. Traditionally, Japanese script was written and read vertically, from the upper right-hand corner of the page, progressing in vertical lines to the left. Today, it's also written horizontally like English, as you've seen in the sample transcriptions next to the illustrations. Virtually all manga continue to use the traditional vertical format.

Hiragana and katakana are collectively called *kana* (the endings *-gana* and *-kana* both come from that same word). These symbols represent all sounds produced in Japanese phonetically— that is, they let you sound out the words, with each symbol indicating a full syllable. Like the letters of the English alphabet, kana have no meaning by themselves; they gain meaning when they are put together to form words and phrases.

Both sets of kana represent the same sounds, but hiragana are the standard script, while katakana are similar to italics in English: they're used for foreign words, for sound effects or other special effects, and also when the writer wants to show particular emphasis or make it clear that a word is being used in an unconventional way. Visually, hiragana have a rounded appearance, while katakana are more angular.

Each set has forty-six symbols, or characters. That may sound like a lot to learn when compared to your English alphabet of only twenty-six letters, but actually, learning to write Japanese phonetically with kana is a snap compared to learning to write English with all its irregular spellings, silent letters, vowel confusion, and so forth. With kana, words are written exactly as they sound—with only a tiny handful of exceptions. It also helps that there are no separate capital letters to learn for either set.

Unfortunately, most Japanese text is not written with kana alone, even though it could be. Kana are usually mixed with kanji, the far more complex and vast set of characters imported from China (the word kanji literally means "Chinese letters"). That means if you want to be able to read anything other than the books first graders use before kanji are introduced or Japanese-as-a-second-language textbooks and supplements that provide romaji help, you ultimately have to tackle kanji as well. And that task, no matter how you slice it, will take some time and effort. Kanji number in the thousands, and most have at least two different pronunciations or "readings" (some have a dozen or more) depending on the context in which they appear.

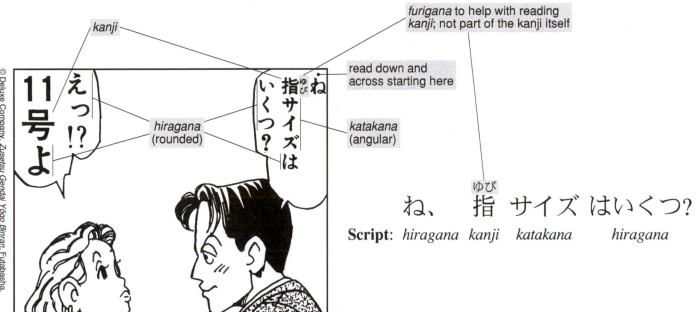

Script: *hiragana   kanji   katakana   hiragana*

Why do the Japanese still use kanji if they can spell everything out in the simple kana syllabaries? Partly it's because kanji are more efficient: since each individual kanji has meaning, a single character can represent a whole word, saving the trouble of writing as many as four or five kana to spell out the word; the meaning indicated by the kanji also clarifies which of several soundalike words (of which Japanese has many) is intended, thus avoiding ambiguities that words spelled only in kana might create.

Another reason, believe it or not, is that text is a lot easier to read when kana and kanji are mixed—at least once you know your kanji. To ease the pain a little until you do, you often get a little help in the form of small kana known as *furigana* or *rubi*, which are written alongside the kanji in the space between the lines to show how it/they should be read. Most books targeted at the general public contain at least some furigana—for difficult, less commonly used kanji, or for unconventional readings. Books for younger readers generally provide more furigana, in many cases providing readings for all kanji, or all but the simplest. Some manga also carry furigana for most or all kanji.

So even if you're one of those who's not so sure about learning thousands of kanji, you'll find it well worth your while to begin learning kana right away. Most learners of Japanese who put off learning kana live to regret their delay. The tables on the next two pages will help you get started.

The hiragana tables

In the table at the top of page xx, first look at the section headed Basic Hiragana Sequence. Since the table is laid out horizontally in this case, read across from the upper left. (In other places you'll often see this same table laid out vertically, and then you'll need to read down from the upper right.)

In Japanese dictionaries and indexes, entries are placed in kana order according to this table, so learning the sequence you see here is as important as learning the alphabet in English. Start by memorizing the vowel order, *a i u e o,* and the order of syllables in the first column on

Hiragana

basic hiragana sequence					voiced syllables					aspirated syllables				
あ a	い i	う u	え e	お o										
か ka	き ki	く ku	け ke	こ ko	が ga	ぎ gi	ぐ gu	げ ge	ご go					
さ sa	し shi	す su	せ se	そ so	ざ za	じ ji	ず zu	ぜ ze	ぞ zo					
た ta	ち chi	つ tsu	て te	と to	だ da	ぢ ji	づ zu	で de	ど do					
な na	に ni	ぬ nu	ね ne	の no										
は ha	ひ hi	ふ fu	へ he	ほ ho	ば ba	び bi	ぶ bu	べ be	ぼ bo	ぱ pa	ぴ pi	ぷ pu	ぺ pe	ぽ po
ま ma	み mi	む mu	め me	も mo										
や ya		ゆ yu		よ yo										
ら ra	り ri	る ru	れ re	ろ ro										
わ wa				を o										
ん n														

Combination Syllables

unvoiced			voiced			aspirated		
きゃ kya	きゅ kyu	きょ kyo	ぎゃ gya	ぎゅ gyu	ぎょ gyo			
しゃ sha	しゅ shu	しょ sho	じゃ ja	じゅ ju	じょ jo			
ちゃ cha	ちゅ chu	ちょ cho	ぢゃ ja	ぢゅ ju	ぢょ jo			
にゃ nya	にゅ nyu	にょ nyo						
ひゃ hya	ひゅ hyu	ひょ hyo	びゃ bya	びゅ byu	びょ byo	ぴゃ pya	ぴゅ pyu	ぴょ pyo
みゃ mya	みゅ myu	みょ myo						
りゃ rya	りゅ ryu	りょ ryo						

Katakana

basic katakana sequence					voiced syllables					aspirated syllables				
ア a	イ i	ウ u	エ e	オ o										
カ ka	キ ki	ク ku	ケ ke	コ ko	ガ ga	ギ gi	グ gu	ゲ ge	ゴ go					
サ sa	シ shi	ス su	セ se	ソ so	ザ za	ジ ji	ズ zu	ゼ ze	ゾ zo					
タ ta	チ chi	ツ tsu	テ te	ト to	ダ da	ヂ ji	ヅ zu	デ de	ド do					
ナ na	ニ ni	ヌ nu	ネ ne	ノ no										
ハ ha	ヒ hi	フ fu	ヘ he	ホ ho	バ ba	ビ bi	ブ bu	ベ be	ボ bo	パ pa	ピ pi	プ pu	ペ pe	ポ po
マ ma	ミ mi	ム mu	メ me	モ mo										
ヤ ya		ユ yu		ヨ yo										
ラ ra	リ ri	ル ru	レ re	ロ ro										
ワ wa				ヲ o										
ン n														

Combination Syllables

unvoiced			voiced			aspirated		
キャ kya	キュ kyu	キョ kyo	ギャ gya	ギュ gyu	ギョ gyo			
シャ sha	シュ shu	ショ sho	ジャ ja	ジュ ju	ジョ jo			
チャ cha	チュ chu	チョ cho	ヂャ ja	ヂュ ju	ヂョ jo			
ニャ nya	ニュ nyu	ニョ nyo						
ヒャ hya	ヒュ hyu	ヒョ hyo	ビャ bya	ビュ byu	ビョ byo	ピャ pya	ピュ pyu	ピョ pyo
ミャ mya	ミュ myu	ミョ myo						
リャ rya	リュ ryu	リョ ryo						

the left: *a ka sa ta na ha ma ya ra wa n*. Once you've done that, you can reproduce the basic kana table in romaji whenever you need, simply by combining the consonants of the first column with each of the vowels (except syllabic *n*, which stands alone), and keeping the following points in mind:

First, there are some irregular consonants—in the syllables *shi, chi, tsu,* and *fu*. Some romaji schemes try to make things more regular by spelling these syllables *si, ti, tu,* and *hu*, but the Hepburn system uses *shi, chi, tsu* and *fu* because those are the spellings that come closest to what English speakers expect for how the syllables actually sound; this lets most people get the sound right without having to think about it or needing any special explanation. But it means that when you start making verb transformations you have to remember this: for *s* row syllables, *s* and *sh* represent the same consonant, and for *t* row syllables, *t, ch,* and *ts* represent the same consonant (*fu* is not affected). So long as you remember these few irregularities of the romaji—and it's not at all hard if you've learned the kana table with the proper pronunciations to begin with—you'll be able to transform the affected verbs correctly. You'll also recognize that the *t* and *ch* in words like *kotchi* ("here") and *matcha* ("powdered green tea") represent the same consonant, so the rules for pronouncing doubled consonants apply (see p. x).

Second, there are some blank spots. There used to be symbols for all fifty possible combinations of consonants and vowels, but two from the *y* row and three from the *w* row are no longer used in modern Japanese. Since the *y* and *w* sounds have been lost from these syllables, they've become plain vowels and are spelled using the kana in the *a* row.

Finally, there's the *o* in the *w* row. Some speakers still pronounce this *wo*, at least in certain contexts, but in most speech the *w* has been lost and the sound is just like the plain vowel *o*. In this case, though, the lost consonant hasn't made the symbol fall out of use; it's been kept active to serve a special grammatical purpose, which you will learn about in Lesson 10.

☞ You can find hiragana help sites on the web with audio files that let you hear the kana pronounced. See Appendix A.2.

Some things to know about kanji

There are 1,945 kanji on the list of characters that the Japanese government has designated for standard use, but a good many more are commonly seen—especially in literary, academic, and other specialized works, but also in ordinary newspapers and magazines and in proper names. Most college graduates probably know another thousand or so kanji beyond the standard list. The largest dictionaries contain tens of thousands, many of them archaic and no longer used.

Kanji originated in China. Some kanji are based on pictures of what they represent (e.g., 𡶳 → 山 = "mountain"; ☉ → 日 = "sun"; 巛 → 川 = "river"); others are based on conceptual diagrams (e.g., ⌣ → 上 = "above"; ⌢ → 下 = "below"; 一、二、三 = "1, 2, 3"). But the vast majority are combinations of two or more previously established kanji, and can't really be thought of as pictures or diagrams of the meanings they represent—at least not in any intuitive sense. Sometimes the parts of the new kanji were chosen for the way their meanings came together to suggest a new meaning (e.g., the kanji for "person" placed next to the kanji for "tree," suggesting someone taking a break in the shade of a tree, became the kanji for "rest"); other times one part was chosen for its meaning and the other for pronunciation (e.g., the Chinese words for "lake" and "ocean" are *hu* and *hai*, so an element meaning "water" plus an already established kanji pronounced *hu* were combined to make a new kanji for "lake," and the same "water" element plus a kanji pronounced *hai* made a new kanji for "ocean").

The simplest kanji have only a single stroke; the most complex have over thirty. Many complicated kanji that are used a lot have been replaced by simpler forms over the years. The Chinese have simplified the characters in different ways from the Japanese, so many of the characters used today by Chinese and Japanese speakers are no longer mutually understood.

When kanji were adopted in Japan, they were used to represent both the original Chinese word they came with and one or more Japanese synonyms for that word. As a result, most Japanese kanji have several pronunciations, some deriving from Chinese, called "*on* readings," and some deriving from Japanese synonyms, called "*kun* readings." Some kanji were created in Japan by combining other kanji, and most of these have only *kun* readings.

Voiced and unvoiced pairs

Now look at the four rows under Voiced Syllables, and compare them with the same rows in the Basic Hiragana Sequence. Notice that the kana characters are identical except for the addition of two "dots" at the upper right, and notice the difference those two dots make in the pronunciation. Most English speakers have probably never thought about it, but *k* and *g*, *s* and *z*, and *t* and *d* are closely related sounds: both sounds in each of these pairs are made with the same mouth, tongue, and throat movements, but the first sound is unvoiced (i.e., made without actually vibrating your vocal chords), while the second is voiced (i.e., made with the help of sound from your vocal chords). Historically, this held true for the sounds in the *h* and *b* rows as well: instead of the open mouth *h* that you're accustomed to in English and that today's Japanese speakers use, the Japanese *h* used to be made with a mouth movement similar to a *b*; it was the unvoiced counterpart to the voiced *b*. To get a better idea of what this voiced/unvoiced distinction means, try sounding each of these eight consonants all by itself—i.e., without a vowel, since vowels are all voiced—and you'll see the difference. Your vocal chords remain silent when you make the *k*, *s*, *t*, and *h* sounds, but you can't produce a *g*, *z*, *d*, or *b* without vibrating your vocal chords.

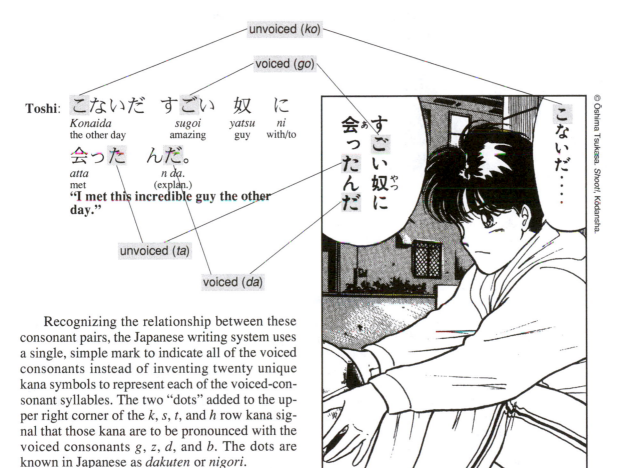

> unvoiced (*ko*)
> voiced (*go*)
> unvoiced (*ta*)
> voiced (*da*)

Toshi: こないだ　すごい　奴　に
Konaida　*sugoi*　*yatsu*　*ni*
the other day　amazing　guy　with/to

会った　んだ。
atta　*n da.*
met　(explan.)

"I met this incredible guy the other day."

Recognizing the relationship between these consonant pairs, the Japanese writing system uses a single, simple mark to indicate all of the voiced consonants instead of inventing twenty unique kana symbols to represent each of the voiced-consonant syllables. The two "dots" added to the upper right corner of the *k*, *s*, *t*, and *h* row kana signal that those kana are to be pronounced with the voiced consonants *g*, *z*, *d*, and *b*. The dots are known in Japanese as *dakuten* or *nigori*.

You should note that in romaji, three of the four irregular spellings for unvoiced sounds carry over to the spellings of the voiced sounds: the voiced partners to *shi*, *chi*, and *tsu* become *ji* (intead of *zi*), *ji* (instead of *di*), and *zu* (instead of *du*), respectively. This also means you need to remember that for *z* row syllables, *z* and *j* represent the same consonant, and for *d* row syllables, *d*, *j*, and *z* represent the same consonant.

Note, too, that the voiced *ji* and *zu* each have two kana options: the *z* row kana are preferred as a rule, but there are a small number of exceptions requiring *d* row kana that you will have to learn individually.

In Japanese dictionaries and indexes, words beginning with が *ga* are intermixed with those that begin with か *ka*, and the same is true for all voiced/unvoiced pairs. The "dots" are ignored except when two words are otherwise the same, in which case the word without the dots is listed first.

The aspirated sounds

Similarly, Japanese recognizes that the *p* sound is made with the same mouth movement as the *b* sound (and, historically, the *h* sound). The difference in this case is that the sound is aspirated—that is, it is created with the help of a small but audible puff of breath following the consonant rather than with help from the vocal chords. A tiny circle similar to the degree symbol (°) is used to show when *h* row kana should be pronounced with the aspirated consonant *p*.

© Ōshima Tsukasa, *Shoot!*, Kōdansha.

aspirated syllable (*pa*)

だから　いっぱい　食べな　よ。
Da kara　　　*ippai*　　　*tabena*　　　*yo*
so/therefore　lots　　　　eat-(command)　(emph.)
"So eat lots."
"So eat all you want."

In dictionaries and indexes, words beginning with aspirated syllables are intermixed with words beginning with their unvoiced and voiced counterparts. For words that are otherwise the same, the word with an aspirated syllable comes after the other word(s).

Small kana

A few of the kana symbols are written smaller for certain purposes. Unlike the differences between capitals and small letters in English, large and small kana have exactly the same shape; and sometimes the size difference is not very obvious, so you need to keep a close eye out.

As noted on page xviii, when you see a doubled consonant in romaji, you stop the sound for a beat with your mouth in position to say the first consonant before proceeding to the next syllable. In kana, a small *tsu* is used to show the same vocal maneuver. For example, a small *tsu* followed by a *te*—i.e., って—means you should form the *t* with your mouth and pause a beat before saying *te*; in romaji, this is written *tte*.

Here are three word pairs that are distinguished only by the small *tsu*:

また　　= *mata* ("again")　　はこ　　= *hako* ("box")　　ほさ　　= *hosa* ("aide")
まった　= *matta* ("waited")　はっこ　= *hakko* ("8 pieces")　ほっさ　= *hossa* ("seizure")

You'll generally encounter a small *tsu* only in the middle of words, but it can occur at the beginning of certain contracted forms, and writers also use it at the end of words to show that the last syllable is spoken sharply, like an exclamation—especially with interjections of surprise or with commands. In the latter case, the small *tsu* essentially fills the role of an exclamation point, so the transcriptions in this book use an exclamation point to represent it. (Many Japanese writers also use the exclamation point, either instead of or together with the small *tsu*.)

まて　　= *mate*　　A normally spoken command, "Wait."
まてっ　= *mate!*　A sharply spoken/shouted command, "Wait!/Stop!/Halt!"

The three *y* row kana are also written in small form, in combination with most but not all of the kana in the *i* column, forming the syllables in the Combination Syllables table at the bottom of page xx. In such cases, the *i* from the first kana drops out, and the combination with small *ya*, *yu*, or *yo* is pronounced as a single syllable. The same kana combination but with full-sized *ya*, *yu*, or *yo* needs to be pronounced as two distinct syllables.

きや = *ki + ya*　　きやく = *ki-ya-ku* (3 syllables)　　　　　= "agreement"
きゃ = *kya*　　　　きゃく = *kya-ku* (2 syllables; *i* drops out) = "guest"

Don't forget that *y* in Japanese is always a consonant and pronounced like the *y* in "year"; it's never pronounced like in English "my," nor can it by itself fill in for the vowel in a syllable

© Kobayashi Makoto. *What's Michael!?*, Kōdansha.

full-sized *ya*, independent syllable

small *ya* combines with preceding syllable (*ji* + small *ya* = *ja*)

small *tsu* means following consonant is doubled

full-sized *ya*　　small *ya*

やめてー! ツメ を といじゃ ダメー! これ 高かった の よー!!
Yametē!　*Tsume*　*o*　*toija*　*damē!*　*Kore*　*takakatta*　*no*　*yō!!*
stop　　　 nails　(obj.)　if sharpen　is no good　this　was expensive　(explan.)　(emph.)

"Stop! Don't sharpen your nails! This was expensive!"

Where hiragana and katakana came from

At the time kanji first arrived in Japan more than 1500 years ago, the Japanese had no writing system of their own. If they wanted to write anything down, they had to do it in Chinese. Not surprisingly, the Japanese soon decided they'd like to be able to write things in their own language. To do that, they began using kanji solely for their sound value. That is, they ignored what the kanji meant in Chinese and used them instead to "spell out" the sounds of their native Japanese words, one kanji to a syllable.

But many of the kanji they applied this way required quite a few strokes, and having to go through all those strokes just to set down one syllable was tedious, so early writers sought to simplify things. One way they achieved this was by writing the kanji in progressively more cursive forms, so that several strokes combined into one. Characters simplified in this manner ultimately became the hiragana syllabary, with no character having more than four strokes; most had two or three strokes, and quite a few had only one. For example, the six-stroke kanji 安 became the three-stroke hiragana あ *a*; the five-stroke 以 became the two-stroke い *i*; and the six-stroke 宇 became the two-stroke う *u*.

Another way early writers reduced their stroke counts was to write only part of the character, like writing an abbreviation of a word; sometimes the part they took as the abbreviation was made slightly simpler as well. Characters "abbreviated" in this way ultimately became the katakana syllabary, also with no character having more than four strokes, most having two or three, and a few having only one. For example, the lefthand component of the kanji 阿 was slightly simplified to make the katakana ア *a* (two strokes, down from eight); the lefthand component of 伊 became the katakana イ *i* (two strokes, down from six); and the top component of 宇 became the katakana ウ *u* (three strokes, down from six).

the way *y* can in English. Japanese *y* is always followed by a vowel, which must be pronounced together with it in a single unit. When it's also preceded by another consonant, that consonant, too, must become part of the single unit.

Shi and *chi* had irregular romaji spellings in the basic hiragana sequence, and that irregularity carries over to their combination syllables as well: these syllables are spelled without using *y* in romaji even though in kana they are written with small *ya*, *yu*, and *yo*. Once again, the Hepburn romaji spellings in the table on page xx correspond to what most English speakers would naturally expect for how the syllables actually sound.

The kana of the *a* row are also sometimes made smaller, but this is more common in katakana than hiragana.

Double-length vowels

The romaji spellings for double-length vowels were shown on page xvi. In hiragana, a double-length vowel is shown by adding the appropriate vowel character (*a*-row kana), as follows:

あ *a* column syllables:	add あ	→	ああ = *ā*; かあ = *kā*; さあ = *sā*; まあ = *mā*
い *i* column syllables:	add い	→	いい = *ii*; きい = *kii*; ちい = *chii*; ひい = *hii*
う *u* column syllables:	add う	→	うう = *ū*; くう = *kū*; ふう = *fū*; ゆう = *yū*

The other two vowels aren't quite so obvious:

え *e* column syllables:	normally add い	→	けい = *kei*; でい = *dei*; れい = *rei*
	sometimes add え	→	ええ = *ē*; ねえ = *nē*; へえ = *hē*
お *o* column syllables:	normally add う	→	おう = *ō*; そう = *sō*; もう = *mō*
	sometimes add お	→	おお = *ō*; とお = *tō*; よお = *yō*

© Ōshima Tsukasa, *Shoot!*, Kōdansha.

double-length vowels in kana

Toshi: 危ない　なあ！
Abunai　　　nā!
is dangerous　(emph.)
"That's dangerous!"

歩道　を　走るな　よ！
Hodō　o　hashiru na　yo!
sidewalk　on/along　don't run/ride　(emph.)
"Don't ride on the sidewalk!"

Kenji: よお、トシ！　部活　楽しい　か？
Yō,　Toshi!　Bukatsu　tanoshii　ka?
hey　(name)　club activity　is fun/enjoyable　(?)
"Hey there, Toshi! Is practice fun?"
"Yo, Toshi! Having fun in practice?"

For the last two vowels, it's the particular word, not the preceding consonant, that determines which is correct, and of course, there's no way for beginners to know beforehand which words are which. You simply need to be aware that you will encounter two different ways of elongating *e* and *o* column syllables in kana. Make note of the exceptions that require え or お when they come up; since manga artists don't always follow standard usage, it's a good idea to check the proper spelling in a dictionary as well.

Katakana

The tables on page xxi show the katakana equivalents of the hiragana, laid out for easy comparison in the same format as the tables on the facing page. The same two dots are used in katakana for the voiced consonants of the *g*, *z*, *d*, and *b* rows, and the same little circle indicates the aspirated consonants of the *p* row.

Since katakana are used to write foreign words that don't conform so neatly to the Japanese sound system, they're sometimes used a little more creatively than hiragana—e.g., the *a* row kana are often made small to show that the vowel should be merged with the previous syllable instead of being pronounced separately—but both sets of kana represent the same sounds. The one significant difference between the two sets is that all five double-length vowels in katakana are usually indicated simply by adding a long dash after the syllable that is to be lengthened. This dash is commonly called "the katakana long mark" (in Japanese, *chōon kigō* or *bō*). When text is written vertically, the long mark is vertical; when text is written horizontally, so is the long mark.

the katakana long mark changes its axis

Uzuratani: サード　でした。
Sādo　deshita.
third　was
"I was third baseman."
"I played third."

Especially in manga but in other forms of writing as well, you will sometimes see the katakana long mark used with hiragana (see panel on page xv), and the hiragana conventions for long vowels used with katakana, but neither practice is considered standard. The wavy long mark used in the panel on page xxv is also non-standard.

Punctuation

The comma for Japanese script is an angled "dot" (、), and the period is a small circle (。). In vertical text, these appear at the upper right of the character square they occupy, while in horizontal text, they appear at the lower left. As you've seen in the illustrations, the question mark and exclamation point familiar to you in English are also used; they appear centered in that character square.

ほう、やるねえ。

You should be aware, though, that most manga artists are quite unconventional in their use of punctuation—placing commas where periods are called for and vice versa, inserting question marks and exclamation points in the middle of sentences, and often skipping punctuation altogether. Short lines and limited space encourage the last option. For native speakers, such liberties work to good effect, but for beginning language learners they can create confusion, making it difficult to determine where sentences begin and end. The punctuation in the transcribed text has been revised along more standard lines, with an eye to helping the beginning student.

Learning to write kana and kanji

One of the best ways to learn to read kana and kanji is to practice writing them. Practicing with grid-marked paper—use graph paper, or make your own—will help you achieve better balance and shape in your characters; learning the proper order of the strokes helps as well. This book does not provide further instructions along those lines, but there are a variety of published guides available for you to choose from, as well as a growing number of web-based resources. A few of each are listed in Appendix A.2.

The Lessons

The Three Basic Sentence Types

Japanese is built on three basic sentence types: verb, adjective, and noun. And the simple sentences of each type could hardly be simpler. A **verb**—an action word, like "go"—all by itself makes a complete sentence. An **adjective**—a describing word, like "cold"—by itself can make a complete sentence, too, because in Japanese the meaning of the verb "to be" is built right in. A **noun**—a word that names a person, place, thing, or idea—must come with a separate verb "to be," but only a single noun has to be stated. So to give English comparisons, the simplest Japanese sentences are like:

Goes. Went. Came. Will come.   (verb type: action)
Is cold. Was fantastic.   (adjective type: describing)
Is phone. Were friends.   (noun type: naming/identifying)

In English, these are sentence fragments, because they don't have **subjects**—that is, they don't say who's doing the action, or what is being described or identified—and a native English speaker who spoke this way would sound rather silly. In Japanese, though, sentences like these sound perfectly normal; in fact, it often sounds quite unnatural to include the subject when it's already obvious from what came before in the conversation, or simply from the situation.

Some people point to these missing subjects and complain that Japanese is a vague language, but it's better to think of the subjects as merely unstated rather than altogether absent. The specific subject isn't always included in English, either; much of the time, a substitute like "he" or "she" fills its place instead. How do you know who "he" or "she" is? By what came before in the conversation, or by the situation. The same holds for the unstated subjects in Japanese. So long as you're paying attention, the context usually fills in the subject for you. Once you get used to this approach, it's actually quite efficient, but you do have to stay on your toes. Keeping tuned in to the context is crucial.

☛ Brief descriptions of the manga series used to illustrate this book are included in Appendix B. You can look a series up by author and title based on the information in the copyright notice next to each example.

Simple verb-type sentences

A verb-type sentence tells of an action. All the verb-type sentences in this lesson consist of only a single verb and nothing else.

Sayuri

1 Yamashita Sayuri has a new boyfriend and doesn't really want to have anything to do with Shin'ichi anymore. Shin'ichi wants to tell her how much she still means to him, and asks for a chance to talk to her. When she seems to think they have nothing to talk about, he pleads:

Shin'ichi: たのむ!
Tanomu!
request/ask/beg
"I request!"
"I beg you!" (PL2)

• *tanomu* means "make a request/ask a favor." When addressed directly to someone, it literally implies "I request this of you," and often serves as an equivalent of "Please"; when asked with strong feeling it can be like "I beg you!"
• it's obvious from the context that the subject of the verb is Shin'ichi himself ("I ～"), so there's no need to state it. In conversation, the speaker and listener are among the first candidates to consider when trying to fill in an unstated subject.

"Non-past" verbs

In fig. 1, *tanomu* is the **plain, dictionary form** of the verb for "request/ask a favor," and in fig. 2 here, *iku* is the plain, dictionary form of the verb for "go." But the context in fig. 2 demands that the verb be translated "will go"—that is, as future tense. In Japanese, the plain, dictionary form of a verb is used to speak of both present and future events, so it's best to call it the **non-past form**.

☞ The dictionary form of a verb is its plain non-past form, but there will be other plain forms to learn as well, such as plain past, plain negative, and so forth.

2 At the bar Lemon Hart, regular patron Matsuda has been rattling on nonstop about the woman who came in for the first time the night before, when that very woman calls to say she has gotten lost trying to find the bar again. The proprietor announces that she wants somebody to come and meet her, and Matsuda leaps at the chance.

Matsuda: 行く!!
Iku!!
will go
"I'll go!" (PL2)

- *iku* is the verb for "go/goes/will go," and the context makes it clear that the speaker is the subject—i.e., the person who will go.

-ます *-masu* changes the politeness level

Japanese verbs don't change for number (how many people or things do the action) or person (whether the speaker, the listener, or someone else does the action). An English speaker has to distinguish between "request" and "requests" or "go" and "goes" to make the verb agree with the subject of the sentence, but a Japanese speaker simply says *tanomu* or *iku* no matter who or how many people are making a request or going somewhere.

Actually, that's not quite true, because the *who* does matter in a different way. Japanese verbs change form to express different **levels of politeness** depending on the situation and the social relationship between the speaker and the listener. The "PL2" you saw in parentheses after the final translation in the first two examples means "Politeness Level 2"—a level used among friends. In more formal situations, a higher level of politeness is called for.

This example illustrates a PL3 verb, which ends in -ます *-masu*. The **-masu** form of *tanomu* is *tanomimasu*, and the *-masu* form of *iku* is *ikimasu*.

3 The leader of the opposition has obtained a copy of a highly classified message that appears to show the U.S. president attempting to influence Japanese policy toward France. At a question and answer session in the Diet (Japan's legislature), he asks the prime minister to confirm that the copy is indeed genuine.

Opposition leader

Prime Minister: 認めます。
Mitomemasu.
acknowledge/confirm
"I confirm it." (PL3)

- *mitomemasu* is the polite, PL3 form of the verb *mitomeru*, which has a range of affirmative meanings: "acknowledge/confirm/admit/accept/approve/recognize."

The four politeness levels

Although many subtler gradations exist, for most purposes it's enough to distinguish four levels of politeness: PL1 = rude/condescending; PL2 = plain/abrupt/familiar; PL3 = ordinary polite; and PL4 = very polite. In this book, you will see mostly the middle two levels.

Most sentences aren't made up of only a single verb and nothing else, of course, and other elements in the sentence can affect the politeness level as well. But if the main verb is in a plain form, it usually makes the sentence PL2, and if it's in one of the forms of *-masu*, it most typically makes the sentence PL3.

4 At a working dinner, the client abruptly gets up to leave when he learns that the ad agency has failed to follow one of his instructions in preparing its proposal.

Client: 帰ります。
Kaerimasu.
will go home/leave
"I will go home."
"I'll be leaving!" (PL3)

- *kaerimasu* is the PL3 form of the verb *kaeru* ("return home/leave"). Depending on the point of view of the speaker, *kaeru* can mean either "go home/leave" or "come home/arrive."

The four politeness levels:

PL1
Rude/condescending; best to avoid.

PL2
Plain/familiar; use with close friends.

PL3
Ordinary polite; your safest overall choice.

PL4
Very polite; use with social superiors (see pp. 38–39).

Only the politeness is different

The dictionary form and *-masu* form differ only in politeness, not meaning, number, person, or tense. *Iku* and its polite form *ikimasu* are both non-past verbs; so are *tanomu* and *tanomimasu*, *mitomeru* and *mitomemasu*, and *kaeru* and *kaerimasu*. Context will tell whether the event/action spoken of is present or future.

Important usage note: PL2 sentences sound quite familiar and even abrupt, so they are reserved for informal situations such as conversations among family and friends/peers, or persons of higher status speaking to persons of lower status. PL3 sentences sound quite a bit more formal, and they are appropriate when speaking to strangers, new or relatively distant acquaintances, and one's elders and social superiors. There's nothing intrinsically rude about PL2 forms, but to avoid the risk of rudeness from using them at the wrong time, beginning learners of Japanese will do best to stick with PL3 forms at first.

5 Shin-chan and his parents have just sat down for a special New Year's meal.

Father: いただきまーす。
Itadakimāsu.
will receive/partake
"I will partake."
"Let's eat!" (PL3)

- *itadakimasu* is the polite form of *itadaku* ("receive"). The verb can be used to speak of receiving anything, but the most common use of its polite form is as a set expression spoken at the beginning of a meal, as seen here, or at other times when being served something to eat or drink. When used this way, *itadakimasu* essentially means "I will partake," but the feeling can range from a very casual "Dig in!" to a formal "Thank you for providing what I am about to eat." In failing to say *itadakimasu* along with his father, little Shin-chan has forgotten his manners, and his mother corrects him in the next frame.
- the elongated *ma* implies he's saying the word with particular gusto/enthusiasm; *-masu* does not normally have a long vowel.

Basic verb facts

The table shows a few other basic verbs worth learning right away. In each case the plain, dictionary form is given first, followed by the polite, *-masu* form, and in each case, either of these by itself can make a complete sentence in the right situation. In the absence of any real-life context, random subjects have been assigned to show what the verbs might mean as sentences.

Most discussion of verb groups can wait until the PL2 past tense and other verb forms are introduced in the second half of the book, but it's worth briefly mentioning them here. Japanese has just **two irregular verbs**, and all the rest fit into one of two groups, as illustrated in the table. For **Group 1** (sometimes called *u*-verbs), the polite form is made by changing the final *-u* of the dictionary form to *-i* and adding *-masu* (owing to the irregular romanization in the *sa* and *ta* rows of the kana table—see Introduction—verbs ending in *-su* are written *-shimasu* rather than *-simasu*, and those ending in *-tsu* are written *-chimasu* rather than *-tsimasu*). For **Group 2** (sometimes called *ru*-verbs), the polite form is made by replacing the final *-ru* with *-masu*.

The part that comes before *-masu* in the polite form (e.g., *kai-* in *kaimasu*) is called the **stem** or **pre-*masu* form** of the verb. In some cases, a conversion pattern is the same for all verb groups if you work from the stem.

This book gives both the plain and polite form for each new verb the first few times it appears. If you learn both forms, you'll easily be able to figure out what kind of verb it is simply by comparing the two. The index entry for each verb also gives its group.

	plain/polite	meaning	as sentences
group 1	買う/買います *kau*/*kaimasu*	buy	"They buy [it]." "I will buy [it]."
group 1	飲む/飲みます *nomu*/*nomimasu*	drink	"He drinks." "Everyone will drink."
group 2	食べる/食べます *taberu*/*tabemasu*	eat	"We eat." "She will eat."
group 2	見る/見ます *miru*/*mimasu*	look at/ watch	"She looks at [it]." "We will watch."
irregular	来る/来ます *kuru*/*kimasu*	come	"He comes." "They will come."
irregular	する/します *suru*/*shimasu*	do	"They do [it]." "I will do [it]."

Simple noun-type sentences with です *desu*

Kōsuke

A noun-type sentence names or identifies something (you will also learn later about a special group of descriptive nouns). Like verb-type sentences, noun-types often occur without explicitly stated subjects, but it's not quite possible to say that a noun makes a sentence all by itself. In PL3 speech the noun normally needs to be followed by です *desu* ("is/are"). It's this **noun + *desu* phrase** that makes a complete sentence by itself even without a stated subject.

6 Kōsuke's landlady is having some remodeling done, and since she needed to run some errands, she asked Kōsuke to serve tea to the workers on their mid-afternoon break. Kōsuke already knows Sada the carpenter, but Sada's helper today is someone new. The situation and Sada's pointing finger make it clear what the subject of his sentence is.

> **Sada:** ムスメ　です。
> *Musume　desu.*
> girl/daughter　is
> **"This is my daughter."** (PL3)
>
> **Kōsuke:** あっ!!
> *A!!*
> (interj.)
> **"Oh!"** (PL2–3)

- *musume* is used both for "girl/maiden/young woman" and for "daughter." Here the context makes it clear that Sada means "my daughter." You'll find more about kinship terms on p. 91.
- depending on what's called for by the situation, *musume* can be replaced by the person's name, his/her professional or corporate title, or any other identifying information.

Desu = the verb "to be"

Desu most commonly corresponds to the verb "to be" in English. It is the non-past form of what linguists call a linking verb, and it's used to name, define, describe, or restate the subject of the sentence; to give the subject's location or time; to indicate an action or something else associated with the subject; and to link words to the subject in a variety of other ways.

As with action verbs, *desu* does not change form for number or person or future tense, so it can be equivalent to "am," "is," "are," or "will be," depending on the context. *Desu* does not change form in all the ways that action verbs do, but it does have separate forms for past ("was/were") and for surmising/guessing ("might be/is surely"), which you will learn in Lesson 3. Unlike action verbs, *desu* cannot stand alone as a sentence.

> **7** Matsuda, a writer, is busy at work when the phone rings.

Matsuda: ハイ、 松田 です。
Hai,   Matsuda desu.
yes/hello (name) is/am
"Hello, this is Matsuda." (PL3)

- *hai*, literally "yes," serves as a "hello" when picking up the phone to answer a call.
- a very common way of identifying or introducing oneself, whether on the phone or in person, is to state one's name followed by *desu*.
- what looks like graph paper in the frames at left is Japanese manuscript paper, known as *genkō yōshi*. The writer writes just one kana or kanji per box in order to keep the characters distinct and legible.

RI-I-ING!

ハイ
松田です

The plain equivalent of *desu* is だ *da*

Desu is polite and represents PL3 speech; its plain, PL2 equivalent is *da*. *Da* can sound quite abrupt, or even rough, so some of its uses are limited to male speakers. Women tend to speak more politely as a matter of custom, sticking with *desu* and *-masu* forms when men would not. Even when they're speaking quite informally, they often shy away from the abruptness of *da*, preferring to replace *desu* not with *da* but with a softer sounding particle, or with a combination of *da* plus a particle. You'll learn about particles in Lesson 2.

Male speakers shouldn't take this as a go-ahead to forget about *desu* and just use *da*. The level of politeness always needs to fit the situation—especially the speaker's relationship to the listener. No matter your gender, the rule still holds: beginners should stick to the polite forms except when you're very confident that being less formal won't cause offense.

> **8** This boy wakes up and opens his window one morning to discover...

Boy: わぁ、 雪 だァ。
Wā,   yuki   dā.
(exclam.) snow is
"Wow! It's snow!"
"Wow! It's snowing!" (PL2)

- the small katakana *a* serves to elongate the vowel of *da*; elongating *da* can give the feeling of an exclamation.
- the speaker here is a male, but when speaking to herself, a female speaker is just as likely to use *da* and other PL2 forms as a male. People speaking to themselves is something you can actually see in manga, even if you wouldn't normally hear it in real life.

わぁ
雪
だァ

The difference is only in politeness

Da and *desu* differ only in the level of politeness, not meaning or tense. They aren't always grammatically interchangeable, but you can assume they are unless you're told otherwise.

9 Based on what he hears and sees in the first two frames, the president of the company concludes that there's a fire in the building. It turns out to be otherwise.

© Ueda Masashi. *Furiten-kun.* Take Shobō.

1   **Employee**: 火事 だー!!
      Kaji   dā!!
      fire   is
      "It's a fire!"
      "Fire!" (PL2)

2   **Employee**: 火事 だー!!
      Kaji   dā!!
      "Fire!" (PL2)

      Furiten-kun: 社長、   火事 です!!
      Shachō,   kaji desu!!
      company president fire   is
      "Sir! It's a fire!" (PL3)

- *kaji* is written with kanji meaning "fire" and "incident," and it's used only for accidental/destructive fires.
- the elongated *da* again represents an exclamation. The president assumes it's an exclamation of alarm.
- *shachō* is written with kanji meaning "company" and "head/chief/leader" to give the meaning "company president." Japanese have traditionally addressed their superiors by title rather than by name—though recent years have seen some movement away from this custom.
- note how Furiten-kun uses PL3 speech when speaking directly to the president of his company.

Some more examples

Two possible translations are given for each sentence. It should not be difficult for you to imagine situations in which either meaning—or still other meanings—might apply.

先生 です。
Sensei desu.
teacher is
"She's a teacher." / **"This is my teacher."** (PL3)

明日 です。
Ashita   desu.
tomorrow is
"It's tomorrow." / **"It will be tomorrow."** (PL3)

- when the situation or a time word points to the future, *desu* can mean "will be."

チョコレート だ。
Chokorēto   da.
chocolate is
"It's chocolate." / **"They're chocolates."** (PL2)

- *chokorēto* is the Japanese rendering of English "chocolate."

学校 です。
Gakkō   desu.
school   is
"It's a school." / **"He's at school."** (PL3)

- *desu* after a place name can imply that's where the subject is.

"EXIT"   **"Where did it break out?"**

"Wow! We can see really well!"

Simple adjective-type sentences

An adjective-type sentence describes something. English speakers are used to having adjectives work in two ways: coming directly before a noun to describe what the noun refers to ("It's a *hot* day"), and coming after the verb "to be" to describe the subject of the sentence ("The day is *hot*"). Japanese adjectives are used in both of these ways, too, but there's one key difference: the adjectives themselves have the meaning of the verb "to be" built in. This means that an adjective by itself can fully replace the verb in a sentence: it can stand alone as a complete sentence just like a verb, with an implied subject, or it can have its own explicitly stated subject.

10 Husband and wife agreed to meet back at the department store entrance in two hours. The husband waits at the appointed time, but his wife fails to appear.

Husband: おそい。
Osoi.
is late/slow
"She's late." (PL2)

- the adjective *osoi* can mean either "is late" or "is slow." In this case, context shows the subject to be "she." If the husband were saying this same sentence directly to his wife when she showed up late, the context would tell us that the intended meaning is "You're late!"

Eventually the clerk at the information counter in the background calls him to the phone, and his wife tells him she unthinkingly went straight home, from force of habit.

The definition of "adjective" for Japanese

In English, any word modifying or describing a noun can be called an adjective, but for Japanese, it's best to restrict the term "adjective" to the kind of words described above, called *keiyō-shi* in Japanese, which contain the meaning of the verb "to be" within them. These words have their own distinct ways of changing form, which you will learn alongside the corresponding verb forms in the second half of the book.

In their plain, dictionary form, all adjectives end with the syllable -い -*i* (but this doesn't mean that all words ending in -*i* are adjectives). Like verbs, the dictionary form of an adjective is non-past, serving as both present and future tense; the dictionary and other plain forms are used to make PL2 sentences. Like verbs, adjectives do not change form for number or person.

There is another group of descriptive words that are sometimes called "*na*-adjectives," "quasi adjectives," or "pseudo adjectives." Although their descriptive nature means they often translate as adjectives in English, they're in fact a special kind of noun in Japanese; like any other noun, they must be followed by *da* (PL2) or *desu* (PL3) to make a complete sentence. You'll learn more about them in Lesson 7.

11 This man has been shoveling snow off of the roof after a heavy snowfall. Now he's done for the day and coming inside.

Man: おー、さむい、さむい。
Ō,　samui,　samui.
(exclam.)　is cold　is cold
"Hooo, it's cold. It's cold."
"Hooo, it's cold out there!" (PL2)

Sound FX: ガタ
Gata
(sound of setting shovel against wall)

- each *samui* is strictly speaking a separate sentence by itself, but they're spoken in quick succession. Doubling up an adjective like this can be a way of adding emphasis.

The polite form of an adjective

The polite form of an adjective, for PL3 speech, is simply its dictionary form plus *desu*: *osoi* → *osoi desu* and *samui* → *samui desu*. As with verbs, this changes only the level of politeness, not the meaning or tense.

Adding *desu* makes a PL3 adjective-type sentence look a lot like a PL3 noun-type sentence. But there's an important difference: since the adjective itself contains the meaning of the verb "to be," *desu* in this case serves purely to raise the level of politeness; it doesn't add any meaning. The *desu* in a PL3 adjective is not the verb "to be"; it's just a polite flourish.

And that explains a second important difference: this *desu* cannot be replaced with *da*. *Da* does not follow directly after an adjective. As seen in the examples on the facing page, it's the unaltered dictionary form that's used for non-past tense in PL2 speech.

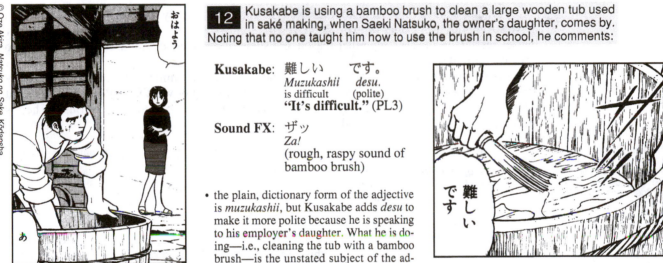

12 Kusakabe is using a bamboo brush to clean a large wooden tub used in saké making, when Saeki Natsuko, the owner's daughter, comes by. Noting that no one taught him how to use the brush in school, he comments:

Kusakabe: 難しい　です。
Muzukashii　desu.
is difficult　(polite)
"It's difficult." (PL3)

Sound FX: ザッ
Za!
(rough, raspy sound of bamboo brush)

- the plain, dictionary form of the adjective is *muzukashii*, but Kusakabe adds *desu* to make it more polite because he is speaking to his employer's daughter. What he is doing—i.e., cleaning the tub with a bamboo brush—is the unstated subject of the adjective.

© Oze Akira, *Natsuko no Sake*, Kōdansha.

おはよう

"Good morning."
"Oh, (hi)."

A usage note on adjectives

The plain form of an adjective doesn't sound quite as abrupt as the noun + *da* combination does, so there's very little difference between the sexes in the use of the two politeness levels for adjectives. Whether you're male or female, you wouldn't normally use the PL3 form when exclaiming how cold it is or mentioning the frigid weather to a peer, but you would if your boss or teacher asked you what the temperature was like outside.

Here are a few commonly occurring adjectives for you to learn. As with the verbs listed on p. 5, the subjects here are chosen at random; in real life, they would depend on the situation. To get the dictionary form of the adjectives in the right two columns, simply remove *desu*.

☛ You can find many of these words used in real manga examples by looking them up in the index (note: the references are to figure numbers, not pages). Make a habit of checking the index to find additional examples of the words you encounter; at first, of course, you may not understand the more advanced sentences the words appear in, but this will change as you proceed. If you don't find an index entry, the word probably does not appear again in the book.

おおきい。	ちいさい。	おいしい　です。	まずい　です。
Ōkii.	*Chiisai*	*Oishii　desu.*	*Mazui　desu.*
is big/large	is little/small	is tasty　(polite)	is bad/unsavory　(polite)
"He's huge."	**"They're small."**	**"It's delicious."**	**"It's awful."**
とおい。	ちかい。	おもしろい　です。	つまらない　です。
Tōi.	*Chikai.*	*Omoshiroi　desu.*	*Tsumaranai　desu.*
is far/distant	is near/close	is interesting　(polite)	is boring/dull　(polite)
"It's a long way."	**"That's nearby."**	**"This is interesting."**	**"They're boring."**
ながい。	みじかい。	やすい　です。	たかい　です。
Nagai.	*Mijikai.*	*Yasui　desu.*	*Takai　desu.*
is long	is short	is inexpensive　(polite)	is high/expensive　(polite)
"It's long."	**"They're short."**	**"They're cheap."**	**"It's expensive."**

Lesson 2

Sentence Particles

Before you can learn about subjects, objects, modifiers, and the like in Japanese, you first need to know about a special class of words called **particles**. Particles serve two basic purposes: they **mark** a word's function—that is, they can tell you what role the word is playing in the sentence—or they express the speaker's feeling about what he or she is saying. Some particles manage to do both.

Particles always come right after the word or phrase they apply to—though they sometimes have strong ties as a matter of expression to what follows as well. They never change form for tense, person, number, or any other reason, but some of them can combine with one another to create different effects.

Like the plot of a good story, a Japanese sentence saves the climax—the crucial verb, adjective, or noun + *da/desu* phrase that tells you what's happening or what's what—for the end. But often there's a little bit of wrapping up to do afterwards with particles and extensions. So here's how a Japanese sentence is shaped:

☛ The example sentences in the early lessons in this book are all "climax" and "wrap-up," without any "development," so it won't look like their climax is at the end, But when the examples start adding other elements, you will soon see that nearly everything else builds onto the front of the sentence.

development (optional)		climax (required)		wrap-up (optional)
Subject, object, place, time, modifiers, etc.—with the appropriate particles to identify or "mark" each element	+	Main verb, adjective, or noun + *da/desu* phrase	+	Particle(s) and extensions

Particles that come at the very end apply to the entire sentence, and so are called **sentence particles**. The particles introduced in this lesson are generally used only in conversation, not in formal writing.

The colloquial particle ね *ne*

Ne is a mildly emphatic sentence particle that expresses common feeling between the speaker and listener. It implies that the speaker expects agreement or sympathy from the listener, similar to a rhetorical tag question in English: "isn't it?/don't they?/right?/ don't you agree?"

Proprietor

13 Noboru has come up to Tokyo with starry-eyed notions of working in the big city, but his Uncle Matsuda (figs. 2, 7) thinks he should go back to his secure job in Kyushu. The proprietor of Matsuda's favorite bar, Lemon Hart, suggests a test: if a glass of clear water placed under a napkin changes color after thirty minutes, Noboru goes home; otherwise he can have a job at the bar. To Noboru's great surprise, the glass glows a magnificent pink when the napkin is removed. Though it's not the result Noboru had expected or hoped for, he accepts it graciously.

© Furuya Mitsutoshi, *Bar Remon Hāto*, Futabasha.

Noboru: きれい　です　ね。
Kirei　desu　ne.
pretty/beautiful　is　(colloq.)
"It's beautiful, isn't it?" (PL3)

• *kirei* is a descriptive noun that can refer either to "beauty" or to "cleanness"; followed by *da* or *desu* ("is/are"), it means "is beautiful/pretty/clean."
• the PL2 equivalent of this sentence is either *Kirei da ne* (both sexes, but more masculine) or *Kirei ne* (feminine; see fig. 16).

Requesting confirmation with *ne*

Ne can also represent an explicit request for confirmation, and in many such cases it carries the force of a genuine question, not merely a rhetorical one. But even then it expects the listener to agree or answer in the affirmative. (Lesson 4 introduces questions that do not assume an affirmative answer.)

© Hirokane Kenshi, Kaji Ryūsuke no Gi, Kōdansha.

14 On a rainy night, this woman is on her way home from the public bath when a private investigator approaches her.

PI:
一ノ関　鮎美　さん　です　ね。
Ichinoseki Ayumi -san desu ne.
(surname) (given name) Mr./Ms. is (colloq.)
"You're Ms. Ichinoseki Ayumi, aren't you?"
"Ms. Ichinoseki Ayumi, I believe?" (PL3)

- context makes it clear that the implied subject is "you," the listener; when a question doesn't specify a subject, a good first candidate to consider is "you."
- *Ichinoseki* is her surname/family name, and *Ayumi* is her given name. The customary order for Japanese names is surname first.
- *-san* is a polite suffix appended to personal names and titles, equivalent to either "Mr." or "Ms." The same suffix is used for both sexes and regardless of marital status. It can be used with both social superiors and inferiors, but it's never used with one's own name.
- the PL2 equivalent of this sentence is *Ichinoseki Ayumi-san da ne?*
- this questioning *ne* is spoken with a slightly rising intonation. You will learn a little more about question intonation in Lesson 4.

Ne as emphasis

In many cases *ne* simply provides light emphasis. When it's elongated to *nē*, it shows stronger emphasis, with the feeling of "It's really ～, isn't it?" or "It really *is* ～, isn't it?" This works whether expressing admiration, excitement, sympathy, or dismay—or when just remarking on the weather.

© Maekawa Tsukasa. Dai-Tōkyō Binbō Seikatsu Manyuaru, Kōdansha.

15 Kōsuke's (fig. 6) landlady takes him to help celebrate the 30th anniversary of "Kiichi-tei," a small restaurant specializing in *tonkatsu* ("pork cutlets") run by a man named Kiichi. As they sit down at the counter, he greets them with cups of tea.

Kiichi: どーも、　いらっしゃい。
Dōmo, irasshai.
(emph.) welcome
"Welcome." (PL3–4)

暑い　です　ねえ。
Atsui desu nē.
is hot (pol.) (colloq. emph.)
"It's really hot, isn't it." (PL3)

- *irasshai*, or more formally *irasshaimase*, is a polite expression shopkeepers and restaurant workers use to greet/welcome customers.
- *atsui desu* is the polite form of the adjective *atsui* ("is hot"). When referring to the weather, *atsui* is written 暑い; when referring to hot foods and beverages, it's written 熱い. In conversation, the context has to tell you which is meant.
- the PL2 equivalent of this sentence is *Atsui nē*—with the particle directly following the plain, dictionary form of the adjective. (Remember: the *desu* after an adjective in PL3 speech does not become *da* in PL2 speech; see fig. 12.)

Ne without *da/desu*

Ne alone sometimes stands in for *da ne* or *desu ne* ("is, isnt' it?") at the end of a noun-type sentence. The informal feeling this gives makes it mostly suitable to PL2 speech. A noun + *ne* sentence that requests confirmation (like the noun + *desu ne* sentence does in fig. 14) can be used by either gender, but the same type of sentence used as an exclamation, as in the example here, has a distinctly feminine ring; a male speaker would generally keep the *da* or *desu*.

16 This young mother is out walking her baby when she sees a sure sign of spring.

Mother : まあ、　ふきのとう。
Mā,　　　fukinotō.
(interj.)　butterbur sprouts
"Oh my! Butterburs!" (PL2)

春　ねえ。
Haru　nē,
spring　(is-colloq.)
"It really is spring!" (PL2)

© Hotta Katsuhiko. *Obatarian*, Take Shobō.

- *mā* is commonly used by women as an interjection of surprise. Men can use *mā* in other ways, but they sound very effeminate if they use it to express surprise.
- *fukinotō* ("butterburs") can be seen as a one-word exclamation here, but it can also be considered a noun-type sentence with *da/desu* omitted. Either gender can omit *da/desu* at the end of an exclamation.
- *Haru nē* is equivalent to *Haru da nē* ("It's spring, isn't it?"). The long *nē* shows strong feeling, like an exclamation. When *nē* is used in an exclamation, a male speaker would not normally drop the *da*.

☞ See p. 15 for a note on the masculine/feminine distinctions made in this book.

な *na*, a masculine *ne*

Both sexes use *ne* in both PL2 and PL3 speech, but male speakers often use *na* instead—especially in PL2 speech. There are other uses of *na* common to both genders, but it's mostly masculine to use it as the equivalent of a rhetorical tag question that expects or solicits agreement, like *ne* in fig. 14. One important difference: *na* cannot be used directly after a noun the way *ne* is used in fig. 16—whether as an exclamation or as a tag question/request for confirmation. It *can* follow directly after an adjective or a verb (for the latter, intonation must distinguish it from the negative command form introduced in fig. 403).

17 Section Head Shima Kōsaku of Hatsushiba Electric Co. has been transferred to a plant in Kyoto. Old friend Tanaka Tetsuo, who joined the company in the same year as Shima, comes to greet him.

Tanaka : よっ、　島。　　久しぶり　　だ　な。
Yo!,　Shima.　Hisashiburi　da　na.
hi/yo　(name)　first time in long time　is　(colloq.)
"Yo, Shima! It's the first time [we meet] in a long time, isn't it?"
"Yo, Shima! It's been a long time, hasn't it?" (PL2)

Shima : おお、　哲ちゃん!
Ō,　　Tet-chan!
hi/hey　(name-dimin.)
"Hey there, Tet-chan!" (PL2)

© Hirokane Kenshi. *Kachō Shima Kōsaku*, Kōdansha.

- *hisashiburi* is a noun that refers to something occurring for the first time in a long time. It's commonly used as a greeting when meeting someone you haven't seen in a while, like "Long time no see." The polite equivalent of the greeting is *Hisashiburi desu ne*; as a PL2 greeting, *Hisashiburi da ne* (both sexes) and *Hisashiburi ne* (feminine) also occur, as does *Hisashiburi* all by itself (both sexes).
- *-chan* is a diminutive equivalent of the polite title *-san* ("Mr./Ms.") that's attached to personal names (fig. 14). It's most typically used with and among children, but can also be used among close adult friends and family. It's commonly attached to just the first syllable or two of a name.

Na for emphasis

Using *na* (or an elongated *nā*) for emphasis rather than as a tag question is less limited to males; female speakers are likely to use it in informal situations, especially amongst themselves. But beginning students will do best to consider this use masculine as well.

18 One day in winter, Tanaka-kun calls in sick with a cold. The boss suspects his ever un-dependable employee is playing hooky.

Boss: あやしい 　なー。
Ayashii 　*nā*.
is suspicious (colloq. emph.)
"That sure sounds suspicious."
"Sounds pretty suspicious to me."
(PL2)

- *ayashii* is an adjective, so *na* connects directly to the plain form (no intervening *da*). The PL3 equivalent of this sentence is *Ayashii desu nē*.
- *-kun* is a more familiar/informal equivalent of *-san* ("Mr./Ms."); though it adds politeness, more often than not it feels a little too casual to be translated as "Mr." or "Ms." Among children and peers, it's mostly used for addressing or referring to males, but superiors at work typically use it for subordinates of both sexes. One should never use it with a superior; it's also never used with one's own name.

More specifically, the boss suspects Tanaka-kun has gone skiing—and he proves to be right. Tanaka-kun wears a full-face ski mask to avoid getting a telltale sunburn, but a broken ankle gives him away.

Tanaka-kun

よ *yo* gives authoritative emphasis

Yo is an emphatic particle used by both sexes. It usually has a gentle, friendly feeling, and that's the case with the examples included here; but in some situations, it can be spoken in a strongly argumentative or angry tone instead. One of its common uses is to emphasize information that the speaker thinks is new to the listener—especially when he thinks the listener particularly needs that information, as when giving a reminder or warning. Although it's used at all levels of politeness, this note of authority means it needs to be used with a certain amount of caution when speaking to your superiors—lest you inadvertently imply that you think your superior is stupid.

19 A heavenly aroma wafts through the air at a late autumn festival, and Kōsuke can't help following it to a booth selling toasty warm brown-rice buns.

Vender: あつい 　よ。
Atsui 　*yo*.
is hot 　(emph.)
"It's hot." (PL2)

FX: ほっほっ
Ho! ho!
(blowing on something hot)

- the adjective *atsui* in this case would be written with the kanji 熱い if kanji were used (fig. 15) ; the PL3 equivalent of this sentence is *Atsui desu yo*.

Situational authority

Although *yo* expresses authority, that authority is often determined more by the situation than by social status. In this example, it's the child who knows something the adult needs to be told, and his use of *yo* is entirely appropriate.

20 Shin-chan's mother has asked him to inform his napping father that dinner is on the table.

© Usui Yoshito. *Kureyon Shin-chan*, Futabasha.

Shin-chan: ごはん　だ　よー。
Gohan　da　yō.
meal/mealtime is (emph.)
"It is mealtime."
"It's time to eeeat!" (PL2)

Sound FX: くかー
Kukā
(effect of sleeping soundly)

• *gohan* means "cooked rice," but it is also the generic term for "meal." The PL3 equivalent of this sentence would be *Gohan desu yo*.

Asserting oneself

In many cases *yo* simply represents the speaker asserting himself a little more strongly than if he made his statement without *yo*, and does not imply any special authority. Here, *yo* is used in a verb-type sentence.

21 This *sarariiman* (from English "salary" and "man") and OL (from English "office" and "lady") are on a date, and he offers to escort her home at the end of the evening.

© Ueda Masashi. *Kariage-kun*, Futabasha.

Salaryman: 送る　よ。
Okuru　yo.
send (emph.)
"I'll see you home." (PL2)

OL: あら、ありがと。
Ara,　arigato.
(interj.) thanks
"Oh, thanks." (PL2)

• *okuru/okurimasu* literally means "send," and is used when sending mail, a package, money, etc. It's not used to speak of sending a person to do something, however; with people, it means "see/send [a person] off" or "escort [a person] home/someplace." The plain form of the verb is being used here for future tense, "will escort home." The PL3 equivalent of this sentence would be *Okurimasu yo*.
• *ara* is a feminine interjection, like "oh," and ありがとう *arigatō* is one of the most common ways to say "thank you"; shortening the final vowel gives it an informal, casual feeling.
• *sarariiman* and OL (pronounced *ō-eru*) refer to male and female office workers, respectively; OL more specifically refers to non–career track female workers who handle most secretarial and menial tasks around the office.

To compare using the verb from fig. 3, *Mitomeru ne?/mitomemasu ne?* (both genders) or *Mitomeru na?* (mostly masculine) means "You admit it, don't you?" or "He'll admit it, won't he?"; the speaker expects the listener to answer "yes," or to share the same feeling/impression about what will happen. By contrast, *Mitomeru yo/mitomemasu yo* asserts one's own position, "I admit it/I do admit it," or informs of someone else's, "He will admit it." For the adjective from fig. 12, *Muzukashii ne/muzukashii desu ne* (both genders) or *Muzukashii na* (mostly masculine) means "It's hard/difficult, isn't it?" and expects the listener's agreement, while *Muzukashii (desu) yo* asserts, "It's (too) hard," or informs, "It's hard, you know."

Yo without *da/desu*

In informal speech, noun-type sentences can end with just a noun + *yo*, omitting the intervening *da*. The kind of exclamatory use seen in this example is feminine; males would say *da yo* (or use *da* plus one of the masculine particles in figs. 25 and 26). But there are other cases where men can omit the *da* as well.

22 These high-school girls are on their way home from school when they see Michael the cat.

Girl: あっ！ 猫 よ。
    A! *Neko* *yo.*
    (interj.) cat (is-emph.)
    "Oh! It's a cat!"
    "Look! A cat!" (PL2)

- *a!* is an exclamation used when one suddenly notices or realizes something.
- a PL3 equivalent of this feminine sentence would be *Ara, neko desu yo*.

The feminine particle わ *wa*

Wa, pronounced with a slightly rising intonation, offers soft, feminine emphasis. Women use this particle a great deal in PL2 speech in order to soften the abruptness of the plain forms of verbs and adjectives, or of *da* at the end of noun-type sentences (which *cannot* be omitted when *wa* is used, the way it can with *ne* or *yo*); they also use it with the inherently much softer-feeling PL3 forms to add a note of femininity.

23 In an industry where women's involvement was traditionally considered taboo and still remains extremely rare, Natsuko is surprised to learn of a saké brewery not only headed by a woman but with a majority of women on its staff. She finds a quiet moment to taste their saké.

Natsuko: おいしい わ。
    Oishii *wa.*
    is tasty/delicious (fem.)
    "It's delicious." (PL2)

- the PL3 version of this sentence would be *Oishii desu wa*.

Usage note: The masculine/feminine distinctions made in this book are seldom, if ever, absolute—whether for particles or for other aspects of usage. Although it's true that women customarily use more polite forms than men (fig. 8), they routinely switch to more casual or even masculine forms when they are among friends and family; many women also adopt more masculine patterns as they grow older or rise to positions of authority. Men can often use feminine forms without sounding particularly effeminate, as well. Crossovers in both directions are generally more common in informal situations. Still, it's a good idea to observe the distinctions given here when you're first learning the language. Most particles are gender-neutral; you may assume they are unless noted otherwise.

Combining particles

You can't go around combining particles at random, but certain particles can be combined with certain others. The feminine *wa* can be combined with both *ne* and *yo*. In such combinations, *wa* always comes first.

24 Kōsuke is playing Othello with the proprietress of a soul music coffeehouse cum pub. If he wins, he gets a Morris White tape; if he loses, he washes dishes during pub time. As he contemplates his next move, a student part-timer arrives earlier than usual because of a cancelled class.

Student: オッス。
Ossu.
(greeting)
"Yo!" (PL2)

Mama: 早い わね。
Hayai | *wa ne.*
are fast/early (fem.-colloq.)
"You're early, aren't you?"
"You're early!" (PL2)

- *ossu* (or *osu*) is a very informal greeting, "Hey!/Yo!" used by males—especially young males.
- *hayai* is an adjective for both "fast/speedy" and "early." A male speaker here would say *Hayai ne* or *Hayai na* (without *wa*). In a polite situation, either sex would say *Hayai desu ne*; a woman might say *Hayai desu wa ne*.

ぞ *zo* gives assertive, masculine emphasis

Zo is an informal, mostly masculine particle that adds strongly assertive emphasis. It usually feels too rough for PL3 speech, so you generally hear it only in PL2 and PL1 speech. Saying that it's rough doesn't mean it necessarily feels belligerent or aggressive, though; when the situation is not contentious, it carries more a tone of familiarity.

Female speakers would use *zo* only in very informal situations, or when speaking to themselves.

25 While in New York on other business, Shima visits two aspiring female vocalists whom Sunlight Records sent there for voice training. They dine at a club suggested by their voice coach because of the singer who is on the bill there. The emcee has just stepped forward to announce the beginning of the show.

Shima: お、 始まる ぞ!
O, *hajimaru* *zo!*
(interj.) begin/will begin (emph.)
"Hey, [the show] will begin!"
"Hey, the show's going to start!" (PL2)

- *o* is an informal interjection used when suddenly noticing something, usually implying that the speaker is pleased or impressed.
- the polite form of *hajimaru* ("[something] begins") is *hajimarimasu*. This verb is only used to speak of something beginning; see the next example for the verb used when speaking of beginning something.
- neither the interjection *o* nor the particle *zo* is very common in polite speech, so the closest PL3 equivalent is perhaps *A, hajimarimasu yo!*

ぜ *ze* is also masculine

Ze is another particle that gives rough, masculine emphasis. Regarding use in PL3 speech and by female speakers, the same restrictions apply as for *zo*.

26 Kamiya is captain of the soccer team at Kakegawa High School. The freshmen have challenged the upperclassmen to a scrimmage in an effort to prove themselves worthy of being considered for the starting lineup.

Kamiya: 始める　ぜ。
Hajimeru　ze.
will begin　(emph.)
"We're going to begin."
"Let's get started." (PL2)

- *hajimeru/hajimemasu* means "begin [something]." Since *ze* is seldom used in PL3 speech, a polite equivalent of this sentence would be *Hajimemasu yo.*

PL2 noun-type sentences require *da*

As with the feminine particle *wa*, in PL2 noun-type sentences, *da* must be kept before *zo* and *ze*. It cannot be omitted.

27 Writer Matsuda turned down a lucrative one-day assignment in favor of going to a reunion of his grade-school class, hoping to see his former best friend there. When his friend Yamazaki fails to show, the disappointed Matsuda remembers how he had made Yamazaki promise to attend.

Matsuda: 絶対　だ　ぞ!!
Zettai　da　zo.
absoluteness　is　(emph.)
"This is absolute, I tell you."
"You absolutely have to come!" (PL2)

Yamazaki: うん。
Un.
"Uh-huh." (PL2)

- *zettai* is a noun referring to "absoluteness" or "absolute certainty." A PL3 equivalent of this sentence would be *Zettai desu yo.*
- *un* is an informal "yes," very much like English "uh-huh."

Summary: Sentence particles

The femine *wa* is used on the left to model how the sentence particles in this lesson link to the words they follow. You can replace *wa* with *ne, na, yo, zo,* and *ze*—though actual usage varies by politeness level, the speaker's gender, the particular word or form being used, the situation, and so forth. For *ne* and *yo* only, you can omit *da* in PL2 noun-type sentences; some such uses are mostly feminine.

☞ Whether a given word is written in kana, kanji, or a mix of the two (see table) makes no difference in its meaning or politeness level.

	verb-type sent.	adjective-type sent.	noun-type sent.	noun-type sent. (omit *da*)	
plain	かう　わ。 *Kau　wa.* will buy　(sent. part.) **"I'll buy one."**	ちいさい　わ。 *Chiisai　wa.* is small　(sent. part.) **"It's [too] small."**	あした　だ　わ。 *Ashita　da　wa.* tomorrow　is　(sent. part.) **"It's tomorrow."**	ほんとう　ね。 *Hontō　ne.* true/truth　(is-colloq.) **"It's true, isn't it."**	本当　よ。 *Hontō　yo.* true/truth　(is-emph.) **"It's true."**
polite	買います　わ。 *Kaimasu　wa.*	小さいです　わ。 *Chiisai desu　wa.*	明日　です　わ。 *Ashita　desu　wa.*		

Lesson 3

です *Desu* and -ます *-Masu*

A full rundown of the different forms that verbs, adjectives, and *desu* take will come later, so as not to muddle your introduction to the basic structure and building blocks of the language. But in polite speech, a few of the forms for verbs and *desu* are amazingly simple, so you might as well learn them right away.

The past form of *desu* is *deshita* (です → でした), which typically corresponds to "was/were" when used in noun-type sentences. (It's not considered good usage to follow an adjective with *deshita*. You'll learn the past form of adjectives in Lesson 18.)

28 In this gag strip based on life at the office, Section Chief Izumiya (on the left) has asked Uzuratani what his fielding position was when he played baseball in high school.

Uzuratani: サード でした。
Sādo deshita.
third was
"I was third baseman."
"I played third." (PL3)

Izumiya: ほう、 やる ねえ。
Hō, yaru nē.
(interj.) do (colloq.)
"Wow, you do [impressive things]."
"Wow, I'm impressed." (PL2)

• *sādo* is the Japanese rendering of English "third," and in the context of baseball always means "third base" or "third baseman," not third in the batting order. English *th* becomes *s* (unvoiced) or *z* (voiced) in Japanese.

© Ōhashi Tsuyoshi. Kaisha-in no Merodii, Take Shobō.

-ました *-mashita* = "did ～" or "～ed"

For any verb, regardless of type, its polite past form is made by changing *-masu* to *-mashita* (-ます → -ました). You can think of this as being like adding *-ed* to a verb to make it past tense in English—except that in Japanese the simple change in the ending works for *all* verbs, not just regular verbs. So long as you know the verb's *-masu* form, you can make this conversion (and the other polite-form conversions in this lesson) confidently for any verb in the language.

29 Natsuko (figs. 12, 23) is determined to fulfill her late brother's dream of bringing a legendary strain of rice back into cultivation, and starting with just 1350 seeds, she has overcome numerous difficulties to nurture her first small crop. Kusakabe has come to look at the paddy where the grain is almost ready to be harvested.

Kusakabe: がんばりました ね、 夏子 さん。
Ganbarimashita ne, Natsuko -san.
persevered/worked hard (colloq.) (name) Ms./Miss
"You persevered, didn't you, Miss Natsuko."
"You really stuck with it [and pulled it off], Miss Natsuko." (PL3)

• *ganbarimashita* is the polite past form of *ganbaru/ganbarimasu* ("persevere/work hard/give it one's all").

© Oze Akira. Natsuko no Sake, Kōdansha.

18

Japanese past is different from English past

Japanese handles time frames differently from English and does not have a past tense as English speakers know it. The form that's generally used to speak of past events doesn't actually imply past; it implies completion. Because speaking of past events and actions—that is, events and actions completed prior to the present moment—is one of that form's most important uses, it's called "past tense" or "the past form" for convenience. But it's important to remember that the way it's used won't always correspond exactly to past tense in English.

30 When Yagi expresses reservations about a cultural project because he thinks the city's demands will wipe out any advertising value for Hatsushiba Electric, he is surprised to hear his boss Shima (fig. 17) tell him not to worry so much about the bottom line.

Yagi: 島　　課長、　かわりました　ね。
Shima   *-kachō*   *kawarimashita*   *ne.*
(name) section head   changed   (colloq.)
"You've changed, Mr. Shima." (PL3)

- *kawarimashita* is the polite past form of the verb *kawaru/kawarimasu* ("[something] changes"). In this case the natural English equivalent is the "have/has ～" form rather than the simple past form.
- *ka* refers to a "section" within a company, and the suffix *-chō* indicates "head/leader," so what he's literally saying is "Section Head Shima" rather than "Mr. Shima."

31 In one of her first setbacks, Natsuko clutches the "Future site of..." signpost that had marked the rice paddy promised to her brother for growing the special crop (fig. 29). The owner has just explained why he can no longer let her use the paddy for that purpose:

Natsuko: わかりました。
Wakarimashita.
understood
"I see." (PL3)

- *wakarimashita* is the PL3 past form of *wakaru/wakarimasu*, which corresponds to English "understand/comprehend," or colloquial equivalents like "see/get/grasp/discern/follow"; in some of its forms it also overlaps with English uses of "know," and it often includes the meaning of "can"—i.e., "can understand/see/follow/know." The past form is used in a context like this because by the time the person speaks, the understanding is complete.

32 Hatsushiba Electric has hired a new driver for its racing team, and the crew is timing his laps on his first spin around the track. After a mediocre first lap, which they dismiss as a warm-up, they are eager to see the split time on his second lap.

Crew Member: お!　来ました　よ。
O!   *Kimashita*   *yo.*
(interj.)   came   (emph.)
"Hey! Here he comes!" (PL3)

- *kimashita* is the polite past form of the irregular verb *kuru/kimasu* ("come"). In PL3 speech, even the two irregular verbs (see table on p. 5) act exactly the same as all other verbs.

In other contexts, any of these verbs could of course be translated very naturally as simple past tense English verbs, but in these contexts they cannot. Since the right equivalent depends on the exact nature of the verb as well as the context and the differences in how time frames are handled, no simple rule can be laid out for you to follow. You just need to be aware of the differences so you will be prepared to encounter them.

-ません -masen = "doesn't/don't ～"

For any verb, its polite negative form is made by changing -masu to -masen (-ます → -ません). In this example, the negative form is equivalent to a present-tense negative verb in English: "doesn't/don't [do the action]."

33 Kakegawa High (fig. 26) is trailing by a point when crack defender Kubo takes the ball and charges down the field, leaving his usual backfield position and dribbling past one opponent after another. As his teammates watch, he keeps on going even after he crosses the center line.

Play-by-play: 止まりませんー!!
Tomarimasen!!
not stop
"He still doesn't stop!!" (PL3)

- *tomarimasen* is the PL3 negative form of *tomaru/tomarimasu* ("[something] stops/halts"). To say "stop [something]" requires a different verb, *tomeru/tomemasu*.
- lenthening *n* is nonstandard; normally only vowels are lengthened, but the artist uses the long mark here to intensify the exclamation.

-Masen = "won't ～"

The -masen form of a verb is non-past, so it is used for both present ("doesn't/don't [do the action]") and future tense ("won't [do the action]"). Here is an example of its use for future tense:

34 The aging brewmaster at the Saeki Brewery is in failing health. His wife explains to Natsuko what the doctor has told her—that the exertions of another season on the job are likely to kill her husband. But she says she can't bring herself to stop him because she knows how much he has been counting on brewing saké with the legendary Tatsunishiki rice Natsuko has cultivated (fig. 29). She asks Natsuko not to tell him what the doctor has said.

Mrs. Brewmaster

言いません

Natsuko: 言いません。
Iimasen.
won't tell
"I won't tell him." (PL3)

- *iimasen* is the PL3 negative form of *iu/iimasu* ("say/speak/tell"); *iu* is pronounced *yū*.

Here are the polite negative forms of several of the other verbs you've already seen:

行きません。	来ません。	かわりません。	わかりません。
Ikimasen.	*Kimasen.*	*Kawarimasen.*	*Wakarimasen.*
not go	not come	not change	not understand/know
"I won't go."	**"They won't come."**	**"It doesn't change."**	**"I don't understand."**

-ませんでした *-masen deshita* = "didn't ～"

For any verb, its polite negative-past form is made by changing *-masu* to *-masen deshita* (-ます → -ませんでした). You will recognize *deshita* as the past form of *desu* ("is/are"), but in this case it serves only to change the tense; it does not add the meaning of the verb "to be."

35 A young reporter from the *Dainichi News* and a secretary in the Prime Minister's Office, who were having an affair, have just been arrested for leaking classified information. *Dainichi's* editor-in-chief asks editorial board members if any of them had prior knowledge of what was going on.

Noda: 知りません　でした。
　　　Shirimasen　　deshita.
　　　not know　　　(past)
　　　"I didn't know about it." (PL3)

Name: 野田　　　　編集局長
　　　Noda　　　henshūkyoku-chō
　　　(surname)　　executive editor
　　　Executive Editor Noda

- *shirimasen deshita* is the PL3 negative-past form of *shiru/shirimasu*. Strictly speaking, this verb means "come to know/learn/find out," but in several of its forms it corresponds to English "know"; its negative form means "not know" rather than "not learn."
- *henshūkyoku* = "editorial board," and the suffix *-chō* means "head/leader"; the correspondence between Japanese and English job titles is seldom exact, but *henshūkyoku-chō* can be considered roughly equivalent to "executive editor."

-ましょう *-mashō* = "let's/I shall/I think I'll ～"

If you change the *-masu* form of a Japanese verb to *-mashō* (-ます → -ましょう), you get a form that expresses intention/determination or a decision to do the action, like "Let's [do the action]" (when the speaker and at least one other person will act together) or "I will/I shall/I think I'll [do the action]" (when the speaker will act alone, in many cases doing something for the listener). Since the form implies a willful decision, not all verbs make sense in this form.

36 Just after Kusakabe has congratulated Natsuko on the impending harvest of her Tatsunishiki crop (fig. 29), she discovers a tiny insect on one of the stalks—and then on countless others. She takes one to the retired farmer who is advising her, and he confirms that the insects could ruin the crop. Natsuko remains determined not to use any chemicals, so she decides to at least remove as many of the insects as she can by hand. Kusakabe offers to help.

Kusakabe: 行きましょう、　夏子さん。
　　　　　Ikimashō,　　　Natsuko-san.
　　　　　let's go　　　　(name-pol.)
　　　　　"Let's go, Miss Natsuko." (PL3)

　　　　　手伝います。
　　　　　Tetsudaimasu.
　　　　　will help
　　　　　"I'll help." (PL3)

- *ikimashō* is the PL3 "let's/I'll ～" form of *iku/ikimasu* ("go").
- among people who are on familiar terms, the polite suffix *-san* ("Mr./Ms."; fig. 14) can be used with given names as well as family names. The feeling can still be quite casual, so it is not always like using "Miss/ Master" with first names in English, but Kusakabe's consistent deference toward his employer's daughter seems to call for such treatment.
- *tetsudaimasu* is the PL3 form of *tetsudau* ("help/will help"). The understood subject is "I."

でしょう *deshō* = "probably/surely is"

Desu can also be given a *-shō* ending, making *deshō* (です → でしょう). But it has a very different meaning from *-mashō* so it's important to keep the distinction clear in your mind. *Deshō* essentially expresses a guess—"is maybe/probably/surely [the stated thing]"; usually the speaker has some evidence/reason for what he is saying but is not certain enough about it to state it with the more categorical *desu* ("is/are"). You'll learn more about this form as well as its plain equivalent in Lesson 26.

37 The proprietor of Lemon Hart is getting ready to close up shop one night when a young guitarist comes in. As the guitarist studies the bottles on the wall behind the bar, the proprietor says he'd like to try guessing what the customer wants to drink.

バーボンでしょう

© Furuya Mitsutoshi. *Bar Remon Hāto*, Futabasha.

Proprietor: バーボン でしょう。
Bābon ・ *deshō.*
bourbon ・ is probably
"It's probably bourbon."
Bourbon, I bet. (PL3)

Summary: *Desu* and *-masu*

Here's a quick reference table for the new forms introduced in this lesson, followed by a table listing each of those forms for a few of the verbs you have seen. Practice the conversions by hiding all but the first column with a sheet of paper, referring as necessary to the quick reference table.

☞ The negative forms of *desu* are introduced in Lesson 21.

	kana	romaji	form (meaning)
desu	です	*desu*	non-past ("is/are/will be")
	でした	*deshita*	past ("was/were")
	でしょう	*deshō*	guess ("probably/surely is")
-masu	-ます	*-masu*	non-past ("do/does/will do")
	-ました	*-mashita*	past ("did do")
	-ません	*-masen*	negative ("don't/doesn't/won't do")
	-ませんでした	*-masen deshita*	negative-past ("didn't do")
	-ましょう	*-mashō*	determination ("let's/I'll/I think I'll do")

non-past	past	negative	negative-past	"let's/I'll ～"
たのみます *tanomimasu* request	たのみました *tanomimashita* requested	たのみません *tanomimasen* doesn't/won't request	頼みませんでした *tanomimasen deshita* didn't request	頼みましょう *tanomimashō* let's request
いきます *ikimasu* go	いきました *ikimashita* went	いきません *ikimasen* doesn't/won't go	行きませんでした *ikimasen deshita* didn't go	行きましょう *ikimashō* let's go
きます *kimasu* come	きました *kimashita* came	きません *kimasen* doesn't/won't come	来ませんでした *kimasen deshita* didn't come	来ましょう *kimashō* let's come
たべます *tabemasu* eat	たべました *tabemashita* ate	たべません *tabemasen* doesn't/won't eat	食べませんでした *tabemasen deshita* didn't eat	食べましょう *tabemashō* let's eat
かいます *kaimasu* buy	かいました *kaimashita* bought	かいません *kaimasen* doesn't/won't buy	買いませんでした *kaimasen deshita* didn't buy	買いましょう *kaimashō* let's buy
はじめます *hajimemasu* begin	はじめました *hajimemashita* began	はじめません *hajimemasen* doesn't/won't begin	始めませんでした *hajimemasen deshita* didn't begin	始めましょう *hajimemashō* let's begin

Interjections

Interjections often occur at the beginning of a sentence, and they can telegraph a great deal about the speaker's frame of mind and where the sentence is going.

In fig. 38, Sayuri's *ā* is in effect a fully voiced sigh; it can express fatigue/weariness as well as dismay/woe, so if you happened to be with her, you would probably know she's tired even before

38 High schooler Sayuri is trying to study, but she's having a tough time keeping her eyes open. She decides to turn on the radio and reaches for the switch.

Sayuri:

あー、	ねむい	なあ。
Ā,	*nemui*	*nā.*
(interj.)	am sleepy	(emph.)

"Darn, I'm so sleepy." (PL2)

Sound FX:
パチ
Pachi
Click (radio switch)

- *nemui* is an adjective for "sleepy."
- as noted at fig. 18, using *nā* for emphasis is not limited to males.

she says she's sleepy. *Sā* in fig. 39 can be used either like "well now/all right" as you yourself move into action, or like "come on" to urge your listener to action, so it expresses Mrs. Nohara's eagerness to get into the pool.

In real life, much of what an interjection conveys is in the speaker's tone and inflection, so you can often get an instant feel for what the word means even if it's your first encounter. In a book, where you can't hear the speaker's voice, you have to rely on the rest of the sentence and the context to help you get a feel for the word's usage and tone.

For the most part, you can simply learn interjections as they come up. But it's worth taking a quick look at a somewhat arbitrary selection here, with special emphasis on those that can have several different meanings or forms.

- besides being a sigh of dismay/woe ("Rats!/Darn!") as in fig. 38, an elongated *ā* can be a sigh of pleasure (as, for example, when you're sinking deep into a hot tub). It's also used when listening, to indicate that you're following what the speaker is saying; and male speakers use it as an informal "yeah." A short *a!* (for female speakers, also *ara!*) expresses surprise or sudden awareness/recognition/recollection, like "Oh!"; it also serves as an informal greeting when you run into someone on the street, like "Oh, hi!"
- *are?*, *ara?* (feminine), and *arya* express surprise or uncertainty/bewilderment at something unexpected.
- an elongated *ē* can mean "yes"; it can be a warm-up word like "well/let's see" (in this case it often becomes *ē to*); or it may simply be a hesitation sound, like "uh/umm." A short *e?* with the intonation of a question (see next page) implies the speaker did not hear clearly ("Huh?/What?"); or if he did hear clearly, that he is surprised or puzzled by what he has heard. An elongated *ē?* with the intonation of a question suggests even greater surprise or shock/disbelief.

- *hai* is a more formal "yes" than *ē*, *un* is less formal (like "uh-huh"), and *sō*, *ā*, *hā*, and *ha!* are some other ways to express the same meaning. A key difference from English "yes" is that all these words confirm the previous statement, so if they are spoken in response to a negative statement, they wind up being equivalent to "no" in English. (Q: "You won't eat?" A: "Yes [I won't].")
- *hai* is also used like "here" when handing something to someone, as well as when responding to a roll call (but it doesn't mean "here" in other situations).
- *iie* is a formal "no" (the counterpart to *hai*), and *iya* is a less formal equivalent. Again, there's a key difference from English "no": the basic meaning of these words is to contradict the previous statement, so they can wind up being equivalent to "yes" in English. (Q: "You won't eat? A: "No [I will].")
- *iya* is also often used merely as a hesitation or warm-up word like "well" or "I mean," without any sense of negation; an elongated *iyā* may simply represent a longer hesitation/warm-up, or it can introduce an exclamation.
- *mā!* spoken as an exclamation is a feminine expression of surprise, whether of alarm or delight: "Oh my!/My goodness!/Dear me!" Spoken more evenly by either sex, *mā* or *ma* can be like "now/come now" when urging the listener to do something; it can show a degree of reservation/reluctance/uncertainty about what the speaker is saying; it can be used to "soften" the expression of an opinion; or it can be a warm-up or pause word that adapts quite broadly to fit the context: "I mean/you know/really/anyway/of course."
- *ne* and *nē* are often used to get someone's attention; male speakers also use *na* or *nā* for the same purpose.
- *o!* expresses surprise or sudden awareness, with an approving tone; a long *ō!* is an exclamation of approval or amazement.
- *oi* is an abrupt "Hey!" or "Yo!" to get someone's attention; a long *ōi* gets the attention of someone farther away.
- *otto* is like "oops," when the speaker realizes he has just made a mistake, or is on the verge of making a mistake; variations include *ototo*, *ottotto*, *tototo*.
- *sā* as used in fig. 39 shows readiness for action, but in reply to a question it expresses uncertainty or ignorance about the answer: "Hmm/It's hard to say/I don't know."

39 Mrs. Nohara has brought Shin-chan to the city pool. As usual the precocious boy causes one delay after another in the dressing room, but now everything is finally under control.

Mrs. Nohara:

さあ、	泳ぐ	ぞ。
Sā	*oyogu*	*zo.*
all right	will swim	(emph.)

"All right, we're [finally] going to swim."
"All right! Let's swim!" (PL2)

- *oyogu/oyogimasu* means "swim/will swim," so she literally only says "I/we will swim," with emphasis. But the context makes "Let's swim!" an appropriate equivalent. In PL3 speech she might well have said *Sā, oyogimashō!* in this situation (see fig. 36).
- *zo* is a mostly masculine particle for emphasis, but female speakers can use it as well in informal situations.
- naturally, it begins to pour down rain in the very next frame.

Lesson 4

Simple Questions with か *Ka*

In Japanese, a sentence can be turned into a yes-or-no question simply by putting the sentence particle か *ka* at the end. There's no need to switch words around or add helping words like "do" or "did" the way English requires. All you have to do is put *ka* at the end—like a verbal question mark. (You'll learn about using question words like "what?" and "who?" in Lesson 17.)

Ka usually replaces other sentence particles, but it can also be used in combination with *ne* or *yo*—in which case it comes immediately after the verb, adjective, or *desu* and before *ne* or *yo*. Also, except in special instances involving indirect questions, *ka* is not added to *da* in a PL2 noun-type question; it replaces *da* instead, as seen in this example:

40 Shima is passing through the hotel lobby after a meeting with some clients when he runs into his ex-wife. He has not seen her in quite some time.

Shima: 元気 <u>か？</u>
Genki | *ka?*
well/healthy | (?)
"Are you well?"
"How've you been?" (PL2)

- *genki* is a noun referring to good spirits and/or to a vigorous state of health/energy. The question *Genki ka?* (PL2) or *Genki desu ka?* (PL3)—literally, "Are you well?"—often serves as the equivalent of "How are you?/How have you been?"

The question of intonation

Plain declarative sentences in Japanese end with the last few syllables at a low pitch, and the final syllable even lower. Questions, on the other hand, are asked with a rising intonation as in English. But there's an important difference: in English, the rising pitch often spans several words at the end of a sentence; in Japanese it occurs only on the final syllable. (The *ne* used for rhetorical tag questions [fig. 14] is also spoken with a slightly rising intonation, but not as much as with *ka*). Here's another example of a noun-type question—this one in PL3 form.

41 Division Head Nakazawa, Shima's boss and strongest ally within Hatsushiba Electric Co., has been picked to join the board of directors. Nakazawa has just told Shima.

Shima: え？ 本当 です <u>か？</u>
Ē? | *Hontō* | *desu* | *ka?*
(interj.) | truth/true | is | (?)
"What? Is that the truth?"
"What? Is that true?" (PL3)

- *e?* spoken with the rising intonation of a question expresses surprise: "What?/Really?" It can also be elongated for stronger effect ranging from pleasant surprise to dismay/protest.
- strictly speaking, *hontō* is a noun for "truth," but followed by *da/desu* it most frequently corresponds to the English adjective "true." Without *ka* on the end, *Hontō desu* is the simple PL3 statement "It is true." The PL2 equivalent of this statement is *Hontō da*; the PL2 question, *Hontō ka?* (*da* is replaced by *ka*).

The subject is often "you"

Obviously it depends on what the speaker is talking about, but a good first guess for the subject of a question is the listener ("you"), just as a good first guess for the subject of a declarative statement is the speaker ("I"). The listener is the subject in the verb-type question seen here:

42 Bonobono the **sea** otter takes Chipmunk to see Fishing Cat, and they find him catching fish for his dinner. When he lands one, he eats half of it himself and offers the other half to his visitors.

Fishing Cat: 喰う か?
Kuu *ka?*
eat (?)
"Will you eat it?"
"Want the rest?" (PL2)

Bonobono: うん。
Un.
"Uh-huh." (PL2)

- *kuu* is an informal, masculine word for "eat"; since the word is inherently informal, it's not very often heard in its polite form, *kuimasu*, but the equivalent question in PL3 speech would be *Kuimasu ka?* The gender-neutral equivalent for "eat" is *taberu/tabemasu*, and the same question using that verb would be *Taberu ka?* (**PL2**) and *Tabemasu ka?* (**PL3**).

The form of the verb makes no difference

The question particle *ka*, like all other sentence particles, can be added to any form of the verb—the polite, past, negative, and "let's/I'll ～" forms, as well as others you will learn in the second half of this book. Here's an example using a polite past verb:

43 When the chairman of the board of Hatsushiba Electric died recently, the president took over as chairman and one of two vice presidents on the board became president. Now these reporters are waiting in the press room while the board meets to fill the vacancy. Suddenly the door opens.

Sound FX: ガチャ
Gacha
(rattle of door knob/latch)

Sound FX: ガタタッ
Gatata!
(clatter of chairs as reporters leap to their feet)

Reporter: 決まりました か?
Kimarimashita *ka?*
decided (?)
"Was [the new VP] decided?"
"Has the new VP been chosen?" (PL3)

- *kimaru/kimarimasu* is the verb used to say "[something] is decided" or "a decision occurs" and *kimarimashita* is its PL3 past form. The verb for "[someone] decides [something]" is *kimeru/kimemasu*. There are a number of verb pairs in Japanese that have similar sounds (sometimes only a single vowel sound differs) and closely related meanings. See figs. 25, 26, and 33 for other pairs; *kawaru/kawarimasu* ("[something] changes") in fig. 30 also has a counterpart, *kaeru/kaemasu* ("change [something]").

An adjective-type question

In informal speech, *ka* follows directly after the plain, dictionary form of an adjective as it does with the plain form of a verb: *Muzukashii ka*? = "Is it difficult?" In polite speech it follows *desu* as it does with a polite noun-type question: *Muzukashii desu ka*? Here's an example of a polite adjective-type question:

44 This TV reporter is covering the new trend in "surfing" this summer. Young people are taking their surfboards to the man-made beach and spending the day on the gentle waves there, soaking up the rays.

Reporter: 楽しい です か?
Tanoshii *desu* *ka?*
is fun (pol.) (?)
"Is it fun?"
"Are you having fun?" (PL3)

Surfer: ほっといて くれ よ。
Hottoite *kure* *yo.*
leave be please (emph.)
"Leave me alone." (PL2)

© Deluxe Company. *Zusetsu Gendai Yōgo Binran*, Futabasha.

- *tanoshii* is an adjective meaning "fun/enjoyable." The PL2 equivalent of this question is *Tanoshii ka?*— though, as noted in the next example, women would normally drop the *ka* and just say *Tanoshii?*
- *hottoite* is a contraction of *hōtte oite*, which comes from *hōtte oku/okimasu* ("leave be"). You will learn about the *-te* form and some expressions that use it in Lessons 19, 25 and 31.

Omitting *ka*

In colloquial speech, *ka* is in fact often omitted, and the question is expressed simply by raising the intonation—just like "You will" in English can be turned into the question "You will?" For example, *Samui ka?* → *Samui?* ("Are you cold?"). The omission occurs among speakers of either gender; for females it can be considered pretty much the norm, since *ka* feels quite abrupt and unfeminine in PL2 speech. *Ka* can also be dropped from PL3 verb-type questions—*Ikimasu ka?* → *Ikimasu?*("Will you go?")—but not PL3 noun- or adjective-type questions. The PL3 usage is mostly feminine.

45 An OL with time on her hands approaches a coworker with a cat's cradle.

OL: できる?
Dekiru?
can do/be able to do
"Can you do this?" (PL2)

© Ueda Masashi. *Furiten-kun*, Take Shobō.

- the polite form of *dekiru* is *dekimasu*. The PL3 equivalent of this question would be *Dekimasu?* The question is indicated solely by a rising intonation on the last syllable.

46 Yamamoto Makio, the head of Kaji Ryūsuke's election committee in his run for the House of Representatives, has just been told that Kaji's brother was seen taking some pills at a banquet the night he fell asleep at the wheel and killed both his father and himself.

Yamamoto: 錠剤? 確か か?
Jōzai? *Tashika* *ka?*
pill(s)? certainty (?)
"Pills? Is it a certainty?"
"Pills? Are you sure?" (PL2)

© Hirokane Kenshi. *Kaji Ryūsuke no Gi*, Kōdansha.

- in the first sentence, the noun alone is spoken with the intonation of a question on the final syllable. In this case, the equivalent PL3 question would have to include *ka*: *Jōzai desu ka?*
- *tashika* is a noun meaning "certainty," but in actual use it often corresponds to the English adjectives "certain" and "sure."

Rhetorical questions

Since *ka* can be omitted in this way, you could say that what really makes a sentence into a question in colloquial speech is the rising intonation. In fact, without that rising intonation, even using *ka* does not make a true question—only a rhetorical one. In the examples on this page, the intonation would be flat or falling on the last syllable. The implied answer to the rhetorical question depends on the context.

47 The man who came in from shoveling snow in fig. 11 has warmed up. He has had dinner and taken a bath and is now ready for bed.

Man: さーて、　寝る　かー。
Sāte,　　　neru　　kā.
(interj.) sleep/go to sleep (?)
"Well then, shall I go to sleep? [Yes I shall.]"
"Well then, I think I'll get to bed." (PL2)

- *sate* or *sāte* is an interjection used when the speaker is about to do something, like "well now/well then."
- the polite form of *neru* ("go to sleep/bed") is *nemasu*.
- when the implied answer to the rhetorical question is affirmative, as here, it's essentially like saying "Is it ～? Yes, it certainly is ～" (in the case of nouns and adjectives), or "Will/shall I ～? Yes, I certainly will/shall ～" (in the case of a verb).

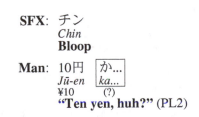

48 Sayū asks one of his coworkers to look at a growth on his face, and then wants to know this:

Sayū: しぬ？
Shinu?
die?
"Will I die?" (PL2)

Coworker: しぬ　かっ！
Shinu　ka!
die　　(?)
"Will you die? [Hardly!]"
"Don't be ridiculous!" (PL2)

- the polite form of *shinu* ("die") is *shinimasu*. Note that Sayū's question is a genuine question, indicated by his intonation even though he does not use *ka*.
- the coworker's question is rhetorical; when the implied answer to a rhetorical question is negative, as here, it is essentially like saying "Is it/will you ～? Hardly!" → "Don't be ridiculous/Give me a break!"
- the small *tsu* after *ka* indicates that the coworker says it very sharply/forcefully.

49 At the cash register, this man asked the clerk to scan his comb-over with the handheld barcode scanner.

SFX: チン
Chin
Bloop

Man: 10円　か...
Jū-en　ka...
¥10　　(?)
"Ten yen, huh?" (PL2)

- ¥ is the symbol for the Japanese monetary unit, "yen." In recent years, ¥10 has been roughly eqivalent to a dime.
- here the *ka* makes a rhetorical tag question: "So it's ～, is it?" As in this case, the form is often used to express disappointment—though it can also be a more neutral response to (or acknowledgement of) whatever the speaker has learned.

A colloquial variant: かい *kai*

In colloquial speech, *kai* is sometimes used instead of *ka* to mark a question. Most commonly it has a softer, friendlier feeling than the abrupt *ka*, but the right tone of voice in a contentious situation can make it even more forceful than *ka*.

50 Kōsuke notices a vintage suitcase, sturdy and well cared for, sitting in front of a resale shop, and he picks it up to see how it feels in his hand. The shopkeeper knows Kōsuke from before and invites him in for a cup of coffee. As Kōsuke continues to admire the suitcase, the shopkeeper says:

Shopkeeper: 買う かい?
    Kau *kai?*
    buy (?)
    "Will you buy it?"
    "Wanna buy it?" (PL2)

Kōsuke: えっ?
   E!?
   huh?/what?
   "Huh?" (PL2)

- the polite form of *kau* ("buy") is *kaimasu*.
- a short *e?* spoken with the rising intonation of a question expresses mild surprise, like "Huh?/What?/Oh?" It's also used when you're not sure you heard clearly.

Questions with かな *ka na*

The particle combination *ka na* implies something of a guess. After a noun or adjective-type sentence, it's like "Is he/she/it perhaps ~?" or "I wonder if he/she/it is ~." After a verb-type sentence it's like "Does/will he perhaps [do the action]?" or "I wonder if he [does/will do the action]?" This usage can be considered mostly informal and somewhat masculine (fig. 52 shows the feminine equivalent). In polite speech, guesses tend to be expressed in other ways.

51 Kōsuke wakes up with a leaden feeling in his head and sneezes when he looks out the window. Lying back down on the *tatami* (the traditional Japanese floor covering of thick, firm straw mats covered with a woven rush facing), he wonders if he's coming down with a cold.

Kōsuke:
カゼ かな?
Kaze *ka na?*
a cold is it perhaps?/I wonder
"Is it perhaps a cold?"
"I wonder if I've caught a cold." (PL2)

FX:
グズグズ
Guzu guzu
(effect of feeling stuffed up/groggy)

- *kaze* refers only to the kind of cold you catch. *Samui* means "cold" when talking about weather/climate/ambient temperature and how you might feel all over (fig. 11); *tsumetai* means "cold" when talking about drinks, food, something cold to the touch, or how a particular part of your body (hands, feet, etc.) feels.
- there is also a homonym *kaze* that means "wind" (fig. 317), but the context tells us that's not the meaning here.

Questions with かしら *kashira*

Women can use *ka na* informally and when alone, but if they want to sound feminine, they use *kashira* instead. Like *ka na*, this particle can be used with polite forms, but it's mostly informal; in polite speech, other forms tend to be used to suggest a guess or uncertainty.

52 Kōsuke decided to try eating a raw egg the way his uncle once showed him—by sucking it out through a small hole in one end. Hiroko, his artistically inclined girlfriend, has just finished drawing a face on the empty shell with a felt-tipped pen.

Hiroko: 立つ　かしら?
Tatsu　*kashira?*
will stand　I wonder
"I wonder if it'll stand."
(PL2)

- the polite form of *tatsu* is *tachimasu*. *Tatsu ka?* (PL2, masculine), *Tatsu?* (PL2) and *Tachimasu ka?* (PL3) simply ask, "Will it stand?" Using *kashira* makes it "I wonder if it will stand?"; the masculine equivalent of this PL2 question is *Tatsu ka na?*

Summary: Simple questions

For quick reference, here are some model questions showing how *ka*, *ka na*, and *kashira* (the latter two imply an element of guesswork) are added to each of the three types of sentences.

		verb-type question		adjective-type question		noun-type question	
plain		いく *Iku*	か?[1] *ka?*	遠い *Tōi*	か?[1] *ka?*	かじ *Kaji*	か?[1] *ka?*
polite		行きます *Ikimasu* will go **"Will you go?"**	か?[2] *ka?* (?)	とおいです *Tōi desu* is far/distant **"Is it far?"**	か?[2] *ka?* (?)	火事です *Kaji desu* fire　is **"Is it a fire?"**	か?[2] *ka?* (?)
masc.		来る *Kuru*	かな? *ka na?*	たかい *Takai*	かな? *ka na?*	本当 *Hontō*	かな? *ka na?*
fem.		くる *Kuru* will come **"I wonder if she'll come?"**	かしら? *kashira?* I wonder if	高い *Takai* is expensive **"I wonder if they're expensive?"**	かしら? *kashira?* I wonder if	ほんとう *Hontō* truth **"I wonder if it's true?"**	かしら? *kashira?* I wonder if it is

[1] In PL2 speech, female speakers would normally omit *ka* and express the question by intonation alone.

[2] In PL3 speech, *ka* can be omitted only for verb-type questions; doing so is mostly feminine.

A note on the question mark: Since *ka* serves quite well all by itself to indicate questions, Japanese writers did not traditionally feel the need for a separate question mark symbol. In recent times, though, manga artists and other writers have found the familiar "?" imported from the West handy when writing colloquial dialogue in which questions are asked without *ka*, and many append it even when *ka* is used. For the sake of consistency and as an aid to the learner, the transcriptions in this book include question marks for all true questions.

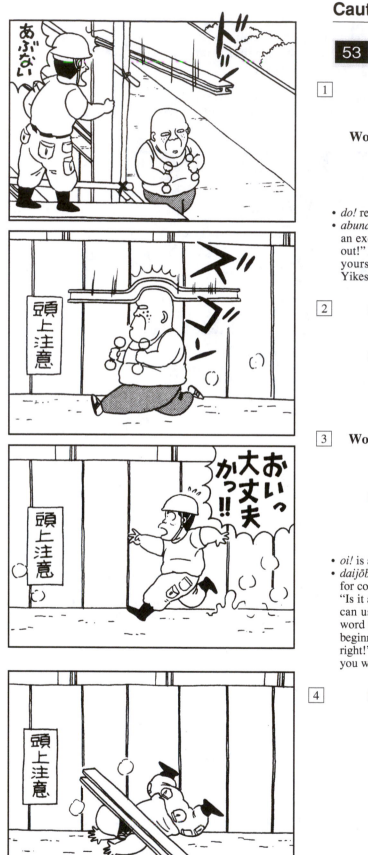

Caution: Falling objects

53 Here's a complete strip from the four-frame, gag manga series *Ojama Shimasu* ("Pardon the Intrusion").

1 **FX**: ドッ
Do!
Zoom

Worker: あぶない!
Abunai!
is dangerous
"It's dangerous!"
"Look out!" (PL2)

- *do!* represents the effect of something large/heavy moving rapidly.
- *abunai* is an adjective meaning "dangerous/perilous." When spoken as an exclamation directed at another person, it's equivalent to "Watch out!" It can also be used as a half-spoken exclamation when you catch yourself on the verge of an accident or mistake ("Oops!/Oh no!/ Yikes!") or having barely escaped one ("That was close!").

2 **SFX**: ズゴン
Zugon
Klonggg

Sign: 頭上　　注意
Zujō　　Chūi
overhead　caution
Watch out overhead
Caution: Falling objects

3 **Worker**: おいっ!　大丈夫　かっ?!
Oi!　　Daijōbu　ka?!
(interj.)　all right/safe　(?)
"Hey! Are you all right?" (PL2)

Sign: 頭上　　注意
Zujō　　Chūi
overhead　caution
Caution: Falling objects

- *oi!* is an abrupt/rough "Hey!" or "Yo!" for getting someone's attention.
- *daijōbu* means "all right/okay" in the sense of "safe and secure/no cause for concern." Using it as a question implies there is cause for concern: "Is it all right/safe?" or "Are you all right?" But don't get the idea you can use *daijōbu* anytime you'd say "all right/okay" in English. The word is *not* used to express willingness ("Okay, I'll do it"), nor when beginning an action ("All right, here goes"), nor as an exclamatory "All right!" when you win the lottery or hit a home run (see fig. 140 for what you would exclaim instead).

4 **Sign**: 頭上　　注意
Zujō　　Chūi
overhead　caution
Caution: Falling objects

Existence

Japanese has two verbs for saying "exist(s)." When speaking of people and other animate things, いる／います *iru/imasu* is used, while ある／あります *aru/arimasu* is the rule when speaking of inanimate things and plants.

In addition to speaking of whether someone or something exists at all, these words are used to speak of whether something or someone exists in a particular place (i.e., "is present/is here/is there") or in someone's possession (i.e., "[I/they] possess/have" or "[he/she] possesses/has"). The place where the thing or person/animal exists is marked with the particle に *ni*. (You'll learn more about *ni* and other phrase particles in Lesson 13.)

When *aru* is used to speak of the existence of events, the meaning often becomes "[an event] occurs/will occur."↗

The location of the event is marked with the particle で *de*. But one important note: there is also a formal/literary form of *desu* that takes the form of *de aru* and *de arimasu*; when *de* comes immediately before *aru/arimasu* in this way, it is usually a form of *desu* (i.e., it means "am/is/are") rather than the location particle *de* plus the verb for "exist(s)/occurs(s)."

Iru and *aru* also play important roles as helper verbs. You'll learn about those uses in Lessons 19 and 25.

54 A student suffering from insomnia comes into the bar Lemon Hart and asks for some warm milk. Learning that he also has an upset stomach, a fellow customer recommends he try an alcoholic drink that he says will both settle his stomach and foster sound sleep. "Does such a drink exist?" the student asks. The proprietor answers:

Student

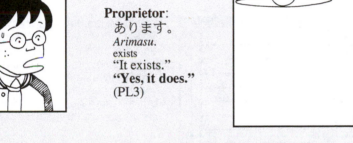

Proprietor:
あります。
Arimasu.
exists
"It exists."
"Yes, it does."
(PL3)

55 Another evening, Matsuda learns that the bar Lemon Hart was named after a brand of rum. He is curious.

Matsuda:
ここ　に　ある　の?
Koko ni aru no?.
here in/at exists/have (explan.-?)
"Do you have some [of that rum] here?" (PL2)

Proprietor:
あります。
Arimasu.
exists/have
"I have some."
"Yes." (PL3)

- *ni* marks the place of existence—in this case, the place where he's asking whether something exists.
- for using *no* to ask an informal question, see Lesson 8.

The proprietor says exactly the same thing in both of the above examples, but in the first case he is stating whether something exists at all, while in the second he is stating whether something exists in his possession/proximity. Because he is talking about beverages, which are inanimate, he uses *arimasu*; he cannot use *imasu*. The following example, on the other hand, requires *iru* or *imasu* because Saeko is asking about the presence of a person.

56 Saeko came running to tell Natsuko that her rice crop is starting to form ears of grain.

Sound FX: ハァハァハァハァ
Hā hā hā hā
(effect of breathing hard)

Saeko: あの、　夏子さん、　います?
Ano, Natsuko-san, imasu?
(interj.) (name-pol.) exists/is present
"Um, is Miss Natsuko here?" (PL3)

- *ano* or *anō* is a warm-up/hesitation word similar to "uhh/um."

Lesson 5

Doing Things with する *Suru*

You could call する *suru* the single most important verb in Japanese. It's one of just two irregular verbs, and its polite form is *shimasu*. The word basically means "do," but it is used in countless special expressions and two-word verb combinations where it often corresponds more closely to English words like "occur," "make," "have," "feel," "go," "change," and still others.

Suru can be added to many nouns to turn them into verbs, commonly referred to as **suru verbs**. Most often, the word is added to a noun that refers to an action or activity, and it creates a verb meaning "do that action/activity"; sometimes it can be added to other kinds of nouns, in which case the meaning becomes "do the action associated with that noun." For example, *dorobō* is a noun that can mean either "thief" or "thievery," so *dorobō suru* makes the verb for "steal"; *kakeochi* means "elopement," so *kakeochi suru* is "elope"; and *tenisu* is the Japanese rendering of English "tennis," so *tenisu suru* means "play tennis."

57 Michael the cat has snatched a fish from the fishmonger, and the man has snatched a shopper's purse, but they get caught in a blind alley as they flee. Michael slips away between the fence and the wall, but the man gets nabbed when he can't squeeze through.

Michael: ウニャ ニャ ニャッ
Unya nya nya!
"Meow-yow-yow."

FX: サッ
Sa!
(effect of quick, agile movement)

Man: むおーっ!
Muō!
"Urggghhh."

FX: バッ
Ba!
(effect of sudden, vigorous action)

Woman: どろぼう!!
Dorobō!
"Thief!!" (PL2)

Policeman: 逮捕 する!!
Taiho suru!!
arrest　do/make
"I arrest you!"
"You're under arrest!"
(PL2)

Man: ひっ!
Hi!
"Aiii!"

• the standard Japanese cat sounds are *nyā* and *nyan*, but there are many variations based on them. The manga *What's Michael* is particularly creative in its variations.

• *taiho* is a noun for "(an) arrest," and adding *suru/shimasu* makes it a verb, "arrest/apprehend/take into police custody." When a Japanese law officer says *Taiho suru* to the person he's arresting, it's essentially equivalent to an American law officer declaring, "You're under arrest."

The Chinese connection

Historically, a great many of the nouns that could become *suru* verbs were loanwords adopted from Chinese. When turned into verbs, the noun part is usually written in kanji—the original Chinese characters—and the appropriate form of *suru* (non-past, past, negative, etc.) is added in hiragana. (Today, most new loanwords come from languages other than Chinese; see fig. 64.)

58 In 1926, when little Kikue's young father dies, the Saeki family patriarch decides to send the girl's mother, Moé, back to her parents' home so they can arrange a new marriage for her; Kikue stays with the Saekis, however, to be raised by her uncle and his wife. Kikue at first does not take to her new mother, Natsu (grandmother of Natsuko, seen in figs. 23, 29, and others), but when they finally become friends, Kikue wants Natsu to promise not to let her forget her real mother.

> **Natsu:** 約束 します。
> *Yakusoku shimasu.*
> promise do/make
> **"I promise."** (PL3)

- *yakusoku* is a noun meaning "promise," so *yakusoku suru* can be thought of literally as "make a promise" → "(to) promise." The subject "I" is understood.

A useful expression: *Shitsurei shimasu*

Shitsurei is written with two kanji meaning "lose" and "politeness/manners," creating a noun that means "rudeness" or "a lapse in manners." Adding a form of *suru* turns it into a verb that literally means "commit a rudeness." The PL3 form, *Shitsurei shimasu,* serves as a polite "Excuse me" when entering someone's office, walking in front of someone, or otherwise intruding on their space; in informal situations or when speaking from a position of rank, the PL2 equivalent for this purpose is a plain *Shitsurei,* without *suru.* The polite *Shitsurei shimasu* is also used when taking leave of someone, especially a superior, as well as to say good-bye on the phone; in less formal situations or when speaking from a position of rank, the PL2 *Shitsurei suru* or a plain *Shitsurei* can serve as a more abrupt "Excuse me/I'm leaving/Good-bye."

59 The head of Kaji Ryūsuke's election committee is visiting Kaji for the first time in his new digs in the House of Representatives Office Building. Kaji's secretary enters with tea.

> **Secretary:** 失礼 します。
> *Shitsurei shimasu.*
> rudeness will do/commit
> **"Excuse me."** (PL3)

- in situations like this, the expression means "Excuse me for intruding," and it's used for politeness even when one has specifically been summoned.

60 The angry client in fig. 4 spits out his good-bye.

> **Client:** 失礼 する!!
> *Shitsurei suru!!*
> rudeness will do/commit
> **"You'll have to excuse me!"** (PL2)

The PL3 past form of *suru*

You've just seen in figs. 58 and 59 that the PL3 form of *suru* is *shimasu*, which tells you that the polite past form of *suru* has to be *shimashita* (review Lesson 3 if you don't remember why). It also tells you that the past form of every *suru* verb has to be *something shimashita*, so the past of *shitsurei suru* is *shitsurei shimashita*.

The polite past *Shitsurei shimashita* serves as a broadly applicable apology for anything you have done wrong or that might have caused offense—burping/sneezing, creating a disturbance, misunderstanding a request/order/situation, mistaking someone's identity, and so forth. In informal situations or when speaking from a position of rank, a plain *Shitsurei* can serve the same purpose.

61 Yamada is being transferred to Germany, so his friend Kimura brings him to the bar Lemon Hart to learn about German beers from the proprietor. After the proprietor holds forth at length, Yamada appreciatively calls him "Professor Beer," but Kimura tells him he is being rude by implying the proprietor only knows about beer, when he is in fact an expert on every imaginable kind of alcoholic beverage. Yamada apologizes and offers up a different title.

Yamada: 失礼 しました、 サケ 博士!!
Shitsurei shimashita, Sake -hakase!!
rudeness　did　wine/spirits　professor/doctor
"I have done you a rudeness, Professor Drink!"
"My apologies, Dr. Drink!" (PL3)

- *sake* can refer specifically to the rice wine for which Japan is famous, or more generically to all varieties of "alcoholic beverage."
- *hakase* (or *hakushi*—both pronunciations are used) officially refers to anyone with a doctoral degree, but it's sometimes used playfully with people who might be termed "walking encyclopedias" in English.

The PL3 negative forms of *suru*

If the PL3 form of *suru* is *shimasu*, then you also know immediately that its PL3 negative form is *shimasen*, and the PL3 negative-past form is *shimasen deshita*.

62 Several times during the growing season, Natsuko has worked herself beyond exhaustion to nurture her crop of Tatsunishiki rice (fig. 36). Today she has stayed out in an approaching typhoon, trying to protect the rice, and her mother scolds her for foolishly overexerting herself again. As she takes off her raincoat, she tells her mother she'll stop being so reckless.

Natsuko: もう 無理 しません。
Mō muri shimasen.
now/already　overexertion　won't do
"I won't overexert myself any longer."
"I won't push so hard anymore." (PL3)

- *mō* can mean either "more" or "now/already" when followed by a regular verb (see figs. 74–75), but when followed by a negative it implies "no longer ～/not ～ anymore."
- *muri*, written with kanji that literally mean "without reason/not reasonable," is a noun referring to something that is impossible—or that is at least beyond what one can expect reasonably to do/accomplish. *Muri shimasen* is the PL3 negative form of the verb *muri suru*, which essentially means to overexert oneself or push oneself too hard attempting the impossible.

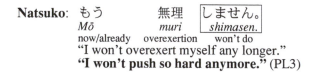

The PL3 "let's/I'll/I think I'll ～" form of *suru*

Completing this mini-review of the polite verb forms introduced in Lesson 3, the PL3 "let's/I'll ～" form of *suru/shimasu* is *shimashō*. By itself, *shimashō* implies "let's do" or "I will/I shall/I think I'll do" the action that we've been talking about (or that is otherwise understood from the context). When combined with a noun to make a *suru* verb, it implies "let's do/I think I'll do" the action indicated by or associated with that noun.

© Hirokane Kenshi. *Kaji Ryūsuke no Gi*, Kōdansha.

63 Tanizaki Kengo, Kaji Ryūsuke's opponent in his run for the Diet (Japan's national assembly), is giving a speech atop his campaign van when Kaji's van drives by. Japanese campaign vans are equipped with large loudspeakers, over which candidates make high-decibel speeches at major intersections or appeal for votes while driving around town. Kaji calls out his best wishes, but Tanizaki challenges Kaji to stop and debate him on the spot. Kaji promptly tells the driver to pull over, but his campaign manager Yamamoto is concerned about getting to his next appearance in time and thinks they'd best drive on.

Yamamoto: 無視　しましょう。
　　　　　Mushi　*shimashō.*
　　　　　ignoring/disregarding　let's do
　　　　　"Let's ignore him." (PL3)

• *mushi*, written with kanji meaning "without a look/not looking," is a noun referring to the act of ignoring/disregarding/paying no attention to something, but it more often occurs in its verb form *mushi suru* ("ignore/disregard").

Some more *suru* verbs

Here are several more *suru* verbs. In each case, the PL3 form follows below the PL2 form; and the first line of translation gives an equivalent English noun + "do," the second gives the corresponding English verb or verb phrase, and the last treats it as a single verb sentence with an arbitrarily chosen subject. (Although these *suru* verbs are almost always written with kanji, some are provided in kana here for kana practice.)

べんきょう する。	感謝　　する。	うんてん する。	電話　　する。
Benkyō　*suru.*	*Kansha*　*suru.*	*Unten*　*suru.*	*Denwa*　*suru.*
勉強　　　します。	かんしゃ します。	運転　　　します。	でんわ　　します。
Benkyō　*shimasu.*	*Kansha*　*shimasu.*	*Unten*　*shimasu.*	*Denwa*　*shimasu.*
studying　do	gratitude　do	driving　do	telephone　do
"study"	"be grateful"	"drive"	"make a phone call"
"We will study."	**"I am grateful."**	**"He will drive."**	**"I will call."**

Many regular Japanese verbs have *suru*-verb counterparts—though the exact range of meaning can be somewhat different, so you can't consider them interchangeable. For example, both *taberu* and *shokuji suru* correspond to "eat" if you're talking about eating a meal, but you can't use the latter if you're only talking about a snack or about eating some particular item in a meal. Also, the *suru* verb generally sounds more formal than its regular verb counterpart, and this can make it more likely to occur in writing than in speech. Here are some *suru* verbs that can be considered synonyms for verbs you've seen before.

食べる/*taberu*/eat	ある/*aru*/exists	頼む/*tanomu*/request	買う/*kau*/buy
しょくじ する。	存在　　する。	いらい　する。	購入　　　する。
Shokuji　*suru.*	*Sonzai*　*suru.*	*Irai*　*suru.*	*Kōnyū*　*suru.*
食事　　します。	そんざい します。	依頼　　します。	こうにゅうします。
Shokuji　*shimasu.*	*Sonzai*　*shimasu.*	*Irai*　*shimasu.*	*Kōnyū*　*shimasu.*
meal　do	existence　do	request　do	purchase　do
"eat a meal"	"exist"	"request"	"make a purchase"
"I will eat."	**"It exists."**	**"He will request it."**	**"I will buy it."**

The European and English connection

Beginning in the mid- to late-nineteenth century, a flood of new loanwords came in from the European languages and English, and most of these are written in katakana. For nouns used as *suru* verbs, the foreign part is written in katakana and *suru* is written in hiragana.

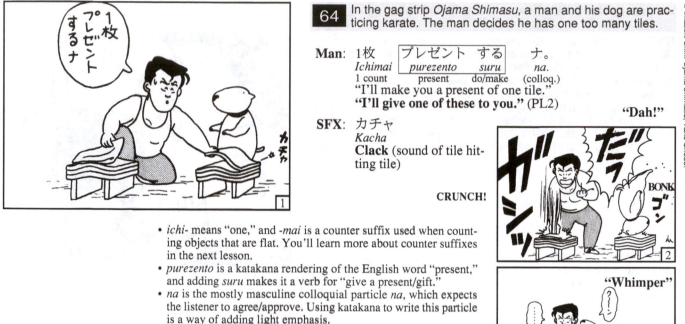

64 In the gag strip *Ojama Shimasu*, a man and his dog are practicing karate. The man decides he has one too many tiles.

Man: 1枚 プレゼント する ナ。
Ichimai   purezento   suru   na.
1 count   present   do/make   (colloq.)
"I'll make you a present of one tile."
"I'll give one of these to you." (PL2)

SFX: カチャ
Kacha
Clack (sound of tile hitting tile)

"Dah!"

CRUNCH!

BONK

"Whimper"

WAG WAG

- *ichi-* means "one," and *-mai* is a counter suffix used when counting objects that are flat. You'll learn more about counter suffixes in the next lesson.
- *purezento* is a katakana rendering of the English word "present," and adding *suru* makes it a verb for "give a present/gift."
- *na* is the mostly masculine colloquial particle *na*, which expects the listener to agree/approve. Using katakana to write this particle is a way of adding light emphasis.

Watch out for false friends

Words borrowed from English may seem familiar to you at a glance, but watch out! The Japanese meaning of a word can be quite different from the meaning you associate with it or the word may be used for only one of several meanings you are accustomed to using it for—and this is true of all loanwords, not just *suru* verbs. Be sure to pay attention to exactly how each word is used in Japanese, as well as its Japanese pronunciation—which can also be quite different from the original pronunciation. Here are a few more English-derived words to give a taste of what you'll encounter.

kana	romaji	English		meaning(s) in Japanese
プレイする	*purei suru*	play	→	play sports
コピーする	*kopii suru*	copy	→	make a photocopy
タイプする	*taipu suru*	type	→	type on a typewriter/computer
サインする	*sain suru*	sign	→	sign a document/autograph; (only in sports) give a hand signal
メモする	*memo suru*	memo	→	make a note/write something down
カンニングする	*kanningu suru*	cunning	→	cheat on an exam
オープンする	*ōpun suru*	open	→	launch a new business/branch/shop; open shop for the day
オーバーする	*ōbā suru*	over	→	go over the limit/exceed
アップする	*appu suru*	up	→	go up/rise
ダウンする	*daun suru*	down	→	go down/decline/become depressed
サービスする	*sābisu suru*	service	→	give a special discount/deal; throw in for free; do something special for someone

Special expressions with *suru*

Suru appears in many common expressions. For example, a noun followed by the pattern *ni suru* means "make it [into] ~" when speaking of changing something from an old state/use to a new state/use. The same pattern is used to express a choice, essentially implying "I'll make my choice ~" → "I'll choose ~."

65 Shin-chan's parents have brought him to the ski slopes for the first time. When his father tells him to walk sideways like a crab in order to climb the hill, he wants to know what kind of crab. His mother says that doesn't matter, to which he responds:

Shin-chan: じゃ、　　　毛ガニ　にする。
Ja,　　　kegani　ni suru.
in that case/then　hair crab　will make it
"In that case, I'll make it a hair crab."
"Then I'll be a hair crab." (PL2)

- *ja* is a connecting word meaning "in that case/then."
- *kegani* is a combination of *ke* ("hair") and *kani* ("crab"); in combinations, the *k* in *kani* changes to *g* for euphony.
- *ni* is one of the most versatile "phrase particles"—particles that mark the function of words and phrases within sentences. One use is to mark the endpoint or result of an action—in this case, the result of a choice. You'll learn more about *ni* and other phrase particles as they come up, as well as in Lesson 13.

Making humble verbs

Suru also plays an important role in honorific language (PL4), which includes a way of turning many regular verbs into humble verbs. When speaking to a social superior in a formal situation, you use humble verbs to refer to your own actions and exalting verbs to refer to your listener's. (The sidebar on the next two pages tells you a little more about honorific language.)

The humble form of a verb is made up of an honorific prefix *o-* followed by the verb's pre-*masu* stem, plus *suru* or *shimasu* (or the past, negative, or other form of *suru* as called for by the context). Unfortunately, this doesn't work with just any verb, so you can't begin transforming verbs at random. But once you've learned to recognize the form, you can begin paying attention to which verbs it does work with.

66 The day after Shima handles an unusual stock trade for Hatsushiba director Usami, the news at noon reports that Hatsushiba Chairman Yoshihara has died of a heart attack. Smelling a rat, Shima has a trusted private-eye friend investigate and confirms that he has unwittingly participated in an insider trading scheme that brought Usami a profit of ¥50 million. When Usami and Shima's own department head Fukuda summon him to give him "his share" of the profits, Shima is prepared with a swift answer. Usami and Fukuda are dumbfounded.

Usami & Fukuda

Shima: お　　断り　します。
O-　kotowari　shimasu.
(hon.)- refuse/decline (hon.)
"I decline." (PL4)

- *o-* is an honorific prefix, *kotowari* is the pre-*masu* form of the verb *kotowaru/kotowarimasu* ("refuse/decline"), and *shimasu* is the polite form of *suru*. Since this makes the humble form of *kotowaru*, you can think of it literally as "I humbly/respectfully decline," but humble forms are used much more widely in Japanese than such locutions are in English.

Honorific Language

To cover all the ins and outs of honorific language would require a book of its own—or several—and, in any case, a full introduction to honorific speech is something best left for later in your study of the language. But since the honorific system can't be avoided altogether even at the beginning, it's worth familiarizing yourself with the basic elements involved. The full honorific system—what this book calls PL4 speech—can be divided into three main sub-divisions: honorific, humble, and formal.

Honorific speech

One way to honor or show special politeness to someone is to place honorific prefixes before nouns that refer to things belonging to or associated with that person. Most words take the prefix お- *o-*, many others take ご- *go-* and a few take み- *mi-*. The prefixes are usually written in hiragana today, but when they are written in kanji, the same kanji is used for all three: 御. As a rule, the three are not interchangeable; only experience will tell you which should be used (or how 御 needs to be read) with a particular word. Also, some words customarily get a prefix regardless of the politeness level, while others never get one; again, only experience can tell you which words fall into these categories. (Even though they're called "honorific," *o-* and *go-* are also used in humble forms, as seen in figs. 66 and 69, and in certain conventional expressions or for touches of politeness at all levels of speech).

Another way to honor someone is to use honorific, or exalting, verbs when referring to that person's actions. With some of the most common verbs, an entirely new verb can be substituted for the regular verb. For example, *suru/shimasu* ("do") becomes *nasaru/nasaimasu*; *iku/ikimasu* ("go"), *kuru/kimasu* ("come"), and *iru/imasu* ("exists" for people and other animate things) all become *irassharu/irasshaimasu*; and *iu/iimasu* ("say") becomes *ossharu/osshaimasu*. For most verbs, though, honorific equivalents are formed by altering the usual verb. For example, *kimeru/kimemasu* ("decide") becomes *kimerareru/kimeraremasu* or *o-kime ni naru/narimasu*; *kaeru/kaerimasu* ("go home") becomes *kaerareru/kaeraremasu* or *o-kaeri ni naru/narimasu*, or yet again *o-kaeri da/desu*. Note that even though these words all belong to an inherently higher level of politeness, each of them still has both a plain form and a polite *-masu* form.

67 As an interesting customer who came in for the first time tonight gets up to leave, the proprietor of Lemon Hart asks him his name.

Proprietor:
お客さん、　お名前　は?
O- kyaku-san,　o- namae　wa?
(hon.)-guest-(pol.)　(hon.)-name　as for
"Honorable guest, as for your name?"
"Sir, could I ask your name?" (PL4)

- *kyaku* is literally "guest/visitor," and is also used for customers/clients of a business. When directly addressing a customer, the honorific prefix *o-* and the polite suffix *-san* ("Mr./Ms.") is always used, even in less polite speech.
- *namae* means "name," and since he is asking for the name of the person he is addressing, he adds the prefix *o-* to honor him. He would never use *o-* in speaking of his own name.
- *wa* ("as for") here creates a shorthand for "As for your name, what is it?" You'll learn about this particle in Lesson 11.

68 The boss endures a bone-chilling walk to the station, a hot and crowded commuter train ride, and another cold walk from station to office. Then he finds the office overheated when he arrives.

Sound FX: ブーン
Būn
Whirrr (hum of heater fan)

Boss: 暑い　な。　やれやれ。
Atsui　na.　Yareyare.
is hot　(colloq.)　(sigh)
"It sure is hot. Boy oh boy." (PL2)

OL: もう　お疲れ　です　か、　課長?
Mō　o-tsukare　desu　ka,　kachō?
already　(hon.)-fatigue　is/are　(?)　section chief
"Are you worn out already, Sir?" (PL4)

- *yareyare* is a verbalized sigh of fatigue, exasperation, or relief—here a combination of the first two.
- *mō* is an adverb meaning "already." See Lesson 6.
- *tsukare* is the pre-*masu* form of the verb *tsukareru/tsukaremasu* ("become tired/worn out"), and *o-* is an honorific prefix. She uses the honorific form because she is speaking to her superior and referring to his state/action. For this verb, *o-tsukare ni naru/narimasu* is the honorific form for "become tired," while *o-tsukare da/desu* implies "has/have grown tired" or "is/are worn out." Adding *ka* to *desu* makes it the question, "Are you worn out?"

69 After Noboru goes back to Kyushu (fig. 13), his uncle Matsuda asks the proprietor why the water in the glass turned pink.

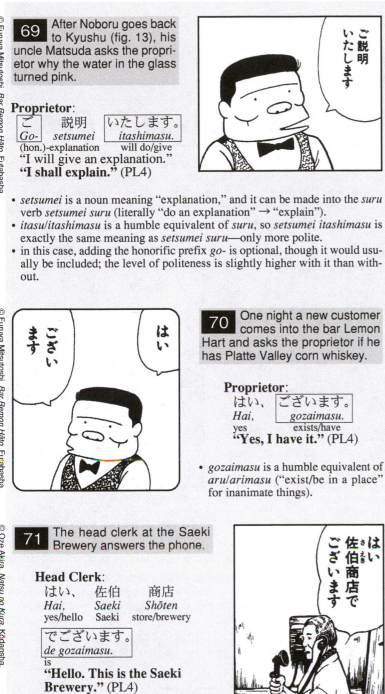

ご説明
いたします

Proprietor:

ご	説明	いたします。
Go-	*setsumei*	*itashimasu.*
(hon.)-explanation		will do/give

"I will give an explanation."
"I shall explain." (PL4)

- *setsumei* is a noun meaning "explanation," and it can be made into the *suru* verb *setsumei suru* (literally "do an explanation" → "explain").
- *itasu/itashimasu* is a humble equivalent of *suru*, so *setsumei itashimasu* is exactly the same meaning as *setsumei suru*—only more polite.
- in this case, adding the honorific prefix *go-* is optional, though it would usually be included; the level of politeness is slightly higher with it than without.

70 One night a new customer comes into the bar Lemon Hart and asks the proprietor if he has Platte Valley corn whiskey.

ございます

はい

Proprietor:

はい、	ございます。
Hai,	*gozaimasu.*
yes	exists/have

"Yes, I have it." (PL4)

- *gozaimasu* is a humble equivalent of *aru/arimasu* ("exist/be in a place" for inanimate things).

71 The head clerk at the Saeki Brewery answers the phone.

はい
佐伯商店で
ございます

Head Clerk:

はい、	佐伯	商店
Hai,	*Saeki*	*Shōten*
yes/hello	Saeki	store/brewery

でございます。
de gozaimasu.
is

"Hello. This is the Saeki Brewery." (PL4)

- in its narrow definition, *shōten* refers to a retail business selling merchandise in a storefront, but the term is also used as a generic label for almost any kind of small business. In this case the business is a saké brewery.
- *de gozaimasu* is a humble equivalent of *desu* ("is/are"). Take care to distinguish it from plain *gozaimasu* (fig. 70), which is equivalent to *aru/arimasu*.

Humble speech

A speaker can also show politeness and respect toward someone else by using verbs that humble the speaker's own actions. Again, with some common verbs, an entirely new verb can be substituted for the standard verb. For example, *suru* ("do") becomes *itasu/itashimasu*, *iku* ("go") becomes *mairu/mairimasu*, and *iu* ("say") becomes *mōsu/mōshimasu*. For many other verbs, humble equivalents are formed by altering the regular verb: *kotowaru/kotowarimasu* becomes *o-kotowari suru/o-kotowari shimasu* ("refuse/decline," fig. 66) and *tetsudau/tetsudaimasu* ("help," fig. 36) becomes *o-tetsudai suru/o-tetsudai shimasu*.

Formal speech

The words in this category neither humble the speaker nor exalt anyone else. Rather, they represent a more general quality of politeness, formality, and refinement. The *desu* and *-masu* forms that characterize PL3 speech are actually part of this category, but a variety of other substitutions occur at the PL4 level. For example, *aru/arimasu* ("exists/be in a place" for inanimate things) becomes *gozaru/gozaimasu*, *taberu* ("eat") becomes *itadaku/itadakimasu*, *desu* becomes *de gozaru/de gozaimasu*, and the adjective *ii/yoi* ("good/fine/OK"; see fig. 76 note on *yoku*) becomes *yoroshii (desu)*.

Additional notes

It's useful to know that an honorific or humble verb often provides its own subject, in effect. If a conversation between two people is only about the two people present, then all honorific verbs must refer to the listener's actions, since a speaker never uses such verbs to speak of his own actions; conversely, all humble verbs must refer to the speaker's actions. If the conversation involves a third person, either as a speaker/listener or as someone being spoken about, things get more complicated.

In any given context, the two most important factors in determining the proper level of politeness are (a) the relative social positions of the speaker, listener, and the person being spoken of (who in many cases is the speaker or listener), and (b) their group identities. Though different groups have different expectations regarding degree of formality, as a general rule, within a given group, plain PL2 forms are reserved for peers and subordinates, and polite forms are used when speaking to or about superiors—PL3 for those closer in the hierachy, with varying doses of PL4 honorific forms for those higher up. When speaking to someone outside the group, however, the outsider and his actions, regardless of his status, receive PL3 or 4 treatment, while humble language is used for referring to those belonging to the speaker's own group—even if they rank far above the speaker or listener.

Lesson 6

Modifying Verbs, Adjectives, & *Desu*

A verb may be **modified**—i.e., described or characterized—by one or more **adverbs**. Among other things, adverbs express the manner (how), timing (when), and degree or extent (how much, how many, how far, how long) of an action. An adverb always precedes the verb it modifies. In the sentence here it comes directly before the verb, but in longer sentences it may come earlier in the sentence, separated from the verb.

72 Michael the cat has been lured into a hostess club by a fetching chinchilla Persian standing outside. She accompanies him in, pours him a drink, and then disappears, to be replaced by a frightful-looking hostess who finishes off half a dozen appetizers at his expense and offers him "special services" for ¥20,000 more. Michael declines.

CHOMP
CHOMP
CHOMP

Michael:	いや、	そろそろ	帰る	よ。
	Iya,	*sorosoro*	*kaeru*	*yo.*
	no	by and by/now	go home/leave	(emph.)

"No, I'll be going on home now." (PL2)

- *iya* is an informal word for "no"; the more formal equivalent is *iie*.
- *sorosoro* is an adverb implying that the action is impending: "by and by/soon/any time now."
- the polite form of the verb *kaeru* ("return home"; fig. 4) is *kaerimasu*.

Adverbs modify adjectives

An adverb can modify an adjective, limiting or qualifying the description it gives, whether the adjective in turn modifies a noun within the sentence or stands alone at the end. The adverb always comes before the adjective modified—most typically right before.

73 Kōsuke's girlfriend Hiroko invited him out for dinner, and he wants to iron his good pants. He goes to borrow his landlady's iron, which was custom-made in the era when an iron's effectiveness depended largely on its sheer weight.

Landlady:	ちょっと	重い	よ。
	Chotto	*omoi*	*yo.*
	a little	is heavy	(emph.)

"It's a little heavy."
"It's pretty heavy." (PL2)

FX: ずしっ
Zushi!
(effect of something being/feeling heavy)

- *chotto* literally means "a little/a bit," but when modifying adjectives it's often more like "quite/pretty ～."
- since *omoi* is an adjective, the PL3 equivalent of the sentence would be *Chotto omoi desu yo.*

Adverbs modify other adverbs

Adverbs can also modify other adverbs. When two adverbs occur in a row, the first adverb is the modifier for the second. Adverbs do not change form for different levels of politeness.

74 Today the neighborhood doctor has asked Kōsuke to reorganize a year's worth of random accumulation in his storeroom, as well as to give the room a general cleaning. The doctor looks in on him when he returns from making house calls. Kōsuke will get a complete physical exam when he's done.

Kōsuke: お帰りなさい。
O-kaeri nasai.
(greeting)
"Welcome back." (PL2–3)

もう	少し	かかります。
Mō	*sukoshi*	*kakarimasu.*
more	a little	will take/require

"[This] will require a little more [time]."
"It's going to take me a little longer." (PL3)

- *o-kaeri nasai,* a form of the verb *kaeru/kaerimasu* ("return home"), is used as the standard greeting for welcoming a person back home from work/school/an errand, or back at the office from an errand or business trip. Informally, it's often shortened to just *o-kaeri.*
- when *mō* comes before a number or quantity, it usually means "[that many/that much] more."
- *sukoshi* can be either a noun or an adverb meaning "a little/a few," so *mō sukoshi* = "a little/few more." As an adverb, *sukoshi* expresses the extent or degree of the verb's action: "[do/act] a little/a few times." *Sukoshi* and *chotto* (fig. 73) can be considered synonyms, and either could have been used in this case (as well as in fig. 73), but they're not always interchangeable; *chotto* feels quite a bit more informal.
- *kakarimasu* is the polite form of *kakaru* ("takes/requires/costs"). The situation makes clear that the verb's tense is future ("will take/is going to take"), and its subject is the work Kōsuke is doing.

Doctor & patient

Adverbs modify noun + *da/desu* phrases

Adverbs can also modify noun + *da/desu* phrases in the same way. When an adverb precedes a noun + *da/desu* phrase, the adverb (including any of its own modifiers) modifies the entire phrase, as in this example. To modify just the noun, an adjective or other noun modifier is usually called for. You will learn about modifying nouns in the next lesson.

75 As he reads something at his desk, Uzuratani suddenly feels hot in the sweatshirt he's wearing.

Uzuratani:
もう	すぐ	夏	だ	な。
Mō	*sugu*	*natsu*	*da*	*na.*
now/already	soon	summer	is	(colloq.)

"Very soon now it is summer, isn't it?"
"I guess it's almost summer." (PL2)

- when it's not used with a number or quantity, the adverb *mō* seen in fig. 74 often means "now/already." This same use appears in fig. 68.
- *sugu* is an adverb that implies close in time or space → "soon/immediately/just ahead."
- ～ *da na* is literally "It's ～, isn't it?"; when making an observation, it can feel like,"It must be/I guess it's/I'll bet it's ～."

Terminology note: Some Japanese adverbs can in fact modify individual nouns. In English, such words would simply be called adjectives when they modify nouns, but in this book the term "adjective" is reserved for the narrower definition stated in Lesson 1.

A few more adverbs

Here are some more adverbs in sample sentences:

かならず 来る。
Kanarazu *kuru.*
definitely will come
"They'll definitely come." (PL2)

まだ 子供 だ わ ね。
Mada *kodomo* *da* *wa* *ne.*
still child is (fem.) (colloq.)
"He's still a child, isn't he?" (PL2)

また 電話 します。
Mata *denwa* *shimasu.*
again telephone will do
"I'll call again." (PL3)

とても むずかしいです。
Totemo *muzukashii desu.*
very much is difficult-(pol.)
"It's very difficult." (PL3)

すっかり 変わりました ね。
Sukkari *kawarimashita* *ne.*
completely has changed hasn't it?
"It has completely changed, hasn't it?" (PL3)

かなり 高い よ。
Kanari *takai* *yo.*
fairly/quite is high/expensive (emph.)
"It's quite expensive." (PL2)

ゆっくり 運転 しました。
Yukkuri *unten* *shimashita.*
slowly driving did
"He drove slowly." (PL3)

もっと 安いです。
Motto *yasui desu.*
more is cheap-(pol.)
"It's cheaper [than that]." (PL3)

Adjectives can become adverbs

Besides the "true" adverbs introduced above, adverbs can also be formed from other parts of speech. Adjectives can be made into adverbs by changing the final -い *-i* to -く *-ku*. As with "true" adverbs, there is no separate polite form.

☞ A word to the wise: The ***-ku* form** of an adjective is important when learning additional forms, so it's well worth getting this simple transformation down cold right at the start.

adjective	adverb form	modifying a verb
はやい *hayai* fast/early	はやく *hayaku* rapidly/quickly/early	はやく食べる *hayaku taberu.* **eat quickly/eat early**
おいしい *oishii* tasty/delicious	おいしく *oishiku* deliciously	おいしく食べる *oishiku taberu.* **eat deliciously/eat with relish**

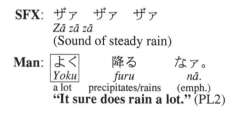

76 The rainy season in Japan, known as *tsuyu*, typically lasts for a month or so starting in early to mid-June. This man sounds like he is getting pretty tired of contending with the constant downpour on his way to and from work.

SFX: ザァ ザァ ザァ
Zā zā zā
(Sound of steady rain)

Man: よく 降る なァ。
Yoku *furu* *nā.*
a lot precipitates/rains (emph.)
"It sure does rain a lot." (PL2)

• *yoku* is the adverb form of an adjective that occurs in two forms, *ii* and *yoi*; the first of these can be considered the more common form in general use (fig. 82), but you'll need to pay attention to when *yoi* is used rather than *ii*. The basic meaning of the adjective is "good/fine/okay," but it also has a variety of special meanings, depending on context. The adverb form is always *yoku*, based on *yoi*, and it, too, has a range of meanings: "[do the action] well/thoroughly/carefully/frequently/a lot."
• the verb *furu/furimasu* refers to the falling not just of rain but of any kind of precipitation, including snow, hail, sleet, etc., and sometimes other things that fall from above as well. Here, the context, illustration, and sound effects make the meaning clear.
• the small katakana *a* elongates the colloquial *na*, adding emphasis and feeling.

Some nouns can become adverbs

Some nouns can act as adverbs, either by themselves or with the addition of に *ni*. *Ni* can be thought of in this case as a particle that indicates manner or extent. Whether *ni* is required depends on the particular noun, and some nouns can be used either with or without. The descriptive "adjectival nouns" introduced in the next lesson require *ni* as a group.

Kashimura

77 Kashimura was having such a good day on the golf course that he worried out loud to Shima whether it portended something bad to follow. Then he gets a hole in one. As they celebrate, Shima remarks:

Shima:
こりゃ 本当に 危ない ぞ。 ハハハハ
Korya *hontō ni* *abunai* *zo.* *Ha ha ha ha.*
as for this truly be in danger/dangerous (emph.) (laugh)
"Based on this, you really are in danger. Ha ha ha ha."
"Now you really know you're in trouble. Ha ha ha ha." (PL2)

- *korya* (lit. "as for this") refers to Kashimura's hole in one, with the feeling of "to judge from what has just happened."
- *hontō* ("truth") appears as a noun in fig. 41, but here it's followed by *ni* to make it an adverb: "truly/really."
- *abunai* is an adjective meaning "dangerous/perilous" (fig. 53), and is also used to speak of something/someone being "in danger/peril."
- the hand to the back of the head is a gesture of embarrassment—in this case, happy embarrassment at his good fortune.

Adverbs with *naru*

Adverbs typically indicate the manner, timing, extent, or some other characteristic of the action of the verb. But with the verb *naru/narimasu* ("become"), adverbs formed from adjectives and nouns (figs. 76–77) indicate the result of the action. For example, the noun *kirei* means "cleanness/prettiness" (fig. 13), and *kirei ni* is its adverb form, so *kirei ni naru* = "become clean/pretty"; *ōkii* is the adjective for "big," and *ōkiku* is its adverb form, so *ōkiku naru* = "become big." (Often these would actually imply "become more ~" → "become cleaner/prettier/bigger").

SQUEAK

78 When Shima is dispatched from Hatsushiba Electric to carry out a reorganization of its struggling affiliate, Sunlight Records, he arranges to have Hoshi Yasuo transferred to the accounting department there—to quietly keep an eye on the company's accounting practices. Here Hoshi arrives at the bar where he and Shima periodically meet after work to discuss what he has learned.

Hoshi: 遅く なりました。
Osoku *narimashita.*
late/slow became
"I became late."
"I'm sorry to be late." (PL3)

- *osoku* is the adverb form of the adjective *osoi* ("late/slow"), and *narimashita* is the PL3 past form of *naru/narimasu* ("become"). The expression *osoku narimashita* is often used as an implicit apology when one arrives late for a meeting or submits/delivers a requested item late.

Another adverb can be added before such statements to express a characteristic of the action. For example, *hayaku* = "quickly" (from *hayai*, "quick"), and *yoku* = "well" (fig. 76), so *hayaku yoku naru* = "become well quickly/get better quickly." In this particular case, *hayaku* modifies the combination of *yoku naru*, but in other cases the first adverb in the sequence may modify only the second adverb. For example, *motto* = "more," and *motto osoku naru* = "become later" or "become even later."

Relative time adverbs

Nouns indicating relative time ("today/yesterday/tomorrow"; "this year/last year/next year") are used as adverbs without any following particles.

Kumiko

79 Ōmachi Aiko is listening as her daughter Kumiko leaves a message on her answering machine. She is unhappy because Kumiko walked out on the *yuinō*—a ceremonial exchange of betrothal gifts between the families of a newly engaged couple—for the marriage she had arranged for her. After apologizing, Kumiko explains that she realized she could not marry a man she did not love. Since her mother does not pick up, she promises to call again.

Kumiko:

明日　また　連絡します。　では！　（プツッ）
Ashita mata renraku shimasu. De wa! (Putsu!)
tomorrow　again　will contact　then/bye　click
"[I'll] be in touch again tomorrow. Bye! (Click!)"
"I'll call again tomorrow. Bye! (Click!)" (PL3)

- *ashita* (the noun "tomorrow" serving as an adverb) and *mata* (the adverb "again") both modify the verb *renraku shimasu*.
- *renraku* is a noun that basically refers to a connection, including connections/contacts made by phone, letter, or other means of communication. Adding *suru/shimasu* makes it a verb for "contact/get in touch."
- *de wa* is literally "then/in that case," but it serves as an informal "good-bye."

Relative time table

Here are some relative time words commonly encountered in colloquial speech. In many cases there are one or more additional forms, but those given here are good ones to start with. The zero row in the center represents the present.

		日 *hi; nichi* day	週 *shū* week	月 *tsuki; getsu* month	年 *toshi; nen* year	朝 *asa* morning[1]	晩 *ban* night[1]
-2		一昨日 *ototoi* day before yesterday	先々週 *sensenshū* week before last	先々月 *sensengetsu* month before last	一昨年 *ototoshi* year before last		
-1	さっき[2] *sakki* a while ago	昨日 *kinō* yesterday	先週 *senshū* last week	先月 *sengetsu* last month	去年 *kyonen* last year		夕べ *yūbe* last night
0	今 *ima* now	今日 *kyō* today	今週 *konshū* this week	今月 *kongetsu* this month	今年 *kotoshi* this year	今朝 *kesa* this morning	今晩 *konban* tonight
+1	あとで[2] *ato de* later	明日 *ashita* tomorrow	来週 *raishū* next week	来月 *raigetsu* next month	来年 *rainen* next year		
+2		あさって *asatte* day after tomorrow	さ来週 *saraishū* week after next	さ来月 *saraigetsu* month after next	さ来年 *sarainen* year after next		
every		毎日 *mainichi* every day	毎週 *maishū* every week	毎月 *maitsuki* every month	毎年 *maitoshi* every year	毎朝 *maiasa* every morning	毎晩 *maiban* every night

Relative time words

[1] for the empty morning and night slots, add *no asa* or *no ban* to the relative day words—e.g., *kinō no asa* = "yesterday morning" and *ashita no ban* = "tomorrow night."
[2] for *sakki* and *ato de* the length of time removed from the present is relatively brief but not a specific unit of time.

The extent of the action

When *sukoshi* ("a little") modifies a verb like *taberu* ("eat"), it indicates the extent of the action—how much the person will eat—in general terms. Words that express a more specific quantity or number also function as adverbs to indicate the extent of the action.

© Maekawa Tsukasa, *Dai-Tōkyō Binbō Seikatsu Manyuaru*, Kōdansha.

80 While taking in the street scene in Shibuya, a trendy section of Tokyo, Kōsuke and his girlfriend Hiroko stop in at a small coffee shop. On the way out, Hiroko buys two bags of Mt. Kilimanjaro coffee and gives one to Kōsuke.

Hiroko: ひとつ あげる わ。
Hitotsu   ageru   wa.
one   will give   (fem. colloq.)
"I'll give you one [bag]."
"One's for you." (PL2)

Kōsuke: ありがと。
Arigato.
"Thanks." (PL2)

- the polite form of *ageru* ("give [away]") is *agemasu*.
- *arigato* is a casual "thanks," already seen in fig. 21. The form for very formal situations is ありがとうございます *arigatō gozaimasu*.

As is true of other quantity words in Japanese, *hitotsu* ("one") can be used as a noun, but here it is an adverb that indicates the extent of the verb's action: how much she will give. This is typical of quantity expressions in Japanese—they modify the verb rather than the related noun, even when the quantity expression precedes an explicitly stated subject or object. The structure for nouns modifying other nouns that you'll learn in Lesson 7 does allow Japanese quantity words to directly modify subjects/objects, but such use is relatively uncommon.

Counter suffixes

When counting or saying how many in Japanese, the number is customarily given a "counter" or "classifier" suffix that expresses the shape or nature of the objects in question. These suffixes are similar to words like "sheets" when you say "ten sheets of paper" or "cups" when you say "three cups of coffee" in English, but in Japanese the system is pervasive rather than being used only for certain select items. There are dozens of different counters, some with rigidly restricted usage, others with a broader range.

The counter in fig. 80 is -つ *-tsu*. Because it can be applied to almost anything except people and other animate things, it serves as a kind of generic counter that you can use when you don't know which of the more specific counters is appropriate; it's also often used for stating the age of small children. This generic counting sequence goes only to 10, with the suffix sometimes changing to -っつ *-ttsu*, and with 10 getting no suffix at all.

If the complete series only goes to 10, what do you do after that? As a matter of fact, it gets easier in this case, because you can then just say the number by itself and have it mean "11 items," "25 items," "50 items," and so forth. The more complete number series is introduced on the next page.

The corresponding word for asking "how many?" is いくつ *ikutsu*. This word is also used to ask ""How old are you/is she?"—especially when speaking to or about a small child, but also for older folks as well (with whom it often becomes *o-ikutsu*, for politeness).

A generic counting sequence

ひとつ	ふたつ	みっつ	よっつ	いつつ
一つ	二つ	三つ	四つ	五つ
hitotsu	*futatsu*	*mittsu*	*yottsu*	*itsutsu*
one	two	three	four	five
むっつ	ななつ	やっつ	ここのつ	とお
六つ	七つ	八つ	九つ	十
muttsu	*nanatsu*	*yattsu*	*kokonotsu*	*tō*
six	seven	eight	nine	ten

いくつ	あります	か?		二つ	食べます。
Ikutsu	*arimasu*	*ka?*		*Futatsu*	*tabemasu.*
how many	exist/have	(?)		2 count	will eat
"How many do you have?" (PL3)				**"I'll eat two."** (PL3)	

いくつ?			五つ	です。
Ikutsu?			*Itsutsu*	*desu.*
how old			5 yrs.	am/is
"How old are you?" (PL2)			**"I'm five."** (PL3)	

A more comprehensive counting system

The generic counter *-tsu* attaches to numbers in a native Japanese counting system whose use is now quite limited. Most counters are used with another number system that derives from Chinese. It's this second system that people use for the vast majority of tasks involving calculations and numerical values: math, statistics, finance, science, engineering, and so forth.

81 This man is trying to teach Michael the cat to fetch like a dog. Not surprisingly, Michael is unimpressed, but the man decides to try again.

Man: よーし、 それじゃ、 もう 一回 いく ぞ!!
Yōshi,   sore ja,   mō   ikkai   iku   zo!!
all right   then   more   one time go/will go (emph.)
"All right, then, here goes one more time!" (PL2)

- *yoshi* or *yōshi* is an interjection used when about to begin an action, and it usually carries a feeling of determination → "OK!/Here goes!/Let's go!/All right!"
- *sore ja* is used at the beginning of sentences as a connecting word, like "then/in that case."
- *mō* before a quantity or number means "[that much/that many] more."
- *ikkai* is a combination of *ichi* ("one") and *-kai*, the counter suffix used for "times/occasions/repetitions."
- the adverb *mō* modifies *ikkai* (*mō ikkai* = "one more time"), and that combination modifies the verb *iku/ikimasu* ("go") to indicate the extent of the action.

1 *ichi + kai = ikkai*
2 *ni + kai = nikai*
3 *san + kai = sankai*
4 *yon + kai = yonkai*
5 *go + kai = gokai*
6 *roku + kai = rokkai*
7 *nana + kai = nanakai*
8 *hachi + kai = hakkai*
9 *kyū + kai = kyūkai*
10 *jū + kkai = jukkai* or *jikkai*

The numbers

The Chinese-derived numbers work very much like English numbers, with the largest unit coming first. For multiples of tens, hundreds, thousands, and ten-thousands, the multiplier precedes the unit: 30 = *san* ("3") × *jū* ("10") → *sanjū*, and 200 = *ni* ("2") × *hyaku* ("100") → *nihyaku*. The values of the next largest units follow in sequence, finishing with the ones, so 230 = *nihyaku* + *sanjū* → *nihyaku-sanjū*, and 235 = *nihyaku-sanjū* + *go* ("5") → *nihyaku-sanjū-go*.

But there's one big difference. Japanese has a distinct "ten-thousands" place, *man*. This means large numbers are grouped by thousands instead of by hundreds. After 100 *man* comes 1000 *man* before moving on to the next group starting at 1 *oku*, then 10 *oku*, 100 *oku*, etc.

The basic numbers and units

Arabic	Kanji	Kana/Romaji
1	一	いち *ichi*
2	二	に *ni*
3	三	さん *san*
4	四	よん *yon* or し *shi*
5	五	ご *go*
6	六	ろく *roku*
7	七	なな *nana* or しち *shichi*
8	八	はち *hachi*
9	九	きゅう *kyū* or く *ku*
10	十	じゅう *jū*
100	百	ひゃく *hyaku*
1,000	千	せん *sen*
10,000	万	まん *man*
100,000,000	億	おく *oku*

How units are combined

十一	二十	四十六
jū-ichi[1]	*nijū*	*yonjū-roku*
11	20	46
百九十九	四百	八百三十七
hyaku-kyūjū-kyū[1]	*yonhyaku*	*happyaku-sanjū-nana*[2]
199	400	837
三千	六千一	八千五百七十
sanzen[2]	*rokusen-ichi*	*hassen-gohyaku-nanajū*[2]
3,000	6,001	8,570
一万	十万	百万	一千万
ichiman	*jūman*	*hyakuman*	*issenman*[1,2]
"1 *man*"	"10 *man*"	"100 *man*"	"1000 *man*"
10,000	100,000	1,000,000	10,000,000

[1] a multiple of one is not explicitly stated for tens and hundreds, and is stated for thousands only in numbers over 10,000,000.
[2] sound changes are quite common when combining numbers: *ichi* + *sen* = *issen* (only in very large numbers); *san* + *hyaku* = *sanbyaku*; *san* + *sen* = *sanzen*; *roku* + *hyaku* = *roppyaku*; *hachi* + *hyaku* = *happyaku*; *hachi* + *sen* = *hassen*.

Another generic counter

For the Chinese-derived system, the most versatile counter is 個 (*-ko* or *-kko*, often written with a katakana コ as in this example). *Ko* is used for a wide variety of objects, usually but not always relatively small, that don't have a more specific counter; it can be thought of as meaning "items" or "pieces."

82 Every year around the time of the spring equinox, Kōsuke gets a craving for *sakura-mochi*—a pounded rice cake filled with sweet bean-jam and wrapped in a cherry leaf—and he makes a trip to the local shop specializing in traditional confections. The lady there always adds something extra, and this time, when he's finished, she asks if he'd like another.

Shop Lady: もう ⎡1コ⎤ 食べる かい?
Mō ⎡*ikko*⎤ *taberu kai?*
more 1 piece will eat (?)
"Will you eat one more?"
"Would you like another?" (PL2)

Kōsuke: もう いい です。
Mō ii desu.
now/already good/fine/enough is
"It's already enough."
"I've had enough, thanks." (PL3)

Customer: ください。
Kudasai.
please
"Excuse me." (PL3)

- *ikko* is *ichi* ("one") plus the counter suffix *-ko*, which changes to *-kko* when combined with *ichi*. Sound changes like those noted on the facing page for combining numbers also occur when combining numbers with counter suffixes. You can see the other sound changes for *ko* at the right.
- the polite form of *taberu* ("eat") is *tabemasu*.
- *kai* is a friendlier-feeling, colloquial version of the question marker *ka* (fig. 50).
- *mō* appears here in both of its meanings, "more" and "already" (figs. 74–75).
- *ii* is an alternative form of the adjective *yoi* ("good/fine/okay"; see fig. 76 note on *yoku*). *Mō ii desu* (lit. "I am/it is already good") is an expression for "I've had enough."
- *kudasai* means "please/please give me," and can be used like this to get a store clerk's attention.

1 *ichi + ko = ikko*
2 *ni + ko = niko*
3 *san + ko = sanko*
4 *yon + ko = yonko*
5 *go + ko = goko*
6 *roku + ko = rokko*
7 *nana + ko = nanako*
8 *hachi + ko = hakko*
9 *kyū + ko = kyūko*
10 *jū + ko = jukko* or *jikko*

Some other common counters

Listed in the box below are a few of the more common counters. Except as noted, simply combine the standard form of the number with the standard form of the suffix. The question mark indicates the form for asking "how many?"; when no special form is indicated for questions, combine *nan-* with the standard form of the suffix.

Yon is generally preferred over *shi* for 4, in part because *shi* sounds the same as the word for "death." *Nana* and *shichi* for 7 are usually both acceptable, but in many cases conventional usage favors one or the other, so you'll want to pay attention to which seems to be more common among native speakers. Wherever *jū-* for 10 changes to a short *ju-, ji-* is also acceptable (e.g., *jippon* instead of *juppon*).

Frequently used counters

-本 **-hon** = things that are long and skinny or cylindrical, like pencils, pens, needles, wires, lines, bottles, teeth (1 = *ippon*, 3 = *sanbon*, 6 = *roppon*, 8 = *happon*, 10 = *juppon*, ? = *nanbon*).

-枚 **-mai** = thin, flat things, like paper, plates, CDs, computer disks, boards/ plywood, mats.

-杯 **-hai** = cupfuls, glassfuls, bowlfuls, boxfuls (1 = *ippai*, 3 = *sanbai*, 6 = *roppai*, 10 = *juppai*, ? = *nanbai*)

-冊 **-satsu** = bound volumes: books, magazines, photo albums (1 = *issatsu*, 8 = *hassatsu*, 10 = *jussatsu*).

-台 **-dai** = machines large and small, including electrical appliances, electronic equipment, telephones, cameras, automobiles, buses, trucks.

-匹 **-hiki** = small- to medium-sized animals (1 = *ippiki*, 3 = *sanbiki*, 6 = *roppiki*, 8 = *happiki*, 10 = *juppiki*, ? = *nanbiki*).

-番 **-ban** = places in numbered series.

-人 **-nin** = persons (1 = *hitori*, 2 = *futari*, 4 = *yonin*).

-才 **-sai** (also written -歳) = years of age (1 = *issai*, 8 = *hassai*, 10 = *jussai*). The generic -つ **-tsu** is also used to count age, especially for small children.

Fun with dates

The gag in this four-frame strip hinges in part on relative time words. The strip also offers a good opportunity to introduce some basic weather terminology, as well as Japanese dates, which are treated in detail on the facing page.

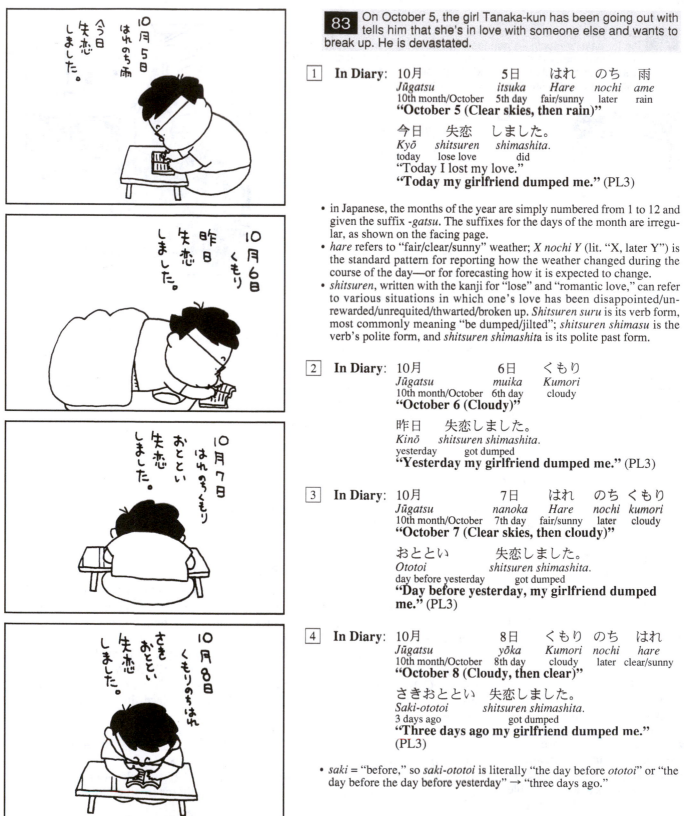

83 On October 5, the girl Tanaka-kun has been going out with tells him that she's in love with someone else and wants to break up. He is devastated.

1 **In Diary:** 10月　　　　　5日　　はれ　のち　雨
Jūgatsu　　　　　*itsuka*　*Hare*　*nochi*　*ame*
10th month/October　5th day　fair/sunny　later　rain
"October 5 (Clear skies, then rain)"

今日　失恋　しました。
Kyō　*shitsuren*　*shimashita.*
today　lose love　did
"Today I lost my love."
"Today my girlfriend dumped me." (PL3)

- in Japanese, the months of the year are simply numbered from 1 to 12 and given the suffix *-gatsu*. The suffixes for the days of the month are irregular, as shown on the facing page.
- *hare* refers to "fair/clear/sunny" weather; *X nochi Y* (lit. "X, later Y") is the standard pattern for reporting how the weather changed during the course of the day—or for forecasting how it is expected to change.
- *shitsuren*, written with the kanji for "lose" and "romantic love," can refer to various situations in which one's love has been disappointed/unrewarded/unrequited/thwarted/broken up. *Shitsuren suru* is its verb form, most commonly meaning "be dumped/jilted"; *shitsuren shimasu* is the verb's polite form, and *shitsuren shimashita* is its polite past form.

2 **In Diary:** 10月　　　　　6日　　くもり
Jūgatsu　　　　　*muika*　*Kumori*
10th month/October　6th day　cloudy
"October 6 (Cloudy)"

昨日　失恋しました。
Kinō　*shitsuren shimashita.*
yesterday　got dumped
"Yesterday my girlfriend dumped me." (PL3)

3 **In Diary:** 10月　　　　　7日　　はれ　のち　くもり
Jūgatsu　　　　　*nanoka*　*Hare*　*nochi*　*kumori*
10th month/October　7th day　fair/sunny　later　cloudy
"October 7 (Clear skies, then cloudy)"

おととい　　　　　失恋しました。
Ototoi　　　　　*shitsuren shimashita.*
day before yesterday　got dumped
"Day before yesterday, my girlfriend dumped me." (PL3)

4 **In Diary:** 10月　　　　　8日　　くもり　のち　はれ
Jūgatsu　　　　　*yōka*　*Kumori*　*nochi*　*hare*
10th month/October　8th day　cloudy　later　clear/sunny
"October 8 (Cloudy, then clear)"

さきおととい　失恋しました。
Saki-ototoi　　　　　*shitsuren shimashita.*
3 days ago　　　　　got dumped
"Three days ago my girlfriend dumped me." (PL3)

- *saki* = "before," so *saki-ototoi* is literally "the day before *ototoi*" or "the day before the day before yesterday" → "three days ago."

Dates and Durations

Years

When the year is given in a Japanese date, it comes first, followed by the month, and then the specific day of the month. Years are indicated by the year number plus the suffix -年 *-nen*:

1984年 =	*Sen kyūhyaku hachijū-yonen*	昭和59年	*Shōwa gojū-kyūnen*	
1989年 =	*Sen kyūhyaku hachijū-kyūnen*	平成元年	*Heisei gannen*	
1990年 =	*Sen kyūhyaku kyūjūnen*	平成2年	*Heisei ninen*	
2000年 =	*Nisennen*	平成12年	*Heisei jūninen*	
2005年 =	*Nisen gonen*	平成17年	*Heisei jūshichinen*	

Common Era dates are widely used in Japan today, but the older tradition of giving each Emperor's reign its own era name also continues. 1989 started out as 昭和64年 *Shōwa rokujūyonen* ("64th year of the Shōwa Era"), but when the Shōwa Emperor died on January 7, the new era name of 平成 *Heisei* ("Attaining Peace") was chosen and the name of the year became *Heisei gannen* ("original/ first year of the Heisei Era"). January 1, 1990 then marked the start of *Heisei ninen* ("second year of Heisei"), 1991 was *Heisei sannen* ("third year of Heisei"), and so on.

A duration of years

The same suffix is used to speak of a duration of time in years. The optional suffix -間 *-kan*, meaning "period/timespan," may also be added:

1 year	一年	*ichinen*	5 years	五年間	*gonen-kan*
3 years	三年	*sannen*	100 years	百年間	*hyakunen-kan*

Months of the year

The months of the year are numbered from 1 to 12 (either in kanji or in Arabic numerals) and given the suffix -月 *-gatsu*:

January	一月	*ichigatsu*
February	二月	*nigatsu*
March	三月	*sangatsu*
April	四月	*shigatsu*
May	五月	*gogatsu*
June	六月	*rokugatsu*
July	七月	*shichigatsu*
August	八月	*hachigatsu*
September	九月	*kugatsu*
October	十月	*jūgatsu*
November	十一月	*jūichigatsu*
December	十二月	*jūnigatsu*

A duration of months

To indicate a duration of time in months, the suffix -カ月 *-kagetsu* is used (for 1, 6, 8, and 10 it becomes *-kkagetsu*). The optional suffix *-kan* ("period/timespan") may be added.

1 month	一カ月	*ikkagetsu*
2 months	二カ月間	*nikagetsu-kan*
3 months	三カ月	*sankagetsu*

Days of the week

Monday	月曜日	*getsuyōbi*
Tuesday	火曜日	*kayōbi*
Wednesday	水曜日	*suiyōbi*
Thursday	木曜日	*mokuyōbi*
Friday	金曜日	*kin'yōbi*
Saturday	土曜日	*doyōbi*
Sunday	日曜日	*nichiyōbi*

In conversation, *-bi* is often omitted. When the day of the week is stated, it is generally stated last, so "Wednesday, December 28, 2005" would be 2005年12月28日水曜日 *Nisen gonen jūnigatsu nijūhachi-nichi suiyōbi*.

A duration of weeks

The word for "week" is either 週 *shū* or 週間 *shūkan* depending on the context. The latter is always used when indicating a duration of time (for 1, 8, and 10, the pronunciation becomes *-sshūkan*):

1 week	一週間	*isshūkan*
2 weeks	二週間	*nishūkan*
10 weeks	十週間	*jusshūkan*

Days of the month

The names and suffixes for the days of the month are irregular—though most fall into one of two patterns ending in *-ka* or *-nichi*.

1	一日	*tsuitachi*
2	二日	*futsuka*
3	三日	*mikka*
4	四日	*yokka*
5	五日	*itsuka*
6	六日	*muika*
7	七日	*nanoka*
8	八日	*yōka*
9	九日	*kokonoka*
10	十日	*tōka*
11	十一日	*jūichinichi*
12	十二日	*jūninichi*
13	十三日	*jūsannichi*
14	十四日	*jūyokka*
15	十五日	*jūgonichi*
16	十六日	*jūrokunichi*
17	十七日	*jūshichinichi*
18	十八日	*jūhachinichi*
19	十九日	*jūkunichi*
20	二十日	*hatsuka*
21	二十一日	*nijūichinichi*
22	二十二日	*nijūninichi*
23	二十三日	*nijūsannichi*
24	二十四日	*nijūyokka*
25	二十五日	*nijūgonichi*
26	二十六日	*nijūrokunichi*
27	二十七日	*nijūshichinichi*
28	二十八日	*nijūhachinichi*
29	二十九日	*nijūkunichi*
30	三十日	*sanjūnichi*
31	三十一日	*sanjūichinichi*

A duration of days

Except for *tsuitachi*, the same forms as above are used to indicate a duration of time in days. The optional suffix *-kan* ("period/time span") may be added.

1 day	一日	*ichinichi*
2 days	二日	*futsuka*
3 days	三日間	*mikka-kan*
8 days	八日間	*yōka-kan*
20 days	二十日間	*hatsuka-kan*
30 days	三十日間	*sanjūnichi-kan*

(For hours and minutes, see p. 93.)

Lesson 7

Modifying Nouns

Nouns can be modified by adjectives, other nouns, and verbs—as well as by certain adverbs that cross over to become noun modifiers.

As with adverbs, the modifier always comes before the noun it modifies. In English, you can say either "the delicious chocolate" or "the chocolate that is delicious," and both mean the same thing; but in Japanese you don't have the second option—not even when the modifier is more complicated, as in "the chocolate that her husband gave her for Christmas last year." It doesn't matter what kind of modifiers are used, or how long or short they are, or how many separate modifiers there may be. The rule remains: modifiers always come first. (This rule does not overturn what you have already learned about adjectives being used like verbs at the end of a sentence. Such adjectives are not being used as modifiers.)

84 This OL has just stepped out of the rain as she arrives for work.

Sound FX: ザー
Zā
(sound of heavy downpour outside)

OL: ひゃー、 ひどい 雨!
Hyā, *hidoi* *ame!*
(exclam.) terrible/horrible rain
"Yikes! [It's] a terrible rain!"
"My goodness! What a downpour!" (PL2)

- this is a noun-type sentence in which the main/final noun is modified by an adjective, and *da* ("is/are")—or *da wa*, since the speaker is female—has been omitted at the end. *Da* is quite commonly omitted at the end of noun-type sentences in colloquial speech—especially in exclamations, and especially among female speakers.

A plain adjective in a polite sentence

Adjectives that modify nouns are always in the plain form, even within a PL3 sentence; *desu* never comes between an adjective and the noun it modifies. A sentence's politeness level is determined primarily by the final verb, adjective, or noun + *da/desu* phrase (the sidebar on pp. 38–39 notes some other factors) and is not affected by plain adjectives being used as modifiers.

Asami

85 Dietman Kaji Ryūnosuke offers congratulations to Asami Tsunetarō when he returns from facing the press for the first time after being selected prime minister.

Kaji: 素晴しい 演説 でした!
Subarashii *enzetsu* *deshita!*
wonderful speech was
"It was a wonderful speech!" (PL3)

- the core statement of the sentence is *enzentsu deshita* ("[it] was a speech"); with the adjective *subarashii* ("wonderful/fantastic") modifying the main noun *enzetsu*, it becomes "[It] was a wonderful speech." The PL3 adjective *subarashii desu* would never occur as a modifier—though it often occurs as a sentence.
- the present-tense equivalent of the sentence, "It is a wonderful speech," would be *Subarashii enzetsu desu* (PL3) or *Subarashii enzetsu da* (PL2).

Modifying the adjective that modifies a noun

An adjective that is modifying a noun can in turn be modified by an adverb. Since modifiers always come first, an adverb precedes the adjective it modifies, which precedes the noun it modifies.

86 In looking over the personnel files for his newly formed section, Shima observes not only that his deputy chief speaks several languages and has won the Hatsushiba President's Award three times, but that he is twice divorced.

Shima: なるほど。 結構 いそがしい 男 だ な。
Naruhodo. Kekkō isogashii otoko da na.
I see/ah-hah quite busy man is (colloq.)
"Ah-hah. He's quite a busy man, isn't he?"
"Ah-hah. Sounds like he's quite a busy man." (PL2)

- *naruhodo* expresses understanding of, or interest in, what one has heard/observed/experienced: "ah-hah/I see/indeed/interesting." It's most commonly used to respond to what another person has said.
- *kekkō* also occurs as an "adjectival noun" (to be introduced in fig. 93), but here it appears as an adverb, modifying the adjective *isogashii*. The combination *kekkō isogashii* ("quite busy") in turn modifies the noun *otoko* ("man/male person") → "quite busy man" → "quite a busy man."
- a PL3 equivalent of this sentence would be *Kekkō isogashii otoko desu ne.* The *da* at the end changes to *desu*, but the modifying adjective remains in plain form.

Nouns modifying nouns with の *no*

The particle の *no* between two nouns makes the first into a modifier for the second, and the first can describe the second in a wide variety of different ways. When the first noun is a personal name or any other noun referring to a person, it most typically describes the next mentioned item as belonging to that person—that is, it indicates possession.

87 As a treat for the carpenters' tea break (fig. 6), Kōsuke's landlady has left some *kinton*, a confection made from mashed sweet potatoes and chestnuts.

Sada: ウマイ きんとん です ね。
Umai kinton desu ne.
good/tasty kinton is (colloq.)
"This is good *kinton*." (PL3)

Kōsuke: 大家さん の 自家製 です。
Ōya-san no jikasei desu.
landlady-(pol.) 's homemade is
"It's my landlady's homemade." (PL3)

- *umai* is an adjective modifying *kinton*; when *umai* describes a food item, it means "tasty/delicious."
- *-san* is usually added for politeness when speaking of one's *ōya* ("landlord/landlady").
- *jikasei*, written with kanji meaning "own + house + made," is a noun in Japanese.

Even when the noun does not refer to a person, it's often easiest to think of the Japanese noun + *no* combination as showing possession.

会社	の	社長		ねこ	の	ごはん		明日	の	クラス		火事	の	勢い
kaisha	*no*	*shachō*		*neko*	*no*	*gohan*		*ashita*	*no*	*kurasu*		*kaji*	*no*	*ikioi*
company	's	president		cat	's	food/meal		tomorrow	's	class		fire	's	intensity
the company's president				**the cat's food**				**tomorrow's class**				**the fire's intensity**

会社 の 社長
kaisha no shachō
company 's president
the company's president

ねこ の ごはん
neko no gohan
cat 's food/meal
the cat's food

明日 の クラス
ashita no kurasu
tomorrow 's class
tomorrow's class

火事 の 勢い
kaji no ikioi
fire 's intensity
the fire's intensity

No can simply show direct modification, or be like "of"

In many cases, *X no Y* is simply equivalent to *XY* in English—as with the "four-leaf clover" in the first frame here. In other cases, *no* is better thought of as equivalent to "of"—as with the "sign of good luck" in the second frame. Be careful, though. In the latter case, the word order is the opposite of English: *X no Y* in Japanese is equivalent to "Y of X" in English.

88 A young couple are out for a leisurely stroll in the countryside when one of them discovers a four-leaf clover.

Woman: あ! 四つ葉 の クローバー。
A!   Yotsuba no   kurōbā.
(interj.) four-leaf (mod.) clover
"Oh! A four-leaf clover!" (PL2)

Man: 幸運 の しるし だ。
Kōun no shirushi da.
good fortune of   sign   is.
"It's a sign of good luck." (PL2)

- *yotsuba* is a compound noun formed by combining *yottsu* ("four") and *ha* ("leaf"; the sound changes to *ba* in combinations).

No = "in/on/at"

The noun marked by *no* may indicate the location of the noun that follows, so it can be equivalent to English words like "in/on/at" that indicate location. In this case, too, the word order is the opposite of English, so Japanese *X no Y* is equivalent to "Y in/on/at X" in English.

89 In the men's room at work, Kariage-kun discovers there is no toilet paper. Then he notices an emergency call button intended for use by someone who feels ill. He presses it and a buzzer goes off in the security office.

Sound FX: ビー
Bii
Bzzz (sound of alarm buzzer)

Guard: 一階 の トイレ だ!
Ikkai no toire da!
first floor on toilet/restroom is
"It's the restroom on the first floor!" (PL2)

- *ikkai* is a combination of *ichi* ("one") and the counter suffix *-kai* used for floors/stories in a building. This counter sounds the same as the one used for "times/occasions/repetitions" in fig. 81, but it is written with a different kanji. In spoken language, the difference has to be understood from the context.

- in this case, "the first-floor restroom" works just as well in English as "the restroom on the first floor," but that won't always be true when the modifying noun indicates a location.

"If you feel unwell, press this button."

No = "who is/that is"

In many cases, *no* indicates that the two nouns refer to the same person or thing, either like "the cat Michael" or like "Michael, who is a cat" (*neko no Maikeru*). Again, it's important to remember that in the latter case, the word order is the reverse of English. Particles don't change for tense, so *no* can be "who is/that is," "who was/that was," or "who will be/that will be" depending on the tense of the verb, adjective, or *da/desu* at the end of the sentence.

90 Shin-chan's parents have brought him skiing for the first time in his life (fig. 65). His mother is excited to be back on the slopes after a long hiatus.

Mother: 久しぶり ｜の｜ スキー だ わ。
Hisashiburi ｜*no*｜ *sukii da wa.*
first time in long time   that is   ski/skiing   is   (fem.)
"This is skiing that is the first time in a long time."
"This is our first time skiing in a long time."
(PL2)

- *hisashiburi* is a noun referring to an event that occurs for the first time in a long time, so *hisashiburi no sukii* = "skiing that is the first time in a long time." The use of *hisashiburi* as a greeting appears in fig. 17.

Modifying the modifier

The modifying noun can in turn be modified by another, placed before it. Theoretically, there is no limit to how many nouns can be strung together with a *no* between each noun.

91 Friends of the bride seated together at a wedding dinner are getting acquainted.

A: みち子 ｜の｜ 会社 ｜の｜ かた です か?
Michiko ｜*no*｜ *kaisha* ｜*no*｜ *kata desu ka?*
(name)   's   company   of/from   person   is/are   (?)
"Are you a person from Michiko's company?"
"Are you from Michiko's work?" (PL3)

B: いえ、あの、学生 ｜の｜ 時 ｜の｜ バイト仲間 です。
Ie,   ano, gakusei ｜*no*｜ *toki* ｜*no*｜ *baito nakama desu.*
no   um   coll. stud.   (mod.)   time   of/from   stud. job friend   am
"No, um, I'm a student job friend from her college days."
"No, um, I worked a part-time job with her in college."
(PL3)

- *kata* is a formal/polite word for "person" The more neutral word is *hito*.
- in A's speech, the first *no* shows possession and the second is like "of" or "from" → "person of/from Michiko's company." Japanese speakers often use *kaisha* ("company") when English speakers would say "work" or "the office."
- *gakusei* most commonly refers to college undergraduates—though it can also include students at other levels. When *toki* ("time") is modified like this, it typically means "the time/days/era when" the specified action occurred or when the state/situation existed: *gakusei no toki* = "time when [someone] was a student" → "student days."
- when three nouns are linked with *no*s, the first two may combine to modify the third, as in both cases here, or the first may modify the combination of the other two. With longer strings of nouns, various groupings can apply; context usually tells you what the groupings should be.
- *baito* is short for the loanword *arubaito* (from German *Arbeit*, "work/job"), which in Japanese refers to jobs done alongside one's main occupation, such as student jobs, moonlighting, and housewives working part time for a little extra cash.

Omission of the modified noun

Sometimes the noun being modified is understood and therefore omitted. In the example here, the *no* indicates possession, but the same omission can occur with other uses of *no* as well.

92 As he's on his way out of the locker room, Toshihiko finds a student ID case on the floor. He recognizes it as belonging to the girl who volunteered to be manager for the Kakegawa High soccer team.

Toshihiko: ん?
N?
huh?/what?
"What's this?"

あの　女　の　だ。
Ano   onna   no   da.
that   girl   's   is
"It's that girl's." (PL2)

• the full sentence would be *Ano onna no gakusei-shō da,* but *gakusei-shō* ("student ID") is understood so it is omitted.

The ways one noun can describe another are virtually limitless. To help zero in on the intended meaning in any given case, start by placing English equivalents of the two nouns together in the same order as the Japanese nouns (as with the four-leaf clover in fig. 88), then adjust the first word to give it a descriptive form that fits the context. For example, if you see or hear *Tōkyō no kata* and think "Tokyo person," the context should quickly tell you whether it means "person who lives in Tokyo," "person going to Tokyo," "person who came from Tokyo," or a person with yet some other relationship to Tokyo.

On the other hand, when you're the speaker, knowing that a single particle can serve for all those meanings makes things wonderfully simple: you don't have to learn different expressions for each; you just put the modifying noun first and follow it with *no.*

Some nouns take な *na*

Most nouns take *no* to become modifiers, but there's a special subgroup that requires *na* instead. They are all descriptive nouns, which typically correspond to English adjectives, and because of this they have variously been called "*na*-adjectives," "quasi adjectives," or "pseudo adjectives," but this book calls them **adjectival nouns**. As the main noun at the end of a sentence, these words require *da* or *desu* just like other nouns (when used this way instead of as a modifier, they sometimes correspond to English verbs rather than adjectives).

93 This couple is all ready for bed when the phone begins to ring. They've apparently had late night calls before.

Sound FX: ルルル　　ルルル　　ルルル
Rururu   rururu   rururu
Ring   ring   ring

Wife: きっと　また　ヘンな　イタズラ　電話　　よ。
Kitto   mata   hen na   itazura   denwa   yo.
probably   again   strange   mischief   phone call   (is-emph.)
"It's probably some weird crank call again." (PL2)

Husband: ヘンタイ　め!
Hentai   -me!
pervert   -(derog.)
"Damn pervert!" (PL1)

• *kitto* can variously mean "maybe/probably/surely."
• *hen* (written 変 in kanji) is an adjectival noun that, when followed by *na,* generally corresponds to English adjectives like "strange/odd/abnormal."
• *itazura* is a noun for "mischief/a trick/a prank," and *denwa* can refer either to the telephone itself or to a phone call—here the latter. *Itazura denwa* is an established compound noun for "crank call."
• *-me* is a derogatory suffix expressing contempt/anger toward the person named.

Don't be fooled by a final *-i*

Some adjectival nouns end in *-i*, like adjectives, and because they are descriptive, they translate as adjectives in English, but that doesn't make them adjectives in Japanese. They require *na* when modifying another noun, and at the end of a sentence they require *da* or *desu* like any other noun. (As with other nouns, *da/desu* may be omitted in exclamations.)

94 Shinnosuke the dog and Poppo the cat have been brought together for an *o-miai*—a formal meeting between the prospective bride and groom in an arranged marriage. The go-between introduced the two families, and then she and the parents excused themselves so that the two young people could get to know each other. After an awkward silence, Shinnosuke tries to break the ice.

Shinnosuke: いやー、 き、 きれいな 方 です ねえ。
Iyā,   ki-   kirei na   kata   desu   nē.
(interj.) (stammer) pretty person is/are (colloq.)
"Uhhh, y- you sure are a pretty person."
"Uhhh, y- you're a very pretty girl." (PL3)

Poppo: そ、 そんな...
So-   sonna...
(stammer) that kind of
"Gr- gracious me..." (PL3 implied)

- *iyā* is a warm-up/hesitation word—like "well/that is/ uhh" spoken while searching for what to say or getting up the nerve to say it.
- *kirei* is an adjectival noun for either "pretty/beautiful" or "clean"—here clearly the former.
- *sonna* here is Poppo's way of modestly brushing off the compliment, essentially implying "That's not true." It's customary in Japan to deny a compliment rather than thank the speaker. *Sonna* has no politeness level of its own, but if Poppo had completed her sentence here, she would have ended it with a PL3 form.

Here are a few more adjectival nouns used as modifiers. Foreign adjectives generally enter Japanese as adjectival nouns.

好きな 人	嫌いな 食べ物	便利な 辞書	ハンサムな 男
suki na hito	*kirai na tabemono*	*benri na jisho*	*hansamu na otoko*
liked person	disliked food	handy/useful dictionary	handsome man
the person I like	**a food I dislike**	**a handy dictionary**	**a handsome man**

☛ Another key difference of adjectival nouns is that they cannot be modified by adjectives or the other usual ways of modifying nouns; they are modified by adverbs.

Some adjectives can also modify with *-na*

For most adjectives, using the plain form ending in *-i* is the only way to modify a noun, but a very small number have an alternative form: the final *-i* can be changed to *-na*. Of the adjectives introduced so far, *chiisai* ("small") can become *chiisana*, and *ōkii* ("large") can become *ōkina*. Two others that have alternative forms are *okashii → okashina* ("strange/funny") and *yawarakai → yawarakana* ("soft"). The *-na* forms of these adjectives cannot be used at the end of a sentence, only as modifiers.

95 In this gag strip, Cat comes upon Dog howling at the moon—or at least he thinks that's what Dog is doing. He asks him if it's because he's lonely. Dog pulls himself erect and sticks out his chest.

Dog: 大きな アクビ でした。 エッヘン。
Ōkina   akubi   deshita.   Ehhen.
big   yawn   was   ahem
"It was a big yawn. Ahem."
"That was just a big yawn. Ahem." (PL3)

- writing *akubi* in katakana is merely the artist's choice; the same is true with *hen*, *itazura*, and *hentai* on the facing page.
- *ehhen* (or *ehen*) is a self-satisfied clearing of the throat sound.

Sukku
(effect of standing up tall)

Compound nouns

As seen with *baito nakama* ("student job" + "friend") in fig. 91 and *itazura denwa* ("mischief" + "phone call") in fig. 93, certain nouns join other nouns to form compound nouns without any intervening *no*. Sometimes it's all right to add the *no* anyway, but depending on the particular word, it may sound unnatural or even alter the meaning, so you will essentially need to learn such compounds one by one. Here is another example.

96 This do-it-yourselfer is building a new brick fence around his house when his wife calls out the window:

Wife: お昼ごはん　　　　よ。
O-hiru-gohan　　*yo.*
(hon.)-noon meal　(is-emph.)
"It is the noon meal."
"It's time for lunch." (PL2)

Husband: オウ。
Ō.
(interj.)
"All right." (PL2)

- *hiru* means "noon," and *gohan* means "meal," so *hiru-gohan* = "noon meal" → "lunch." Similarly, *asa* = "morning," and *ban* = "evening/night," so *asa-gohan* = "morning meal" → "breakfast," and *ban-gohan* = "evening meal" → "supper."
- the honorific *o-* is commonly added to *hiru* or *hiru-gohan* even in PL2 speech, especially by female speakers; it is never added to *asa-gohan* or *ban-gohan*.
- the particle *yo* often serves all by itself as *da yo* or *desu yo* ("is/are" + emphasis).
- the interjection *ō* here acknowledges that he heard and expresses approval.

Verbs can modify nouns, too

If Japanese adjectives can act like verbs, perhaps it won't be too much of a surprise to learn that Japanese verbs can act like adjectives. Place any verb in front of a noun, like an adjective, and the verb becomes a modifier for the noun.

97 At their *o-miai*, Poppo asks Shinnosuke what his favorite pastime is, and he says it's to race vigorously about the fields. When Shinnosuke returns the question, the differences in their tastes begin to emerge:

Poppo: 寝る　　　こと　です。
Neru　　*koto*　*desu.*
to sleep　thing/activity　is
"[My favorite pastime] is the activity of sleeping."
"I like to nap." (PL3)

- the polite form of *neru* ("to sleep/go to bed") is *nemasu*.
- *koto* refers to an intangible "thing" such as a "question/fact/matter/event/situation/purpose/activity," so *neru koto* is literally "the activity of sleeping."

In Japanese, almost any verb in almost any form can be placed before a noun to modify it—past, non-past, and negative, as well as the other forms introduced in the second half of this book; the one crucial qualifier is that the polite *-masu* forms aren't generally used this way. By comparison, relatively few verbs in relatively few forms can do the same in English, so the frequency with which verbs modify nouns in Japanese can take some getting used to for English speakers. But once you've picked up how it works, you'll find it a very efficient and straightforward means of expression.

Nouns

Japanese nouns are pretty uncomplicated. They don't have gender, and they don't change form according to where they appear in the sentence, nor depending on how many items are being spoken of, so for the most part you learn one form and that's it. Still, there are a few things worth knowing and keeping in mind.

◆**Plurals:** Not having separate forms for plural nouns certainly can cause ambiguity at times, but usually it doesn't. When context isn't sufficient to make clear whether the number of items involved is one or more than one, the specific number is stated or a more general quantity word like *sukoshi* ("a little/a few") or *takusan* ("a lot/many") is used.

◆**Plurals for people:** Words that refer to people can be made explicitly plural by adding **-tachi** (neutral), **-gata** (formal/polite), or **-ra** (informal).

子供	子供たち	先生	先生方
kodomo	*kodomo-tachi*	*sensei*	*sensei-gata*
child/children	children	teacher/teachers	teachers

When attached to the name of an individual, these suffixes imply "[that person] and his group/associates."

山田	山田ら / 山田たち
Yamada	*Yamada-ra/Yamada-tachi*
Yamada [alone]	Yamada and his associates/cohorts

Of the three suffixes, *-tachi* is the most common and can be used across all politeness levels—though *-ra* takes over quite often in PL2 speech and usually in PL1 speech. *-Gata* belongs to PL4 speech and is used only with *anata* ("you"—see "Personal Pronouns," p. 63) and relatively few regular nouns.

◆**Doubling up:** In a few cases it's possible to make a noun plural by repeating it (often a sound change is involved). This doesn't work for just any noun, but when you encounter doubled-up nouns like these, you know you're dealing with more than one of the item. (Note: 々 is a repeat character for kanji.)

山	山々	人	人々
yama	*yama-yama*	*hito*	*hito-bito*
mountain/mountains	mountains	person/people	people

◆**Nouns from adjectives:** Adjectives can be turned into nouns by replacing the final -い -*i* with -さ **-sa**, or sometimes -み **-mi**.

寒い	寒さ	暑い	暑さ
samui	*samusa*	*atsui*	*atsusa*
(is) cold	coldness/chill	(is) hot	hotness/heat
ありがたい	ありがたみ	悲しい	悲しみ
arigatai	*arigatami*	*kanashii*	*kanashimi*
(is) grateful	value/appreciation	(is) sad	sadness/sorrow

98 Kakegawa High is still a new school, and most people gave its soccer team little chance against its first-round opponent, which, though recently down on its luck, has been a longtime powerhouse. Even the players themselves had their doubts as game time approached—in spite of their confidence in practice. But they take the game easily, 5-0.

掛川	の	強さ	は	本物	だ!!
Kakegawa	*no*	*tsuyosa*	*wa*	*honmono*	*da!!*
Kakegawa	's	strength	as for	real thing	is

"Kakegawa's strength is the real thing!"
"Kakegawa's strength is for real!" (PL2)

- *tsuyosa* is the noun form of the adjective *tsuyoi* ("is strong"), so it means "strength."
- *wa* ("as for") in this case marks *Kakegawa no tsuyosa* ("Kakegawa's strength") as the subject of the sentence. You will learn more about the particle *wa* in Lesson 11.

◆**Nouns from verbs:** With many verbs, the stem, or pre-*masu* form, can be used as a noun. There's no easy way to know which ones, though, so you'll simply have to learn them as you encounter them.

帰る	帰ります	帰り
kaeru	*kaerimasu*	*kaeri*
go home	go home	"the way home" or "his/her return"
始める	始めます	始め
hajimeru	*hajimemasu*	*hajime*
begin	begin	the beginning

◆**Suru-verb nouns:** For *suru* verbs, the part before *suru* is a noun. As a rule, foreign verbs enter Japanese as nouns, and they must be followed by *suru* to turn them back into verbs in Japanese.

逮捕する	逮捕	約束する	約束
taiho suru	*taiho*	*yakusoku suru*	*yakusoku*
to arrest	an arrest	to promise	a promise
コピーする	コピー	メモする	メモ
kopii suru	*kopii*	*memo suru*	*memo*
to photocopy	a photocopy	make a note	a note

Lesson 8

Explanatory の *No*

Many sentences in Japanese get a special extension consisting of the particle *no* plus *da* or *desu* in the "wrap-up" position where sentence particles optionally appear (see p. 10). Because it occurs when giving or seeking explanations, the particle is called **explanatory *no*** and *no da/ desu* is called the **explanatory extension**. The feeling can be like English explanations that begin, "It's that ∼," or, "The situation/explanation is that ∼." But the form also occurs in sentences that English speakers won't think of as explanations, and sometimes all that the so-called explanatory *no* does is add emphasis.

99 This scholar began by describing the flehmen reaction in cats in relatively formal scientific language, noting that it is associated with the inhalation of odors and the stimulation of the olfactory organ, and so forth, but then he boils it down to its essence:

Scholar: くさい ｜のです。｜
   Kusai ｜*no desu.*｜
   is smelly (explan.)
   "It's that [something] is smelly."
   "Something stinks." (PL3)

© Kobayashi Makoto, *What's Michael!?*, Kōdansha.

- his core statement is the one word adjective-type sentence *Kusai*, but he adds the explanatory extension because he is explaining what is going on when a cat makes the face known as a flehmen reaction.

Combining with sentence particles

The extension can occur together with the various sentence particles introduced in Lesson 2; any such particle(s) included are placed after *no da* or *no desu*, not before.

As seen in this example, explanatory *no* can be shortened to *n*, changing the extension to *n da* or *n desu*. This occurs very commonly in both PL2 and PL3 speech. In fact, using the full *no* can sound quite stiff: although *no desu* in fig. 99 simply reflects the formal, academic tone of the scholar's entire speech, in most conversational situations it would sound stilted.

100 Kōsuke's landlady grows *hechima* ("loofah") vines to use the leaves in a folk remedy for rheumatism. Since the liquid that flows from the vine when it's cut is valued as a cosmetic lotion, she asks Kōsuke to help draw it into bottles. Kōsuke asks why she wants to collect so much.

Landlady: 近所 に 配る ｜んだ よ。｜
   Kinjo *ni* *kubaru* ｜*n da* *yo.*｜
   neighborhood to/among will distribute (explan.) (emph.)
   "I'm going to distribute it to the neighborhood."
   "I'm going to share it with the neighbors." (PL2)

© Maekawa Tsukasa, *Dai-Tōkyō Binbō Seikatsu Manyuaru*, Kōdansha.

- *kinjo* literally means "nearby place" → "neighborhood/vicinity," but it often refers to the homes/families/residents of the neighborhood → "neighbors."
- *ni* marks the target of the action: "to."
- the PL3 form of *kubaru* ("distribute/hand out") is *kubarimasu*.
- *Kinjo ni kubaru* is a complete sentence ("I will distribute it to the neighborhood") without the extension, but *n da yo* adds the feeling of "The explanation [for why I want to collect so much] is that ∼." In English, the explanatory feeling is implicit from the situation, but in Japanese an explanation like this sounds funny without the extension.

For noun-type sentences

What comes before *n(o) da* or *n(o) desu* can be any kind of complete sentence, but it usually ends in a plain, PL2 form. For verb- and adjective-type sentences, this simply means the familiar dictionary form, or the PL2 version of any of the various forms to be introduced later. For noun-type sentences, however, the final *da/desu* is replaced by *na*, and this is followed by *n(o) da* or *n(o) desu* → ~ *na n(o) da/* ~ *na n(o) desu*. *Na* essentially serves as the verb "to be" in this pattern, and it does so for *all* nouns (i.e., it has nothing to do with nouns that require *na* when modifying other nouns). Here's a noun-type sentence with a PL3 extension.

101 The doctor is discussing the results of the patient's annual physical. He tells the patient that his blood pressure is high for his age.

Doctor: **"Please ask your wife to watch the salt in your diet."** (PL3)

Patient: 独身　　なんです。
Dokushin　*na n desu.*
single　　am-(explan.)
"I'm single." (PL3)

- without the extension, the patient's complete sentence would be *Dokushin desu*. The final *desu* in this simple sentence is replaced by *na* and then the extension *n desu* is attached (in PL2 speech, *n da* would be attached, as in the next example).
- the patient adds the extension because he is explaining that his circumstances are a little different from what the doctor has assumed.

A noun-type sentence with a PL2 extension

The politeness level of the sentence as a whole is determined mostly by whether the speaker uses *da* or *desu* in the extension—not by the politeness of the word that precedes it. Here's another noun-type sentence, this time with a PL2 extension.

102 Kōsuke's girlfriend Hiroko had put her name on a bottle of high quality Scotch at her favorite bar and invited Kōsuke to join her for a drink. He knows his limit is one drink, but he enjoys the good Scotch so much he can't resist having a second, and afterwards Hiroko has to prop him up as they make their way home by train. When they come out of the station near his apartment, Kōsuke remembers that he borrowed his neighbor's bicycle to come to the station.

Kōsuke: あ、　　自転車　なんだ。
A,　　*jitensha*　*na n da.*
(interj.)　bicycle　is/was-(explan.)
"Oh, I came by bike." (PL2)

Sound FX: ガチャ
Gacha
(rattle of bike lock)

- the basic sentence is *Jitensha da*, which often would simply mean "It's a bike," but here implies "[My means of transportation] is a bike" → "I came by bike." Kōsuke uses the *na n da* extension because he's explaining the circumstances that determine how they must proceed from here.

You will learn as you proceed that the *da* and *desu* in the explanatory extension can change form in all the same ways that any noun-type sentence changes form.

Omitting *da*

In informal speech, *no* (never just *n*) or *na no* (after nouns) can be used by itself, without adding *da*. This practice is more common among women and children, but it's heard among men as well. Ending a sentence with *no* or *na no* usually sounds quite a bit softer than ending with *n da* or *na n da*, so long as the tone of voice is benign. But *no/na no* can also be used very forcefully, as in this example where both speakers try to get their way by "explaining" in no uncertain terms what they want/intend to do.

TURN

"Urrrmph." "Urghgh."

103 Shin-chan and his mother are at the supermarket, and Shin-chan has just spotted the candy and snack food section. He leaps from the cart and starts trying to push the cart in that direction while his mother tries to turn it away.

Shin-chan:
お菓子　　コーナー　に　行く　[の!!]
O-kashi　　kōnā　ni　iku　no!!
candy/snack food corner　to　will go (explan.)
"We're going to the candy section!" (PL2)

Mother:
魚　　　　コーナー　に　行く　[の!!]
Sakana　　kōnā　ni　iku　no!!
fish　　　corner　to　will go (explan.)
"We're going to the seafood section!" (PL2)

© Usui Yoshito, Kureyon Shin-chan, Futabasha.

- *o-kashi* refers to sweets and snack foods of all kinds—candy, cookies, cakes, pastries, crackers, chips, etc. The *o-* is honorific but almost always used.
- *kōnā*, from English "corner," is often used to refer to a section/department/aisle in a store.
- *ni* marks the destination of a movement.
- *Okashi kōnā ni iku* and *Sakana kōnā ni iku* are both complete sentences ("We will go to the candy/fish section") without *no*, but mother and Shin-chan both add *no* because they're explaining their actions/intentions.

A plain *no* with a particle

Adding *ne* or *yo* to a plain *no* or *na no* (without *da* or *desu*) tends to sound more distinctly feminine—though this can't be considered exclusively female speech either.

Endo

104 As the newest member of the Kakegawa High soccer team, Toshihiko has been assigned to wash uniforms while the upperclassmen take a day off from practice. Just then Endō shows up to ask if she can be the team manager. When she realizes Toshihiko has been left to do the laundry while the others are off taking it easy, she draws her own conclusion.

Endō: よっぽど　　　　　へた　[なの]　ね。
Yoppodo　　　　heta　na no　ne.
greatly/considerably lacking in skill are-(explan.) (colloq.)
"It's that you are considerably unskilled [at soccer], isn't it?"
"You must be a really lousy player." (PL2)

Toshihiko

© Ōshima Tsukasa, Shoot!, Kodansha.

- *yoppodo* is a colloquial variation of *yohodo* ("considerably/greatly/very much").
- *heta* is an adjectival noun that refers to being "awkward/clumsy/all thumbs" at a particular skill—in this case, at playing soccer.
- the main sentence is *Yoppodo heta da* ("You are considerably unskilled"), and she uses the explanatory extension because she thinks she has found the explanation for the situation she observes. Since *heta* is a noun, the plain extension is *na no*; adding the particle *ne*, which seeks confirmation or agreement from the listener ("right?/isn't that so?") gives the feeling that she's guessing/surmising ("You must be ~") rather than stating a definite conclusion ("You are ~").

Asking for an explanation politely

When asking for an explanation in PL3 speech, *ka* follows the full extension, including *desu*, so the extension ends with *n(o) desu ka?* or *na n(o) desu ka?* After a verb, this essentially asks "Is the explanation that 〜?" or "Is it the case that 〜?" (with someone's/something's action filling the blank). After a noun or adjective, it asks, "Is the explanation that it's/I'm/you're/they're 〜?" or "Is it the case that it's/I'm/you're/they're 〜?" (with a name or description filling the blank). Here are a verb- and noun-type sentence.

105 When Kaji stops his campaign van in fig. 63, he says he would welcome a debate but does not think they should have it right there on the street. His opponent Tanizaki immediately questions him about a flier that links him with underworld figures. Kaji denies the link and reiterates that this is not the place to debate such groundless rumors. When he gets back into his van, Tanizaki calls after him.

Tanizaki: 加治さん、 逃げる ｜んです か?｜
 Kaji-san, nigeru | n desu ka? |
 (name-pol.) run away (explan.) (?)
 "Are you running away, Mr. Kaji?" (PL3)

- the polite form of *nigeru* ("flee/run away") is *nigemasu*.

- he uses the explanatory extension because he's in effect seeking an explanation for why he should run into her here.

106 Itō runs into Ms. Yoshida from the accounting department at work as he comes out of a video rental store.

Ito: うち、 この辺 ｜なんです か?｜
 Uchi, kono hen | na n desu ka? |
 home this vicinity is-(explan.) (?)
 "Is your home around here?"
 "Do you live around here?" (PL3)

Yoshida: **"Uh-huh. Up the hill just past Hi-kawa Shrine."** (PL2)

Asking for an explanation informally

When asking for an explanation in PL2 speech, *ka* replaces *da* in the extension: *(na) no da → (na) no ka?* (You will recall that *ka* also replaces *da* in making ordinary PL2 noun-type questions; see fig. 40). *(Na) no ka?* sounds quite abrupt, and can be considered mostly masculine. In the example here, the speaker asks for an explanation by adding *no ka?* to an adjective-type sentence.

107 Cat finds Dog howling at the moon—or at least he thinks that's what Dog is doing. He wonders why, so he asks this question. Dog's answer appears in fig. 95.

Cat: さびしい ｜の か?｜
 Sabishii | no ka? |
 lonely (explan.) (?)
 "Is it that you're lonely?"
 "Are you howling because you're lonely?" (PL2)

- the PL3 form of this question would be *Sabishii n(o) desu ka?*
- a straightforward *Sabishii ka*, without *no*, would be simply, "Are you lonely?" Adding the explanatory extension gives it the feeling of "Is it because you're lonely [that you're howling]?"

Asking more gently

Asking for an explanation with *(na) no ka?* sounds very abrupt, so when women are speaking informally, they usually use only *no?* or *na no?* with the intonation of a question, omitting *ka*.

108 Natsuko's high-school classmate Hashimoto Saeko lived for a time in Tokyo before returning to the village and coming to work for the Saeki Brewery. Here she tells Natsuko that she plans to go back to the city, and shows her the letter she has received from a man who promises to leave his wife for her.

Natsuko: 好き 　なの?
Suki 　 *na no?*
like/love 　(explan.-?)
"Do you love him?" (PL2)

- *suki* is an adjectival noun rather than a verb, so strictly speaking it refers to a state of liking/fondness rather than to an action; but it's much easier to think of the phrase *suki da/desu* as equivalent to the English verb "like." In interpersonal relationships, *suki da/desu* often implies the more intense emotion of "love." Because *suki* is a noun, *da/desu* changes to *na* when the explanatory *no* is added: *Suki na no* = "It's that I love him"; with the intonation of a question, the same sentence becomes, "Is it that you love him?" → "Do you love him?"

Not limited to women

Asking for an explanation with just *no?* or *na no?* may be more common among women and children, but it's also heard a good deal from men in informal speech.

109 When Kōsuke goes next door to borrow some butter, he finds his friend, a college student, putting on his jacket.

Kōsuke: 出かける　の?
Dekakeru 　 *no?*
go out 　(explan.-?)
"Are you going out?" (PL2)

Student: バイト　です。
Baito 　 *desu.*
part-time job　is
"It's my part-time job."
"To work." (PL3)

- *dekakeru/dekakemasu* means "leave the house/office (to run an errand, shop, go on a date, etc.)."
- *baito* is short for *arubaito* ("part-time job"; fig. 91).

Some final notes on *no da/desu*

N(o) da/desu is used a great deal more in Japanese than locutions like "The explanation is that ∼" or "It's that/It's because ∼" are used in English, so when going from Japanese to English, it's relatively rare that you really need to use such phrasings; the context is usually enough to provide the explanatory impact in English. On the other hand, when going the other way, *n(o) da/desu* is often required in Japanese when you'd never think of using locutions like "The explanation is that ∼" or "It's that/It's because ∼" in English, so it's important to keep your ears tuned to actual Japanese usage and not merely rely on translating from your English thought.

Japanese also has some particles that specifically mean "because," which are introduced in Lesson 14. But in many cases, only the *n(o) da/desu* or *na n(o) da/desu* extension is needed when making an explanation.

Personal Pronouns

No personal pronouns (words used in place of people's names) have appeared in the manga examples so far—though they are ubiquitous in the English translations. That's mainly because context has always made them unnecessary in the Japanese. But even when the context doesn't sufficiently identify a person and an explicit reference is indeed called for, Japanese speakers tend to avoid using pronouns; they prefer to use the person's name or title instead. The result is that personal pronouns are heard relatively rarely in Japanese, and English speakers accustomed to using them constantly must rein in the impulse to do the same in Japanese if they want their speech to sound natural. Still, sometimes pronouns are needed. Here is a brief introduction to the most important personal pronouns:

110 The proprietor of Lemon Hart asked a new customer his name in fig. 67. Here is his answer.

わたし	です	か?	仁	です。
Watashi	*desu*	*ka?*	*Jin*	*desu.*
I/me	is	(?)	(name)	is

"Me? Jin." (PL3)

First Person

わたし **watashi** is used for both "I" and "me" by adult speakers of both sexes; *watashi-tachi* = "we/us." あたし **atashi** and *atashi-tachi* are informal feminine variations. ぼく **boku** and おれ **ore** = "I/me" for male speakers only; both are less formal than *watashi*, and *ore* can have a rough feeling—though among friends and family it is merely familiar. *Boku-tachi/boku-ra* and *ore-tachi* = "we/us" for males only. *Watashi no/atashi no/boku no/ore no* = "my/mine." (For more on the plural forms, see "Nouns" on p. 57.)

111 The wife of Hatsushiba Electric's President Ōizumi has dropped in on a "Spring Fiesta" sales event that Shima is in charge of. She has not met Shima before, but she recognizes his name when he greets her and identifies himself.

Ōizumi:
そう...	あなた	が	島さん	ね。
Sō...	*Anata*	*ga*	*Shima-san*	*ne.*
I see	you	(subj.)	(name-pol.)	(colloq.)

"I see... So you're Mr. Shima." (PL2)

• *ga* marks the subject of a sentence. See next page.

Second Person

あなた **anata** (plural: *anata-gata/anata-tachi*) means "you"; in informal speech this can become あんた **anta** (plural: *anta-gata/anta-tachi/anta-ra*). Though *anata* is quite formal, you should avoid using it with social superiors, whom you should address and refer to by name or title instead. *Anata no/anta no* = "your/yours." きみ **kimi** (plural: *kimi-tachi/kimi-ra*) is an informal "you," generally used only by males when addressing equals or subordinates. おまえ **omae** (plural *omae-tachi/omae-ra*) is the second person counterpart to *ore*; it is very informal/familiar, can feel quite rough, and is generally used only by males. *Kimi no/omae no* = "your/yours."

Third Person

かれ **kare** = "he/him" and かのじょ **kanojo** = "she/her," but these should not be used when speaking of social superiors or of one's own family members. *Kare-tachi/kare-ra* = "they/them" when speaking of a male and his cohorts (male or female), while *kanojo-tachi/kanojo-ra* = "they/them" when speaking of a female and her cohorts (male or female). *Kare no* = "his" and *kanojo no* = "her/hers."

(For some other important pronouns, see Lesson 12.)

112 An OL catches a co-worker sneaking a peek at a special picture.

• *kare* ("he/him") and *kanojo* ("she/her") also double as words for "boyfriend" and "girlfriend" when the context is right.

• *kare no* can show possession (fig. 87), so *kare no shashin* could also mean "his picture" in the sense of "belonging to him," but the context tells us otherwise in this case.

• *miisētē* is an elongated *mise-te*, a form of the verb *miseru/misemasu* ("show"). The *-te* form of a verb, formally introduced in Lesson 19, can be used to make informal requests.

OL:
あーっ!	彼	の	写真?	みーせーてー。
Ā!	*Kare*	*no*	*shashin?*	*Miisētē.*
(interj.)	he/him	of	photo	show-(request)

"Oh! Is that a picture of him? Show me!"
"Oh! Is that a picture of your boyfriend? Let me see it!" (PL2)

Lesson 9

が *Ga* Marks the Subject

The subject of a sentence tells you who or what the main verb, adjective, or noun at the end is talking about. In all but one (fig. 111) of the examples you've seen so far, the subject was already clear enough from the context that the speakers did not feel they needed to state their subjects explicitly. But that's certainly not always the case. When the subject does need to be spelled out, it's usually marked with the particle が *ga*.

A verb-type sentence tells of an action, and *ga* marks who or what does/did/will do that action.

113 Uzuratani thinks his boss shouldn't have to prepare his own tea.

Uzuratani: 課長、 私 が やりますよ。
Kachō, | *watashi ga* | *yarimasu yo.*
sec. chief　　I　(subj.)　do/will do　(emph.)
"Boss, I'll do that." (PL3)

Boss: いい、　　　　いい。
Ii,　　　　　　　*ii.*
good/fine/okay　good/fine/okay
"That's okay, that's okay." (PL2)

- *ga* marks *watashi* ("I/me") as the subject—the doer.
- *yaru/yarimasu* means "do." *Yaru* and *suru* are sometimes interchangeable, as they are in this case (→ *Watashi ga shimasu yo*), but in many cases the usage is a matter of custom and the other cannot be substituted. When they are interchangeable, *yaru* feels less formal than *suru*.
- *ii* is an adjective meaning "good/fine/okay," but when used in response to an offer, *Ii* (or *Ii desu/Ii yo/Ii wa*) means "That's okay/Never mind."

© Ōhashi Tsuyoshi. *Kaisha-in no Merodii*, Take Shobō.

Subject of an adjective-type sentence

Since Japanese adjectives have the meaning of the verb "to be" built in, the subject of an adjective-type sentence is the subject of the adjective itself, not of a separate verb.

An adjective-type sentence describes something, and *ga* marks who or what it describes.

114 This man has woken up with a searing hangover the morning after a night on the town.

Man: ふぁー
Fuā
(Yawn)

あー、 頭 が 痛い。
Ā, | *atama ga* | *itai.*
(interj.)　head　(subj.)　is painful
"Ohh, my head hurts."
"Ohh, what a headache!" (PL2)

- *ga* marks *atama* as the subject—what *itai* describes.
- *itai* is an adjective meaning "(is) painful," but its use with a subject often corresponds more naturally to the English "~ hurts," or the expression "have a ~ ache."
- the PL3 equivalent of this sentence is *Atama ga itai desu.* If responding to the question "What's wrong?" one would add the explanatory extension: *Atama ga itai n da/desu.*

© Imazeki Shin. *Ojama Shimasu*, Take Shobō.

64

Subject of a noun-type sentence

A noun-type sentence names or identifies something, and *ga* marks who or what it names or identifies. If the main noun before *da/desu* at the end of the sentence is an adjectival noun, the sentence is usually describing something, and *ga* marks who or what it describes.

Megane

115 Ever since hearing on the bar radio that heavy rains are expected to continue through the night, with flooding likely, Matsuda has been fretting about getting home. Then he checks outside again and sees that the rain has stopped. He speaks to his friend Megane.

Matsuda:
帰りましょう。 いま が チャンス。
Kaerimashō. | *Ima* | *ga* | *chansu.*
let's go home | now | (subj.) | chance
"Let's go home. Now's our chance." (PL3)

- *kaerimashō* is the PL3 "let's/I'll ～" form of *ka-eru/kaerimasu* ("return home"). See fig. 36.
- the relative time word *ima* ("now") is used as a noun here, with *ga* marking it as the subject. The sentence essentially identifies "now" as the moment of opportunity.
- *chansu* is the Japanese rendering of the English word "chance." *Desu* ("is") has been omitted at the end of the sentence, giving it an informal note—though in cases like this the PL of the first sentence tends to carry over to the second.

Even with the subject explicitly stated, you may find that you still need to turn to context to fill in some of the details. In fig. 114, context reveals that it is the speaker's head that hurts ("my head"), but in another situation (e.g., in a question or as part of a longer sentence), *atama ga itai* could refer to the listener's or someone else's head hurting. Similarly, in this example, the context reveals that Matsuda is talking about a chance for himself and his friend ("our chance").

Omitting *ga*

Even when the speaker deems it a good idea to specify a subject, he or she doesn't necessarily have to use *ga*. In colloquial speech, the particle is often omitted when the context or structure of the sentence makes it sufficiently clear which word is the subject.

GULP

116 Kōsuke's cousin Masabō is on summer vacation, and he asks Kōsuke to go hiking with him in the hills on the far outskirts of Tokyo. They take along a picnic lunch of *o-nigiri* ("rice balls") and *mugi-cha* ("roasted barley tea," popular as a chilled drink in summer).

Kōsuke: あー、 もう ムギ茶 ぬるい や。
Ā, | *mō* | *mugicha* | *nurui* | *ya.*
(interj.) | already | barley tea | is lukewarm | (emph.)
"Oh, the barley tea is already lukewarm."
"Oh well, the *mugicha* isn't cold anymore." (PL2)

Masabō: あれー。
Arē.
"Darn." (PL2)

- Masabō's *o-nigiri* is partly covered with a sheet of dried seaweed called *nori*—familiar to many as the wrapping used for sushi rolls.
- *mugicha* is the subject of the adjective *nurui* ("is lukewarm"), which refers to when something either isn't as hot as desired or isn't as cold as desired.
- *ya* is a mildly emphatic sentence particle that carries a note of disappointment or resignation, used only in informal speech.
- *are?* is an interjection of surprise or bewilderment: "Huh?/What?/What the—?" An elongated *arē* feels like a dismayed "Wha-a-at?/Oh no-o-o!/Dar-r-rn!"

A modified subject

The subject of a sentence is always a noun or noun substitute, and it can be modified in any of the ways shown for modifying nouns in Lesson 7. In this example, the subject's modifier is another noun.

117 The minister of foreign affairs has scheduled a press conference the day after reports appeared in the media about a ship transporting plutonium to Japan—supposedly under a strict veil of secrecy.

Aide: 大臣、 | 記者会見　の　用意　が | ととのいました!
Daijin, | *kisha kaiken　no　yōi　ga* | *totonoimashita!*
minister　press conference　of preparations　(subj.)　arranged/completed
"Mr. Minister, preparations for the press conference have been completed!"
"Mr. Minister, we're all ready for the press conference!" (PL3)

- *daijin* refers to a cabinet minister. The Ministry of Foreign Affairs is called 外務省 *Gaimu-shō*, and 外務大臣 *gaimu daijin* is the full title of the person who heads the ministry.
- *kisha* means "reporter/journalist," and *kaiken* means "interview/audience" → *kisha kaiken* = "press conference."
- *totonoimashita* is the PL3 past form of *totonou/totonoimasu* ("[something] is arranged/set/put in order," or in the case of preparations, "be completed"). *Yōi ga totonoimashita* = "Preparations have been completed" → "Everything is ready/We're all ready."

Mixed modifiers

This example includes modifiers both for the subject and for the main verb. Although some adverbs can modify nouns, and therefore the subject, most of the time an adverb that comes before the subject modifies the verb, adjective, or noun + *da/desu* phrase at the end of the sentence; or it modifies the entire rest of the sentence as a whole.

118 Hatsushiba Electric has planned a special countdown event at the Tokyo Tower for New Year's Eve, and turnout has been even better than expected. At midnight, the structure's usual lighting will be extinguished so that the tower can be bathed in a rainbow of color.

Yada: よし、 　　大　成功　だ!
Yoshi, 　　*dai- seikō　da!*
good/all right　big　success　is
"Great! It's a huge success!" (PL2)

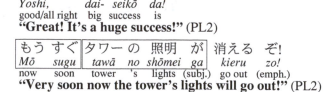

もう　すぐ | タワーの　照明　が | 消える　ぞ!
Mō　sugu | *tawā no shōmei ga* | *kieru　zo!*
now　soon　tower　's　lights　(subj.)　go out　(emph.)
"Very soon now the tower's lights will go out!" (PL2)

- *yoshi* is an interjectory form of the adjective *ii/yoi* ("good/fine/okay"); among its several uses, it can express satisfaction with the way something is going.
- *dai* means "big/large"; as a noun prefix it implies large either in size or in degree.
- *mō sugu* ("very soon now"; fig. 75) is an adverb phrase modifying the verb *kieru/kiemasu* ("[a light/fire] goes out/is extinguished"); modifiers like this can also appear between the subject and the verb: e.g., *Tawā no shōmei ga mō sugu kieru zo!*
- the particle *no* makes *tawā* (from English "tower") a noun-modifier for *shōmei* ("lights"), which *ga* marks as the subject—what will do the action.

Subject of *aru/arimasu*

The subject of the verb of existence *aru/arimasu* (figs. 54–55) in Japanese may in fact be what you think of as the direct object (see next page) in English, as this example illustrates.

119 Kōsuke's girlfriend Hiroko has returned from a trip home to see her family, and they go out for a sumptuous meal at a Chinese restaurant. When Kōsuke loosens his belt afterwards, it reminds Hiroko that she brought something for him.

Hiroko: そうそう、 おみやげ が ある の。
Sō sō, *o-miyage* *ga* *aru* *no.*
that's right (hon.)-gift (subj.) exists/have (explan.)
"That's right. I have a present [for you]."
"Oh, that reminds me. I brought you a present." (PL2)

- *sō sō* is used as an interjection like "oh yeah/that's right" when remembering something.
- *o-miyage* (the honorific prefix *o-* is almost always used) refers to a gift or souvenir brought back from a trip/outing, or to a "housegift" when paying someone a visit; other traditional gifts have their own special names, and birthday and Christmas gifts are usually called *purezento* (from English "present").
- *ga* marks *o-miyage* as the subject of *aru/arimasu* ("exists"), so the sentence literally says "A present exists"; but in this context it corresponds to "I have a present for you."

The subject of *suru*

Sometimes the subject of the verb *suru* is exactly what you would expect: who or what is doing something. But there are a number of expressions in the pattern ～ *ga suru* in which *ga* follows a noun phrase describing a kind of sensation or feeling. To make the phrase work as the subject of the sentence in English, *suru* can be translated as "occurs": *hen na oto* = "strange sound," and *Hen na oto ga suru* = "A strange sound occurs." But often it's more natural to think of the phrase marked by *ga* as something other than the subject: e.g., "It makes a strange noise," or "I hear a strange noise," or even "It sounds strange" (in the last case, the sensation noun has been turned into its corresponding verb). Let context help you determine the best English subject—i.e., what is creating or feeling the sensation.

120 Kōsuke is eating his annual *sakura-mochi* (fig. 82). The cherry-leaf wrapper, salted and preserved since this same time last year, gives it a very distinctive aroma, which Kōsuke associates with spring.

Kōsuke: 春 の 香り が する。
(thinking) *Haru* *no* *kaori* *ga* *suru.*
spring of scent/fragrance (subj.) does/occurs
"The scent of spring occurs."
"It smells like spring." (PL2)

Additional examples:

- *oishii* = "tasty/delicious" and *nioi* is another word for "smell/aroma," so *Oishii nioi ga suru* (lit. "A delicious smell occurs") might mean "This place smells delicious" if the speaker is walking past a bakery; or it might mean "I smell something good" if the speaker is merely sitting in her apartment when a tasty smell of unknown origin wafts in through the window.

- *iya na* is an adjectival noun meaning "unpleasant/disagreeable," and *yokan* = "premonition," so *Iya na yokan ga suru* = "A bad premonition occurs" → "I have a bad premonition."

を *O* Marks the Direct Object

Many verb-type sentences include a word or phrase known as the **direct object**, which tells what or whom the action of the verb most directly affects or acts upon. For example, if you begin a game (fig. 26), the game is what gets begun; if you eat a fish (fig. 42), the fish is what gets eaten; if you ignore a rival (fig. 63), the rival is who gets ignored. In each of these previous examples, the Japanese sentence does not state the direct object—what or who is affected by the action— because the situation provides that information. But when that information isn't already obvious and needs to be spelled out, it's usually marked by the particle *o*, written を (see note on kana usage below).

Since ～*o* phrases tell what is affected by an action, and actions are expressed by verbs, ～*o* phrases cannot link up with sentence adjectives or noun + *da/desu* (though, as you will see, this does not mean they never appear in adjective- or noun-type sentences). Also, not all verbs take ～*o* phrases, so you will need to pay attention to which ones do.

The word or phrase that *o* follows is not always exactly the same as the direct object in English, but for most purposes it's convenient to speak of it as the direct object.

121 Michael is being tested as a baggage-sniffing cat for the customs service, and this suitcase draws his attention.

Customs Agent:

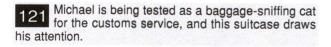

中 を 確かめます!!
Naka o tashikamemasu!!
inside/contents (obj.) will check/examine/verify
"[I] will check the inside."
"I'm going to inspect the contents." (PL3)

FX: バッ
Ba!
(Effect of flipping lid open)

Michael: ウニャ ニャ ニャー
Unya nya nyā
"Meow-yow-yow."

Traveler: は、 はあ...
Ha- hā...
(stammer) yes/okay
"O- okay..." (PL3)

- *naka* is a noun meaning "inside/the inside," and it's often used to refer to "contents."
- *tashikamemasu* is the polite form of *tashikameru* ("check/examine/ verify").
- *hā* is a very tentative/uncertain *hai* ("yes/okay"), giving the feeling that he's a bit baffled why the customs agent has suddenly become so eager to inspect his luggage.

Kana usage alert!

In hiragana, the independent syllable *o* has always been written お until now (figs. 67, 68, 74, 96, and others), but in the above sentence, the particle *o* appears as を. The hiragana character を makes its debut here because this is the first example containing an explicitly stated direct object. Although the character saw wider use in classical Japanese writing, を is reserved solely for use as the object-marking particle *o* in modern Japanese. The character is from the *w* row of the kana tables, and you may encounter some speakers who actually say *wo*, but the *w* sound is no longer pronounced by the vast majority.

For reading, this simplifies things: any time you see an を, you know the word or phrase immediately before it is acting as a direct object. For writing, though, it means you need to be on your toes and always distinguish whether *o* is part of another word (write お) or is a particle marking a direct object (write を).

A direct object with modifier

© Oze Akira, *Natsu no Kura,* Kōdansha.

そして立派な精米機を入れる……

Direct objects, like subjects, are nouns or noun substitutes, and they can be modified in all the same ways as any other noun. Here the modifier for the direct object is an adjectival noun.

122 When Natsuko's grandfather Zenzō returns from the city to take over the Saeki Brewery after his older brother's death in 1928, he immediately sees the limitations of the rice-polishing capabilities of the saké brewery's waterwheel-driven mill. Here he tells his young wife that he intends to bring electricity to the village and to the brewery.

Zenzō:	そして	立派な	精米機	を	入れる。
	Soshite	*rippa na*	*seimai-ki*	*o*	*ireru.*
	and/then	fine/powerful	rice-cleaning machine	(obj.)	put in/install

"And then I'll install a powerful rice miller." (PL2)

- *soshite* is a connecting word meaning "and/and then/and as a result."
- *rippa* is an adjectival noun corresponding to English adjectives like "imposing/grand/fine/powerful/worthy."
- *seimai* is a noun referring to the cleaning/polishing of brown rice into white rice, and *-ki* is a suffix meaning "machine."
- the polite form of *ireru* ("put in/install") is *iremasu.*

An adverb before the direct object

Although some adverbs can modify nouns, and therefore the direct object, most of the time an adverb right before the object modifies the verb or the rest of the sentence as a whole. Adverbs can also come between the object and the verb.

123 As Natsuko tends her first small crop of Tatsu-nishiki rice, she calls a meeting of neighboring farmers to ask them to grow the rice next year, using the grain she will harvest as seed. The meeting grows contentious when discussion turns to the viability of the organic methods Natsuko wants them to use. Natsuko's father decides nothing can be gained by prolonging the meeting.

© Oze Akira, *Natsuko no Sake,* Kōdansha.

Father:	どうも	ありがとう	ございました。
	Dōmo	*arigatō*	*gozaimashita.*
	(emph.)	thank you	(hon.)

"Thank you very much for coming." (PL4)

いずれ	あらためて	会合	を	開きます。
Izure	*aratamete*	*kaigou*	*o*	*hirakimasu.*
in time	again/anew	gathering	(obj.)	will open/hold

"We'll call another gathering sometime later." (PL3)

- *dōmo* is an intensifier like "indeed/quite/very much" that's used with expressions of apology, thanks, and greeting.
- *izure* is an adverb meaning "in time" → "eventually/sooner or later/someday/some other time/one of these days"; it implies the action will take place after some time has passed—not necessarily a long time. Here the word modifies the rest of the sentence.
- *aratamete* is an adverb meaning "again" or "anew/afresh," here modifying *hirakimasu.*
- *o* marks *kaigō* ("a gathering/meeting") as the direct object of *hirakimasu,* which is the polite form of *hiraku* ("open," or when speaking of certain events, "call/organize/hold/convene/commence").

Omitting *o*

Even when the speaker needs to specify the object, the particle *o* may be omitted if the context makes it clear what the word or phrase is.

124 The head priest of the local Buddhist temple has asked Kōsuke to deliver a congratulatory gift to a fellow priest who has been newly appointed to head a temple on the island of Shikoku in western Japan. Kōsuke expects to stay there awhile, so as Hiroko sees him off at the station, she tells him she'll write.

Hiroko: 手紙 書く わね。 行ってらっしゃい。
        Tegami kaku wa ne. Itterasshai.
        letter   will write   (fem. colloq.)   go and come
        "I'll write letters. Have a nice trip."
        "I'll write. Have a nice trip." (PL2)

- she omits the particle *o* because it's obvious that *tegami* ("letter") is the direct object of *kaku/kakimasu* ("write"). In Japanese you must specify the direct object when speaking of writing letters; you cannot just say *kaku* or *kakimasu* the way you can say "I'll write" in English.
- *itterasshai* is the standard phrase used to send off someone leaving for work, school, an errand, or any other excursion/trip from which the person will ultimately return home, so depending on the situation it can be equivalent to "have a nice day/see you later" or "have a nice trip." The expression is actually a contraction of the PL4 verb phrase *itte irasshai* (lit. "go and come"), but it's used in PL2 and PL3 speech as well without changing the form.

"Normal" word order is subject-object-verb

As the longer sentences in the examples are finally beginning to show, the crucial verb, adjective, or noun + *da/desu* phrase that tells you what's happening or what's what comes last in a Japanese sentence (except for the optional "wrap-up" items). Apart from this one rigid rule, word order in the "development" part of the sentence is quite flexible and can be adjusted according to what the speaker wants to emphasize. But the "normal" order—the most likely order when all other factors are equal—is subject-object-verb, with modifiers for each element preceding that element.

125 When Saeko comes running to tell Natsuko that her Tatsunishiki crop is forming ears of grain in fig. 56, this is what she says:

Saeko: 龍錦 が 穂 を 出しました。
        Tatsunishiki ga ho o dashimashita.
        (name)   (subj.)   ears/heads   (obj.)   put out
        "The Tatsunishiki has put out ears."
        "The Tatsunishiki is forming ears." (PL2)

- *ho* refers to "ears/heads" of grain.
- *dashimashita* is the polite past form of *dasu/dashimasu*, which can mean either "put [something] out" or "take [something] out" depending on the context and the perspective of the speaker or subject.

O can mark a starting point

The particle *o* can mark the point where a movement begins. For example, *deru/demasu* means "to exit" or "come/go out," so ～ *o deru* means "to exit (from) ～" or "come/go out of ～."

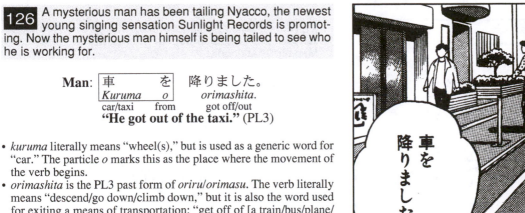

126 A mysterious man has been tailing Nyacco, the newest young singing sensation Sunlight Records is promoting. Now the mysterious man himself is being tailed to see who he is working for.

Man:	車	を	降りました。
	Kuruma	*o*	*orimashita.*
	car/taxi	from	got off/out

"He got out of the taxi." (PL3)

- *kuruma* literally means "wheel(s)," but is used as a generic word for "car." The particle *o* marks this as the place where the movement of the verb begins.
- *orimashita* is the PL3 past form of *oriru/orimasu*. The verb literally means "descend/go down/climb down," but it is also the word used for exiting a means of transportation: "get off of [a train/bus/plane/boat/bicycle]" or "get out of [a car/cab/truck]."

© Hirokane Kenshi. Buchō Shima Kōsaku, Kōdansha.

O can mark where a movement occurs

The particle *o* can also mark the place in/on/across/through/along which a movement takes place. For example, *kaidan* = "stairs/steps," so, using the verb seen in fig. 126, *kaidan o oriru* = "descend the stairs." In this case, the movement takes place on/along the stairs rather than starting from it. In the example below, the movement takes place on/along the sidewalk.

127 Toshihiko is walking home after joining the Kakegawa High soccer team on the first day of school, when his friend Kenji rides his motorcycle right up onto the sidewalk.

Toshihiko:	危ない		なあ!
	Abunai		*nā!*
	is dangerous		(emph.)

"That's dangerous!" (PL2)

歩道	を	走るな	よ!
Hodō	*o*	*hashiru na*	*yo!*
sidewalk	on/along	don't run/ride	(emph.)

"Don't ride on the sidewalk!" (PL2)

Kenji:	よお、	トシ!	部活	楽しい	か?
	Yō,	*Toshi!*	*Bukatsu*	*tanoshii*	*ka?*
	hey	(name)	club activity	is fun/enjoyable	(?)

"Hey there, Toshi! Is practice fun?"
"Yo, Toshi! Having fun in practice?" (PL2)

© Ōshima Tsukasa. Shoot!, Kōdansha.

- *hashiru na* is the negative command form ("don't ～") of *hashiru/hashirimasu* ("run [on foot]"; or when speaking of motor vehicles, "ride/drive"). *O* marks *hodō* ("sidewalk") as the place along which the riding occurs. Command forms are formally introduced in Lesson 27.
- *yō* is an informal greeting like "Hi!/Hey!/Yo!" used by male speakers.
- in a high school, *bu* refers to a student activity group, including the athletic teams as well as a wide variety of clubs. *-Katsu* is short for *katsudō* ("activities"), so *bukatsu* refers to whatever the club does as a group. In the case of an athletic team it typically means "practice," but it also includes any other official team activity. (The particle *wa*, to mark this as the "topic" of the sentence, has been omitted; you will learn about *wa* and sentence topics in the next lesson.)

に *ni* may mark the direct object

With some verbs, *ni* is used instead of *o* to mark what English speakers may think of as the direct object of the verb. In many cases, this *ni* will mark the end point/destination/target of a movement or action (in contrast to *o* marking the starting point, as in fig. 126).

128 This newly hired OL is ready to make her first call to a client after prepping herself with a "Telephone Manners" handbook.

New OL: よし。　（ごく）
Yoshi.　(Goku)
all right　(gulping FX)
"All right! (Gulp)" (PL2)

取り引き先　に　電話する　ぞ。
Torihiki-saki　ni　denwa suru　zo.
client　(obj.)　will telephone　(emph.)
"I'm going to call the client." (PL2)

Book: でんわ　の　マナー
Denwa　no　Manā
telephone　(mod.)　manners
Telephone Manners

© Akizuki Risu, *OL Shinkaron*, Kōdansha.

- *yoshi* is often used when the speaker thinks the right moment has arrived for action. Here it carries a feeling of determination. See fig. 118 for another use.
- *ni* marks *torihiki-saki* ("client") as the party she is going to call—in essence the target of her action.
- *zo* is a rough masculine particle (see fig. 25), and in conversation it tends to sound even rougher when coming from a woman. But females often use masculine forms when speaking to themselves. In this case the *zo* emphasizes her determination.

が *ga* may mark the direct object

As already noted for *aru/arimasu* in Lesson 9 (fig. 119), with some verbs, *ga* is used instead of *o* to mark what English speakers may think of as the direct object. One such word is *wakaru/wakarimasu* ("understand/comprehend"), illustrated in this example. In addition, some of the verb forms introduced in the second half of the book require the object-marker *o* to be replaced with *ga* (see Lessons 23, 25, and 28).

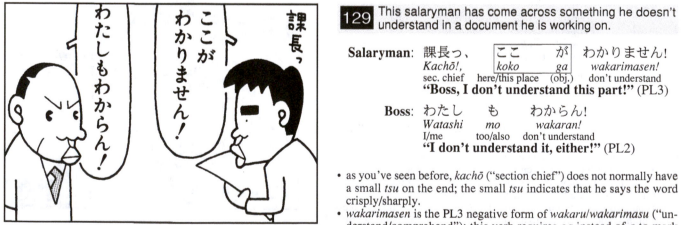

129 This salaryman has come across something he doesn't understand in a document he is working on.

Salaryman: 課長っ、　ここ　が　わかりません！
Kachō!,　koko　ga　wakarimasen!
sec. chief　here/this place　(obj.)　don't understand
"Boss, I don't understand this part!" (PL3)

Boss: わたし　も　わからん！
Watashi　mo　wakaran!
I/me　too/also　don't understand
"I don't understand it, either!" (PL2)

© Ōhashi Tsuyoshi, *Kaisha-in no Merodii*, Take Shobō.

- as you've seen before, *kachō* ("section chief") does not normally have a small *tsu* on the end; the small *tsu* indicates that he says the word crisply/sharply.
- *wakarimasen* is the PL3 negative form of *wakaru/wakarimasu* ("understand/comprehend"); this verb requires *ga* instead of *o* to mark what is understood (or in this case, what is not understood).
- *wakaran* is a contraction of *wakaranai*, the PL2 negative form of *wakaru*, so its meaning is the same as *wakarimasen*; only the politeness level is different. You will learn about PL2 negative verbs in Lesson 20.
- *mo* marks something as being in addition to something else, so *watashi mo* = "I, too." *Watashi mo wakaran* = "I, too, don't understand it" → "I don't understand it, either."

でも *de mo* may mark the direct object

When offering food or drink as well as when making other kinds of suggestions or invitations, speakers may mark the object with *de mo* instead of *o*. In this use, ～ *de mo* literally means "～ or something." Often, as here, this simply adds a note of casualness; in other cases it can be used for politeness, since the Japanese generally consider it more polite to express themselves indirectly or to leave things a little bit vague. (*De mo* can also be used in combination with certain other particles to give meanings like "or someplace," "or sometime," etc.).

130 Mrs. Nohara has asked her neighbor to look after Shin-chan while she attends a funeral.

Neighbor: お菓子　　　　　　　でも　食べる　かい?
O-kashi   *de mo*   *taberu*   *kai?*
(hon.)-sweets/snack foods   or something   eat   (?)
"Will you eat some sweets or something?"
"Would you like a snack?" (PL2)

Shin-chan: ほい。
Hoi.
(interj.)
"Sure." (PL2)

- the PL3 form of *taberu* ("eat") is *tabemasu*. The sentence is essentially equivalent to *O-kashi o taberu kai?* ("Will you eat some sweets?")
- *hoi* is an interjection that goes with putting out one's hand; here it also reflects his eagerness to accept the offered snack, without any polite reserve.

Suru verbs and *o*

As you learned in Lesson 5, *suru* verbs are made up of a noun followed by *suru* and imply "do the action associated with that noun." In essence, the noun in these combinations is the direct object of the verb *suru*, and you will in fact often see the noun and *suru* with the particle *o* inserted between them. But the meaning is basically the same either way: *denwa* = "telephone," and *denwa suru* = *denwa o suru* (both mean "make a phone call," or just "call"); *unten* = "driving," and *unten suru* = *unten o suru* (both mean "drive").

131 With baby daughter Tamami reaching the age of greater mobility, Michael the cat's owners will have their hands full keeping her away from Michael's food dish and litter box.

"Gooo."

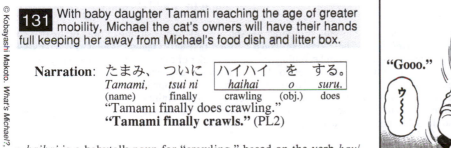

Narration: たまみ、　ついに　ハイハイ　を　する。
Tamami,   *tsui ni*   *haihai*   *o*   *suru.*
(name)   finally   crawling   (obj.)   does
"Tamami finally does crawling."
"Tamami finally crawls." (PL2)

- *haihai* is a babytalk noun for "crawling," based on the verb *hau/haimasu* ("crawl"). Whether in the form *haihai suru* or *haihai o suru*, the verb created with *haihai* usually means "a baby crawls."

So long as the noun part of a *suru* verb is not marked with *o*, the verb can often take a separate direct object. For example, 勉強する *benkyō suru* ("study") can have a ～ *o* phrase stating *what* is being studied: 日本語を勉強する *Nihongo o benkyō suru* = "study Japanese."

When the noun part of a *suru* verb is marked with *o*, as in 勉強をする *benkyō o suru* (lit. "do studying"), that noun becomes the object of the independent verb *suru* ("do") and there cannot be a second ～ *o* phrase to go with the same verb. In such a case, the way to indicate *what* is being studied (or whatever the activity in question may be) is to modify the direct object; if the chosen modifier is a noun (such as *Nihongo*), it must be marked with *no* (see Lesson 7) instead of *o*: 日本語の勉強をする *Nihongo no benkyō o suru* = "do studying of Japanese " → "study Japanese." Of course, *benkyō* can take an adjective or verb as a modifier as well, in which case no particle is necessary: むずかしい勉強をする *muzukashii benkyō o suru* = "do difficult studying" → "study something difficult."

Lesson 11

は *Wa* Marks the Topic

An important part of Japanese sentence structure is something called the **topic**, which is grammatically distinct from the subject. There's no real equivalent to the topic in English, but the basic concept should be fairly easy to grasp because it's exactly what the name suggests: the topic of a sentence is a word or phrase that says what that sentence is fundamentally about.

As with subjects and objects, once the topic has been stated it's generally not repeated in subsequent sentences on the same topic, and context can often make it unnecessary to state the topic to begin with. But when it *is* necessary to state the topic, it's usually marked with the particle *wa*, written は (see note on kana usage below).

To approximate the effect of the Japanese topic in English, you can translate *wa* as "speaking of ～," or "as for ～." But when you're actually translating into natural-sounding English, these phrases usually disappear.

132 Aosugi Kanji is only in his second term in the House of Representatives, the lower but more powerful chamber of Japan's Diet, but he is highly ambitious and has already caught the attention of the prime minister's circle. Now he has been appointed a minister without porfolio to spearhead electoral reforms. He intends to use his new position to really shake things up—as well as to launch himself to the top.

© Hirokane Kenshi, *Kaji Ryūsuke no Gi*, Kodansha.

Aosugi:

天下	は	俺	が	とる!
Tenka	*wa*	*ore*	*ga*	*toru!*
the world/country	as for	I/me	(subj.)	will take

"As for [power over] the country, I am going to take it!"
"I'm going to rule!" (PL2)

- *tenka* is literally "under heaven," implying "all under heaven" → "all the world/the entire country," and *toru/torimasu* means "take/seize." The expression *tenka o toru* ("take/seize the world/country"; *o* marks *tenka* as the direct object of *toru*) refers to becoming the supreme ruler of the known world (in early times) or of a country (in more recent times). The expression harkens back to the era when it implied seizing power by force of arms, but in spite of the sword in Aosugi's hand, that is not implied here.
- in this example, *wa* marks *tenka* as the topic of the sentence: "As for the entire country, ～."
- *ore* is an informal/rough word for "I/me" used by males. *Ga* marks this as the subject of the verb *toru*. Note that the topic and the subject are separate elements in this sentence.

Kana Usage Alert!

In hiragana, the sound *wa* has always been written わ until now. You've seen it in words like わかります *wakarimasu* ("understand"; figs. 31, 129), and in the feminine sentence particle わ *wa* (figs. 23, 24). But the topic marker *wa* is an exception: it's written は. When は appears anywhere else, it's read *ha*, as in はい *hai* ("yes"; fig. 70), but as a topic marker, it's read *wa*.

In reading, you never have to puzzle over わ: it's always read *wa*. But when you encounter a は you have to determine whether it's marking the topic (read it *wa*) or it's part of another word (read it *ha*).

In writing, you never have to wonder how to write the sound *ha*: it's always written は. But when you want to write *wa*, you have to distinguish between whether you're using it as a topic marker (write は) or as something else (write わ).

The topic can be the subject

Much of the time, the word or phrase that's marked with *wa* is also the subject of the sentence, as in this example. But as you have seen in fig. 132, the topic and subject may be completely separate. In fact, the topic can be virtually anything—whatever the central focus of discussion in the sentence is. And since the focus of the sentence is not always the subject in Japanese, it's very important to keep the topic and the subject separated in your thinking.

When the subject is also the topic, *wa* replaces *ga* rather than being added to it.

133 *Obatarian* became a colloquial/slang term for "pushy middle-aged woman" as a result of this long-running four-frame gag manga of the same name. The woman seen here is one of several recurrent characters in the strip who epitomize their kind. In this episode she is shown watching a late-night rerun of the classic spy drama, "The Man from U.N.C.L.E."

Narration: オバタリアン は 深夜 テレビ を みる。
Obatarian wa shin'ya terebi o miru.
mid.-aged women as for late night TV (obj.) watch
"As for *obatarians*, [they] watch late-night TV."
"*Obatarians* watch late-night TV." (PL2)

Sound FX: ドギュン ドギュン バン バン
Dogyun dogyun Ban ban
(sounds of gunfire)

Napoleon Solo: 行く ぞ、イリヤ。
Iku zo, Iriya.
will go (emph.) (name)
"Here we go, Illya." (PL2)

- *shin'ya* is literally "deep night" and *terebi* is shortened from *terebijon*, the Japanese rendering of "television." The combination makes a compound noun meaning "late-night TV," and *o* marks that noun as the direct object.
- the polite form of *miru* ("see/watch") is *mimasu*.

Wa vs. *ga*

There's no simple rule about when you should treat the subject as a topic and replace *ga* with *wa*. But it's worth keeping in mind that using *ga* generally focuses attention on who or what does the action, or on who or what is being described—that is, on the subject itself: Uzuratani in fig. 113 is focused on *who* will make the tea, and the man in fig. 114 is focused on *what part* of his anatomy hurts. By contrast, using *wa* focuses attention on what is being said about the subject—that is, on what the subject is, is like, or is doing: the *wa* in fig. 133 focuses attention on Obatarian's action (what it is that she does) rather than on who does that action.

When *wa* is used with verbs of existence (*aru/iru*; figs. 54–56) the attention is not on who or what exists/is present, but on *whether* the person or thing exists/is present. In this example, the issue is whether the magazine in question exists in the bookstore's possession/stock.

134 With the Japanese stock market in the doldrums, a salaryman in the financial district goes to a nearby bookstore to see if he can get some job information—only to discover that many others in his industry must have had the same idea before him.

Man: すみません。 『就職情報』 は あります か?
Sumimasen. "Shūshoku Jōhō" wa arimasu ka?
sorry/excuse me (magazine name) as for exist/have (?)
"Does 'Employment Classifieds' exist [in your stock]?"
"Excuse me. Do you have 'Employment Classifieds'?" (PL3)

Clerk: 売り切れ です。
Urikire desu.
sold out is/are
"It's sold out." (PL3)

- *sumimasen* is a polite "excuse me," for getting someone's attention to ask a question; it's also used for apologies ("I'm sorry").
- English makes the magazine the direct object here, but in Japanese the magazine is the subject of the verb *aru/arimasu*. With the same verb in fig. 119, the emphasis is on *what* Hiroko has, so she uses *ga* to mark

o-miyage ("present") as the subject; here the emphasis is on *whether* the store has the magazine, so the man treats the subject as the sentence topic, and uses *wa* instead of *ga*.

The topic can be the direct object

The topic is a noun or noun substitute, and it typically comes at or near the beginning of the sentence. This means that when the topic is also the subject, the "normal" word order remains the same as the order noted at fig. 125 (subject-object-verb). But if the topic is the object—as it often is, including here and in fig. 132—the so-called "normal" order of subject and object gets reversed (object-subject-verb).

When the object is also the topic, *wa* replaces the object marker *o* rather than being added to it.

135 At a second-hand bookstore that he frequents, Kō-suke occasionally watches the store while the owner runs errands. On this day, a man comes in wanting to sell one of his books. It is Kōsuke's first time having to deal with this kind of customer, but the man apparently knows the owner and feels the owner would agree to the price he asks.

Customer: 値段　は　私　が　決める。
Nedan wa | *watashi* | *ga* | *kimeru.*
price　as for　I　(subj.)　will decide
"As for the price, I will decide it."
"I will set the price." (PL2)

- *nedan* ("price") is both the topic of the sentence and the direct object of the verb *kimeru/kimemasu* ("decide/choose [something]").
- *ga* marks *watashi* ("I") as the subject of the verb.

The topic can be a time

In this example, the topic is a time—indicated by the relative time word *kyō* ("today"; see p. 44). Relative time words used as adverbs don't require a particle, but when they become the topic, they are acting as nouns, so they are usually marked with *wa*. Absolute time words (e.g., "Tuesday/noon/three o'clock") can also be used as topics in the same way.

"Hey! That's my wallet!"

136 Uzuratani and his colleage Sayū often eat lunch together, and Uzuratani is apparently feeling generous today.

Uzuratani: 今日　は　おれ　が　払う　よ。
Kyō wa | *ore* | *ga* | *harau* | *yo.*
today　as for　I　(subj.)　will pay　(emph.)
"As for today, I will pay."
"I'll get it today." (PL2)

Sayū: おっ、　かっくいー!
O! | *Kakku ii!*
(interj.)　cool/hip
"Hey, you're cool!"
"Aren't you cool!" (PL2)

- *ore* is an informal/rough "I/me" used by males, and *ga* marks it as the subject of *harau*.
- *harau/haraimasu* means "[to] pay"; this verb takes an *o* phrase, but here it does not need to be stated because it's obvious that he's talking about the bill for the meal they have just eaten.
- *kakku ii* is a variation of *kakko ii*, a colloquial expression for "look good/cool/hip." It often refers to how one is dressed, but also can refer to one's actions, as in this case. Showing his generosity makes Uzuratani cool—except it turns out that he's paying with his colleague's wallet. (For a note on Sayū's response, see fig. 321.)

The topic can be a place

To illustrate just one more of the many possibilities, the topic of the sentence in this example is a place. But the important point to remember is that the topic can be nearly anything: a situation, a condition or state, an activity, a quality or characteristic, an idea, a feeling, a hope, and so on; and sometimes it will be the subject or object of the sentence as well, while at other times it will be neither.

137 Two OLs have decided to spend their holiday at the swimming pool in an amusement park.

A: 遊園地　の　プール　は　子供　が　多い　ね。
Yūenchi　no　pūru　wa　kodomo　ga　ōi　ne.
amus. park (mod.)　pool　as for　children (subj.)　are many (colloq.)
"As for amusement park pools, the children are many, aren't they?"
"Amusement park pools really bring in the little ones, don't they?" (PL2)

B: うん。
Un.
yes
"Uh-huh." (PL2)

SFX: キャー　　　ワー
Kyā　　　　Wā
(scream/squeal)　(crowd noise)

- *no* makes *yūenchi* ("amusement park") a modifier for *pūru* (from English "pool"), and *wa* marks the phrase as the topic of the sentence.
- *ga* marks *kodomo* ("children/kids") as the subject of *ōi*, which is an adjective meaning "is a lot/are numerous" → *kodomo ga ōi* = "children are numerous."

Multiple particles

The first *wa* here is another example in which *wa* marks a place as the topic, but in this case the *wa* follows and works together with the particle *ni*, which indicates the location where something or someone exists (see p. 31). Although *wa* does not combine with *ga* or *o* (it always replaces them instead), *wa* can indeed combine with a number of other particles, and when it does, it always comes after the other particle.

138 Kōsuke discovers that a library book he has borrowed is overdue. When he goes to return it, the library turns out to be closed, and he is relieved that he can just drop the book in the slot without having the librarian give him a hard time.

Narration:
ここ　の　図書館　には　ちょっとうるさい　司書　が　いる。
Koko no toshokan　ni wa　chotto　urusai　shisho ga　iru.
here (mod.) library　at as for　a little　noisy/fussy librarian (subj.) exists/there is
"As for at the library here, there is a somewhat noisy [about overdue books] librarian."
"The librarian here is a bit fussy." (PL2)

Sign:
本日　は　休館します。
Honjitsu wa　kyūkan shimasu.
today　as for　will close
Closed today. (PL3)

- the adjective *urusai* literally means "is noisy," often implying the person "is a stickler/fussy" about something. *Chotto* modifies *urusai*, which in turn modifies *shisho*.
- the verb *iru/imasu* means "exists/be in a place" (for people and other animate things), and *ni* marks *toshokan* ("library") as the place of existence. *Ga* marks *shisho* ("librarian") as the subject—the person who is in/at that place.
- *honjitsu* is a formal word for "today," used mostly on signs or advertising fliers and in public announcements. *Wa* marks this as the topic of the sentence on the sign.
- *kyūkan shimasu* is the polite form of *kyūkan suru* ("close/will close/will be closed"); *kyūkan* is written with kanji meaning "rest" and "hall," and is the word for "closed" used by libraries, meeting halls, theaters, and other public buildings.

More than one topic

A sentence is not necessarily limited to a single topic. If two phrases are marked with *wa*, the first establishes a broad topic and the second narrows it down to a more specific case or defines a subtopic.

139 Toshihiko wants to join the soccer team right away on his first day at Kakegawa High, but when he gets to the club room he finds it locked. Then Kamiya, acting captain of the team, comes along, and Toshihiko states his purpose. Kamiya tells Toshihiko he's welcome to join, but adds:

Kamiya

© Ōshima Tsukasa. *Shoot!*, Kōdansha.

Kamiya:
今日	は		部活	は	休み	だ。
Kyō	*wa*		*bukatsu*	*wa*	*yasumi*	*da.*
today	as for		club/team activities	as for	day off	is/are

"As for today, as for team activities, it's a day off."
"The team doesn't practice today." (PL2)

- for *bukatsu* ("club activities"), see fig. 127.
- *yasumi* is the stem or pre-*masu* form of the verb *yasumu/yasumimasu* ("rest/take time off"). With many verbs, the pre-*masu* form can be used as a noun (see p. 57).

Omitting *wa*

Like many other particles, *wa* can be omitted if the context makes the topic word or phrase obvious. In this example, *omae* ("you") is the topic of the sentence, but the *wa* to mark it has been omitted.

140 Kōsuke has come to the pachinko (Japanese pinball) parlor with a message for the greengrocer's elderly mother. Her son wants her to come home and help with the store. Just after Kōsuke gives her the message, Granny hits the jackpot.

SFX:
チーン	ジャラジャラ
Chiin	*Jara-jara*
Din-n-ng	**Rattle rattle** (sound of bell followed by pachinko balls pouring out)

Granny: やったあ!!
Yattā!!
did
"All right!" (PL2)

おまえ、	福	の	神	だ	ね!
Omae,	*fuku*	*no*	*kami*	*da*	*ne!*
you	good fortune	of	god	is/are	(colloq.)

"You're the god of good fortune!" (PL2)

© Maekawa Tsukasa. *Dai-Tōkyō Binbō Seikatsu Manyuaru*, Kōdansha.

- *Yattā!* is a common exclamation of joy, similar to "All right!" or "Hooray!" It is the plain past form of *yaru/yarimasu*, an informal word for "do."
- *omae* is an informal word for "you" that is best considered masculine. Men use *omae* to address one another familiarly among friends, but the word feels very rough when used with people other than friends. Women's use is generally restricted to addressing their husbands or children; the tone can range from endearing to rough; some older women will also use it with other close acquaintances, generally with a tone of familiarity/endearment.
- *omae* is both topic and subject in this case, but if a particle were stated, it would be *wa* instead of *ga* because the focus is on what is being said about Kōsuke, and not on who the god of good fortune is (see fig. 134).

A topic by itself

To add a new twist to the Japanese penchant for omitting parts of sentences, it's sometimes possible to state just a topic and omit the rest of the sentence. Most commonly, the stand-alone topic is a question—made so by simply raising the intonation on *wa*. It's like saying "As for ～, please answer the obvious question I have about it."

Besides when the question is obvious, this kind of topic-only question can be pressed into service when you aren't quite sure exactly how to formulate your question. It allows you to ask generally about the status, condition, nature, location, and so forth, of the topic—leaving the other person to determine which specific aspect(s) should be addressed in the response.

141 Tanaka-kun and his friend are taking a break at a coffee shop.

Waitress: ご注文　は？
Go-chūmon　wa?
(hon.)-order　as for
"As for your order?"
"What can I get you?" (PL4)

Friend: コーヒー。
Kōhii.
"Coffee." (PL2)

Tanaka-kun: ぼく　も。
Boku　mo.
I/me　also
"Me, too." (PL2)

- *chūmon* refers to an "order" for food or merchandise. *Go-* is honorific.
- the particle *mo* implies "too/also."

Wa = "at least"

When *wa* follows a quanity, it means "at least" that much.

142 As soon as Hanba orders his bowl of noodles, he immediately breaks apart his disposable chopsticks and poises himself at the ready, as if he expects the food to arrive instantly. The waiter thinks maybe he'd better set him straight.

SFX: パキ
Paki
(sound of breaking chopsticks apart)

Waiter: あの...
Ano...
(interj.)
"Umm..."

10分　ぐらい　は　かかります　よ。
Juppun　gurai　wa　kakarimasu　yo.
10 min.　about　at least　will take/consume　(emph.)
"It's going to take at least 10 minutes or so." (PL3)

- *-fun* is the counter suffix for "minutes," but a sound change occurs when combined with *jū* ("ten") → *juppun* (see p. 93).
- *gurai* (or *kurai*) after a number or quantity indicates it is an approximation: "about ～/～ or so."
- *kakarimasu* is the polite form of the verb *kakaru* ("to take/require/consume/cost").

Adverbs can come before or after the topic

Adverbs modifying the verb, adjective, or noun + *desu* phrase at the end of the sentence may come either before or after the topic. In the first example here, an adverb follows the topic and modifies the verb that comes next; in the second example, an adverb precedes the topic, but it skips over the topic to modify the adjective at the end of the sentence. Adverbs may also modify the subject, object, topic, or another element instead of the sentence's final statement—as seen in fig. 138, where *chotto* modifies an adjective that modifies the subject. Context must be your guide.

143 Soon after Natsuko's grandmother, Natsu (fig. 58), marries into the Saeki family, curiosity gets the better of her and she decides to break the taboo against women entering the brewhouse. As she is coming down the steps from the platform around the massive fermentation vats, she trips and falls, wrenching her back and spraining her ankle. She must stay off her feet for a time, and here her husband comes to ask how she is faring.

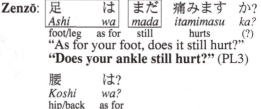

Zenzō: 足　　は　　まだ　痛みます　か?
Ashi　wa　mada　itamimasu　ka?
foot/leg　as for　still　hurts　(?)
"As for your foot, does it still hurt?"
"Does your ankle still hurt?" (PL3)

腰　　　は?
Koshi　wa?
hip/back　as for
"How about your back?" (PL3)

- *ashi* can refer to any part of the leg or foot or both; context reveals that it refers to her ankle in this case.
- *itamimasu* is the polite form of *itamu* ("hurt/ache/be painful"). The adverb *mada* ("still") modifies this verb.
- *koshi* refers to the rear midsection of a person's body, roughly from a little above the waist down through the hips. What English speakers typically think of as lower back pain is attributed to the *koshi* in Japanese.

144 The period from April 29 through May 5 each year is called Golden Week in Japan because workers can sometimes get as many as ten continuous days off by combining a couple of vacation days with weekends, three national holidays, and May Day, for which many companies close down. But some workers find the time off more exhausting than being at work. These men are back at work on May 6.

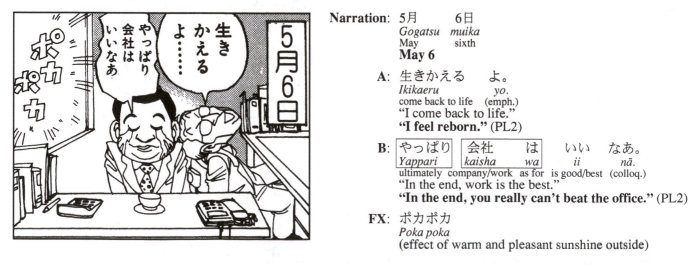

Narration: 5月　　　6日
Gogatsu　muika
May　sixth
May 6

A: 生きかえる　　よ。
Ikikaeru　yo.
come back to life　(emph.)
"I come back to life."
"I feel reborn." (PL2)

B: やっぱり　会社　　は　　いい　なあ。
Yappari　kaisha　wa　ii　nā.
ultimately　company/work　as for　is good/best　(colloq.)
"In the end, work is the best."
"In the end, you really can't beat the office." (PL2)

FX: ポカポカ
Poka poka
(effect of warm and pleasant sunshine outside)

- the polite form of *ikikaeru* ("come back to life/be reborn") is *ikikaerimasu*.
- *yappari* (and the more formal *yahari*) implies that a situation/outcome fits one's expectations or common sense: "as you might expect/after all/in the end."
- the adjective *ii* basically means "good/fine/okay," but sometimes, as here, saying "~ is good" implies "~ is better/best."

The *wa-ga* group

As figs. 132 and 135–37 show, the pattern *A wa B ga C* is very common in Japanese. Most of the time, *wa* marks A as the topic (it may be a direct object, place, time, or anything else a topic can be except a subject) and *ga* marks B as the subject of C.

For a few words that appear in the C position of this *A wa B ga C* construction, A represents the subject and B represents what English speakers think of as the direct object. These words can collectively be called the **wa-ga group**. Most often, though by no means always, A is a person, and B *ga* C expresses that person's ability, how he feels (as in the example here), or what he wants.

Members of the *wa-ga* group include verbs, adjectives, and adjectival nouns. For the latter two, you can usually see that the word or phrase marked with *ga* is structurally the subject of the adjective or adjectival noun in Japanese, even if it turns into a direct object in the English translation. For verbs, it's easiest just to think of *ga* as marking the direct object in this pattern.

145 While drawn to Natsuko's idealism, neighboring brewery heir Kuroiwa Shingo never thought he was worthy of her. Now he has decided to focus completely on making a batch of saké that rejects the shortcuts his father has adopted, and he doesn't want to see Natsuko again until he is finished. But to make sure she doesn't misunderstand, he tells her how he feels about her.

Shingo: おれ は 夏ちゃん が 好きだ。
Ore | *wa* | *Nat-chan* | *ga* | *suki da.*
I/me | as for | (name-dimin.) | (subj.) | like
"As for me, I like Nat-chan."
"I like you, Nat-chan." (PL2)

おれは夏ちゃんが好きだ

- following the customary preference (see p. 63), Shingo uses his listener's name when an English speaker would use "you."
- *suki* is an adjectival noun for "liking/fondness," but it's usually easier to think of *suki da* as equivalent to the English verb "like." *Wa* marks the person who does the liking, and *ga* marks the object of affection. The opposite of *suki* is 嫌い *kirai* ("dislike"), which also belongs to the *wa-ga* group.

Some usage notes on *wa*

Here are a few other things to remember about the use of *wa*:

- When you're confused about whether to use *wa* or *ga*, one way out is to simply omit the particle. But don't let this become your permanent escape. Even though native speakers often omit particles, they don't do it at random. Omitting the wrong ones will make your Japanese sound forever foreign.
- *Wa* is generally used to single out the chosen subject, object, etc. among previously mentioned (or implied) items in the conversation—not to introduce new items. This should be easy to grasp if you remember that one of the suggested translations for *wa* is "Speaking of ～." A typical pattern is for a subject, object, time, place, etc. to first appear under the previous topic with their usual particles marking them, then get singled out as the new primary topic of discussion using *wa*. For example, *Hiru-gohan wa o-nigiri o tabemasu* ("As for lunch, I eat rice balls"; *hiru-gohan* is the topic, and *o-nigiri* is the direct object) might be followed by *O-nigiri wa oishii desu ne* ("Speaking of rice balls, they are delicious, aren't they?"; *o-nigiri* is the new topic).
- Once a topic has been introduced, it's not normally repeated in subsequent sentences on the same topic; only when switching to a new topic or subtopic is another *wa* phrase used. On the other hand, it's not uncommon for new topics to appear several sentences in a row depending on the nature of what is being said.
- Since *wa* is used for singling out, its effect is often like "Speaking of this item as opposed to other items"—that is, it can express a contrast.
- It's worth engraving in your mind that the structure **topic + *wa* + discussion** represents a fundamental pattern underlying Japanese expression—even when the topic is not explicitly stated. It is how Japanese tend to structure things in their minds as they put their thoughts into words. When going from Japanese to English, knowing this will help you understand why sentences come out the way they do, and why English translations need to be restructured if they are to sound natural. When going the other way, keeping this in mind will help you restructure your English thoughts into more natural-sounding Japanese.

Lesson 12

Ko-so-a-do Words

Japanese has a number of pronouns (words that stand in for nouns) and modifiers (words that describe other words) occurring in groups of four words that are alike except for their first syllable. The first syllables are こ *ko*, そ *so*, あ *a*, and ど *do*, so together they're called *ko-so-a-do* words.

The こ- *ko-* words imply close to the speaker

The *ko-* word in each group of four implies closeness to the speaker. *Kore* corresponds to the pronouns "this" or "these," and refers to an object or objects close at hand (context tells whether it's singular or plural). In fig. 73, for example, the landlady could have said *Kore, chotto omoi yo* ("This is pretty heavy"; PL3 equivalent: *Kore wa chotto omoi desu yo*). Here's another example:

146 Kōsuke's girlfriend Hiroko visited him at his apartment. Since the time was getting late, he offered to take her to the train station by bike. Hiroko didn't think Kōsuke owned a bicycle, so she asks him about it.

> **Hiroko:** これ あなた の 自転車?
> *Kore anata no jitensha?*
> this you 's bicycle
> **"Is this your bicycle?"** (PL2)
>
> **Kōsuke:** いや。
> *Iya.*
> **"No."** (PL2)

- *wa*, to mark *kore* as the topic of the sentence, has been omitted.
- Hiroko omits *na no?* (informal) or *desu ka?* (polite) at the end, and asks her question using only intonation.
- *anata* is a formal word for "you," used with equals or subordinates. Adding *no* makes it show possession: "your."

The そ- *so-* words imply close to the listener

The *so-* word in each group implies distance from the speaker and closeness to the listener. *Sore* corresponds to the pronouns "that" or "those." In fig. 50, for example, the shopkeeper could have asked *Sore, kau kai?* ("Want to buy that?"; PL3 equivalent: *Sore o kaimasu ka?*), and in fig. 112 the OL could have said *Ā, sore, kare no shashin?* ("Oh, is that your boyfriend's picture?"; PL3 equivalent: *A, sore wa kare no shashin desu ka?*).

Like their English counterparts, *kore* and *sore* can be used to refer not only to concrete objects, but to abstract things, such as ideas and actions. As seen here, *sore* often refers to what the other person has just said.

147 Raccoon's father is angry because Raccoon disappeared all day after peeing in their den. When he finally sees Raccoon, he barks out, "Where've you been?"

> **Raccoon:** それ は 秘密 です。
> *Sore wa himitsu desu.*
> that as for secret is
> **"That's a secret."** (PL3)

The あ- *a-* words imply away from both speaker and listener

The *a-* words in each group of four implies distance from both the speaker and the listener. *Are* will most often translate into English as "that" or "those," but its full meaning is "that/those over there, away from both of us," so it's important to distinguish its usage from *sore*.

148 This couple is looking out the window of an airplane as they approach their landing in Hong Kong.

He: ほら、 あれ が 香港 の
　 Hora, 　*are* 　*ga* 　*Honkon* 　*no*
　 look 　that 　(subj.) 　Hong Kong 　's

　 100万ドル の 夜景 だ よ。
　 hyakuman-doru 　*no* 　*yakei* 　*da* 　*yo.*
　 million dollar 　(mod.) 　nightscape 　is 　(emph.)
　 "Look. That's the million-dollar nightscape of Hong Kong." (PL2)

She: きれい ねー。
　 Kirei 　*nē.*
　 pretty 　(emph.)
　 "It's so pretty!" (PL2)

- *hora* is an interjection for calling the listener's attention to something.
- *nē* with a long vowel at the end of a sentence is like a mild exclamation.

The ど- *do-* words are for questions

The *do-* words in each group of four makes an associated question word. *Dore* corresponds to "which?" or "which one(s)?" and is usually used when there are three or more alternatives from which to choose. (For selecting between just two items, see figs. 152–53.)

kore
"this/these"

sore
"that/those"

are
"that/those over there"

dore
"which?"
"which [of many]?"

(The plural suffix -*ra* is sometimes added to *kore, sore,* and *are,* but it's usually not necessary.)

149 While traveling on a writing assignment, Lemon Hart denizen Matsuda drops in to see an old college friend. The friend happens to be researching an essay on *shōchū,* a kind of liquor distilled from various grains and sweet potatoes, and he invites Matsuda to help him taste the many selections he has gathered.

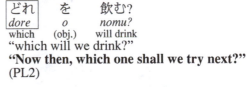

Friend:
さてと 次 は
Sate to 　*tsugi* 　*wa*
now then 　next 　as for
"Now then, as for next,

どれ を 飲む?
dore 　*o* 　*nomu?*
which 　(obj.) 　will drink
"which will we drink?"
"Now then, which one shall we try next?"
(PL2)

- *sate to* (or just *sate*) is used when contemplating or beginning an action: "let's see/well now/well then."
- the polite form of *nomu* ("drink") is *nomimasu.*

Here are some more examples:

これ を もう 一つ ください。
Kore 　*o* 　*mō* 　*hitotsu* 　*kudasai.*
this/these 　(obj.) 　more 　1 count 　please give me
"I'd like one more of these." (PL3)

あれ が 私 の 車 です。
Are 　*ga* 　*watashi* 　*no* 　*kuruma* 　*desu.*
that over there 　(subj.) 　I/me 　's 　car 　is
"That [car] over there is my car." (PL3)

それ は 危ない です。
Sore 　*wa* 　*abunai* 　*desu.*
that 　as for 　is dangerous 　(pol.)
"That is dangerous." (PL3)

あなた の は どれ です か?
Anata 　*no* 　*wa* 　*dore* 　*desu* 　*ka?*
you 　's 　as for 　which 　is 　(?)
"Which one is yours?" (PL3)

"This" and "that" for modifying

kono
"this/these ～"

sono
"that/those ～"

ano
"that/those ～ over there"

dono
"which ～?"

The *kore* group words are stand-alone pronouns meaning "this/that" and "these/those"; the *kono* group are modifiers that can only occur together with a noun or noun substitute: "this/these ～" and "that/those ～." The *a-* word again implies "over there," so *ano* ～ is literally "that/those ～ over there."

150 Earlier in the pursuit of Michael the cat and the purse snatcher (fig. 57), the woman whose purse was taken and the fishmonger whose fish Michael made off with point out the thieves to a policeman.

© Kobayashi Makoto. *What's Michael!?*, Kōdansha.

4 あの 猫 です!
Ano neko desu!
that cat is
"It's that cat!" (PL3)

3 なに?!
Nani?!
what
"What?!" (PL2)

2 あの 男 です よ!
Ano otoko desu yo!
that man is (emph.)
"It's that man!" (PL3)

1 あいつ だー!
Aitsu dā!
that guy is
"It's that guy!" (PL2)

koitsu
"this guy"

soitsu
"that guy"

aitsu
"that guy over there"

doitsu
"which guy?"

(For plurals in this set, the suffix *-ra* is usually added. *Koitsu* and *soitsu* are also used to refer to things: "this/that one," or when speaking more roughly, "this damn thing/that sucker.")

Aitsu in the above example represents another, mostly masculine *ko-so-a-do* set, which offers a casual, often rough way of referring to another person: *koitsu* = "this guy," *soitsu* = "that guy," and *aitsu* = "that guy over there." Depending on the situation, the feeling can be quite rough/rude/derogatory, like saying "this knucklehead" or "that rat/bum" or worse, so these words should be used with great caution. The words are pronouns, so *no* must be added when they are used to modify a noun: e.g., *soitsu no* ～ = "that guy's ～."

Place

The *koko* group are pronouns used to indicate relative place: "here," "there," "over there," and "where?" *Soko* refers to a place that is near the listener but away from the speaker. The *a-* word in this set is irregular and gains an extra syllable: *asoko*. Because the words in this group are pronouns, *no* must be added when they are used to modify a noun (*koko no* ～, *soko no* ～, etc.).

koko
"this place/here"

soko
"that place/there"

asoko
"that place over there"

doko
"which place/where?"

151 With his friends helping from the sidelines, the blindfolded man tries to hit the watermelon. He strikes something solid, but it turns out to be the head of a burrowing aardvark.

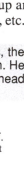

© Imazeki Shin. *Ojama Shimasu*, Take Shobō.

Friends: 少し 前っ! もっと 右。
Sukoshi mae! Motto migi.
a little front/forward more right
"A little forward! More to the right." (PL2)

FX: モコモコモコ
Moko moko moko (burrowing effect)

Friends: よしっ、 そこ だっ!
Yoshi! Soko da!
good/all right that place/there is
"All right, it is there!"
"That's good! Right there!" (PL2)

• the small *tsu* after *mae*, *yoshi*, and *da* indicate that the words are spoken sharply/forcefully.

Direction, formal

The *kochira* group are pronouns that indicate direction: "this way/that way/over that way," and "which way?" By extension, the words are also used to refer to relative place: "here/there/over there," and "where?" Both uses feel quite polite/formal, and usually occur in PL3 or PL4 speech.

Three of the words are also brought into service as polite/formal personal pronouns: *kochira* = "I/we"; *sochira* = "you"; and *achira* = "he/she/they." Similarly, *dochira-sama* (*-sama* is a more formal equivalent of the polite suffix *-san* that's attached to names) is used to politely ask "who?" On the other hand, *dochira* (without *-sama*) can be used to politely ask "which?" when there is a choice between two items/alternatives (contrast this with *dore*, which asks "which [of many items/alternatives]?").

The words in this group are pronouns, so *no* must be added when they modify a noun (*kochira no* ～, *sochira no* ～, and so forth).

kochira
"this way/direction"
"here"
"I/we"

sochira
"that way/direction"
"there"
"you"

achira
"over that way"
"over there"
"he/she/they"

dochira
"which way/direction?"
"where?"
"which [of two]"

152 Wooden fermentation tanks are the standard of the time, but as an experiment Zenzō has installed an enamel tank. A wholesaler comes to taste the results.

© Oze Akira, *Natsu no Kura*, Kōdansha.

Wholesaler: その 琺瑯タンク は どこ に?
Sono hōrō tanku wa doko ni?
that enamel tank as for where at
"As for that enamel tank, where is it?"
"Where is the enamel tank you mentioned." (PL3 implied)

Zenzō: こちら です。
Kochira desu.
this way is
"It's this way." (PL3)

- *sono hōrō tanku* is literally "that enamel tank," implying "the enamel tank you spoke of."
- *ni* marks the place of existence and the verb *aru* ("exists") is understood, so ～ *wa doko ni?* implies ～ *wa doko ni arimasu ka?* = "Where does ～ exist?" → "Where is ～?"

Direction, less formal

The *kochira* group sounds quite formal, so they generally feel out of place in informal speech. The *kotchi* group has essentially the same meanings and uses, but feels much less formal; they are the words of choice for indicating direction, place, person, or "which [of two]?" in PL2 speech, and they are often used in PL3 speech as well.

kotchi
"this way/direction"
"here"
"I/we"

sotchi
"that way/direction"
"there"
"you"

atchi
"over that way"
"over there"
"he/she/they"

dotchi
"which way/direction?"
"where?"
"which [of two]"

153 This strip includes many gags about trying to get to sleep by counting sheep jumping over fences. In this case, one sheep keeps running and running, but he never reaches a fence to jump over. Finally another sheep points out what his problem is.

© Imazeki Shin, *Ojama Shimasu*, Take Shobō.

FX: たったったったったっ
Tattattattatta!
(effect of running swiftly)

Sheep 1: ずいぶん 遠い 柵 だ なあ。
Zuibun tōi saku da nā.
very/awfully far/distant fence is (colloq.)
"It's an awfully distant fence."
"It sure is a long way to the fence." (PL2)

Sheep 2: 柵 は あっち だ ヨ。
Saku wa atchi da yo.
fence as for over that way is (emph.)
"The fence is over that way." (PL2)

- *zuibun* is an adverb meaning "quite/very much/extremely/awfully," here modifying the adjective *tōi* ("far/distant"), which in turn modifies *saku* ("fence").

Manner

The *kō* group are adverbs indicating manner. *Kō* is used when the speaker is actually demonstrating an action or showing its result: "[do something] this way/like this." *Sō* is used when speaking of more "distant" actions, such as the speaker's past or future actions, or actions done by the listener or others: "[do it] that way/like that." *Ā* (the *a-* is simply elongated instead of adding an *-o*) is like *sō*, except with a feeling of greater distance. *Dō* basically asks "[do it] in what manner/how?"—but you will also learn about some exceptions on the facing page.

The *kono yō ni* group also function as adverbs that indicate manner: Their meanings are the same as the *kō* group, but they have a somewhat more formal feeling.

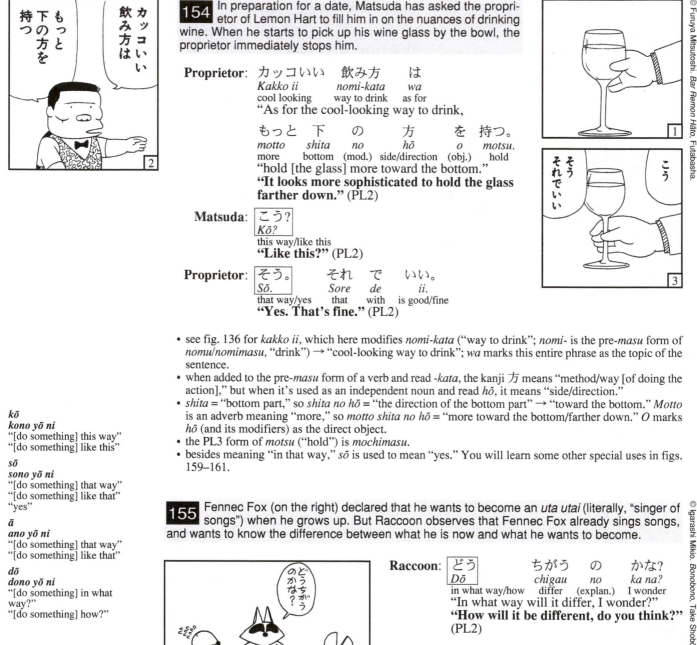

154 In preparation for a date, Matsuda has asked the proprietor of Lemon Hart to fill him in on the nuances of drinking wine. When he starts to pick up his wine glass by the bowl, the proprietor immediately stops him.

Proprietor: カッコいい 飲み方 は
Kakko ii   *nomi-kata*   *wa*
cool looking   way to drink   as for
"As for the cool-looking way to drink,

もっと 下 の 方 を 持つ。
motto   *shita*   *no*   *hō*   *o*   *motsu.*
more   bottom   (mod.)   side/direction   (obj.)   hold
"hold [the glass] more toward the bottom."
"It looks more sophisticated to hold the glass farther down." (PL2)

Matsuda: こう？
Kō?
this way/like this
"Like this?" (PL2)

Proprietor: そう。 それ で いい。
Sō.   *Sore*   *de*   *ii.*
that way/yes   that   with   is good/fine
"Yes. That's fine." (PL2)

- see fig. 136 for *kakko ii*, which here modifies *nomi-kata* ("way to drink"); *nomi-* is the pre-*masu* form of *nomu/nomimasu*, "drink") → "cool-looking way to drink"; *wa* marks this entire phrase as the topic of the sentence.
- when added to the pre-*masu* form of a verb and read *-kata*, the kanji 方 means "method/way [of doing the action]," but when it's used as an independent noun and read *hō*, it means "side/direction."
- *shita* = "bottom part," so *shita no hō* = "the direction of the bottom part" → "toward the bottom." *Motto* is an adverb meaning "more," so *motto shita no hō* = "more toward the bottom/farther down." *O* marks *hō* (and its modifiers) as the direct object.
- the PL3 form of *motsu* ("hold") is *mochimasu*.
- besides meaning "in that way," *sō* is used to mean "yes." You will learn some other special uses in figs. 159–161.

kō
kono yō ni
"[do something] this way"
"[do something] like this"

sō
sono yō ni
"[do something] that way"
"[do something] like that"
"yes"

ā
ano yō ni
"[do something] that way"
"[do something] like that"

dō
dono yō ni
"[do something] in what way?"
"[do something] how?"

155 Fennec Fox (on the right) declared that he wants to become an *uta utai* (literally, "singer of songs") when he grows up. But Raccoon observes that Fennec Fox already sings songs, and wants to know the difference between what he is now and what he wants to become.

Raccoon: どう ちがう の かな？
Dō   *chigau*   *no*   *ka na?*
in what way/how   differ   (explan.)   I wonder
"In what way will it differ, I wonder?"
"How will it be different, do you think?" (PL2)

- *chigau* is a verb for "differ/be different." Its polite form is *chigaimasu.*
- *no* is the explanatory *no*, and *ka na* asks a question like "I wonder who/what/how 〜?" but in this case both can be thought of mainly as softeners, to make his question—which is actually an indirect way of asserting that there is no difference—feel less abrupt.

どう dō is sometimes "what?"

Sometimes *dō* can be equivalent to English "what?" instead of "how?" For example, the line in fig. 155 could also have been translated "What's the difference?" You will encounter other cases where good English equivalents can be formed using either "how?" or "what?"

There are also a number of expressions in which the only natural English translation of *dō* is "what?" Here are some examples:

156 After making dietman Aosugi a minister without portfolio to oversee political reform (fig. 132), Prime Minister Asami is having second thoughts. Aosugi has been asserting himself much more aggressively than expected. Here Asami asks his closest colleague, Kaji Ryūnosuke, what he thinks about the situation.

Asami: 加治君、 どう 思う?
Kaji-kun, *dō* *omou?*
(name-fam.) how/what think
"What do you think, Kaji?" (PL2)

• *Dō omou?* (or in polite speech, *Dō omoimasu ka?*) looks literally like "How do you think?" but it's equivalent to English "What do you think?"

157 Natsuko's brother was managing day-to-day operations of the Saeki Brewery when he died. At his wake, the owner of the neighboring Kuroiwa Brewery asks Natsuko's parents what their plans are for the future with their son gone.

Kuroiwa: これから どう する ね?
Kore kara *dō* *suru* *ne?*
from now how/what do (colloq.)
"What will you do now?" (PL2)

Saeki: どう する?
Dō *suru?*
how/what do
"What will we do?" (PL2)

• the pronoun *kore* ("this") plus the particle *kara* ("from/beginning with") can simply mean "from this," but most often it implies "from this time forward/from now on." The other members of this *ko-so-a-do* group are shown to the right.

• *suru* means "do," so *Dō suru?* looks literally like "How will you do?" But if you recast that as "In what manner will you act/proceed?" you can see a little better how it comes to mean "What will you do?" The polite form of this expression is *Dō shimasu ka?*

• Saeki echoes the question with the feeling of "What will we do about what?" because at this point it's not yet clear exactly what Kuroiwa is asking about.

kore kara
"from this/these"
"beginning with this/these"
"from this time forward"
"from now on"

sore kara
"from that/those"
"after that"
"from that time on"
"and then/since then"
"next/in addition"

are kara
"since that time"
"since then"

dore kara
"beginning with which?"
"from which?"

158 These two samurai guerrillas are making their way through the underbrush when the one in the lead stops to ponder something.

Hachi: どう しました、 親分?
Dō *shimashita,* *oyabun?*
how/what did boss
"What's the matter, boss?" (PL3)

• *shimashita* is the PL3 past form of *suru* ("do"), so *Dō shimashita?* looks literally like "How did you do [it]?" but it's actually an expression for "What's the matter?/What's wrong?" The PL2 equivalent is *Dō shita?*

It's important to remember, though, that *dō* still basically means "in what manner?/how?" You will learn another word for "what?" in Lesson 17, where other kinds of question words are introduced. These examples merely represent instances where Japanese and English usage does not match.

Special uses of そう *sō*

Sō also has some special uses that diverge (or at least seem to) from its basic meaning of "in that manner/that way/like that." You have seen one such use in fig. 154, where *sō* serves as "yes." It's worth noting that *sō* (or its polite equivalent, *sō desu*) can be used quite broadly to mean "yes," even when the question has nothing to do with "how/in what manner" the action occurs.

There are far too many variations on the uses of *sō* to illustrate them all, but here are a few to get you started:

159 Sunlight Records singing star Yatsuhashi Shinko collapsed during a New Year's concert. Shima was among the few who knew that she had been fighting terminal cancer. The doctor has just told him that she is hemorrhaging so badly they can barely keep up with transfusions, and that he cannot offer much hope.

Shima: そう です か。
Sō desu ka.
that way is (?)
"I see." (PL3)

• spoken with the rising intonation of a question, this sentence literally asks, "Is it that way?" and is like the English "Really?/Is that true?" But when it's spoken with a falling intonation at the end, it's an expression of comprehension/understanding, like "I see." The context and look of grim acceptance on Shima's face show this is a case of the latter.

160 A headhunter approached Shima, claiming that rival company Solar Electric was interested in hiring him away from Hatsushiba Electric. Just before Shima is to give him an answer a week later, he learns that the headhunter has been seen consulting with one of Shima's enemies within Hatsushiba.

Shima: そう か!!
Sō ka!!
that way (?)
"I get it!" (PL2)

これ は 罠 だ!
Kore wa wana da!
this as for trap is
"This is a trap!" (PL2)

• *Sō ka?* can also be a question ("Is that right/true?" or "Is it really that way?"), but here it expresses a sudden understanding/realization: "So that's it!/Oh, I get it!/That explains it!"

161 Bonobono the otter and his friends are trying to figure out what they can do for some fun. Bonobono suddenly has an idea.

Bonobono: あっ、 そう だ!
A!, sō da!
oh that way is
"Oh, I know!" (PL2)

• *Sō da* is literally "It is so/It is that way," but it's often used like "Oh, I know!/Oh, that's right!/Oh, yeah" when you have a sudden thought/idea, or when you remember something you intended/needed to do. When the phrase expresses this kind of sudden idea or recollection, it's often preceded by an interjection like *a!*

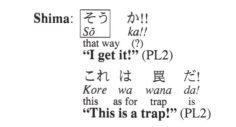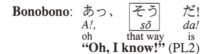

Nature/kind

The *kō iu* group are noun modifiers indicating nature or kind: "this/that kind of ～," "～ like this/that," or "such (a) ～." They must always be followed by a noun or noun substitute. As you would expect, *dō iu* ～ often asks "what kind of ～?" (as illustrated here). But in other situations, *dō iu* ～ can also be just a roundabout (and more polite) way of asking "what ～?"

162 The day after Asami Tsunetarō is elected as prime minister by the House of Representatives, members of the media fan out in his home district to see what people who've known him since childhood have to say about him

Reporter:

どういう	少年時代	でした	か?
Dō iu	*shōnen jidai*	*deshita*	*ka?*
what kind of	boyhood	was	(?)

"What kind of boyhood was it?"
"What kind of boyhood did he have?"
(PL3)

- because of a slight ambiguity, the reporter could be asking for either a description of Asami's character as a boy, or a description of his life as a boy. The person being interviewed here takes it to be the former (his response is in fig. 228).

Another set of noun modifiers that indicate nature or kind is the *kono yō na* group. Their meaning and usage is the same as the *kō iu* group except that the *kono yō na* group feels a little more formal.

Nature/kind, less formal—and even pejorative

The *konna* group is distinctly less formal than either *kō iu* or *kono yō na,* above, but it covers essentially the same ground. In addition, in some contexts and depending on the tone of voice, the *konna* group can take on a belittling/pejorative tone, in which case they are like "this stupid/lousy ～" or "that stupid/lousy ～." One exception: the question word *donna* does not take on this negative feeling regardless of the context.

163 At their *o-miai,* after learning that Poppo likes to spend her days sleeping instead of gamboling energetically about the fields (fig. 97), Shinnosuke ventures to ask Poppo about her taste in men.

Shinnosuke:

そ、	それで、	ポッポさん	は
So-	*sore de,*	*Poppo-san*	*wa*
(stammer)	so	(name-pol.)/you	as for

"S- so, as for Miss Poppo/you,

どんな	男性	が	好み	です	か?
donna	*dansei*	*ga*	*konomi*	*desu*	*ka?*
what kind of	male/man	(subj.)	preference	is	(?)

"what kind of man is your preference?"
"S- so, what kind of man do you like, Miss Poppo?" (PL3)

- *sore de* is often used as a connecting word at the beginning of a sentence, like "so" or "and so."
- Shinnosuke uses Poppo's name when an English speaker would say "you."
- *dansei* refers to males; 女性 *josei* is the corresponding word for females. For children, the words 男子 *danshi* and 女子 *joshi* are also used.
- Poppo gives her response in fig. 220.

kō iu
kono yō na
konna
"this kind of ～"
"～ like this"

sō iu
sono yō na
sonna
"that kind of ～"
"～ like that"

ā iu
ano yō na
anna
"that kind of ～"
"～ like that"

dō iu
dono yō na
donna
"what kind of ～?"
"～ like what?"

Amount/extent

The *konna-ni* group are adverbs indicating amount or extent: "this many/that many" or "this much/that much." They modify adjectives and verbs, and usually imply that the amount/extent is quite large: "so many/so much."

164 Natsuko and a fellow organic farmer declare that growing rice is an art, and so is the production of fine saké. The vice-president of the local farmer's cooperative (Gotō) immediately bursts out laughing, but to his surprise, the president of the cooperative (Hirooka) doesn't think it's so funny.

Gotō: お酒 が 芸術? ヒャハハハハ
O-sake ga geijutsu? Hya ha ha ha ha
(hon.)-saké (subj.) art (laugh)
"Saké's an art? Hyuk hyuk hyuk!" (PL2)

Hirooka: そんなに おかしい かね?
Sonna-ni okashii ka ne?
that much funny (?-colloq.)
"Is it that funny?"
"You think it's that funny?" (PL2)

© Oze Akira, Natsuko no Sake, Kōdansha.

- *okashii* is an adjective that means "funny"—either in the humorous sense or the strange/odd sense, depending on the context. Here it is quite clearly the former. In other contexts, its meanings range to "improper/illogical/unreasonable/preposterous/wrong."
- asking a question with *ka ne* is mostly reserved for males, and for superiors speaking to subordinates. Using only *ka* sounds very abrupt, and *ne* has a softening effect.

Approximate amount/extent

The *kore kurai* and *kono kurai* groups indicate approximate amount or extent: "about this many/that many" or "about this much/that much." The words in these groups can function as adverbs, to modify adjectives and verbs; or they can function as pronouns and be made into noun modifiers by adding *no* (*kore kurai no ～*, *sore kurai no ～*, and so forth).

165 Walking by a flower shop after a hard day at work, this OL thinks she deserves a little reward and stops to buy a large bouquet.

OL: このくらい の ぜーたく、
Kono kurai no zeitaku,
about this much of extravagance
"[As for] an extravagance of about this much,

たまに は いい わ よ ね
tama ni wa ii wa yo ne.
occasionally as for is fine/okay (fem.) (emph.) (colloq.)
"as for occasionally, it's fine, right?"
"This much of an extravagance is all right now and then, right?" (PL2)

© Akizuki Risu, OL Shinkaron, Kōdansha.

- the standard way of writing *zeitaku* ("extravagance") in hiragana is ぜいたく. *Wa* to mark *zeitaku* as the overall topic has been omitted.
- *tama ni* means "occasionally/now and then"; *wa* marks this as a second topic: "as for occasionally."

Kinship Terms

Japanese has two main sets of terms for addressing or referring to family members—a neutral set, and a polite set. Both sets are used in both PL2 and PL3 speech, but the appropriate set to use depends on the situation and the specific person you are referring to.

When speaking to someone outside the family, the neutral set is used to refer to members of your own family and the polite set is used to refer to members of your listener's or a third person's family.

Within the family, the polite set is used for those who are older than the speaker (except spouses). Even among siblings, the younger usually address or refer to the older using these "titles" instead of their given names, as Natsuko does in the example here—though in larger families it's sometimes necessary to combine names with the titles. The honorific o- may or may not be used; some families stand on formality more than others, and even those that tend to be

("uncle") or *obasan* ("aunt"). Adults often address/refer to young strangers as *o-niisan* or *o-nēsan*, and older strangers (roughly speaking, those past their mid-twenties—but the demarcation is fluid) as *ojisan* and *obasan*. *O-jiisan* and *o-bāsan* are used by one and all for addressing/referring to those who have entered their golden years.

There are many other kinship terms besides those listed in this table—both more formal/polite (e.g., for use in PL4 speech) and less formal/polite (including even insulting/derogatory terms). The ones given here are the key ones to learn first.

© Oze Akira, Natsuko no Sake, Kōdansha

166 When still working for a Tokyo ad agency, Natsuko learns that copy she wrote for a saké company ad—her first really big project—will run nationwide in the newspaper. She wants to tell her brother about her accomplishment.

Natsuko:
もしもし？　あ、　お母さん？
Moshi-moshi?　A,　o-kāsan?
hello　oh　(hon.)-mother
"Hello? Mother?" (PL3)

あたし、　夏子　です。
Atashi,　Natsuko　desu.
I/me　(name)　is
"It's me. Natsuko. (PL3)

兄さん、　　　いる？
Niisan,　　　iru?
older brother　exists/is present
"Is Brother there?" (PL2)

- *moshi-moshi* is the traditional telephone "hello"; it can be spoken either by the person initiating the call or by the person answering, but in the latter case it would usually be preceded by *hai*.
- *atashi* is a mostly feminine variation of *watashi* ("I/me").
- she makes *iru/imasu* ("exist/be in a place") a question by raising the intonation on the last syllable.
- Natsuko says *niisan* when an English speaker would use the brother's name; Natsuko seems to always use the honorific *o-* with her mother, but uses it only some of the time in addressing or referring to her older brother.

more formal may not use the *o-* consistently all the time. Family members younger than the speaker are usually addressed or referred to by name, but also at times with the neutral set. Spouses address each other as *o-tōsan* ("father") and *o-kāsan* ("mother"), as "you" (husbands use *omae*; wives use *anata* and sometimes *omae*), or sometimes by name or name + -*san*. When speaking to their children, parents typically refer to each other as *o-tōsan* and *o-kāsan*.

Some of the polite set (those marked with asterisks in the table) are also used as generic terms of address/reference for people outside the family. Children may address/refer to any older child or young adult as *o-niisan* ("older brother") or *o-nēsan* ("older sister") according to gender, and in the same way, any adult as *ojisan*

	neutral	polite[1]
father[2]	父 *chichi*	お父さん *o-tōsan*
mother[2]	母 *haha*	お母さん *o-kāsan*
son	息子 *musuko*	息子さん *musuko-san*
daughter	娘 *musume*	娘さん *musume-san*
older brother	兄 *ani*	お兄さん* *o-niisan*
older sister	姉 *ane*	お姉さん* *o-nēsan*
younger brother	弟 *otōto*	弟さん *otōto-san*
younger sister	妹 *imōto*	妹さん *imōto-san*
siblings	兄弟 *kyōdai*	ご兄弟 *go-kyōdai*
uncle[3]	伯父/叔父 *oji*	おじさん* *ojisan*
aunt[3]	伯母/叔母 *oba*	おばさん* *obasan*
grandfather	祖父 *sofu*	おじいさん* *o-jiisan*
grandmother	祖母 *sobo*	おばあさん* *o-bāsan*
husband	夫/主人 *otto/shujin*	ご主人 *go-shujin*
wife	妻/家内 *tsuma/kanai*	奥さん *okusan*

[1] For use of the polite forms within the family, the honorific prefix *o-* is often dropped, and the diminutive suffix -*san* often replaces -*san* (e.g., *o-tōsan* becomes *tōsan* or *tōchan*; *o-nēsan* becomes *nēsan* or *nēchan*). The *o-* at the beginning of *otōto*, *ojisan*, and *obasan* are not honorific and can never be omitted.
[2] The imported パパ *papa* and ママ *mama* are also widely used, especially by young children and parents speaking to their young children.
[3] Only in writing, a distinction is made between aunts/uncles who are the parents' older siblings (伯父/伯母) and those who are their younger siblings (叔父/叔母); in spoken Japanese, *oji* and *oba* simply mean "uncle" and "aunt," without regard to relative age.

Lesson 13

Some High-Traffic Particles

There aren't enough pages in this book to devote entire lessons to all of the particles used in Japanese. But now that you know about the all-important *ga*, *o*, and *wa* and have a basic understanding of how particles work—by marking whatever precedes them—you should be able to pick up on the basic usage of others simply by studying the examples and notes whenever they happen to appear. Use the index to find other examples for comparison, and you can even begin to get a sense of the gradations and subtleties of nuance. This lesson is designed to give you a running start on "the best of the rest"—a few of the most versatile and frequently used particles—by giving them more focused attention than a take-them-as-they-come approach allows.

The first particle that deserves a bit of a closer look is *ni*, which has already popped up quite a few times. In fig. 65 it marked the choice made; in figs. 100 and 128, the target of an action; and in fig. 103, the destination of a movement. Consider these examples closely, and you will see a common thread: *ni* marks the endpoint (of a decision, an action, a movement). But you have also seen a completely different use for *ni* in figs. 55, 138, and 152, where it marks the place of existence, and this lesson will show you a few more. *Ni* is in fact one of the most versatile particles around, and you will continue to discover new uses for it as you proceed with your study.

に *ni* marks purpose

The obvious endpoint of a movement from one place to another, represented by such verbs as *iku* ("go"), *kuru* ("come") or *kaeru* ("return home"), is the destination. But as the English expression "ends and means" implies, the purpose or aim of a movement can also be considered an endpoint—what the movement is intended to accomplish in the end—and indeed, with verbs indicating this kind of movement from one place to another, *ni* often marks the purpose: "for the purpose of/in order to ～," or simply "for/to ～." The purpose itself is expressed with a noun that represents an activity (e.g., *kaimono* = "shopping" → *kaimono ni iku* = "go to shop/go shopping"), or with the pre-*masu* form of a verb, as in this example.

167 In spite of her history of getting lost because she has no sense of direction, Yun-chan is often the one asked to deliver completed work to clients. This time she found her way there without trouble.

Client: やあ、ゆんちゃん。
Yā,   Yun-chan.
hi   (name-dimin.)
"Hi, Yun-chan." (PL2)

Yun-chan: 図面　届け　に　きました。
Zumen todoke ni kimashita.
drawings deliver (purpose) came
"I came to deliver the drawings." (PL3)

Sign: 土木　　　　　課
Doboku   -ka
civil eng./pub. works section
Public Works Section

- *yā* is an informal "hi/hello" used by male speakers.
- *todoke* is the pre-*masu* form of the verb *todokeru/todokemasu* ("deliver"), and *ni* marks this as the purpose of coming.
- *kimashita* is the PL3 past form of *kuru/kimasu* ("come").

Ni marks absolute time

As noted in Lesson 6, relative time words such as *kinō* ("yesterday"), *kyō* ("today"), and *ashita* ("tomorrow") do not need a particle, but if an absolute time word is used to indicate when an action takes/took place, it is marked with the particle *ni*. This is true when indicating a specific hour on the clock, as in the example below, as well as for other kinds of time references: *nichi-yōbi ni* = "on Sunday"; *Kurisumasu ni* = "at Christmas"; *natsu ni* = "in the summer"; *dai-gaku jidai ni* = "during my college years."

Yoshihara

168 Usami, executive director of the Hatsushiba Electric Sales Division, has come to see Chairman of the Board Yoshihara on a business matter. As he prepares to leave, they make final arrangements for a planned golf outing the next day.

Usami: はい！ では、 明日 10時 に
Hai! De wa, ashita jūji ni
yes/okay in that case/then tomorrow 10:00 at

お迎え に 参ります。
o-mukae ni mairimasu.
(hon.)-pick up (purpose) will come

"**Yes sir! Well then, I will come to pick you up at 10:00 tomorrow.**" (PL4)

- *de wa* at the beginning of a sentence literally means "in that case/if that is the case," but it often corresponds to words like "then/well then/so" at the beginning of English sentences.
- *ni* marks *jūji* ("10:00") as the time when the action will take place.
- *o-* is honorific, and *mukae* is the pre-*masu* form of *mukaeru/mukaemasu*, which implies either going or coming to "meet/receive/welcome" someone.
- *mairimasu* is the polite form of *mairu*, a PL4 humble verb that can mean either "go" or "come" depending on the context, so *o-mukae ni mairimasu* here is a PL4 equivalent of *mukae ni kuru* (lit. "come to meet/receive [you]" → "come to pick you up").

Telling time

The hours of the day are indicated with a number plus the suffix 時 *-ji*; minutes get the suffix 分 *-fun* (which sometimes changes to *-pun* or *-ppun*); and seconds get the suffix 秒 *-byō*. As in English, the hour is stated first, then minutes, then seconds. The times are given in kanji at the top here, but today it's more common to see Arabic numerals, as in the examples at the bottom (the suffixes remain in kanji).

When necessary, 午前 *gozen* precedes the time to indicate "a.m.," and 午後 *gogo* precedes the time for "p.m." (they occur both with and without a trailing *no*). *Asa (no)* ("in the morning"), *hiru (no)* ("in the afternoon/daytime"), and *yoru (no)* ("in the evening/at night") can also be used.

The half hour can be indicated either as *-ji sanjuppun* ("〜 thirty") or by adding the suffix *-han* ("half"): *-ji-han* ("half past 〜").

The suffix *-kan* ("period/timespan")

Hours and minutes

1:00	一時	*ichiji*		:01	一分	*ippun*
2:00	二時	*niji*		:02	二分	*nifun*
3:00	三時	*sanji*		:03	三分	*sanpun*
4:00	四時	*yoji*		:04	四分	*yonpun*
5:00	五時	*goji*		:05	五分	*gofun*
6:00	六時	*rokuji*		:06	六分	*roppun*
7:00	七時	*shichiji*		:07	七分	*nanafun*
8:00	八時	*hachiji*		:08	八分	*happun, hachifun*
9:00	九時	*kuji*		:09	九分	*kyūfun*
10:00	十時	*jūji*		:10	十分	*juppun, jippun*
11:00	十一時	*jūichiji*		:11	十一分	*jūippun*
12:00	十二時	*jūniji*		:12	十二分	*jūnifun*

1時10分	午後4時30分	11時59分59秒
ichiji juppun	*gogo yoji sanjuppun*	*jūichiji gojūkyūfun gojūkyūbyō*
1:10	**4:30 p.m.**	**11:59:59**
午前8時25分	6時半	5時間 / 20分間
gozen hachiji nijūgofun	*rokuji-han*	*gojikan* / *nijuppun-kan*
8:25 a.m.	**6:30/half past six**	**5 hours** / **20 minutes**

used to indicate durations of years, months, weeks, and days (p. 49) is also used for shorter timespans: *-jikan* = "〜 hours" (*jikan* is also the word for "time" in general); *-fun-kan* = "〜 minutes"; and *-byō-kan* = "〜 seconds." The suffix is always required when indicating hours, but optional for durations of minutes and seconds.

Gōda

Ni marks a source

In statements about something received, *ni* can mark the source. With the verb *kariru/karimasu* ("borrow") appearing in this example, *ni* marks the source from which the borrowing takes place. Compare this with fig. 100, where the verb is "distribute" and *ni* marks the target of the distribution. The nature of the verb determines which meaning it must be.

169 When organic farmer Gōda sees Natsuko using an antique weeding tool to tend to her field of Tatsunishiki, he stops to watch. At first he doesn't say anything, but then he asks her where she found such an old-fashioned contraption.

Natsuko:	近所	の	おじいさん	に	借りました。
	Kinjo	*no*	*o-jiisan*	*ni*	*karimashita.*
	neighborhood	of	(hon.)-old man	from	borrowed

"I borrowed it from an old man who lives nearby." (PL3)

Sound FX:	ジャバジャバ	
	Jaba jaba	(gentle splashing in flooded rice paddy)

- within the family, *o-jiisan* is a polite word for addressing or referring to "Grandfather"; outside the family, it's used to address or refer to any elderly man. The honorific *o-* tends to be kept even in informal speech because dropping it can sound too abrupt/rough and impolite.
- *karimashita* is the PL3 past form of *kariru/karimasu* ("borrow"). The source from which borrowing takes place can be marked either with *ni*, as here, or with *kara* ("from"; fig. 176).

Ni marks a surface

Ni can mark the surface on/against which an action takes place, such as writing or drawing on a sheet of paper (*kami ni kaku*, from *kami* = "paper" and *kaku/kakimasu* = "write/draw"), or reflecting in a mirror (*kagami ni utsuru*, from *kagami* = "mirror" and *utsuru/utsurimasu* = "reflect"), or setting something on a shelf (*tana ni oku*, from *tana* = "shelf" and *oku/okimasu* = "set down"). As in fig. 100 and others cited above, *ni* can be thought of as marking the endpoint of an action in these cases.

Anchor:	次	の	ニュース	です。
	Tsugi	*no*	*nyūsu*	*desu.*
	next	(mod.)	news	is

"Now the next news." (PL3)

	今日、	坊主	が	びょうぶ	に	しょうずに
	Kyō,	*bōzu*	*ga*	*byōbu*	*ni*	*jōzu ni*
	today	priest	(subj.)	folding screen	on	skillfully

	ボウズ	の	絵	を	書きました。
	bōzu	*no*	*e*	*o*	*kakimashita.*
	priest	's	picture	(obj.)	drew

"Today a priest skillfully drew a picture of a priest on a folding screen." (PL3)

	中継さん。
	Chūkei-san.
	live reporter-(pol.)

"Mr. Live Reporter."
"Let's go to our reporter at the scene." (PL3)

170 If this news item sounds nonsensical, that's because it's like an American anchorman saying, "In other news, Peter Piper picked a peck of pickled peppers today. Let's go to the scene." The line he speaks is a well-known Japanese tongue twister.

NEWS NEWS NEWS 5:00

- *bōzu* is an informal, sometimes even derogatory, word for "priest/monk."
- *ni* marks *byōbu* ("folding screen") as the surface on which the drawing took place.
- *jōzu ni* ("skillfully") is the adverb form of the adjectival noun *jōzu*, which in the form *jōzu da/desu* typically means "is skillful." *Jōzu ni* here modifies the verb *kakimashita*, the PL3 past form of *kaku/kakimasu* ("write/draw"). When *jōzu da/desu* appears in the sentence final position, it follows the *wa-ga* construction (fig. 145).
- *chūkei* refers to a live broadcast or report. The word is not normally followed by *-san*, but adding it here creates a generic stand-in for the reporter's name.

Ni can also be "and"

You will sometimes see and hear *ni* being used like "and" to connect nouns. Often there will be three or more items listed, and the items will belong to a set of some kind—either of like items, such as the hot drinks in this example, or of unlike items that have been assembled for some common purpose (e.g., items in a picnic basket). *Ni* is also used as "and" between pairs of items that always go together, such as *gohan ni misoshiru* ("rice and miso soup"). The particle *to*, coming up in fig. 179, can also be used in these cases, but *ni* tends to carry a stronger sense of the items belonging together.

171 A group of coworkers went out for karaoke one evening, and since she lived nearby, this OL invited the entire crew to her place for coffee afterwards. Here she summarizes everyone's hot drink orders.

OL: コーヒー 4つ に 紅茶 二つ に ウーロン茶 ね。
Kōhii yottsu ni kōcha futatsu ni ūroncha ne.
coffee 4 count and black tea 2 count and oolong tea (is-colloq.)
"So that's 4 coffees and 2 black teas and an oolong tea."
(PL2)

SFX: ワイワイ
Wai wai
  (clamor/chatter of large group of people.)

* though written with kanji meaning "red/crimson" and "tea," *kōcha* refers to what English speakers know as "black tea."

© Akizuki Risu. OL Shinkaron, Kodansha.

へ *e* marks direction/destination

The particle へ, read *e* (see note on kana usage below), marks a direction or destination: *migi e iku* = "go right"; *Nihon e iku* = "go to Japan." It's also used with certain verbs to indicate the target or recipient of the action: *gakkō e denwa suru* = "telephone the school." In all these uses *e* is generally interchangeable with *ni*, but *e* primarily emphasizes the direction, while *ni* emphasizes the person/point reached.

© Furuya Mitsutoshi. Bar Remon Hāto, Futabasha.

172 Noboru soberly accepts the verdict of the pink water that emerged from under the napkin in fig. 13.

Noboru: 故郷 へ 帰ります。
Kuni e kaerimasu.
hometown to will return
"I'll return to my hometown."
"I'll go home." (PL3)

* when written with this kanji, *kuni* refers to one's "hometown/native place/birthplace," usually when one is away from it. *Kuni* can also mean "country/nation" (referring to the whole of Japan or to other countries of the world), in which case it's written 国.

Kana Usage Alert!

Until now, the independent syllable *e* has always been written え in hiragana (figs. 50, 140, 144, and others), and the hiragana character へ has been read *he* (fig. 104). But the particle *e* for marking a destination is an exception. It's written へ.

When you're reading, え is always *e*, but with へ you have to determine whether it is a particle (read it *e*) or part of another word (read it *he*). When you're writing, if the sound *e* represents a particle, write へ; if it's part of another word, write え.

で *de* marks where an action occurs

When speaking of a place in English, it doesn't matter whether it's the place where something *is* or where something *occurs*, but in Japanese you have to make a distinction. You've already learned that *ni* marks a place of existence—where something is located (figs. 55, 138, 152); for actions, the particle *de* marks the place of occurrence—where the action takes place. Words like "at/on/in" work as English equivalents for both particles.

173 Kōsuke has been going to the library periodically to read Ernest Hemingway's *Islands in the Stream*. It looks like he'll finish it today, but he takes a break for lunch.

Narration:
昼　　は　　地下　　の　　食堂　　で
Hiru　　wa　　chika　　no　　shokudō　　de
noon/lunch　as for　basement　(mod.)　cafeteria　at

300円　　　の　　定食　　を　　食べる。
sanbyaku-en　no　teishoku　o　taberu.
¥300　　　　that is　set meal　(obj.)　eat

"As for noon, I eat a ¥300 set meal at the cafeteria in the basement."

"For lunch, I go to the cafeteria in the basement and eat one of their set meals for ¥300." (PL2)

- *hiru* literally means "noon," but it's often used to mean "noon meal/lunch."
- *shokudō* can refer to a variety of relatively inexpensive "eateries/restaurants"; when it refers to a room within a larger building it means "dining room/cafeteria." *De* marks this word as the place where Kōsuke eats.
- *teishoku* refers to the traditional Japanese "set meal" of steamed rice, miso or other soup, an entree, and pickles. The PL3 form of *taberu* ("eat") is *tabemasu*.

De can mark a tool or means

The particle *de* is also used to mark a tool or means: "with/using/by means of ～." In most cases whether *de* marks a place or a tool/means will be obvious from the nature of the word it marks, but sometimes the marked word can be either a place or a tool/means; in such cases, the nature of the verb and the rest of the context must be your guide. To take *kuruma* ("car") as an example, if the verb is *neru* ("sleep"), you know *kuruma de* refers to the place of action—"sleep in the car"; if the verb is *kuru* ("come"), you know *kuruma de* refers to the means—"come by car."

174 Igarashi has decided to marry Stella, a dancer from the Philippines. He has just told Shima about his plans and introduced him to her. Shima asks Stella if her parents know about her wedding plans. (The horizontal script is intended to show that she's actually speaking entirely in English.)

Stella: **"Oh, yeah."**

2ヵ月　　前、　　電話　で　伝えました。
Nikagetsu　mae,　denwa　de　tsutaemashita.
2 mos.　before/ago　phone　by　told/informed
"I told them by phone two months ago." (PL3)

OK　　してくれました。
Ōkē　shite kuremashita.
okay　　　　did for me
"They okayed it for me."
"They gave their consent." (PL3)

- *-kagetsu* is the counter suffix for counting months (p. 49), so *nikagetsu* = "2 months"; *mae* after a timespan means "that much time ago/before." *Ni* to mark this as the time of action has been omitted.
- *de* marks *denwa* as the tool used in doing the action.
- *tsutaemashita* is the PL3 past form of *tsutaeru/tsutaemasu* ("tell/inform").
- *OK* is also commonly written in katakana: オーケー. *OK shite kuremashita* is a PL3 past form coming from the *suru* verb, *OK suru* ("to okay"); the *-te kureru/kuremasu/kuremashita* form of a verb is formally introduced in Lesson 31; it implies that the action is/was done for the speaker.

De can indicate scope

After words that express a quantity, *de* marks that quantity as the scope of something. If *de* follows a timespan, it implies that's how long the action takes (*gofun de taberu* = "eat in five minutes"); it if follows an amount of money, it implies that's how much it costs (*sen-en de kau* = "buy for ¥1000"); if it follows a count of objects or people, it implies that's how many are required or included (*sannin de benkyō suru* = "study in a group of three people").

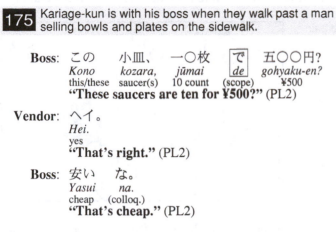

175 Kariage-kun is with his boss when they walk past a man selling bowls and plates on the sidewalk.

Boss: この　　小皿、　一〇枚　で　五〇〇円?
Kono　　kozara,　jūmai　de　gohyaku-en?
this/these　saucer(s)　10 count　(scope)　¥500
"These saucers are ten for ¥500?" (PL2)

Vendor: ヘイ。
Hei.
yes
"That's right." (PL2)

Boss: 安い　な。
Yasui　na.
cheap　(colloq.)
"That's cheap." (PL2)

- *kozara* combines the prefix *ko* ("small") with *sara* ("plate"; the *s* changes to *z* in combinations).
- *de* marks *jūmai* ("ten plates"; *-mai* is the counter suffix for thin, flat objects—see p. 47) as the number included in the price.
- *hei* is an informal *hai* ("yes") often used by male shopkeepers/tradesmen/laborers.

から *kara* = "from"

The particle *kara* after a noun (or noun substitute) indicates a place or time at which something begins/originates or the source from which it comes, usually corresponding to "from" or "begin(ning) at/with" in English: *koko kara* = "from here"; *gogo ichiji kara* = "from 1:00 p.m."; *sensei kara* = "from the teacher."

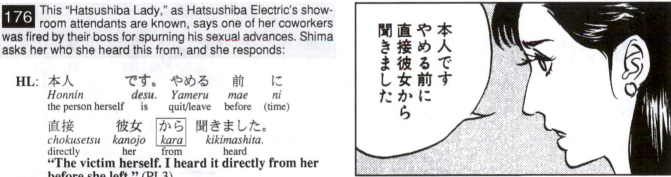

176 This "Hatsushiba Lady," as Hatsushiba Electric's showroom attendants are known, says one of her coworkers was fired by their boss for spurning his sexual advances. Shima asks her who she heard this from, and she responds:

HL: 本人　　　です。やめる　前　　に
Honnin　　desu.　Yameru　mae　ni
the person herself　is　quit/leave　before　(time)

直接　　　彼女　から　聞きました。
chokusetsu　kanojo　kara　kikimashita.
directly　her　from　heard
"The victim herself. I heard it directly from her before she left." (PL3)

- *honnin* = "the very person" or "the person himself/herself," in this case referring to "the victim herself."
- *yameru/yamemasu* means "quit/stop," but in this case the woman was fired, so the sense is more like "leave the company."
- *mae* is a noun meaning "front" or "[a time/place] before"; when it follows a verb, it means "before [the described action takes/took place]" → *yameru mae* = "before she quit/left." *Ni* marks this as the time when the action of the main verb (*kikimashita*) took place.
- *kikimashita* is the PL3 past form of *kiku/kikimasu* ("hear/listen").

Kara can also occur after the *-te* form of a verb (you will learn about this form in Lesson 19), in which case it implies "after/since [the action takes/took place]" or "[the action takes/took place] and then ～"; and it can occur after a complete sentence as a connecting word meaning "because/so" (fig. 198).

まで *made* = "to/up to/until"

The particle *made* is used to indicate how far an action extends in place or time. After a place word, it implies "to/as far as [the stated place]": *koko made* = "to here/this far"; *Tōkyō made* = "to Tokyo." After a time word it means "to/until [the stated time]": *goji-han made* = "until 5:30"; *rainen made* = "until next year." After a number or price it means "up to [the stated number/price]": *sanko made* = "up to 3 pieces"; *goman-en made* = "up to ¥50,000." In some contexts it can mean "even" in the emphatic sense of "even to the extent of" or "even including."

177 Shin-chan's mother looks at the fare map at the train station to see how much it costs to go to S.

Mother: えーと、　S駅　まで　210円　か。
Ē to,　Esu-eki　made　nihyaku jū-en　ka.
(interj.)　S train station　to/as far as　¥210　(?)
"Umm, as far as S Station is ¥210, is it?"
"Let's see, to S is ¥210, I guess." (PL2)

- *ē to* is a pause/hesitation phrase, like "uhh/well/let me see."
- *ka* literally makes a question, "Is it ¥210 to S Station?" But the question form is often used rhetorically when observing/confirming something for oneself, with the feeling of "So it's ～, is it?/I guess/it seems."

For verbs describing movement from one place to another (e.g. *iku*, "go"), *made* essentially marks the destination, so it can sometimes be used interchangeably with *ni*; but *made* tends to place emphasis on the distance to the destination and the route taken (the example here feels like: "To go as far as S is ¥210, I guess"), while *ni* focuses on the destination reached, so the effect of the two particles can be quite different.

☞ Not surprisingly, *kara* and *made* often appear together to make an expression for "from ～ to ～": *Amerika kara Nihon made* = "from America to Japan."

Made after a verb

Made after a verb means "until [the described action takes/took place]": *kuru made* = "until he/she comes/came." The verb before *made* is usually in the plain, non-past form. If the person or thing doing the action needs to be specified, it precedes the verb and is marked as its subject with *ga*: *chichi ga kuru made* = "until my father comes/came." This creates a small complete sentence embedded as a time phrase within the larger sentence.

178 Before Igarashi brings Stella home, Shima gently breaks the news to Igarashi's son about his father's plans to remarry (fig. 174). Even so, Ryūsuke runs to his room when his father and Stella arrive. Shima goes to talk to him some more, but the boy remains adamant.

Ryūsuke: 島さん!　僕　は　あの　人　が　帰る　まで
Shima-san!　Boku　wa　ano　hito　ga　kaeru　made
(name-pol.)　I/me　as for　that　person　(subj.)　leave/go home　until

この　部屋　から　出ません。
kono　heya　kara　demasen.
this　room　from　won't exit
"Mr. Shima, I will not leave this room until that person goes home." (PL3)

- *ano* = "that" for referring to things that are close to neither the speaker nor the listener, so *ano hito* here feels like "that person in the other room." *Ga* marks this as the subject of *kaeru*, creating a small embedded sentence, *ano hito ga kaeru* ("that person goes home"), and *made* adds the meaning of "until ～."
- *demasen* is the PL3 negative form of *deru/demasu* ("exit").
- *kara* ("from") marks *heya* ("room") as the place from which he will not exit.

When *made* is combined with *ni*, it means "by [the stated time/event/place]" → *Goji made ni kaerimasu* = "I'll be home by 5 o'clock." When *made* is combined with *wa*, it means "at least until [the stated time]/at least as far as [the stated place]/at least as much as [the stated amount]" → *Goji made wa imasu* = "I'll be here until at least 5 o'clock."

と *to* = "and," but only between nouns

There are several different ways to say "and" in Japanese, and *to* is the most commonly used "and" for linking nouns (or noun substitutes). It is *not* used for linking two sentences into a single longer sentence, though, so don't let your English habit of applying the same word to both purposes spill over into your Japanese.

179 Matsuda, who generally drinks distilled spirits, wants to learn about wine in order to impress a date (fig. 154), so the proprietor of Lemon Hart asks him what he already knows. He knows wine is made from grapes, and just this much more:

ワインには赤と白がある

Matsuda: ワイン に は 赤 と 白 が ある。
Wain   ni   wa   aka   to   shiro   ga   aru.
wine   in/among   as for   red   and   white   (subj.)   exist
"As for among wines, red and white exist."
"Among wines, there are reds and whites." (PL2)

- *ni* marks *wain* ("wine") as the place of existence. The "place" in this case is an abstract one—the category of drinks known as wines. (Figs. 55, 138, and 152 show more concrete places of existence.)
- *wa* marks *wain ni* as the topic of the sentence: "as for in the category of drinks called wine."
- the pattern ～ *ga aru* means "～ exist(s)" or "there is/are ～," and in this case *aka to shiro* ("red [wine] and white [wine]") fills the blank.

To = "with"

To often marks the person with whom an action is done/was done/will be done.

180 Little Kikue has been sleeping with Shizu, one of the maids, ever since her father died and her mother was sent back to her parents' home so she could remarry (fig. 58). Tonight she was supposed to sleep in Natsu's room for the first time, but she got up to go to the bathroom and sneaked off to be with Shizu. As Shizu urges her to return to Natsu, Kikue clings to her and to the doll her mother left her.

菊江はしずと寝る！

しずと……

おっかさまと……

3人で……

Kikue: 菊江 は しず と 寝る!
Kikue   wa   Shizu   to   neru!
(name)   as for   (name)   with   will sleep

しず と... おっかさま と... 3人 で...
Shizu   to...   okkasama   to...   sannin   de...
(name)   and   mother   with   three persons   (scope)
"Kikue will sleep with Shizu! With Shizu...and Mother...the three of us."
"I'm going to sleep with you! With you and Mother and me, the three of us." (PL2)

- it is not uncommon for little children to refer to themselves by name.
- the polite form of *neru* ("sleep/go to bed") is *nemasu*. The same verb is understood at the end of the second sentence.
- *de* marks *sannin* ("three persons") as the size/scope of the group included in the action of sleeping together.
- *okkasama* is an archaic variation of *o-kāsama*, a more formal equivalent of *o-kāsan* ("mother"). Here she is referring to her doll, which is the only keepsake she has of her real mother.

Compare:

わたし と むすめ は かえります。
Watashi   to   musume   wa   kaerimasu.
I/me   and   daughter   as for   will go home
"My daughter and I will go home." (PL3)

私 は 娘 と 帰ります。
Watashi   wa   musume   to   kaerimasu.
I/me   as for   daughter   with   will go home
"I will go home with my daughter." (PL3)

To marks a comparison

To is also used to mark what something is being compared to. Its English equivalent varies according to context. For example, if the two things are the same, it is like "as" in "the same as," and if the two things are similar, it is like "to" in "similar to." If the items are not the same or similar, it can be like "from" in "different from," or, as in the second example here, like "of" in "the opposite of."

181 Toshihiko and Kazuhiro were talking with a soccer player from Fujita East High School about the upcoming tournament in which they will meet. The player mentions his playing position just before he leaves, and afterwards Toshihiko ponders the implications as Kazuhiro notes:

Toshihiko

Kazuhiro: センターフォワード...
(off panel) *Sentā fowādo.*
center-forward
"Center-forward."

お前　と　同じ　ポジション　だ　な。
Omae | *to* | *onaji* | *pojishon* | *da* | *na.*
you (compare) same position is (colloq.)
"It's the same position as you."
"He plays the same position as you." (PL2)

182 As Natsuko prepares to return to her ad agency job in Tokyo after her brother's funeral, she remarks to Kusakabe that she got fed up with her tiny country village at an early age and always knew she would escape to the big city the first chance she had.

Kusakabe: じゃあ、　おれ　と　は　逆　です　ね。
Jā, | *ore* | *to* | *wa* | *gyaku* | *desu* | *ne.*
then me (compare) as for opposite is/are (colloq.)
"Then you're the opposite of me." (PL3)

• *ore* is an informal masculine word for "I/me." *To* marks *ore* as the basis of comparison, and *wa* marks that combination as the topic of the sentence: "as for compared to me."

だけ *dake* = "only/just"

Dake after a noun means "only/just [the stated item]"; after a number or amount it means "only that much/many"; after a word referring to a person (name, title, pronoun, etc.) it means "[that person] alone"; after a word referring to a group of things or people it means "only [those things/people]"; after a verb it means that's the only action that is/was/will be/needs to be done: "do only ～ and nothing else."

Big Size Choco Balls

183 At the grocery store (fig. 103), Mrs. Nohara tells Shin-chan he can go pick out just one treat in the candy aisle. When Shin-chan gets to the aisle, he immediately grabs a ¥50 lollypop, but then he sees boxes of chocolate balls for ¥200 and ¥1000. Here he replays in his mind exactly what his mother said, and decides he should be able to get away with picking the ¥1000 box.

Mother: 一コ　だけ　よ。
Ikko | *dake* | *yo.*
one count only (emph.)
"Only one, now." (PL2)

• the range of the counter suffix *-ko* (fig. 82) is broad, from very small things to quite large things, including boxes of all sizes. Shin-chan knows his mother's *ikko* really meant "one piece" of something like a lollypop; but the ¥1000 box of chocolate balls would also be counted *ikko*, so it falls within the letter of her instructions. Note that once the box is opened, each individual chocolate ball would also be counted *ikko*.

か *ka* can indicate a choice: "either ～ or ～"

The particle *ka* between two nouns instead of at the end of a sentence means "or": *kyō ka ashita* = "today or tomorrow." *Ka* repeated after two (or sometimes more) nouns or sentences in sequence means "either ～ or ～," indicating a choice between alternatives.

184 This man is driving on an expressway, and as he approaches a split in the road, he ponders his choice down to the last possible moment.

Driver: 右 か 左 か? どっち を 選ぶ か?!
Migi ka hidari ka? Dotchi o erabu ka?!
right or left or which (obj.) choose (?)
"Right or left—which shall I choose?!"
"Right or left—which will it be?!" (PL2)

一 か 八 か。 よーし...
Ichi ka bachi ka. Yōshi...
one or eight or okay/here goes
"Nothing ventured, nothing gained. Here goes..." (PL2)

左 の 道 だ!!
Hidari no michi da!
left (mod.) road is
"It's the left road!"
"It's left!" (PL2)

- the polite form of *erabu* ("choose/select") is *erabimasu*.
- *ichi ka bachi ka* is an expression for "take a chance/test one's luck/hope for the best/go for broke" when one is uncertain of success. According to one theory, the phrase originally meant "Will it be odd or even?" in a popular form of dice gambling.
- *yōshi* (or a short *yoshi*, a form of the adjective *ii/yoi*, "good/fine/okay") is often used to express determination and muster one's strength/concentration/courage when ready to begin a challenge or do something daring.

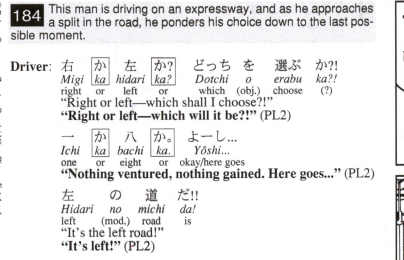

SQUEEEAL!!

も *mo* = "too/also/as well"

As seen in figs. 129 and 141, when the particle *mo* follows a noun it implies that that item is in addition to something else: "[the specified item] too/also/as well" → *watashi mo* = "I/me too." When two or more nouns in sequence are each followed by *mo*, the effect is emphatic, like "not only A, but B (and C), too."

Mrs. A: ウチの マンション、 両どなり も
Uchi no manshon, ryōdonari mo
our condo both neighbors too/also

上 も 下 も 空家 なの よ。
ue mo shita mo akiya na no yo.
above too/also below too/also empty home is/are-(expl.) (emph.)
"In our building, not only the units on both sides of us but above and below us as well are empty." (PL2)

Mrs. B: あらー。
Arā.
(interj.)
"Goodness gracious!" (PL2)

185 Two homemakers are catching up over tea at a coffee shop.

- *uchi no* means "of or belonging to our house/shop/company"—or simply "our."
- *manshon* (from English "mansion") refers to a high-class apartment or condominium building.
- *ryō-* is a prefix meaning "both," and *tonari* (it changes to *-donari* in combinations) is a noun referring to an adjacent/neighboring location, so *ryōdonari* = "both neighbors" → "the units on both sides."
- *akiya* (written with kanji meaning "empty" and "house/home") refers to a vacant residence, and sometimes to other kinds of vacant buildings as well.
- a short *ara* is a feminine interjection of surprise; elongating it can express a feeling of sympathy or chagrin/disappointment.

Lesson 14

Connecting Words

All of the sentences you've seen so far have had only one main part, but sometimes two or more such sentences are joined into a single longer sentence. In Japanese, certain particles and verb forms fill the role of English connecting words like "and," "but," "because," "so," and others.

A form of the verb, adjective or *desu* called **the -te form** is often used like "and" between two sentences to join them into one. In fact, this is probably the single most common way of saying "and" between two sentences. (Remember: the particle *to* you saw in Lesson 13 also means "and," but it's only used between two nouns or noun substitutes, not to link full sentences.)

186 Kōsuke looks down from the window of his one-room apartment and sees the student who lives next door going out with his Waseda University jacket on.

Kōsuke: 学校　ですか?
Gakkō　desu ka?
school　is it?
"Are you going to school?" (PL3)

Student: ラグビー　の　　　早慶戦　| 見て、| そのあと　コンパ　なんです。
Ragubii　no　Sōkei-sen　mite,　sono ato　konpa　na n desu.
rugby　of　Waseda-Keiō game　see-and　after that　party　is-(explan.)
"I'm going to see the Waseda-Keiō rugby game, and then there's a party afterwards." (PL3)

- 早慶 *Sōkei* comes from the first kanji of 早稲田 *Waseda* and of 慶応 *Keiō*, two private universities in Tokyo that can be described as the Harvard and Yale of Japan. The suffix *-sen* refers to a "contest/battle," or in sports, a "game." The particle *o*, to mark *Sōkei-sen* as the direct object of *mite*, has been omitted.
- *mite* is the *-te* form of *miru/mimasu* ("see/watch"); as an independent sentence, the first half would be *Ragubii no Sōkei-sen o miru/mimasu* ("I will watch the Waseda-Keiō rugby game"). Using the *-te* form of *miru* connects this to the second half (another full sentence) like using "and" in English.
- *konpa* (from English "company") generally refers to parties/socials held by student groups.

Linking individual adjectives/verbs

This lesson focuses mainly on linking two sentences to make them one, but it's worth noting that the *-te* forms of verbs and adjectives can also be used to link individual words with the meaning of "X and Y." This should be no surprise when you consider that a single verb or adjective by itself can be a complete sentence.

187 The narrator is needling *obatarians* for some of the uncool things they do at fast-food restaurants.

Sound FX: ガラガラ
Gara gara
Rattle rattle (sound of ice rattling)

Narration: アイスコーヒー　の　フタ　　で
Aisu kōhii　no　futa　de
iced coffee　of　lid　with/using

氷　を　| かき出して | かじる。
kōri o　kakidashite　kajiru.
ice (obj.)　scrape out-and　bite/chew
She scoops out ice with the lid of her iced coffee and chews on it. (PL2)

- *kakidashite* is the *-te* form of *kakidasu/kakidashimasu* ("scrape out"), and *kajiru/kajirimasu* = "bite/chew," so *kakidashite kajiru* = "scrapes out and chews."

The -て -te form sometimes ends in -で -de

With some verbs, the -te form ends in -de, the voiced counterpart to -te. The -te form is formally introduced in Lesson 19, where you will find details about how it is created and examples of several of its uses; Lessons 25 and 31 cover some additional uses.

188 These *obatarians* are on a cruise with a tour group to an unspecified destination.

Narration: オバタリアン　は　　騒ぐ　　　だけ　　騒いで...
Obatarian   wa   sawagu   dake   sawaide...
mid.-aged women as for make noise as much as make noise-and
Obatarians carry on for all they're worth, and...

Sound FX: キャッキャッ　ワイワイ　ギャーギャー
Kya! kya!   Wai wai   Gyā gyā
(screaming, gabbing, shouting noises)

Narration: 船酔いする。
funa-yoi suru.
become seasick
[then] they get seasick. (PL2)

Sound FX: うえーっ
Uē!
(retching sound)

- *sawaide* is the -te form of *sawagu/sawagimasu* ("clamor/make noise/make merry"). As an independent sentence, the first half would be *Obatarian wa sawagu dake sawagu/sawagimasu*.
- *dake* here means "as much as," so *sawagu dake sawaide* means "make merry as much as [they care to] make merry" → "carry on for all they're worth." This usage is distinct from the usage introduced in fig. 183.
- *funa-yoi* (literally, "boat-intoxication") = "seasickness," and *funa-yoi suru* = "get seasick." (This can also occur as *funa-yoi o suru*, with the particle *o* marking *funa-yoi* as the direct object of *suru* → "experience seasickness"; see fig. 131.) As an independent sentence, this second half would be *Obatarian wa funa-yoi suru*, but the topic does not need to be restated once it is established.

The -te form of *desu*

In ordinary conversation, the -te form of *da* and *desu* is usually *de*—the same for both politeness levels. You will also occasionally encounter *deshite* (from *desu*) in PL3 speech, but this is usually reserved only for very formal situations.

VROOM

189 When Natsuko rushes home to the country after learning of her brother's death, Kusakabe meets her at the station. She asks him about the funeral plans.

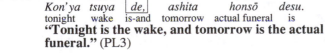

Natsuko: 葬式　　　　は?
Sōshiki   wa?
funeral service as for
"As for the funeral?" (PL2–3)
"What are the funeral plans?"

Kusakabe: 今夜　　通夜　で、　明日　　本葬　です。
Kon'ya   tsuya   de,   ashita   honsō   desu.
tonight   wake   is-and   tomorrow actual funeral is
"Tonight is the wake, and tomorrow is the actual funeral." (PL3)

- as an independent sentence, the first half would be *Kon'ya tsuya desu* ("Tonight is the wake").
- *hon-* as a prefix has a range of meanings, from "this/the current ～" (fig. 138: *honjitsu* = "this/the current day" → "today"), to "main ～," "full-fledged ～," "real/actual ～," and "official ～." *Honsō* combines this prefix with the first character of *sōshiki* ("funeral ceremony") to mean "the actual funeral."

The pre-*masu* form or -*ku* form = "~ and"

When the first of two sentences being combined is a verb-type sentence, the stem or pre-*masu* form of the verb can serve as "[do the action] and": *Ichiji ni arubaito kara kaerimasu* ("He comes home from his part time job at one o'clock") + *Sugu neru* ("He goes to bed right away") → *Ichiji ni arubaito kara kaeri, sugu neru* ("He gets home from his part time job at one o'clock and goes straight to bed.").

When the first of two sentences being combined is an adjective-type sentence, the -*ku* form of the adjective (fig. 76) can serve as the equivalent of "and": *Yūenchi no pūru wa kodomo ga ōi* ("At the amusement park pool, children are many") + *Totemo urusai* ("It is very noisy") → *Yūenchi no pūru wa kodomo ga ōku, totemo urusai* ("There are lots of children at the amusement park pool, and it is very noisy").

190 Hiroko thought Kōsuke wasn't getting enough exercise, so she suggested they play badminton at the park. After working up a sweat, they take a break for a snack. Kōsuke has brought some *ohagi* (sweet rice cakes), and Hiroko goes to get some hot oolong tea from a vending machine.

Both of these patterns are mostly used in writing rather than in spoken Japanese. An example using the pre-*masu* form of a verb appears in the narration here.

- *tabe* is the pre-*masu* form of *taberu/tabemasu* ("eat").
- *chōsen* = "a challenge," and *shita* is the plain past form of *suru* (fig. 259). The verb *chōsen suru* can mean either "issue a challenge (to)" or "take up a challenge/make an attempt (at)." *Ni* marks the target of the challenge or attempt.

Narration: 熱い ウーロン茶 と おはぎ を 食べ、 再び バドミントン に 挑戦した。
Atsui   ūroncha   to   ohagi   o   tabe,   futatabi   badominton   ni   chōsen shita.
hot   oolong tea   and   (food)   (obj.)   eat-and   once again   badminton   (target)   took up the challenge
We ate some hot oolong tea and *ohagi*, and once again took up the challenge of badminton.
We had some hot oolong tea and ohagi, and then gave badminton another go. (PL2)

し *shi* = "and" or "because/so"

The particle *shi* is a fairly emphatic "and" for joining two sentences into one, often feeling like "and moreover" or "and besides that." In other cases, the same particle means "because/so."

As illustrated in the example here, *shi* can be used to join more than two sentences in sequence, such as when listing up multiple causes/reasons in an explanation or observation; in such cases, the last *shi* in a sequence means "so"—like saying "A, and B, and C, so D."

191 Looking at new houses, this couple sound like they are ready to make a decision. As sometimes happens with married couples everywhere, the husband finishes the sentence his wife starts.

Wife: 出窓 も ある し、
Demado   mo   aru   shi,
bay window   also   has   and
"It has a bay window, and..."

Husband: 明るい し、 いい な。
akarui   shi,   ii   na.
is bright   and/so   is good/fine   (colloq.)
"...it's bright, so it's good, isn't it?" (PL2)

- *mado* = "window" and *de-* as a prefix often implies "protruding," so *demado* = "protruding window/bay window."
- *aru* means "exists," but it's often equivalent to English "have/has": "A bay window exists [in the house]" → "The house has a bay window."
- *akarui* is an adjective meaning "bright/full of light."

けど *kedo* = "but" (or "and")

The particle *kedo* marks the preceding as background information for what follows, and it's most typically equivalent to "but." In some contexts, though, it is more like "and"; in others, it can be like punctuating with a colon, semicolon, or dash in English, or like simply juxtaposing two sentences without any connecting word or punctuation (see next example).

Alternative forms of *kedo* include *keredo*, *keredomo*, and *kedomo*, all of which sound a little more formal than *kedo*.

© Nonaka Nobara, *Ai ga Hoshii*, Futabasha.

192 The young man breaks into a cold sweat when his fiancée places the engagement ring he gave her on the table.

Woman: 悪い けど、 この 指輪 返す わ。
Warui kedo, kono yubiwa kaesu wa.
is bad　but　this　ring　will return　(fem.)
"[It] is bad [of me], but I will return this ring."
"I'm sorry, but I have to return this ring." (PL2)

Sound FX: コト
Koto
(sound of setting ring box on table)

Man: えっ?
E!?
"What?" (PL2)

- *warui* is an adjective that literally means "is bad," but it's often used as an informal apology, implying "it is/was bad of me."
- *o* or *wa*, to mark *yubiwa* ("ring") as the direct object or topic, has been omitted.
- the polite form of *kaesu* ("return [something]") is *kaeshimasu*.

He wants to know if this means the wedding is off. "I... was lying to you," she says with some difficulty, then blurts out, "The truth is, well, my finger size isn't a 7 but a 10."

Da/desu kedo and *da/desu shi*

Shi and *kedo* in the previous two examples both follow one complete sentence and link it to another. When the first sentence is a noun-type sentence, whatever form of *da/desu* appears at the end of the sentence remains unchanged, and *shi* or *kedo* follows: *Goji da/desu* ("It's five o'clock") → *Goji da/desu kedo, kaerimasen* = "It's 5:00, but I'm not going home"; *Goji da/desu shi, kaerimasu* = "It's 5:00, so I'm going home."

© Kobayashi Makoto, *What's Michael?*, Kōdansha.

193 When Michael is being tested as a baggage-sniffing cat (fig. 121), he sniffs out a crescent-shaped, driftwood-like object, and the customs agent demands to know what it is.

Traveler: カツオブシ です けど、 いけません か?
Katsuobushi desu kedo, ikemasen ka?
dried bonito　is　but　unacceptable　(?)
"It's dried bonito, but is it unacceptable?"
"It's dried bonito. Is that a problem?" (PL3)

Agent: い、 いえ。
I- ie.
(stammer)　no
"N-no." (PL2–3)

- *katsuobushi* refers to bonito that has been dried until it becomes as hard as wood; the dried bonito is then shaved into flakes and used to make stocks for soups and sauces in Japanese cookery.
- although the most common translation for *kedo* is "but," always remember that its key function is to mark the preceding as background for what follows, so its equivalent in English will vary according to the precise context.
- *ikemasen* is the polite form of *ikenai*, which expresses disapproval: "is no good/not permitted/unacceptable."
- *ie* is a shortened *iie* ("no").

が *ga* = "but" (or "and")

The particle *ga* is used as a more formal equivalent of *kedo*. It marks the preceding as background information for what follows, most typically implying "but"; but like *kedo*, it is sometimes more like "and," like using a colon/semicolon/dash, or like simply juxtaposing two sentences without a connecting word or special punctuation.

194 Kōsuke is waiting for Hiroko, who was supposed to meet him at 4:30. The place usually closes from 5:00 to 6:00 to make the switch from coffee shop to pub, but the proprietor lets Kōsuke stay on. It is now well past 5:00.

Proprietor:
失礼 です が、 トーホク の かた です か?
Shitsurei desu ga, Tōhoku no kata desu ka?
rudeness is but (place) of person is/are ?
"It is rude of me, but are you a person from the Tōhoku region?"
"Excuse me, but are you from Tōhoku?" (PL3)

- *shitsurei desu ga* literally means "It is a rudeness, but ～." It's equivalent to "Excuse me, but ～" in English.
- Tōhoku (東北 when written in kanji) is literally "northeast," and as the name of a region refers to the northern part of the main Japanese island of Honshu, including the prefectures of Aomori, Iwate, Akita, Miyagi, Yamagata, and Fukushima.
- *kata* is a formal/polite word for "person." The more neutral word is *hito*.
- *ha?* (not transcribed) is a more formal equivalent of *e?*, which shows surprise or confusion about what the other person has said: "Huh?/What?/Pardon?"
- the proprietor later explains that he guessed Kōsuke was from Tōhoku because he was willing to wait so long for his friend to show up.

© Maekawa Tsukasa. Dai-Tōkyō Binbō Seikatsu Manyuaru, Kōdansha.

Kedo or *ga* at the end of a sentence

Sometimes *kedo* or *ga* occurs at the end of a sentence instead of after just the first half. In some cases this is because the background information has been added as an after thought—i.e., the sentence is inverted. In others the speaker may intend a general question like "but/and how do you respond to that?"; or he may simply think his implied meaning is clear enough without his having to finish the sentence. In still other cases its purpose may be merely to make the end of the sentence feel "softer" or less abrupt.

195 This *obatarian* was looking for Ikari Sauce—a name-brand Worcestershire-type sauce—but it's out of stock. When the storekeeper points her to a new brand, saying that it has been well received, she declares histrionically that she has always used only Ikari and won't settle for anything less. Then comes this exchange:

Storekeeper: ご試食 セール で 半額 です が。
Go-shishoku sēru de hangaku desu ga.
(hon.)-tasting sale is-and half price is but
"We're having an introductory sale, and they're half price." (PL3–4)

Obatarian: 2本 ちょうだい。
Nihon chōdai.
2 count give me/let me have
"Give me two bottles."
"I'll take two." (PL2)

- *shishoku* (lit. "trial eating") refers to tasting a food to see if you like it; *shishoku sēru* is a sale aimed at getting people to try a new food item.
- *de* is the *-te* form of *da/desu* being used as a connecting "and" (see fig. 189).
- *-hon* is the counter suffix for long, skinny objects (p. 47).
- *chōdai* is an informal word for "[please] give me/let me have"; the more formal/polite equivalent is ください *kudasai*.

© Hotta Katsuhiko. Obatarian, Take Shobō.

Kedo or *ga* at the beginning of a sentence

As with "but" in English, *kedo* and *ga* can be used at the beginning of a sentence to refer back to the previous sentence without actually joining the two sentences. The plain *kedo* and *ga* can be used this way, but *da kedo* and *da ga* are the more common forms in this position, regardless of how the previous sentence ends. They can be thought of as literally meaning "although it is so." *Da kedo* is heard frequently in conversation, while the more formal *da ga* occurs mostly in writing or formal speeches; in polite speech, *desu kedo* and *desu ga* are also heard.

196 Gōda, who found Natsuko using an antique weeding implement in fig. 169 because she doesn't want to use chemicals on her small crop of Tatsunishiki, is an organic farmer himself. He quickly becomes Natsuko's strongest ally in a village of farmers who depend heavily on chemical fertilizers and weed killers.

Gōda: 有機農法　　　　は　　世界　　を　　席巻する。
Yūki nōhō　　　　wa　　sekai　　o　　sekken suru.
organic farming methods　　as for　　world　　(obj.)　　will conquer
"Organic farming will take over the world." (PL2)

だが、　　その前　　に　　戦争　　が　　ある。
Da ga,　sono mae　ni　sensō　ga　aru.
but　　before that　(time)　war　(subj.)　will exist/occur
"But before that, a war will occur."
"But first there will be a war." (PL2)

- *mae* is a noun meaning "front" or "[a time/place] before" → *sono mae* = "before that."
- when speaking of events, *aru* ("exists") can often be thought of as equivalent to "occur(s)."

Is that *ga* a subject marker or "but/and"?

When *ga* follows a noun or noun substitute directly, it's a subject marker, but when *ga* follows a verb, adjective, or noun + *da/desu* phrase, it's serving as a connecting word.

197 Hatsushiba President Nakazawa wants Shima to take a post with Hatsushiba Trading Company and get the firm into the business of importing wines. He thinks boosting the wine business in Japan could be just the shot in the arm the stagnant economy needs.

Shima:
はい、　　わかりました!
Hai,　　wakarimashita!
yes/all right　　understood
"Yes, sir. I'd be pleased to do it!" (PL3)

私の　　力　　が　　及ぶ　　かどうか　　わかりません　が。
Watashi no　chikara　ga　oyobu　ka dō-ka　wakarimasen　ga.
my　　strength　(subj.)　is up to　whether or not　not know　but
"I don't know whether or not my strength is up to [the task], but..."
"Though I don't really know whether I have what it will take." (PL3)

- *wakarimashita* is the polite past form of *wakaru/wakarimasu* ("understand"); in response to requests/instructions/commands, *wakarimashita* implies "I understand what you are asking and I will do it."
- *ga* directly after the noun *chikara* marks it as the subject of the verb *oyobu/oyobimasu* ("reach/extend to/be equal to") → *chikara ga oyobu* = "strength is up to [the task]"; the pattern ∼ *ka dō-ka* means "whether ∼ or not," so *chikara ga oyobu ka dō-ka* = "whether my strength is up to [the task] or not."
- *wakarimasen* is the polite negative form of *wakaru*. The negative forms of this verb can mean either "not understand" or "not know," depending on the context.
- *ga* after the verb *wakarimasen* is the connecting word "but"; in this case, the rest of his thought remains unstated, but it's clear that it is something like "I will do my best."

から *kara* = "because/so"

When the particle *kara* connects two sentences, it means "because." But be careful: in English the cause is stated after the word "because," but in Japanese the cause is what comes *before* the word *kara*. Since the normal order is for the *kara* statement to come first, the structure is closest to the English "Because X, Y" or "X, so Y"—where X states the cause and Y states the result or consequence.

If the *kara* statement is a noun-type sentence, *da/desu* must be retained at the end, making it *da kara* or *desu kara*. Without that *da* or *desu*, *kara* after a noun is the particle meaning "from" (fig. 176). In the example here, the *kara* statement is an adjective-type sentence.

198 Hiroko visited Kōsuke at his apartment, and in spite of his extremely limited kitchen equipment, they managed to put together a satisfying spaghetti dinner. Now it is late.

Kōsuke: 遅い から 駅 まで 送る よ。
Osoi kara eki made okuru yo.
is late because/so station to see off (emph.)
"It's late, so I'll see you to the station."
(PL2)

Hiroko: ありがと。
Arigatō.
thanks
"Thanks." (PL2)

SFX: チャラ
Chara
(rattle of bike lock)

• *osoi* is an adjective that means "is late/slow."
• *made* = "as far as," or simply "to" (fig. 177).
• the polite form of *okuru* ("see off/escort/accompany"; fig. 21) is *okurimasu*.

だから *da kara* at the beginning = "because it is so"

Da kara (or *desu kara*, but never just *kara*) is used at the beginning of a sentence to mean "because it is so"—referring back to what has just been stated or observed. It's often like "so," "therefore," or "that's why" in English.

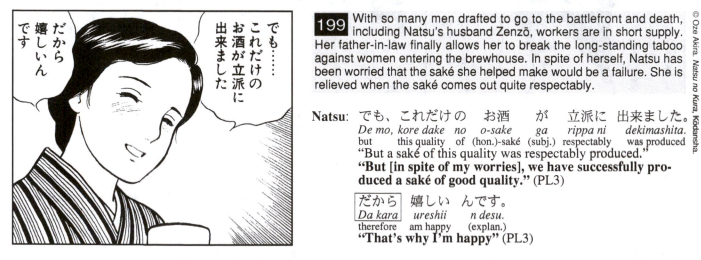

199 With so many men drafted to go to the battlefront and death, including Natsu's husband Zenzō, workers are in short supply. Her father-in-law finally allows her to break the long-standing taboo against women entering the brewhouse. In spite of herself, Natsu has been worried that the saké she helped make would be a failure. She is relieved when the saké comes out quite respectably.

Natsu: でも、これだけの お酒 が 立派に 出来ました。
De mo, kore dake no o-sake ga rippa ni dekimashita.
but this quality of (hon.)-saké (subj.) respectably was produced
"But a saké of this quality was respectably produced."
"But [in spite of my worries], we have successfully produced a saké of good quality." (PL3)

だから 嬉しい んです。
Da kara ureshii n desu.
therefore am happy (explan.)
"That's why I'm happy" (PL3)

• *dake* = "just/only," and *kore dake* can be used to mean "only this." But *kore dake* can also mean "this much/many" or "this degree/extent"—in this case implying "(of) this quality" or "this good."
• *rippa ni* is the adverb form of the adjectival noun *rippa*, which ranges in meaning from "excellent/grand/splendid/imposing" to "admirable/respectable/creditable."
• *dekimashita* is the PL3 past form of *dekiru/dekimasu* ("be completed/be produced"). This usage of the verb is distinct from the usage seen in fig. 45.

ので *no de* = "because/so"

No de (or its shortened form, *n de*) also means "Because X, Y" or "X, so Y." *No de* sounds somewhat more formal than *kara*, but both words are used at all politeness levels, and they are often interchangeable. *No de* implies that the cause given is objective and certain, though, so it's a little more limited than *kara*. For example, since it implies certainty, *no de* cannot be used after forms that express guesses or uncertainty ("perhaps/probably ～"; fig. 37 and Lesson 26).

200 Kariage-kun is visiting his boss's house, located on a busy street. His boss shows off the special windows he had put in so as to dampen the noise. Kariage has the same noise problem, but can't afford the windows.

Boss: うるさい ┃んで┃
Urusai ┃*n de*┃
is noisy ┃because┃

二重窓 に した んだ よ。
nijū-mado *ni* *shita* *n da* *yo.*
two-layered windows into made them (explan.) (emph.)
"Because it was noisy, we made them double-paned windows."
"Because of all the noise, we had double-glazed windows put in." (PL2)

Kariage: いい です ねー。
Ii *desu* *nẽ.*
is good/nice (pol.) (colloq.)
"That sure is nice."
"I'm envious." (PL3)

- *～ ni shita* is the plain past form of *～ ni suru*, which means "make it *～*" in the sense of making a choice or making a change (fig. 65). You will learn about plain past forms in Lesson 18.
- *ii desu nẽ* (in PL2 speech, *ii nẽ/ii nā*) can be an expression of envy. *Ii* ("good/nice") in this case essentially means "You have it good/nice," implying "You're so lucky/I'm envious."

なので *na no de* = "because it is"

When the *no de* statement is a noun-type sentence, the final *da/desu* changes to *na*, making it X *na no de* Y = "Because it is X, Y" or "It's X, so Y." As with the explanatory *no*, *na* serves as the verb "to be" (fig. 101) in this pattern, and it does so for all nouns, not just those that require *na* when modifying other nouns. In PL3 and PL4 speech you will also hear *desu no de*.

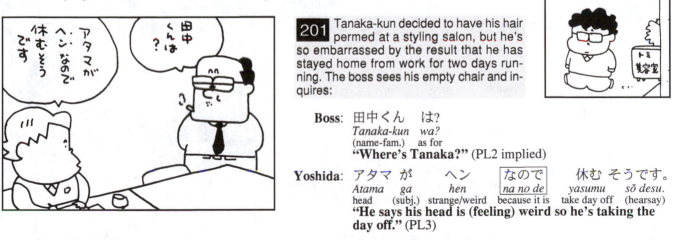

Tomi Hair Salon

201 Tanaka-kun decided to have his hair permed at a styling salon, but he's so embarrassed by the result that he has stayed home from work for two days running. The boss sees his empty chair and inquires:

Boss: 田中くん は?
Tanaka-kun *wa?*
(name-fam.) as for
"Where's Tanaka?" (PL2 implied)

Yoshida: アタマ が ヘン ┃なので┃ 休む そうです。
Atama *ga* *hen* ┃*na no de*┃ *yasumu* *sō desu.*
head (subj.) strange/weird because it is take day off (hearsay)
"He says his head is (feeling) weird so he's taking the day off." (PL3)

- *hen* is an adjectival noun, and *hen da/desu* = "is strange/odd/weird." *Atama ga hen da* is most commonly an expression for how one's own head feels or a judgment of another person's sanity; though there's no reason it can't be used to describe the way a person's head/hair looks, Tanaka-kun was obviously counting on his boss taking it the other way.
- *yasumu/yasumimasu* means ("rest/take the day off [from work/school]"), and *sō desu* implies that she's relaying hearsay information—what Tanaka-kun told her. Hearsay forms are presented in Lesson 32.

Kara and *no de* at the end

Although the standard order is for *kara* or *no de* to appear at the end of the first half of a complex sentence, you will also encounter them at what seems to be the end of the sentence—or of a separate second sentence. This typically means either that the speaker is offering an explanation for something that's obvious from the context, or that the normal order has gotten turned around because the speaker decided to state the cause/reason as an afterthought. Both situations are quite common in real-life conversations.

202 Managing Director Fukuda thinks Showroom Section Chief Konno has done sufficient penance for the sexual harassment incident (fig. 176) that led to his exile within the company, and he is eager to bring him back. Nakazawa won't hear of it.

Nakazawa:　ダメ　です。あの　男　は　無能　です　から。
Dame desu. Ano otoko wa munō desu kara.
no good　is　that　man　as for　incompetent　is　because/so
"That will be no good. Because that man is incompetent."
"It's out of the question. The man is incompetent." (PL3)

- *dame* is an adjectival noun referring to a thing/situation/circumstance that is "unacceptable/no good" or that "won't do." Other English equivalents for *Dame da/desu* include "You may not" (when asked for permission), "It's no use" (when repeated attempts at something fail), and "I refuse" (in response to a request).
- the standard word order here would be: *Ano otoko wa munō desu kara dame desu.*

のに *no ni* = "even though"

When the particle *no ni* connects two sentences, it means "even though/in spite of [the preceding]." As with *kara* and *no de*, the standard order is for the *no ni* statement to come first, followed by a sentence stating what is true in spite of all: *X no ni Y* = "Even though/in spite of X, Y" or "X, but nevertheless/in spite of that, Y."

203 Toshihiko (fig. 181) has been beating up on himself after failing to complete a hat trick in the final seconds of Kakegawa High's last soccer game. In today's practice, though, he seems to be back to normal form.

Kenji:　あんなに　落ちこんでた　のに　さ、
Anna-ni ochikondeta no ni sa,
that much　was depressed　even though　(colloq.)
"Even though he was acting so depressed, you know,

立ち直り　だけ　は　早え　な、　あいつ　は。
tachinaori dake wa haē na, aitsu wa.
recovery　at least　as for　is quick　(colloq.)　that guy　as for
"as for his recovery at least, it was [admirably] quick, that guy."
"You know, you at least gotta give the guy credit for getting back on his feet this quickly in spite of being so down in the dumps." (PL2)

- *ochikondeta* is a contraction of *ochikonde ita* ("was depressed"), from *ochikomu/ochikomimasu* ("become depressed/sink into depression"). You'll learn about the *-te/-de ita* form in Lesson 19.
- *sa* in the middle of a sentence is a kind of verbal pause to draw the listener's attention to what the speaker is saying, somewhat comparable to a teen's use of "like/you know" in colloquial English.
- ~ *dake* usually means "just/only ~," but ~ *dake wa* = "at least ~" (or if followed by a negative, "at least not ~").
- 早え *haē* is a rough, slangy slurring of the adjective 早い *hayai* ("fast/quick").

なのに *na no ni* = "even though it is"

When the *no ni* statement is a noun-type sentence, the final *da/desu* changes to *na*, making it *X na no ni Y* = "Even though it is X, Y" or "It's X, but nevertheless/in spite of that, Y." As with *na no de* in fig. 201, *na* serves as the verb "to be" in this pattern.

In the example here, X and Y have been reversed and split up, making *na no ni* appear at the end of the second sentence intead of its standard mid-sentence position.

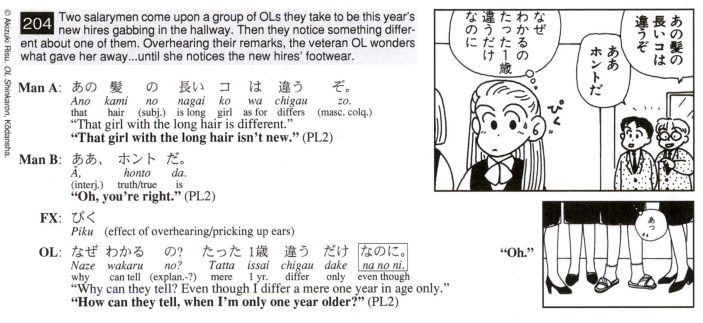

204 Two salarymen come upon a group of OLs they take to be this year's new hires gabbing in the hallway. Then they notice something different about one of them. Overhearing their remarks, the veteran OL wonders what gave her away...until she notices the new hires' footwear.

Man A: あの　髪　の　長い　コ　は　違う　ぞ。
Ano   kami   no   nagai   ko   wa   chigau   zo.
that   hair   (subj.) is long   girl   as for   differs   (masc. colq.)
"That girl with the long hair is different."
"That girl with the long hair isn't new." (PL2)

Man B: ああ、　ホント　だ。
Ā,   honto   da.
(interj.)   truth/true   is
"Oh, you're right." (PL2)

FX: ぴく
Piku   (effect of overhearing/pricking up ears)

OL: なぜ　わかる　の?　たった　1歳　違う　だけ　なのに。
Naze   wakaru   no?   Tatta   issai   chigau   dake   na no ni.
why   can tell   (explan.-?)   mere   1 yr.   differ   only   even though
"Why can they tell? Even though I differ a mere one year in age only."
"How can they tell, when I'm only one year older?" (PL2)

"Oh."

- *no* marks *kami* ("hair") as the subject of the adjective *nagai* ("long"), which modifies *ko* ("girl"). See fig. 227.
- the polite form of *chigau* ("differ/be different") is *chigaimasu. Tatta* (often in tandem with *dake*) emphasizes the smallness/minuteness of a number or amount, so *tatta issai chigau* = "differ a mere one year." The standard word order for the OL's sentence would be: *Tatta issai chigau dake na no ni, naze wakaru no?*

Expressing disappointment with *(na) no ni*

Sometimes when *no ni* or *na no ni* appears at the end of a sentence, it is simply a case of things getting turned around, as in the above example. But quite often *(na) no ni* at the end of a sentence carries a note of disappointment, regret, or discontent; such sentences imply "even though/in spite of ～, [something undesirable/unwanted nevertheless is true]," and the feeling is that a phrase like "What a shame!/What a disappointment!/That's really too bad/I'm so sorry to hear it" is being left unsaid.

Nat-chan: 牛乳、　いやん。
Gyūnyū,   iyan.
milk   disagreeable
"I hate milk." (PL2)

205 Little Nat-chan wanted something to drink, but she apparently isn't very fond of milk.

Mother: 体　に　いい　のに。
Karada   ni   ii   no ni.
body   for   is good   even though
"Even though it's good for your body, [you dislike it. What a shame.]"
"That's a shame—when it's so good for you." (PL2)

- *iyan* is a feminine/childish variation of *iya*, an adjectival noun that expresses distaste or objection. As a noun modifier in the form *iya na*, the word typically corresponds to English adjectives like "disagreeable/distasteful/repugnant/unbearable"; in the form *Iya da/desu* it has a range of meanings, including "No, I won't/I refuse," "I hate it/I can't stand it/I'm fed up with it," and "Oh, gross!/How disgusting!" as well as a more lighthearted "That's/you're silly."
- *karada* = "body," so *karada ni ii* = "good for your body/health," or just "good for you."

Lesson 15

Quoting with と *To*

In Lesson 13 you saw examples of the particle *to* used to mean "and" or "with," as well as to mark an object of comparison, but another important use of *to* is for quoting. *To* follows the content of the quote, which can range from just a single word to a complete sentence, and it embeds that content in a larger sentence that ends with a verb appropriate for quoting, such as *iu/iimasu* ("say"), *yomu/yomimasu* ("read"), or *kiku/kikimasu* ("ask" or "hear"). Sometimes the sentence can end in other kinds of verbs as well. Thus:

quoted content		particle		quoting verb
Word, phrase, or complete sentence	**+**	*to*	**+**	*iu, yomu, kiku,* and others

Since *to* marks the end of the quoted content, you can think of it as a kind of "unquote" mark—except that it's actually spoken, and there is never any corresponding word to mark the beginning of the quote. *To iu* never precedes the quote the way "she says/said" can in English, and any words or phrases coming after *to* and before the verb at the end belong to the larger, embedding sentence, not to the quote.

Same structure for direct and indirect quotes

The same *to iu* structure is used for both direct quotes ("She said, 'I will come'" or "'I will come,' she said") and indirect quotes ("She said that she would come"). In conversational Japanese, the general custom is to quote indirectly, which means that pronouns and references to place are changed to fit the quoter's perspective ("She said she would come here" instead of "She said, 'I will go there'").

In formal situations, such as newspaper quotes, the quoted content will be set off with special brackets, like so: 「......」 (see the balloon in the panel here for how the orientation of the brackets changes in vertical text), and in such cases direct quotes are more common; but these brackets are often used even with indirect quotes and paraphrases, or simply to highlight a word or phrase (in which case there would be no *to*, as in the example here), so their presence does not guarantee a direct quote.

206 Kōsuke bought a sandwich and a liter of milk for lunch, and he also asked the baker for some free bread crusts so he can make some "bread gruel" later. He sees that that leaves him with just ¥22 to his name.

Kōsuke: オレ は 20円 で カノジョ に 電話した。
(narrating) *Ore wa nijū-en de kanojo ni denwa shita.*
I/me as for ¥20 using her/girlfriend to telephoned
"I telephoned my girlfriend using ¥20." (PL2)

カノジョ は 夕方 オレの アパート へ 来る と 言った。
Kanojo wa yūgata ore no apāto e kuru to itta.
she as for evening my apartment to will come (quote) said
"She said she would come to my apartment in the evening." (PL2)

Kōsuke: 夜、 「パンがゆ」 やる んだ。
(on phone) *Yoru, pan-gayu yaru n da.*
evening/tonight bread gruel will do (explan.)
"I'm gonna make 'bread gruel' tonight." (PL2)

- *denwa shita* is the plain past form of *denwa suru* ("to telephone"), and *itta* is the plain past form of *iu/iimasu* ("say/speak"). The plain past forms of verbs are formally introduced in Lesson 18.
- *Kanojo wa...itta* ("She said/spoke") is the larger sentence in which the quoted sentence, *Yūgata ore no apāto e kuru* ("[She] will come to my apartment in the evening"), is embedded.
- *kayu* (it becomes *-gayu* in combinations) refers to a "gruel/porridge" usually made with rice; the quote brackets here are merely highlighting the slightly unconventional term rather than indicating a quote. The polite form of *yaru* (an informal "do") is *yarimasu.*

Relating hearsay with *to*

The phrase or sentence followed by *to iu/iimasu*, especially in the non-past form, may be a general description/idea/paraphrase or un-attributed hearsay rather than a specific statement: "They say ～."

207 After getting his degree in fermentation sciences from the Agricultural College, Natsu's son Hiroo returns home to the brewery. Three years later he successfully revives the premium *ginjō*-style saké that his late father had worked so hard to develop before he was killed in the war. The narrator here is Shizu, one of Natsu's maids, who was apparently not actually present at the tasting.

Shizu: その　酒　を　口　に　して　奈津さま　は
Sono sake o kuchi ni shite Natsu-sama wa
that　saké　(obj.)　mouth　into　do/put-and　(name-hon.)　as for

涙　が　とまらなかった　と　言います。
namida ga tomaranakatta to iimasu.
tears　(subj.)　didn't stop　(quote)　say

"As for Madame Natsu, she tasted that saké, and her tears did not stop, they say."
"They say that when she tasted the saké, Madame Natsu wept endless tears of joy." (PL3)

- *shite* is the *-te* form of *suru*, and *kuchi ni suru* literally implies "take/put into one's mouth" → "taste." The *-te* form is being used as "and" (fig. 186).
- *-sama* has the same meaning as *-san* ("Mr./Ms.") but is more polite.
- *tomaranakatta* is the past form of *tomaranai* ("not stop"), which is the plain negative form of *tomaru/tomarimasu* ("[something] stops"). Negative verbs are formally introduced in Lesson 20.

って *tte* or て *te* = an informal *to*

In informal speech, *tte* (and somewhat less often, *te*) is commonly used in place of *to* to mark quotes. Both *to iu* and *tte iu* (or sometime just *tte* alone) can mean "be named/called/termed/known as."

208 Mother is asking Daughter, newly employed as an OL, how things are going at work. Daughter assures her all is well, everyone's been nice to her, but Mother presses on.

Mother: セクハラ　って　いう　の?
Sekuhara tte iu no?
sexual harassment　(quote)　say/called　(explan.-?)
"Is it called sexual harrassment?" (PL2)

ほら、　上司　が　いやらしい　マネ　したり...
Hora, jōshi ga iyarashii mane shitari...
(interj.)　superiors　(subj.)　disagreeable/indecent　behavior　do things like
"You know, where your superiors behave indecently..."
(PL2)

Daughter: ない、　ない。
Nai, nai.
not exist　not exist
"No, no (there's nothing like that)." (PL2)

- *sekuhara* is the Japanese adaptation of the English "sexual harassment," abbreviated from the full katakana rendering, *sekushuaru harasumento*. Such abbreviation of foreign words is quite common.
- *iyarashii* is an adjective meaning "disagreeable/offensive," often implying the offensiveness is of an "indecent/lascivious" nature.
- *shitari* is a form of *suru*; *mane* by itself means "imitation/mimicry," but an adjective followed by *mane (o) suru* makes an expression meaning "behave [in the described manner]." A *-tari* verb followed immediately or later by a form of *suru* (here she breaks her sentence off, but it's implicit) means "do such a thing as/do things like ～"; it can be used as a way of being less direct and "softening" the impact of the verb.

To iimasu/to mōshimasu in introductions

When meeting someone for the first time, whether you are being introduced by a mutual acquaintance or you are introducing yourself, it is common practice to state your name followed by *to iimasu* or its humble equivalent *to mōshimasu*. (*Tte iimasu* can be used in introductions, too, but usually only in very informal situations.)

© Hirokane Kenshi. *Kaji Ryūsuke no Gi*, Kōdansha.

209 After regaining his seat in the House of Representatives of the Diet, Kaji introduces his journalist friend Ōmori Yōichirō to two newly elected members of his party. Ōmori then greets the two this way:

Ōmori: 初めまして。　大森　と　申します。
Hajimemashite. *Ōmori* *to* *mōshimasu.*
(greeting)　(name)　(quote)　say/am called
"I'm pleased to meet you. My name is Ōmori." (PL4)

• *hajimemashite* is a standard part of introductions/first meetings. It comes from the verb *hajimeru* ("begin") and literally means "for the first time," but it typically corresponds to English phrases like "I'm pleased to meet you" or "How do you do?"
• the verb *mōsu/mōshimasu* ("say") is equivalent to *iu*, but has both humble and polite/formal uses (see pp. 38–39). It is commonly used in introductions regardless of the status of the other party, since formality is generally called for with new acquaintances. When speaking with persons of higher status, it's used as a humble verb to quote your own or your peers' statements; the corresponding honorific/exalting verb, *ossharu/osshaimasu* ("say") must be used for the statements of your listener or others of higher status.

Describing with *to iu*

The phrases *to iu* and *tte iu* (or sometimes just *tte*) are often used when describing—especially when the description involves sound or something verbal, but in other cases as well. In effect, *to iu/tte (iu)* makes what comes before it into a modifier for what comes after. The description preceding *to iu/tte (iu)* can be just a single word, a several-word phrase, or a complete sentence.

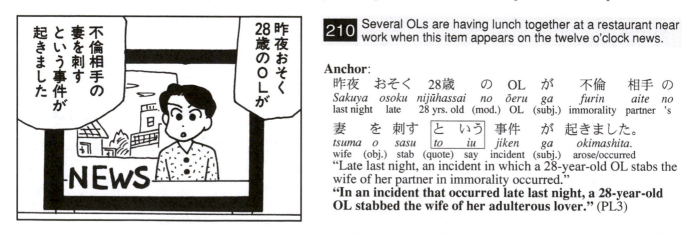

© Akizuki Risu. *OL Shinkaron*, Kōdansha.

210 Several OLs are having lunch together at a restaurant near work when this item appears on the twelve o'clock news.

Anchor:
昨夜　おそく　28歳　の　OL　が　不倫　相手　の
Sakuya *osoku* *nijūhassai* *no* *ōeru* *ga* *furin* *aite* *no*
last night　late　28 yrs. old　(mod.)　OL　(subj.)　immorality　partner　's

妻　を　刺す　と　いう　事件　が　起きました。
tsuma *o* *sasu* *to* *iu* *jiken* *ga* *okimashita.*
wife (obj.)　stab　(quote)　say　incident　(subj.)　arose/occurred
"Late last night, an incident in which a 28-year-old OL stabs the wife of her partner in immorality occurred."
"In an incident that occurred late last night, a 28-year-old OL stabbed the wife of her adulterous lover." (PL3)

• the larger sentence here is *Sakuya osoku...jiken ga okimashita* ("Late last night an incident occurred"), and this larger sentence frames a complete embedded sentence ending at *to iu* that describes the *jiken* ("incident"): *Nijūhassai no OL ga furin aite no tsuma o sasu* = "A 28-year-old OL stabs the wife of her partner in immorality."
• *osoku* is the adverb form of the adjective *osoi* ("late/slow").
• the polite form of *sasu* ("stab/pierce") is *sashimasu*.
• *okimashita* is the polite past form of *okiru/okimasu* ("arise/occur").

"Quoting" thoughts/opinions

The same *to* is used when stating one's thoughts, opinions, ideas, beliefs, expectations, and the like, and in such cases *to* is followed by verbs like *omou/omoimasu* ("think/hold/believe/feel"), *kangaeru/kangaemasu* ("think/contemplate"), and *shinjiru/shinjimasu* ("believe").

A complete quoted sentence before *to*—whether it represents a statement or thought—usually has a plain, PL2 ending. The politeness level of the larger sentence is determined by its own ending and other elements in the sentence.

211 Zenzō is about to go out for the evening because he has a meeting. He lets Natsu know that she should not expect him to be home early.

Zenzō: 今夜　　は　遅く　　　なる　　と　　思う。
Kon'ya　wa　osoku　naru　to　omou.
tonight　as for　late　will become　(quote)　think
"As for tonight, I will become late, I think."
"I expect to get home pretty late tonight." (PL2)

- *osoku* is the adverb form of the adjective *osoi* ("slow/late"; fig. 78).
- the polite form of *naru* ("become") is *narimasu. Osoku naru* = "become slower" or "become late."
- *to* marks the complete sentence *Kon'ya wa osoku naru* ("Tonight I will be late") as the "quoted" content of Zenzō's thinking/expectations.

Asking about a person's thoughts

To ask a simple yes-or-no question about a person's thoughts or opinions, the speaker "quotes" the thought and adds *to omou (ka)?/to omoimasu ka?* ("Do you think ～?") or *to omotta (ka)?/ to omoimashita ka?* ("Did you think ～?"). In PL2 speech, using *ka* is mostly masculine; female speakers would normally just say *to omou?/to omotta?* with the rising intonation of a question.

212 In spite of his father's initial opposition, Zenzō has been lobbying the mayor and other villagers to have the electrical grid extended to the village. Now he must persuade his father, who is concerned not only about his own costs at a time when the brewery has suffered losses, but the burden that regular electricity bills will place on the villagers:

Father:
それでも　おまえ　は　電気　が
Sore de mo　omae　wa　denki　ga
even so　you　as for　electricity　(subj.)

この　村　の　将来　に　役立つ　と　思う　か?
kono　mura　no　shōrai　ni　yakudatsu　to　omou　ka?
this　village　's　future　to　will be useful　(quote)　think　(?)
"Despite that, do you think that electricity will be beneficial to the future of this village?" (PL2)

- *sore de mo* = "even so/even considering that/despite that"; *sore* ("that") refers to what has just been said—in this case the concerns about ongoing costs that Zenzō's father has raised.
- the polite form of *yakudatsu* ("be useful [to]") is *yakudachimasu*. The expression also occurs in the form *yaku ni tatsu/tachimasu*.
- *Sore de mo omae wa...omou ka?* ("Even so do you think...?") is the framing sentence, and *Denki ga kono mura no shōrai ni yakudatsu* ("Electricity will be useful to the future of this village") is an embedded sentence representing the content of Zenzō's thoughts/views that his father is asking about.

Quoted questions

A PL2 or PL3 question ending in *ka* followed by a form of *to iu/iimasu* ("say") or *to kiku/kikimasu* ("ask") provides a direct quote of the question: *Shima-san desu ka to iimashita* = "She said, 'Is it/Are you Mr. Shima?'"

A plain PL2 question ending in *ka* followed by *to omou/omoimasu* ("think") creates a somewhat tentative statement that is like "I think perhaps/maybe/possibly/probably ~." In spite of the question form used for the embedded sentence, ~ *ka to omou* creates an assertion, so it's important not to confuse it with ~ *to omou ka* (fig. 212).

213 Despite the brewmaster's deteriorating health, Natsuko's father asks him to return for the next season, when the first batch of Tatsunishiki saké will be made. The brewmaster accepts, but if anything happens to him, he wants the young Kusakabe to be the one to replace him—even though he is not really ready yet to be a brewmaster. The Tatsunishiki project represents the future of the brewery, he says, and goes on:

Brewmaster: 若い　力　が　必要　か　と　思います。
Wakai chikara ga hitsuyō ka to omoimasu.
young　strength　(subj.)　necessity/need　(?)　(quote)　think
"I think, 'Does the brewery need young strength?'"
"I think the brewery needs young energy." (PL3)

- *hitsuyō* is an adjectival noun for "necessity/need," and *hitsuyō da/desu* means "is necessary/needed"; the word belongs to the *wa-ga* group (fig. 145), which means its subject marked with *ga* is easier to think of as the direct object of "need" in English. The understood topic is the brewery, so *Wakai chikara ga hitsuyō da* = "The brewery needs young strength," and the question *Wakai chikara ga hitsuyō ka?* = "Does the brewery need young strength?"
- the tentative *ka to omou* is mostly for politeness here, to soften a statement that might otherwise sound too assertive, but in many cases the tentativeness would be real.

To with other verbs

A quoting *to* can also be followed by verbs that you may not think of as having anything to do either with speaking/reading/hearing or with thoughts/beliefs/feelings. In many such cases, *to* can be thought of as marking what precedes it as the "content" (in a very broad sense) of the action of the verb that follows—much as it marks the content of a statement or thought when used with *iu* or *omou*. In other cases it may mark an idea or thought associated with the action—such as the motivation for it, or the conclusion drawn from it.

In the example here, "Michael" is the content of the naming action, which in Japanese is expressed using the verb *tsukeru/tsukemasu* ("stick/affix/attach").

214 In a letter to a private eye, Michael's owner Tachibana Reiko relates how she first found her pet, still a little kitten, and took him home.

Reiko: 名前　は　マイケル　と　つけました。
Namae wa Maikeru to tsukemashita.
name　as for　(name)　(quote)　attached
"As for a name, I affixed [the name] Michael."
"I named him Michael." (PL3)

- *tsukemashita* is the PL3 past form of *tsukeru/tsukemasu* ("stick/attach [to something]"). The verb for "[something] sticks/attaches" is *tsuku/tsukimasu*.

© Oze Akira, Natsuko no Sake, Kodansha.

© Kobayashi Makoto, What's Michael!?, Kodansha.

Tte at the end of a sentence

The informal *tte* is often used at the end of a sentence without a verb, implying "that's what someone says/is saying/said." It may or may not be followed by a sentence particle (*yo, sa,* and sometimes *ne* or *na*). *To* can also be used this way, almost always with a following particle like *na/ne/sa/yo,* but it occurs less commonly than *tte.*

This use of *tte* often occurs without any speaker specified, even by the context—in which case it is like "They say (that) ～."

215 This young woman's boyfriend is scheduled to come today to formally ask her father for her hand in marriage, but he has just called to say he's going to be late.

Woman: パパ、あのー、 ユウジさん
Papa, anō, Yūji-san
papa/dad um (name-pol.)

今日 遅く なる って。
kyō osoku naru | *tte.*
today late will become (quote)
"Dad, um, Yūji says he's going to be late today."
(PL2)

Father: 何?!
Nani?!
"What?!" (PL2)

SFX: ピッ
Pi!
Bip (turning off phone)

• for *osoku naru,* see fig. 211.

Tte = *wa*

The informal *tte* is quite a versatile particle. Besides being equivalent to both *to* and *to iu,* it can also be equivalent to the longer quoting phrase *to iu no wa* (lit. "as for what is called ～"). Since this phrase is often just a fancy way of setting up the topic, *tte* can in effect serve as the topic marker *wa* ("as for ～") in colloquial speech.

Shima

216 Shima has never been a fan of bread, but when he's put in charge of advertising his company's consumer bread machines, he decides he'd better learn the difference between good and indifferent bread, and he begins eating some every day for lunch. Suzukamo Katsuko, the proprietress of an exclusive bar, is sure this will make a good impression on his new subordinates, but Shima says he eats in private so no one sees him having to make such special efforts.

Suzukamo: うふっ。 男の人 の そういう 見栄 って 可愛い わ。
Ufu! Otoko no hito no sō iu mie | *tte* | *kawaii wa.*
(chuckle) men 's that kind of vanity as for is cute (fem. colloq.)
"(Chuckle) As for men's that kind of vanity, it is cute."
"(Chuckle) It's so cute when men show their vanity like that." (PL2)

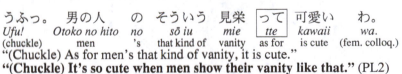

• *ufu!* represents a stifled feminine giggle/chuckle.
• *otoko* ("male/man") feels rather abrupt in spoken Japanese; saying *otoko no hito* (lit. "male/man person") softens it and makes it more polite.
• *mie* is a noun that refers to one's efforts to "look good/keep up appearances" → "vanity."

Complete Sentence Modifiers

In English, longer and more complex modifiers for nouns usually come after the word modified and begin with words like "that," "who," "when," and "where"—e.g., "the man *who is standing at the bus stop*"; "the place *where I met my future bride*." In Japanese, the modifier always comes first, no matter how complex, so the same meaning would be conveyed as "the *standing-at-the-bus-stop* man" or "the *I-met-my-future-bride* place."

To illustrate the underlying principle, the first three examples in this lesson show the same noun with different modifiers, starting with the simplest. These are only modified nouns, not complete sentences.

217 An episode entitled "The Essentials of Michael" illustrates some of Michael's favorite mannerisms.

Narration:

うれしい	とき
Ureshii	*toki*
is happy	time

[he]-is-happy time
When he's happy

- *ureshii* is an adjective meaning "(is) happy/pleased/delighted."

FX: ゴロ ゴロ ゴロ ゴロ
Goro goro goro goro (effect of rolling)

At first glance, *ureshii toki* looks like nothing more than an adjective modifying a noun—"[a] happy time"—and that's indeed the easiest way to think about it if you're dealing with just a single adjective. But when you consider that a Japanese adjective contains the meaning of the verb "to be" (*ureshii* = "is happy") and can be a complete sentence all by itself (*ureshii* = "I am/he is happy"), *ureshii toki* can be thought of literally as "[a] he-is-happy time." That is, it can be thought of as being a complete sentence modifying a noun, not just a single adjective.

The same is true when the adjective is in turn modified by an adverb, as here:

218 "The Essentials of Michael" episode continues with this panel.

Narration:

もっと うれしい	とき
Motto ureshii	*toki*
more is happy	time

[he]-is-more-happy time
When he's even happier

FX: ゴロロン ゴロロン
Gororon gororon
(effect of dancing)

Narration: (ウソ です けど。)
(Uso desu kedo.)
lie is but/although
(It's a lie, but.)
(Though it's a lie.) (PL3)

Since this is still a relatively simple modifier, the easiest way to think of it in English may be as an adverb modifying an adjective modifying a noun—"[a] more happy time" → "[a] happier time"—as similar examples were presented in Lesson 6. But once again, *motto ureshii* can be thought of as a complete sentence modifying a noun. As an independent sentence, if you spell out the understood subject and the verb "to be" in the translation, *Motto ureshii* means "He is more happy " → "He is even happier"; this sentence has been used, without alteration, to modify *toki*, making it literally like "[a] he-is-even-happier time."

217, 218 © Kobayashi Makoto. *What's Michael!?*, Kōdansha.

With an explicit subject

The concept of the modifier being a full sentence should come even clearer when you see the subject of the modifying sentence spelled out even in the Japanese.

219 Another panel from "The Essentials of Michael" shows Michael scratching with his forepaw like a human. (The next panel notes that cats don't actually scratch with their forepaws.)

Narration:
頭　　が　　かゆい　とき
Atama   ga   kayui   toki
head   (subj.) is itchy time
[his]-head-is-itchy time
When his head itches

FX: ボリ ボリ
Bori   bori
(effect of scratching)

Narration: (これ　も　ウソ です　けど。)
(Kore   mo   uso desu   kedo.)
this   too   lie   is   but/although
(Though this is a lie, too.) (PL3)

- *ga* marks *atama* ("head") as the subject of *kayui* ("is itchy").
- *atama ga kayui* is a complete sentence, "[his] head is itchy." This adjective-type sentence, without any linking word or alteration in form, modifies the noun *toki* ("time").

The episode does not go on to illustrate *atama ga motto kayui toki* ("when his head itches even more"; *motto* = "more"), but it could have. The crucial point to grasp is that a single adjective can in fact be replaced by any complete sentence ending in an adjective. No matter how complex the modifying sentence may be, it stays in front of the noun it modifies and keeps the same form it would have as an independent sentence; there is no change in word order, nor any need to add words like "that," "who," "when," or "where."

In a complete sentence

Figs. 217–19 show only sentence fragments: nouns with modifiers. In another context, these exact same phrases could be seen as complete sentences that simply have *da*/*desu* omitted at the end. But in this context, the illustration completes the thought, so the implied complete sentence is "When ～, this is what Michael does"—with the modified noun serving as the sentence's time phrase. In general writing and conversation, of course, the overall sentence is more typically stated in full, as here:

220 At their *o-miai*, when Shinnosuke asks about her taste in men (fig. 163), this is Poppo's response:

Poppo:
木登り　　が　　うまい　　方　　が　　好きです。
Ki-nobori   ga   umai   kata   ga   suki desu.
tree climbing (subj.) is skillful person (subj.)   [I] like
"A [he]-is-skillful-at-tree-climbing person [I] like."
"I like a man who's good at climbing trees." (PL3)

- *ki* = "tree" and *nobori* is the pre-*masu* form of the verb *noboru*/*noborimasu* ("climb"); *ki-nobori* is a noun for "tree-climbing."
- *umai* is an adjective for "is skillful/good at," and depending on the context, *ga* can mark either the skill that the person in question is good at, or the person who is good at the skill in question—in this case the former. *Umai* belongs to the *wa-ga* group introduced in fig. 145.
- *ki-nobori ga umai* ("[he] is skillful at tree-climbing") is a complete sentence modifying *kata*, a formal/polite word for "person."
- *suki* is an adjectival noun, but *suki da*/*desu* is easiest to think of as equivalent to the verb "to like" (fig. 145); the word belongs to the *wa-ga* group, and when the thing or person liked is mentioned (in this case *kata*, together with its modifier), it is marked with *ga*.

Verb-type sentences as modifiers

The four previous examples all have adjectives and adjective-type sentences as modifiers, but any verb can be placed in front of a noun as a modifier as well. And just as with adjectives, that verb-type modifier can in fact be anything from a single verb to a full verb-type sentence with a subject, object, time and place phrases, adverbs, and more. The example here shows a noun modified by a relatively simple verb-type sentence:

221 Kyōko and her father are looking out the window and enjoying the quiet snow scene in their garden. Father notes in wonderment that when he listens very closely, he can actually hear the snow falling. Then Kyōko remarks on a rather more distinct sound they have just heard.

Sound FX: ズ...ズズン
Zu...zuzun
Thudududd

Kyōko: あ、 お母さん が こける 音。
A,　o-kāsan　ga　kokeru　oto.
(interj.) mother (subj.) fall/tumble sound
"Ahh, a Mother-tumbles sound."
"Ahh, the sound of Mother taking a tumble."

- *kokeru/kokemasu* is an informal word for "trip/fall/take a tumble," and *o-kāsan* is its subject; *o-kāsan ga kokeru* is a complete verb-type sentence ("mother tumbles") modifying *oto* ("sound/noise").
- *da/desu* has been omitted from the end of the overall sentence.

Separating modifier and sentence

When dealing with modifying sentences that are embedded in larger sentences, context must be your guide in sorting out which part of the sentence belongs to the modifier and which to the larger sentence; in spoken conversations, the speech rhythms can also help. In figs. 220 and 221, the *ga* phrases are the subjects of the embedded modifying sentences; in the example here, the *ga* phrase is the subject of the larger sentence in which the modifier is embedded.

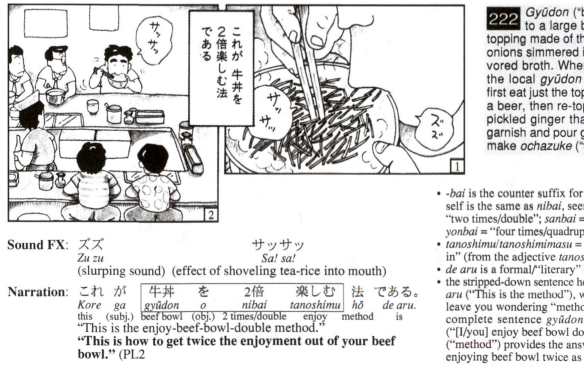

222 *Gyūdon* ("beef bowl") refers to a large bowl of rice with a topping made of thin-sliced beef and onions simmered in a soy-sauce flavored broth. When Kōsuke goes to the local *gyūdon* shop, he likes to first eat just the topping while he has a beer, then re-top the rice with the pickled ginger that's provided as a garnish and pour green tea over it to make *ochazuke* ("tea rice").

Sound FX: ズズ　　　　　　　　　サッサッ
Zu zu　　　　　　　　*Sa! sa!*
(slurping sound) (effect of shoveling tea-rice into mouth)

Narration: これ が 牛丼 を 2倍 楽しむ 法 である。
Kore　ga　gyūdon　o　nibai　tanoshimu　hō　de aru.
this (subj.) beef bowl (obj.) 2 times/double enjoy method is
"This is the enjoy-beef-bowl-double method."
"This is how to get twice the enjoyment out of your beef bowl." (PL2

- *-bai* is the counter suffix for multiples; *bai* by itself is the same as *nibai*, seen here, which means "two times/double"; *sanbai* = "three times/triple," *yonbai* = "four times/quadruple," and so forth.
- *tanoshimu/tanoshimimasu* = "enjoy/take pleasure in" (from the adjective *tanoshii*, "is enjoyable").
- *de aru* is a formal/"literary" equivalent of *desu*.
- the stripped-down sentence here is *Kore ga...hō de aru* ("This is the method"), which by itself would leave you wondering "method of/for what?" The complete sentence *gyūdon o nibai tanoshimu* ("[I/you] enjoy beef bowl double") modifying *hō* ("method") provides the answer: "the method for enjoying beef bowl twice as much."

A modified object

In fig. 220, the subject (*kata*) receives a complete sentence modifier; in fig. 222, it is the noun (*hō*) in the main noun + *de aru* phrase at the end of the sentence that does. In fact, any noun anywhere in the sentence can be modifed by a complete embedded sentence. Here's an example where the direct object gets a complete sentence modifier.

Garcia

223 Garcia left his family behind in Colombia and came to work in Japan. He found a job at a flower shop, where he does all of the menial tasks. Here, the owner's little boy watches as Garcia scrubs out a flowerpot. "I really admire you, Garcia," he says. Then he explains:

Boy:

みんな	が	嫌がる	仕事	を
Minna	*ga*	*iyagaru*	*shigoto*	*o*
everyone	(subj.)	finds distasteful	work/job	(obj.)

一生懸命	やる	んだ	もん。
isshōkenmei	*yaru*	*n da*	*mon.*
diligently	do	(explan.)	because

"Because you diligently do everyone-finds-[it]-distasteful work."
"Because you really work hard doing the jobs no one else wants to do." (PL2)

- *iyagaru* combines the adjectival noun *iya* that expresses distaste (fig. 205) with the suffix *-garu*, which attaches to certain adjectives and adjectival nouns of feeling to mean "show signs of [being happy/sad/pleased/disgusted/in pain/etc.]." So *iyagaru* = "show signs of distaste" → "find distasteful." You'll find more on *-garu* at fig. 348.
- *minna ga iyagaru* is a complete sentence ("everyone finds [it] distasteful") modifying *shigoto* ("work/job"): "work that everyone finds distasteful" → "work no one else wants to do."
- *o* marks *shigoto* (along with its full modifier) as the object of the verb *yaru/yarimasu* ("do"; see fig. 113).
- *isshōkenmei (ni)* implies doing an action "very hard/diligently/with all one's might/for all one is worth."
- *n da mon* is a contraction of *no da mono* (the explanatory *no da* plus *mono*), which altogether can be thought of as "because." This ending is often used when giving an explanation for something one has just said.

☛ Don't worry if some of the longer sentences in this lesson seem like complete puzzles at first. Just plan to come back to them again later. They're here to illustrate a basic feature of the language, but some of them are pretty complicated for this stage of your learning.

A modifed time word

In this example, it is the time word that is modifed by a complete sentence modifier.

224 Hiroko was supposed to meet Kōsuke at this coffee shop cum pub at 4:30, but she still hasn't shown up at 5:00, when the proprietor needs to close the shop for an hour. (This panel comes before fig. 194, where the proprietor has decided to let Kōsuke stay on.)

Proprietor:

まことに　　申し分けありません。
Makoto ni 　　*mōshiwake arimasen.*
truly/extremely 　　(apology)
"I'm terribly sorry." (PL4)

5時	から	パブタイム	が	始まる	6時	まで
Goji	*kara*	*pabu-taimu*	*ga*	*hajimaru*	*rokuji*	*made*
5:00	from	pub time	(subj.)	begins	6:00	until

店	を	閉めます	ので...
mise	*o*	*shimemasu*	*no de...*
shop	(obj.)	will close	because/so

"I will be closing the shop from 5:00 until 6:00, when pub time begins, so..." (PL3)

- *makoto* = "sincerity/truth," and *makoto ni* = "truly/sincerely." The latter is often used as an emphasizer, "extremely/terribly." *Mōshiwake arimasen* is a very polite/formal apology.
- *pabu-taimu ga hajimaru* ("pub time begins") is a complete sentence modifying *rokuji* ("6:00") → "6:00, when pub time begins."
- *shimeru/shimemasu* = "close [something]"; the verb for "[something] closes" is *shimaru/shimarimasu.*
- ending his sentence with *no de* ("because/so") and leaving the understood conclusion ("I need you to leave") unsaid is a form of politeness.

A modified destination/place

In this example, the word modified by a complete-sentence modifier refers to a destination—the roller coaster at an amusement park.

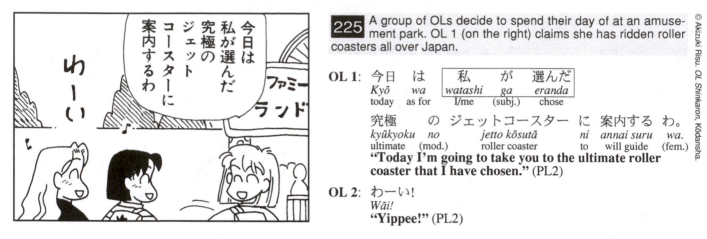

225 A group of OLs decide to spend their day of at an amusement park. OL 1 (on the right) claims she has ridden roller coasters all over Japan.

OL 1: 今日　は　│私　が　選んだ│
Kyō   wa   watashi   ga   eranda
today as for I/me   (subj.) chose

究極　　の　ジェットコースター　に　案内する　わ。
kyūkyoku   no   jetto kōsutā   ni   annai suru   wa.
ultimate (mod.) roller coaster to   will guide (fem.)
"Today I'm going to take you to the ultimate roller coaster that I have chosen." (PL2)

OL 2: わーい!
Wāi!
"Yippee!" (PL2)

- *eranda* is the PL2 past form of the verb *erabu/erabimasu* ("select/choose"), and *ga* marks *watashi* as its subject: *watashi ga eranda* = "I chose [it]." This sentence modifies the noun phrase *kyūkyoku no jetto kōsutā*.
- *kyūkyoku* is a noun for "the extreme/the ultimate," but it most typically occurs with *no* to modify another noun—in this case *jetto kōsutā* (from English "jet" and "coaster"; "jet coaster" is the standard Japanese term for "roller coaster"): *kyūkyoku no jetto kōsutā* = "the ultimate roller coaster." Combining this with its preceding sentence modifier makes it "the ultimate roller coaster that I chose." In English the modifiers are split before and after the word modified, but in Japanese all modifiers come before.
- *annai* is a noun meaning "guidance/information"; *suru* makes it a verb for "guide/lead/show the way."

A modified noun-modifier

In this example, a complete verb-type sentence modifies a noun that is itself modifying another noun.

226 The story of the man in fig. 11 starts by noting the many hardships snow brings during the winter to all those who live in the "snow country."

Narration:
これ　は　│そんな　　雪国　　で　強く　　たくましく
Kore   wa   sonna   yukiguni   de   tsuyoku   takumashiku
this   as for that kind of snow country in   strongly   hardily

生きる│男　　の　　物語　　　である。
ikiru   otoko   no   monogatari   de aru.
live(s) man   of   story   is
As for this, it is the story of a lives-strong-and-hardy-in-that-kind-of-snow-country man.
This is the story of a man who lives strong and hardy in just such snow country. (PL2)

- *tsuyoku* is the adverb form of the adjective *tsuyoi* ("strong"), and *takumashiku* is the adverb form of the adjective *takumashii* ("robust/hardy/resilient").
- *ikiru/ikimasu* = "[to] live"; *sonna yukiguni de tsuyoku takumashiku ikiru* ("[he] lives strong and hardy in that kind of snow country") is a complete sentence modifying *otoko* ("man").
- the stripped-down sentence here is *Kore wa...monogatari de aru* ("This is a story"). When *otoko no* is added, it becomes "This is the story of a man." The long, complete sentence modifier further modifies *otoko* to indicate what kind of man the story is about.

It's worth making special note of the difference between the two examples on this page. In fig. 225, the sentence modifier (*watashi ga eranda*) modifies the combination of noun 1 and noun 2 (*kyūkyoku no jetto kōsutā*); in fig. 226, the combination of the sentence modifier and noun 1 (*sonna yukiguni de tsuyoku takumashiku ikiru otoko*) modifies noun 2 (*monogatari*).

の *no* as a subject marker

The subject of an embedded modifying sentence is often marked with *no* instead of the usual *ga*. Whether to use *no* or *ga* can be considered essentially a stylistic choice. The subject of an embedded modifying sentence cannot be marked with *wa*.

The subject of the larger embedding sentence must still be marked with *ga* or, if the subject is also the topic, *wa*; it cannot be marked with *no*.

227 Maintaining the longstanding taboo against women entering the brewhouse, Zenzō's father turns down his request to let Natsu enter. Here Zenzō tries to give Natsu a sense of the layout of the interior by describing it from the outside.

Zenzō: そして　ここら　　が
Soshite kokora ga
and   this area (subj.)
"And this area

麹室　　　の　　ある　ところ　だ。
kōji-muro no aru tokoro da.
kōji room (subj.) exists place is
"is the place where the *kōji* room exists."
"And right about here is where the *kōji* room is located." (PL2)

"The *kōji* room?"

- *soshite* is often used at the beginning of a sentence like "and/then/and then/and now."
- *kokora* is a *ko-so-a-do* word that can mean either "hereabouts/this area" or "about this much" depending on the context; in the latter use it is a synonym for *kono kurai/kore kurai* (see fig. 165).
- *ga* marks *kokora* as the subject of the sentence as a whole; the stripped-down sentence is *Soshite kokora ga...tokoro da* ("And this area is the place"), which by itself would leave you wondering, "What place?"
- *kōji* is a mold used for converting starch to sugar in the saké brewing process, and *muro* can refer to a wide variety of climate-controlled rooms or buildings for growing, culturing, drying, preserving, storing, etc. The *kōji-muro* is a room that's heated to foster growth of the *kōji*.
- *kōji-muro no aru* ("the *kōji* room exists") is a complete sentence modifying *tokoro* ("place") → "the place where the *kōji* room exists/is located." Because this sentence is an embedded modifier rather than an independent statement, *no* marks *kōji* as the subject of *aru* ("exists") instead of the standard *ga*; as a statement on its own, the sentence would read *Kōji-muro ga aru* ("A *kōji* room exists/there is a *kōji* room.").

Double sentence modifiers

In this example, there are two complete sentences modifying the main noun at the end. In this particular case, the structure is lost in the final English translation, so an extra intermediate translation has been added to show how the English might come out in other, similar situations. It is not unusual for there to be two or more sentence modifiers for a single noun.

228 When Asami Tsunetarō is elected prime minister, reporters fan out to interview constituents in his home district. This constituent responds to a question about Asami's childhood (fig. 162).

Constituent:
とても　頭　の　いい、　心　　の　優しい　少年　でした。
Totemo atama no ii, kokoro no yasashii shōnen deshita.
very much head (subj.) is good heart (subj.) is kind boy was
"He was very much a head-is-good, heart-is-kind boy."
"He was a boy whose head was very good and heart was very kind."
"He was a very intelligent, kindhearted boy." (PL3)

- *totemo* is an adverb that adds emphasis, like "very/very much"; in this position, its emphasis gets added to both of the modifying sentences.
- *atama no ii* and *kokoro no yasashii* are both complete sentences modifying *shōnen* ("boy/youth"). In both cases, *no* marks the subject of the modifying sentence. In a non-modifying situation *atama no ii* would be *Atama ga ii* ("[His] head is good" → "He is smart/intelligent"); similarly, *kokoro no yasashii* would be *Kokoro ga yasashii* ("[His] heart is kind" → "He is kindhearted").

Two generic nouns: もの *mono* and こと *koto*

Two words meaning "thing," *mono* and *koto*, often receive elaborate sentence modifiers. In general use, *mono* tends to refer to concrete, tangible things, while *koto* refers to intangibles and abstract things—questions, facts, matters, events, situations, aims, actions, and so forth. But the line between the two words can't be drawn too sharply, since *mono* can also be quite abstract. Here are examples of the two words in action.

229 At the office, Ms. Yoshida asks Tanaka-kun what he is writing so intently, and he says he is making an entry in his diary. After her response here, he promptly puts his head down on his desk and falls asleep.

Yoshida:
やー　ネー!　日記　と　いう　[もの]　は
Yā　nē!　Nikki　to　iu　mono　wa
weird/silly (colloq.) diary (quote) say/called thing as for
"That's silly! As for a diary,

寝る　　前に　つける　[もの]　よー。
neru　mae ni　tsukeru　mono　yō.
go to bed/sleep before enter thing (is-emph.)
"it's something you make entries in before going to sleep."
"Silly! A diary is something you write in before going to bed." (PL2)

- *yā* is a variation of *iya* or *iyā*, the word that expresses distaste or objection seen in figs. 205 and 223. When the objection is to something the speaker considers merely strange rather than distasteful, it can be like "that's silly." The long *nē* gives an emphatic, exclamatory effect.
- *nikki to iu* (lit. "[it] is called 'a diary'"; *to* is the particle for quoting—see fig. 208) is a complete sentence modifying *mono* ("thing"), so *nikki to iu mono* means "a/the thing called a diary," and *wa* marks this as the topic of the sentence. In fact, the whole phrase ～ *to iu mono wa* is often just a fancy way of marking the topic ("as for ～") → "as for a diary." *Mono* can be modified by much more elaborate sentences, and takes any role in the sentence a noun can fill.
- *neru* = "go to bed/sleep," and *mae* after a verb means "before [the action takes/took place]." The particle *ni* marks *neru mae* ("before going to bed/sleep") as the time when the action occurs.
- when speaking of various kinds of records and documents, including diaries, *tsukeru/tsukemasu* means "make an entry." *Neru mae ni tsukeru* is a complete sentence ("[you] make entries [in it] before going to bed") modifying *mono* ("thing").
- in colloquial speech, the emphatic particle *yo* can by itself serve as *da/desu yo* ("is/are" + emphasis). Here she lengthens it for further emphasis.

230 Through no fault of his own (apart from trying to be discreet), Shima offended the president's wife (fig. 111), and now he has suddenly been reassigned to the Philippines. His mentor, Nakazawa, is chagrined: he had had high hopes for Shima's advancement in the company. Shima assures him that he really doesn't mind being sent abroad, but inwardly he admits having certain regrets.

Shima:　確かに　　中沢　部長　と　離れる　[こと]　は　　残念　だ。
(thinking) *Tashika ni　Nakazawa buchō　to　hanareru　koto　wa　zannen　da.*
certainly/definitely (name) dept. hd. from separate thing as for disappointment is
"Certainly, as for the separate-from-Department-Head-Nakazawa thing, it is a disappointment."
"I'll definitely regret the separation from Mr. Nakazawa." (PL2)

- *tashika ni* ("certainly/assuredly/definitely/indeed") is an adverb modifying the sentence as a whole.
- *hanareru/hanaremasu* = "separate (from)," and *to* marks the person he will be separating from. *Nakazawa buchō to hanareru* is a complete sentence modifying *koto* ("thing"), and *wa* marks this modified noun as the topic of the sentence (as reflected in the intermediate translation). A verb + *koto* is often simply a way of turning a verb into a noun, so *hanareru koto* can also be translated simply as "a separation" → "the separation from Mr. Nakazawa."
- *zannen* is an adjectival noun meaning "disappointment"; depending on the context, ～ *wa zannen da* may translate variously as "I regret/lament ～"; "I'm sorry/mortified that ～"; "It's a pity that ～"; etc.

の *no* as "thing/one"

Similarly *no* can be like a generic "thing," or the pronoun "one." But there is a key difference: while *koto* and *mono* can stand alone as nouns in many cases, *no* cannot; it must always be preceded by a modifier.

231 One morning, Kōsuke flags down the milkman for some fresh milk, and then heads for the bakery to buy the rest of his breakfast.

Narration:
牛乳 に 合う ［の］ は アンパン だ。
Gyūnyū ni au no wa an-pan da.
milk with fits thing as for (food) is
The goes-with-milk thing is *an-pan*.
What goes with milk is *an-pan*. (PL2)

Sign:
おいしい パン 菓子 ジュース 牛乳
Oishii Pan Kashi Jūsu Gyūnyū
delicious bread sweets/pastries juice milk
Tasty Bread   Pastries   Juice   Milk

Awning:
いろは 屋
Iroha -ya
(name) store/shop
Iroha Bakery

- *au/aimasu* written with this kanji means "fits/matches."
- *gyūnyū ni au* ("it fits milk") is a complete sentence modifying *no*, which in this case can be thought of as "thing" → "the thing that fits/goes with milk."
- *an* (or *anko*) is a thick, heavily sweetened paste made of adzuki beans, and *pan* (from Portuguese *pāo*) is the generic word for breads of all kinds; *an-pan* is a bread roll filled with *an*.
- *i*, *ro*, and *ha* are the first three syllables of the old Japanese syllabary order from classical times, so *iroha* is equivalent to "ABC" in English. Since the suffix *-ya* designates a shop, eatery, or other small business, *Iroha-ya* is like "The ABC Bakery."

☞ When the complete sentence modifier ends with an adjectival noun, this *no* becomes *na no*: *Sakkā ga jōzu da* = "[He] is good at soccer" → *Sakkā ga jōzu na no wa Tanaka-san desu* = "The one who is good at soccer is Tanaka."

No as noun-maker

It's often easier to think of *no* as a "noun-maker" that turns what precedes it (i.e., the word, phrase, or complete sentence that modifies it) into a noun—similar to the way many English verbs can be made into nouns simply by adding *-ing* ("run" → "running").

232 At their *o-miai*, Poppo asks Shinnosuke what his favorite pastime is, and this is his answer. (Poppo's answer to the same question appears in fig. 97.)

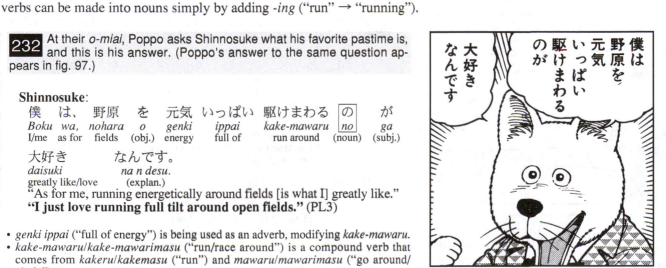

Shinnosuke:
僕 は、 野原 を 元気 いっぱい 駆けまわる ［の］ が
Boku wa, nohara o genki ippai kake-mawaru no ga
I/me as for fields (obj.) energy full of run around (noun) (subj.)
大好き なんです。
daisuki na n desu.
greatly like/love (explan.)
"As for me, running energetically around fields [is what I] greatly like."
"I just love running full tilt around open fields." (PL3)

- *genki ippai* ("full of energy") is being used as an adverb, modifying *kake-mawaru*.
- *kake-mawaru/kake-mawarimasu* ("run/race around") is a compound verb that comes from *kakeru/kakemasu* ("run") and *mawaru/mawarimasu* ("go around/circle").
- *no* makes the complete sentence *nohara o genki ippai kake-mawaru* ("run around the fields energetically") act like a single noun: "running around the fields energetically."
- *daisuki* is the prefix *dai-*, meaning "great/greatly," plus the adjectival noun *suki* ("like"). It belongs to the *wa-ga* group, so *ga* marks the thing that is liked—which is structurally the subject of *daisuki* in Japanese, but corresponds to what you think of as the direct object in English.

Tsumori = "intention" = "intend to ～"

This and the facing page illustrate several nouns that usually occur with modifiers, but that are used in ways not readily translated as modified nouns in English. In some cases they translate better as the corresponding verb form of the noun. For example, *tsumori* is a noun that refers to someone's "intention/plan," but with a non-past verb-type modifier, ～ *tsumori da/desu* is best thought of as meaning "[someone] intends/plans to [do the described action]."

233 Zenzō asked village headman Kurashige to see about bringing electricity to the village, but did not want to tell his father until the plans were further along. Having done the groundwork, Kurashige says he now needs a firm financial commitment from Zenzō's father.

Zenzō: 父 に は これから 相談する つもり です。
Chichi ni wa kore kara sōdan suru | *tsumori* | *desu.*
father to/with as for from now consult intention is
"As for with my father, it is my intention to consult beginning now."
"I plan to consult with my father about it now." (PL3)

Kurashige: は？
Ha?
"Pardon?" (PL3)

- *chichi* is the proper way to refer to one's own father when speaking to someone outside the family (see p. 91).
- *kore kara* (lit. "from this") often means "from now (on)/beginning now." *Chichi ni wa kore kara sōdan suru* is a complete sentence ("I will consult with my father beginning now") modifying *tsumori* ("intention").
- *ha?* shows surprise or confusion about what the other person has said: "Huh?/What?/ Pardon?" It is more formal than the *e?* seen in fig. 50. Kurashige is suprised that Zenzō hasn't discussed the plan with his father because Kurashige himself already has.

Hazu = "expectation" = "should/ought" or "expect/believe"

Hazu is a noun referring to an "expectation" or "presumption"—what the speaker "believes/ feels sure" is/was the case, or what she "expects" to occur/to have occurred. With a non-past verb-type modifier, *hazu da/desu* typically means "[the action] should/ought to occur"; with a past verb-type modifier, it means the speaker "believes [the action] did occur/has occurred."

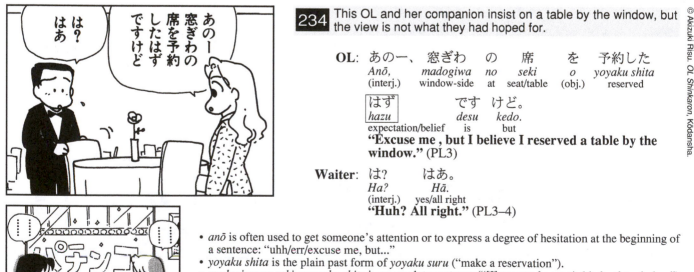

234 This OL and her companion insist on a table by the window, but the view is not what they had hoped for.

OL: あのー、 窓ぎわ の 席 を 予約した
Anō, madogiwa no seki o yoyaku shita
(interj.) window-side at seat/table (obj.) reserved

はず です けど。
hazu desu kedo.
expectation/belief is but
"Excuse me , but I believe I reserved a table by the window." (PL3)

Waiter: は？ はあ。
Ha? Hā.
(interj.) yes/all right
"Huh? All right." (PL3–4)

- *anō* is often used to get someone's attention or to express a degree of hesitation at the beginning of a sentence: "uhh/err/excuse me, but..."
- *yoyaku shita* is the plain past form of *yoyaku suru* ("make a reservation").
- *madogiwa no seki o yoyaku shita* is a complete sentence ("[I] reserved a seat/table by the window") modifying *hazu*.
- *kedo* ("but") "softens" the end of the sentence and implies she wants a response (see fig. 195).
- for the short *ha?*, see fig. 233. *Hā* with a long vowel and a low/flat intonation is a rather uncertain/ tentative-sounding "yes/I see/all right." The waiter, of course, knows that all they'll see from the window is the garish neon facade of the pachinko (Japanese pinball) parlor across the street.

Neon sign: Pachinko

© Oze Akira, *Natsu no Kura*, Kōdansha.

© Akizuki Risu, *OL Shinkaron*, Kōdansha.

Stating a purpose or reason with *tame*

Tame after a non-past verb-type modifier means "in order to do [the described action]" or "for the purpose of [the described action]"; after a past verb-type modifier it means "because of/ owing to [the described action]."

Note: 人生 を 考える ┃ため┃ に 旅 に 出ます。
Jinsei o kangaeru tame ni tabi ni demasu.
life (obj.) contemplate purpose (purpose) trip to/on will depart
"I'm going on a trip to reflect on life. " (PL3)

とーさん を よろしく。
Tōsan o yoroshiku.
father (obj.) [treat] well
"Please take good care of Dad." (PL2–3)

Father: あさめし は?
Asa-meshi wa?
morning meal as for
"Where's my breakfast?" (PL2)

- *kangaeru/kangaemasu* = "think about/contemplate/ponder."
- *jinsei o kangaeru* is a complete sentence ("[I] will think about/reflect on life") modifying *tame* ("purpose"): "for the purpose of reflecting on life" → "to reflect on life."
- *tame* occurs both with and without the particle *ni* for indicating purpose (see fig. 167).
- in the context of travel, *deru/demasu* ("go/come out") means "depart."
- *yoroshiku* (lit. "well/favorably") is short for *yoroshiku onegai shimasu* ("I request your favorable treatment"), a formal phrase used when asking a favor. In this case, *tōsan* ("Father") is the direct object, so it becomes "I request your favorable treatment of Father" → "Please take good care of Father."
- *meshi* is an informal, mostly masculine word for "meal."

235 When Mother tells Daughter she needs to start thinking seriously about getting married, Daughter gets a little carried away listing things she doesn't find so attractive about marriage—using her own parents as examples. The next morning she finds a note from Mother on the table.

Stating what is greater/better/preferable

The greater/better/preferable side of a comparison in Japanese is expressed using the noun *hō* ("side/direction") plus *ga*. The word or sentence modifying *hō* is the specific item or action or quality that is deemed superior, and what follows *ga* expresses how it is superior.

The expression ～ *(no) hō ga ii* (featuring the adjective *ii* = "good/fine") makes a generic statement of superiority: "～ is better."

236 These OLs are planning to go to a hot springs resort for the weekend, and the two on the left are reluctant to invite a fourth OL, whom they don't know so well. Moéko says "Grow up," which seems to imply she thinks they are being small-minded, but then she adds:

Moéko: 人数多く で 行った ┃方┃ が
Ninzū ōku de itta hō ga
large no. of people (scope) went side/direction (subj.)

安く すむ んだ から ね。
yasuku sumu n da kara ne.
cheaply ends (explan.) because (colloq.)
"Going with more people makes it cheaper [for each person], you know." (PL2)

- *ōku* is the *ku*-form of the adjective *ōi* ("are many/numerous"); here it combines with *ninzū* ("number of people") to make a compound noun meaning "a large(r) number of people."
- *itta* is the plain past form of *iku/ikimasu* ("go"); *ninzū ōku de itta* ("[we] went with a large number of people") is a complete sentence modifying *hō* (lit. "side/direction").
- *yasuku* is the adverb form of *yasui* ("cheap"); ～ *hō ga yasui* = "～ is cheaper."
- *sumu/sumimasu* = "end/finish," so *yasuku sumu* is literally "ends cheaply" → "ends/turns out/will be cheap(er)."
- the explanatory *n da* and the connecting word *kara* often combine to mean "because"; here her implication is, "Because it is so, you should stop being childish and invite her."

Lesson 17

Question Words

In the *ko-so-a-do* sets introduced in Lesson 12, the *do-* words are all question words: "which one?" "where?" "how?" "how much?" and so forth. This lesson introduces some of the other common question words.

The simplest question asked with most of these words is merely the question word by itself, spoken with or without the rising intonation of a question. This makes an informal, PL2 query. (The particle *ka* is added directly to question words only in special contexts, and sometimes the combination forms another noun instead of a question; see figs. 251–52.)

237 Kōsuke's landlady gave him some of the *hechima* ("loofah") vine water she asked him to draw into bottles (fig. 100). He has divided it into two small bottles—one for himself, to use as aftershave, and one for his girlfriend Hiroko, to use as hand lotion.

Kōsuke: これ あげる。
Kore   ageru.
this   will give you
"I'll give you this."
"This is for you." (PL2)

Hiroko: 何?
Nani?
what
"What is it?" (PL2)

- *ageru/agemasu* means "give" when speaking of giving something to your listener or a third party → "give you/him/her/them"; it's never used for "give me/us." Lesson 31 explains more about verbs of giving and receiving.
- *nani?* can be a simple "What?" or "What is it?/What's up?/What happened?" depending on the context.

なに *nani* = なん *nan* = "what?"

Directly before *da* or *desu*, *nani* is customarily shortened to *nan*. This contraction occurs in other grammatical situations as well, so you will want to keep your ears tuned to whether *nani* or *nan* is used in any given situation.

238 At their *o-miai*, Poppo asked Shinnosuke about his favorite pastime, and he responded as shown in fig. 232. Here Shinnosuke returns the question, and Poppo hesitates a moment before responding as shown in fig. 97.

Shinnosuke: ポッポさん の ご趣味 は なん です か?
Poppo-san   no   go-shumi   wa   nan   desu   ka?
(name-pol.)/you   's   (hon.)-hobby as for   what   is/are   (?)
"As for Miss Poppo's hobby, what is it?"
"What is your favorite pastime, Miss Poppo?" (PL3)

Poppo: え... ええ...
E...   ē...
(interj.)   (interj.)
"Uhh... urr..."

- he uses his listener's name when an English speaker would use "you." Adding *no* shows possession, so *Poppo-san no* is effectively the same as "your."
- *shumi* has a broader meaning than English "hobby," referring to more general interests and tastes—anything one finds pleasure in—in addition to the specific kinds of activities English speakers think of as hobbies.

128

© Maekawa Tsukasa. *Dai-Tōkyō Binbō Seikatsu Manyuaru, Kōdansha.*

© Kobayashi Makoto. *What's Michael?, Kōdansha.*

Question words as nouns

Most question words function as nouns (some can also be adverbs), and they can appear any-where a noun would appear except as a topic (i.e., they can't be marked with *wa*). In figs. 237 and 238, *nan/nani* is essentially the main noun at the end of the sentence—though in the first case there happens to be nothing else before it. In the example here, *nani* is the direct object, so it's marked with *o* and appears in a normal direct-object position. No special word order is required; word order remains as flexible in questions as in declarative sentences (see fig. 125).

© Maekawa Tsukasa. Dai-Tōkyō Binbō Seikatsu Manyuaru, Kōdansha.

239 Kōsuke goes hiking in the mountains intending to camp out, but he runs into a Buddhist priest meditating under a waterfall, and the priest invites him to stay at his small temple. In lieu of payment, Kōsuke helps in the vegetable garden.

Kōsuke: ここ に 何 を まく んです か?
Koko ni nani o maku n desu ka?
here to/in what (obj.) sow/plant (explan.) (?)
"What are we going to plant here?" (PL3)

Priest: インゲン です。
Ingen desu.
beans is
"Beans." (PL3)

- *maku/makimasu* = "sprinkle/scatter," or when gardening, "sow/plant." *Ni* marks *koko* ("here") as the target of the action—the place where the seeds will end up when planted.
- if the priest were voluntarily explaining his plans instead of answering a question, he might say *Koko ni ingen o maku n desu* ("I'm going to plant beans here"). Kōsuke has simply inserted *nani* in place of the information he is missing/asking about and added *ka* to the end of the sentence to make it a question. The question word has the same position in the sentence as the item it asks about.

Asking questions with *da/desu*

Yes-or-no questions can end with *ka* or *no* (Lessons 4 and 8), or with just a noun/verb/adjective spoken with the intonation of a question, but they cannot normally end with *da* or *desu*. By contrast, questions asked with question words *can* end with *da* or *desu*. Using *da* this way is mostly masculine, and depending on the tone of voice can sound very rough. In PL2 speech, female speakers would more likely just end the query with the question word itself spoken with rising intona-tion (e.g., for the illustration here, *Kore wa nani?*); men can use this pat-tern, too. In PL3 speech asking a question with just *desu* at the end (*Kore wa nan desu?*) sounds gentler and is mostly feminine—though tone of voice can make it sound quite sharp in this case, too; male speakers would usually use *ka* (*Kore wa nan desu ka?*).

240 Michael the baggage-sniff-ing cat pulls a bag contain-ing some kind of plant material out of the suitcase that drew his atten-tion in fig. 121. The customs agent angrily confronts the passenger, only to be told it is *matatabi* ("sil-vervine"), an East Asian plant with the same effect on cats as catnip.

© Kobayashi Makoto. What's Michael?, Kōdansha.

Michael: ウニャン
Unyan
"Meow."

Agent: ん?!
N?!
"Huh?!" (PL2)

これ は なん だ?!
Kore wa nan da?!
this as for what is
"What's this?!" (PL1–2)

Michael: ウニャッ
Unya!
"Meow!"

Nan- = "how many ～?"

Nan- is combined with the appropriate counter suffix (pp. 45–47) to ask "how many [of the indicated item]?" Such question words can function either as nouns or as adverbs, depending on the context.

241 Vertically challenged Tanaka-kun is impressed by how tall his colleague is.

© Tanaka Hiroshi. *Naku na! Tanaka-kun*, Take Shobō.

Tanaka-kun: 背　　　が　高い　んです　ネー。
Se　　ga　takai　n desu　nē.
height/stature　(subj.)　is high　(explan.)　(emph.)
"Your height is high, isn't it?"
"You sure are tall!" (PL3)

何　　　センチ　です　か?
Nan　-senchi　desu　ka?
how many　centimeters　is/are　(?)
"How many centimeters are you?" (PL3)

Colleague: 一九〇センチ。
Hyaku-kyujussenchi.
190 centimeters
"190." (PL2)

- *se* refers to "the back" of something, including a person's back, but it's also commonly used to speak of "[a person's] height/stature"; the adjective *takai* means "is high" so *se ga takai* = "is tall." For Tanaka-kun the adjective would be *hikui* ("is low"): *se ga hikui* = "is short [in stature]."
- *nē* with a long vowel gives the feeling of a mild exclamation.
- *senchimētoru*, the full Japanese rendering of "centimeter," is usually shortened to *senchi*, and a person's height is customarily stated in centimeters only. 190 cm is roughly 6'3".
- it's not uncommon to see kanji numbers written without 十, 百, 千, or 万 (p. 46), using only the kanji for 1 through 9 plus 〇 in the same way as Arabic numerals: e.g., 20 = 二〇 (instead of 二十); 46 = 四六 (instead of 四十六); 8,570 = 八五七〇 (instead of 八千五百七十). Thus, 一九〇 = 190. Another example of this usage appears in fig. 175.

Nanji = "what time?"

Combining *nan-* with the counter suffix for the hours of the day, *-ji* (p. 93), yields the question word for "what time?" *Nanji* is a noun, so *no* is added when it modifies another noun (*dēto* = "date," so *nanji no dēto* = "a date for/at what time"), and *ni* is added when it's used to ask about the timing of a verb—i.e., to ask when something is going to happen (*tsuku*/*tsukimasu* = "arrive," so *nanji ni tsuku* = "arrive at what time").

242 When Shin-chan decides to help his father out by shaving his day-old beard while he's sleeping in on Sunday morning, he gets distracted by the TV and winds up shaving off his eyebrows as well. He is still trying different things to cover up his mistake, including a thick magic marker—hence the long thick mark over Father's eyes—when his father stirs. Shin-chan tries to get him to go back to sleep by lying about the time.

© Usui Yoshito. *Kureyon Shin-chan*, Futabasha.

Father: 今　何時?
Ima　nanji?
now　what time
"As for now, what time is it?"
"What time is it?" (PL2)

Shin-chan: し、7時　　ぐらい...
Shi- shichi-ji　gurai...
(stammer)　7:00　about
"About seven o'clock." (PL2)

- in Japanese, one typically includes *ima* ("now") when inquiring about the present time. In a complete PL3 sentence, the question would be: *Ima nanji desu ka?*

いくつ *ikutsu* = "how old/how many/what size?"

Ikutsu is the question word that goes with the counter suffix *-tsu* introduced on p. 45, and it serves as a generic word for asking about a number or quantity: "what number?" or "how many?" It's also used to ask about a size (essentially implying "what number size?"), and it's a common way to ask a person's age, especially for small children (essentially implying "how many years of age"). *Ikutsu* can be either a noun or an adverb depending on the context.

243 This young man and woman have apparently been going out for quite a while. After asking this question, he tells her there's something he wants to give her the next time they meet.

He: ね、 指サイズ は　いくつ？
Ne, yubi-saizu wa ikutsu?
say   finger size as for   what number/what size
"Say, as for your finger size, what number is it?"
"Say, what's your finger size?" (PL2)

She: えっ?!　　11号　　よ。
E!? Jūichigō yo.
what?/huh?   No. 11   (is-emph.)
"Huh? It's size 11." (PL2)

- *-gō* is a counter suffix used broadly for designating numbers in a sequence, including such things as issues of newspapers or magazines, flu viruses, train/bus numbers, and the sizes of certain things.

えっ!? 11号よ

ね 指（ゆび）サイズは いくつ？

いくら *ikura* = "how much?"

Ikura can ask "what quantity" or "how much?" for just about anything, but it most often means "How much does/did it cost?" *Ikura* can be either a noun or an adverb.

オバタリアンは すぐ値段を聞く

あら それ いくら？

244 The young woman in the middle is showing off her brand new jacket to the oohs and ahhs of her friends when this *obatarian* (fig. 133) comes along.

Obatarian: あら、　それ　いくら？
Ara, sore ikura?
(interj.)   that   how much
"Oh my, how much was that?" (PL2)

Narration: オバタリアン　は
Obatarian wa
middle-aged women   as for

すぐ　　値段　を　聞く。
sugu nedan o kiku.
right away   price   (obj.)   ask
***Obatarians* immediately ask the price.** (PL2)

- *ara* is an interjection used mainly by female speakers when suddenly recognizing or noticing something: "Oh!/Oh, my!/Hey!"
- in PL2 speech, *Ikura?* can be either "How much is it?" or "How much was it?" depending on the context. If she asked in a complete sentence here, she would use *datta* or *deshita* (the past forms of *da* and *desu*; see next chapter).
- the polite form of *kiku* is *kikimasu*; the verb can mean either "hear/listen to" or "ask [a question]" depending on the context. Here it's the latter.

だれ *dare* = "who?"

The standard word for "who?" is *dare*, which is a noun. *Donata* is used by both genders in very polite speech, and *doitsu* is used by men in very informal speech (fig. 150).

As this example illustrates, a query containing a question word can end with the explanatory *n da/desu* or *na n da/desu*, without the question particle *ka*. And as with *da/desu* questions (fig. 240), using the PL2 ~ *(na) n da?* to ask something is mostly masculine (in PL2 speech, female speakers would more likely say ~ *[na] no?*), while using the PL3 ~ *(na) n desu?* is mostly feminine (in PL3 speech, male speakers would generally say ~ *[na] n desu ka?*).

245 Shima gets transferred to the Philippines for offending the wife of Hatsushiba President Ōizumi Yūsuke. Upon arrival, he learns that Hatsushiba Japan has only a minority position in Hatsushiba Philippines, Inc. He's curious who the Philippine owner of the company is.

Shima: オーナー は 誰 なんだ?
Ōnā   wa   dare   na n da?
owner   as for who   is-(explan.)
"As for the owner, who is it?"
"Who's the owner?" (PL2)

- *ōnā* is from the English word "owner."
- a female speaker would more likely say *Ōnā wa dare na n desu?* or use the more complete form *Ōnā wa dare na n desu ka?*
- if it did not follow another question word, なんだ *na n da* might look/sound like the question *Nan da?*—that is, the contraction of *nani* ("what") + *da* seen in fig. 240, meaning "What is it?" But the question *Nan da?* never directly follows another question word or noun, so you generally should have no trouble distinguishing it from the explanatory ~ *na n da?* after a question word—as here. When the explanatory extension follows *nani*, the question becomes なんなんだ *Nan na n da?*—which is easier to understand at a glance if it's written with kanji: 何なんだ?

いつ *itsu* = "when?"

The word for "when?" is *itsu*. It can also be an adverb, but in this example it is functioning as a noun.

246 Sayuri thinks she is pregnant, so she goes to the doctor for a pregnancy test.

Doctor: 前の 生理 は いつ でした か?
Mae no seiri   wa itsu deshita ka?
previous period as for when was (?)
"When was your last period?" (PL3)

Sayuri: えーっと...
Ē   tto
umm   (quote)
"Umm..."

- in speaking of time, *mae* = "before," and *mae no* = "previous." In speaking of physical space, *mae* means "(in) front (of)."
- *seiri* is the common term for "menstrual period." The more technical term is 月経 *gekkei*.
- *deshita* is the PL3 past form of *da/desu* ("is/are").
- *ē tto* is a verbal pause that implies, "Umm, let me think..."

なぜ *naze* = "why?"

The word for "why?" is *naze*, which mostly occurs as an adverb—though it can also be used like a noun with *da/desu*.

247 Veterinarian and fugitive Richard Kimbley is looking for the buck-toothed man who was seen leaving the scene of the murder for which Kimbley has been wrongfully convicted. One day he recognizes the man singing at a karaoke contest in San Francisco, but by the time Kimbley reaches the stage the buck-toothed man is already off and running.

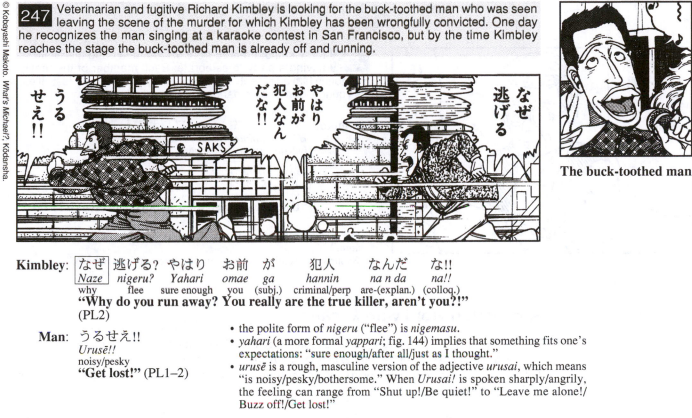

The buck-toothed man

Kimbley: なぜ 逃げる? やはり お前 が 犯人 なんだ な!!
Naze nigeru? Yahari omae ga hannin na n da na!!
why　flee　sure enough　you　(subj.)　criminal/perp　are-(explan.)　(colloq.)
"Why do you run away? You really are the true killer, aren't you?!"
(PL2)

Man: うるせえ!!
Urusē!!
noisy/pesky
"Get lost!" (PL1–2)

- the polite form of *nigeru* ("flee") is *nigemasu*.
- *yahari* (a more formal *yappari*; fig. 144) implies that something fits one's expectations: "sure enough/after all/just as I thought."
- *urusē* is a rough, masculine version of the adjective *urusai*, which means "is noisy/pesky/bothersome." When *Urusai!* is spoken sharply/angrily, the feeling can range from "Shut up!/Be quiet!" to "Leave me alone!/Buzz off!/Get lost!"

どうして *dōshite* and なんで *nande* also mean "why?"

Dōshite is a less formal *naze*—though it can still be used at all politeness levels; *nande*, another synonym, is quite informal and can only be used in PL1 and PL2 speech.

Proprietor

248 When Natsuko says she probably won't be coming again, the proprietor of a pub specializing in regional saké labels from around Japan asks why.

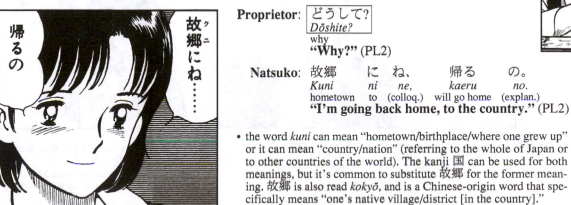

Proprietor: どうして?
Dōshite?
why
"Why?" (PL2)

Natsuko: 故郷 に ね、 帰る の。
Kuni ni ne, kaeru no.
hometown　to　(colloq.)　will go home　(explan.)
"I'm going back home, to the country." (PL2)

- the word *kuni* can mean "hometown/birthplace/where one grew up" or it can mean "country/nation" (referring to the whole of Japan or to other countries of the world). The kanji 国 can be used for both meanings, but it's common to substitute 故郷 for the former meaning. 故郷 is also read *kokyō*, and is a Chinese-origin word that specifically means "one's native village/district [in the country]."
- using *ne* in the middle of a sentence is a kind of verbal pause, somewhat similar to the use of words like "you know/you see/I mean/like" in English.

A question word with *ka na*

Asking a question with *ka na* has the feeling of a guess, and without a question word it is like "I wonder if it ～?" or "Is/does it perhaps ～?" With a question word it becomes "I wonder what/who/when/how ～?" In both cases, it is mostly informal and can be considered somewhat masculine. As with *kashira* below, the question word can come anywhere in the sentence—not only right before *ka na,* as in this example.

249 Mr. Okamoto retired from his job today and his family is having a party to celebrate. Each member of the family has gotten him a present, and after a toast to kick off the festivities, his younger son Saburō hands him his first gift to open.

Okamoto: ほう、 三郎 の プレゼント は
Hō, Saburō no purezento wa
(interj.) (name) 's/from present as for

なに かな?
nani ka na?
what I wonder
"Hmm, I wonder what Saburō's present is?" (PL2)

- *hō* is an interjection that shows interest or mild surprise, like "well, well/hmm."
- "Saburō's present" in this case means "present from Saburō."

A question word with *kashira*

As you saw when simple yes-or-no questions were introduced in Lesson 4, the feminine equivalent of *ka na* is *kashira.* Here is an example of *kashira* used with a question word; in this particular case the question word appears at the beginning of the sentence as the subject rather than right before *kashira.*

250 Conventional farmer Yoshida says it's only natural for farmers to conduct themselves as businessmen and seek the greatest personal financial gain; organic farmer Gōda insists that farmers should concern themselves above all with the careful stewardship of nature and the food supply, and do so in a spirit of cooperation and sharing, without regard for profits. In spite of her own idealism, Gōda's view seems so far removed from the realities of modern farm life that Natsuko is left wondering as she and Kusakabe make their way home.

Natsuko: どちら が 真実 かしら?
Dochira ga shinjitsu kashira?
which (subj.) truth I wonder
"I wonder which is the truth?" (PL2)

Kusakabe: 豪田さん です。
Gōda-san desu.
(name-pol.) is
"It is Mr. Gōda."
"It is Mr. Gōda's view." (PL3)

- *dochira* asks "which [of two alternatives]?" See fig. 152.
- her question could instead have been phrased *Shinjitsu wa dochira kashira?*

Question words + *-ka*

A question word followed immediately by *ka*, especially if it's not at the end of the sentence, is usually a compound word rather than a question. The resulting word refers to an indefinite person, place, thing, number, amount, time: "something/someone/sometime/etc."

251 This OL has learned during a doctor's visit that she has Type A blood instead of Type B—which surprises her because she has always thought of herself as a Type B personality. When the doctor confirms that Type A is correct, she seems to immediately take on a little of the Type A personality, which includes being a compulsive worrier.

OL: あの、 | 何か | 気をつける ことって
  Ano, *nani-ka* *ki o tsukeru* *koto* *tte*
  (interj.) something be careful/concerned thing as for
  "Umm, as for something to be concerned about

あります?
arimasu?
exists
"does it exist?"
"Umm, is there anything I needed to be concerned about?" (PL3)

Doctor: べつに。
  Betsu-ni.
  not particularly
  "Not really." (PL2)

- *ano* is a hesitation word similar to "uhh/um."
- *nani* = "what" and *nani-ka* = "something."
- *ki* means "mind/heart/spirit," and *tsukeru/tsukemasu* means "attach": to attach one's mind to something is to "be careful/concerned" about it. The complete sentence *nani-ka ki o tsukeru* ("be careful about something") modifies *koto* ("thing") → "something to be careful about."
- *tte* = *wa* ("as for"; see fig. 216), and *arimasu* is the polite form of *aru* ("exists"), here spoken with the rising intonation of a question.
- *betsu-ni* normally combines with a negative later in the sentence to mean "not particularly." Here, *betsu-ni* by itself implies the negative.

252 A ship transporting plutonium from France to Japan has been taken over by terrorists, but a counterterror agent remains in hiding on board. He is spied from the bridge as he moves into action.

Terrorist:
おい! | 誰か | いる ぞ!!
Oi! *Dare-ka* *iru* *zo!!*
hey someone exists/is there (emph.)
"Hey! Someone is there!"
"Hey! There's someone out there!" (PL2)

- *dare* = "who" and *dare-ka* = "someone."

Some common question-word + *ka* forms

なに *nani* what	なにか *nani-ka* something	どこ *doko* where	どこか *doko-ka* somewhere	いくつ *ikutsu* how many	いくつか *ikutsu-ka* some number/a certain number/several
だれ *dare* who	だれか *dare-ka* someone	どう *dō* how	どうか *dō-ka* somehow	どちら/どっち *dochira/dotchi* which direction/which side/which [of 2]	どちらか/どっちか *dochira-ka/dotchi-ka* some direction/somewhere/one or the other [of 2]
いつ *itsu* when	いつか *itsu-ka* sometime/someday	いくら *ikura* how much	いくらか *ikura-ka* some amount/a certain amount/to some degree	どれ *dore* which [of 3 or more]	どれか *dore-ka* some item/one or another [of 3 or more]
なぜ *naze* why	なぜか *naze-ka* for some reason				

"Or something/someone/somewhere"

A noun + *ka nani-ka* means "〜 or something." Similarly, 〜 *ka dare-ka* means "〜 or someone," and 〜 *ka doko-ka* means "〜 or somewhere." *Nani*, *dare*, and *doko* are the three question words that occur most commonly in this pattern, but some of the others can occur as well, in the right context. One important note: 〜 *ka dō-ka* after a verb or verb-type sentence looks similar but has a completely different meaning: "whether or not 〜" (fig. 197).

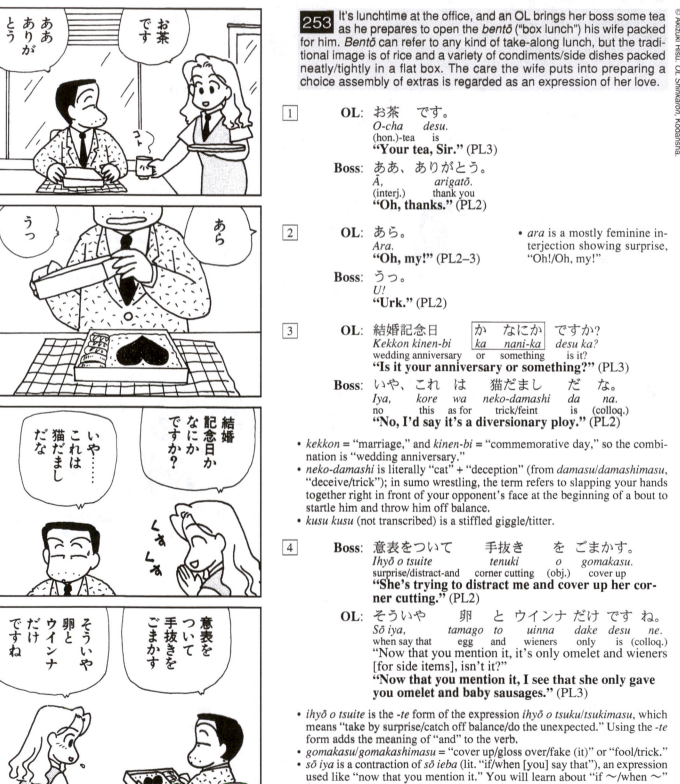

253 It's lunchtime at the office, and an OL brings her boss some tea as he prepares to open the *bentō* ("box lunch") his wife packed for him. *Bentō* can refer to any kind of take-along lunch, but the traditional image is of rice and a variety of condiments/side dishes packed neatly/tightly in a flat box. The care the wife puts into preparing a choice assembly of extras is regarded as an expression of her love.

1　OL:　お茶　です。
O-cha　desu.
(hon.)-tea　is
"Your tea, Sir." (PL3)

Boss:　ああ、ありがとう。
Ā,　arigatō.
(interj.)　thank you
"Oh, thanks." (PL2)

2　OL:　あら。
Ara.
"Oh, my!" (PL2–3)

• *ara* is a mostly feminine interjection showing surprise, "Oh!/Oh, my!"

Boss:　うっ。
U!
"Urk." (PL2)

3　OL:　結婚記念日　か　なにか　ですか?
Kekkon kinen-bi　ka　nani-ka　desu ka?
wedding anniversary　or　something　is it?
"Is it your anniversary or something?" (PL3)

Boss:　いや、これ　は　猫だまし　だ　な。
Iya,　kore　wa　neko-damashi　da　na.
no　this　as for　trick/feint　is　(colloq.)
"No, I'd say it's a diversionary ploy." (PL2)

• *kekkon* = "marriage," and *kinen-bi* = "commemorative day," so the combination is "wedding anniversary."
• *neko-damashi* is literally "cat" + "deception" (from *damasu/damashimasu*, "deceive/trick"); in sumo wrestling, the term refers to slapping your hands together right in front of your opponent's face at the beginning of a bout to startle him and throw him off balance.
• *kusu kusu* (not transcribed) is a stiffled giggle/titter.

4　Boss:　意表をついて　手抜き　を　ごまかす。
Ihyō o tsuite　tenuki　o　gomakasu.
surprise/distract-and　corner cutting　(obj.)　cover up
"She's trying to distract me and cover up her corner cutting." (PL2)

OL:　そういや　卵　と　ウインナ　だけ　です　ね。
Sō iya,　tamago to　uinna　dake desu　ne.
when say that　egg　and　wieners　only　is　(colloq.)
"Now that you mention it, it's only omelet and wieners [for side items], isn't it?"
"Now that you mention it, I see that she only gave you omelet and baby sausages." (PL3)

• *ihyō o tsuite* is the -te form of the expression *ihyō o tsuku/tsukimasu*, which means "take by surprise/catch off balance/do the unexpected." Using the -te form adds the meaning of "and" to the verb.
• *gomakasu/gomakashimasu* = "cover up/gloss over/fake (it)" or "fool/trick."
• *sō iya* is a contraction of *sō ieba* (lit. "if/when [you] say that"), an expression used like "now that you mention it." You will learn about "if 〜/when 〜" forms in Lesson 24.

An indirect question

A complete PL2 question containing a question word and ending in *ka* can be followed by another verb, embedding the question in a larger sentence. If the embedded question is a noun-type sentence, it can end in either noun + *ka* or noun + *da ka* (but don't forget that in independent PL2 questions, *ka* always replaces *da*, never follows it; see fig. 40).

In the example here, the larger sentence is also a question, but it does not have to be. The larger sentence cannot end with just any verb, of course, since it must have something to do with asking the question or giving/knowing/pondering/learning/deciding the answer. Some commonly used verbs are *kiku* ("ask"), *iu* ("say"), *wakaru* ("understand"), *kangaeru/kangaemasu* ("think about"), *shiraberu/shirabemasu* ("investigate"), and *kimeru/kimemasu* ("decide").

254 Some of Saeki Natsuko's idealism has rubbed off on neighboring brewery heir Kuroiwa Shingo (fig. 145), who can't believe his ears when he learns of the tactics his father has been using to persuade retailers to stock the Kuroiwa brand and stop carrying the Saeki brand. He confronts his father. His father responds by telling him how many breweries fail each year, and continues:

Father:
なぜ	潰れる	か	わかる	か?
Naze	*tsubureru*	*ka*	*wakaru*	*ka?*
why	fail	(?)	understand/know	(?)

"Do you know why they fail?" (PL2)

- *tsubureru/tsuburemasu* = "be crushed/collapse," or when speaking of a business, "fail/go bankrupt."
- *naze tsubureru ka?* asks "Why do they fail?"; *naze tsubureru ka wakaru* = "[I/you/he] understand(s) why they fail," and *naze tsubureru ka wakaru ka?* = "Do you understand/know why they fail?"

Summary: Question-word sentence structure

	plain (PL2)	plain (PL2)	polite (PL3)	polite (PL3)
	何? *Nani?* **What?/What is it?**	何だ?[1] *Nan da?* **What?/What is it?**	何です?[2] *Nan desu?* **What?/What is it?**	なんですか? *Nan desu ka?* **What?/What is it?**
	何なの? *Nan na no?* **What is it?**	何なんだ?[1] *Nan na n da?* **What is it?**	なんですの?[2] *Nan desu no?* **What is it?**	何なんですか? *Nan na n desu ka?* **What is it?**
		なにかな?[1]/何かしら?[2] *Nani ka na?/Nani kashira?* **I wonder what it is?**		何でしょうか? *Nan deshō ka?* **I wonder what it is?**

		plain (PL2)	plain-explan. (PL2)	polite (PL3)	polite-explan. (PL3)
qw as subject	verb-type sent.	だれが行く?[3] *Dare ga iku?* **Who will go?**	誰が行くの? *Dare ga iku no?* **Who will go?**	誰が行きますか? *Dare ga ikimasu ka?* **Who will go?**	誰が行くんですか? *Dare ga iku n desu ka?* **Who will go?**
	noun-type sent.	誰が先生(だ)?[4] *Dare ga sensei (da)?* **Who is the teacher?**	誰が先生なの? *Dare ga sensei na no?* **Who is the teacher?**	誰が先生ですか? *Dare ga sensei desu ka?* **Who is the teacher?**	誰が先生なんですか? *Dare ga sensei na n desu ka?* **Who is the teacher?**
	adj.-type sent.	誰がうまい?[3] *Dare ga umai?* **Who is skillful?**	誰がうまいの? *Dare ga umai no?* **Who is skillful?**	誰がうまいですか? *Dare ga umai desu ka?* **Who is skillful?**	誰がうまいんですか? *Dare ga umai n desu ka?* **Who is skillful?**

other	direct object	何を食べますか? *Nani o tabemasu ka?* **What will you eat?**	time phrase	いつ食べますか? *Itsu tabemasu ka?* **When will you eat?**	place phrase	どこで食べますか? *Doko de tabemasu ka?* **Where will you eat?**

multiple								
いつ	どこ	で	誰	が	何	を	食べます	か?
Itsu	*doko*	*de*	*dare*	*ga*	*nani*	*o*	*tabemasu*	*ka?*
when	where	at	who	(subj.)	what	(obj.)	will eat	(?)

Who will eat what, when, and where?
Who will eat what, at what time and place?

➡ The PL3 examples in this lesson all end with the question particle *ka*, while none of the PL2 examples do, and this is quite typical for questions that contain question words. When *ka* is used with a PL2 question containing a question word, it is usually an indirect question or a rhetorical one.

[1] Used mainly by males.

[2] Used mainly by females.

[3] Used by both sexes, but females tend to favor the PL2 explanatory pattern over the plain PL2.

[4] *Da* is used mainly by males.

Lesson 18

The Past Forms

Now that you know the basic building blocks for Japanese sentences and how they fit together, it's time to begin looking at the detail work. The rest of this book will focus primarily on the different forms that verbs, adjectives, and *desu* can take.

Lesson 3 already introduced the easiest of the verb transformations. There you learned that the polite past, negative, negative-past, and "let's/I'll ～" forms of a verb require only very simple changes to its *-masu* form, and that the rules for making the changes are the same for all verbs, including the two irregular ones. You also learned the simple transformations for the polite past and "maybe/probably/surely" forms of *desu*.

For each of the forms you encounter in the rest of this book, you will need to learn the differences for PL2 and PL3 speech. In the case of verbs, you will also need to learn distinct rules for converting Group 1 and Group 2 verbs, and memorize the two irregular verbs. Most of the rules about how the verb changes shape will be based not on the polite *-masu* form, as in Lesson 3, but on the dictionary form. Still, some of the verb transformations will be easier if you base them on the pre-*masu* stem of the verb (the part that comes before *-masu* in the polite form); and comparing the dictionary and polite forms of a verb will let you figure out its group as well—a key step, if you don't already know it. So the *-masu* form will remain very important in mastering the new forms.

This lesson introduces the rest of the past forms: all of the PL2 past forms, and the PL3 past form for adjectives. As you proceed, keep in mind that Japanese past is different from English past tense because it only implies completion of the action, not that the action necessarily took place in the past (see figs. 30–32).

PAW PAW "Meow" POKE POKE "Meow" POKE "Meow"

The past forms of *da/desu*

In Lesson 3 as well as a number of examples since (figs. 85, 162, 228, and others), you've seen that the past form of *desu* in polite, PL3 speech is でした *deshita*. In plain, PL2 speech, the equivalent of *desu* is *da* (figs. 8, 9, 17, and others), and the past form of *da* is だった *datta*.

255 Michael's owner Reiko has a tendency to oversleep, but the reader soon discovers that Michael and his hungry siblings have learned how to get her up.

Narration: この　　女　　は　　朝寝坊　だった。
Kono　onna　wa　asanebō　datta.
this　woman　as for　oversleeper　was
"This woman was an oversleeper."
"This woman tended to oversleep." (PL2)

• *asanebō* refers either to a person who tends to oversleep in the morning or to the act of oversleeping itself. *Asa-* ("morning") can be omitted, and the verb form is often just *nebō suru* ("oversleep/sleep in").

© Kobayashi Makoto. *What's Michael?,* Kodansha.

138

The past form of an adjective

The plain non-past form of an adjective (which is also the dictionary form), always ends in -い -i; the plain past form of an adjective is made by changing that final -i to -かった -katta.

Past adjectives occur more commonly at the end of a sentence than as modifiers. Adjectives used to modify nouns within the sentence typically remain non-past even when the end of the sentence is in past tense—unless there's a particular need to use past tense in describing the noun.

☞ The part of the adjective that doesn't change when making conversions like this is called the **adjective stem**: e.g., *atsu-* is the stem of *atsui*, and *oso-* is the stem of *osoi*.

256 On a hot summer day, Hiroko comes to visit Kōsuke at his apartment, bearing gifts of cold beer and potato chips.

Hiroko: こんにちは。
Konnichi wa.
(greeting)
"Hello." (PL2–3)

きょう　は　| 暑かった |　わね。
Kyō　wa　| atsukatta |　wa ne.
today　as for　was hot　(fem. colloq.)
"It was hot today, wasn't it?" (PL2)

- *konnichi wa* is the standard daytime (mostly afternoon) greeting, like "hello/good day/good afternoon."
- *atsukatta* is the past form of the adjective *atsui* ("is hot"; see fig. 15 for a note on kanji usage). She uses past tense because she is arriving quite late in the afternoon, after the worst of the heat is over.

© Maekawa Tsukasa, *Dai-Tōkyō Binbō Seikatsu Manyuaru*, Kōdansha.

For the polite past form of an adjective, add *desu*

When the situation calls for greater politeness, *desu* is added to the plain past form of the adjective: *atsukatta → atsukatta desu. Desu* is added only to sentence adjectives, never to an adjective being used as a modifier.

As with the *desu* used to make non-past adjectives more polite (fig. 12), this *desu* is strictly for politeness. Since the *-katta* form of an adjective already expresses past tense, there's no need to change *desu* to *deshita* when it follows *-katta.*

You may sometimes encounter the dictionary form of an adjective plus *deshita*—e.g., *atsui deshita*—as an alternative form for PL3 past adjectives, but this is not generally considered good usage. Be sure to learn and use the *-katta* form.

257 Some OLs called the noodle shop to have bowls of noodles delivered for their lunch, but the wait has been unusually long. When the delivery man finally arrives, one of the OLs remarks by way of complaint:

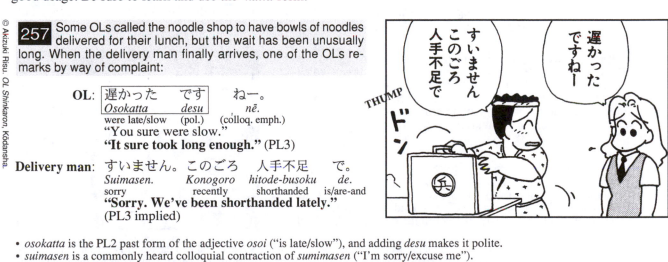

OL: | 遅かった |　です |　ねー。
| *Osokatta* |　*desu* |　*nē.*
were late/slow　(pol.)　(colloq. emph.)
"You sure were slow."
"It sure took long enough." (PL3)

Delivery man: すいません。このごろ　人手不足　で。
Suimasen.　Konogoro　hitode-busoku　de.
sorry　recently　shorthanded　is/are-and
"Sorry. We've been shorthanded lately."
(PL3 implied)

© Akizuki Risu. *OL Shinkaron*, Kōdansha.

- *osokatta* is the PL2 past form of the adjective *osoi* ("is late/slow"), and adding *desu* makes it polite.
- *suimasen* is a commonly heard colloquial contraction of *sumimasen* ("I'm sorry/excuse me").
- *hitode* is written with kanji meaning "person(s)" + "hand(s)" and refers to "worker(s)."
- *-busoku* is from *fusoku* ("insufficiency/shortage"; the *f* sound changes to *b* in combinations), so *hitode-busoku* = "worker shortage" → "shorthanded." *De* is the *-te* form of *desu* ("is/are"); using the *-te* form often adds the meaning of "and" to the verb, adjective, or *da/desu* (fig. 186); something to the effect of "and it's a real problem" is left unsaid.

きた *kita* = "came"

Japanese has only two irregular verbs: *kuru/kimasu*, "come," and s*uru/shimasu*, "do." That's pretty good news when you consider how much irregularity there is among English verbs. It's nice, too, that even these two verbs are completely regular in PL3 speech: you make their polite past forms exactly the same way as all other verbs—by changing the final *-masu* to *-mashita*. But when it comes to PL2 speech, there's just no getting around memorizing each of the forms individually.

The plain past form of 来る *kuru* ("come") is 来た *kita*. Note that even though the first syllable changes from く *ku* to き *ki*, the same character is used when writing in kanji; you must simply learn to pronounce it differently by recognizing the complete word.

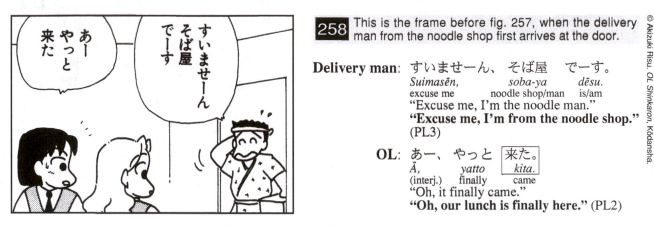

258 This is the frame before fig. 257, when the delivery man from the noodle shop first arrives at the door.

Delivery man: すいませーん、 そば屋　でーす。
Suimasēn,　soba-ya　dēsu.
excuse me　noodle shop/man　is/am
"Excuse me, I'm the noodle man."
"Excuse me, I'm from the noodle shop."
(PL3)

OL: あー、 やっと 来た。
Ā,　yatto　kita.
(interj.)　finally　came
"Oh, it finally came."
"Oh, our lunch is finally here." (PL2)

- *soba* = "buckwheat" or "buckwheat noodles," and the suffix *-ya* refers to a shop, eatery, or other small business. It can also refer to the individuals who run that business or work for it.
- *yatto* is an adverb meaning "finally/at long last."
- as in this example, *kita* ("came/has come") and its PL3 equivalent *kimashita* sometimes translate just as well (or better) as "～ is here."

した *shita* = "did"

The plain past form of する *suru* ("do") is した *shita*. In the example here, *suru* is used as an independent verb, but in Lesson 5 you saw how important this word is because of the way it combines with many nouns to turn them into verbs. In one sense, that means Japanese has countless irregular verbs. Fortunately, all it takes to master the transformations of those untold numbers is to learn the forms of the single verb *suru*.

259 While working in private industry prior to becoming a diet-man, Kaji sees some of his colleagues on break watching the news with great interest. According to the report, derogatory remarks made by Japan's minister of education while traveling in the American South are threatening to erupt into an international firestorm. Since he came in late, Kaji asks his colleagues for details.

Kaji:
どういう 内容 の 失言 を した んだ?
Dō iu　naiyō　no　shitsugen　o　shita　n da?
what kind of　content　(mod.)　slip of tongue　(obj.)　did/made　(explan.)
"He made a slip of the tongue of what kind of content?"
"Exactly what sort of slip of the tongue did he make?" (PL2)

- *shitsugen* is a noun for the act of sticking one's foot in one's mouth: "slip of the tongue/verbal lapse/misstatement." The word can also be used as a *suru* verb (*shitsugen suru*), but here it appears as the direct object of the independent verb *suru* (see fig. 131).
- *no* marks *dō iu naiyō* ("what kind of content") as a modifier for *shitsugen*. He could also have said more simply, *dō iu shitsugen* ("what kind of slip of the tongue"), but including *naiyō* focuses attention on the specific nature/content of the statement made.

The plain past form of Group 2 verbs: -る -ru → -た -ta

Don't worry, Group 1 verbs are next; it's just easier to start with Group 2. In their dictionary form, all Group 2 verbs end in -iru or -eru. But not all verbs ending in -iru and -eru are Group 2 verbs—for example, *kaeru* (fig. 4), *hashiru* (fig. 127), and *kajiru* (fig. 187) are all Group 1 verbs—so to make the proper transformations you either have to know which ones belong to Group 2 or have a way of figuring it out. More on that below.

To make the plain past form of a Group 2 verb, replace the final -る -ru of the dictionary form with -た -ta. Or if you're starting from the polite form, replace -ます -masu with -た -ta.

Some other Group 2 verbs you've already seen:

-ru	→	-ta	
dekiru		dekita	(fig. 45)
oriru		orita	(fig. 126)
iru		ita	(fig. 166)
kariru		karita	(fig. 169)
ikiru		ikita	(fig. 226)
ageru		ageta	(fig. 80)
nigeru		nigeta	(fig. 105)
deru		deta	(fig. 178)
tsukeru		tsuketa	(fig. 214)
kangaeru		kangaeta	(fig. 235)

260 Nat-chan says she dreamed that she was soaring high among the clouds and wishes she could really fly.

Grandma: あたしも 空とぶ 夢 みた よ。
Atashi mo sora tobu yume mita yo.
I/me too/also flying dream saw (emph.)
"I saw a flying dream, too."
"I dreamed of flying, too." (PL2)

Nat-chan: えっ? おばあちゃん もっ?
E? O-bāchan mo?
(interj.) (hon.)-grandma too/also
"Really? You did, too?" (PL2)

- *atashi* is a mostly feminine variation of *watashi* ("I/me").
- an *o* to mark *sora* ("sky") as the place across/through which a movement occurs (see fig. 127) has been omitted. *Tobu/tobimasu* can mean either "jump" or "fly," but specifying *sora* makes it unambiguously "fly." *Sora (o) tobu* is a complete sentence modifying *yume* ("dream") → lit. "an [I]-fly-through-the-sky dream."
- *mita* is the PL2 past form of *miru/mimasu* ("see/watch")—the final -る -ru of the dictionary form has changed to -た -ta. O to mark *yume* as the direct object of *mita* has been omitted. *Yume (o) miru* (lit. "see a dream") is the standard expression for "(to) dream/have a dream" in Japanese.

Identifying a verb's type

It's easy to figure out what group a verb belongs to so long as you've been learning the plain and polite forms of each verb together: simply compare the two forms to see which part of the final -ru in the dictionary form changes. If the full syllable -ru has disappeared before -masu, it's a Group 2 verb (e.g., *neru/nemasu* = "sleep"); if only the final -u has changed, it's a Group 1 verb (e.g., *neru/nerimasu* = "knead").

Since all Group 2 verbs end in either -iru or -eru, you only have to go through this comparison for verbs with those endings. All other endings automatically signal Group 1 verbs. The verb in fig. 260 ends in -iru; here's a Group 2 verb ending in -eru:

☛ With a Group 2 verb, the full final syllable -ru simply disappears when connecting to -masu to make the polite form. With a Group 1 verb, just the final -u changes to -i, which is then followed by -masu. But with the Hepburn romaji used in this book, it looks like the full final syllable changes for Group 1 verbs ending in -す -su and -つ -tsu. That's because the romanizations for the さ sa and た ta row kana are irregular (see Introduction), and not because those verbs are irregular.

261 New baby Tamami (fig. 131) is getting all of her parents' love. The cats have tried everything they can think of to win back the attention they used to get, but without success.

Michael: ま、 負けた。
Ma- maketa.
(stammer) lost/were defeated
"We lost."
"We've been defeated." (PL2)

- *maketa* is the PL2 past form of *makeru/makemasu* ("lose/be defeated"). Comparing the plain and polite forms shows that the full final syllable -ru disappears before -masu; this tells you it's a -ru verb, and you can make the PL2 past form by replacing the final -ru with -ta: *makeru → maketa*.

The plain past form of Group 1 verbs: -る -ru → -った -tta

The plain past form of a Group 1 verb depends on the last syllable of its dictionary form, so it's a little more complicated: five different endings for past tense replace nine different dictionary-form endings. Even so, your task is a lot simpler than what English-as-a-second-language students have to go through with irregular verbs in English. Just memorize one model verb for each ending—you can use the ones given in the summary table at the end of this chapter, on p. 147—and you will know how to transform every other verb with that ending. Still looking for better news? This is as hard as verb transformations get; it'll be all downhill from here.

To make the plain past form of a Group 1 verb whose dictionary form ends in -る -ru, replace -ru with -った -tta. Be sure not to miss that small *tsu*: the Group 2 verb *neru* ("sleep") becomes ねた *neta*, while the Group 1 verb *neru* ("knead") becomes ねった *netta*, so the small *tsu* makes a very big difference in the meaning.

262 At the vet, Michael climbs all over Reiko, trying to escape an injection. Finally he crawls under her blouse to hide, but that gives the exasperated Reiko a chance to restrain him, and the vet quickly gives the shot. Here, Reiko lets him know it's all over, and he dashes quickly into his carrying case.

Reiko: 終わった わよ、マイケル。 帰る わよ!!
Owatta   *wa yo,*   *Maikeru.*   *Kaeru*   *wa yo!!*
is finished (fem. emph.) (name) will go home (fem. emph.)
"It's finished, Michael. We're going home!"
"We're done, Michael. Time to go home!" (PL2)

FX: サァッ
Sā!   (effect of quick, deft movement)

- *owatta* is the plain past form of *owaru/owarimasu* ("[something] ends/finishes/is over"). The final syllable -る -ru of the dictionary form has changed to -った -tta in the plain past form. (You can tell *owaru* isn't a Group 2 verb even without comparing its two non-past forms because it doesn't end in either -iru or -eru.)
- the two sentence particles *wa yo* in combination give a distinctly feminine kind of emphasis that typically feels quite soft/gentle; but tone of voice can also make it quite sharp/firm, as in this case.

[caption, right margin, top comic:] © Kobayashi Makoto. *What's Michael?*, Kōdansha.

-う -u → -った -tta

To make the plain past form of a Group 1 verb whose dictionary form ends in an independent syllable -う -u, replace -u with -った -tta. Caution: When written in romaji, all verbs end in -u; the rule here applies only to verbs ending in -う, like 買う (*kau*, "buy") and 言う (*iu*, "say").

263 Toshihiko is practicing his ball handling in the street when Endō, the team manager, comes along. She asks if he's been practicing so much lately because the first string is scheduled to be announced the next day. Toshihiko says that's not it, and tells her about the player he met from Fujita East (fig. 181).

Toshihiko: こないだ すごい 奴 に 会った んだ。
Konaida   *sugoi*   *yatsu*   *ni*   *atta*   *n da.*
the other day amazing guy with/to met (explan.)
"I met this incredible guy the other day." (PL2)

- *konaida* is a contraction of *kono aida* ("the other day/some time ago/not long ago/recently").
- *yatsu* is an informal/slang word for "guy/fellow/person"; *ni* marks this as the person met.
- *atta* is the PL2 past form of 会う/会います *au/aimasu* ("meet/see [a person]"). The final syllable -う -u of the dictionary form has changed to -った -tta in the plain past form.

[caption, right margin, bottom comic:] © Ōshima Tsukasa. *Shoot!*, Kōdansha.

-つ -tsu → -った -tta

To make the plain past form of a Group 1 verb whose dictionary form ends in a large -つ -tsu, replace -tsu with -った -tta.

264 Two classes at Shin-chan's kindergarten are about to begin a softball game, and the captains are playing paper-scissors-rock to determine who will bat first. Even though he's not supposed to, Shin-chan joins in and declares himself the winner.

Captains: ジャンケンポイ。
Janken poi.

Shin-chan: ほい。
Hoi.
(interjection to go with sticking his hand out)

Shin-chan: わーい、 | 勝った、勝った！
Wāi, | *katta, katta!*
(exclam.) | won won
"Yippee! I won, I won!"
(PL2)

- *janken* is the name of the paper-scissors-rock game in Japan, and *janken poi* (or *pon*) is the standard formula chanted when playing the game—with all players sticking their hands out on *poi*.
- *katta* is the plain past form of *katsu*/*kachimasu* ("win"). The final syllable -つ -*tsu* (a large *tsu*) has changed to -った -*tta* (small *tsu* plus *ta*).

Some Group 1 verbs whose plain past forms end in -*tta*:

-ru	→ -tta	
kaeru	kaetta	(fig. 4)
okuru	okutta	(fig. 21)
wakaru	wakatta	(fig. 31)
aru	atta	(fig. 54)
mairu	maitta	(fig. 168)

-u	→ -tta	
iu	itta	(fig. 34)
kau	katta	(fig. 50)
omou	omotta	(fig. 156)
chigau	chigatta	(fig. 204)

-tsu	→ -tta	
tatsu	tatta	(fig. 52)
motsu	motta	(fig. 154)
yakudatsu	yakudatta	(fig. 212)

So three different non-past Group 1 verb endings get the same plain past ending, -*tta*. This means that if you encounter a verb for the first time in its plain past form and it ends in -*tta*, you have three possible endings to consider for its dictionary form: -*ru*, -*u*, and -*tsu*.

-ぶ -bu → -んだ -nda

To make the plain past form of a Group 1 verb whose dictionary form ends in -ぶ -*bu*, replace -*bu* with -んだ -*nda*.

265 Lemon Hart regular Megane (fig. 115) gave Kenji a paper airplane folded a special way to make it fly better. Kenji tries it out.

Kenji: わあー、 すごい！
Wā, *sugoi!*
(exclam.) is amazing/incredible
"Wow! Incredible!" (PL2)

飛んだ、飛んだ！
Tonda, tonda!
flew flew
"It flew, it flew!" (PL2)

- *tonda* is the plain past form of *tobu*/*tobimasu*, which means either "jump" or "fly." The final syllable -ぶ -*bu* of the dictionary form has changed to -んだ -*nda* in the plain past form. Repeating the verb here gives an emphatic/exclamatory feeling, implying "It really flew well/far!" so a looser translation in this context could be the exclamation, "Look how far it flew!" (In the context of airplanes, even paper ones, there's usually no need to specify *sora* with *tobu*; see fig. 260).

-む -mu → -んだ -nda

To make the plain past form of a Group 1 verb whose dictionary form ends in -む -mu, replace -mu with -んだ -nda. The past verb in this example is being used as a modifier; most forms of a verb can appear in a modifying position before a noun.

266 At the bar Lemon Hart, with Noboru waiting outside, Matsuda has enlisted the proprietor's help in persuading Noboru to go back to his secure job in the country (fig. 13). As he rises to call Noboru inside, Matsuda reminds the proprietor of his promise.

© Furuya Mitsutoshi, *Bar Remon Hāto*, Futabasha.

Matsuda: さっき 頼んだ こと、
Sakki   *tanonda*   *koto,*
a while ago   requested/asked   thing

お願い だ よ、 マスター。
onegai   *da*   *yo,*   *Masutā.*
request   is   (emph.)   master/proprietor
"The thing I requested a while ago, it's my request, Chief."
"Now Chief, about what I asked a while ago, I'm counting on you." (PL2)

- *tanonda* is the plain past form of *tanomu/tanomimasu* ("make a request/ask a favor"); the final syllable -む -mu of the dictionary form has changed to -んだ -nda in the plain past form.
- *sakki tanonda* is a complete sentence modifying *koto* ("thing") → "the thing/favor I asked of you a while ago."
- *onegai* is a noun that comes from the verb *negau/negaimasu* ("desire/wish for"), so *onegai da* is literally "It is my desire/wish"; it's often used for making requests/asking favors. Adding *yo* makes it feel more like "I'm counting on you."
- *masutā* is the katakana rendering of the English word "master"; it's commonly used as a title for owners/proprietors of Western-style eating and drinking establishments.

Some Group 1 verbs whose plain past forms end in *-nda*:

-bu	→	-nda	
erabu		eranda	(fig. 184)
oyobu		oyonda	(fig. 197)
yobu		yonda	(fig. 279)
asobu		asonda	(fig. 413)

-mu	→	-nda	
itamu		itanda	(fig. 143)
nomu		nonda	(fig. 149)
yasumu		yasunda	(fig. 201)
tanoshimu		tanoshinda	(fig. 222)

-nu	→	-nda	
shinu		shinda	
(category of one)			

-ぬ -nu → -んだ -nda

To make the plain past form of a Group 1 verb whose dictionary form ends in -ぬ -nu, replace -nu with -んだ -nda. Actually, in modern Japanese, this is a category of one: *shinu/shinimasu* ("die") is the only verb that ends in -nu: *shinu* → *shinda*.

267 When Natsuko phones home to tell her brother Yasuo that an ad she wrote will run in one of the national dailies (fig. 166), her mother answers with shocking news.

© Oze Akira, *Natsuko no Sake*, Kōdansha.

Mother: 夏子、 泰男 は 死んだ わ。
Natsuko,   *Yasuo*   *wa*   *shinda*   *wa.*
(name)   (name)   as for   died   (fem.)
"Natsuko, Yasuo has died." (PL2)

Natsuko: え?
E?
huh?/what?
"What?!" (PL2)

So three different non-past Group 1 verb endings get the same plain past ending, *-nda*. Since the last is a category of one, if you encounter a verb first in its plain past form and it ends in *-nda*, you only need to consider the other two possibilities for its dictionary form: *-bu* or *-mu*.

-す -su → -した -shita

To make the plain past form of a Group 1 verb whose dictionary form ends in -す -su, replace -su with -した -shita.

268 This man is having a very bad day. As his misfortunes continue and he wonders what happened to the good luck promised by the charm he bought, the gods look down on him, snickering that life's not that easy.

Man: あ、　　サイフ　落とした!
A,　saifu　otoshita!
(interj.) wallet/purse dropped/lost
"Oh no! I dropped my wallet!" (PL2)

定期　忘れた!
Teiki　wasureta!
pass　forgot
"I forgot my pass!" (PL2)

FX: ザバ
Zaba
Splash! (mud kicked up by passing car)

Arrow: ウンコ　を　ふんでいる。
Unko　o　funde iru.
poop (obj.) is stepping on
Stepping on doggie doo. (PL2)

• *otoshita* is the plain past form of *otosu/otoshimasu* ("drop [something]"); the final syllable -す -su of the dictionary form has changed to -した -shita in the plain past form. (The corresponding verb for "[something] drops" is *ochiru/ochimasu*.)
• the particle *o*, to mark *saifu* ("wallet/purse") as the item dropped, has been omitted.

Some Group 1 verbs whose plain past forms end in -shita, -ita, and -ida:

-su	→	-shita	
dasu		dashita	(fig. 125)
kaesu		kaeshita	(fig. 192)
mōsu		mōshita	(fig. 209)
sasu		sashita	(fig. 210)

-ku	→	-ita	
itadaku		itadaita	(fig. 5)
kaku		kaita	(fig. 124)
ochitsuku		ochitsuita	(fig. 354)
oku		oita	(fig. 469)

-gu	→	-ida	
sawagu		sawaida	(fig. 188)
fusegu		fuseida	(fig. 300)
isogu		isoida	(fig. 328)
yusugu		yusuida	(fig. 409)

• *teiki* can refer to any kind of commuter pass—for bus, train, ferry, etc.
• *wasureta* is the plain past form of the Group 2 verb *wasureru/wasuremasu* ("forget"). *O*, to mark *teiki* as the item forgotten, has again been omitted.
• *unko* is a baby-talk word for "poop/doo-doo," but it's widely used by/with all ages; a clinical/adult equivalent is *daiben*, which is more like "excrement/feces/stool." *Funde iru* is from the verb *fumu/fumimasu* ("step on"); you'll learn about the *-te iru/-de iru* form of a verb in the next lesson.

-く -ku → -いた -ita

To make the plain past form of a Group 1 verb whose dictionary form ends in -く -ku, replace -ku with -いた -ita. The example below illustrates this rule, and the next one shows the single exception.

269 When one of the "Hatsushiba Ladies" who used to be under Shima's direction tells him that their new boss fired one of their colleagues for refusing his sexual advances, Shima asks who she heard it from. The woman's response is shown in fig. 176.

Shima: それ　は　誰　から　聞いた　話　だ?
Sore　wa　dare　kara　kiita　hanashi　da?
that as for who from heard story is
"As for that, it is a [you]-heard-[it]-from-whom story?"
"Who did you hear that from?" (PL2)

• *kiita* is the plain past form of *kiku/kikimasu* ("hear/listen"). In this case, changing the final syllable -く -ku of the dictionary form to -いた -ita results in a long vowel, *ii*, but that occurs only when the syllable before *ku* ends in *-i*. For what happens in other cases, see the verbs shown to the right.
• *dare kara kiita* ("[you] heard [it] from whom?") is a complete sentence modifying *hanashi* ("story") → "a story that you heard from whom?" The stripped-down sentence is *Sore wa...hanashi da* ("That is a story"); the question word *dare* ("who/whom") in the sentence modifier turns the overall sentence into a question ("That is a story that you heard from whom?").

One exception: いく *iku* → いった *itta*

There's just one very important exception among Group 1 verbs ending in -*ku*: the verb 行く *iku* ("go") becomes 行った *itta* ("went"). *Iku* is otherwise an entirely regular Group 1 verb.

270 Tanaka-kun is away from his desk, and his boss has a pretty good idea where he's gone.

Boss: あいつめ。
Aitsu-me.
that guy/fellow-(derog.)
"That twit." (PL1)

また パチンコ に 行った な?
Mata pachinko ni itta na?
again　pinball　to　went　(colloq.)
"He went to *pachinko* again, didn't he?"
"I bet he went to play *pachinko* again." (PL2)

DING! CLATTER CLATTER

- *aitsu* is from *ano yatsu*, a rough way of saying "that guy/fellow"; -*me* after a word referring to a person shows contempt or derision, so *aitsu-me* is like "that twit/jerk/idiot."
- *pachinko* is the name of Japan's most popular form of legalized gambling, a kind of pinball played on upright machines. The player buys some 11-mm diameter steel balls to get started, feeds them into a machine that feels lucky to him, and starts propelling them to the top of the machine to try to get them to drop into winning slots on their way down; each hit makes the machine discharge more balls. The objective is to amass large quantities of the balls to trade in for prizes ranging from food and cigarettes to household goods, fashion accessories, and more.
- *ni* here can be thought of as indicating either destination or purpose.
- when making an observation/drawing a conclusion like this, *na* can give the feeling of a guess, like "That must be it" or "I'll bet that's it."

-ぐ *-gu* → -いだ *-ida*

To make the plain past form of a Group 1 verb whose dictionary form ends in -ぐ *-gu*, replace -*gu* with -いだ *-ida*.

DIT!

CLAP CLAP CLAP CLAP CLAP

271 Michael and companion are channel surfing on a TV set that can receive feline signing in a corner of the screen. They happen upon a singing show featuring an *aidoru kashu* ("teen idol singer").

Singer: 季節はずれ　の　湘南　で、ラララ、
Kisetsu-hazure no Shōnan de, ra ra ra,
off-season　(mod.)　(place name)　at/in　la la la
"In off-season Shōnan, la la la,

泳いだ もん だ からー...
oyoida mon da karā...
swam　thing　is　because
"because I swam..."
"Because I went swimming, la la la, when it was out of season in Shōnan..." (PL2)

- *kisetsu* = "season" and *hazure* is the stem of *hazureru* ("be/go off the mark"), so *kisetsu-hazure* makes a noun for "off-season."
- *oyoida* is the plain past form of *oyogu/oyogimasu* ("swim"); the final syllable -ぐ *-gu* of the dictionary form has changed to -いだ *-ida* in the plain past form.
- *mon* is a contraction of *mono* ("thing"), which here is part of an explanatory form: ～ *mon(o) da kara* as a whole is best thought of simply as meaning "because ～" (strictly speaking, *mon* is being modified by the complete sentence that ends with the verb *oyoida*).
- the overall sentence is incomplete in this panel; it continues in the next line of the song to reveal, predictably, that she caught a nasty cold.

Summary: Past forms

In each case, the non-past form is on top and the past form underneath it. For *da/desu*, simply memorize the plain and polite past forms. For all adjectives, the plain past form is the adjective stem plus *-katta*; adding *desu* to this makes the polite past form.

For all verbs, the polite past form is the pre-*masu* stem plus *-mashita*. The plain past form depends on the group: for the irregular verbs, simply memorize each form; for Group 2 verbs, replace the final *-ru* of the dictionary form with *-ta*; for Group 1, nine dictionary-form endings become five plain-past endings, so you need to memorize one of each as a model. To determine a verb's group, compare the end of its dictionary form with its *-masu* form (*-u* → *-imasu* = Group 1; *-ru* → *-masu* = Group 2), or look it up in a learner's dictionary (see Appendix A.4).

☛ If you have only the *-masu* form to start with, the dictionary form will be either the pre-*masu* stem plus *-ru*, or the pre-*masu* stem with the final *-i* changed to *-u*. If you find both versions in a glossary or dictionary, you will need to rely on context in deciding which is the one you're looking for.

	plain form (PL2)		meaning	polite form (PL3)		pre-*masu* stem
desu	だ	*da*	am/is/are	です	*desu*	
	だった	*datta*	was/were	でした	*deshita*	
adj.	さむい	*samui*	is cold	さむいです	*samui desu*	
	さむかった	*samukatta*	was cold	さむかったです	*samukatta desu*	
irreg. verbs	くる	*kuru*	come	きます	*kimasu*	き-/ki-
	きた	*kita*	came	きました	*kimashita*	
	する	*suru*	do	します	*shimasu*	し-/shi-
	した	*shita*	did	しました	*shimashita*	
group 2 verbs	みる	*miru*	see	みます	*mimasu*	み-/mi-
	みた	*mita*	saw	みました	*mimashita*	
	たべる	*taberu*	eat	たべます	*tabemasu*	たべ-/tabe-
	たべた	*tabeta*	ate	たべました	*tabemashita*	
group 1 verbs	とる	*toru*	take	とります	*torimasu*	とり-/tori-
	とった	*totta*	took	とりました	*torimashita*	
	かう	*kau*	buy	かいます	*kaimasu*	かい-/kai-
	かった	*katta*	bought	かいました	*kaimashita*	
	もつ	*motsu*[1]	hold	もちます	*mochimasu*[1]	もち-/mochi-
	もった	*motta*	held	もちました	*mochimashita*	
	よぶ	*yobu*	call	よびます	*yobimasu*	よび-/yobi-
	よんだ	*yonda*	called	よびました	*yobimashita*	
	のむ	*nomu*	drink	のみます	*nomimasu*	のみ-/nomi-
	のんだ	*nonda*	drank	のみました	*nomimashita*	
	しぬ	*shinu*	die	しにます	*shinimasu*	しに-/shini-
	しんだ	*shinda*	died	しにました	*shinimashita*	
	おとす	*otosu*[1]	drop	おとします	*otoshimasu*[1]	おとし-/otoshi-
	おとした	*otoshita*	dropped	おとしました	*otoshimashita*	
	かく	*kaku*[2]	write	かきます	*kakimasu*	かき-/kaki-
	かいた	*kaita*[2]	wrote	かきました	*kakimashita*	
	およぐ	*oyogu*	swim	およぎます	*oyogimasu*	およぎ-/oyogi-
	およいだ	*oyoida*	swam	およぎました	*oyogimashita*	

[1] For Group 1 conversions in romaji, in *t* row syllables, *t* = *ch* = *ts*, and in *s* row syllables, *s* = *sh*. See Introduction.

[2] One exception for Group 1 verbs ending in *-ku*: 行く *iku* ("come") → 行った *itta* ("came")

Lesson 19

The -て -*Te* Form

The -て -*te* form appeared briefly in Lesson 14 as an equivalent to "and." This lesson looks at some of its other uses, and still more will come in Lessons 25 and 31.

The -*te* form of a verb is a snap once you know the plain past past form: just change the final vowel sound of the plain past form from -*a* to -*e*. This means -た -*ta* becomes -て -*te* and -だ -*da* becomes -で -*de*; everything before -*te*/-*de* remains exactly the same as in the plain past form, so -った -*tta* becomes -って -*tte*, -んだ -*nda* becomes -んで, and so forth.

The -*te* form of an adjective is every bit as easy: just add -*te* to the -*ku* form introduced in Lesson 6: -く -*ku* → -くて -*kute*. And the -*te* form of *da/desu* is simply で *de*.

Though you will occasionally come across *deshite* or *de gozaimashite* as the -*te* form of *desu* in very formal PL3 and PL4 speech, -*te* forms otherwise remain unchanged across politeness levels.

☞ If you happen to encounter a verb first in its -*te* form, simply reverse the process described here to find its plain past form.

Manner

Using a -*te* form verb can mean that that verb (or the sentence it completes) describes the manner in which the following was done/is being done/will be done. A -*te* form does not have any tense of its own, so tense is determined by other elements in the sentence.

272 Electoral districts have been re-shaped, altering the political landscape for many. Party Chairman Uzugami has just told Kaji who his opponent will be in the next election.

Kaji: はい!
Hai!
yes

全力 を つくして 闘います!
Zenryoku o | *tsukushite* | *tatakaimasu!*
all strength (obj.) exhaust-(manner) will fight
"Yes, sir! I will fight with every ounce of strength I have!" (PL3)

- *zenryoku o tsukusu/tsukushimasu* means "exhaust one's strength [towards achieving a goal]." The plain past form of the Group 1 verb *tsukusu* is *tsukushita*, so its -*te* form is *tsukushite* (the final vowel changes from -*a* to -*e*).
- the plain form of *tatakaimasu* ("fight") is *tatakau*. Its plain past form is *tatakatta*, so its -*te* form is *tatakatte*.

Sequence

Using a -*te* form verb often implies a chronological sequence: what precedes the -*te* form takes place first, and what follows the -*te* form takes place next.

273 One day in the park, Shin-chan overhears a man reviewing the plans he has made for a hot date. Just as the man begins to fantasize what might happen after a movie and a fancy Italian dinner, Shin-chan butts in.

Shin-chan: はみがきして ねる。
Hamigaki shite | *neru.*
brush teeth-and go to bed
"Brush your teeth and go to bed." (PL2)

- *hamigaki shite* is from *hamigaki (o) suru/shimasu*, "brush teeth." As a *suru* verb, its plain past form is *shita*, so its -*te* form is *shite*. Another way to say "brush teeth" is *ha o migaku/migaki-masu* ("teeth" + object marker + "polish/clean"); the plain past form of *migaku* is *migaita*, and its -*te* form is *migaite*, so another way to say "Brush your teeth and go to bed" is *Ha o migaite neru* (PL2).

Cause/reason

A -te form can imply that the preceding states the cause or reason for what follows. In colloquial speech it's not unusual for the parts of the sentence to be turned around, in which case the cause/reason is stated second; but this should not create confusion so long as you remember that the part ending in the -te form states the cause or reason.

In English, cause-effect relationships are sometimes stated explicitly by using connecting words like "because," "since," and "so"; other times the cause-effect relationship is shown more loosely by linking sentences with a simple "and" or merely juxtaposing them without any special connecting word. Using a -te form to show cause and effect tends to feel more like the latter, while using *kara* or *node* (figs. 198, 200) feels more like the former—though it ultimately depends on the precise context.

274 Hiroko takes a sniff of the *hechima* water lotion Kōsuke gave her in fig. 237, then tries it out on her hands.

Hiroko: すべすべして 　気持ち　が　　いい。
Sube-sube shite 　　*kimochi*　*ga*　　*ii.*
feels smooth/slippery-(cause)　feeling　(subj.)　is good/nice
"It's slippery and [therefore] the feeling is good."
"It makes my skin smooth and feels nice." (PL2)

- *sube-sube shite* is the -te form of *sube-sube suru* ("be [or feel] smooth/slippery/velvety").
- *kimochi ga ii* is literally "the feeling is good/nice" → "feels good/nice."

The *-te* form of an adjective

Here's another example showing cause/reason, but this time with the -te form of an adjective. In Lesson 6 you learned the -ku form of an adjective as its adverb form; the -ku form plus -te gives you the -te form: *hayai* (adjective: "is quick/fast") → *hayaku* (adverb: "quickly/rapidly") → *hayakute* (-te form, various uses).

275 As autumn advances toward winter, the mornings are getting colder in Kōsuke's unheated apartment. A deep chill wakes him one morning, telling him it's about time to add a blanket, but he also finds the bracing air invigorating and decides to go for a walk.

Kōsuke (narrating):
息　が　白く　なる　の　が　うれしくて、
Iki　*ga*　*shiroku*　*naru*　*no*　*ga*　*ureshikute,*
breath　(subj.)　white　becomes　(noun)　(subj.)　was joyful/delightful-(cause)
My breath becoming white was delightful [to me], so

オレ　は　外　へ　出る　こと　に　した。
ore　*wa*　*soto*　*e*　*deru*　*koto*　*ni*　*shita.*
I/me　as for　outside　to　go out　thing/situation　to　made it
I decided to go outside.
I enjoyed seeing my breath turn white, so I decided to go outside. (PL2)

- *shiroku* is the adverb form of the adjective *shiroi* ("is white"), and *naru/narimasu* = "become"; *iki ga shiroku naru* is a complete embedded sentence ("my breath becomes white"), and *no* makes it act as a single noun (fig. 232); *ga* marks this noun as the subject of *ureshikute*.
- *ureshikute* is the -te form of the adjective *ureshii* ("is joyful/delightful/gratifying" or "be happy/pleased/delighted"). *Ureshii* belongs to the *wa-ga* group, so when the thing that brings joy/delight is mentioned, it is marked with *ga*.
- *e* marks *soto* ("outside") as the destination of *deru/demasu* ("go out/come out").
- *koto ni shita* is the plain/abrupt past form of *koto ni suru* (lit. "make it the thing/situation"), which after a verb or verb-type sentence means "decide to [do the described action]" → "I decided I would go outside." Structurally, *koto* is a noun modified by the complete sentence *ore wa soto e deru* ("I will go outside").

Requesting something politely

To politely ask for a material thing, you say the name of the item and add *kudasai* ("please give me"). Strictly speaking, the desired item should be marked with *o*, but in colloquial speech the *o* is often dropped. (Don't look for a *-te* form here; it's in the next example.)

276 When he gets outside on the chilly autumn morning (fig. 275), Kōsuke spies the milk truck coming a short distance behind the newspaper delivery boy. He raises his hand to stop the truck, and the milkman hops out.

Kōsuke: 牛乳　　2本　　ください。
Gyūnyū　nihon　　kudasai.
milk　　2 count　please give me
"I'd like 2 bottles of milk, please." (PL3)

Milkman: 2本?!
Nihon?!
2 count
"2 bottles?!" (PL2)

- *o*, to mark *gyūnyū* ("milk") as the direct object, has been omitted.
- *-hon* is the counter suffix for long slender things, including bottled drinks (see p. 47).

Requesting/urging an action politely

To politely ask or urge someone to *do* something, you state the action using the *-te* form of the verb and add *kudasai*: e.g., *tetsudau* = "help" → *Tetsudatte kudasai* = "Please help"; *kubaru* = "distribute/dole out" → *Kubatte kudasai* = "Please distribute."

277 Kaji's father, a highly respected Diet member from Kagoshima, is killed in an automobile accident. Kaji, who is still in private industry at this point, rushes home as his older brother, the driver of the ill-fated vehicle, continues to cling to life. His brother has been their father's right-hand man—expected ultimately to take over his seat in the Diet. But during the visitation for their father, Kaji is called away to his brother's bedside. As he reemerges from the ICU, his father's political aides want to know how his brother is faring.

Kaji: 死にました。　詳しい　こと　は
Shinimashita.　Kuwashii　koto　wa
died　　　　　detailed　things　as for
"He died. For further details,

先生　　から　きいて下さい。
sensei　kara　　kiite kudasai.
doctor　from　　ask/hear-(request)
"please ask the doctor."
"He died. Please get the details from the doctor." (PL3)

- *shinimashita* is the PL3 past form of *shinu/shinimasu* ("die").
- *kuwashii* is an adjective meaning "detailed/minute," and *kuwashii koto* is an expression for "the details" or "further information." *Wa* marks this as the topic of the sentence.
- *sensei*, already seen as the word for "teacher," is also used as a term of address or reference for a variety of people considered worthy of respect, including doctors, politicians, writers, artists, and musicians in addition to teachers. The actual word for "doctor" is 医者 *isha*, which is very frequently used in the form *o-isha-san* (with the honorific prefix *o-* and the polite suffix *-san*) when speaking of doctors, but usually gives way to *sensei* when directly addressing a doctor.
- *kiite* is the *-te* form of *kiku/kikimasu*, which can mean either "hear/listen" or "ask/inquire." Adding *kudasai* to the *-te* form makes a request: "please ask [the doctor]."

Requesting an action informally

In informal speech, the *-te* form of a verb by itself is often used to ask that the action be done. Depending on the context and tone of voice, the feeling can range from an informal but still relatively polite request to an urgent plea, a gentle command, or even a very abrupt demand.

278 When Hiroko is seeing Kōsuke home because he has had one too many, Kōsuke remembers that he came by bike (fig. 102). He manages to undo the chain lock, but then falls on his behind, so Hiroko decides he's in no condition to pedal and steer.

Hiroko:
あたし が こぐ ワ。
Atashi ga kogu wa.
I/me (subj.) will pedal (fem.)
"I'll pedal." (PL2)

しっかり つかまって。
Shikkari tsukamatte.
firmly hold onto-(request)
"Hold on tight." (PL2)

- *atashi* is a mostly feminine variation of *watashi* ("I/me").
- the polite form of *kogu* ("to pedal") is *kogimasu*.
- *tsukamatte* is the *-te* form of *tsukamaru/tsukamari-masu* ("grab/grasp/hold onto"; the plain past form is *tsukamatta*). The *-te* form makes an informal request or gentle command.

A relatively gentle command

A very common way for male speakers to ask for something to be done in PL2 speech is to use the *-te* form of a verb plus *kure*. This generally makes a relatively abrupt request or gentle command—though elongating the final vowel can also give it a pleading tone.

The *-te kure* combination sounds too abrupt for feminine speech, so female speakers tend to use just the *-te* form by itself, as seen above.

279 Suzuka Hiroshi is secretary-general of the ruling Democratic Harmony Party—a fictitious political party modeled on Japan's Liberal Democratic Party. His aide has just announced the return of the man they sent to America to obtain the secretly recorded tape of the education minister's remarks (fig. 259).

Suzuka: おう！ 呼んでくれ。
Ō! Yonde kure.
(exclam.) call-(command)
"All right! Call him in."
"All right! Tell him to come in."
(PL2)

- *ō* is an interjection/exclamation of approval/delight.
- *yonde* is the *-te* form of *yobu/yobimasu* ("call/summon"; the plain past form is *yonda*), and *kure* makes it a gentle command.

-ている -te iru = "is/are ～ing"

The -te form of a verb plus iru makes a two-verb combination that's often used to express an action in progress, like "am/is/are ～ing" in English.

You learned on p. 31 that iru means "exists/is here/is there" only when speaking of people or animals, and aru must be used instead when speaking of inanimate things. This limitation to animate things doesn't apply when iru is a helping verb after a -te form instead of a verb standing on its own: the -te iru combination is used to speak of an action associated with anything—animate or inanimate. (But be careful: this does not mean that iru and aru are interchangeable after a -te form; -te aru has an entirely different meaning, which you will learn in Lesson 25.)

280 Based on the Japanese folk belief that when you sneeze it means someone is talking about you somewhere, a bout of sneezing delights this woman. But she has actually been having an allergy attack.

私　　は　うわさ　の　女。
Watashi wa   uwasa   no   onna.
I/me　as for　talk/rumor　of　woman
"I am a woman being talked about."
"I'm on everybody's lips." (PL2)

世の中　　の　男　が　みんな
Yo no naka no otoko ga minna
the world　of　men　(subj.)　all
"The men of the world all

私　　の　こと　を　うわさしている　わ。
watashi no   koto   o   uwasa shite iru   wa.
I/me　of　things　(obj.)　are talking　(fem.)
"are talking about me."
"All the men in the world are talking about me." (PL2)

- uwasa is a noun for "gossip/rumor/common talk," and uwasa no ～ means "a/the ～ that everyone's talking about."
- ～ no koto is literally "things of/about ～," which typically can be reduced to just "about ～."
- uwasa shite iru ("are talking/gossiping") comes from the verb uwasa suru; the plain past form is uwasa shita, so the -te form is uwasa shite.
- ホホホ ho ho ho (sometimes オホホ o ho ho, without an h on the first syllable, as in this case) is most typically a demure, feminine laugh—nothing at all like the boisterous, Santa Claus laugh those syllables suggest in English. The laugh can also carry a smug, gleeful note, as here.

-ている -te iru contracts to -てる -teru

In colloquial speech, the i- in iru often gets dropped when following a -te form, leaving the contraction -teru. The meaning does not change.

281 When Ms. Yoshida sees Tanaka-kun busily writing in a notebook, she asks him what he's doing. He explains here. Ms. Yoshida's next response appears in fig. 229.

Tanaka: 日記　を　つけてる　んだ　よ。
Nikki o   tsuketeru   n da   yo.
diary (obj.) am entering/keeping (explan.) (emph.)
"I'm entering in my diary."
"I'm writing in my diary." (PL2)

- tsuketeru is a contraction of tsukete iru, from tsukeru/tsukemasu, which means "make an entry" when speaking of various kinds of records/documents. With a diary, the verb is used both to speak of making a particular entry, as here, and to speak more generally of "keeping a diary."

-*Te iru* acts like any individual verb

The *iru* in -*te iru* can occur in the various forms that *iru* takes as an independent verb. Using the plain past form of *iru* makes -*te ita*, meaning "was/were ～ing." In polite speech, you will hear -*te imasu* ("is/are ～ing") and -*te imashita* ("was/were ～ing"). The plain forms of -*te iru* can be used as modifiers (e.g., *mite iru hito* = "the person who is looking/watching"); as with all verbs, the polite forms are not usually used for modifying purposes.

In the same way as for the plain, non-past -*te iru*, the *i*- can be dropped from any of these other forms to make a contraction: the polite non-past -*te imasu* becomes -*temasu*, and the past forms -*te ita* and -*te imashita* similarly become -*teta* and -*temashita*.

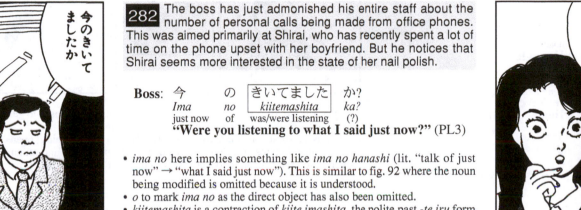

282 The boss has just admonished his entire staff about the number of personal calls being made from office phones. This was aimed primarily at Shirai, who has recently spent a lot of time on the phone upset with her boyfriend. But he notices that Shirai seems more interested in the state of her nail polish.

Boss: 今　　の　きいてました　か?
Ima　　no　kiitemashita　ka?
just now　of　was/were listening　(?)
"Were you listening to what I said just now?" (PL3)

- *ima no* here implies something like *ima no hanashi* (lit. "talk of just now" → "what I said just now"). This is similar to fig. 92 where the noun being modified is omitted because it is understood.
- *o* to mark *ima no* as the direct object has also been omitted.
- *kiitemashita* is a contraction of *kiite imashita*, the polite past -*te iru* form of *kiku*/*kikimasu* ("hear/listen") → "was/were listening."

Shirai: "Huhhh?"

-*Te iru* = "has/have done the action"

Besides being used to express an action in progress, the -*te iru* form can also mean "has/have done the action." For many verbs, the difference is a matter of context. For example, *kiite iru* can mean either "is/are listening [now]" or "has/have heard [before now]"; the past form *kiite ita* can be either "was/were listening [at a particular time]" or "had heard [before then].

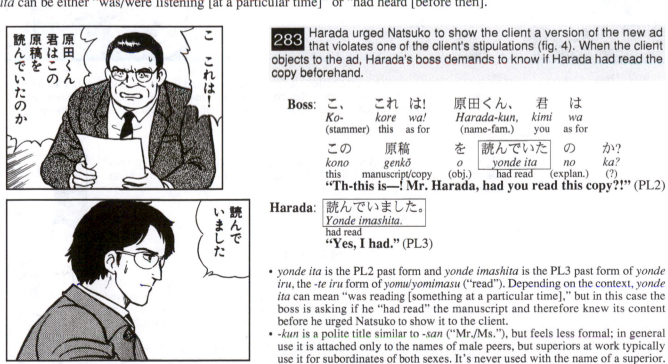

283 Harada urged Natsuko to show the client a version of the new ad that violates one of the client's stipulations (fig. 4). When the client objects to the ad, Harada's boss demands to know if Harada had read the copy beforehand.

Boss: こ、　これ　は!　原田くん、　君　は
Ko-　kore　wa!　Harada-kun,　kimi　wa
(stammer)　this　as for　(name-fam.)　you　as for

この　　原稿　　を　読んでいた　の　か?
kono　genkō　o　yonde ita　no　ka?
this　manuscript/copy　(obj.)　had read　(explan.)　(?)
"Th-this is—! Mr. Harada, had you read this copy?!" (PL2)

Harada: 読んでいました。
Yonde imashita.
had read
"Yes, I had." (PL3)

- *yonde ita* is the PL2 past form and *yonde imashita* is the PL3 past form of *yonde iru*, the -*te iru* form of *yomu*/*yomimasu* ("read"). Depending on the context, *yonde ita* can mean "was reading [something at a particular time]," but in this case the boss is asking if he "had read" the manuscript and therefore knew its content before he urged Natsuko to show it to the client.
- -*kun* is a polite title similar to -*san* ("Mr./Ms."), but feels less formal; in general use it is attached only to the names of male peers, but superiors at work typically use it for subordinates of both sexes. It's never used with the name of a superior.

-Te iru and momentary verbs

In effect, the use of *iru* ("exists") as a helping verb implies either that the action of the *-te* form verb "exists" (i.e., continues in progress: "is/are 〜ing") or that the result of its action "exists" (i.e., the action has resulted in a change of state that persists: "has/have 〜"). With certain verbs, especially those that represent momentary actions like those seen on this page, the English equivalent may need to vary ("is/are 〜" or ordinary present/past tense, etc.).

284 The morning Noboru arrives from Kyushu wanting to seek his fortune in Tokyo (fig.13), Matsuda is still in bed.

Matsuda: ウーン。
Ūn.
(moan)
"**Unnngh.**"

Noboru: ごめんください。
Gomen kudasai.
(greeting)
"**Hello.**" (PL3)

Matsuda: ハーイ、ドア 開いてる よ。
Hāi, doa aiteru yo.
yes door is open (emph.)
"**Ye-e-es, the door is open.**" (PL2)

• *gomen kudasai* (lit. "pardon please") is the traditional phrase used to get a home occupant's or shopkeeper's attention when arriving.
• *aiteru* is a contraction of *aite iru*, from *aku/akimasu* ("[something] opens"). The *-te iru* form implies "the door has opened/has been opened and remains in an open state" → "is open/unlocked"; this form is not used to mean "is opening."

285 Shima and Hatsushiba Electric's racing team manager Ono are relaxing at a bar after a test run at the track and discussing their chances of victory, when rival Solar Electric's driver Inagaki sits down.

Ono

Inagaki:
あ、 小野さん、 来てた んです か?
A, Ono-san, kiteta n desu ka?
(interj.) (name-pol.) had come (explan.) (?)
"**Oh, Mr. Ono. You were here?**" (PL3)

Ono:
や。
Ya.
(greeting)
"**Hey.**" (PL2)

• *kiteta* is a contraction of *kite ita*, the plain past form of *kite iru*, from the irregular verb *kuru* ("come"; the plain past form is *kita*). *Kite iru* is literally "has come," but it's usually better thought of as "is/are here"; it never means "is coming," which is expressed in other ways. Similarly, *kite ita* is usually best thought of as "was/were here."

286 Kazuhiro learned today that he is to play the position of forward on his soccer team. When he tells his parents, his father notes that their first opponent will be no pushover.

Kazuhiro: わかってる さ!
Wakatteru sa!
know (emph.)
"**I know that!**" (PL2)

• *wakatteru* is a contraction of *wakatte iru*, from *wakaru* ("comprehend/understand"). Comprehension is a momentary action, so *wakatte iru* literally means "I have comprehended/understood, and I am in a continuing state of comprehension"—all of which can usually be reduced to the more natural "I know." *Wakatte iru* never means "am/is/are understanding."
• *sa* is a sentence particle used in informal speech mostly by males; it gives authoritative/confident (and sometimes cocky) emphasis.

Context and experience will be your guide

Although "am/is/are ～ing" and "has/have ～" are your best first guesses for understanding -te iru verbs, always be prepared to try other things that fit the context. Although the root verb in the example here is aisuru ("love"), the natural English equivalent for the -te iru form is neither "am loving" nor "have loved" but simply "love."

Another important use of the -te iru form is to speak of habitual actions. Words like mai-nichi ("every day") and itsu mo ("always") often help establish the habitual meaning, but are not required: Hiru wa (itsu mo) rāmen o tebete imasu = "I (always) eat ramen for lunch."

287 Igarashi tells Shima that he has fallen in love with Stella (fig. 174).

© Hirokane Kenshi. Kachō Shima Kōsaku, Kōdansha.

Igarashi: 彼女　を　愛している。
Kanojo　o　aishite iru.
she/her　(obj.)　love
"I love her." (PL2)

Summary: -te forms

-Te forms have no tense of their own; tense is determined by the context. The -te form of da/desu is simply de. For adjectives, add -te to the -ku form. For all verbs, the -te form is identical to the plain past form except for the final vowel, which changes to -e (-ta → -te; -da → -de). The past verbs have been included in the table for easy comparison.

da/desu	だ/です	da/desu	am/is/are
	で	de	am/is/are-and
adj.	さむい	samui	is cold
	さむくて	samukute	is cold-and
irregular verbs	くる	kuru	come
	きた	kita	came
	きて	kite	come-and
	する	suru	do
	した	shita	did
	して	shite	do-and
group 2 verbs	みる	miru	see
	みた	mita	saw
	みて	mite	see-and
	たべる	taberu	eat
	たべた	tabeta	ate
	たべて	tabete	eat-and
group 1 verbs	とる	toru	take
	とった	totta	took
	とって	totte	take-and
	かう	kau	buy
	かった	katta	bought
	かって	katte	buy-and

group 1 verbs (continued)	もつ	motsu	hold
	もった	motta	held
	もって	motte	hold-and
	よぶ	yobu	call
	よんだ	yonda	called
	よんで	yonde	call-and
	のむ	nomu	drink
	のんだ	nonda	drank
	のんで	nonde	drink-and
	しぬ	shinu	die
	しんだ	shinda	died
	しんで	shinde	die-and
	おとす	otosu	drop
	おとした	otoshita	dropped
	おとして	otoshite	drop-and
	かく	kaku	write
	かいた	kaita[1]	wrote
	かいて	kaite	write-and
	およぐ	oyogu	swim
	およいだ	oyoida	swam
	およいで	oyoide	swim-and

[1] 行く iku ("come") was noted as an exception in Lesson 18 because its plain past form is 行った itta. For its -te form, it acts like any verb whose plain past form ends with -tta: the final -a changes to -e, making it 行って itte.

Lesson 20

Negative Verbs

In Lesson 3, you learned that the polite negative form of any verb is formed simply by changing the *-masu* ending to *-masen* (for non-past) or *-masen deshita* (for past). Forming negatives in PL2 speech is similar—you simply change the ending. There are slight differences in how the ending changes, depending on the verb type, so there's a little more to learn for PL2 negatives than for PL3, but not as much as you had to learn for the past forms.

There's one exception to the rule about changing just the ending, and it's best to begin with this exception. In polite speech, the verb *aru* ("exists" for inanimate things) is like any other verb: the negative is formed by changing its PL3 form *arimasu* to *arimasen*. But in PL2 speech, the negative of *aru* is ない *nai*, which by itself means "doesn't/don't exist" or "isn't/aren't present." When speaking of whether or not something "exists/is present" in one's possession, as in the example here, the more natural English equivalent for *nai* is "doesn't/don't have."

チェッ
マッチがないや

288 Caught in a sudden downpour while in Gion, one of Kyoto's oldest and most celebrated entertainment districts, Shima ducks under the eaves of a small members-only bar to wait for the rain to let up. He takes out a cigarette, but then discovers that he has no matches.

Shima: チェッ、　マッチ　が　　ない　　　や。
Che!,　　matchi　ga　　nai　　　ya.
darn/drat　match(es)　(subj.)　not exist/not have　(emph.)
"Darn, I don't have any matches." (PL2)

- *che!* is an expression of disgust or chagrin: "Rats!/Dang!/Shoot!/ Sheesh!"
- *matchi* is a katakana rendering of the English word "match."
- the informal particle *ya* adds light emphasis; it often carries a note of disappointment/resignation and is mostly masculine.

ない *nai* acts like an adjective

Except for its special negative form, *aru* is a standard Group 1 verb. *Nai*, however, acts like an adjective, so to make its plain past form, the final *-i* is replaced with *-katta*: ない *nai* → なかった *nakatta* ("didn't exist/was not present/didn't have"). Also, since adding *desu* to an adjective makes it polite, you often hear *nai desu* and *nakatta desu* as PL3 forms equivalent to the polite negative forms *arimasen* ("doesn't/don't exist" or "doesn't/don't have") and *arimasen deshita* ("didn't exist/have").

289 When the OL who decided to be a little extravagant in fig. 165 gets home with her flowers, she realizes she has nothing to put them in. She improvises with a tea kettle.

OL: 花ビン　が　　なかった。
Kabin　ga　　nakatta.
vase　(subj.)　didn't have
"I didn't have a vase." (PL2)

- in kanji, *kabin* is written 花瓶—a combination of "flower" and "jar/bottle."

……
花ビンが
なかった

Negative of *kuru*

Nai stands by itself as the PL2 negative form of *aru*; for all other verbs, it serves as the ending of the PL2 negative form. The plain negative form of the irregular verb *kuru* ("come") is こない *konai* ("not come"—including both present tense "doesn't/don't come" and future tense "won't come"), and the plain negative-past form is こなかった *konakatta* ("didn't come").

290 When Mother Brown Bear came out of hibernation, someone had left food for her and her cub. Since Fishing Cat has sometimes helped them out, she asks if he was the one, but he denies it. "Then maybe the jerk's been back," she says, referring to the frequently absent Father Brown Bear. Here Mother Bear and Fishing Cat are waiting to see if Father Bear shows up.

Fishing Cat: 来ない な。
Konai *na.*
not come (colloq.)
"He doesn't come."
"He's not coming." (PL2)

Mother Bear: オス って なんで そんなに 自分 の
Osu *tte* *nande* *sonna-ni* *jibun* *no*
males as for why that much oneself 's
力 を 見せたがる の かしら ね?
chikara *o* *misetagaru* *no* *kashira* *ne.*
strength (obj.) want to show (explan.) I wonder (colloq.)
"Why are males always so bent on showing off their strength, I wonder?" (PL2)

- *tte* here is a colloquial equivalent of *wa* ("as for"; fig. 216).
- *nande* is a colloquial/informal *naze* or *dōshite*, "why?"
- *jibun* refers to "oneself," so depending on the context it becomes "me/myself," "he/himself," "you/yourself," "they/themselves," etc.; *no* shows possession, so *jibun no* = "my/his/your/their."
- *misetagaru* is the verb *miseru/misemasu* ("show") plus *-tagaru* ("express/show a desire [to] ～") → "want to show/be bent on showing." For more about *-tagaru*, see fig. 348.

Negative of *suru*

The plain negative form of the irregular verb *suru* ("do") is しない *shinai* ("doesn't/don't do" or "won't do"), and the plain negative-past form is しなかった *shinakatta* ("didn't do").

291 Shin-chan's mother is scolding him for always forgetting to feed his dog, Shiro. At one point she asks him whether he likes Shiro or not. Still trying to get out of having to feed Shiro, Shin-chan gives a rather incongruous reply.

Shin-chan: 好きだ けど 結婚 は しない。
Suki da *kedo,* *kekkon* *wa* *shinai.*
like but marriage as for won't do
"I like him, but as for marrying, I won't do it."
"I like him, but I'm not going to marry him." (PL2)

Mother: あたりまえ だ!!
Atarimae *da!!*
common sense/matter of course is
"That's a matter of course."
"Of course not!!" (PL2)

- *kekkon* is a noun for "marriage" or the act of "getting married," and *kekkon suru* is its verb form. Shin-chan's line echoes what a commitment-shy young person might say about his/her marital intentions.
- *atarimae* is an adjectival noun meaning "common sense/a matter of course/an obvious thing." *Atarimae da* in response to an affirmative statement means "of course"; in response to a negative statement, "of course not." Although most adjectival nouns require *na* when modifying another noun, *atarimae* occurs with both *na* and *no* → *atarimae na* ～/*atarimae no* ～; when modifying a verb it takes *ni* → *atarimae ni* ～.

CHOMP CHOMP   CHOMP CHOMP

Group 2 verbs

The plain negative form of a Group 2 verb is made by replacing the final -る *-ru* of the dictionary form with -ない *-nai*.

292 Michael's owner, Reiko, overslept again, and in her great rush to make up for lost time, she inadvertently trapped Michael between folds of her futon when she put her bedding away in the closet. She finally notices that he's missing when she gives her cats their breakfast.

Reiko:
あら？　　1、2、3、4...
Ara?　　*Ichi, ni, san, shi...*
(interj.)　　(counting)
"Huh? One, two, three, four..."

い、　　1匹　　たりない!!
I-　　*ippiki*　　*tarinai!!*
(stammer)　1 count　insufficient
"There's one missing!!" (PL2)

マイケル　が　　いない　　わ!!
Maikeru　*ga*　　*inai*　　*wa!!*
(name)　(subj.)　not present　(fem.)
"Michael isn't here!" (PL2)

- *ara?* is a mostly feminine interjection of surprise.
- *-hiki* is the standard form of the counter suffix for small to medium-sized animals, but in some combinations it changes to *-ppiki* or *-biki*.
- *tarinai* is the negative form of the Group 2 verb *tariru/tarimasu* ("be sufficient").
- *inai* is the the negative form of the Group 2 verb *iru/imasu* ("exist/be present" for humans and animals).

Another Group 2 verb

It shouldn't be necessary to go on illustrating them separately for every new form, but always keep in mind that Group 2 verbs in their dictionary form have two possible endings when written in romaji: they end in either *-iru* or *-eru*. That means the plain negative forms can end in either *-inai* or *-enai*. (In fact, except for *shinai*, from *suru*, any time you encounter a negative verb ending in *-inai*, you automatically know it's a Group 2 verb; unfortunately, the same doesn't hold for *-enai*.)

Here's an example of a plain negative Group 2 verb ending in *-enai*:

293 Kazuhiro insists that he can prepare for college entrance exams and also play soccer, but when his father discovers that he has been skipping cram school in favor of soccer practice, he lays down the law. Kazuhiro remains determined.

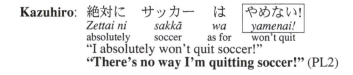

Kazuhiro:　絶対に　　サッカー　　は　　やめない!
　　　　　Zettai ni　*sakkā*　　*wa*　　*yamenai!*
　　　　　absolutely　soccer　as for　won't quit
"I absolutely won't quit soccer!"
"There's no way I'm quitting soccer!" (PL2)

- *zettai* is a noun for "absoluteness" or "the absolute," and *zettai ni* is its adverb form, "absolutely." Actually, the word often serves as an adverb even without the *ni*.
- *yamenai* is the negative form of the Group 2 verb *yameru/yamemasu* ("quit").

The negative form of a Group 1 verb

The plain negative form of a Group 1 verb is made by changing the final -*u* to -*a* and adding -*nai*, so the new negative ending is -*anai*. In kana, change the final syllable to the *a* sound in the same row—if it's く, make it か; if it's む, make it ま, and so forth—and add -ない -*nai*.

294 Akaiwa, the man waiting for his date in fig. 273, thinks he has gotten rid of nosy Shin-chan. But when his date, Ms. Shirakawa, finally arrives, Shin-chan suddenly reappears and greets her as if he's with Akaiwa.

Shirakawa: 誰?
Dare?
who
"Who's this?" (PL2)

Akaiwa: 知らない、 知らない。
Shiranai, shiranai.
not know   not know
"I don't know him, I don't know him." (PL2)

Shin-chan: オラ、しんのすけ。
Ora, Shinnosuke.
I/me   (name)
"I'm Shinnosuke." (PL2)

- *shiranai* is the plain negative form of *shiru/shirimasu*, which means "learn/come to know"—but its negative form always means "not know" (fig. 35).
- *ora* is a variation of *ore*, a rough/masculine word for "I/me." When used by adults, *ora* has a provincial or lower-class feeling.

The plain negative form can be a good way to first encounter a new verb:
- if it ends in -*anai*, you automatically know it's a Group 1 verb: change the -*anai* to -*u* and you have the dictionary form; change it to -*imasu* and you have the polite form. (If the negative form ends in -*wanai*, you also need to drop the *w* when making the conversion; see below.)
- if it ends in -*inai*, you automatically know it's a Group 2 verb: change -*nai* to -*ru* and you have the dictionary form; change it to -*masu* and you have the polite form.
- if it ends in -*enai*, you'll have to apply another test; it could be either the negative form of a Group 2 verb or the "can't ～" form of any verb but *suru* (see Lesson 28).

One special subgroup

All Group 1 verbs have negative forms ending in -*anai*, but for one subgroup, that's not quite the whole story. Verbs that end in the independent syllable -う -*u* pick up a new consonant: -*u* changes to -わ -*wa*, making the negative form end in -*wanai*: e.g., 思う *omou* ("think") → 思わない *omowanai* ("not think").

295 After team captain Kubo dies, his girlfriend turns to Toshihiko (fig. 263) for comfort. At first he is flattered, but now he has grown uncomfortable with the relationship.

Toshihiko: もう 会わない 方がいい と 思う んだ。
Mō awanai hō ga ii to omou n da.
anymore   not meet   is better   (quote)   think   (explan.)
"To not meet anymore is better, I think."
"I think it'd be better if we stopped seeing each other." (PL2)

- *awanai* is the plain negative form of *au/aimasu* ("meet/see").
- *hō ga ii* after a negative verb implies "is/would be better not to [do the action]."
- for the use of *to* with *omou/omoimasu* ("think"), see fig. 211.

Negative-past for all verbs

Just like the independent word *nai*, the verb-ending *-nai* acts as an adjective, and that means all plain negative verbs act as adjectives. To make the plain past form of any negative verb, change -ない *-nai* to -なかった *-nakatta*.

Maruyama

296 Shima is visiting Maruyama, whose career has been languishing in a Shikoku backwater for five years. Here Shima ponders why as they eat lunch together. In talks between the company union and management, most men on the verge of promotion to section chief (*kachō*)—at which point they would leave the union and join management—begin currying favor with their future non-union colleagues.

© Hirokane Kenshi, *Kachō Shima Kōsaku*, Kōdansha.

Shima (thinking):
それ を 丸山 は やらなかった。
Sore o Maruyama wa yaranakatta.
that (obj.) (name) as for didn't do
"That, as for Maruyama, [he] didn't do [it]."
"Maruyama didn't do that." (PL2)

• *yaranakatta* is the past form of *yaranai*, the PL2 negative form of *yaru/yarimasu* ("do").

Summary: Negative verbs

For the polite negative form of all verbs, replace *-masu* with *-masen*; to make the past form of the negative, add *deshita* → *masen deshita*. For the plain negative form of a Group 2 verb, replace the final *-ru* with *-nai*; for a Group 1 verb, change the final *-u* to *-a* and add *-nai*. To make the negative-past form in each case, use *-nakatta* instead of *-nai*.

Sometimes *-nai desu* and *-nakatta desu* are used as PL3 alternatives to *-masen* and *-masen deshita*, respectively. Exception: for the independent *nai* (negative of *aru*), *nai desu = arimasen* and *nakatta desu = arimasen deshita*.

[1] For verbs with final syllable -う *-u*, the connecting syllable becomes -わ *-wa*.

[2] For romaji conversions, in *t* row syllables, *t = ch = ts*. See Introduction.

		dictionary form		negative form		
irreg. *aru*	ある	*aru*	exist/have	ない	*nai*	not exist/have
	くる	*kuru*	come	こない	*konai*	not come
	する	*suru*	do	しない	*shinai*	not do
gr. 2	みる	*miru*	see	みない	*minai*	not see
	たべる	*taberu*	eat	たべない	*tabenai*	not eat
group 1 verbs	とる	*toru*	take	とらない	*toranai*	not take
	かう	*kau*[1]	buy	かわない	*kawanai*[1]	not buy
	もつ	*motsu*[2]	hold	もたない	*motanai*[2]	not hold
	よぶ	*yobu*	call	よばない	*yobanai*	not call
	のむ	*nomu*	drink	のまない	*nomanai*	not drink
	しぬ	*shinu*	die	しなない	*shinanai*	not die
	おとす	*otosu*	drop	おとさない	*otosanai*	not drop
	かく	*kaku*	write	かかない	*kakanai*	not write
	およぐ	*oyogu*	swim	およがない	*oyoganai*	not swim

The negative verb-ending *-nai* can contract to *-ん -n*

In PL2 speech, the *-nai* ending for verbs often gets shortened to just *-n*—especially among male speakers.

297 Section Chief Izumiya seems to be very worried about some documents that are missing.

Izumiya: おい、ここ に あった 重要 書類
Oi, koko ni atta jūyō shorui
hey here at existed important documents
"Hey, [as for] the important documents that were here,

知らん か?
shiran ka?
not know (?)
"do you not know?"
"Hey, does anyone know what happened to the important documents that were sitting here?" (PL2)

- *atta* is the PL2 past form of *aru* ("exist/be in a place"); *koko ni atta* ("[they] were here") is a complete sentence modifying *jūyō shorui* ("important documents"). *O*, to mark this as the direct object of *shiran*, has been omitted.
- *shiran* is a contraction of *shiranai*, from *shiru/shirimasu* ("learn/come to know"), so the standard PL2 ending of this sentence would be *shiranai ka?* and the PL3 equivalent is *shirimasen ka?* or *shiranai desu ka?*
- the negative question *X (o) shiranai (ka)/shirimasen (ka)?* (with or without the final *ka*) is often use to ask if someone knows where X is, rather than what/who X is: *Okāsan shiranai?* = "Do you know where Mom is?"

Inviting or suggesting with *-masen ka*

The way to politely invite your listener to do something is to use the *-masen* form of a verb plus the particle *ka*, making the question "Won't you [do the action]?"—much like you might say "Won't you have some tea?" or "Won't you come with me?" as invitations in English.

If the speaker will also be involved in the action, *-masen ka* often is more like a suggestion, "Shall we not [do the action]?" → "Why don't we/how about we [do the action]?"

-Masen ka can of course also be used as a straightforward question: "Don't you/doesn't he/don't they [do the action]?" or "Won't you/he/they [do the action]?"

298 An old Japanese folktale tells of Urashima Tarō, who rescues a turtle from some mischievous children, and is then taken by the grateful turtle to a magnificent undersea palace, where he is entertained lavishly. In this send-up of that story, Shinnosuke the dog (fig. 94) rescues a kitten from a gang of malicious monkeys and is taken to a dazzling underground "Catbaret." After a floor show featuring comely chinchilla Persian dancers, one of the hostesses invites Shinnosuke to join in some karaoke.

Hostess: ねえ、 ねえ、 伸之助さん も
Nē, nē, Shinnosuke-san mo
say say (name-pol.)/you too/also

なにか 歌いません か?
nani-ka utaimasen ka?
something won't [you] sing (?)
"Say, Mr. Shinnosuke, won't you sing something, too?"
"Say, Mr. Shinnosuke, wouldn't you like to sing something, too?" (PL3)

Shinnosuke: え?
E?
"Huh?" (PL2–3)

Songbook: カラオケ
Karaoke

- *nē* at the beginning of a sentence is to get the listener's attention, like "say/hey/look here/you know."
- she could have used a pronoun to refer to her listener, but following the general Japanese preference, she uses his name instead.
- *utaimasen* is the polite negative form of *utau/utaimasu* ("sing"). Since *utau* ends with the single-vowel syllable う *u*, its plain negative form is *utawanai*.

-*Nai ka?* or -*nai?* as informal invitation

To invite or suggest an action informally, the PL2 -*nai* form of a verb plus *ka* works the same way—except that it generally sounds a little too abrupt for female speakers even in informal speech. Female speakers simply use -*nai?* with the intonation of a question instead, omitting the final *ka*. Males can omit the *ka*, too, without sounding effeminate.

299 This OL and salaryman worked late today finishing up a project, and now they are on their way home. The OL suggests they stop for a bite to eat.

OL: 焼き肉 | 食べない?
Yakiniku | *tabenai?*
barbecued meat not eat?
"Won't you eat *yakiniku* [with me]?"
"Why don't we stop for some *yakiniku*?" (PL2)

Salaryman: あ、 いい ね。
A, *ii* *ne.*
(interj.) is good (colloq.)
"Sure, sounds great." (PL2)

© Akizuki Risu. *OL Shinkaron,* Kōdansha.

- *yakiniku* (lit. "broiled/grilled meat") is thin-sliced beef, pork, or chicken together with sliced onions and some other vegetables cooked on a grill or iron griddle in the middle of the table. The meat is marinated before cooking and also dipped in a spicy sauce after cooking.
- for the adjective that occurs both as *ii* and *yoi* ("is good/fine/OK"), *ii* is the more commonly used non-past form (as in the example here), but *yoi* is the basis of the word's other forms, including the adverb *yoku*, the -*te* form *yokute*, the past form *yokatta* ("was good"), the negatives *yokunai* ("isn't good") and *yokunakatta* ("wasn't good"), and other forms yet to come.

A negative verb with explanatory *no*

The explanatory extension ～ *no,* ～ *n da/desu,* or ～ *no da/desu* (Lesson 8) can be used with a negative sentence just as with any other, making it correspond to an English explanation like "It's that he isn't/doesn't/won't ～," or "The situation/explanation is that she isn't/doesn't/won't ～." Most typically, the PL2 -*nai* form is used before the extension, and the politeness of the sentence is determined by the form the extension itself takes, but the polite -*masen* + *no* is also heard in PL3 feminine speech.

A negative question that ends with ～ *no?* or ～ *no ka?* or ～ *n desu ka?* is asking for an explanation regarding the situation ("Is it that she isn't/doesn't/won't ～?"), and is never an invitation or suggestion. In fact, in many cases, this is precisely the way to ask a straightforward negative question that won't be misunderstood as an invitation.

300 Natsuko's first crop of Tatsunishiki rice has been doing well, but now a typhoon is on its way, and her father warns her that Tatsunishiki is particularly susceptible to blowover because it has taller stalks and heavier ears.

Natsuko:
防ぐ 方法 は | ない | んです か?
Fusegu *hōhō* *wa* | *nai* | *n desu* *ka?*
prevent method/means as for not exist (explan.) (?)
"Is it that a means to prevent it doesn't exist?"
"Isn't there some way to prevent it?" (PL3)

© Oze Akira. *Natsuko no Sake,* Kōdansha.

- *fusegu/fusegimasu* ("protect against/prevent") modifies *hōhō* ("method/means") → "a means to prevent/some way to prevent."
- *nai* is the plain negative form of *aru* ("exist[s]").

Negative questions in English are not the same

A negative question in Japanese doesn't necessarily translate as a negative question in English. Fig. 297 has already shown one such instance: the question "Don't you know ～?" in English implies that the listener should know the answer but probably doesn't, whereas the Japanese question *Shiranai ka?* carries a fairly strong expectation that the listener must know the answer. Here's another example where translating as a negative question in English would give the wrong impression.

301 Rie, an old friend of Kōsuke's from junior high, has become a hair stylist, and she recently moved to a salon near Kōsuke's apartment. Kōsuke decides to have her cut his hair. As she gives him a shampoo, she asks:

Rie: かゆい ところ は ｜ありません か?｜
Kayui tokoro wa arimasen ka?
itchy spot as for not exist/have (?)
"Don't you have any itchy spots?"
"Do you have any itchy spots?" (PL3)

Kōsuke: 全部。
Zenbu.
all
"Everywhere." (PL2)

- the English question "Don't you have any itchy spots?" carries the presumption that the listener surely must have itchy spots, or expresses surprise that he doesn't. Rie's question here, however, presumes that Kōsuke probably does not have any itchy spots; she is only asking just in case, as part of her standard routine, and is no doubt used to getting a simple "No" most of the time. In fact, in the next frame she reacts to Kōsuke's response with the equivalent of "Oh, gross! No one's ever said that before."

A negative question with *ka na/kashira*

Negative questions can end with *ka na* (somewhat masculine) or *kashira* (feminine) just like any other question. With action verbs, questions ending in *-nai ka na/kashira* literally ask "Does/Will the action perhaps not occur?" or "I wonder if the action doesn't/won't occur?" With the independent *nai* (PL2 negative of *aru*, "exists"), questions ending in *nai ka na/kashira* literally ask "Does [the specified item] perhaps not exist?" or "I wonder if [the specified item] doesn't exist." For such questions, too, context will determine whether or not it's appropriate to translate into a negative question in English.

302 Matsuda is experiencing writer's block while trying to get started on a mystery thriller, and the insufferably hot and sticky summer weather doesn't help. Regretting that he didn't buy an air conditioner with his last paycheck, he decides to head for his favorite bar, Lemon Hart, where he poses this question to the proprietor.

Matsuda: ねえ、マスター。ミステリー に ぴったり の
Nē, masutā. Misuterii ni pittari no
say master mystery for perfect (mod.)
なにか いい プロット ｜ない かな?｜
nani-ka ii purotto nai ka na?
something good plot not exist/have I wonder if
"Say, Chief. I wonder if you don't have some good plot perfect for a mystery?"
"Say, Chief. Can you think of a good plot idea that's perfect for a mystery?" (PL2)

- *pittari* is an adverb meaning "perfectly/exactly" used with verbs like "suit" and "fit" → "suit/fit perfectly"; adding *no* allows it to modify a noun directly, and effectively includes the meaning of the missing verb: *pittari no purotto* = "perfectly suited plot."
- *nani-ka* ("something") + *ii* ("good") also modifies *purotto*: "something [that will make a] good plot" → "some good plot."
- although literally it sounds like he's only wondering if "some good plot doesn't exist," he is in fact asking the proprietor if he has any ideas for one.

The *-te form* of *nai*

The *-te* form of the independent word *nai* ("not exist/not be present") is *nakute*—formed by adding *-te* to the *-ku* form of *nai*, as for all adjectives. *X ga nakute Y* implies that the lack/absence/nonexistence of X is the cause or reason for Y; if the *X ga* phrase has been omitted because the subject is understood, then the lack/absence/nonexistence of the understood subject is the cause/reason for Y.

For the verb-ending *-nai*, *-nakute* is one of two *-te* forms. This *-te* form implies that the lack/absence/nonexistence of an action—expressed by the negative verb—is the cause or reason for what follows.

SFX: ガチャン
Gachan
(setting phone
down hard)

303 The call is about a lucrative one-day writing assignment that Matsuda would like to have accepted, but it can only be done on June 1, the day of Matsuda's class reunion (fig. 27). Matsuda declines the job.

Matsuda: お役　　に　　│立てなくて│　すみません。
　　　　　O-yaku　ni　　tatenakute　　sumimasen.
　　　　　(hon.)-role　for　can't stand/fill-(reason)　(apology)
"I'm sorry I can't be of service." (PL3–4)

- *o-* is honorific, and *yaku* means "role/function"; *yaku ni tatsu/tachimasu* (lit. "stand for the role/function" or "fill the role/function") is an expression for "be useful/helpful/of service" or "serve a purpose" (it can be used to speak of tools as well as people). The plain negative form of the expression is *yaku ni tatanai* ("am/is/are not useful"); its "can't" form is *yaku ni tatenai* ("can't be useful"), and the *-te* form of that is *yaku ni tatenakute*.
- the *-nakute* form indicates a cause/reason, so *yaku ni tatanakute* (with the standard form of the verb) means "because I'm not useful/of service" and *yaku ni tatenakute* (with the "can't" form of the verb) means "because I can't be useful/of service"). In effect, he is stating the reason for his apology, which immediately follows.
- the "can" and "can't" forms of verbs are formally introduced in Lesson 28.

A second *-te* form for the verb-ending *-nai*

The verb-ending *-nai* (but not the independent *nai*) has a second *-te* form, *-naide*, so many verbs have two "negative *-te* forms"; it depends on the particular verb whether one or both can be used. *-Nakute* is used to indicate cause or reason, and also in certain special expressions; *-naide* is called upon for the other uses of the *-te* form illustrated in Lesson 19, and also sometimes to show cause/reason. Just like a non-negative *-te* form, *-naide* can link two verbs to imply that the first action indicates something about the manner or circumstances of the second; since it's negative, it typically implies doing the second action "without [doing the first action]" or "instead of [doing the first action]."

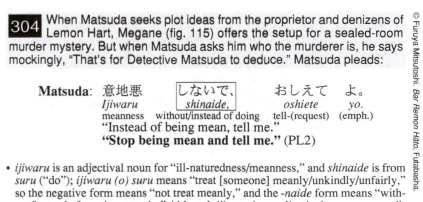

304 When Matsuda seeks plot ideas from the proprietor and denizens of Lemon Hart, Megane (fig. 115) offers the setup for a sealed-room murder mystery. But when Matsuda asks him who the murderer is, he says mockingly, "That's for Detective Matsuda to deduce." Matsuda pleads:

Matsuda: 意地悪　　│しないで、│　　おしえて　　よ。
　　　　　Ijiwaru　　shinaide,　　　oshiete　　yo.
　　　　　meanness　without/instead of doing　tell-(request)　(emph.)
"Instead of being mean, tell me."
"Stop being mean and tell me." (PL2)

- *ijiwaru* is an adjectival noun for "ill-naturedness/meanness," and *shinaide* is from *suru* ("do"); *ijiwaru (o) suru* means "treat [someone] meanly/unkindly/unfairly," so the negative form means "not treat meanly," and the *-naide* form means "without/instead of treating meanly." Although *ijiwaru* is an adjectival noun, as a modifier it also occurs in the form of an adjective, *ijiwarui*.
- *oshiete* is the *-te* form of *oshieru/oshiemasu* ("tell/inform"); this *-te* form is being used to make an informal request (fig. 278).

A negative request or command

The *-naide* form of a verb by itself is used to make negative requests ("Please don't ～") or relatively gentle negative commands ("Don't ～")—though the feeling can in fact be quite sharp depending on the tone of voice.

As with non-negative *-te* forms, adding *kudasai*, as seen here, makes it a polite request.

305 The gray box located somewhat improbably right in front of the pet shop entrance is a mail box. This man is about to drop his letter in the slot when he notices the sign next to it and pauses to wonder if it perhaps applies to the mailbox.

In Window: ペット　ショップ
Petto　　　　shoppu
Pet Shop

Sign: エサ　　を　　与えないで　下さい。
Esa　　o　　ataenaide　kudasai.
food/feed　(obj.)　don't give-(request)　please
Please do not give feed.
Please do not feed. (PL3)

- *esa* refers to "food/feed" given to animals/pets. It's also used for "bait" when fishing or setting a trap.
- *ataenaide* is a negative *-te* form of *ataeru/ataemasu* ("give/bestow/award").

Negatives with *-te iru*

The helping verb *iru* in *-te iru* combinations can occur in negative form just like any other verb: *-te inai/-te imasen*. This most typically implies either "am/is/are not [doing the action]" or "has/have not [done the action]," but as noted with the non-negative form in Lesson 19, context may call for some other English rendering.

In some instances, the *-te* form itself (rather than *iru*) may be negative: *-naide iru* or *-naide imasu* (never *nakute*). This use implies deliberately leaving the action undone.

306 Shortly after the accident that killed their father (fig. 277), Kaji's brother Haruhiko appears to be on the road to recovery, and the doctor tells Kaji he can speak with him. "If I die," Haruhiko says, "you have to take over Dad's constituency." Kaji says he isn't interested, but he does want to know whether there's any truth to recent media reports about their father accepting large sums of money that could be perceived as bribes.

Haruhiko:
誓ってもいい。　オヤジ　は　受け取っていない。
Chikatte mo ii.　Oyaji　wa　uketotte inai.
willing to swear　Dad　as for　has not received
"I'm willing to swear it. Dad has not received [such money]."
"I swear. He accepted no such money." (PL2)

- *chikatte* is the *-te* form of *chikau/chikaimasu* ("swear/vow/pledge/take an oath"). The verb pattern *-te mo ii* (or just *-te ii*) expresses a willingness to do the action (see fig. 364), so *chikatte mo ii* is like "I'm willing to swear" → "I swear/upon my word."
- *oyaji* is a mostly masculine, informal word for "Dad." In adult speech it's usually reserved for one's own father, and *oyaji-san* is used for someone else's father. Even with the polite suffix, though, the word feels quite informal/familiar, so it should be used with caution. The corresponding word for "Mom" is *ofukuro*, which also gets the suffix *-san* when referring to someone else's mother.
- *uketotte* is from *uketoru/uketorimasu* ("receive/accept"), and *inai* is the negative form of *iru*; *uketotte iru* = "has received/accepted," and *uketotte inai* = "has not received/accepted."

Lesson 21

Kuroiwa Shingo

SCRITCH
ポリ

Negative Adjectives & *Desu*

The negative form for *desu* in polite speech is じゃありません *ja arimasen* ("is/are not"); the negative-past form is じゃありませんでした *ja arimasen deshita* ("was/were not"). When *arimasen* follows immediately after particles like *wa*, *ga*, *ni*, and *mo*, it's generally the polite negative form of the verb *aru* ("exist"), but when used like this in combination with *ja* (or its equivalents on the facing page), it's the polite negative form of *desu*.

黒岩さん
ゲームじゃ
ありませんよ

307 Saké dealer Yasumoto is sponsoring a tasting. When Kuroiwa Shingo starts trying to persuade Yasumoto to carry his brand, Yasumoto lays down a challenge. If Kuroiwa can identify three of ten brands in a tasting contest, Yasumoto will buy his brand. Kuroiwa protests that he sees no need to play games. Yasumoto responds:

Yasumoto:
黒岩さん、　ゲーム　じゃありません　よ。
Kuroiwa-san,　gēmu　ja arimasen　yo.
(name-pol.)　game　is not　(emph.)
"It's not a game, Mr. Kuroiwa." (PL3)

The plain equivalent of *ja arimasen*

You learned in the last lesson that the plain equivalent of *arimasen* is *nai*, so it should be no surprise that the plain equivalent of *ja arimasen* is じゃない *ja nai* ("is/are not"), and its plain past form is じゃなかった *ja nakatta* ("was/were not").

308 When the elevator is stuck between the fourth and fifth floors, everyone wonders who might be trapped in it. Most likely Tanaka-kun, they all agree. He's the one this sort of thing always happens to. Then the elevator finally moves.

Victim: いやー、　こわかったー。
Iyā,　kowakattā.
(exclam.)　was scary
"Man, that was scary!" (PL2)

Yoshida: あれ?　田中くん　じゃない。
Are?　Tanaka-kun　ja nai.
(interj.)　(name-fam.)　is not
"Huh? It's not Tanaka-kun." (PL2)

Boss: じゃ、　田中くん　は　どこ　に　いる　んだ?
Ja,　Tanaka-kun　wa　doko　ni　iru　n da?
in that case　(name-fam.)　as for　where　at　exists　(explan.)
"Then where *is* Tanaka-kun?" (PL2)

- *iyā* is a kind of warm-up word for exclamations of either consternation or delight/approval, here the former.
- *kowakatta* is the past form of the adjective *kowai* ("is scary").
- *are?* spoken with the intonation of a question is an interjection of surprise/bewilderment when something is wrong or not as expected: "Huh?/What?/What's going on?"
- the boss's *ja* is a connecting word used like "in that case/then/well" at the beginning of a sentence.
- *doko* = "where/what place," *ni* marks a place of existence, and *iru* = "exists," so *doko ni iru?* = "Where does he/she exist?" → "Where is he/she?"

166

じゃ *ja* = では *de wa*

The *ja* in *ja nai/ja arimasen* is actually a contraction of *de wa* (for reasons that need not concern you here, *wa* is the topic marker and therefore written は), so you will also encounter *de wa nai* and *de wa arimasen*. *Nai* or *arimasen* after other 〜 *wa* phrases means "not exist/have," with *wa* marking the thing that is nonexistent/missing; but *nai* or *arimasen* in combination with *de wa* is almost always the polite negative of *desu* ("is/are not").

309 Natsu is not a drinker, but on several occasions she has demonstrated a discerning nose and palate for good saké—something her husband Zenzō knows he lacks. Her mother-in-law, however, has threatened to take her child away if she touches another drop, so Natsu refuses to taste the new saké when Zenzō asks her to. "Then was it a lie," he asks, "when you said you'd help me in any way you could?"

Natsu: 嘘 | ではありません！
Uso | *de wa arimasen!*
lie | is not
"It is not a lie!"
"It was not a lie!" (PL3)

- in Japanese, there is no dissonance between Zenzō asking his question using the past form (*Uso datta no ka*, "Was it a lie?"), and Natsu's use of a non-past form in response.

☛ Like *da* and *desu*, *ja nai* and *ja arimasen* most commonly follow a noun or adjectival noun. But they can also sometimes follow a plain adjective or verb, as you will learn in figs. 323 and 324.

De wa is also shortened to *de*

The *wa* in *de wa nai/arimasen* ("is/are not") is often omitted in colloquial speech, so *de nai* is another common equivalent of the PL2 *ja nai/de wa nai*, and *de arimasen* is equivalent to the PL3 *ja arimasen/de wa arimasen*.

The full form with *de wa* is standard in written Japanese and in very polite, formal speech. The shortened *ja* and *de* are generally the rule in colloquial spoken use—especially in PL2 speech, but also in most PL3 speech.

310 This episode of *What's Michael?* notes that Michael and his mate Poppo have different tastes in food. Using the narrative past tense, the narrator observes, for example, that Michael loved dried sardines, but Poppo hated them and wouldn't touch them. By contrast, Poppo loved milk.

Narration: だけど マイケル は
Da kedo Maikeru wa
but (name) as for

ミルク が 好き でなかった。
miruku ga suki de nakatta.
milk (subj.) like/be fond of was not
"But Michael was not fond of milk."
"But Michael was not fond of milk." (PL2)

- *de nakatta* is the plain past form of the PL2 negative *de nai*. The polite equivalent is *de arimasen deshita*.

De mo nai/arimasen = "not entirely" or "not either"

In some cases, the pattern ∼ *de mo nai* or ∼ *de mo arimasen* means "is/are not entirely ∼"; in other cases it means "is/are not ∼ either." Where there are two (or more) phrases ending in *de mo* with the final one concluding *de mo nai/arimasen*, as in this example, it is like "is neither ∼ nor ∼."

311 Kaji is visiting the United States as a member of the Japanese cabinet, and here he is consulting with Japan's ambassador to the U.S. regarding a meeting with the secretary of defense the next day. The ambassador sizes the secretary up for Kaji.

Ambassador:

タカ派 | でも | ハト派 | でもありません | ね。
Taka-ha | *de mo* | *hato-ha* | *de mo arimasen* | *ne.*
hawk faction | nor | dove faction | is not either | (colloq.)

"He's neither a hawk nor a dove." (PL3)

- *ne* often implies that the speaker expects the listener to concur/agree with what he is saying, but here it's used just for light emphasis. In this case, Kaji is in no position to know one way or the other; that's the very reason the ambassador is offering his assessment.

Negative questions

A negative question is made by adding *ka* to the end of a negative sentence: ∼ *ja nai (desu) ka/ja arimasen ka?* asks "∼, is it not?" or "Isn't it ∼?" In PL2 speech, ∼ *ja nai ka?* tends to sound quite abrupt, though, so ∼ *ja nai no?* (with the explanatory *no*) or just ∼ *ja nai?* (using neither *ka* nor *no*) with a rising intonation on the last syllable is often preferred. Omitting *ka/no* in the same way after ∼ *ja arimasen?* in PL3 speech has a distinctly feminine ring. Usually, when *ka* is omitted, *ja* is used rather than *de wa*.

As noted at fig. 289, *nai desu* is often heard as a PL3 negative form equivalent to *arimasen*. Similarly, *ja nai desu* is frequently used instead of *ja arimasen*; and for questions, *ja nai desu ka?* is used instead of *ja arimasen ka?*

312 After Kaji's father dies, his chief of staff Tanizaki Kengo vies with Kaji to win the elder Kaji's seat, and here they are participating in a televised debate. Tanizaki considers a representative's principal responsibility to be bringing home the pork, while Kaji believes a representative to the central government must place the national interest first. "Sometimes local interests have to be sacrificed for the good of the country as a whole," Kaji declares at one point, and Tanizaki responds:

Tanizaki:

加治さん、 | それ | は
Kaji-san, | *sore* | *wa*
(name-pol.) | that | as for

全体主義 | じゃないです | か?
fashizumu | *ja nai desu* | *ka?*
fascism | is not | (?)

"Isn't that fascism, Mr. Kaji?" (PL3)

- although the reading ファシズム ("fascism") is provided in furigana, implying that's what Tanizaki actually said, the proper reading for 全体主義 is *zentai shugi*; since *zentai* means "totality" and *shugi* means "doctrine/principle/-ism," the more standard translation of this four-kanji combination is "totalitarianism."

Ja nai/arimasen with explanatory no

The explanatory extension *n da/desu*, *no da/desu*, or just plain *no* after a negative *ja nai* (or the other plain equivalents, *de wa nai* and *de nai*) makes a sentence like "It's that he/she/it isn't ～" or "The situation is that he/she/it isn't ～." If just *ja nai no* (without the full extension) is spoken with the intonation of a question, the sentence is like "Is it that he/she/it isn't ～?" or "Is the situation that he/she/it isn't ～?"—which often boils down to "Isn't he/she/it ～?"

Usually, the plain *ja nai* is the form used before the explanatory extension, and the politeness level of the sentence as a whole is determined by the extension itself; but in PL3 feminine speech, you will also sometimes hear *ja arimasen no*.

313 Ever since Sayuri found out she's pregnant, her boyfriend Yōji has been very supportive. But she thinks about how badly her friend Sakata's guy treated her when she went through the same thing, and tears come to her eyes. Yōji asks her what's wrong, and Sayuri tells him about Sakata.

Sayuri: その こ ね、 しあわせ 　じゃない　 の。
Sono ko ne, shiawase ja nai no.
that girl (colloq.) happy is not (explan.)
"That girl—it's that she isn't happy."
"The girl's been having some hard times." (PL2)

• *ko* = "child/young person" or more specifically (according to context), "boy/girl."
• *ne* in the middle of a sentence is a kind of verbal pause.
• *shiawase* is an adjectival noun meaning "happiness," and its usage usually corresponds to the English adjective "happy." But it often refers more to a person's objective quality of life than to how he or she feels, and in such cases *shiawase da/desu* = "has a good life" and *shiawase ja nai* = "has an unhappy/hard/miserable life."

314 When Noboru comes to Tokyo saying how determined he is to make a go of it in the big city, Matsuda's first response is this:

Matsuda: いわゆる　5月病　じゃない　の?
Iwayuru gogatsu-byō ja nai no?
so-called May fever is not (explan-?)
"Isn't this just a case of the so-called 'May Fever'?" (PL2)

• *gogatsu-byō* (literally, "May sickness") refers to the let down/depression that sets in a month or so after a freshman begins college or a new college graduate begins his first full-time job. The Japanese school year begins in April, and so do new jobs after graduation.

Ja nai/arimasen can also come *after* an explanatory *no* or *na no*. In casual speech, *(na) no* used in this position usually gets shortened to *(na) n*, resulting in ～ *(na) n ja nai/arimasen*; in more formal speech you will hear *(na) no de wa nai/arimasen*. In this example, an adjective is followed by *no*, which is in turn followed by *ja nai*?

Bride-to-be　　　　　**Friend**

315 An OL who will soon be married (the one seen in profile here) asks a friend to help her pick out a wedding dress. By the time she emerges from the dressing room to ask her friend's opinion, the friend has tried on a dress, too, and seems to have forgotten the real reason she came.

Friend: あ、 うん、 いい 　ん　 じゃない?
A, un, ii n ja nai?
(interj.) uh-huh good/fine (explan.) is not-?
"Oh, uh-huh, it's good, isn't it?"
"Oh, right, it's probably fine." (PL2)

• *n ja nai?* after an adjective is literally like "It's ～, is it not?" but it can have the feeling of "It's probably/surely ～," or "Don't you think it's ～?" It can have a similar feeling after a verb or noun as well.

With *ka na* or *kashira*

When *ka na* (somewhat masculine) or *kashira* (feminine) is used after *ja nai*, it makes a question like "Perhaps he/she/it isn't ～," or "I wonder if he/she/it isn't ～?" When the explanatory *no* follows *ja nai* as well, it must always precede *ka na/kashira*. The question ～ *ja nai no ka na/kashira?* is like "Is the situation/explanation perhaps that he/she/it isn't ～?" → "Perhaps he/she/it isn't ～" or "I wonder if he/she/it isn't ～."

316 Garcia from Colombia has been in Japan long enough to ask for directions in Japanese, but the man he asks responds only in an incomprehensible attempt at English.

Garcia: 日本人 │じゃない　の　　かな？│
(thinking) *Nihon-jin* │*ja nai　　no　　ka na?*│
Japanese person │ is not　(explan.)　perhaps │
"Is it perhaps that he isn't Japanese?"
"I wonder if he's not Japanese?" (PL2)

Man: クソォー、　もっと　　高い　　テキスト　を　　買う　ぞォ。
(thinking) *Kusō,　　motto　　takai　　tekisuto　o　　kau　　zō.*
(chagrin)　more　high/expensive　textbook　(obj.)　will buy　(emph.)
"Dammit! I'm gonna buy a more expensive textbook!" (PL1–2)

- *kuso* (here lengthened for emphasis) is widely used as a curse of chagrin/aggravation: "Damn!/Confound it!/Crap!/Arggh!" It's actually a relatively crude word for "excrement/feces," but is not considered unprintable like a certain English counterpart.
- the man is referring, of course, to a textbook for studying English.

Negative adjectives

Adjectives also have negative forms that use the ending *-nai*. Just add *-nai* to the *-ku* form (or adverb form) of the adjective: *hayai* ("is fast/early") → *hayaku* ("quickly/early") → *hayakunai* ("isn't fast/early").

317 During the brief cherry blossom season each spring, crowds of revelers flock to famous flower-viewing spots on evenings and weekends to picnic and party under the blossoms. Kōsuke has been sent ahead to reserve a choice spot for his apartment building's party. As he settles comfortably against the base of a giant cherry tree, a gentle spring breeze stirs the air and the sunshine warms his toes.

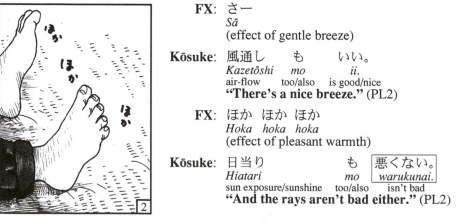

FX: さー
Sā
(effect of gentle breeze)

Kōsuke: 風通し　　も　　　いい。
Kazetōshi　mo　　　ii.
air-flow　too/also　is good/nice
"There's a nice breeze." (PL2)

FX: ほか　ほか　ほか
Hoka　hoka　hoka
(effect of pleasant warmth)

Kōsuke: 日当り　　　　　も　│悪くない。│
Hiatari　　　　mo　│warukunai.│
sun exposure/sunshine　too/also　│isn't bad │
"And the rays aren't bad either." (PL2)

- *kazetōshi* (from *kaze* = "wind," plus *tōshi*, the stem of *tōsu/toshimasu* = "let through/let pass") is a noun referring to the way a room or a particular spot catches the wind/breeze. *Kazetōshi ga ii* = "air-flow is good" → "is well ventilated/airy," and *kazetōshi ga warui* = "air-flow is bad" → "is airless/close/stuffy."
- *hiatari*, similarly, is a noun referring to the way a room or place catches the sunshine. *Hiatari ga ii* = "sunshine exposure is good" → "is bright and sunny/gets plenty of sunshine," and *hiatari ga warui* = "sunshine exposure is bad" → "is dark/doesn't get much sunshine."
- *warukunai* is the negative form of the adjective *warui* ("is bad") → "is not bad."

© Takeuchi Akira, *Garushia-kun*, Futabasha.

© Maekawa Tsukasa, *Dai-Tōkyō Binbō Seikatsu Manyuaru*, Kōdansha.

Negative adjectives in polite speech

In polite speech, the negative form of an adjective is made using *arimasen* instead of *nai* after its -*ku* form: *hayakunai* ("is not fast/early"; PL2) → *hayaku arimasen* (PL3). An alternative form is to simply add *desu* to the PL2 form: *hayakunai* → *hayakunai desu*.

Since -*nai* acts as an adjective, the same -*nai desu* pattern also occurs for negative verbs: *iku* ("go") → *ikanai* ("not go," PL2) → *ikanai desu* (PL3; same as *ikimasen*). But -*nai desu* forms generally don't sound quite as refined as the -*ku arimasen* form of an adjective or -*masen* form of a verb.

318   When Natsuko goes home for her brother's funeral and Kusakabe picks her up at the train station (fig. 189), they are meeting for the first time. As they drive home, Natsuko remarks that it's unusual these days to meet someone so young who wants to work at a saké brewery.

Kusakabe:
いやあ、 | 若くない | です。
Iyā, | *wakakunai* | *desu.*
(interj.) | am not young | (pol.)
"No, I'm not young."
"Actually, I'm not so young." (PL3)

先輩 と みっつ 違い です から。
Senpai to mittsu chigai desu kara.
(title) (compare) 3 count difference is/am because/so
"Because I'm [only] three years different from *senpai*."
"I'm only three years younger than *senpai*." (PL3)

- *iyā* is an elongated *iya*, which is an informal "no"; the elongated form is used as a warm-up/hesitation word ("well/really/urr/uhh/I mean") at the beginning of affirmative sentences as well as negative sentences, so the negative meaning is often lost, but here it retains the feeling of "no/not really."
- *senpai* is a title that refers to a person of more senior standing within a given group by virtue of having become a member of the group first. Later arrivals often address or refer to their predecessors/seniors as *senpai* rather than using their names. When Natsuko asks if by *senpai* he means her brother, Kusakabe explains that he went to the same college as her brother.

A negative adjective in a question

Questions ending in a negative adjective take the form of -*kunai ka?* (PL2) and -*ku arimasen ka?* or -*kunai desu ka* (PL3). In PL2 speech, explanatory *no* can be inserted before *ka* in the appropriate situations. Since -*nai ka*/-*nai no ka* sounds quite abrupt, female speakers in PL2 situations usually just say the negative adjective with the intonation of a question (*Hayakunai?*), or they use -*nai no?* without a *ka* on the end (*Hayakunai no?*)—both of which patterns are used by male speakers as well.

319   Garcia finds an inebriated man sitting against a utility pole at the side of the road and decides to help him home. He lifts him onto his back and heads down the narrow residential street.

Garcia: 寒くない | です | か?
Samukunai | *desu* | *ka?*
not cold | (pol.) | (?)
"Are you not cold?"
"Are you cold?" (PL3)

Man: うん。
Un.
uh-huh
"No." (PL2)

- *samukunai* is the plain negative form of the adjective *samui* ("cold"), and adding *desu* makes it polite—the same as asking *Samuku arimasen ka?*
- *un* is an informal "uh-huh/yes." In Japanese, *un* or *hai* in answer to a negative question implies "yes, that negative statement is correct," so the man is in effect saying, "Yes, I am not cold." This is a case where a Japanese "yes" is equivalent to "no" in English.

Rhetorical questions

Questions ending in *ja nai ka, ja arimasen ka,* and *ja nai desu ka* are often used rhetorically, in fact acting as mild assertions—or even quite strong ones. The rhetorical question essentially assumes an affirmative answer: "Is it not ～?" "Yes, it (most certainly) is!" Rhetorical questions end in the falling intonation of a regular sentence rather than the rising intonation of a question.

320 On his way back from a business trip to New York, Shima spends three days on vacation in Paris, and he decides to drop in on Hirase Ken'ichi, president of Hatsushiba France. Hirase and Shima joined Hatsushiba the same year.

Hirase: よう!　島　|じゃない　か。|
　　　Yō!　*Shima*　|*ja nai*　*ka.*|
　　　(greeting)　(name)　is not　(?)
"Hey! Is it not Shima?
"Hey! If it isn't Shima!" (PL2)

• *yō* is an informal greeting, "Hi!/Hey!/Yo!" used by male speakers.

For objecting/complaining or scolding/admonishing

A rhetorical question ending in *ja nai ka, ja arimasen ka,* or *ja nai desu ka* is often used to express an objection or complaint: "Is it not [something objectionable]?" "Yes it (most certainly) is!" If spoken in the presence of the person involved in the offense, the rhetorical question can be used to admonish or scold the listener, with a feeling something like "Don't you know that ～?" or "You know very well that ～."

In PL2 speech, female speakers tend to avoid the abrupt sounding ～ *ja nai ka* and instead say ～ *ja nai no* or just ～ *ja nai* (see next example), both of which patterns can be used by male speakers as well.

321 Prime Minister Hatomura is expected to resign shortly, and that means an election will be held to select a new party president. As Kaji and his aides discuss the convoluted electoral math involved, someone notes that large sums of money can be expected to change hands in pursuit of votes.

Aide:
それ　は　完全な
Sore　*wa*　*kanzen na*
that　as for　complete

選挙違反　|じゃないです　か。|
senkyo ihan　|*ja nai desu*　*ka.*|
election violation　is not　(?)
"As for that, it's a complete electoral violation, is it not?"
"But that's a complete violation of electoral laws!" (PL3)

• *kanzen* is an adjectival noun; when followed by *na*, it corresponds to English adjectives like "complete/utter/full/perfect."

• *senkyo* = "election" and *ihan* = "violation" → *senkyo ihan* = "violation of election laws."

• it may literally look like he is asking a question, but the question is rhetorical and, as his use of *kanzen na* ("complete") underscores, he is in fact making a strong assertion/objection.

• a PL2 example of this use appears in the punch line of fig. 136. *Ore* = "I/me" (masculine), *saifu* = "wallet/purse," and *ja nē ka* is a slurred, masculine equivalent of *ja nai ka,* so *Ore no saifu ja nē ka* is literally "Is that not my wallet?" Sayū speaks this very assertively as a rhetorical question, in effect implying "Yes, that *is* my wallet, and I object!"

Ja nai as a true or rhetorical question

Yama-chan

It's not unusual in PL2 speech for just *ja nai*—without *ka* or *no*—to be used as either a true or rhetorical question. If *ja nai* has the rising intonation of a question, it's a genuine question ("Isn't it ～?/Aren't you ～?"); if it's spoken with a falling intonation and an accented *nai*, it's a simple negative statement ("It isn't ～/You aren't ～"); with a falling intonation and unaccented *nai*, it's a rhetorical question that actually makes an assertion and expects agreement from the listener ("It is ～, isn't it?/You are ～, aren't you?"). Besides intonation and accent, context will usually help you decide which meaning is intended.

322 Cameraman Yama-chan has just returned from location shoots in Guam and Hawaii. These coworkers don't know where he has been.

Shades: なん　だー?
Nan　dā?
what　is
"What's this?"

山ちゃん、　　まっ黒　┃じゃない。┃
Yama-chan　makkuro　ja nai.
(name-dimin.)　(emph.)-black　is/are not
"You're completely black, are you not?"
"That's quite a tan you've got, Yama-chan!" (PL2)

* *Yama* here represents the first kanji of the cameraman's surname, which could be Yamada or Yamazaki or Yamamoto, etc. It's quite common for adult friends/associates to call each other by the first kanji (or first syllable or two) of their surname plus the diminutive *-chan*.
* まっ *ma!* is an intensifying prefix, which when used with colors implies "red as red can be," "black as black can be," and so forth.
* *makkuro ja nai* can also mean "[someone/something] is not completely black," but here it's a rhetorical question: "You are completely black, are you not? [Yes, you are!]" → "You're completely black!")

Rhetorical question with an adjective

This lesson began by showing *ja nai (desu)* and *ja arimasen* to be the negative forms of *da* and *desu* in the noun + *da/desu* pattern. But the rhetorical uses seen in figs. 320–22 can occur with adjectives and verbs as well.

An adjective in the non-past, past, or negative plain forms (never the polite forms) followed by *ja nai (ka)*, *ja arimasen (ka)*, or *ja nai desu ka* (in this last case, *ka* cannot be dropped) spoken with a falling intonation makes a rhetorical question: *Osoi ja nai (ka)!* = "You are late, are you not? [Yes, you are]!" → "You're late!" The rhetorical *ja nai (ka)* (and PL3 equivalents) make the statement much more assertive than just saying *Osoi ne* or *Osoi na* ("It's late/You're late"), and it's often used to express a complaint/protest, or to take someone to task (though the example seen here is good natured).

Important note: An adjective followed by the negative *ja nai* (without *ka*) is the same as the rhetorical question ～ *ja nai ka* and means "is/are ～." It must be clearly distinguished from the negative form of the adjective itself, which ends in *-kunai* and means "is/are not ～": *Samui ja nai* = "It's cold"; *Samukunai* = "It's not cold."

323 Shima had a longer day than Nakazawa, and Nakazawa has already been at the bar quite a while when Shima arrives.

Nakazawa:
よう、　　島君。　┃遅い　じゃない　か。┃
Yō,　Shima-kun.　Osoi　ja nai　ka.
(greeting)　(name-fam.)　late　are not　(?)
"Hey, Shima. You're late, are you not?"
"Hey, Shima. You're late!" (PL2)

Rhetorical question with a verb

Similarly, a verb in the non-past, past, or negative plain forms (never the polite forms) followed by *ja nai (ka)*, *ja arimasen (ka)* or *ja nai desu ka* (the *ka* is required for the last) spoken with a falling intonation makes a rhetorical question: *Shinu ja nai (ka)!* = "He will die, will he not? [Yes, he will!]" → "He'll die/It'll kill him!" Again, a rhetorical question of this kind is more assertive than just saying *Shinu/shinimasu yo* or *Shinu zo* ("He'll die/It'll kill him"), and it's often used to object/complain/admonish/scold; in the example seen here, it expresses a light-hearted protest.

Important note: A plain verb followed by only *ja nai* (without *ka*) is the same as the rhetorical question ~ *ja nai ka* and means "does/did/will do/is doing [the action]." It must be clearly distinguished from the negative form of the verb itself, which means "does not/did not/will not do/is not doing [the action]."

Father

☞ See remarks at fig. 321 about female use of the abrupt-sounding ~ *ja nai ka*.

> **324** When Natsuko leaves Tokyo for good and arrives home, her father is out at a business dinner, so the women of the house decide to have a little party of their own. Later, her father finds them rosy-cheeked and merry, and he is outraged that they have gotten drunk in his absence. Natsuko's mother and her sister-in-law respond:

© Oze Akira, *Natsuko no Sake*, Kōdansha.

Mother: 父さん　だって　酔ってる　じゃありません　か。
Tōsan　datte　yotteru　ja arimasen　ka.
dad/you　also　are drunk　are not　(?)
"You, too, are drunk, are you not?"
"But you're drunk, too!" (PL3)

Kazuko: これ　で　互角　よ　ね。
Kore　de　gokaku　yo　ne.
This　with　even　(is-emph.)　(colloq.)
"This makes us even." (PL2)

- *datte* here is a colloquial equivalent of the particle *mo* ("too/also").
- *yotteru* is a contraction of *yotte iru* ("is drunk"), from *you/yoimasu* ("become drunk"). The negative *ja arimasen ka* makes a rhetorical question.

Expressing delight

Besides objecting/complaining or admonishing, the rhetorical *ja nai/arimasen (ka)* can also be used to express delight.

> **325** When the OL serves her boss some tea, he notices that she has brought it in a new teacup.

© Ishii Hisaichi, *Ishii Hisaichi Senshū*, Futabasha.

Boss: おや、新しい　湯のみ　だ　な。
Oya,　atarashii　yunomi　da　na.
(interj.)　new　teacup　is　(colloq.)
"Oh, it's a new teacup, isn't it?" (PL2)

OL1: ホホ。　　いえ、まー。
Ho ho.　　Ie,　mā.
(fem. laugh/chuckle)　(interj.)　(interj.)
"(laugh) Oh, you mustn't." (PL2–3)

Boss: 気がきく　じゃない　か。
Ki ga kiku　ja nai　ka.
is thoughtful　is not　(?)
"It is thoughtful of you, is it not?"
"That's very thoughtful of you!" (PL2)

- *oya* is an interjection of sudden awareness/mild surprise.
- *ho ho* represents a gentle, feminine laugh (fig. 280).
- *ki ga kiku/kikimasu* (lit. "thoughts/attentions are effective") is an expression for "thoughtful/considerate."
- *ie* is a shortened *iie*, "no," and *mā* is a soft/gentle/agreeable/self-effacing interjection that adapts to fit the context. It can be used to avoid giving too straight an answer, which is what she is doing here. For the final frame and punch line of this gag manga, see fig. 349.

Ja nai ka after a negative

As noted at figs. 323 and 324, the rhetorical *ja nai (ka)* can follow a negative plain (never polite) form. For a negative noun-type sentence (∼ *ja nai/janakatta*), the full rhetorical ending becomes ∼ *ja nai ja nai ka* (non-past) or ∼ *ja nakatta ja nai ka* (past); for a negative adjective-type sentence (*-kunai/-kunakatta*), the full rhetorical ending becomes *-kunai ja nai ka* (non-past) or *-kunakatta ja nai ka* (past). The feeling in these cases is often like "[It] isn't/wasn't [the named thing/the described quality] at all!" For a negative verb-type sentence (*-nai/-nakatta*), the full rhetorical ending becomes *-nai ja nai ka* (non-past) or *-nakatta ja nai ka* (past), and it often feels like "[It] doesn't/didn't [do the action] at all!"

326 The boss doesn't like any of the ideas his subordinate has presented for a poster that will urge citizens to use resources wisely and reduce waste.

Boss: なん だ よ？ なん だ よ？
Nan da yo? Nan da yo?
what is (emph.) what is (emph.)
"What is this? What is this?" (PL2)

ロクな アイデア ｜ない じゃない か。
Roku na aidea ｜ *nai ja nai ka.*
decent idea ｜ not exist is not (?)
"A decent idea doesn't exist—isn't that so?"
"There's not a single decent idea here!" (PL2)

FX: ポイ ポイ ポイ
Poi poi poi
(effect of tossing away one sheet after the other)

• *roku na* is an adjectival noun meaning "satisfactory/proper/decent," and *aidea* is the Japanese rendering of the English word "idea." *Ga*, to mark this as the subject of *nai*, has been omitted.

Summary: Negative *da/desu* and adjectives

Ja nai forms have many uses, and the kind of brief treatment given them in this lesson can't show all the different twists. But being aware of the uses introduced here will help you grasp the underlying meaning when you encounter new expressions. This table summarizes the basic negative forms for *da/desu* and adjectives.

	negative of *da/desu* (follows a noun or adjectival noun)		negative of adjective (follows the adjective stem)		meaning
	plain	polite	plain	polite	
non-past	*ja nai*[1] *de wa nai* *de nai*	*ja arimasen* *de wa arimasen* *de arimasen* *ja nai desu* *de wa nai desu* *de nai desu*	*-kunai*[1]	*-ku arimasen* *-kunai desu*	is not ∼[2]
past	*ja nakatta*[1,3]	*ja arimasen deshita* *ja nakatta desu*	*-kunakatta*[1]	*-ku arimasen deshita* *-ku nakatta desu*	was not ∼[2]
question	*ja nai ka?*[4] *ja nai?*[4]	*ja arimasen ka?*[4] *ja nai desu ka?*[4] *ja arimasen?*[4]	*-kunai ka?* *-kunai?*	*-ku arimasen ka?* *-ku nai desu ka?* *-ku arimasen?*	isn't it ∼?[2]
question	*ja nakatta ka?* *ja nakatta?*	*ja arimasen deshita ka?* *ja nakatta desu ka?* *ja arimasen deshita?*	*-kunakatta ka?* *-kunakatta?*	*-ku arimasen deshita ka?* *-kunakatta desu ka?* *-ku arimasen deshita?*	wasn't it ∼?[2]
explan.	*ja nai no*[4]	*ja arimasen no* *ja nai n(o) desu*	*-kunai no*	*-ku arimasen no* *-ku nai n(o) desu*	it's that it isn't ∼[2,5]
explan.	*ja nakatta no*	*ja arimasen deshita no* *ja nakatta n(o) desu*	*-kunakatta no*	*-ku arimasen deshita no* *-ku nakatta n(o) desu*	it's that it wasn't ∼[2,5]

[1] The plain negative forms (both past and non-past) can be used in a modifying position as well as at the end of a sentence: *gakusei ja nai/ja nakatta hito* = "the person who isn't/wasn't a student"; *samukunai/samukunakatta hito* = "the person who isn't/wasn't cold."

[2] For a regular noun, fill in the blank with an equivalent English noun; for an adjective or adjectival noun, fill in with an equivalent English adjective.

[3] In the remainder of the table, *ja* can be replaced with *de* or *de wa*.

[4] Also commonly used as a rhetorical question—in which case it can follow the plain form of an adjective or verb as well as a noun.

[5] The forms ending in *no* can be used with rising intonation to ask, "Is the situation that it isn't ∼?"—which often boils down to "Isn't it ∼?"

Lesson 22

Let's Do It!

You learned in Lesson 3 that changing a polite verb's -ます -*masu* ending to -ましょう -*mashō*—a simple conversion that works for all verbs—creates a form that expresses intention/determination or a decision to do the action, like "Let's [do the action]" (when the speaker and at least one other person will act together), or "I will/I shall/I think I'll [do the action]" (when the speaker will be acting alone—often, though not always, doing something for the listener). The first of these uses has already been illustrated in figs. 36, 63, and 115. Here's an example of the latter use.

327 The customer who comes into the second-hand book-store while Kōsuke is minding the store (fig. 135) says he wants ¥5000 for the book. Kōsuke takes a look at the book and agrees.

Kōsuke:
わかりました。　その　値段　で　買いましょう。
Wakarimashita.　Sono nedan de　kaimashō.
understood　　　that price at　I'll buy
"All right. I'll buy it at that price." (PL3)

- in response to a request or command, *wakarimashita* and *waka-tta*—i.e., the past forms of *wakaru* ("understand")—imply "I understand what you are asking [and I will do it]" → "all right."
- *kaimashō* is the polite "let's/I'll ~" form of *kau/kaimasu* ("buy").

Group 1 verbs

To make the plain equivalent of -*mashō* for a Group 1 verb, change the final -*u* of the dictionary form to a long -*ō*: *iku* ("go") → *ikō* ("let's go"). In kana, change the last syllable to the *o* sound in the same row—if it's す make it そ; if it's つ make it と—and lengthen it by adding う).

328 Just before flying to the U.S. for meetings with American congressmen, Kaji learned that a man he and his aides suspect of being involved in his father's death is now in Washington D.C. He's asked two friends to join him there to see if they can find the man and learn who he's working for. The friends are arriving by train from New York.

Kaji: いそごう！　そろそろ　ワシントン駅　へ　到着する　頃　だ。
Isogō!　Sorosoro Washinton-eki e tōchaku suru koro da.
let's hurry　soon (name)-station to/at arrive approx. time is
"Let's hurry. Soon it is approximately [they]-arrive-at-Washington-Station time."
"Let's hurry. It's about time the train's supposed to get in at the station." (PL2)

- *isogō* is the plain "let's/I'll ~" form of the Group 1 verb *isogu/isogimasu* ("hurry/make haste").
- *sorosoro* is an adverb implying that the action is impending: "by and by/soon/now."
- *tōchaku* is a noun for "arrival," and adding *suru* makes it a verb.
- *koro* (also pronounced *goro* when used right after a time word) is a noun referring to an approximate point in time; *koro* after a verb means "about when [the action occurs/occurred/will occur]."

Irregular verbs

The plain equivalents of -*mashō* for the irregular verbs both end in -よう -*yō*: the form for *kuru* is こよう *koyō*, and the form for *suru* is しよう *shiyō*. For the latter, although the difference can be very slight, *shi* and *yō* should be pronounced as separate syllables to distinguish it from しょう*shō*, with a small よ *yo*.

329 Although only about one percent of the Japanese population is Christian, Christmas has become a trendy commercial and social holiday. Since December 25 is a regular work day, celebrations center on Christmas Eve, which is regarded as the most romantic date night of the year.

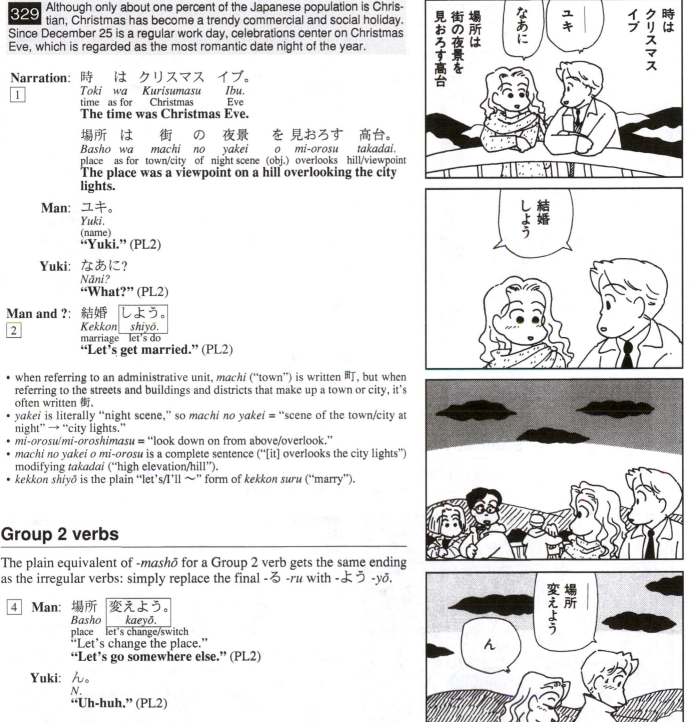

Narration: 時　は　クリスマス　イブ。
1
Toki wa Kurisumasu Ibu.
time as for Christmas Eve
The time was Christmas Eve.

場所　は　街　の　夜景　を　見おろす　高台。
Basho wa machi no yakei o mi-orosu takadai.
place as for town/city of night scene (obj.) overlooks hill/viewpoint
The place was a viewpoint on a hill overlooking the city lights.

Man: ユキ。
Yuki.
(name)
"Yuki." (PL2)

Yuki: なあに?
Nāni?
"What?" (PL2)

Man and ?: 結婚 しよう。
2
Kekkon shiyō.
marriage let's do
"Let's get married." (PL2)

- when referring to an administrative unit, *machi* ("town") is written 町, but when referring to the streets and buildings and districts that make up a town or city, it's often written 街.
- *yakei* is literally "night scene," so *machi no yakei* = "scene of the town/city at night" → "city lights."
- *mi-orosu/mi-oroshimasu* = "look down on from above/overlook."
- *machi no yakei o mi-orosu* is a complete sentence ("[it] overlooks the city lights") modifying *takadai* ("high elevation/hill").
- *kekkon shiyō* is the plain "let's/I'll ～" form of *kekkon suru* ("marry").

Group 2 verbs

The plain equivalent of -*mashō* for a Group 2 verb gets the same ending as the irregular verbs: simply replace the final -る -*ru* with -よう -*yō*.

4　**Man**: 場所 変えよう。
Basho kaeyō.
place let's change/switch
"Let's change the place."
"Let's go somewhere else." (PL2)

Yuki: ん。
N.
"Uh-huh." (PL2)

- *kaeyō* is the plain "let's/I'll ～" form of *kaeru/kaemasu* ("change/switch [something]"). *O*, to mark *basho* as the direct object (i.e., the thing being changed/switched), has been omitted.
- *n* is the same as *un*, an informal "yes/uh-huh."

Summary: The "let's/I'll/I think I'll ～" forms of verbs

To make the polite "let's/I'll ～" forms for all verbs, simply change -*masu* to -*mashō*. The table shows the model plain forms: Group 2 verbs and irregular verbs end in -*yō* (replacing the final -*ru* of the dictionary form), while Group 1 verbs end in just a long -*ō* (replacing the final -*u*). Knowing that Group 1 verbs don't get the *y* sound will help you distinguish verbs that sound the same in the dictionary form but are of different types: *kaeyō* is from the Group 2 verb *kaeru/ kaemasu*, which means "change/switch" (fig. 329), while *kaerō* is from the Group 1 verb *kaeru/ kaerimasu*, which means "return home" (figs. 4, 72).

Since this form implies that a willful decision is being/has been made, it will not ordinarily make sense for some verbs.

¹ For romaji conversions, in *t* row syllables, *t* = *ch* = *ts*. See Introduction.

² Refers to dropping a material object; cannot be used in the English sense of "Let's stop discussing the subject."

		dictionary form			plain "let's/i'll" form	
irreg.	くる	*kuru*	come	こよう	*koyō*	let's come
	する	*suru*	do	しよう	*shiyō*	let's do [it]
gr. 2	みる	*miru*	see	みよう	*miyō*	let's see
	たべる	*taberu*	eat	たべよう	*tabeyō*	let's eat
group 1 verbs	とる	*toru*	take	とろう	*torō*	let's take
	かう	*kau*	buy	かおう	*kaō*	let's buy
	もつ	*motsu*¹	hold	もとう	*motō*¹	let's hold
	よぶ	*yobu*	call	よぼう	*yobō*	let's call
	のむ	*nomu*	drink	のもう	*nomō*	let's drink
	しぬ	*shinu*	die	しのう	*shinō*	let's die
	おとす	*otosu*	drop	おとそう	*otosō*	let's drop [it]²
	かく	*kaku*	write	かこう	*kakō*	let's write
	およぐ	*oyogu*	swim	およごう	*oyogō*	let's swim

"Shall we?"

The effect of a "let's/I'll ～" form on questions is quite varied. Perhaps most typically -*mashō ka?* or -*ō/-yō ka?* makes a question like "Shall we [do the action]?"

330 Kōsuke and Hiroko have been taking in the street scene in trendy Shibuya as part of Hiroko's artistic interest in postmodernism. She suggests they stop for a break.

Hiroko: お茶 でも 飲もう か?
O-cha   de mo   nomō   ka?
(hon.)-tea or something shall drink (?)
"Shall we drink tea or something?"
"Shall we stop for tea or something?" (PL2)

- *cha* ("tea") almost always gets the honorific prefix *o*-, regardless of the politeness level. It often carries the generic meaning of "something to drink."
- *de mo*, "or something," is often added to invitations/offers/suggestions to lend a touch of polite vagueness. In the case of an offer, it may or may not mean that the person truly has a choice of something besides the item mentioned.
- *nomō* is the PL2 "let's/I'll ～" form of the Group 1 verb *nomu/nomi-masu* ("drink").

A rhetorical question

A question asked with *-mashō ka* or *-ō/-yō ka* is sometimes mostly or entirely rhetorical. It can in fact mean "Let's [do the action]," rather than "Shall we [do the action]?"

331 Yata arrives late when Shima asks him to meet him at a bar, and then apologetically says he needs to make a few more calls before he can relax for the evening. Ten minutes later he is finally ready to kick back.

Yata: ケイタイ を 切ります!
Keitai o kirimasu!
portable (obj.) will turn off
"I'm turning off my mobile phone." (PL3)

さあ、 │飲みましょう か!│
Sā, nomimashō ka!
(interj.) let's drink (?)
"Let's drink!" (PL3)

- *keitai* (written 携帯 in kanji) used to occur mainly as a *suru* verb (*keitai suru* = "carry along") or as a modifier (*keitai terebi* = "portable television"), but *keitai* by itself has now become shorthand for *keitai denwa* ("portable/mobile/cell phone").
- *kirimasu* is the polite form of the Group 1 verb *kiru*, which literally means "cut." *Kiru* is used to speak of turning off all kinds of switches (i.e., cutting the power); with land-line phones it refers to hanging up the phone (i.e., cutting off the transmission), and with mobile phones it can refer either to ending a call or turning the handset completely off. Context tells us it's the latter meaning here.
- *nomimashō* is from *nomu/nomimasu* ("drink"); in another context, *nomimashō ka* could be a genuine question, "Shall we drink?" but here the question is merely rhetorical.

Making an offer

A question asked with *-mashō ka* or *-ō/-yō ka* can be used when offering to do something for or with another person: "Shall I ～ for/with you?"

332 Nat-chan sees this stranger struggling with heavy-laden plastic grocery bags and asks if she can help.

Shopper: あーあ、 おもい、 おもい。 あー...
Ā-a, omoi, omoi. Ā...
(interj.) is heavy is heavy (interj.)
"Ohhh, this stuff is so heavy, so heavy. Ohhh..." (PL2)

Nat-chan: おばあさん、 にもつ │持ちましょう│ か?
O-bāsan, nimotsu mochimashō ka?
(hon.)-grandma bags shall carry (?)
"Shall I carry the bags, Granny?"
"Shall I help you with your bags, Granny?" (PL3)

Shopper: 男 だ よ。
Otoko da yo.
man am (emph.)
"I'm a man." (PL2)

- *ā-a* is an interjection that can express a variety of unhappy sentiments: lament/woe/disappointment/fatigue.
- *o-bāsan* means "grandmother/elderly woman," and is used to address or refer to any elderly woman, not just one's own grandmother.
- *mochimashō* is the polite "let's/I'll ～" form of the Group 1 verb *motsu/mochimasu* ("hold/carry").

With question words

When question words are used, the question particle *ka* is sometimes omitted at the end of a *-mashō* or *-ō/-yō* sentence.

333 This couple happened upon the bar Lemon Hart when they were out walking, and they are amazed by the huge selection of bottles they see lining the shelves.

Proprietor: なに を 差し上げましょう?
Nani   o   sashiagemashō?
what (obj.)   shall give you
"What shall I give you?"
"What can I get you?" (PL4)

Customer: ちょっと まって。 いま 考えている から。
Chotto   matte.   Ima   kangaete iru   kara.
a little   please wait   now   am/are thinking   because
"Wait just a second. We're still thinking." (PL2)

- *sashiagemashō* is the polite "let's/I'll ～" form of *sashiageru/sashiagemasu* (an honorific word for "give you").
- *matte* is the *-te* form of *matsu/machimasu* ("wait"); the *-te* form is being used as an informal request.
- *kangaete iru* ("am/are thinking") is from *kangaeru/kangaemasu* ("think about/consider/ponder").

With *ka na* or *kashira*

A question ending with *-ō/-yō* plus *ka na* (somewhat masculine) or *kashira* (feminine) asks, "I wonder if I should ～?" or implies, "Perhaps I should ～/Maybe I will ～." Since *ka na* and *kashira* are informal, they're not generally used with the polite *-mashō*—though you may hear an occasional exception.

334 Like so many others, something has inspired this OL to consider joining an English conversation class.

OL1: 私 も 英会話 やろう かな?
Watashi   mo   eikaiwa   yarō   ka na?
I/me   too/also   Eng. conv.   shall do   I wonder if
"I wonder if I, too, should do English conversation?"
"I wonder if I should take English conversation classes?" (PL2)

これ は イス です。
Kore   wa   isu   desu.
this   as for   chair   is
"This is a chair." (PL3)

OL2: プ
Pu
(stifled laugh)

- she uses *mo* ("too/also") because taking English conversation classes is tremendously popular in Japan, and she would be joining countless others who have preceded her.
- *yarō* is the plain "let's/I'll ～" form of the Group 1 verb *yaru/yarimasu* ("do," informal).
- female speakers often use the somewhat masculine *ka na* in informal situations where there's no particular need to express their femininity.
- the horizontal text implies she's saying the sentence in English. *Isu* means "chair," but it is also the way many Japanese pronounce the English word "is," and she apparently intends a bilingual pun: "This *isu* a chair."

With a question word + *ka na/kashira*

A question containing a question-word and ending with *-ō/-yō ka na* or *-ō/-yō kashira* asks "I wonder who/what/when/how much I should 〜?"

335 Shin-chan's mother had to wait a long time in line before it was her turn at the cash machine. She has been so aggravated about how much time the people ahead of her were taking that she forgot to think about exactly how much money she needs to withdraw.

Mother: やっと　　私　の　番。
Yatto　　watashi　no　ban.
at last/finally　I/me　's　turn
"**It's finally my turn.**" (PL2)

いくら　　おろそう　　かな?
Ikura　　orosō　　ka na?
how much　shall withdraw　I wonder
"**I wonder how much I should withdraw?**"
(PL2)

- something like *da wa* ("is/are" + fem.) is understood after *ban* ("turn"): *Watashi no ban da wa* = "It's my turn."
- *orosō* is the plain "let's/I'll 〜" form of *orosu/oroshimasu*, which more generally means "take [something] down/put [something] down"; but when speaking of money in the bank, it means "withdraw."
- female speakers often use *ka na* when speaking to themselves.

Stating one's intent or decision

Although the *-ō/-yō* form of a verb by itself can mean "I think I'll [do the action]," it's also sometimes followed by *to omou/omoimasu* (the quoting *to* + "think"). This makes an expression that feels more like declaring, "I plan/intend to [do the action]" or "I have decided to [do the action]." The polite *-mashō* form does not ordinarily occur in this pattern.

A plain *-ō/-yō* form followed by *ka to omou/omoimasu* makes a somewhat more tentative expression of intent, like "I'm thinking I might [do the action]/I'm considering [doing the action]."

Since normally only the plain forms are used in these patterns, the politeness level is determined by the form that *omou* takes at the end of the sentence.

336 Natsuko has come to thank Jinkichi after he plowed the small paddy she was preparing for her crop of Tatsunishiki rice. He offers to lend her his weed-spraying equipment next, but she declines. She wants to stick with organic methods, she says. But she also knows she's going to need help from others—especially next year, when the seed produced by this year's crop should fill a lot more than one paddy.

Natsuko:
仁吉くん、　あたし　ね、
Jinkichi-kun,　atashi　ne,
(name-fam.)　I/me　(colloq.)

栽培会　　を　つくろう　と　思う　の。
saibai-kai　o　tsukurō　to　omou　no.
cultivation grp.　(obj.)　I'll make　(quote)　think　(explan.)
"**Jinkichi, I'm planning to start a Tatsunishiki grower's group.**" (PL2)

Jinkichi:
栽培会?
Saibai-kai?
"**A grower's group?**" (PL2)

- *tsukurō* is the plain "let's/I'll 〜" form of *tsukuru/tsukurimasu* ("make/create").

Compare for *ongaku* = "music" and the verb *kiku/kikimasu* ("hear/listen"):
Ongaku o kikō = "Let's listen to some music" or "I think I'll listen to some music."
Konban ongaku o kikō to omoimasu = "I intend/plan to listen to some music tonight."
Konban ongaku o kikō ka to omoimasu = "I'm thinking I might listen to some music tonight."
Kore kara wa mainichi ongaku o kikō to omoimasu = "I've decided to listen to music everyday from now on."

Lesson 23

Hyman

Desire

How to express desire in Japanese depends on whether what you want is a thing or an action. If you want to obtain or possess a thing—either tangible, like an apple, or intangible, like love—you express it by saying 〜がほしい 〜 *ga hoshii*. *Hoshii* is an adjective, so its plain past form is ほしかった *hoshikatta*, and adding *desu* to either the non-past or past form raises its politeness level to PL3. The word usually occurs in a *wa-ga* construction, which means the person who wants (when mentioned) is marked with *wa* and the thing wanted is marked with *ga*.

337 Journalist Jackie Hyman spied fellow journalist Linda Simmons walking with Japanese Defense Minister Kaji by the reflecting pool on the Capitol Mall in Washington D.C. at 5:00 A.M. At a meeting with Hyman, Simmons assumes there will be a cost involved in getting him to keep quiet.

Simmons: あなた　何　が　欲しい　の?
Anata nani ga hoshii no?
you　what　(subj.)　is wanted　(explan.)
"As for you, what is wanted?"
"What is it you want?" (PL2)

- *wa*, to mark *anata* as the topic (the person who wants something), has been omitted.
- as seen here, *hoshii* may be followed by the explanatory extension *no*—and that can make either a statement or a question depending on the intonation. Here her use of a question word makes it clearly a question, the full PL3 version of which would be *Anata (wa) nani ga hoshii no desu ka?* Without a question word, 〜 *ga hoshii (no) (desu ka)?* asks "Do you want 〜?" With a question word, it is typically "What/which one/how many/etc. do you want?" depending on the particular word and its role in the sentence.

Don't want/didn't want

Following the standard rule for adjectives, the plain negative form of *hoshii* is *hoshikunai* ("don't want"), and the plain negative-past form is *hoshikunakatta* ("didn't want"). These can be used in negative questions the same way the English phrasing "Don't/didn't you want 〜?" is used to imply "You surely do want 〜, don't you?" or "You surely did want 〜, didn't you?"

338 An odd-looking man who calls himself "the masked protector of foreign laborers" approaches Garcia (figs. 223, 316) and offers to grant him one wish. When Garcia says he wants Japanese friends, the man pulls out a book entitled *How to Make Japanese Friends*, and says it'll be ¥15,000. Garcia balks at the steep price, but the man presses the sale.

Salesman:
日本人　　の　友達　が　欲しくない　の　か?
Nihon-jin no tomodachi ga hoshikunai no ka?
Japanese person　(mod.)　friend　(subj.)　not want　(explan.)　(?)
"Don't you want Japanese friends?" (PL2)

Garcia:
売って下さい。
Utte kudasai.
sell-(request)
"Please sell [me one]."
"I'll take one." (PL3)

- *utte* is the *-te* form of *uru/urimasu* ("sell"), and *kudasai* makes it a polite request, "Please sell." The context makes it obvious that he means "Please sell one to me" → "I'll take one."

© Hirokane Kenshi, *Kaji Ryūsuke no Gi*, Kodansha.

© Takeuchi Akira, *Garushia-kun*, Futabasha.

As a modifier

Like any adjective, *hoshii* often occurs before a noun or pronoun as a modifier—either for the item wanted (*hon* = "book" and *hoshii hon* = "the wanted book" → "the book that I/you want"), or for the person who wants it (*hito* = "person," and *hoshii hito* = "the wanting person" → "the person who wants [it/something]").

339 While out walking, this woman discovers a shop called "Alice's Room" that's filled with cute merchandise. She can't resist stopping in.

Shopper: きゃー、　かーわいーい!
Kyā,　　　kāwaiiii!
(exclam.)　　cute/darling
"Oooo, how da-a-arling!" (PL2)

ほしい　もの　が　いっぱい　あるー!
Hoshii　mono　ga　ippai　arū!
wanted　thing(s)　(subj.)　lg. quantity　exist/there are
"Things that I want exist in large quantity!"
"There's lots of things I want!" (PL2)

- the adjective かわいい *kawaii* ("is cute/darling") often gets elongated in exclamations, especially among young female speakers.
- lengthening *aru* ("exists") is also exclamatory.

When you want an action

When you want your listener or someone else to *do* something, you use the *-te* form of a verb plus *hoshii*. The same form is used when asking what your listener wants done. The particle *ni* marks the person whom the speaker would like to have perform the action. The *wa-ga* construction that applies to *hoshii* does not apply to *-te hoshii*, so the direct object of the desired action (the thing it is/will be/was performed on) is marked with *o*.

If the person you want to perform the action is a social superior, you should use *-te itadaki-tai (n) (desu)* instead, from *itadaku/itadakimasu* (a polite word for "receive"). The *-tai* form is introduced next in this lesson, and you'll find more on the *-te itadaku* form in Lesson 31.

Mrs. Hirai

340 Corporate warrior Hirai's wife has been having an affair with a mobster, who is now threatening to publish photos of their sexcapades and ruin Hirai's reputation unless he comes up with ¥50 million. Here Hirai confronts his wife with the evidence.

Hirai: おまえ　に、まず、この　写真　を
Omae　ni,　mazu,　kono　shashin　o
you　(doer)　first　these　photos　(obj.)

見て欲しい。
mite hoshii.
want [you] to look
"First, I'd like you to take a look at these pictures." (PL2)

- *ni* marks *omae* ("you") as the person whose action is desired. In general usage, *omae* is a masculine word, used mostly with peers and subordinates. Among friends it carries a feeling of familiarity, but when used with strangers it feels quite rough. Within the family, husbands typically use *omae* when speaking to their wives or children; wives can also use *omae* (often *omae-san*, with an endearing tone like "dear/honey") for their husbands, but the more formal *anata* ("you") is generally preferred.
- *mazu* is an adverb meaning "first of all/to begin with."
- *mite* is the *-te* form of *miru* ("see/watch/look at"); adding *hoshii* to the *-te* form makes it "[I] want [you] to look," and *o* marks *shashin* ("pictures") as what he wants her to look at.

-Te hoshii = "please"

When expressing a desire for the listener to do something, the *-te hoshii* form can be like saying, "Please [do the action]."

341 This young man thought he'd found the right moment to pop the question, but he has apparently caught his sweetheart a little by surprise.

Man: 結婚　| してほしい。|
Kekkon　| *shite hoshii.* |
marriage　want [you] to do
"I want you to marry [me]."
"Please marry me." (PL2)

Woman: えっ?
E?
huh?/what?
"Huh?" (PL2–3)

- *kekkon shite* is the *-te* form of *kekkon suru* ("marry/get married"). It's obvious from the context that he wants her to marry him and not someone else.
- *e?* spoken with the rising intonation of a question is an interjection like "Huh?/What?/Oh?" when you haven't heard clearly or are surprised/startled by what you've heard.

Saying what you want to do: -たい *-tai*

A verb's -たい *-tai* **form** is used to state what you yourself want to do, or to ask what your listener wants to do. The *-tai* form is easy to make so long as you know a verb's *-masu* form: for any verb, simply replace *-masu* with *-tai*.

For a verb that takes an *o* phrase, the direct object of its *-tai* form can usually be marked either with *o*, the normal marker for a direct object, or with *ga*, in the *wa-ga* pattern (fig. 145). The example here shows a case of the latter. But in certain cases, the marking particle must remain *o*. For example, *ga* is not an option for the kind of *o* phrases illustrated in figs. 126 or 127 even when the *-tai* form is used (*kuruma o oritai*; = "want to get out of the car"; *hodō o hashiri-tai* = "want to run/ride/drive on the sidewalk").

342 When the Saeki Brewery entry fails to win any honors at all at a saké fair in which almost half of the nearly 4000 entries received some kind of award, Zenzō goes on a bender and begins asking everyone around if the saké he made is really so terrible. Natsu finally decides to ignore her mother-in-law's objections (fig. 309) and take a taste. When her mother-in-law immediately starts to fly off the handle, Zenzō cuts her off.

Zenzo:
私　　は　　奈津　の　　意見　　が　| 聞きたい。|
Watashi　wa　Natsu　no　iken　ga　| kikitai. |
I/me　as for　(name)　's　opinion/view　(obj.)　want to hear
"I want to hear Natsu's opinion."
"I want to know what Natsu thinks." (PL2)

- *kikitai* is from the verb *kiku* ("hear"), and *ga* marks *iken* ("view/opinion") as its direct object. Normally, the direct object of *kiku* is marked with *o*, but when the verb is in the *-tai* form, either *ga* or *o* may be used.

-*Tai* acts as an adjective

The -*tai* form of a verb acts as an adjective, so its polite form is made simply by adding *desu*: e.g., *miru* ("see/watch") → *mitai* ("want to see/watch"; PL2) → *mitai desu* (PL3). If the explanatory extension is used, it follows directly after -*tai*: *mitai no* or *mitai n(o) da* (PL2), and *mitai n(o) desu* (PL3).

343 Zenzō's last letter from the battlefield before he is killed in action asks Natsu to show their little daughter Aya inside the brewhouse so that she can see what kind of work her father did. When she takes the letter to her father-in-law, he asks her, "Do you still want to see inside the brewhouse?"

Natsu: 入りたいです。
Hairitai desu.
want to enter-(pol.)
"I want to enter."
"Yes, I do." (PL3)

• *hairitai* is from the Group 1 verb *hairu/hairimasu* ("enter"). Adding *desu* raises the politeness to PL3.

The past forms of -*tai*

Since -*tai* acts as an adjective, its plain past form is -たかった -*takatta* ("wanted to ～"), and the polite past form is made by adding *desu* (never *deshita*) to that: e.g., *mitakatta* ("wanted to see"; PL2) → *mitakatta desu* (PL3). With the explanatory extension, the past forms become -*takatta no* or -*takatta n(o) da* (PL2) and -*takatta n(o) desu* (PL3).

344 The first OL here (on the right) had a two-day escape with her boyfriend planned, but a sudden change in his work schedule forced him to cancel for the second night. Since it's too late to cancel the reservation, she decides to see if another friend would like to come.

A: ...と いう わけ。
...to iu wake.
(quote) say situation
"So that's the story." (PL2)

2日目、 あんた 来ない?
Futsuka-me, anta konai?
second day you not come
"The second day, won't you come?"
"Would you like to come the second night?" (PL2)

B: 行く! この ホテル 泊まりたかった んだ。
Iku! Kono hoteru tomaritakatta n da.
will go this hotel wanted to stay (explan.)
"I'll go! I wanted to stay at this hotel."
"You bet! I've been wanting to stay at this hotel sometime." (PL2)

• *to iu wake* (starting with the *to* for quoting) is a common way to conclude an explanation or a description of events; here it implies she has been explaining how the second night became available.

• *konai* is the negative form of *kuru* ("come"). She uses a negative question as an invitation (see figs. 298–99).

• *tomaritakatta* is the plain past form of *tomaritai* ("want to stay/spend the night"), from the Group 1 verb *tomaru/tomarimasu* ("stay/spend the night"). *Ni*, to mark *hoteru* (from English "hotel") as the place where she wanted to stay, has been omitted.

Saying what you don't/didn't want to do

A verb's negative *-tai* forms are made the same way as an adjective's negative forms. The negative non-past forms are *-takunai* ("don't want to 〜"; PL2) and *-takunai desu* or *-taku arimasen* (PL3). The negative-past forms are *-takunakatta* ("didn't want to 〜"; PL2), and *taku nakatta desu* or *-taku arimasen deshita* (PL3). With the explanatory extension the negative forms become: *-takunai no* or *-takunai n(o) da* (PL2 non-past); *-takunai n(o) desu* (PL3 non-past) or *-taku arimasen no* (PL3 non-past, feminine); *-takunakatta no* or *-takunakatta n(o) da* (PL2 past); and *-takunakatta n(o) desu* (PL3 past) or *-taku arimasen deshita no* (PL3 past, feminine).

あたし……農家に嫁ぎたくありません

345　Jinkichi (fig. 336) has asked Natsuko and Shingo to act as his *nakōdo* ("go-betweens") in proposing to Shizue, and the four of them are having dinner at a restaurant. When Jinkichi goes to the restroom, Shingo and Natsuko tell Shizue what he has in mind. Shizue responds that she's very fond of Jinkichi but she doesn't think it would work out. Natsuko asks why not, and Shizue answers:

"Wh-why not?"

Shizue: あたし、　農家　　に　┃嫁ぎたくありません。┃
Atashi,　nōka　　ni　┃totsugitaku arimasen.┃
I/me　farm family　into　not want to get married
"I don't want to marry into a farm family." (PL3)

- なぜ *Naze?* = "Why?"—but in response to a negative statement it becomes "Why not?"
- *nōka* ("farm" + "house/family") can refer either to the farm itself, or to the family that owns/runs it.
- *totsugitaku arimasen* is the PL3 negative form of *totsugitai* ("want to marry"), from the verb *totsugu/totsugimasu* ("marry"). The word can be considered a synonym for *kekkon suru*, which has appeared in fig. 329 among others, but *totsugu* has an old-fashioned ring to it, evoking the traditional matrimonial system in which a woman doesn't so much marry a husband as "marry into" her husband's family, where she effectively becomes her mother-in-law's servant in tending to the extended family's domestic needs. Many young women today resist this model of marriage.

-Tai as a noun modifier

Not surprisingly, a *-tai* verb in any of its plain forms (*-tai, -takatta, -takunai, -takunakatta;* never the polite forms) can occur as a modifier for a noun. This associates that noun with the desired action in a variety of ways, depending on the relationship between the modifying verb and the noun: e.g., *tabetai mono* = "something [I] want to eat"; *tabetai resutoran* = "restaurant [I] want to eat [at]"; *tabetai hito* = "person who wants to eat"; *tabetakunai hito* = "person who doesn't want to eat"; and so forth.

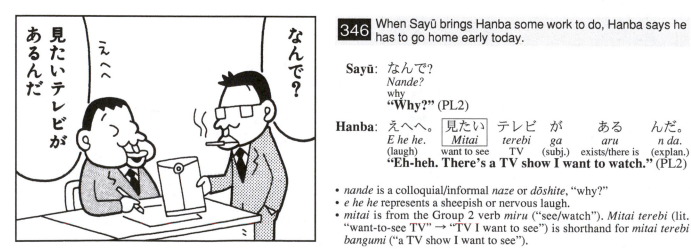

見たいテレビがあるんだ　えへへ　なんで？

346　When Sayū brings Hanba some work to do, Hanba says he has to go home early today.

Sayū: なんで？
Nande?
why
"Why?" (PL2)

Hanba: えへへ。　┃見たい┃　テレビ　が　　ある　　んだ。
E he he.　┃Mitai┃　terebi　ga　　aru　　n da.
(laugh)　want to see　TV　(subj.)　exists/there is　(explan.)
"Eh-heh. There's a TV show I want to watch." (PL2)

- *nande* is a colloquial/informal *naze* or *dōshite*, "why?"
- *e he he* represents a sheepish or nervous laugh.
- *mitai* is from the Group 2 verb *miru* ("see/watch"). *Mitai terebi* (lit. "want-to-see TV" → "TV I want to see") is shorthand for *mitai terebi bangumi* ("a TV show I want to see").

With *to omou*

There are a great many situations—especially polite and formal ones—in which Japanese prefer to avoid being too direct, and one of them is when expressing desires. In such situations, *-tai* forms often appear in a pattern with *to omou/omoimasu* (the *to* for quoting + "think"), making an expression that literally means "I think that I want to ～." In most cases, this is simply a more roundabout way of saying "I want/wish/would like to ～." The same preference for indirection shows when asking about another person's desires in a polite/formal situation, as here:

347 At their *omiai*, Shinnosuke and Poppo continue to search for an interest or goal they have in common.

Shinnosuke: ポッポさん　　は　　どんな　　家庭　　を
Poppo-san　　wa　　donna　　katei　　o
(name-pol.)/you　as for　what kind of　home　(obj.)

作りたい　　と　　思います　か?
tsukuritai　　to　　omoimasu　ka?
want to make　(quote)　think　(?)

"What kind of home do you think you would like to make?"
"What kind of home do you dream of having?" (PL3)

Poppo え...　ええ...
E...　ē...
"Uh...yes, well..."

• *tsukuritai* is from *tsukuru/tsukurimasu* ("make/build").

-tai + -garu
PL2
-tagaru (non-past)
-tagatta (past)
-tagaranai (negative)
-tagaranakatta (neg.-past)

PL3
-tagarimasu (non-past)
-tagarimashita (past)
-tagarimasen (negative)
-tagarimasen deshita (neg.-past)

hoshii + -garu
PL2
hoshigaru (non-past)
hoshigatta (past)
hoshigaranai (negative)
hoshigaranakatta (neg.-past)

PL3
hoshigarimasu (non-past)
hoshigarimashita (past)
hoshigarimasen (negative)
hoshigarimasen deshita (neg.-past)

The suffix -がる *-garu*

The suffix -がる *-garu* attaches to *-tai* and *hoshii* to create verbs that literally mean "show signs of wanting (to) ～" or "show a desire to/for ～." In this case, *-garu* replaces the final *-i*: *-tai* → *-tagaru* and *hoshii* → *hoshigaru*. This is generally just a way of saying "He/she wants (to) ～" or "They want (to) ～"—that is, it is the proper way to talk about what a third person wants, without presuming to speak too directly for him/her. The thing wanted is marked with *o*. An example of *-tagaru* appears in fig. 290; an example of *hoshigaru* is presented here.

The *-garu* suffix also attaches to various other adjectives (replaces the final *-i*) and adjectival nouns (attaches directly to the noun, without *da/desu* or *na*) that describe feelings—either emotional/psychological or physical. In such cases, *o* marks the thing that gave rise to the feeling. For an example used as a modifier, see *iyagaru* in fig. 223.

The *-garu* suffix acts as a Group 1 verb, so the polite forms are based on *-garimasu*; the plain past form is *-gatta*, while the plain negative forms are *-garanai* (non-past) and *-garanakatta* (past).

348 When this man's twelve-year-old son asks for a massage chair for Christmas, it strikes him as odd. He decides to ask at the office to find out whether it's just him, or if his son's request really is odd.

Salaryman:
なあ、　12歳　の　男　の　子　は、
Nā,　jūni-sai　no　otoko　no　ko　wa,
(interj.)　12 yrs. old (mod.) male (mod.) child as for
"Say, as for twelve-year-old boys,

クリスマス　に　何　を　欲しがる　かなあ?
Kurisumasu　ni　nani　o　hoshigaru　ka nā?
Christmas　at/for　what　(obj.)　show desire for　I wonder
"for Christmas, what do they want, I wonder?"
"Say, what sort of thing does a twelve-year-old boy usually want for Christmas?" (PL2)

• *nā* used at the beginning of a sentence like "say/hey" is mostly masculine. Women would usually use *nē*.

Lesson 24

If and When

Japanese has several different ways of establishing one thing or action as a condition for another. The condition can be expressed in terms of a verb-, adjective-, or noun-type sentence.

The -ば -*ba* **form** of a verb establishes the action of that verb (or the sentence it completes) as a condition for what follows, like "If ～, [then ～]." To make the -*ba* form of a Group 1 verb, change the final -*u* of the dictionary form to -*e* and add -*ba*. In kana, change the last syllable to the *e* sound in the same row—if it's く, make it け; if it's る, make it れ—and add ば *ba*.

TEE HEE HEE

349 The OL in fig. 325 is inclined to let her boss continue to think the teacup is new, but a coworker happens by and spills the beans.

OL: 洗えば　きれい　に　なる　もの　ねー。
　　Araeba　*kirei*　*ni*　*naru*　*mono*　*nē.*
　　if wash　clean/pretty　(result)　becomes　thing　(is-emph.)
　　"If you wash it, it becomes quite pretty, doesn't it?"
　　"It really cleans up nicely, doesn't it?" (PL2)

- *araeba* is from *arau/araimasu* ("wash") → "if [you] wash [it]."
- *kirei* is an adjectival noun that can mean either "pretty/beautiful" or "clean/neat," and an example like this illustrates why those two meanings might go together in the same word: making the cup clean also brings out its beauty. *Naru/narimasu* = "become," so *kirei ni naru* = "becomes clean/pretty" (see fig. 78).
- *ne* by itself often replaces *da ne/desu ne* ("is, isn't it/are, aren't they?"), especially in feminine speech; elongating the vowel makes it like a mild exclamation.

© Ishii Hisaichi. Ishii Hisaichi Senshū, Futabasha.

The -ば -*ba* form of Group 2 and irregular verbs

Linda

The rule for the -*ba* forms of Group 2 verbs and the irregular verbs is the same as for Group 1 verbs: change the final -*u* to -*e* and add -*ba*. To be consistent with other Group 2 conversion rules, you can think of it as replacing the final -る -*ru* with -れば -*reba*, but it amounts to the same thing.

リンダ ちょっと
聞きたいことが
あるんだ

出来れば社外の
電話を使ってくれ

350 Shortly after Kaji finds a hidden microphone in the Japanese delegation's suite at an Asia-Pacific Economic Cooperation Summit, the *Washington Journal* publishes a report about the CIA having bugged the Japanese trade representative offices during auto talks held some time before. Kaji decides to call a reporter he knows at the *Journal*.

Kaji: リンダ、ちょっと　聞きたい　こと　が　ある　んだ。
　　Rinda,　*chotto*　*kikitai*　*koto*　*ga*　*aru*　*n da.*
　　(name)　a little　want to ask　thing　(subj.)　exists　(explan.)
　　"Linda, there's something I want to ask you about." (PL2)

出来れば　社外　の　電話　を　使ってくれ。
Dekireba　*shagai*　*no*　*denwa*　*o*　*tsukatte kure.*
if possible　out of office　that is　phone　(obj.)　use-request
"If possible, call me from a phone that is outside the office." (PL2)

© Hirokane Kenshi. Kaji Ryūsuke no Gi, Kodansha.

- *kikitai* ("want to ask") is from *kiku/kikimasu* ("ask"); *kikitai koto* = "something I want to ask."
- *dekireba* is from the Group 2 verb *dekiru/dekimasu* ("can/be able to do") → "if [you] can/if possible."
- *sha* = "company/office" and *gai* = "outside"; *shagai no denwa* = "a phone that is outside the office."
- *tsukatte* is from *tsukau/tsukaimasu* ("use"); the -*te* form of a verb plus *kure* makes a relatively abrupt request or gentle command (fig. 279).

"When ～"

The *-ba* form of a verb is usually like "if ～," but sometimes the context makes it more natural to think of it as "when ～" in English.

351 This salaryman was feeling pretty low as he walked home after another of his endless late nights at the office, but then he sees Garcia (fig. 223 and others) and thinks of how much more fortunate he is than foreign laborers who have only empty apartments to go home to.

Man: 家 に 帰れば 自分の 家 と 家族 が
Uchi ni kaereba jibun no ie to kazoku ga
home to when return my own house and family (subj.)

待ってる んだ もん な。
matteru n da mon na.
are waiting (explan.) because (colloq.)

"After all, when I go home, I have my own house and family waiting for me." (PL2)

SFX: ガチャ
Gacha
Rattle (sound of latch on gate)

- *kaereba* is from *kaeru* ("return") → "if/when [I] return"; in many contexts, *kaeru* by itself implies "go/come home," but it's also very common (and sometimes necessary) to precede it with *uchi ni* ("to home") → *uchi ni kaeru* = "return (to) home" or "go/come home."
- 家 can be read either *ie* or *uchi*, both meaning "house/home"; the readings are often interchangeable, but *ie* tends to be favored for referring to the building/physical structure itself.
- *jibun* = "oneself" (fig. 290), and *jibun no* = "oneself's/one's own" → "my/my own."
- *matteru* is a contraction of *matte iru* ("is/are waiting"), from *matsu/machimasu* ("wait").
- *n da mon* is a contraction of *no da mono*, which altogether can be thought of as "because it's ～." A sentence ending in ～ *n da mon na* typically offers an explanation for something one has just said/observed, with the feeling of "After all, ～ [is the case/situation]."

☛ PL3 verbs rarely occur in *-ba* forms, and PL3 negatives never do; the politeness level is determined by the form used at the end of the sentence.

The *-ba* form of adjectives and negatives

To make the *-ba* form of an adjective, change the final -い *-i* to -ければ *-kereba*: *atsui* ("is hot") → *atsukereba* ("if it is hot").

Since the negative *-nai* acts as an adjective, the same rule holds for the *-ba* form of all negative verbs and adjectives—though it may be easier to think in terms of replacing -ない *-nai* with -なければ *-nakereba*: *atsukunai* → *atsukunakereba* ("if it isn't hot"); *kawanai* ("not buy") → *kawanakereba* ("if [he] doesn't buy [it]"). Negative *-ba* forms give the meanings, "if [he/she/it] isn't ～," "if [he/she/it] doesn't ～," and "if [he/she/it] won't ～."

352 Yamamoto wants Kaji to run for his late father's seat in the Diet. He urges Kaji to make a quick decision, since he expects the current prime minister to call for new elections in the fall.

Yamamoto:
その 時 を にらんで 今 から
Sono toki o nirande ima kara
that time on fix eyes-(manner) now from

準備 を しなければ 遅い んです。
junbi o shinakereba osoi n desu.
preparations (obj.) if don't do will be late (explan.)

"If we don't begin preparations now with our eyes fixed on that time, it will be too late." (PL3)

- *nirande* is the *-te* form of *niramu/niramimasu* ("glare/stare [at]" or "fix one's eyes [on]"). The *-te* form is being used to indicate manner: how the preparations must be advanced.
- *shinakereba* is the *-ba* form of *shinai* ("not do"), from *suru* ("do") → "if [we] don't do/make [preparations]." Here, *o* marks *junbi* ("preparations") as the direct object of *suru*, but the *suru* verb *junbi suru* ("prepare") is also very common.

The *-ba* form of *desu*

The *-ba* form of *da/desu* is based on *de aru*, the formal/literary equivalent of *desu* seen in figs. 222 and 226: *de aru → de areba* ("if it is ～").

The negative *-ba* form of *desu* is based on *ja nai/de (wa) nai*, so it follows the same pattern as for negative verbs and adjectives noted in fig. 352: *ja nai → ja nakereba* or *de (wa) nai → de (wa) nakereba* ("if it is not ～").

353　Kaji and his close aides have just begun to suspect that the car crash in which his father and brother died was not an accident at all, but the result of a plot to murder them. Nishi is Kaji's chief aide.

© Hirokane Kenshi, *Kaji Ryūsuke no Gi*, Kodansha.

Nishi:

もし　それ　が　本当　であれば、
Moshi　sore　ga　hontō　de areba,
if　that　(subj.)　truth/true　if it is

犯人　　は　どういう　連中　でしょう　か?
hannin　wa　dō iu　renchū　deshō　ka?
criminal(s)/culprit(s)　as for　what kind of　group　probably is　(?)

"If that's true, as for the criminals, what kind of people might they be?"

"If that's true, then who could be behind it?" (PL3)

- *moshi* often appears at the beginning of a sentence that expresses a condition; it reinforces the meaning of "if."
- *renchū* is an informal, and often even derogatory, word for referring to a group of people: *dō iu renchū* = "what kind of people" or "what kind of rabble/scoundrels/scum."

Summary: *-ba* forms

For all verbs, change the final *-u* of the plain, dictionary form to *-e* and add *-ba*. The *-ba* form of a *-masu* verb is *-masureba*—but occurs only rarely, in very formal speech.

For adjectives, replace the final *-i* with *-kereba*.

Negative *ba*-forms are all based on *-nai*:

　*ja **nai** →*
　*ja **nakereba***

　*samuku**nai** →*
　*samuku**nakereba***

　*tabe**nai** →*
　*tabe**nakereba***

[1] The pronouns used as subjects in the English translations are assigned at random; in real life, context will determine the subjects if they are not stated explicitly.

[2] For romaji conversions, in *t* row syllables, *t = ch = ts*. See Introduction.

	dictionary form		-ba form		
adj. *desu*	だ/です	*da/desu*	であれば	*de areba*	if it is[1]
adj.	寒い	*samui*	寒ければ	*samukereba*	if it is cold
	いい/良い	*ii/yoi*	よければ	*yokereba*	if it is good/OK
irreg.	来る	*kuru*	来れば	*kureba*	if he comes
	する	*suru*	すれば	*sureba*	if I do
gr. 2	見る	*miru*	見れば	*mireba*	if we see
	食べる	*taberu*	食べれば	*tabereba*	if they eat
group 1 verbs	取る	*toru*	取れば	*toreba*	if I take
	買う	*kau*	買えば	*kaeba*	if you buy
	持つ	*motsu*[2]	持てば	*moteba*	if she holds
	呼ぶ	*yobu*	呼べば	*yobeba*	if I call
	飲む	*nomu*	飲めば	*nomeba*	if we drink
	死ぬ	*shinu*	死ねば	*shineba*	if he dies
	落とす	*otosu*	落とせば	*otoseba*	if I drop [it]
	書く	*kaku*	書けば	*kakeba*	if you write
	泳ぐ	*oyogu*	泳げば	*oyogeba*	if we swim

Stating conditions with と *to*

"If/when 〜" conditions can also be stated by following most non-past forms of a verb with the particle と *to*. This includes negatives and *-te iru* forms as well as other forms yet to be introduced, and it includes all politeness levels. (*To* after the *-ō/-yō* ["let's/I'll 〜"] form of a verb has other special uses.) Likewise, non-past adjectives followed by *to* and nouns followed by *da to* or *desu to* can be equivalent to "if/when it is 〜."

Agent: 床下　　収納　ベッド　です。
Yukashita　shūnō　beddo　desu.
under floor　storage　bed　is
"It's an underfloor bed." (PL3)

慣れる　　　と　　落ちつきます　よー。
Nareru　to　ochitsukimasu　yō.
grow used to　if/when　become relaxed　(emph.)
"When you grow used to it, you will become relaxed."
"Once you get used to it, you'll find it very relaxing." (PL3)

Renter: 慣れたくない　　です。
Naretakunai　desu.
not want to get used to　(pol.)
"I don't want to get used to it." (PL3)

354 This potential tenant is worried that there won't be much room left in the apartment for anything else once she moves her bed in. The rental agent tells her about this space-saving design.

- the polite form of *nareru* ("become accustomed to/grow used to") is *naremasu*; adding *to* makes the meaning "if/when [you] grow used to [it]."
- *ochitsukimasu* is the polite form of *ochitsuku* ("settle/relax" or "become calm/relaxed").
- *naretakunai* is the negative form of *naretai* ("want to grow used to"), from *nareru*. Adding *desu* makes it polite.

-たら/-だら *-tara/-dara* = "if/when"

"If/when 〜" conditions can also be stated using the **-tara form** of a verb. This is the verb's past form plus *-ra*, so for verbs whose past forms end in *-da*, the *-tara* form is *-dara*. The equivalent for *da* is *dattara*; for *desu*, *deshitara*; and for adjectives, *-kattara* (*hayai* ["is fast"] → *hayakatta* ["was fast"] → *hayakattara* ["if he/she/it is fast"]). Negatives usually occur in the form of *-nakattara*, from the past form of *-nai*, but in very polite speech they can take the form of *-masen deshitara*.

Being based on the past form of the verb, the suffix *-tara* implies that the action of that verb is/was/will be/must be completed first, before the action of the main verb (or, as in the example here, the action noun) at the end of the sentence.

355 Michael and fellow youngsters are in school. The teacher warned the first time Michael yawned that any student who yawns three times will be sent home. Now he has caught Michael in a second yawn.

Teacher:
マイケル!!　あと　　　　1回　　あくび　を
Maikeru!!　Ato　ikkai　akubi　o
(name)　remaining　1 time/occasion　yawn　(obj.)
したら　　　退場　　だ　ぞ!!
shitara　taijō　da　zo!!
if do　withdrawal/ejection　is　(emph.)
"Michael! If you yawn one more time, you're outta here!" (PL2)

- *ato* before a number or quantity means "[that much] remains/is left over."
- *shitara* is the *-tara* form of *suru*. *Akubi (o) suru* is literally "do a yawn" → "yawn."
- *taijō* is a noun for "leaving/withdrawing" from the site of an event/activity (a room, hall, stadium, etc.), and its usual verb form is *taijō suru* ("leave/withdraw"). *Taijō da* shouted directly at a person like a command means, "You're ejected!/You're out of here!" In this case, he states a condition first, so it's merely a warning.

なら *nara* = "if ～" or "if it is ～"

Nara after a verb means "if ～," and after a noun or adjective, "if it is ～." *Nara* follows a noun directly, without an intervening *da* or *desu* (*hontō nara* = "if it is the truth"); it can follow a verb or adjective directly, or with an intervening explanatory *no*—i.e., the pattern can be either *iku nara* or *iku n(o) nara* = "if [you] are going."

356 Distraught by their breakup, Yōji's former girlfriend Shirai (fig. 282) calls to tell him she has turned the gas on in her apartment and wants to say good-bye. Yōji (fig. 367) rushes over to find her lying motionless on her bed, but then notices that the window is open. When he starts to leave, she presses something to her wrist.

© Uchida Shungicu, *Maboroshi no Futsū Shōjo*, Futabasha.

Shirai: 帰る　　ん　ボ　なら、　死ぬ　わ。
Kaeru　　*n*　　*nara,*　*shinu*　*wa.*
go home/leave　(explan.)　if　will die　(fem.)
"If you go home, I'll die."
"If you leave, I'll kill myself!" (PL2)

- *n* is a contraction of explanatory *no*.
- *shinu/shinimasu* usually means "die," but it can also be used like this to mean "kill oneself." The usual verb for "kill" is *korosu/koroshimasu* (figs. 426, 459), but it's not normally used to speak of killing oneself.
- it turns out that she only has a cheese knife.

では *de wa* (or じゃ *ja*) = "if it is"

De wa (or its contraction *ja*) after a noun can sometimes express a condition, like "if it is ～." The equivalent for verbs and adjectives is the *-te* form plus *wa* (see following examples).

357 A Mr. Smith from the United States is visiting, and he is a very large man. This OL wonders if they need to find something bigger to serve his coffee in than their usual coffee cups.

© Ueda Masashi, *Kariage-kun*, Futabasha.

OL:
こんな　カップ　じゃ　小さくない　かしら?
Konna　*kappu*　*ja*　*chiisakunai*　*kashira?*
this kind of　cup　if it is　not small　I wonder
"If it is this kind of cup, is it not [too] small, I wonder?"
"I wonder if a cup like this isn't too small?" (PL2)

Kariage:
そう　　ねー。　でっかい　人　だ　　から。
Sō　　*nē.*　*Dekkai*　*hito*　*da*　*kara.*
that way　(is-colloq.)　big/huge　person　is　because/since
"I suppose you're right, since he's a big man." (PL2)

- *chiisakunai* is the negative form of the adjective *chiisai* ("is small"). It's not unusual for the adjective to imply not just "small" but "too small."
- *sō ne* expresses agreement or acceptance, like "That's true, isn't it?"; with a long *nē*, the feeling can be either more emphatic ("That's really true, isn't it?") or more tentative ("Maybe so/I suppose so") depending on the context and how it's said.
- *dekkai* (or *dekai*) is an informal/slang word for "big/huge."
- normal order would put the *kara* ("because") statement first—*Dekkai hito da kara, sō (da/desu) ne*—but in this case Kariage gives his basic response first and then adds his reasoning as an afterthought. Such inversions are common in colloquial speech.

-Te wa ikenai/naranai = "must not"

The "must not" forms of verbs and adjectives—there are several—are based on their "if" forms. One way to say "must not" is to follow -*te wa* or -*de wa* with *ikenai*, which literally means "It is no good/it won't do": -*te wa ikenai* = "If [you do the action], it is no good/it won't do" → "[You] must not [do the action]."

Another way is to follow -*te wa* or -*de wa* with *naranai*. Using *naranai* instead of *ikenai* makes the prohibition feel a little stronger, but the basic meaning is the same: -*te wa naranai* = "[You] must not [do the action]."

In these patterns, -*te wa* often gets shortened to -*cha*, and -*de wa* gets shortened to -*ja* → -*cha ikenai/naranai* and -*ja ikenai/naranai*.

358 Nat-chan has been saying nasty things about her friends behind their backs.

Mother:

人 の 事、 陰 で 悪く 言っちゃ いけない わ。
Hito no koto, kage de waruku itcha ikenai wa.
people of things shadows in badly/ill if speak it's no good (fem.)
"It's no good if you speak badly about people in the shadows."
"You mustn't speak ill of people behind their backs." (PL2)

- ∼ *no koto* is literally "things of/about ∼," which typically can be reduced to just "about ∼."
- *kage* is literally "shade/shadows," and *de* marks it as the place where an action occurs: "in the shadows"; *kage de* is an expression for "behind a person's back" or "in secret."
- *waruku* is the adverb form of the adjective *warui* ("is bad"); *waruku iu* = "speak badly/ill of."
- *itcha* is a contraction of *itte wa*, the -*te* form of *iu* ("say/speak") plus *wa* → "if [you] say/speak."

-Te wa dame = "must not"

Yet another way to say "must not" is to follow -*te wa*/-*de wa* with *dame* instead of *ikenai* or *naranai*. *Dame* is an adjectival noun referring to a thing/situation/circumstance that is "unacceptable/no good/bad" or "won't do." Again, -*te wa* often gets shortened to -*cha* and -*de wa* gets shortened to -*ja*.

359 Michael's family decided to buy wicker furniture for the living room, and to their dismay, he immediately begins using it as a scratching post.

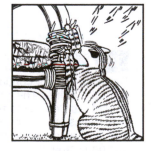

やめてー! ツメ を といじゃ ダメー! これ 高かった の よー!!
Yametē! Tsume o toija damē! Kore takakatta no yō!!
stop nails (obj.) if sharpen is no good this was expensive (explan.) (emph.)
"Stop! Don't sharpen your nails! This was expensive!" (PL2)

- *yamete* is the -*te* form of *yameru/yamemasu* ("stop/quit"), used here as a command. See fig. 278.
- *toija* is a contraction of *toide wa*, from the verb *togu/togimasu* ("sharpen/hone"); *toide wa dame* = "you mustn't sharpen/don't sharpen."
- *takakatta* is the past form of the adjective *takai* ("high"), here meaning "high in cost/expensive," as it often does (context is your guide).

-Nakute wa ikenai/naranai/dame = "must/have to"

For the patterns with *ikenai*, *naranai*, and *dame* illustrated in figs. 358 and 359, if the *-te* form is negative, the meaning for a verb becomes "must [do the action]" or "have/has to [do the action]" (*yamenakute wa ikenai* = "if you don't stop, it is no good" → "must stop"), and the meaning for an adjective becomes "must be/has to be [the described quality]" (*ōkikunakute wa ikenai* = "if it is not big, it is no good" → "must be big"). The equivalent forms for a noun + *da/desu* phrase are *ja nakute wa ikenai/naranai/dame* or *de (wa) nakute wa ikenai/naranai/dame*, meaning "must be/has to be [the stated thing]" (*Nihongo ja nakute wa ikenai* = "if it is not Japanese [language], it is no good" → "must be Japanese").

Once again, *-nakute wa* often shortens to *-nakucha* → *-nakucha naranai/ikenai/dame*.

360 Natsuko finds out that her late brother left a bottle of saké especially for her, saying it was the best he had been able to make. But when she tastes it, she is disappointed. It's very good, she says, but that's all. Her brother's saké was supposed to be more than just "very good."

Natsuko:
これ　は　　特別な　　酒 | でなくてはいけない | んです。
Kore wa tokubetsu na sake | *de nakute wa ikenai* | *n desu.*
this as for special saké | must be/has to be | (explan.)
"This has to be a special saké."
"This is supposed to be a really special saké." (PL3)

- *tokubetsu* occurs both as an adjectival noun and as a regular noun that takes *no* when modifying other nouns: *tokubetsu na ～* or *tokubetsu no ～*. Either way, its usage usually corresponds to the English adjectives "special/exceptional/extraordinary."

-Nakereba naranai = "must/have to"

The negative *-ba* form of a verb or adjective can also be used with *naranai*, *ikenai*, and *dame* to mean "must/have to/has to [do the action]" (*yamenakereba naranai* = "must stop"), or "must be/has to be [the described quality]" (*ōkikunakereba naranai* = "must be big"). The equivalents for a noun + *da/desu* phrase are *ja nakereba naranai/ikenai/dame* or *de (wa) nakereba naranai/ikenai/dame*, meaning "must be/has to be [the stated thing]" (*Nihongo ja nakereba naranai* = "must be Japanese").

361 Sales have fallen at Cat Corp. while rival Dog Enterprises continues to make gains. The president of Cat Corp. exhorts his executives to pull together and find a way to turn the company around.

President: いい　か?!　とにかく　なんとしても　この　　ピンチ　　を | きりぬけなければならない!!
Ii ka?! Tonikaku nan to shite mo kono pinchi o | *kirinukenakereba naranai!!*
good/OK (?) in any case whatever it takes this pinch/crisis (obj.) | must get through
"Now listen! Absolutely no matter what it takes, we have to make it through this crisis!" (PL2)

- *ii ka* is literally the question "Is it OK?" but it's also used when beginning admonitions/instructions like "Are you ready?/Now, pay attention!/Listen up!"
- *pinchi* is from English "pinch" (in the sense of being in a pinch).
- *kirinukenakereba* is the negative *-ba* form of *kirinukeru/kirinukemasu*, a verb meaning "to get out of [trouble]/find one's way out of [difficulty]/pass safely through [dangers]": *kirinukereba* = "if [we] get through"; *kirinukenakereba* = "if [we] don't get through"; *kirinukenakereba naranai* = "If [we] don't get through, it is unacceptable" → "[We] must get through."

-Nakya = -nakereba

In colloquial speech, *-nakereba* often gets shortened to *-nakya*.

362 On the trip to S (fig. 177), Shin-chan wants to hold his mother's ticket. His mother admonishes him not to lose it, and explains why:

SCREEECH CLICKETY-CLACK CLACK

Mother: おりる 時 に キップ
Oriru toki ni kippu
get off time at ticket

見せなきゃいけない の よ。
misenakya ikenai no yo.
must show (explan.) (emph.)
"We have to show the ticket when we get off." (PL2)

Shin-chan: あ、 そう。
A, sō.
(interj.) that way
"Oh, I see." (PL2)

- the polite form of *oriru* ("get off") is *orimasu*. A verb followed by *toki ni* means "at the time when [the action takes place]" or just "when [the action takes place]." Structurally, the verb is modifying the noun *toki* ("time").
- *misenakya* is a contraction of *misenakereba*, the negative *-ba* form of *miseru/misemasu* ("show"). *Misenakya ikenai* is a "must/have to" form of *miseru*.
- *a* is an interjection like "Oh," and *sō* here is short for *sō (desu) ka*, "Is it that way?/Is that so?"—a rhetorical question that essentially means "I see" (fig. 159).

-ても -te mo = "even if/when"

When the *-te* form is followed by *mo* instead of *wa* it expresses a more "emphatic" condition, like "even if," or depending on the context, "even when," "even after," and "even though."

363 The balloons in this panel show the words of the caller, who started by saying in a threatening tone that he was willing to wait only 30 minutes—sounding very much like a kidnapper or extortionist. The man answering the phone breaks into a sweat as the caller continues.

Caller: もし 30分 たっても 来なければ
Moshi sanjuppun tatte mo konakereba
if 30 minutes even when pass if don't come

わかってる だろー な。
wakatteru darō na.
know/understand probably/surely right?
"If you don't come even when 30 minutes pass, you surely know [what will happen]."
"I suppose you know what'll happen if you're not here in 30 minutes." (PL2)

- *moshi* often appears at the beginning of a sentence that expresses a condition; it reinforces the meaning of "if."
- *tatte mo* is the "even if/when" form of *tatsu/tachimasu* ("[time] passes"), and *konakereba* is the negative *-ba* form of *kuru* ("come"): "if [you] don't come even when 30 minutes pass" → "if you don't come within 30 minutes."
- *wakatteru* is a contraction of *wakatte iru* ("know"), from *wakaru* ("understand/comprehend").
- *darō* is the PL2 equivalent of *deshō*, which implies an element of guesswork ("probably/surely"). This form is formally introduced in Lesson 26.
- it turns out the man taking the call here is the owner of a pizza parlor and this happens to be how one of his regular customers likes to order his pizza.

-てもいい -te mo ii expresses willingness or permission

Takaichi

Following *-te mo* with the adjective *ii* ("is good/fine/okay") expresses the speaker's willingness to do the stated action ("I could/I'd be willing to/I'd be happy to ～"; fig. 306). The same form is used to grant permission for the listener to do the action ("You may ～"). The *mo* is often dropped for the latter use: *-te ii*.

364 At Kyoto Station, Shima's secretary Takaichi Chizuru is boarding the bullet train to return to the office in Tokyo. She asks when Shima will be returning.

今日の夜遅くだ
キミは先に
帰っていい

© Hirokane Kenshi. *Buchō Shima Kōsaku*, Kōdansha.

Shima:
今日 の 夜 遅く だ。
Kyō no yoru osoku da.
today 's night late is/will be
"It will be late tonight." (PL2)

キミ は 先に 帰っていい。
Kimi wa saki ni | *kaette ii.*
you as for first/before | may go home
"As for you, you may go home before [my return]."
"You may go on home without waiting for me." (PL2)

- *osoku* is from the adjective *osoi* ("late"); the *-ku* form of an adjective most commonly serves as an adverb (fig. 76), but as in this case, with certain adjectives the *-ku* form can also be used as a noun.
- *kimi* is an informal word for "you" that's generally used only by males when addressing equals or subordinates/juniors. The word is more typically written with the kanji 君.
- *saki ni* is an adverb for "[do] first" or "[do] before something/someone else."
- *kaette* is the *-te* form of *kaeru* ("go home"); *-te (mo) ii* in this case literally implies "it is good/fine if you [go home]" → "you may [go home]."

-てもいい？ -te mo ii? asks permission

To request permission, the *-te (mo) ii* form is used in a question—either by simply raising the intonation, or by adding *ka?* or *desu ka?* The request for permission can be "softened" by using *ka na?/kashira?* (PL2) or *deshō ka?* (PL3) instead. *Mo* is often omitted.

365 The fetching chinchilla Persian who lured Michael into the hostess club (fig. 72) excuses herself almost as soon as his drink arrives. The hostess who comes to replace her urges Michael to take a drink, then asks if she can order something, too. It's understood that whatever she orders will go on his bill.

うう
ん……

わたしも
なにか
いただいて
いいかしら

Hostess:
わたし も なにか いただいていい かしら？
Watashi mo nani-ka | *itadaite ii kashira.*
I/me too/also something | may eat/drink I wonder if
"May I, too, have something to eat/drink, I wonder."
"I wonder if I could order something, too?" (PL2)

Michael:
う、 うん。
U- un.
(stammer) uh-huh.
"S- sure." (PL2)

© Kobayashi Makoto. *What's Michael?*, Kōdansha.

- *itadaite* is the *-te* form of *itadaku/itadakimasu*, which literally means "receive," but is also used as a polite word for "eat/drink." *Itadaite ii* in a question asks "May I eat/drink?"—or in this context, "May I order something to eat/drink?"

-ばいい *-ba ii*

The adjective *ii* after the *-ba* form of a verb literally means "If [you do the action], it is/will be good," but it has quite a broad range of meanings. Sometimes it's used to suggest a possible action; other times it states more definitively what you're supposed to do or are required to do; still other times the emphasis is that just the specified action is enough—it's all you have to do. (*To ii* and *-tara ii* are used in some of the same ways, but are not always interchangeable.)

366 Prime Minister Aosugi (fig. 132) says he thinks Japan should move toward ending its security treaty with the United States now that the cold war is over. He acknowledges that Japan still faces outside threats, but he no longer sees a need to rely on the American nuclear umbrella for security.

Aosugi:
いざ と いう 時　に　は
Iza to iu toki   ni   wa
pinch/crisis time   at/in   as for
"As for in a time of crisis,

国連　　の　　力　　を　借りれば　　いい　　んだ。
Kokuren no chikara o karireba   ii   n da.
U.N.   's strength (obj.) if borrow is good/fine (explan.)
"all we have to do is borrow the strength of the United Nations."
"In a pinch, we can simply get the United Nations to help us." (PL2)

- *iza to iu toki* is an expression that implies a critical do-or-die situation or moment of truth: "in an emergency/ when one's back is to the wall/when push comes to shove."
- 国際連合 *Kokusai Rengō* is the full Japanese name for the United Nations, but the name is usually shortened to *Kokuren*.
- *karireba* is the *-ba* form of *kariru/karimasu* ("borrow"); *chikara o kariru* ("borrow strength") is an expression for "get help."

Informal suggestions

In colloquial speech, the *-tara* and *-ba* forms by themselves, without the addition of *ii* but spoken with the intonation of a question, are often used for suggesting or urging an action. The feeling is like the English questions, "Why don't you ～?/How about if you ～?"

Sakata

367 Sakata has come over hoping to have a chance to talk privately with Sayuri about her boyfriend problems just as the Yamashitas are about to sit down to a meal prepared by Sayuri's boyfriend, Yōji.

Sayuri:
ヨージ　が　めし　つくってる　から　　さ、
Yōji   ga meshi tsukutteru   kara   sa,
(name) (subj.) meal   is making because/so (emph.)

いっしょ　に　くえば?
issho   ni kueba?
together   with   if eat
"Yōji's making dinner, so why don't you eat with us?" (PL2)

Yōji:
こんちは。
Konchi wa.
"Hi." (PL2–3)

- *meshi* is an informal and mostly masculine word for "rice/meal." Here Sayuri is among close friends and family, but elsewhere a woman using the word is likely to sound a little rough.
- *tsukutteru* is a contraction of *tsukutte iru*, the "is ～ing" form of *tsukuru/tsukurimasu* ("make").
- *sa* is a colloquial particle that provides light emphasis; in the middle of a sentence it often serves as a kind of verbal pause, similar to "like/you know."
- *kueba* is the *-ba* form of *kuu*, an informal, mostly masculine word for "eat."
- *konchi wa* is a contraction of *konnichi wa*, the standard daytime (usually afternoon) greeting, "hello."

Lesson 25

More -*Te* Form Expressions

The -*te* form of a verb is one of its most versatile forms, and Lesson 19 served only as a first taste. This lesson presents several more ways in which the -*te* form of a verb combines with a helping verb that comes after it.

To review briefly, the -*te iru* combination implies that the action is continuing/in progress ("is/are ～ing"), or that the action occurred/was done and a state resulting from it continues ("has/have ～" or "is/are ～"). Even though *iru* as an independent verb is restricted to speaking about the existence/presence of people and animate things, the -*te iru* form of a verb can be used to speak of any action, whether the doer is animate or inanimate.

The counterpart of *iru* for speaking of the existence/presence of inanimate things is *aru*, and it, too, can be used as a helping verb after a -*te* form. Like -*te iru*, the -てある -*te aru* form of a verb can speak of both animate and inanimate things—though much more commonly the latter. It's used almost exclusively with verbs that take an *o* phrase (see Lesson 10; this restriction makes its use much more limited than -*te iru*), but what would be marked with *o* for other forms of the verb is usually marked with *ga* for the -*te aru* form. -*Te aru* never indicates a continuing action; it indicates that the action of the verb "has been done" and the result "exists" (i.e., remains as it was when the action was completed); in addition, it clearly implies, without specifying who, that someone did the action that created the observed result (this also limits its use compared to -*te iru*).

368 When this inebriated salaryman arrives home after an office party and begins changing for bed, his wife asks him if he has a habit of taking his clothes off when he gets drunk. He admits that he sometimes does, as a kind of joke, but then wants to know how she found out.

Wife: 背中 に マジック で ｜書いてある｜ わ。
Senaka ni majikku de kaite aru wa.
back on magic ink with has been written (fem.)
"It's written with magic ink on your back."
"It says so in Magic Marker on your back." (PL2)

Man: えっ? いつ の ま に?
E!? Itsu no ma ni?
huh?/what? when of interval in
"What? When the heck—?" (PL2)

On Back: 課長 は 酔うと 裸 になる ので、
Kachō wa you to hadaka ni naru no de,
section chief as for when gets drunk naked becomes so

奥さま から 注意して 下さい。
okusama kara chūi shite kudasai.
wife/you from caution/warn please
When your husband gets drunk, he takes off his clothes, so please caution him. (PL3)

- *majikku* here is short for *majikku inki*, from the English words "magic" and "ink" → "Magic Marker/felt-tip pen." *De* marks this as the tool used to do the action.
- *kaite aru*, from *kaku/kakimasu* ("write"), implies not only "it has been written" but that the writing is still there → "is written."
- *itsu* is the question word "when," and *ma* means "interval [in time]," so *itsu no ma ni* is literally "in the interval of when?" The expression is used when something has occurred without your notice—especially when it seems like you should have noticed.
- *to* makes *you/yoimasu* ("become drunk") a condition for what follows: "when [he] becomes drunk."
- *okusama* (or the slightly less formal *okusan*) is the proper way to address or refer to someone else's wife; when directly addressing the woman, it can be like "ma'am," and as with other titles, it's often used when an English speaker would refer to his/her listener (in this case, the reader) as "you."
- *chūi shite* is the -*te* form of the verb *chūi suru* ("caution/warn/reprimand"); *kara* ("from") marks *okusama* as the source of the caution. *Kudasai* after a -*te* form makes a polite request (fig. 277).

-てみる *-te miru* = "try/attempt"

Adding *miru* ("see") to the *-te* form of a verb literally means "do the action and see," and it corresponds closely to the usage of "try" or "make an attempt" in English.

369 In becoming a candidate for the House of Representatives for the first time, Kaji wants to run strictly on national and global issues, not on the usual platform of pork-barrel campaign promises. His friends tell him it's a prescription for certain defeat: the voters only care about what he can do for them and their district. But Kaji thinks that makes it all the more important as an exercise in raising the electorate's consciousness.

Kaji: だから　　あえて　それ　を　やってみる。
Da kara　　aete　sore　o　yatte miru.
because it is so　daringly　that　(obj.)　will try doing
"Because it is so, in spite of the likelihood of failure, I will try doing it."
"That's exactly why I'm going to try it." (PL2)

- *aete* is an adverb that implies "daringly/venturesomely" taking up a challenge in spite of adversity or likely failure.
- *yatte* is the *-te* form of *yaru* ("do," informal).

-Te miru changes form just like the independent verb *miru*, so *-te mita/mimashita* = "tried"; *-te minai/mimasen* = "not try"; *-te minakatta/mimasendeshita* = "didn't try"; *-te mitai (desu)* = "want to try"; *-te mitakunai (desu)* or *-te mitaku arimasen* = "don't want to try"; *-te miyō/mimashō* = "let's try/I'll try/I think I'll try"; *-te miyō/mimashō ka?* = "shall I/we try?"; *-te mireba/-te miru to/-te mitara* = "if/when one tries"; and so forth.

All of the helping verbs in this lesson can theoretically change form in all the same ways that they can change as independent verbs—though not every form will necessarily make sense when combined with the *-te* form of a particular verb.

-Te miru = "try it and see"

As with English "try," *-te miru* doesn't always refer to attempting something you're not sure you can do successfully. Often, as in this example, the issue is not whether you can do the action, but rather what will result or what you will discover from doing it.

370 Michael is lying on the couch trying to go to sleep, but he can't seem to doze off.

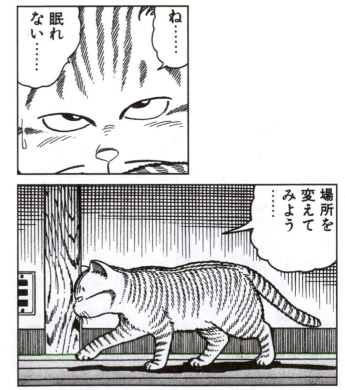

Michael: ね、　　眠れない。
Ne-　　nemurenai.
(stammer)　can't sleep
"I- I can't sleep." (PL2)

場所　を　変えてみよう。
Basho　o　kaete miyō.
place　(obj.)　I'll try changing
"I think I'll try changing my spot [and see if that helps]."
"I think I'll try going someplace else." (PL2)

- *nemurenai* is the negative form of *nemureru*, the "can/be able to" form of *nemuru/nemurimasu* ("sleep"). The "can/be able to" form is formally introduced in Lesson 28.
- *kaete* is the *-te* form of *kaeru/kaemasu* ("change/switch [something]"), and *miyō* is the plain "let's/I'll/I think I'll ～" form of *miru*.

-てしまう -te shimau can imply "completely/without delay"

Shimau/shimaimasu by itself means "finish/close/put away," but when it follows the *-te* form of another verb it often implies that the action is done completely or is completed without delay. For example, *yomu* = "read," so *yonde shimau* = "read it all/through to the end/completely," or "go ahead and read it now/read it and get it over with." In the panel here, both meanings apply—though the time phrase makes the latter sense stronger.

和尚にたのまれていた肉体労働も今のうちに片づけてしまう

KLONK KLONK

371 Summer is getting too hot for strenuous exercise, so Kōsuke decides he'll suspend his jogging until cooler days arrive in the fall. He also figures he should take care of the wood he'd promised to chop for the priest at the nearby temple before it gets any hotter.

Kōsuke (narrating):
和尚 に たのまれていた 肉体労働 も
Oshō ni tanomarete ita nikutai rōdō mo
priest by had been asked manual labor too/also

今 のうちに ☐片づけてしまう。☐
ima no uchi ni katazukete shimau.
now while/during dispose of/deal with-(complete w/o delay)
The physical labor that the priest had asked me to do, too, I will dispose of completely now.
I'll also go ahead and finish off that physical labor the priest asked me to do. (PL2)

• *tanomarete ita* is from *tanomareru/tanomaremasu* ("be asked a favor"), which is the passive form of *tanomu/tanomimasu* ("ask a favor"; fig. 1). Passive forms are formally introduced in Lesson 29.
• ～ *no uchi ni* means "while it's still [the indicated day/week/month/year]" or "during/within [the timeframe of the indicated action/event]," so *ima no uchi ni* is literally "while it's still now"—implying "now without delay/now beforehand/now while the time is ripe." In this case he means "now before the weather gets even hotter."
• *katazukete* is from *katazukeru/katazukemasu* ("dispose of/deal with/put in order") → *katazukete shimau* = "dispose of/finish off [a task] without delay."

-Te shimau can imply regret or undesirability

The same form often implies that the action is regrettable or unwanted/undesirable. It can also convey a number of other related nuances depending on the context, implying the action is unfortunate, inappropriate, problematic, embarrassing, irreversible, etc.

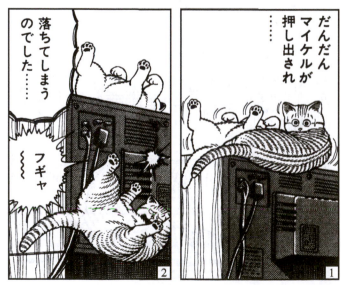

落ちてしまうのでした……
フギャ
だんだんマイケルが押し出され……

"Yeeagh!"

372 Michael likes to sleep on top of the TV, and Poppo likes to join him there, but since she tends to toss and roll in her sleep...

Narration: だんだん マイケル が 押し出され、
Dandan Maikeru ga oshidasare,
bit by bit (name) (subj.) is pushed out-and

☐落ちてしまう☐ のでした。
ochite shimau no deshita.
falls-(regret) (explan.)
"Little by little, Michael would get pushed over and fall off." (PL3)

• *dandan* = "gradually/by degrees/bit by bit."
• *oshidasare* is the pre-*masu* stem of the passive form of *oshidasu/oshidashimasu* ("push out"—in this case, out toward the edge of the TV top); the pre-*masu* stem is being used like "[do the action] and ～" (fig. 190).
• *ochite* is the *-te* form of the verb *ochiru/ochimasu* ("[something] falls/drops"); *shimau* adds the feeling that this is a regrettable/undesirable action or result.

-Te shimau can express surprise

Shimau after the *-te* form of a verb can also express surprise or imply the action was unexpected/unintended. In many cases, the unexpected action or event is cause for regret, as in fig. 372, but it can also be cause for rejoicing, or it can be neutral, as in the example here.

In colloquial speech, *-te shimau* often gets shortened to *-chau*, and the past form *-te shimatta* gets shortened to *-chatta*. For verbs whose *-te* forms end in *-de*, the corresponding contractions are *-jau* and *-jatta*. These contractions can occur for any of the various uses of *-te shimau/shimatta*.

373 Sayuri's boyfriend Yōji has discovered that Yamashita Tomiko, who often brings customers to his club, is Sayuri's mother, but Tomiko doesn't know yet that Yōji and Sayuri are seeing each other. One day as she arrives at Yōji's club, Tomiko notices that he has cut his formerly shoulder-length hair.

Tomiko: あら、ヨーちゃん、　髪　切っちゃった　の　ね。
　　　　　Ara,　Yō-chan,　kami　kitchatta　no　ne.
　　　　　(interj.) (name-dimin.) hair cut-(surprise) (explan.) (colloq.)
　　　　　"Oh! You cut your hair, Yō-chan!" (PL2)

Yōji: えっ?　えー、　そう　なんす　よ、　ハハハ。
　　　　E?　Ē,　sō　nansu　yo,　ha ha ha
　　　　huh?/what? yes that way is-(explan.) (emph.) (laugh)
　　　　"Huh? Oh, yes. I did. Ha ha ha." (PL3)

- *kitchatta* is a contraction of *kitte shimatta*, the past form of *kitte shimau*, from *kiru/kirimasu* ("cut"). Using the *-te shimau* form here implies the action is unexpected/a surprise.
- *o*, to mark *kami* ("hair") as the direct object of *kitchatta*, has been omitted.
- *nansu* is a colloquial contraction of *na no desu* (explanatory *na no* plus *desu*—see fig. 101). The expression *Sō da/desu* serves broadly as an affirmative response ("Yes/That's right"); making it *Sō na no da/desu* tends to give it a slightly weightier feeling, like "It is indeed so/I'm afraid so."

-Te shimau can imply an impulsive/involuntary action

The *-te shimau* form of a verb can also imply that the action occurs spontaneously/automatically/involuntarily, or that the subject does the action impulsively, without being able to help him/herself or in spite of his/her better judgment.

374 This OL saw some lingerie on display in a window that she just had to have.

On door: ランジェリー　ショップ
　　　　　Ranjerii　Shoppu
　　　　　lingerie　shop
　　　　　The Lingerie Shop

OL: へへっ。　買っちゃったー。
　　　Hehe!　Katchattā.
　　　(laugh) bought-(impulse)
　　　"Tee hee. I went and bought it!" (PL2)

- *hehe!* is a sheepish but self-satisfied laugh.
- *katchatta* is a contraction of *katte shimatta*, the past form of *katte shimau*, from *kau* ("buy"). Adding the past form of *shimau* to the verb expresses the impulsiveness of what she has done—something like "I can hardly believe I actually bought it!" Here the tone is obviously one of glee, but the same form can be used with a tone of regret —i.e., the feeling that one really shouldn't have been so impulsive/rash.

-ておく -te oku = "do in advance"

CLAP CLAP

Adding *oku/okimasu* ("set down/lay/emplace") to the *-te* form of a verb literally says "do the action and leave it in place"—usually meaning "leave the result in place." The form is used to speak of actions done in advance, to serve some later purpose; or done immediately, to serve an ongoing/unfolding purpose. Usage of *-te oku* in some ways overlaps with *-te aru* (fig. 368) but *-te aru* focuses on an existing state, while *-te oku* focuses on the action that creates/created it, so they are not generally interchangeable. In colloquial speech, *-te oku* often gets shortened to *-toku*, and *-de oku* gets shortened to *-doku*.

375 Kōsuke and Hiroko have come to the shrine for an observance marking the end of New Year's festivities. It's also Kōsuke's *hatsumōde*—his first shrine visit of the new year. Before praying, he drops his offering into the box at the front of the shrine.

Narration:
さい銭　は　貯めておいた　1円玉　　　361枚　　だ。
Saisen　wa　tamete oita　ichien-dama　sanbyaku rokujūichimai　da.
offering　as for　accumulated/saved　1-yen coins　　361 count　　is
My offering was 361 one-yen coins I'd saved up [for this purpose].
(PL2)

Sound FX:
ザー　チャリ　チャリ
Zā　Chari chari
(sounds of cascading coins, and of some of them "clinking" against the bars across the top of the offering box)

• *tamete* is from *tameru/tamemasu* ("collect/accumulate," or when speaking of money, "save"), and *oita* is the plain past form of *oku/okimasu*. *Tamete oita* ("[I] saved [them] in advance") modifies *ichien-dama* ("one-yen coins").
• coins are counted with *-mai*, the counter suffix for thin, flat things, or with *-ko*, the more generic counter for small objects regardless of shape.
• *zā* represents the pouring/rushing of water as well as of small hard objects such as rice, dried beans, plastic pellets, or in this case, aluminum coins.

-Te oku = "do for future use/need/reference"

The *-te oku* form is also used to speak of actions that leave no concrete result, but are done with a mind to future eventualities, whether for specific anticipated developments or for more general future reference and potential usefulness. For example, *oboeru* = "learn/memorize," and *oboete oku* = "learn/memorize/remember in case it comes in handy sometime."

376 Already finished with most of her packing, Natsuko, calls to tell her mother that she has quit her advertising job in Tokyo and is coming home to work at the brewery. When she first went to Tokyo, her father told her not to come back until she'd made something of herself; her mother warns her that he won't be pleased.

Natsuko: ハイハイ、お父さん　の　おこごと　は
Hai hai,　o-tōsan　no　o-kogoto　wa
yes, yes,　(hon.)-father　's　(hon.)-scolding　as for

覚悟して　　　おきます。
kakugo shite　okimasu.
prepare/brace for　ahead/in advance
"Yes, yes, I'll mentally prepare myself in advance for Father's scolding."
"I know, I know, I'll be bracing myself for Father's lecture." (PL3)

• *o-kogoto* is the honorific prefix *o-* plus *kogoto* ("scolding/rebuke/faultfinding").
• *kakugo* is a noun referring to one's "readiness/willingness" to accept the undesirable consequences of something (in this case, her own action), and the verb *kakugo suru* implies "mentally preparing/bracing/steeling oneself for," or sometimes "resigning oneself to," those consequences. *Kakugo shite* is the *-te* form of *kakugo suru*, and *okimasu* adds the sense that the action is done now in preparation for a future eventuality.

© Maekawa Tsukasa. *Dai-Tōkyō Binbō Seikatsu Manyuaru*, Kōdansha.

© Oze Akira. *Natsuko no Sake*, Kōdansha.

-てくる *-te kuru* implies movement toward the speaker

The *-te* form of a verb plus *kuru* ("come") often indicates that the action of the verb moves toward the speaker or a place associated with the speaker, including his/her current location.

377 Japan's minister of education predictably denies the allegation that he made derogatory remarks about anyone (fig. 259), but Suzuka Hiroshi (fig. 279) gets wind that there is a secretly recorded tape of the remarks. He sends a man to the U.S. to try to pay off the reporter and obtain the tape. At Suzuka's office, his aide announces that the man has returned. (Fig. 279 is the panel that follows this one.)

Aide: 鈴鹿　先生、アメリカ　に　行っていた　森本君　　が
Suzuka sensei, Amerika ni itte ita Morimoto-kun ga
(name) (title) (place) to had gone (name-fam.) (subj.)

帰って　　きました。
kaette kimashita.
return(ed) home came
"Mr. Suzuka, Morimoto who was in America has returned." (PL3)

- *sensei* is the word for "teacher/instructor," but it is also used as a respectful title and term of address for a variety of other people considered worthy of respect, including artists, writers, doctors, and members of the Diet.

- *itte ita* is the past form of *itte iru*, from *iku* ("go"). As was noted with *kite iru/ita* ("has/had come" → "is/was here"; fig. 285), *itte iru/ita* is literally "has/had gone [to the stated place]," but it's usually better thought of as "is/was in [the stated place]." Since *ni* marks America as the destination, in this case it becomes "was in America."

- *kaette* is the *-te* form of *kaeru* ("return" or "go/come home"), and *kimashita* is the polite past form of *kuru*. Since the verb *kaeru* can be either "go home" or "come home," using the *-te kuru* form clarifies the direction. In this case, the aide is saying that Morimoto has "come home" to Japan.

☞ Remember: *-te* forms do not have any tense of their own, so tense is determined by the helping verb.

-ていく *-te iku* implies movement away from the speaker

The *-te* form of a verb plus *iku* ("go") similarly can indicate that the action of the verb moves away from the speaker or a place associated with the speaker, including his/her present location.

378 At the station after their date when Kōsuke has had one too many (fig. 102), Hiroko decides Kōsuke probably can't get home on his own.

Hiroko: 送って　　いく　ワ。
Okutte iku wa.
escort/accompany go (fem.)
"I'll see you home." (PL2)

- *okutte* is from *okuru/okurimasu* ("send/escort/accompany"); as seen previously in figs. 21 and 198, *okuru* can mean "see off/send off"—i.e., accompany someone to his/her departure point, such as the bus stop or the station—or it can mean "see someone all the way to his/her destination/home." Adding *iku* reflects the fact that Hiroko and Kōsuke will be moving away from their present location. On the other hand, a person waiting at the destination would speak of the escort's action as *okutte kuru/kita* because the act of escorting moves toward him/her.

In some cases, *-te kuru* and *-te iku* merely reflect the direction of movement that is already apparent. In other cases, they can be crucial for clarifying the intended direction of ambiguous words like *deru* ("go/come out"), *hairu* ("go/come in"), *kaeru* ("go/come home"), and even *okuru* ("escort"): *dete iku* = "go out" and *dete kuru* = "come out"; *haitte iku* = "go in" and *haitte kuru* = "come in"; *kaette iku* = "go home" and *kaette kuru* = "come home"; *okutte iku* = "escort/accompany away from here" and *okutte kuru* = "escort/accompany to here."

Moving toward or away from the present

The *-te kuru* form of a verb can imply that the action moves toward the speaker in time—i.e., that it occurred continuously or repeatedly from sometime in the past up to the present: "has/have done up to now." The *-te iku* form can similarly imply that the action moves away from the speaker in time—i.e., that it will proceed from now into the future: "go on doing" or "do from now on." With verbs indicating a process or change, these forms typically imply "[do the action] progressively/increasingly" as time moves toward or away from the present.

379 One day Natsu sees a woman lingering at a small roadside shrine near the Saeki Brewery. Guessing it must be Kikue's mother Moé (fig. 58), she approaches her. Moé tells her story, including how both her in-laws and her own parents made her promise not to see Kikue again.

Moé: わたし は その 約束 を 守って きました。
Watashi wa sono yakusoku o mamotte kimashita.
I/me   as for   that   promise (obj.)   keep/kept   until now
"I have kept that promise until now." (PL3)

• *mamotte* is the *-te* form of *mamoru/mamorimasu*, which when speaking of a promise means "keep"; when speaking of rules or laws means "observe/obey/abide by"; and when speaking of a person, place, or thing means "defend/protect."
• *kimashita* is the PL3 past form of *kuru*. Using a *-te kuru* form implies that she kept her promise from sometime in the past up to the present.

Moé goes on to explain that she is now about to remarry and move away, and she couldn't bear the thought of leaving without seeing her daughter one last time, even if only from afar. That is why she has come, even though she knows it violates the promise she made.

-Te kuru = "begin to do"

With some verbs, the *-te kuru/kimasu* form can mean "begin to [do the action]." Since the expression describes a process or change that is in progress, the past form, *-te kita/kimashita*, typically corresponds to "has/have begun to ～"—or simply "is/are ～ing," which is the natural English way to express an action in progress.

380 Just when Natsuko thinks nothing more can stand in the way of a successful Tatsunishiki harvest, she discovers that her crop is infested with a harmful pest (fig. 36). Then, while she and Kusakabe are trying desperately to remove as many of the insects as they can by hand, a typhoon approaches.

Kusakabe: 暗く なって きました。 帰りましょう!!
Kuraku natte kimashita.   Kaerimashō!!
dark   become   has begun to   let's go home/leave
"It has begun to grow dark. Let's go home!"
"It's getting dark. Let's get on home!" (PL3)

• *kuraku* is the adverb form of the adjective *kurai* ("dark"), and *natte* is the *-te* form of *naru* ("become"): *kuraku naru* = "become/grow dark" (fig. 78); the non-past *kuraku natte kuru/kimasu* = "begins to grow dark"; and the past *kuraku natte kita/kimashita* = "has begun to grow dark" or "is growing dark."
• *kaerimashō* is the polite "let's/I'll ～" form of *kaeru* ("go home").

-Te kuru = "do before coming/on the way"

Since the -te form can add the meaning of "and" to a verb, the -te form of a verb plus *kuru* can literally be translated as "do the action and come," and sometimes it means precisely that. Close variations include "do the action before coming" and "do the action on the way here."

An action before coming may imply a simple sequence of events, or it may state what caused/allowed/made it possible for the person to come. An action on the way may refer to a stop the person made, as in the example here; it may describe the action that brought him/her (*hashiru* = "run," and *hashitte kita* = "ran here/came running"); or it may say something else about his/her manner of coming.

381 On a winter day, Hiroko comes to visit Kōsuke in his apartment, bearing a gift of fruit.

Hiroko: 寒い わ ね。
Samui　wa　ne.
is cold　(fem.)　(colloq.)
"It's cold, isn't it?" (PL2)

Sound FX: ガチャ
Gacha
(rattle of door latch)

Hiroko: 柔軟体操?
Jūnan taisō?
limbering exercises
"Doing some stretching?" (PL2)

Kōsuke: あっ。
A!
(interj.)
"Oh, [hi]." (PL2)

Hiroko: リンゴ 買ってきた わ。
Ringo　katte kita　wa.
apples　bought-and-came　(fem.)
"I bought some apples on my way." (PL2)

-Te iku = "do before going/on the way"

The -te form of a verb plus *iku* can similarly mean "do the action and go," "do the action before going," "do the action on the way there," "go in such-and-such a way," "do the action in order to go," and so forth.

As noted at fig. 282, -te iru often gets shortened to -teru in colloquial speech. The same happens with -te iku, which becomes -teku; similarly, the plain past -te itta becomes -tetta, the plain negative -te ikanai becomes -tekanai, etc. (Don't try to use -teku as a contraction of -te kuru, though; -te kuru does not have a short form.)

382 As Shima leaves an evening of entertainment in Kyoto's Gion district, he gets caught in a downpour. He ducks under some eaves and takes out a pack of cigarettes. (Fig. 288 is the panel that follows this one.)

Shima: 少し この 軒 で 雨やどり を していこう。
Sukoshi　kono　noki　de　amayadori　o　shite ikō.
a little　this/these　eaves　at/under　rain sheltering　(obj.)　I'll do-and-go
"I think I'll do rain sheltering under these eaves a little before I go [any further]."
"I think I'll take shelter from the rain under these eaves for a while." (PL2)

• *amayadori o suru* is an expression for "take shelter from the rain"; the *o* is often omitted to make it a standard *suru* verb, *amayadori suru*. *Shite* is the -te form of *suru*, and *ikō* is the plain "let's/I'll/I think I'll ～" form of *iku*. The contraction for *shite ikō* would be *shitekō*.

-Te kuru = "go do"

You may be surprised to learn that -te kuru—not -te iku—is the correct equivalent for English "go do [something]." For example, in fig. 381, if Hiroko were already visiting and Kōsuke went out to buy some fruit for them to eat, he would say *Ringo (o) katte kuru* ("I'll go buy some apples") as he leaves, or *Ringo (o) katte kita* ("I went and bought some apples") when he arrives back. In both languages, the full thought behind the expression is "go to do the action and come back," but Japanese uses *kuru* ("come") to stand for the round trip, while English uses "go."

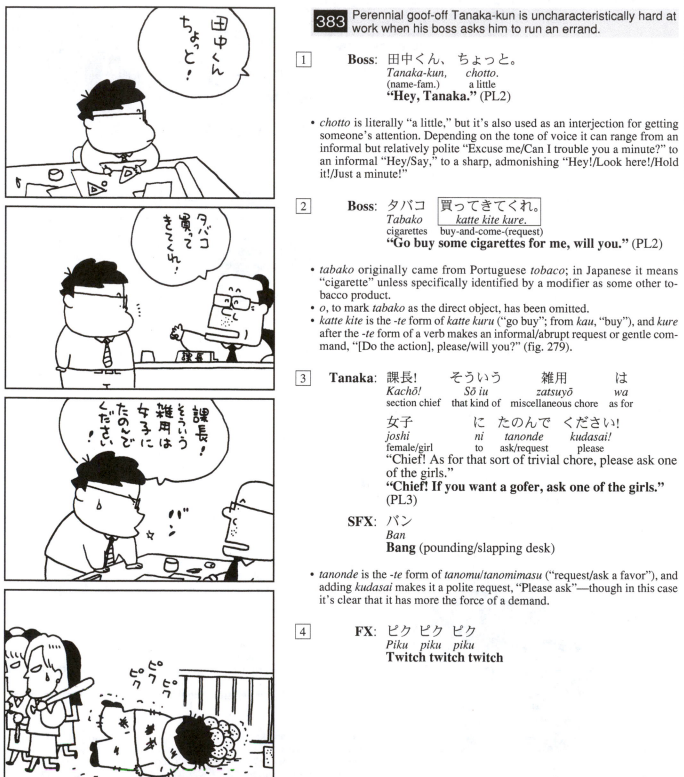

© Tanaka Hiroshi. Naku na! Tanaka-kun, Take Shobō.

383 Perennial goof-off Tanaka-kun is uncharacteristically hard at work when his boss asks him to run an errand.

1   **Boss**: 田中くん、 ちょっと。
    Tanaka-kun,   chotto.
    (name-fam.)   a little
    "Hey, Tanaka." (PL2)

- *chotto* is literally "a little," but it's also used as an interjection for getting someone's attention. Depending on the tone of voice it can range from an informal but relatively polite "Excuse me/Can I trouble you a minute?" to an informal "Hey/Say," to a sharp, admonishing "Hey!/Look here!/Hold it!/Just a minute!"

2   **Boss**: タバコ 買ってきてくれ。
    Tabako   katte kite kure.
    cigarettes   buy-and-come-(request)
    "Go buy some cigarettes for me, will you." (PL2)

- *tabako* originally came from Portuguese *tobaco*; in Japanese it means "cigarette" unless specifically identified by a modifier as some other tobacco product.
- *o*, to mark *tabako* as the direct object, has been omitted.
- *katte kite* is the -te form of *katte kuru* ("go buy"; from *kau*, "buy"), and *kure* after the -te form of a verb makes an informal/abrupt request or gentle command, "[Do the action], please/will you?" (fig. 279).

3   **Tanaka**: 課長! そういう 雑用 は
    Kachō!   Sō iu   zatsuyō   wa
    section chief that kind of miscellaneous chore as for

    女子 に たのんで ください!
    joshi   ni   tanonde   kudasai!
    female/girl   to   ask/request   please
    "Chief! As for that sort of trivial chore, please ask one of the girls."
    "Chief! If you want a gofer, ask one of the girls." (PL3)

  SFX: バン
    Ban
    Bang (pounding/slapping desk)

- *tanonde* is the -te form of *tanomu/tanomimasu* ("request/ask a favor"), and adding *kudasai* makes it a polite request, "Please ask"—though in this case it's clear that it has more the force of a demand.

4   **FX**: ピク ピク ピク
    Piku piku piku
    Twitch twitch twitch

Itte kimasu

Sayonara is familiar to most English speakers as the Japanese word for "good-bye," but, actually, how you say good-bye in Japanese depends a lot on the situation. When leaving home to go to work or school, or to go on a relatively brief errand or excursion, the proper "good-bye" is *Itte kimasu*—literally "I will go and come." The same phrase is used when leaving your workplace or other temporary "home base" on an errand from which you'll return (but not when you're going home at the end of the day).

Besides "good-bye," the phrase can be thought of as equivalent to English expressions like "I'm on my way," "I'm off," "I'll be going then," "See you later," "I'll be back," and the like. It's most commonly used in the polite form, but the plain *Itte kuru* also occurs in informal situations.

384 Shin-chan's mother asked him to take the neighborhood *kairanban*—a clipboard or folder containing information of interest to the community and passed from neighbor to neighbor—to the next person in the rotation. As he heads for the door, he forgets to take the all-important circular.

Shin-chan: いってきまーす。
Itte kimāsu.
will go-and-come
"I'm on my way." (PL2–3)

Mother: 肝心な 物 わすれてる よ。
Kanjin na mono wasureteru yo.
crucial/essential thing are forgetting (emph.)
"You're forgetting the most important thing." (PL2)

- the *ma* in *Itte kimasu* often gets elongated.
- *kanjin* is an adjectival noun; when followed by *na*, it usually corresponds to English adjectives like "crucial/essential/all-important."
- *wasureteru* is a contraction of *wasurete iru* ("is/are forgetting" or "has/have forgotten"), from *wasureru/wasuremasu* ("forget").

☞ *Itte kimasu* and *Itterasshai* typically occur as a pair, as the last thing said by the persons leaving and staying. Either phrase can come first, and the almost automatic response is the other phrase—though there are exceptions like in the case of Shin-chan here.

Itterasshai

Those staying behind when someone else leaves home or office for work, school, or on an errand have their own special good-bye as well, and it is *Itterasshai*. This is a contraction of *itte irasshai*, in which *itte* is the *-te* form of *iku*, and *irasshai* is a command form of the honorific verb *irassharu/irasshaimasu* ("come"; see p. 38), so it literally makes the command "Go and come." In spite of the honorific verb, the word is used at all politeness levels.

Besides "good-bye," *Itterasshai* can be considered equivalent to "Have a nice day" when sending someone off to school or work, or to expressions like "See you later," "Take care," "Good luck," "Have fun," "Hurry back," etc., that you might use in other situations.

385 Sayuri's mother and Yōji both work in nightclubs, so after their early dinner (fig. 367) they head to work. Sayuri sends them off.

Sayuri: いってらっしゃあい。
Itterasshāi.
go-and-come
"Good-bye!" (PL2–3)

- the *sha* in *Itterasshai* often gets elongated.

Lesson 26

Probably, Surely, Maybe

When a speaker is less than completely certain about the accuracy or impact of what he is saying, he can use the PL3 *deshō* to show an element of tentativeness or guesswork in his statement. This form corresponds to words and expressions like "maybe/probably/most likely/surely/must/should/I suppose/I guess/I expect/I bet" in English.

In PL3 noun-type sentences, for non-past, *deshō* replaces *desu* to give the meaning "is/are probably ～" (*daijōbu deshō* = "is/are probably all right"); but for past, *deshō* is added to the plain past *datta* (less commonly to the polite past *deshita*) to give the meaning "was/were probably ～" (*daijōbu datta deshō* = "was probably all right"). *Deshō* itself never changes form—though it does have a plain equivalent (see facing page).

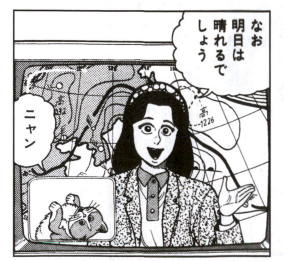

386 When Michael and companion sit down to watch some TV (fig. 271), the first thing that comes on is the weather report. Since weather forecasting is an inexact science, *deshō* is the sentence ending of choice when Japanese weathercasters are giving the forecast.

Weathercaster:
関東　地方　は　今夜　おそく　まで　雨　でしょう。
Kantō chihō wa kon'ya osoku made ame deshō.
(name) region as for tonight late until rain probably is
"As for the Kantō region, it will probably be rain until late tonight."
"Rain will continue throughout the Kantō region until late tonight." (PL3)

Cat:
ウニャニャ
"Unya nya."

- the Kantō region includes Tokyo and six surrounding prefectures.
- *osoku*, from the adjective *osoi* ("late"), is being used as a noun (fig. 364); *osoku made* = "until late."

In PL3 verb-type sentences, *deshō* is added as an extension to the verb. It creates the meaning "probably [will do/did/is doing the action]": *taberu deshō* = "probably will eat"; *tabeta deshō* = "probably ate"; *tabete iru deshō* = "is probably eating." Generally the verb preceding *deshō* is in one of its plain forms, but polite forms are sometimes used, too, especially by women.

Weathercaster:
なお、　　　明日　は　晴れる　でしょう。
Nao, ashita wa hareru deshō.
further/however tomorrow as for will clear up probably
"However, as for tomorrow, it will probably clear up."
"However, we expect fair skies tomorrow." (PL3)

Cat:
ニャン
"Nyan."

- *nao* is used to introduce additional information, so it often means "furthermore," but when what follows is contrasting information, it's more like "however."
- the polite form of *hareru* ("become clear/sunny") is *haremasu*.

In PL3 adjective-type sentences, *deshō* is added as an extension to a plain form of the adjective: *samui deshō* = "is probably cold"; *samukatta deshō* = "was probably cold"; *samukunai deshō* = "probably isn't cold."

In informal speech: だろう *darō*

The PL2 equivalent of *deshō* is *darō*. It works the same way *deshō* does in each of the three types of sentences and gives the same meanings; only the politeness level is different.

In a non-past noun-type sentence, *darō* replaces *da* (*Uso da* = "It's a lie" → *Uso darō* = "It's probably a lie"); in a past noun-type sentence, *darō* is added to *datta* rather than replacing it (*Uso datta* = "It was a lie" → *Uso datta darō* = "It was probably a lie"). *Datta darō* sometimes gets shortened to *dattarō*.

387 When Hatsushiba Electric's Chairman Kino tells Nakazawa (fig. 202) that he wants him to join the board of directors, Nakazawa can hardly believe his ears. He has always been his own man within the company, and can expect no support from any of the leading board members or their factions.

Kino: 私　　と　　社長　　が　　後押しする。
Watashi to   shachō   ga   ato-oshi suru.
I/me   and   co. pres. (subj.)   will support/back
"The president and I will back you." (PL2)

それ　　なら　　充分　　だろう。
Sore   nara   jūbun   darō.
that   if it is   plenty/sufficient   is probably
"That should probably be sufficient." (PL2)

- *ato-oshi* (lit. "pushing from behind") is a noun for "support/backing," and adding *suru* makes it a verb, "[to] support/back [someone]."
- *jūbun* is an adjectival noun; when followed by *da/desu*, it means "is plenty/sufficient," so *jūbun darō* = "is probably plenty/should be plenty."

Negative guesswork

Since neither *darō* nor *deshō* changes form, negative guesswork is expressed simply by adding *darō* or *deshō* to a negative statement. Generally, the negative statement itself is in a plain form (*-nai/-nakatta*) and the politeness level is determined by whether *darō* or *deshō* follows: *-nai darō/deshō* = "probably isn't/doesn't/won't ～"; *-nakatta darō/deshō* = "probably wasn't/didn't ～."

TRICKLE TRICKLE

388 Kōsuke's mother sent him a watermelon from the country, and since he doesn't have a refrigerator he decides to try chilling it by running cold water over it in the communal sink down the hall in his apartment building. Back in his room he ponders the situation.

Kōsuke (thinking):
あれ　じゃ　なかなか　　冷えない　だろー　な。
Are   ja   nakanaka   hienai   darō   na.
that   if it is   [not] easily/well   won't become chilled   probably   (colloq.)
"If it is that [method], it probably won't chill very easily."
"I don't suppose it's going to get very cold that way." (PL2)

- *are* and *sore* both mean "that," but *are* is used for things that are relatively farther away. Things that are in an altogether different location (e.g., a different room) also usually get *are*. Other differences between the two are noted at figs. 147 and 148.
- *ja* is a contraction of *de wa* ("if it is"; fig. 357).
- when *nakanaka* is followed by a negative, it means "[not] easily/readily/quickly," which in this context implies "not very well." (Also see fig. 393.)
- *hienai* is the negative form of *hieru/hiemasu*, which means "[something] chills/becomes chilled." *Hiyasu/hiyashimasu* is the corresponding verb that takes an *o* phrase, meaning "chill [something]."

Questions with *darō ka/deshō ka*

Ending a sentence with *darō ka* or *deshō ka* asks a question like "I wonder if 〜?" or "Is it perhaps 〜?" Such questions are asked with normal sentence intonation—without the rising intonation on the final syllable that otherwise signals a question.

389 Shortly after Hatsushiba sends Shima to Sunlight Records to carry out a reorganization, a recording star invites Shima to a birthday gala. When he wonders what he should take as a gift, Managing Director Tokiwa Kazuo says flowers should be fine, and no one disagrees. But Kajiwara catches up with Shima later:

Kajiwara: 私　　ちょっと　思った　んです　が、
Watashi chotto omotta n desu ga,
I/me a little thought (explan.) but/and

花束　　だけ　で　　いい　　ん　でしょう　か?
hanataba dake de ii n deshō ka?
bouquet only with is good/fine (explan.) I wonder if (?)
"I was just thinking, and I wonder if just a bouquet is enough."
"It occurred to me that maybe just flowers isn't really enough." (PL3)

- the topic marker *wa* has been omitted after *watashi* ("I/me"). The feeling is like "As for me [in contrast to the others], 〜"—i.e., this is the contrastive use of the topic mentioned in the usage notes on p. 81. It's not strictly necessary to say *watashi (wa)* here, but doing so helps politely set himself apart, since he's disagreeing with the view Shima seems to have accepted, along with the rest of the board.
- *omotta* is the plain past form of *omou* ("think/feel"), and *chotto omotta n desu ga* is literally "I thought a little, and 〜"; the expression has the feeling of "I was just thinking/It occurred to me that 〜." *Chotto* ("a little") serves mainly to soften the fact that he is contradicting someone else.
- *ga* marks the preceding as background for what follows (fig. 194).
- 〜 *dake* = "just 〜/only 〜," so *hanataba dake* = "a bouquet of flowers only." Fig. 366 shows how the *-ba* form of a verb plus *ii* can mean "[the stated action] is enough/is all that's needed." A noun plus *de ii* gives much the same meaning for what the noun refers to, so 〜 *de ii* = "〜 is enough," and 〜 *dake de ii* = "just 〜 is enough"; if the noun expresses a quantity, it means "just that much/many is enough" (*de* essentially indicates scope; fig. 175).

With a question word

Ending a sentence containing a question word with *darō ka* or *deshō ka* makes a question like "I wonder who/what/where/how 〜?" or "Who/what/where/how might 〜?" When using these forms, the speaker may only be wondering out loud, but if the question is specifically directed at someone it often has the feeling of "I wonder if you could tell me who/what/where/how 〜?" Again, normal sentence intonation is used rather than question intonation.

390 During a scientific experiment on cat behavior, Michael pauses to scratch behind his ear. The experiment has been videotaped with a running commentary.

Observer:
おっと、頭　を　かいております!!
Otto, atama o kaite orimasu!!
(interj.) head (obj.) is scratching
"Oh, he's scratching his head!" (PL3–4)

こ、これ　は　何　を　意味している　の　でしょう　か?!
Ko- kore wa nani o imi shite iru no deshō ka?!
th- this as for what (obj.) means (explan.) I wonder (?)
"As for this, it means what, I wonder?"
"Wh- what might this signify?" (PL3)

- *orimasu* is the polite form of *oru*, a humble equivalent of *iru*, so *-te oru/orimasu* = *-te iru/imasu*.
- *imi shite iru* ("means") is from the noun *imi* ("meaning") plus the verb *suru* ("do").

Using *deshō ka* for politeness

When an English speaker feels that a point-blank "What's that?" might be too blunt, he can soften his question by asking "What might that be?" Much the same happens in Japanese with *deshō ka*: in PL3 and higher speech, if asking with *desu ka* seems too direct and blunt, the speaker can replace it with the less direct *deshō ka* to make the question feel "softer" and more polite. In fact, many speakers switch quite routinely from *desu ka* to *deshō ka* when speaking to their social superiors in order to sound like they are asking respectfully for an answer rather than demanding one.

Although it's not as polite, *darō ka* is sometimes used for the same softening effect.

391 President Nakazawa of Hatsushiba Electric is relieved to learn that he does not have throat cancer as he feared, but he's not quite sure what to make of the doctor's diagnosis of adenomatous goiter.

Nakazawa:
それ　は　重大な　病気　でしょう　か?
Sore　wa　jūdai na　byōki　deshō　ka?
that　as for　serious　disease　might be/is　(?)
"Might that be a serious disease?"
"Is it a serious illness?" (PL3)

- *jūdai* is an adjectival noun; when followed by *na*, it generally corresponds to the English adjectives "serious/grave/weighty/important."
- there is no absolute reason why Nakazawa needs to use *deshō ka?* here instead of *desu ka?*, but since he is speaking to a doctor, he chooses the less direct form for greater politeness.

Without *ka*

Questions ending in *darō* or *deshō* are often asked without the question particle *ka*. If the query contains a question word, as in the example here, the intonation remains flat. Otherwise the question is indicated by using the rising intonation of a question on the last syllable.

392 Akebono Manufacturing, a former subcontractor for Hatsushiba Electric run by Sugita Rokurō, is being threatened with a hostile takeover, and President Nakazawa has sent Shima to rescue the company. Sugita explains how a man named Arima has been buying up the company's stock with the intention of gaining control of the board of directors.

Sugita

Shima:　有馬　は　一体　いくら　つぎこんだ　の　でしょう?
Arima　wa　ittai　ikura　tsugikonda　no　deshō?
(name)　as for　(emph.)　how much　poured in　(explan.)　I wonder
"Just how much do you suppose Arima has poured into your stock?" (PL3)

- *ittai* is an emphasizer for question words, so it can be like "[what] in the world?/[how] on earth?/[where] the blazes?/just [how much]?"
- *tsugikonda* is the plain past form of *tsugikomu/tsugikomimasu*, which literally means "pour into" and is commonly used to mean "spend/invest."

Darō/deshō as a tag question

Ending a sentence with *darō* or *deshō* spoken in normal sentence intonation in Japanese can be equivalent to a tag question like "〜, isn't it?/don't you?/aren't they?" spoken with a falling intonation in English—that is, it expects agreement or confirmation. Or it can be like "It's/they're 〜, don't you think?"

393 For about a year now, Shima's job has been to get Hatsushiba Trading Company into the business of importing fine wines from Europe, and in his usual fashion he has acquitted himself well. Nakazawa and the new president of Hatsushiba Electric, Mangame Kentarō, now want him to take on the reorganization of the loss-plagued Sunlight Records, another company in the Hatsushiba Group, and they have called him in to discuss it. They start by asking him about his current job.

© Hirokane Kenshi. *Buchō Shima Kōsaku*, Kōdansha.

Nakazawa:
どう だ、 ワイン 業界 は?
Dō da, wain gyōkai wa?
how is wine industry as for
"As for the wine industry, how is it?"
"How's the wine business?" (PL2)

なかなか 面白い だろう?
Nakanaka omoshiroi **darō?**
remarkably is interesting isn't it
"It's pretty interesting, isn't it?" (PL2)

- normal word order for the first sentence would be *Wain gyōkai wa dō da?*
- *nakanaka* means "quite/very/considerably"—usually implying "more than/better than you might expect." (See fig. 388 for when *nakanaka* is followed by a negative.)
- *omoshiroi* is an adjective that can mean either "(is) interesting/exciting/enjoyable" or "(is) amusing/funny"—here the former.

Darō/deshō = "right?"

Darō? or *deshō?* spoken with the rising intonation of a question can be like a rising "right?" at the end of a sentence in English. In this case the final vowel is often shortened: *daro?/desho?*

394 Natsuko is talking to Old Man Miyakawa about her plan to grow a crop of Tatsunishiki with the seeds her brother left behind. Miyakawa has effectively retired from growing rice, but Natsuko knows he was considered a master cultivator in his day and asks him to advise her. The advice he immediately gives her is to forget it, and he quickly lists all the reasons Tatsunishiki is so difficult to grow.

© Oze Akira, *Natsuko no Sake*, Kōdansha.

Natsuko:
でも 方法 は ある ん でしょ?
De mo hōhō wa aru n **desho?**
but method/way as for exists (explan.) right?
"But there is a way, right?"
"But it can be done, right?" (PL3)

- *de mo* at the beginning of a sentence is like "but."

Miyakawa

To soften an assertion

Much in the way they soften questions, *darō* and *deshō* are commonly used to keep strong assertions and statements of belief/opinion from sounding too abrupt, rough, or overweening. In this use, the "probably/perhaps" tentativeness associated with *darō* and *deshō* disappears, since they are actually standing in for *da* or *desu*; and even with the softening effect of using *darō* and *deshō*, the assertion can still sound quite forceful depending on the tone of voice.

395 Kaji is talking to his two most trusted friends about what kind of issues he wants his campaign to focus on if he decides to run for the House of Representatives. (The panel shown in fig. 369 follows shortly after this one.)

Kaji:

国民	全体	の為に	何	を	すべき	か?
Kokumin	*zentai*	*no tame ni*	*nani*	*o*	*subeki*	*ka?*
citizenry/population	totality	for	what	(obj.)	should do	(?)

"What should be done for the population as a whole?" (PL2)

日本	の為に	何	を	すべき	か?
Nihon	*no tame ni*	*nani*	*o*	*subeki*	*ka?*
Japan/the nation	for	what	(obj.)	should do	(?)

"What should be done for Japan as a nation?" (PL2)

それ	が	国政	レベル	の	公約	だろう。
Sore	*ga*	*kokusei*	*reberu*	*no*	*kōyaku*	*darō.*
that	(subj.)	national gov.	level	of/at	campaign promise	is surely

"I believe those are the campaign promises [one must make] at the national level." (PL2)

- *no tame ni* is literally "for the purpose/benefit of" → "for."
- *subeki* is equivalent to *suru beki* ("do" + "should/ought to/must"), and *ka* makes it a question: *Subeki ka?* = "Should one do [it]?" and *Nani o subeki ka?* = "What should one do?"
- even among friends, ending with just *da* would sound quite abrupt here.

かもしれない *ka mo shirenai* = "might ～"

The standard way to say "might ～" or "may possibly ～" is with *ka mo shirenai*. The polite non-past equivalent is *ka mo shiremasen*.

The phrase is added directly after a noun, or after a verb or adjective in one of its various plain forms: *dorobō* = "thief," so *Dorobō ka mo shirenai* = "It might be a thief" (noun); *hareru* = "[skies] become clear," so *Hareru ka mo shirenai* = "It might clear up" (verb); *omoshiroi* = "is interesting," so *Omoshiroi ka mo shirenai* = "It might be interesting" (adjective).

Ka mo shirenai expresses a higher level of uncertainty than *darō/deshō*. Sometimes you will hear *darō* or *deshō* added to *ka mo shirenai* as a tag question (～ *ka mo shirenai darō* = "might/may possibly ～, right?"), or to add politeness/softness.

396 Many larger Japanese firms have regularly scheduled annual or semiannual "shake-ups" because they want to have their employees experience a wide variety of jobs within the company. This man tells his wife what he has heard about his possible fate in the next such shake-up.

Husband:	春	の	異動	で
	Haru	*no*	*idō*	*de*
	spring	(mod.)	shake-up	in

	転勤	に	なる	かもしれない。
	tenkin	*ni*	*naru*	*ka mo shirenai.*
	transfer	(result)	become	might/may

"I may get transferred in the spring shake-up." (PL2)

Wife:	えっ?
	E!?

"What?" (PL2)

- *idō* written with these kanji means "a shift/change/reshuffle." The more complete term for the periodic corporate shake-ups is 人事異動 *jinji idō* (lit. "personnel reshuffle").
- *tenkin* refers to a transfer within the company that requires the employee to move to another city: "job relocation"; *tenkin ni naru* = "be transferred/relocated."

Lesson 27

Commands

As illustrated in Lesson 19, the *-te* form of a verb by itself or in combination with *kure* can make a relatively gentle command. But verbs also have a more abrupt **command form**. The abrupt command form of a Group 1 verb is made by changing the final *u* of the dictionary form to *e*; no additional ending is needed. In kana, simply change the final syllable to the *e* sound in the same row—if it's ぶ, make it べ; if it's む, make it め.

397 Kōsuke's landlady calls up to him from the yard below to get help drawing the liquid from her *hechima* vines (fig. 100). The landlady seldom wastes politeness on Kōsuke.

Landlady: ヘチマ　　の　　水とり　 手伝え!!
Hechima　no　mizu-tori　tetsudae!!
loofah　of　water-drawing　help
"Help me draw the water from the *hechima* vines!" (PL2)

- *tori* is the noun form of *toru/torimasu* ("take/get/draw [from]"), so *mizu-tori* is a noun referring to the act of drawing water/liquid from the vines. *O*, to mark this as the direct object of *tetsudae*, has been omitted.
- *tetsudae* is the abrupt command form of *tetsudau/tetsudaimasu* ("help/assist").

© Maekawa Tsukasa, *Dai-Tōkyō Binbō Seikatsu Manyuaru*, Kōdansha.

Emphasizing with よ *yo*

The particle *yo* is commonly used with commands to provide emphasis that can range from strong to gentle to pleading, depending on how the *yo* is spoken. With some commands, including those in the abrupt command form, a short, unaccented *yo* spoken with falling intonation actually manages to soften the sound of the command even as it emphasizes it.

In most contexts, the abrupt command form would be considered too rough for female speakers to use (they would use the *-te* form instead). If they nevertheless choose to be abrupt, as in this example, they're especially likely to add a falling *yo* in order to take the edge off.

398 Woman A wanted advice about whether she should choose marriage and go with her boyfriend on his overseas assignment, or choose career and continue with the work she has been enjoying more and more lately. Her friend B told her that she shouldn't be asking someone who is currently unemployed and has no boyfriend. A's comeback in this panel does not amuse B:

A: あら、野球　ヘタ　　でも　　審判　は　できる　よ。
Ara, yakyū heta de mo shinpan wa dekiru yo.
(interj.) baseball unskilled even if you are umpire as for can do (emph.)
"But even if you're lousy at baseball, you can still be an umpire." (PL2)

B: 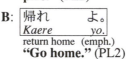 帰れ　　　　よ。
Kaere　　yo.
return home (emph.)
"Go home." (PL2)

© Akizuki Risu, *OL Shinkaron*, Kōdansha.

- *de mo* after a noun makes an expression like "even if I am/it is/you are ～."
- *shinpan* can refer either to "umpire" (the person) or "umpiring" (the activity).
- *kaere* is the abrupt command form of *kaeru* ("go home").

Group 2 verbs

The abrupt command form of a Group 2 verb is made by replacing the final -る -ru with -ろ -ro: *taberu* ("eat") → *Tabero* ("Eat!"); *miru* ("see/watch") → *Miro* ("Look!"). Again, *yo* is often added for emphasis and/or softening: *Tabero yo* and *Miro yo*. (There is also a second command form for Group 2 verbs made by replacing the final -ru with -yo—as in *tabeyo*—but this remnant of classical/literary Japanese is not normally used in spoken Japanese.)

399 Bonobono the otter gets flustered when he has to catch something. Fishing Cat picks up a stone and holds it out toward him saying he's going to suck all of Bonobono's easily flustered parts into the stone so he can throw them away. After a few moments he says he's done and hands the stone to Bonobono.

Fishing Cat: むこう　に　投げろ。
Mukō　ni　nagero.
other side　to　throw
"Throw it over there." (PL2)

FX: ぱいっ　　　　ざさ
Pai!　　　　Zasa
(effect of throwing)　(rustle of underbrush)

- *mukō* means "the other side/the other end" or simply "over there."
- *nagero* is the abrupt command form of the verb *nageru/nagemasu* ("throw/toss").

-ていろ -te iro → -てろ -tero

Iru is a Group 2 verb, so its command form is *iro*, and the command form of every -te iru verb is -te iro. The form -te iro commands someone to "be doing/continue doing [the action]" or "remain in [the described state]." As illustrated here, -te iro often gets shortened to -tero.

400 The whole family is busy cleaning the house from top to bottom, but Michael the cat keeps getting in the way.

Michael: ウニャニャニャ
Unya nya nya
"Meow-yow-yow"

FX: バタバタ
Bata bata
(effect of batting at ball of twine)

Father: あ、　こらー、　あっち　行ってろー！
A,　korā,　atchi　itterō!
(interj.)　(interj.)　over there　go-and-stay
"Hey! Stop that! Go over there!"
"Hey! Cut that out! Scram!" (PL1–2)

FX: ダッ
Da!
(effect of sprinting off)

- *kora!* (often lengthened to *korā!*) is an interjection for scolding, something like "Hey, none of that!/Stop it!/Cut that out!" or any other interjection uttered loudly and sharply to make the offender freeze.
- *ittero* (here elongated into an exclamation) is a contraction of *itte iro*, the -te form of *iku* ("go") plus the abrupt command form of *iru*. The plain non-past *itte iru* is typically "has gone to/is in [the stated place]" (fig. 377); its command form *itte iro* implies "go [to the stated place] and be/stay there," and when the place stated is *atchi* ("over there"), it essentially means "go anywhere other than here and stay there."

Kuru → こい *koi*

The abrupt command form of the irregular verb *kuru* ("come") is *koi*.

401 When his mother sends him to get a couple of things at the greengrocer, Shin-chan forgets to take along the money she gave him. The produce man winds up driving him home with his purchases. Here he says good-bye after dropping Shin-chan off and collecting payment from his mother.

Grocer: また 来い よ。
Mata koi yo.
again come (emph.)
"You come again now." (PL2)

Shin-chan: 体 に 気をつけて ね。
Karada ni ki o tsukete ne.
body/health with be careful (colloq.)
"Take care of yourself." (PL2)

- *karada* is literally "body," but in certain expressions it can be equivalent to "health" in English.
- *ki o tsukete* is the *-te* form of the expression *ki o tsukeru/tsukemasu* ("be careful/take care"); the *-te* form is being used as an informal request or gentle command. *Ki* corresponds closely to the English "mind/attention," and *tsukeru* means "attach/affix," so the expression *ki o tsukeru* literally means "affix one's mind/attention [to]." *Ki o tsukete* is a standard phrase spoken to the person leaving when saying good-byes, implying "Go with care," or if the person is traveling by car, "Drive carefully." The expression *Karada ni ki o tsukete* literally means "Take care of your body/health," and can be said by/to either party, staying or leaving; but it would generally be reserved either for long-term partings or for a person who is in fact having health problems, so Shin-chan's use here is somewhat incongruous.
- since *tsukeru* is a Group 2 verb, its abrupt command form is *tsukero*, and a sharp *Ki o tsukero!* is equivalent to "Be careful!/Watch out!"

Suru → しろ *shiro*

The abrupt command form of the irregular verb *suru* ("do") is *shiro*.

402 Natsuko is returning to Tokyo after what turns out to be the last time she sees her ailing brother Yasuo. He is doing well enough at the moment to see her off at the train.

Yasuo: いい 男 見つけたら 報告しろ よ。
Ii otoko mitsuketara hōkoku shiro yo.
good man if find report (emph.)
"If you find a good man, report to me."
"If you find that special someone, be sure to let me know." (PL2)

Natsuko: ばか ね。
Baka ne.
foolish/silly (colloq.)
"You're silly." (PL2)

- *ii otoko* is literally "good/nice man," but it's often more specifically an expression for "good-looking/handsome man." Since Kazuo goes on in the next frame to say he'll be the judge of whether the man is good enough for Natsuko, a broader meaning seems called for in this context.
- *mitsuketara* is an "if" form of *mitsukeru/mitsukemasu* ("find").
- *hōkoku shiro* is the abrupt command form of *hōkoku suru* ("to report/inform"). *Hōkoku* by itself is a noun for "a report/briefing/account."

Here are some more abrupt commands, using verbs you've seen before:

もっと 急げ! 山田 に 頼め。 よく 聞け。 待て! 逃げる と 撃つ ぞ!
Motto isoge! Yamada ni tanome. Yoku kike! Mate! Nigeru to utsu zo!
more hurry (name) to request good/well listen wait flee/run if will shoot (emph.)
"Hurry faster!" **"Ask Yamada."** **"Listen carefully."** **"Halt! If you run, I'll shoot!"**

Summary: The abrupt command forms of verbs

Here are the abrupt command forms of the model verbs. For Group 2 verbs, the final *-ru* is replaced with *-ro*; for Group 1 verbs, the final *-u* is replaced with *-e*.

Since they are inherently abrupt, there are no polite versions of these forms. This does not mean polite speech is devoid of command forms—in fact, even honorific verbs have abrupt command forms. But situations that demand politeness also tend to demand that you express the desired action in the form of a request rather than a command.

	dictionary form			abrupt command form	
irreg.	来る	*kuru*	come	来い	*koi*
	する	*suru*	do	しろ	*shiro*
gr. 2	見る	*miru*	see	見ろ	*miro*
	食べる	*taberu*	eat	食べろ	*tabero*
group 1 verbs	取る	*toru*	take	取れ	*tore*
	買う	*kau*	buy	買え	*kae*
	持つ	*motsu*[1]	hold	持て	*mote*[2]
	呼ぶ	*yobu*	call	呼べ	*yobe*
	飲む	*nomu*	drink	飲め	*nome*
	死ぬ	*shinu*	die	死ね	*shine*
	落とす	*otosu*	drop	落とせ	*otose*
	書く	*kaku*	write	書け	*kake*
	泳ぐ	*oyogu*	swim	泳げ	*oyoge*

[1] For romaji conversions, in *t* row syllables, *t* = *ch* = *ts*. See Introduction.

[2] Compare this with the verb's *-te* form, 持って *motte*. For all verbs whose dictionary form ends in -つ *-tsu*, be sure to distinguish the command form, which ends in -て *-te*, and the *-te* form, which ends in -って *-tte*.

Making a negative command with な *na*

To make an abrupt negative command or prohibition ("Don't ～"), simply follow the dictionary form of a verb with *na*: *nageru* ("throw") → *Nageru na* ("Don't throw [it]"); *tetsudau* ("help") → *Tetsudau na* ("Don't help"). In most cases, context and intonation make it immediately clear whether the *na* represents a prohibition ("Don't ～") or a tag question ("～, isn't it?/right?"; see fig. 17).

The *na* for prohibition can also occur after a verb in its non-past causative form ("make [someone do the action]"), which is introduced in Lesson 30: *taberu* ("eat") → *Tabesaseru na* ("Don't make [him/her] eat [it]"). And more rarely, it can occur after the non-past *-masu* or *-te iru* forms: *okoru/okorimasu* ("become angry") → *Okorimasu na* = "Don't be angry"; *damaru/damarimasu* ("become silent/shut up") → *damatte iru* = "be silent" → *damatte iru na* ("Don't be silent" or "Say something").

The abruptness of this form makes it mostly masculine. Female speakers generally use the form illustrated in the next example instead.

403 After a "Meet the Press" style television interview in which Kaji feels his views were distorted by the media panel, he and his chief aide Nishi discuss the state of the news media in Japan, focusing in particular on the frequency with which anchors and reporters allow their personal views to color the news. Finally, Kaji says to Nishi:

Kaji: 日本 の テレビ の 報道 を │信用 するな。│
Nihon no terebi no hōdō o │*shin'yō suru na.*│
Japan 's TV 's reporting (obj.) trust don't do
"Don't trust the reporting you see on Japanese TV." (PL2)

新聞 も │信じるな。│
Shinbun mo │*shinjiru na.*│
newspapers too/also don't believe
"Don't believe the newspapers, either." (PL2)

- *shin'yō* = "trust/confidence," and *suru na* is the abrupt negative command form of *suru* ("do"), so *shin'yō suru* = "(to) trust/have confidence in," and *shin'yō suru na* = "don't trust [it]."
- *shinjiru na* is the abrupt negative command form of *shinjiru/shinjimasu* ("believe/accept as true") → "don't believe [it]."

A gentler negative command: -ないで *-naide*

Since the *-te* form of a verb can make an informal request or relatively gentle command (fig. 278), it stands to reason that a negative verb's *-te* form might make a negative command/prohibition ("don't 〜"). But of the two *-te* forms for negative verbs introduced on p. 164, only *-naide* can be used to make negative commands: *hashiru* = "run," so *hashiranai* = "not run," and *hashiranaide* = "don't run."

Adding *kudasai* to this turns it into a polite negative request, "please don't 〜": *hashiranaide kudasai* = "please do not run." *-Naide kudasai* is the best negative command for beginners to use: it's a safe way to ask/tell a person not to do something in nearly any situation.

404 It's finally time to harvest the first crop of Tatsunishiki, and Natsuko wants to do the job herself, with only her sister-in-law Kazuko's help. When Bunkichi grabs his sickle and runs toward the field shouting that he's going to help, Natsuko shouts back:

Natsuko:
いい　　　　の!　｜来ないで!!｜
Ii　　　*no!*　　*Konaide!!*
fine/okay　(is-explan.)　don't come
"That's okay! Don't come!" (PL2)

刈り取り　は　あたし　と　義姉さん　だけ　で
Karitori　*wa*　*atashi*　*to*　*nēsan*　*dake*　*de*
harvest　as for　I/me　and　sister-in-law　only　with

やる　　の!　　そう　　決めてた　　の!!
yaru　*no!*　*Sō*　*kimeteta*　*no!!*
will do　(explan.)　that way　had decided　(explan.)
"As for the harvest, we will do it just with me and Kazuko! I had decided it that way [all along]!"
"Just Kazuko and I are going to harvest the rice. That's what I always wanted!" (PL2)

• *konaide* (the command, "don't come") is from *konai* ("not come"), the negative form of *kuru*.
• the two kanji used here to write *nēsan* ("older sister") mean "(older) sister-in-law," reflecting Kazuko's actual relationship to Natsuko, but in speech the same word is used for both "sister" and "sister-in-law."
• *kimeteta* is a contraction of *kimete ita*, the plain past form of *kimete iru* ("has/have decided," from *kimeru*, "decide"). The past form implies "had decided from before" or "had intended all along."

Commanding with -なさい *-nasai*

Commands can also be made by adding *-nasai* to the pre-*masu* stem of a verb. Or to put it another way, simply replace *-masu* in the polite form with *-nasai*: *damarimasu* ("become silent"; Group 1 verb) → *Damarinasai* ("Be quiet!"); *tabemasu* ("eat"; Group 2 verb) → *Tabenasai* ("Eat!").

This form is used especially by adults speaking to children and superiors/persons of authority speaking to those under their direction. Appending a firm, accented *yo* adds authority (*Tabenasai yo!*), but a gentle, falling *yo* can soften the command for use among equals. (Inferiors speaking to superiors would instead use the polite *-te kudasai* and make it a request.)

Father & Mother

405 Kazuhiro is supposed to be going to *juku* ("cram school") classes after school to prepare for his college entrance exams, but his father has learned of his frequent absences. He guesses correctly that Kazuhiro has been going to soccer practice instead. He hits the roof.

Father: すぐ　　部活　　は　｜やめなさい!｜
(off panel) *Sugu*　*bukatsu*　*wa*　*yamenasai!*
immediately　club activities　as for　quit-(command)
"Stop club activities immediately!"
"Quit the team immediately!" (PL2–3)

Kazuhiro

• for *bukatsu*, see fig. 127.
• *yamenasai* is from *yameru/yamemasu* ("stop/quit"). The exclamation point indicates that Kazuhiro's father is being very abrupt.
• *juku* ("cram school") refers to the private after-school or Saturday academies many young Japanese students attend in an effort to get a leg up on the entrance exams for high school and college.

The same for all types of verbs

Since -*nasai* always connects to a verb's pre-*masu* stem, replacing -*masu* in the polite form, the conversion works exactly the same way for all verbs, including the irregular verbs: *kuru/kimasu* ("come") → *kinasai; suru/shimasu* ("do") → *shinasai*.

How abrupt or sharp a command sounds ultimately depends on the tone of voice, but that being equal, -*nasai* commands sound gentler than the abrupt command forms and a little more authoritarian than commands made with a verb's -*te* form.

406 A burglar is holding Michael the cat hostage with a kitchen knife. He has demanded a ransom of ¥50 million and a car for his getaway.

Detective: よし!! 車 は 用意した ぞ。 人質 を 解放しなさい。
Yoshi!! Kuruma wa yōi shita zo. Hitojichi o kaihō shinasai.
(interj.) car as for prepared/readied (emph.) hostage (obj.) release-(command)
"All right! As for the car [you demanded], we've readied it! Release the hostage!"
"All right! The car you demanded is ready! Release the hostage!" (PL2–3)

- *yōi* is a noun for "preparations/readiness," and *shita* is the plain past form of *suru*, which makes it a verb: *yōi suru* = "prepare/get ready/arrange for."
- *kaihō* is a noun for "release/liberation," and its verb form is *kaihō suru* ("release/liberate").

-*Nasai* often reduces to -な -*na*

The suffix -*nasai* often gets shortened to -*na* in informal speech. This means that it's crucial to pay attention to what comes before *na*: a verb's pre-*masu* stem plus *na* is an abbreviation of the -*nasai* command form (*Oyogina* = "Swim!"; *Tabena* = "Eat!"); the dictionary form (or sometimes a certain other non-past form) plus *na* is a prohibition/negative command (*Oyogu na* = "Don't swim"; *Taberu na* = "Don't eat"). Neglect this distinction and you could wind up doing the exact opposite of what you're being told to do, or telling someone else to do the opposite of what you want him/her to do.

The short -*na* doesn't carry the feeling of authority that the full -*nasai* does, and often feels more like a suggestion than a command. It's widely used among peers as well as by superiors speaking to inferiors.

407 After the first-string players are announced for the Kakegawa High soccer team, team manager Endō invites the usual bunch to the fast-food chicken shop. When they ask her if she's sure she wants to pay for the whole group, she says, "Sure, it's from team funds."

Endō: だから いっぱい 食べな よ。
Da kara ippai tabena yo.
so/therefore lots eat-(command) (emph.)
"So eat lots."
"So eat all you want." (PL2)

- *tabena* is short for *tabenasai*, from *taberu* ("eat").
- the *yo* here is spoken gently, with a falling intonation.

Commands with -たまえ -tamae

Adding -tamae to the pre-masu stem of a verb (i.e., replacing -masu with -tamae) makes a strong, authoritarian command. This use is restricted to the superior in a clear superior-subordinate relationship. It's not generally used with children the way -nasai is.

408 Ever since Shima's arrival at Sunlight Records, Tokiwa Kazuo has been trying to embarrass him and sabotage his efforts to turn the company around. This time Tokiwa has gone too far, bringing scandal on the entire company and precipitating a sharp drop in sales.

Shima:
あなた を 解任 する。 速やかに 出ていきたまえ!
Anata o kainin suru. Sumiyaka ni dete ikitamae!
you (obj.) dismissal do promptly go out/leave-(command)
"I dismiss you. Leave promptly."
"You're fired. I want you to leave promptly." (PL2)

- *sumiyaka ni* is an adverb for "quickly/speedily/promptly."
- *dete* is the -te form of *deru* ("go/come out"), *iki* is the stem of *iku* ("go"), and -tamae makes it a command. As here, *iku* after the -te form of a verb often implies movement away from the speaker.

Commands with dictionary form and *n da/desu*

Sometimes the plain dictionary form of a verb spoken firmly or sharply can serve as a command.

409 This girl has come to the dentist to have some stubborn baby teeth pulled.

Dentist: 口 ゆすぐ。
Kuchi yusugu
mouth rinse
"Rinse your mouth." (PL2)

- the polite form of *yusugu* ("rinse") is *yusugimasu*. *O*, to mark *kuchi* ("mouth") as the direct object, has been omitted.

Similarly, following the dictionary form of a verb with a sharp *n da* or *n desu*—the explanatory extension—can serve as an abrupt command. Using *n da* this way should be considered masculine, though adding *yo* can soften it for female speakers; *n desu* is mostly feminine and not as common. *N da/desu* can have the same effect after a non-past causative verb (see Lesson 30), and in rare cases, other non-past verbs; the verb itself must always be in a plain form, even in the feminine usage when the command ends with *n desu*.

410 A girl Nishi and his friend met in Seoul turns out to be a North Korean agent. When they corner her, they see her put something in her mouth and then she begins spitting up blood.

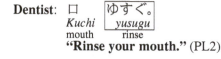

Nishi:
大変 だ! 毒 を 飲んだ! 救急車 を 呼ぶ んだ!!
Taihen da! Doku o nonda! Kyūkyūsha o yobu n da!!
terrible is poison (obj.) drank/took ambulance (obj.) call (explan.)
"Damn! She took poison! Call an ambulance!" (PL2)

Futatsugi:
了解!
Ryōkai!
"All right!" (PL2)

- *taihen* refers to a "serious/terrible/troublesome situation," and the exclamation *Taihen da!* is like "Oh no!/Oh my God!/This is terrible!/Damn!"
- *nonda* is the plain past form of *nomu* ("drink," or in this case "take/swallow").
- the polite form of *yobu* ("call") is *yobimasu*.

N ja nai/arimasen as a negative command/prohibition

Similarly, a sharp ~ *n ja nai* (mostly masculine) or ~ *n ja arimasen* (mostly feminine) can serve as an abrupt negative command or prohibition: "Don't ~."

411 Michael likes to walk along the railing of the veranda, several stories off the ground, and Reiko is always afraid he's going to fall. Today, a sparrow has come to perch on some utility wires just a foot or two away, and Michael seems intent on capturing it.

CHIRP CHIRP

Reiko: 気 に する ん じゃありません!!
Ki ni suru n ja arimasen!!
mind (target) do/put (explan.) do not
"Don't mind [it]!"

そんな スズメ!!
Sonna suzume!!
like that sparrow
"A sparrow like that!!"
"Don't pay any attention to that stupid sparrow!!" (PL3)

- *ki* = "mind/spirit" and *suru* = "do," so the expression *ki ni suru* can be literally translated as "do [it] mind" — i.e., "to mind [something]" or "to let [something] bother you."
- *sonna* ~ literally only means "that kind (of) ~" or "~ like that," but it's often used in a belittling/pejorative way: "that stupid/ lousy ~" (see comments on the *konna* group at fig. 163).
- normal order here would be *Sonna suzume (o) ki ni suru n ja arimasen!*

No yo as a command

In similar circumstances, *no yo*—the explanatory *no* plus the emphatic particle *yo*—makes a distinctly feminine command. It tends to be spoken quite gently—though, as always, it depends on the context. The negative equivalent in this case is *-nai no yo*.

Male speakers can also make commands using *no* and *-nai no*, but without the particle *yo*. Men who include the particle *yo* in this pattern sound effeminate—though *yo* does not carry any effeminacy with other command forms.

412 It's a busy time of day at the cash machine, and the long wait is putting everyone on edge. When Shin-chan's mother finally gets her turn (fig. 335), Shin-chan makes her enter the wrong PIN number. She has to start over, and now she's really feeling the heat from all the eyes behind her. She "commands" herself to be calm.

Mother: おちつく の よ。
Ochitsuku no yo.
relax/calm down (explan.) (emph.)
"Relax." (PL2)

気 を 集中する の よ。
Ki o shūchū suru no yo.
mind (obj.) concentrate (explan.) (emph.)
"Concentrate." (PL2)

私 は プロ の 主婦。
Watashi wa puro no shufu.
I/me as for pro (mod.) homemaker
"I'm a professional homemaker." (PL2)

- the polite form of *ochitsuku* ("relax/calm down") is *ochitsukimasu.*
- *puro* is from the English "pro/professional."

Lesson 28

Can Do

Instead of always requiring a separate helping word or phrase, a Japanese verb has its own special form for saying "can [do the action]" or "be able to [do the action]. For a Group 1 verb, the "can/be able to" form is made by changing the final *-u* to *-e* and adding *-ru* (PL2) or *-masu* (PL3): *oyogu* ("swim") → *oyogeru/oyogemasu* ("can swim"). In kana, change the final syllable to the *e* sound in the same row—if it's す, make it せ; if it's む, make it め—and add る or ます.

413 As he rejoices over passing his college entrance exams, his first thought is to toss his books aside and start having some fun.

Student: やった! 合格 だっ!
Yatta! Gōkaku da!
did it pass is
"I did it! I passed!"
"Hooray! I got in!" (PL2)

これ で 女の子 と バンバン 遊べる ぞー。
Kore de onna no ko to banban asoberu zō.
this with girls with unreservedly can play (masc. emph.)
"With this, I can play with girls all I want."
"Now I can go out with girls all I want!" (PL2)

- *yatta* is the plain past form of *yaru* ("do"). *Yatta!* is like the English exclamation of success, "I did it!" and it also serves as a broader exclamation of joy/delight: "All right!/Yeah!/Hooray!"
- *kore de* means "with this [achievement/development]" → "now that I have done this/now that that's over/now that this has come to pass."
- *asoberu* is the "can ～" form of *asobu/asobimasu* ("play/have fun") → "can play/can have fun/can goof off."
- the young man is next seen back at his desk poring over books like *How to Pick Up Chicks* and *Dating in Tokyo*.

For Group 2 verbs and *kuru*

The "can/be able to" form of a Group 2 verb is made by replacing the final *-ru* with *-rareru* (PL2) or *-raremasu* (PL3): *taberu* ("eat") → *taberareru/taberaremasu* ("can eat").

For the irregular *kuru*, the "can come" forms are *korareru* (PL2) and *koraremasu* (PL3). The endings are the same as for Group 2 verbs, but in this case the first syllable changes as well.

414 Kaji goes to his favorite fishing spot with his son while waiting for election returns to come in. Just when they are about to give up, Kaji feels a powerful pull on the line. He immediately realizes it's the massive *koi* that has gotten away from him three or four times before, and settles in for a long contest with the "King of the River." When his son says he's going to the car to listen to the radio, Kaji stops him.

Kaji: 待て。 もう 少し で 上げられる。
Mate. Mō sukoshi de agerareru.
wait more a little (scope) can raise/land
"Wait. I'll be able to land him in just a little more [time]."
"Wait. I've almost got him." (PL2)

網 を 用意しろ!!
Ami o yōi shiro!!
net (obj.) prepare
"Get the net ready!" (PL2)

- *mate* is the abrupt command form of *matsu/machimasu* ("wait"; be sure to distinguish the verb's *-te* form, which is *matte*), and *yōi shiro* is the abrupt command form of *yōi suru* ("prepare/get ready").
- *mō sukoshi* = "a little more" and the expression *mō sukoshi de* often means "in a little more time/soon."
- *agerareru* is the "can ～" form of the Group 2 verb *ageru* ("raise," or in the context of fishing, "land").

222

An alternative form for Group 2 verbs and *kuru*

The language police frown on it, but in common usage, especially among younger Japanese, the *ra* in *-rareru* is often dropped for both Group 2 verbs and *kuru*, so the endings become *-reru* (PL2) and *-remasu* (PL3): *taberu* → *tabereru/taberemasu*; *kuru* → *koreru/koremasu*. Dropping *ru* like this helps avoid confusion between the "can/be able to" form and the passive form, which is introduced in the next chapter.

415 Michael likes to nap on top of the warm TV, but he keeps draping his tail down over the edge in front of the picture. The family has to yell at him repeatedly, until finally the little girl chases him away and the screen is free of obstruction.

Father: やれやれ、 これ で やっと おちついて テレビ を 見れる な。
Yareyare, kore de yatto ochitsuite terebi o mireru na.
(relief) this with finally in relaxed manner TV (obj.) can watch (colloq.)
"Whew. Now we can finally watch TV in peace." (PL2)

- *yareyare* is a verbal sigh of relief used when something exasperating/worrisome or tiring is over.
- *ochitsuite* is the *-te* form of *ochitsuku/ochitsukimasu* ("settle/relax/become calm"); the *-te* form is being used to indicate the manner of the next mentioned action: "in a relaxed/settled manner" → "in peace."
- since *miru* ("see/watch") is a Group 2 verb, the proper form for saying "can see/watch" is *mirareru*, but the speaker here uses *mireru* instead (the polite equivalent is *miremasu*).

Suru → できる *dekiru*

The "can do/be able to do" form of *suru* ("do") is *dekiru/dekimasu*, and that means the "can/be able to" form of all ～ *suru* verbs is ～ *dekiru*. When the *suru* verb appears in the form of ～ *o suru* (fig. 131), the "can ～" form is usually ～ *ga dekiru*—with *ga* marking the thing that can be done (a *wa-ga* construction). When the thing that can be done is made the topic by marking it with *wa* instead of *ga*, as here, the effect is to emphasize it. *Dekiru* acts as a regular Group 2 verb, but with a somewhat limited set of forms.

☛ *Dekiru* has another important set of meanings besides "can do." It can also mean "[something] is formed/produced/completed" (fig. 199).

416 In a confrontation that occurs prior to the one shown in fig. 405, Kazuhiro lies to his father, saying that he is still attending cram school classes in addition to going to soccer practice. This is what he tells himself afterwards.

Kazuhiro: わかってる!
Wakatteru!
know
"I know it!"
"I'm positive!" (PL2)

予備校 に 行かなくたって
Yobikō ni ikanaku-tatte
cram school to even if [I] don't go

勉強 は できる んだ!
benkyō wa dekiru n da!
studies as for can do (explan.)
"Even if I don't go to cram school, I can do my studies."
"I can keep up my studies without going to cram school." (PL2)

- *wakatteru* is a contraction of *wakatte iru* ("know"), from *wakaru* ("understand/comprehend"). Here the feeling is of a very strong "know" → "I'm sure/positive!"
- *ikanaku-tatte* is a colloquial equivalent of *ikanakute mo*, an "even if" form of *ikanai* ("not go," negative of *iku*), so it means "even if [I] don't go." For *-te mo*, see fig. 363.
- the explanatory extension *n da* is being used purely for emphasis in this case.

"Can't/be unable to"

The "can ～" form of a verb always acts as a Group 2 verb whether it began life as a Group 1 verb, Group 2 verb, or irregular verb, so its negative form ("can't ～/be unable to ～") is made by replacing the final *-ru* with *-nai* (PL2) or *-masen* (PL3): *nomu* ("drink"; Group 1) → *nomeru* ("can drink"; Group 2) → *nomenai/nomemasen* ("can't drink"); *miru* ("see"; Group 2) → *mirareru* ("can see"; Group 2) → *mirarenai/miraremasen* ("can't see/watch"). In romaji, this means that all "can't ～" forms except *dekinai/dekimasen* end in *-enai/-emasen*.

417 While still at the advertising agency in Tokyo, Natsuko's assignment is to write a saké ad that does not mention the word alcohol, even though the ad is for a kind of saké defined by its added raw-alcohol content. She has tried, but inspiration has failed her, and her supervisor finds all her ideas wanting.

Natsuko: あたし 書けません。
Atashi *kakemasen.*
I/me can't write
"I can't write [an ad like that]." (PL3)

- *atashi* is a feminine equivalent of *watashi*.
- *kakemasen* is the PL3 "can't ～" form of *kaku* ("write"). The PL2 equivalent is *kakenai*. *Wa*, to mark *atashi* as the topic, has been omitted.

418 When Hatsushiba Chairman Kino tells Nakazawa that he and President Ōizumi want him on the board of directors (fig. 387), Nakazawa is caught completely by surprise.

Nakazawa:
ど、 どうして? 私 に は 信じられません。
Do- dōshite? Watashi ni wa shinjiraremasen.
(stammer) why I/me to as for can't believe/is unbelievable
"Wh-why? As for to me, this is unbelievable."
"Wh-why? I can't believe this." (PL3)

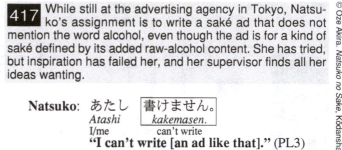

- *shinjiraremasen* is the PL3 "can't ～" form of the Group 2 verb *shinjiru/shinjimasu* ("believe"). The PL2 equivalent is *shinjirarenai*. The affirmative, "can ～" forms are *shinjirareru* and *shinjiraremasu*.

419 Little Nat-chan's grandmother has come for a visit, but Grandpa couldn't make it this time.

Grandma:
来れない から って、 写真 だけ。
Korenai kara tte, shashin dake.
can't come because (quote)-and picture only
"He said, 'Because I can't come,' and [sent] just his picture."
"Since he couldn't come, he sent his picture." (PL2)

Dad:
これ は これ は。
Kore wa kore wa.
this as for this as for
"Well, well." (PL2–3)

- *korenai* is a PL2 "can't ～" form of *kuru*. The PL3 equivalent is *koremasen*. This is the alternative form mentioned in fig. 415; the more proper "can't ～" form for *kuru* is *korarenai/koraremasen*.
- *tte* can be a contraction of several different quoting patterns in colloquial speech, and here it's a contraction of *to itte* (the quoting *to* plus the *-te* form of *iu*, "say"). Since *-tte* makes a quote, ～ *kara tte* is literally "[Someone] said, 'Because ～,'" but it can often be reduced to just "Because ～."
- *shashin dake* (lit. "just a picture") here implies something like "[he] sent/told me to bring just his picture."

"Could/was able to"

To make a past-tense "can ～" statement in English, you change "can" to "could"; similarly, "is able to" becomes "was able to." In Japanese, you replace the final *-ru* of the "can ～" form with the past endings *-ta* or *-mashita*—exactly as you would for any Group 2 verb. In romaji, this means all "could/was able to" forms except *dekita/dekimashita* (for *suru*) end in *-eta/-emashita*: *kaku* ("write"; Group 1) → *kakeru* ("can write"; Group 2) → *kaketa/kakemashita* ("was able to write"); *miru* ("see/watch"; Group 2) → *mirareru* ("can see"; Group 2) → *mirareta/miraremashita* ("was able to see").

English "could" is not simply the past form of "can"; it's also used to mean "might/may be able to" as well as "would be able/willing to." When using "could" to translate *-eta/-emashita* forms, always be sure you're thinking of it in the "was able to" sense; when going from English to Japanese, use *-eta/-emashita* only when "could" means "was able to."

420 Kaji is visiting the home district of Uzugami Saburo to support his bid for the party presidency. Though Kaji had originally made his own overnight arrangements, Uzugami's staff wants to get him a room at a hotel owned by a major supporter.

Staff: とれました。   402号室   です。
Toremashita,   *Yonhyaku nigōshitsu*   *desu.*
was able to get   room no. 402   is
"I was able to get [a room/reservation]. It's Room 402."
"I got a room. He'll be in Room 402." (PL3)

• *toremashita* is the polite past form of *toreru/toremasu* ("can/be able to get"), from *toru/torimasu*, which basically means "take/get/obtain"; but it has a range of other meanings in common expressions. *Toru* is the verb used to speak of getting/making various kinds of reservations.

© Hirokane Kenshi, Kaji Ryūsuke no Gi, Kōdansha.

Wa-ga construction

Sometimes the direct object of a "can/be able to" verb is marked with *o*, as in fig. 415, where *terebi* ("TV") is the direct object of *mireru* ("can see"). But more typically, these verbs occur in the *wa-ga* construction, with the *wa* phrase (often omitted, of course) representing the subject (the person or thing that is able to do the action) and the *ga* phrase representing the direct object (the thing most directly affected or "acted on" by the action).

Yatsuhashi

421 Aging diva Yatsuhashi Shinko's sales have been declining, and Shima wants to see if getting her off her pedestal and giving her a more down-to-earth image might spark sales among younger music fans. She is not very warm to the idea when he floats it during a round of golf, so she suggests an improbable test.

Yatsuhashi:
もし   イーグル   が   とれたら
Moshi   *iiguru*   *ga*   *toretara*
if   eagle   (obj.)   if can get/score
あなた の 言う こと を 聞いてもいい わ。
anata   *no*   *iu*   *koto*   *o*   *kiite mo ii*   *wa.*
you   (subj.)   say   thing   (obj.)   willing to listen   (fem.)
"If I can get an eagle, I am willing to listen to what you say."
"If I can score an eagle, I'll do as you say." (PL2)

• *toretara* is an "if" form of *toreru* ("can take/get," or in sports, "can score"), from the verb *toru* ("take/get/score"). In the *wa-ga* construction, *ga* marks *iiguru* (from English "eagle") as the direct object—i.e., as what she may be able to get/score.

• *iu koto* ("say" + "thing") implies "the thing you say" → "what you say," and *kiite* is the *-te* form of *kiku* ("listen [to]"), so *iu koto o kiku* is literally "listen to what you say"; but it's also an expression for "do as you say."

• to Shima's delight and Yatsuhashi's chagrin, her ball bounces off a rock by a creek and drops in for an eagle.

© Hirokane Kenshi, Buchō Shima Kōsaku, Kōdansha.

ことができる *koto ga dekiru*

Another way to say "can/be able to ～" is to add the phrase *koto ga dekiru/dekimasu* to the dictionary form of a verb of any type. In this case *koto* ("thing") refers to the action described by the preceding verb, so it's literally like saying "can do the action of ～." In actual usage, this "one size fits all" pattern can't quite be considered the same as the individualized "can/be able to" forms; there are sometimes subtle differences in nuance, and it can sound stiff. But for students still learning the language, it serves nicely in a pinch—if you find yourself drawing a blank on how to make the individualized form.

422 Kōsuke has come to the shrine with Hiroko on the day of the local shrine's *dondoyaki*—a ceremonial burning of New Year's decorations in a great bonfire. After making an offering and praying in front of the shrine (fig. 375), they go to warm themselves at the fire.

Narration:

この　火　に　あたると
Kono　hi　ni　ataru to
this　fire　at　if warm oneself
If you warm yourself at this fire,

1年間　　　　健康に
ichinen-kan　　kenkō ni
one/whole year　healthily

過ごす　ことができる　と　言う。
sugosu　koto ga dekiru　to　iu.
pass　can do　(quote)　say
you can pass the whole year in good health, they say.

They say that if you warm yourself at this fire, you'll stay healthy all year long. (PL2)

- *hi ni ataru/atarimasu* is an expression for "warm [oneself] at a fire"; *to* makes it a condition for what he says next: "If ～, then ～."
- *ichinen-kan* = "one year period" → "a/the whole year" or "all year."
- *kenkō ni* is the adverb form of *kenkō* ("health") → "healthily/in good health."
- *sugosu/sugoshimasu* means "pass [the days/months/years/time]"; *koto ga dekiru* has been added to its dictionary form to give the "can" meaning: "can pass [the year]." The verb's individualized "can ～" forms are *sugoseru* and *sugosemasu*.

ことはできない *koto wa dekinai*

The negative equivalent of ～ *koto ga dekiru/dekimasu* is ～ *koto wa dekinai/dekimasen*. Since *wa* marks *koto* as the topic, this is literally like "as for the action of ～, [someone/something] can't do it" → "can't do the action of ～."

423 After Kaji's father is killed in a car accident, the head of his campaign organization, Yamamoto Makio (fig. 352), seeks Kaji out in Tokyo. He wants Kaji to quit his job in private industry and return home to the district to run for the Diet seat that his father's death left vacant.

Kaji:

少し　時間　を　下さい。
Sukoshi　jikan　o　kudasai.
a little　time　(obj.)　please give me
"Please give me a little time."

"I'll need some time to think it over." (PL3)

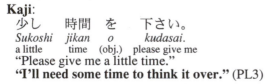

私　の　人生　の　こと　です　から、　今　ここ　で　即断する　ことは出来ない。
Watashi　no　jinsei　no　koto　desu　kara,　ima　koko　de　sokudan suru　koto wa dekinai.
I/me　's　life　about　thing　is　because/so　now　here　at　immediately decide　cannot do
"This is about my [entire] life, so here and now, I cannot immediately decide."

"This will affect the rest of my life, so I can't make a snap decision right here and now." (PL2–3)

- *sokudan* refers to an "instant/immediate/on the spot decision," and *sokudan suru* is its verb form.

Some special verbs

The verbs *mirareru* (from *miru*, "see/look at/watch") and *kikeru* (from *kiku*, "hear/listen to") mean "can see/hear" or "can be seen/heard" in the sense that the object/performance is available for viewing or listening—such as a movie that can be seen at a particular theater or a song that can be heard on the radio. There are separate verbs for "can see/hear" when you mean that something is visible (見える *mieru*) or audible (聞こえる *kikoeru*)—such as an object that is large enough or close enough to see, or sound that is loud enough or clear enough to hear. These latter verbs are also used when speaking of whether the person's eyes and ears are functional. Since they are Group 2 verbs, they convert to past, negative, etc. the same way as all other "can/be able to" verbs.

424 Kōsuke knows he can see (*mirareru*) the movie *The Sting* on TV tonight if he goes to one of his favorite neighborhood eateries. But when he arrives, a raucous party is in progress. He can see (*mieru*) the picture but he can't hear the dialogue.

"Chugulug! Chugulug!"

"Chugulug! He did it!" CLAP CLAP CLAP CLAP

Kōsuke きこえない。
(thinking) *Kikoenai.*
can't hear
"I can't hear." (PL2)

- いっき *ikki* is from the adverb *ikki ni*, which means "[do the action] all at once/without pause/in a single go."
- *kikoenai* is the plain negative form of *kikoeru/kikoemasu* ("can hear").

Summary: The "can/be able to 〜" forms of verbs

Here are the "can/be able to 〜" forms of the model verbs. For Group 2 verbs, the form is made by changing the final *-ru* to *-rareru* or *-raremasu*; for Group 1 verbs, it's made by changing the final *-u* to *-e* and adding *-ru* or *-masu*. This form of a verb acts as a Group 2 verb for any further transformations.

	dictionary form			"can/be able to"		
irreg. verbs	来る	*kuru*	come	来られる	*korareru*	can come
				来れる[1]	*koreru*[1]	can come
	する	*suru*	do [it]	できる	*dekiru*	can do [it]
gr. 2 verbs	見る	*miru*	see	見られる	*mirareru*	can see[2]
				見れる[1]	*mireru*[1]	can see
	食べる	*taberu*	eat	食べられる	*taberareru*	can eat
				食べれる[1]	*tabereru*[1]	can eat
group 1 verbs	取る	*toru*	take	取れる	*toreru*	can take
	買う	*kau*	buy [it]	買える	*kaeru*	can buy [it]
	持つ	*motsu*[3]	hold	持てる	*moteru*[3]	can hold
	呼ぶ	*yobu*	call	呼べる	*yoberu*	can call
	飲む	*nomu*	drink	飲める	*nomeru*	can drink
	死ぬ	*shinu*	die	死ねる	*shineru*	can die
	落とす	*otosu*	drop	落とせる	*otoseru*	can drop
	書く	*kaku*	write	書ける	*kakeru*	can write
	泳ぐ	*oyogu*	swim	泳げる	*oyogeru*	can swim

[1] Widely used, but not officially sanctioned; avoid when being graded on a test!

[2] Special verbs: みえる *mieru* = "is visible" きこえる *kikoeru* = "is audible"

[3] For romaji conversions, in *t* row syllables, *t* = *ch* = *ts*. See Introduction.

Passive Verbs

The **passive form** of a verb is used to speak of the subject being on the receiving end of the action instead of doing the action: The secret message *was stolen*. The students *were scolded*. His family *is cursed*. In these English sentences, "was stolen," "were scolded," and "is cursed" are passive forms of the active verbs "steal," "scold," and "curse."

It's worth noting right away that Japanese and English don't always mirror each other in their usage of passive forms. When translating, passive verbs in Japanese sometimes need to become active verbs in English, and vice versa, active verbs sometimes need to become passive. So be ready to think flexibly.

For Group 1 verbs, the passive forms are made by changing the final -*u* to -*a* and adding -*reru* (PL2) or -*re-masu* (PL3). In kana, change the final syllable to the *a* sound in the same row—if it's く, make it か; if it's つ, make it た—and add -れる or -れます.

425 This *What's Michael* episode focuses on the typical behavior of cats, especially as relates to smells.

Narration: ネコ は チチチチ と 呼ばれる と、 つい ふりむいてしまう。
Neko wa chi chi chi chi to yobareru to tsui furimuite shimau.
cat(s) as for chi chi chi chi (quote) is/are called if/when instinctively turn head-(involuntary)
As for a cat, if it is called with a *chi chi chi chi*, it instinctively turns its head.
If a cat hears someone calling *chi chi chi chi*, it instinctively turns to look. (PL2)

さらに 指 を 出される と、 つい におい を かいでしまう。
Sara ni yubi o dasareru to, tsui nioi o kaide shimau.
in addition finger (obj.) is/are offered if/when instinctively scent/odor (obj.) sniff-(involuntary)
If it is then offered a finger, it instinctively sniffs at it. (PL2)

- *yobareru* is the passive form of *yobu/yo-bimasu* ("call/call out to/hail"). The preceding *to* marks *chi chi chi chi* as a quote, to show the specific content/manner of calling to the cat; the *to* that comes after *yobareru* makes the action a condition for what follows: "If/when it is called with a *chi chi chi chi*, [then] 〜" (fig. 354).
- *tsui* modifying a verb implies the action is/was done "inadvertently/unintentionally/automatically/instinctively." *Tsui* often occurs with a *-te shimau* verb when that form implies that the action was done involuntarily/spontaneously (fig. 374), in effect emphasizing the instinctive, "can't help it" nature of the action.
- *furimuite* is the *-te* form of *furimuku/furimukimasu* ("turn one's head/look over one's shoulder").
- *dasareru* is the passive form of *dasu/dashimasu* ("put out/extend/offer"). The *to* again makes the verb a condition for what follows: "If/when it is offered [a finger], 〜."
- *nioi* is a noun for "smell/scent/odor," and *kaide* is the *-te* form of *kagu/kagimasu*, a verb for the act of deliberately smelling/sniffing at something. When a smell is simply present in the air, you would say 〜 *(no) nioi ga suru* (fig. 120); the blank can be filled either with the name of the thing that smells (*piza* = "pizza," so *Piza no nioi ga suru* = "I smell pizza") or a description of the smell (*hen na* = "strange/weird/funny," so *Hen na nioi ga suru* = "I smell something weird").

Passive past form

A passive verb acts as a Group 2 verb whether it started out as a Group 1 verb, Group 2 verb, or irregular verb, so the past form of any passive verb is made by replacing the final *-ru* with *-ta* (PL2) or *-mashita* (PL3): *tanomu* ("ask a favor"; Group 1) → *tanomareru* ("be asked a favor"; Group 2) → *tanomareta/tanomaremashita* ("was/were asked a favor").

The person or thing that receives the action of the passive verb—the subject—is marked with *wa* or *ga*. Since the main focus is usually on what is done to the subject rather than who or what does it to him/her, the doer of the action often goes unmentioned, as in the example here; when the doer is mentioned, he/she/it is marked with *ni* (see fig. 427, below), or sometimes *kara*.

426 Kokunō, a former business colleague, is serving as Kaji's interpreter and guide while he is in Washington D.C. On the way to the station to meet two other friends (fig. 328), Kaji fills Kokunō in on why he asked the men to come.

Kokunō:

え?　　　加治元春　　先生　　は　　殺された　んです　か?
E?　　　Kaji Motoharu　sensei　wa　korosareta　n desu　ka?
huh?/what?　(name)　　(title)　as for　was killed　(explan.)　(?)
"What? Was the Honorable Kaji Motoharu murdered?"
"What? Are you saying your father was murdered?" (PL3)

• *korosareta* is the plain past form of *korosareru* ("be killed"), which is the passive form of the Group 1 verb *korosu/koroshimasu* ("kill").

One special Group 1 subgroup

As with Group 1 negative forms (fig. 295), Group 1 verbs that end in the independent syllable -う *-u* pick up a new consonant on the way to becoming passive verbs: the *-u* changes to -わ *-wa*, and then *-reru/-remasu* is added: 言う *iu* ("say") → 言われる *iwareru* ("be told").

427 When the samurai asks the ninja to decode the secret message he delivered, the ninja discovers a postscript that says the messenger should be killed, so he pretends he cannot decipher the code. The samurai decides he'll have to protect himself by making it look like the message never arrived. This will be his story:

GLINT

Samurai:

忍者　は　　斬られ、
Ninja　wa　　kirare,
ninja　as for　was cut/killed-and
"The ninja was cut down, and

密書　　は　　何者か　　に　　うばわれた。
missho　wa　nanimono-ka　ni　ubawareta.
secret message　as for　someone　by　was stolen
"the secret message was stolen by someone."
"The messenger was killed, and the secret message was stolen by an unknown agent." (PL2)

"Yikes!"

• *kirare* is the pre-*masu* form of the passive *kirareru* ("be cut down/killed"), from the Group 1 verb *kiru/kirimasu* ("cut"; when written with the kanji used here, "cut down with a sword"). The pre-*masu* form of a verb can join two sentences into one as with "and": "[do the action], and ～" (fig. 190).
• *nanimono* (literally "what person") can be considered a synonym for *dare* ("who?"), but it carries a mysterious or even sinister feeling; *dare-ka* is simply "someone" (fig. 252), but *nanimono-ka* implies "some unidentified/mysterious person." *Ni* marks the person who does/did the action of the passive verb—in this case, the (purported) stealing.
• *ubawareta* is the plain past form of *ubawareru* ("be stolen"), from the Group 1 verb うばう *ubau* ("to steal"; polite form *ubaimasu*). Because the final syllable is -う *-u*, that syllable changes to -わ *-wa* in making the passive form: うばわれる *ubawareru*.

Group 2 passive is the same as Group 1

The passive forms of Group 2 verbs are made exactly the same way as the passive forms of Group 1 verbs: by changing the final *-u* to *-a* and adding *-reru* or *-remasu*. To be consistent with other Group 2 conversion rules, you can think of this change as replacing the final *-ru* with *-rareru* or *-raremasu* instead, but it amounts to the same thing. The resulting form is identical to the same verb's "can/be able to" form: *wasureru* ("forget") → *wasurerareru/wasureraremasu* ("be forgotten" or "can forget"). Which meaning the speaker intends usually comes clear from the context—though not always readily.

428 Here's how Shima tells Suzukamo Katsuko (fig. 216) that he doesn't want his subordinates to know about his efforts to learn the difference between good and mediocre bread.

Shima:

いや、　そんな　　ところ　を　見られる　の　は
Iya,　*sonna*　*tokoro*　*o*　*mirareru*　*no*　*wa*
no　that kind of　place/action　(obj.)　be seen　(noun)　as for

イヤ　　　　　　　　　　　なんだ。
iya　　　　　　　　*na n da.*
disagreeable/unwanted　is-(explan.)

"No, as for that kind of action being seen, it is disagreeable [to me]."
"No, I don't want to be seen doing it." (PL2)

なんか　努力する　　姿　　を　他人　　　に
Nanka　*doryoku suru*　*sugata*　*o*　*tanin*　*ni*
something　make effort　figure　(obj.)　other people　by

見られる　って　恥ずかしい　でしょう?
mirareru　*tte*　*hazukashii*　*deshō?*
be seen　as for　is embarrassing　isn't it?

"It's kind of embarrassing for others to see you having to make an effort at something, don't you think?" (PL3)

- *tokoro* literally means "place," but it's often used abstractly to refer to a situation/action/time/part.
- *mirareru* is the passive form of the Group 2 verb *miru* ("see"); *no* makes the complete sentence *sonna tokoro o mirareru* ("that kind of action is seen") act as a single noun (fig. 232), and *wa* marks it as the topic: "as for that kind of action being seen." For the second instance of *mirareru*, the particle *ni* marks the person/people who will see his efforts (i.e., who will do the action of the passive verb).
- *nanka doryoku suru* ("[one] makes an effort at something") is a complete sentence modifying *sugata* ("figure/appearance") → "the figure of one making an effort at something."
- the colloquial *tte* acts like the topic marker *wa*; see fig. 216, which shows the panel that follows this one.

☞ For passive, Group 2 verbs have no alternative form like the one introduced for "can ～" in fig. 415. Using *-reru/-remasu* for the "can ～" form is one way to avoid ambiguity, but you need to be sure to keep *-rareru/-raremasu* for the passive form.

Group 1 verbs that end in *-ru*

A Group 1 verb that ends in *-ru* has the same passive ending as a Group 2 verb: *-rareru/-raremasu*. But it's important to remember that the "can ～" form for the Group 1 verb is different: e.g., for *okuru* ("send"), the passive form is *okurareru* ("be sent"), but the "can ～" form is *okureru* ("can send"). The two forms are identical only for Group 2 verbs.

"Sorry."

429 Young brewhouse worker Yasuichi got a telegram saying his father is dying, and the brewmaster urges him to go home right away. But Yasuichi says his father told him when he first became a brewer's apprentice that learning the craft was an absolute commitment and he should not plan to come home even if his parents fell ill or died.

Yasuichi:　今　帰ったら　　おやじ　に　しかられます。
Ima　*kaettara*　*oyaji*　*ni*　*shikararemasu.*
now　if go/went home　old man　by　will be scolded

"If I went home now, I'd be scolded by my old man."
"If I went home now, my old man would give me hell." (PL3)

- *kaettara* is an "if" form of *kaeru* (fig. 355).
- *oyaji* is an informal word for "dad/old man" (fig. 306).
- *shikararemasu* is the PL3 passive form of the Group 1 verb *shikaru/shikarimasu* ("to scold"). *Ni* marks the person who will do the scolding. The "can ～" form of the verb is *shikareru/shikaremasu*.
- *sunmasen* (not transcribed) is a contraction of *sumimasen* ("I'm sorry"); he apologizes for disobeying the brewmaster.

The passive forms of *kuru* and *suru*

The passive forms of *kuru* are *korareru* (PL2) and *koraremasu* (PL3), which are identical to the verb's "can come" forms; context must tell you which meaning is intended. Passive *korareru/koraremasu* is quite rare, and usually occurs in the adversative use that will be noted in figs. 434 and 435.

The passive forms of *suru* are *sareru* and *saremasu*, so for all ～ *suru* verbs, the passive forms are ～ *sareru/saremasu* ("～ is done [to the subject]"). In this case there is no resemblance at all to the "can do" form, which is *dekiru/dekimasu* (fig. 416).

430 The evening news reports that the existence of the Loch Ness monster has finally been confirmed.

Anchor: では　　次　　の　　ニュース　です。
De wa tsugi no nyūsu desu.
now then next that is news is
"Now the next news." (PL3)

スコットランド　の　　ネス湖　で
Sukottorando no Nesu-ko de
Scotland in Loch Ness at

ついに　ネッシー　が　発見されました。
tsui ni Nesshii ga hakken saremashita.
finally Nessie (subj.) was discovered
"At Loch Ness in Scotland, Nessie has finally been found." (PL3)

- *tsui ni* = "finally" in the sense of "after much effort/waiting/anticipation."
- *hakken* = "discovery" and *hakken suru* = "discover/find"; *saremashita* is the polite past form of the passive *sareru/saremasu* ("be done"), from *suru*, so *hakken saremashita* = "was discovered/found."

Negative passive

Since the passive form of a verb acts as a Group 2 verb, the negative forms of any passive verb are made by replacing the final *-ru* with *-nai/-masen* (non-past) or *-nakatta/-masen deshita* (past). For example, *kau* ("buy"; Group 1) → *kawareru* ("be bought"; Group 2) → *kawarenai* or *kawaremasen* ("not be bought/is not bought"), and *kawarenakatta* or *kawaremasen deshita* ("was not bought").

431 Freelance cameraman Miyajima received a tip about a secret assignation between a famous kabuki actor and the proprietress of an exclusive club. After tailing her from her club to a hotel, he tells his assistant to follow her in and find out what room she goes to. When the assistant comes back, they enter the hotel together intending to ask for the room across the hall.

Miyajima: 同じ　フロア　で　　降りて
Onaji furoa de orite
same floor on get off-(cause)

あやしまれなかった　か?
ayashimarenakatta ka?
was/were not suspected (?)
"You were not suspected by getting off [the elevator] on the same floor?"
"Are you sure getting off on the same floor didn't raise any suspicions?" (PL2)

CLICK CLICK CLICK

- *orite* is the *-te* form of *oriru/orimasu* ("get down" or "get off/out [of a conveyance]"); the *-te* form is being used to state the (possible) cause for raising suspicions (fig. 274).
- *ayashimarenakatta* is the past form of *ayashimarenai* ("not be suspected"), which is the negative form of *ayashimareru* ("be suspected"), from *ayashimu/ayashimimasu* ("to suspect/view with suspicion").

The *-te* form of a passive verb

A passive verb can be used in a *-te* form, either by itself or with the various helping verbs shown in Lessons 19 and 25. Like all Group 2 verbs, the *-te* form of a passive verb is made by replacing the final *-ru* with *-te*. The example here illustrates a passive verb in a *-te iru* ("is/are ～ing) form:

432 Shinnosuke thought he was being very diligent about his responsibilities as a watchdog when he barked at everyone who came, including the postman.

Narration:
だけど　いつも　おこられている　のだった。
Da kedo   itsu mo   okorarete iru   no datta.
but   always   was getting scolded   (explan.)
"But he was always getting yelled at." (PL2)

Shinnosuke:
ハッハッハッハッ
Hah hah hah hah
(panting)

- *okorarete* is the *-te* form of the passive *okorareru* ("be scolded"), from the Group 1 verb *okoru/okorimasu* ("get angry/scold"). Although the active form of *okoru* can mean "get angry/be angered" as well as "to scold/reprimand," the passive form always means "be scolded." (The synonym *shikaru*, whose passive form is seen in fig. 429, is not used for "get angry"; it only means "scold/reprimand.")
- *-te iru* often makes the "is ～ing" form of a verb, so *okorarete iru* = "is being scolded"; *no datta* (the plain past form of the explanatory extension *no da*) adds past tense, changing it to "was being scolded," and *itsu mo* ("always") makes it "was always being scolded."

A passive verb as modifier

Like any other verb, a passive verb (or the sentence it completes) can be used to modify a noun. When a plain passive verb is used as a modifier, it typically implies "[the thing/person] that is/was/will be ～ed." For example, *yobu* means "call," and *yobareru* is its passive form, "be called," so *yobareru hito* = "the person who is/will be called," and *yobareta hito* = "the person who was called"; if mentioned, the person who does the calling (or other action of the passive verb) is marked with *ni*, as in *sensei ni yobareta hito* = "the person who was called by the teacher."

GLUG GLUG

433 With this year's saké left to age in tanks until fall, the brew-house workers have gone home, and Kusakabe is about to leave as well. An evening with Natsuko turns into a drinking contest as Kusakabe tells how his father and grandfather died young and his brother suffers from liver damage as well, all due to an excessive fondness for saké. Rather than trying to turn over a different leaf, Kusakabe seems resigned to follow the same fate as he drinks saké from a large bowl.

Kusakabe:　のろわれた　家系　です。
Norowareta   kakei   desu.
cursed   lineage   is
"It is a cursed lineage [that I come from]"
"I come from a cursed lineage." (PL3)

- *norowareta* is the plain past form of *norowareru* ("be cursed"), which is the passive form of the Group 1 verb *norou/noroimasu* ("to curse"). Although *norowareta* is literally "was/were cursed," as a modifier it often simply means "(is) cursed." For this verb, using the non-past *norowareru* as a modifier would mean "lineage that will be/is destined to be cursed."

Passives used to express adversity

The passive form in Japanese is very commonly used to speak of actions that have an unwanted/adverse effect on the subject of the sentence (often the speaker)—whether this amounts merely to unpleasant/unwelcome feelings, or to actual inconvenience and suffering. This is sometimes called the **adversative passive** use. Although other uses of the passive occur widely with inanimate subjects, this use is generally reserved for animate. Most typically, the action is not actually directed at the subject, but rather the subject is unfavorably affected by a generalized action (like the rain falling in the example here), or suffers inconvenience/distress/harm as an indirect consequence of someone else's action.

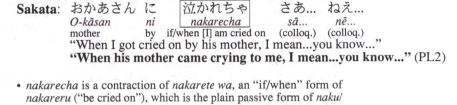

"Whew!"

434 The weather was dry when Nigashima left on his errand, but he apparently got caught in the rain somewhere along the way.

Nigashima: いやー、 途中で 降られちゃいました よ。
Iyā, *tochū de* *furare-chaimashita* *yo.*
(interj.) en route was rained on-(regret) (emph.)
"What a drag! I was rained on en route."
"What a drag! I got caught in the rain on my way."
(PL3)

- *tochū* is a noun referring to any point between start and finish, either in time (in which case *tochū de* means "during/partway through [the timespan/event/process]") or in space (in which case *tochū de* means "en route/on the way [from point A to point B]").
- *furare-chaimashita* is a contraction of *furarete shimaimashita*, which is a passive form of the verb *furu/furimasu* ("[rain/snow/sleet] falls"; fig. 76). The plain, non-past passive form of *furu* is *furareru* ("be fallen on [by rain]" → "be rained on"), and its *-te* form is *furarete*; *shimaimashita* is the polite past form of the helping verb *shimau*, which after the *-te* form of a verb often implies that the action was undesirable/unfortunate (fig. 372): "Unfortunately/to my chagrin, [I] was rained on."
- *ame ni* is understood before *furare-chaimashita*, with *ame* = "rain" and *ni* marking it as the doer of the action (the rain is what does the falling). The speaker is of course the subject, which in a passive sentence is the person or thing on the receiving end of the action.

Understanding adversative passive

This use of passive often involves verbs you wouldn't expect to see and hear used as passive verbs in English, and it means that the standard "is/was ～ed" formula for translating passive verbs will often give the wrong meaning or won't make sense at all. Instead, try using the active form of the verb with a phrase like "on me/him/her," "to me/him/her," or with some other phrasing that shows the action has an effect on the subject of the original Japanese sentence.

Hideki's mother

435 Sakata is explaining to Sayuri after dinner (fig. 367) why she hasn't been able to break up with Hideki. First she felt guilty because he blamed her for making him fail his college entrance exams; and then Hideki's mother, who knows very well that her son has only his own slacker habits to blame, tearfully begged her to help straighten him out. The understood subject of the Japanese sentence is Sakata, the speaker.

Sakata: おかあさん に 泣かれちゃ さあ... ねえ...
O-kāsan *ni* *nakarecha* *sā...* *nē...*
mother by if/when [I] am cried on (colloq.) (colloq.)
"When I got cried on by his mother, I mean...you know..."
"When his mother came crying to me, I mean...you know..." (PL2)

- *nakarecha* is a contraction of *nakarete wa*, an "if/when" form of *nakareru* ("be cried on"), which is the plain passive form of *naku/nakimasu* ("cry/weep"). She leaves her thought unfinished, but implies that faced with Hideki's weeping mother she had no choice but to agree—and to continue going out with Hideki.

Honorific forms

As mentioned briefly on p. 38, some verbs have special honorific substitutes that are used to talk about the actions of one's social superiors, but most verbs simply change form. One honorific form is in fact the same as a verb's passive form. This may seem confusing at first, but you'll find that so long as you consider the nature of the verb (many make no sense in passive form, or rarely do) and keep in mind the relative social positions of the speaker(s) and the actor(s) (which you always need to pay attention to anyway in Japanese), context usually makes it clear which way the verb is being used.

436 Shizue comes to the village to find out what's wrong with Jinkichi, who has been missing work, but she's nervous about seeing him because she thinks he might be moping over her rejection of his marriage proposal (fig. 345). When she runs into Natsuko, she asks her to come along for moral support, but Natsuko says she has an appointment to keep. Shizue loses her nerve and decides to go with Natsuko instead.

Shizue: 夏子さん、 どこ に 行かれる んです か?
    Natsuko-san   *doko*   *ni*   *ikareru*   *n desu*   *ka?*
    (name-pol.)   where   to   will go   (explan.)   (?)
    "Where are you going, Miss Natsuko?" (PL4)

* *ikareru* is the honorific form of the verb *iku* ("go"). Shizue mixes different politeness levels in speaking with Natsuko, but there are several reasons she might use extra politeness: they have only met once before, and a person is generally more polite with new acquaintances; that meeting was at the time of Jinkichi's proposal to Shizue, when Natsuko in effect acted as a *nakōdo* (a go-between for arranging a marriage), and *nakōdo* must be treated with respect; and Shizue is also aware of the high status of Natsuko's family within the village as owner-operators of a saké brewery.

© Oze Akira. Natsuko no Sake, Kōdansha.

437 Following recent electoral reforms, Kaji's party has only 156 incumbent candidates to field in the 300 newly apportioned districts nationwide. After telling Kaji who his opponent will be in Kagoshima District 1 (fig. 272), party president Uzugami asked him to find two new candidates to run under the party banner in other Kagoshima districts. As Kaji is discussing campaign strategy with his staff, his chief aide Nishi brings up the issue.

Nishi:
ところで 新しい 候補者 を
Tokoro de   *atarashii*   *kōhosha*   *o*
by the way   new   candidates   (obj.)

二人 立てる と いう 件 は
futari   *tateru*   *to*   *iu*   *ken*   *wa*
2 count   make stand/field   (quote)   say   matter   as for

どう される つもり です か?
dō   *sareru*   *tsumori*   *desu*   *ka?*
how/what   do   intention   is   (?)
"By the way, as for the matter of fielding two new candidates, what do you intend to do?"
"By the way, what do you intend to do about getting two new candidates for the party to field?" (PL4)

© Hirokane Kenshi. Kaji Ryūsuke no Gi, Kōdansha.

* *tateru/tatemasu* typically means "erect/make stand" or "put in an upright/vertical position," but when speaking of a party's candidates in an election, it means "field/run [candidates]."
* *to iu* is a quoting form, but it often serves to mark the preceding as the specific content or description of what follows. Here it marks *atarashii kōhosha o futari tateru* ("field two new candidates") as the specific content of *ken* ("the matter"): "the matter of fielding two new candidates."
* *wa* marks *ken* (and its full modifier) as the topic of the sentence.
* *sareru* is the honorific form of *suru*, so *dō sareru* = *dō suru* ("what will you do?"; fig. 157). Structurally, this modifies the noun *tsumori* ("intention"; fig. 233).

Summary: The passive and honorific forms of verbs

The passive forms of a verb and one of its honorific forms are made in exactly the same way, and the rule is the same for both Group 1 and 2 verbs: change the final *-u* to *-a* and add *-reru* (PL2) or *-remasu* (PL3). The table lists only the PL2 forms; for PL3, change the final *-ru* to *-masu*.

	dictionary form			passive/honorific form		passive meaning[1]	honorific meaning[2]
irreg.	来る	*kuru*	come	来られる	*korareru*	comes, to S's distress	an exalted person comes
	する	*suru*	do	される	*sareru*	is done to S	an exalted person does [it]
gr. 2	見る	*miru*	see	見られる	*mirareru*	S is seen	an exalted person sees
	食べる	*taberu*	eat	食べられる	*taberareru*	S is eaten	an exalted person eats
group 1 verbs	取る	*toru*	take	取られる	*torareru*	S is taken	an exalted person takes [it]
	買う	*kau*[3]	buy	買われる	*kawareru*[3]	S is bought	an exalted person buys [it]
	持つ	*motsu*[4]	hold	持たれる	*motareru*	S is held	an exalted person holds [it]
	呼ぶ	*yobu*	call	呼ばれる	*yobareru*	S is called	an exalted person calls
	飲む	*nomu*	drink	飲まれる	*nomareru*	S is drunk	an exalted person drinks
	死ぬ	*shinu*	die	死なれる	*shinareru*	dies, to S's distress	an exalted person dies
	落とす	*otosu*	drop	落とされる	*otosareru*	S is dropped	an exalted person drops [it]
	書く	*kaku*	write	書かれる	*kakareru*	S is written	an exalted person writes
	泳ぐ	*oyogu*	swim	泳がれる	*oyogareru*	swims, to S's distress	an exalted person swims

[1] S = the subject; some of the meanings given will make sense only in very limited contexts; the adversative meaning is probably possible for all in the right context, but is indicated here only if a more straightforward meaning is impossible. In Japanese as in English, not all verbs make sense in passive form.

[2] Many of the meanings given here would more likely be expressed with an entirely different verb in PL4 speech (see p. 38), but when these forms are used as honorific verbs, this is what they mean.

[3] For verbs with the final syllable -う *-u*, the connecting syllable becomes -わ *-wa*.

[4] For romaji conversions, in *t* row syllables, *t* = *ch* = *ts*. See Introduction.

Comparing passive and "can/be able to" verbs

Here's a separate table comparing Group 2 verbs with Group 1 verbs that end in *-ru*. The passive forms of both groups end identically. Properly speaking, the "can/be able to" endings of the two groups are different, but these, too, become identical if *ra* is dropped from the Group 2 forms. (Remember, though: Group 1 verbs whose dictionary forms don't end in *-ru* are still a little different; their "can ～" forms end not in *-reru* but *-xeru*, where *x* stands for a consonant other than *r*—see the table on p. 227.)

For Group 1 verbs, there is always a clear distinction between the passive/honorific form and the "can ～" form, but no distinction exists for Group 2 verbs—until *ra* is dropped from the "can ～" form. Considering this, it's easy to see why some speakers drop the *ra* in Group 2 "can ～" verbs. Doing so not only makes the verbs sound the same as their Group 1 counterparts ending in *-ru*; it also creates a useful distinction between the passive and "can ～" forms of Group 2 verbs.

	dict.	passive/hon.	"can ～"	"can"—omit ra
group 2	見る *miru* see	見られる *mirareru* be seen	見られる *mirareru* can see	見れる *mireru* can see
	食べる *taberu* eat	食べられる *taberareru* be eaten	食べられる *taberareru* can eat	食べれる *tabereru* can eat
group 1	帰る *kaeru* go home	帰られる *kaerareru* go home (detrim.)	帰れる *kaereru* can go home	n.a.
	切る *kiru* cut	切られる *kirareru* be cut	切れる *kireru* can cut	n.a.
	取る *toru* take	取られる *torareru* be taken	取れる *toreru* can take	n.a.

Lesson 30

Making It Happen

The form of the verb for saying that the speaker or subject *causes* an action to take place is called the **causative** form. The actual meaning can range according to context from coercion ("make it happen/make [someone] do it"), to permission or acquiescence ("allow [someone] to do it/let it happen"), to something in between ("have [someone] do it").

For Group 1 verbs, this form is made by changing the final *-u* to *-a* and adding *-seru* (PL2) or *-semasu* (PL3): *yomu* ("read") → *yomaseru/yomasemasu* ("make/let [someone] read"). In kana, change the final syllable to the *a* sound in the same row—if it's ぶ, make it ば; if it's る, make it ら, and so forth—and add -せる or -せます. (See fig. 444 for one special subgroup.)

438 The manager of the housing complex sees some ladies hard at work in the flower beds and lauds them for pitching in to help beautify the grounds. What he doesn't know is that the ever-pragmatic ladies are actually planting greens for their tables.

Mgr.: 皆さんの　　団地　を　愛する　気持ち　が
Minasan no 　*danchi* 　*o* 　*aisuru* 　*kimochi* 　*ga*
everyone's/your 　housing complex 　(obj.) 　love 　feelings 　(subj.)

きっと　美しい　花　を　咲かせます　よ。
kitto 　*utsukushii* 　*hana* 　*o* 　*sakasemasu* 　*yo.*
surely 　beautiful 　flowers 　(obj.) 　will make bloom 　(emph.)
"Your love for your housing complex will surely bring us beautiful flowers." (PL3)

- *danchi o aisuru* is a complete sentence ("[you] love the housing complex") modifying *kimochi* ("feelings") → "feelings that you love the housing complex" → "love for the housing complex." *Minasan no* ("everybody's" = "your") also modifies *kimochi*, so it becomes "your love for the housing complex."
- *sakasemasu* is the polite form of the causative *sakaseru* ("make bloom/cause to bloom"), from *saku/sakimasu* ("bloom").

The causative form of Group 2 verbs

The causative form of a Group 2 verb is made by replacing the final -る *-ru* with -させる *-saseru* (PL2) or -させます *-sasemasu* (PL3): *tsukeru* ("to attach") → *tsukesaseru/tsukesasemasu* ("make/let [some-one] attach").

439 As he helps gather the thriving Tatsunishiki seedlings into bunches for planting, Miyakawa Tōru tells Natsuko that his father has finally agreed to come live with him in the city. "He's going to abandon the land he worked so hard to put me through college," he says, and continues:

Miyakawa: おれ　が　捨てさせる　んです。
Ore 　*ga* 　*sutesaseru* 　*n desu.*
I/me 　(subj.) 　will make [him] abandon 　(explan.)
"I'm making him abandon it." (PL3)

- *sutesaseru* is the plain causative form of *suteru/sutemasu* ("discard/throw away/abandon"). The polite causative form is *sutesasemasu*.
- *ga* marks *ore* ("I/me," the speaker) as the person who causes the doer to do the stated action.

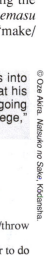

236

が *ga* marks the causer, に *ni* marks the doer

When the person or thing that causes the action—i.e., orders it or otherwise makes/lets it happen—is mentioned, he/she/it is marked with the subject marker *ga*; this can be an abstraction, as seen in fig. 438 on the facing page, or a specific person/thing, as seen in fig 439.

When the person or thing that actually does the action is mentioned, he/she/it is marked with *ni*, as seen here.

440 This *kachō* ("section chief") is talking with a client on the phone about the delivery of some important documents.

Boss:
あー、 うち の 女の子 に [もたせます] から。
Ā,   uchi   no onna no ko ni   motasemasu   kara.
(interj.) our office of/from girl (doer) will make/have carry because/so
"Oh, I'll have a girl from our office carry [them to you], so..."
"Oh, I'll have one of our girls deliver them, so..." (PL3)

• *uchi* often means "our house/shop/office." *Uchi no* means "of/belonging to our house/shop/office," or simply, "our."
• using *onna no ko* ("girl") to refer to female coworkers and subordinates has come to be considered insensitive in Japanese as it has in English.
• *motasemasu* is the polite form of the causative *motaseru*, from the verb *motsu* ("hold/carry"); here *motaseru* implies "will make [her] carry [the documents to you]" → "will have her deliver them to you."
• he leaves his sentence unfinished, but *kara* ("because/so") here implies something like "so please review them/handle them as appropriate."

The causative forms of the irregular verbs

The causative forms of the irregular verbs are also made with *saseru* and *sasemasu*. In fact, those are the causative forms of *suru*, just like that, without being tacked onto the end of anything: *suru* ("do") → *saseru/sasemasu* ("make/let/have [someone] do").

The causative forms of *kuru* ("come") are *kosaseru* and *kosasemasu* ("make/let/have [someone] come").

Like any other verb, a causative verb (or the sentence it completes) can be used to modify a noun, as illustrated here. As modifiers, they usually occur in a PL2 form.

441 On their train excursion to S, Shin-chan's mother buys just one ticket. When Shin-chan asks "What about mine?" she tells him he doesn't need one. As they go through the ticket gate, Shin-chan embarrasses his mother with this remark:

Shin-chan:
ただ乗り [させる] 親。
Tada-nori   saseru   oya.
free ride cause/make do parent
"A parent who has [her kid] ride without paying."
"A parent who doesn't pay for her kid." (PL2)

Mother:
幼児 は 無料 なの!!
Yōji   wa muryō na no!
toddler/preschooler as for no charge is-(explan.)
"Preschoolers are free!" (PL2)

• *tada* means "free/no charge," and *nori* is the noun form of *noru/norimasu* ("ride"); *tada-nori* usually implies an illegal free ride. *Tada-nori saseru* is the plain causative form of the verb *tada-nori (o) suru*: "ride without paying." *Muryō* is a more formal synonym for *tada*; it clearly implies that there is no charge to begin with.
• *tada-nori saseru* ("[she] makes [me/her kid] ride free") modifies *oya* ("parent") → "a parent who makes/has her kid ride without paying." Structurally, Shin-chan's statement is just a modified noun, not a complete sentence.

Past and *-te* forms

All causatives act as Group 2 verbs whether they started out as Group 1 verbs, Group 2 verbs, or irregular verbs. The past form of a causative verb is made by replacing the final *-ru* with *-ta* (PL2) or *-mashita* (PL3): *nomu* ("drink"; Group 1) → *nomaseru* ("make [someone] drink"; Group 2) → *nomaseta* or *nomasemashita* ("made [someone] drink"). The *-te* form is made by replacing the final *-ru* with *-te*: *nomasete* ("make/made [someone] drink, and 〜").

WHOMP!

442 In a scrimmage between the freshmen and upperclassmen (fig. 26), Kazuhiro clears the ball to his own goalie in order to prevent a shot by the other team. But to his dismay, the ball spins and bounces away from the goalie right to where the opposing player, Kubo, is waiting to kick it into the goal. Kubo had gently popped the ball off the ground just before Kazuhiro kicked it, and Kazuhiro now understands why.

Kazuhiro:

ボール を ｜浮かせて｜ わ、 わざと オレ に
Bōru o ukasete wa- wazato ore ni
ball (obj.) make/made float-and (stammer) purposely I/me (doer)

スピンボール を ｜蹴らせた｜ んだ。
supin-bōru o keraseta n da.
spinball (obj.) made kick (explan.)

"He made the ball float, and purposely made me kick a spinball."
"He deliberately popped the ball off the ground so my kick would make it spin!" (PL2)

- *ukasete* is the *-te* form of *ukaseru*, which is the plain causative form of *uku/ ukimasu* ("float [in midair/on water]").
- *keraseta* is the past form of *keraseru*, which is the plain causative form of *keru/ kerimasu* ("kick"). *Ni* marks the person who does the action of the causative verb, so *ore ni...keraseta* = "made me kick."

© Ōshima Tsukasa. Shoot!. Kōdansha.

Negative form, "don't/won't make"

The negative form of a causative verb is created by replacing the final *-ru* with *-nai* (PL2) or *-masen* (PL3): *matsu* ("wait") → *mataseru* ("make [someone] wait") → *matasenai* or *matasemasen* ("not make [someone] wait"). The example here shows a negative *-te* form.

443 Michael is only at the vet for an overnight stay, but when the delivery man notices the litter box and asks about him, it triggers what sounds like an outburst of grief.

Reiko: せっかく 忘れかけてた のに
Sekkaku wasure-kaketeta no ni
finally had started to forget in spite of

｜想い出させないで!｜
omoidasasenaide!
don't make [me] remember

"Just when I'd finally started to forget, please don't make me remember!" (PL2)

Man: す、 すみません。死んだ んです か?
Su- sumimasen. Shinda n desu ka?
(stammer) (apology) died (explan.) (?)
"I'm sorry. Did he die?" (PL3)

- *sekkaku* implies a situation that is special/long awaited/precious/ accomplished with much difficulty: "Just when finally 〜." It's often followed later in the sentence with *no ni* ("even though/in spite of") to express frustration/disappointment that "in spite of" the special situation, something undesirable has happened.
- *wasure-kaketeta* is a contraction of *wasure-kakete ita*, the plain past form of *wasure-kakete iru* ("have started to forget"), from *wasure-kakeru/kakemasu* ("start to forget"; *wasureru* = "forget").
- *omoidasasenaide* is the negative *-te* form of *omoidasaseru* ("make [someone] recall"), from *omoidasu/ omoidashimasu* ("recall/remember"). The negative *-te* form is being used as a request, "Please don't 〜."

© Kobayashi Makoto. What's Michael!?. Kōdansha.

-Te form as "(please) let me ～"

The *-te* form of a causative verb can make a request like "Let me [do the action]": *noru* = "ride" and *noraseru* = "let [someone] ride," so *Norasete* = "(Please) let me ride." Male speakers often add *kure* → *Norasete kure*. In polite speech, all speakers add *kudasai* → *Norasete kudasai.*

The verb in this example belongs to the subgroup of Group 1 verbs that end in -う *-u*. As when forming negative and passive verbs, the verbs with this ending pick up a new consonant when they become causative verbs: the *-u* changes to -わ *-wa* and then *-seru/-seta/-sete/-senai/* etc. is added: 言う *iu* ("say") → 言わせる *iwaseru* ("make/let [someone] say/speak").

444 The girl only goes out with him because he gives her presents and pays for things, and he knows it, so on their New Year's visit to the local shrine, he throws a ¥10 coin into the offering box and prays that this year he can become her true love. "You're asking a lot for only ¥10," she says, and thinking maybe she's right, he drops a ¥1000 bill in the box. The girl rushes to get her own prayer in before he has a chance to repeat his.

FX: ハラリ
Harari (effect of ¥1,000 bill fluttering down)

Girl: あっ、 それ、 私 に ┃つかわせて。┃
    A!, sore, watashi ni ┃*tsukawasete.*┃
    (interj.) that I/me (doer) let use-(request)
"Oh, let *me* use that." (PL2)

Guy: えっ?
    E!?
"Huh?" (PL2)

Girl: グッチ、 エルメス、 ヴィトン、 シャネル。
(praying) *Gutchi, Erumesu, Viton, Shaneru.*
    (brand names)
Gucci, Hermes, Louis Vuitton, Chanel.

- *tsukawasete* is the *-te* form of the causative *tsukawaseru* ("make/let use"), from *tsukau/tsukaimasu* ("use"); the *-te* form is being used as a request. *Ni* marks *watashi* ("I/me"—the speaker herself) as the doer of the action, so she is saying "let me use [it]"—meaning "let me apply that ¥1000 to *my* wish/prayer."

With a condition

In the right contexts, any of the ways for stating an "if/when" condition can work with causative forms. Like all Group 2 verbs, the final *-ru* of the causative form can be changed to *-reba* or *-tara* or *-te wa*; or the plain, non-past form can be followed by *to* or *nara*. See Lesson 24.

445 The owner of the flower shop where Garcia works apologizes for having to ask Garcia to do all the dirty and demanding drudge work, but explains that the shop is simply too short-handed. When Garcia notes that Japan has so many people, the owner laments that Japanese workers are useless. Then he elaborates:

Owner:
こんな 仕事 ┃やらせたら┃ すぐ やめちゃう よ。
Konna shigoto ┃*yarasetara*┃ *sugu yamechau yo.*
this kind of work if made [them] do immediately quit-(undesirable) (emph.)
"If I made them do this kind of work, they'd quit right away." (PL2)

Garcia:
ん?
N?
"Huh?" (PL2)

- *yarasetara* is an "if" form of *yaraseru* ("make [someone] do"), from *yaru/yari-masu* ("do"), so *yarasetara* = "if [I] make/made [them] do [it]."
- *yamechau* is a contraction of *yamete shimau*, the *-te* form of *yameru/yamemasu* ("stop/quit"), plus the suffix *shimau*, indicating that the action or its result is/would be regrettable/undesirable."

With passive

A causative verb can occur in a passive form when the speaker or subject is the person being made to do something. To make the passive form of a causative verb, change the final *-ru* to *-rareru* (PL2) or *-raremasu* (PL3): *motsu* = "carry" and *motaseru* = "make [someone] carry," so *motaserareru* = "[someone] is made to carry." Although the literal meaning becomes "[the doer] is made to [do the action]," this is often better rephrased with the active form of the verb in English: "[someone] makes [the doer do the action]" (e.g., "[I] made him carry [it].").

446 After being called down to help with his landlady's *hechima* vines (fig. 397), Kōsuke explains in his narration that she asks him to do this sort of thing quite frequently.

Kōsuke: オレ は よく 大家 の 手伝い を させられる。
(narrating) *Ore wa yoku ōya no tetsudai o saserareru.*
I/me as for often landlady 's help (obj.) am made to do
"I am often made to do the landlady's help."
"My landlady often makes me help her." (PL2)

- *yoku* is the adverb form of *ii/yoi*; the adverb form can mean either "well/carefully/thoroughly" or "frequently/a lot"—in this case the latter.
- *ōya* can be either "landlord" or "landlady," but in this manga the *ōya* is a woman.
- *tetsudai* is a noun meaning "help/assistance," and *tetsudai o suru* (lit. "do help") makes a verb phrase meaning "provide help/render assistance." *Saserareru* here is the passive form of *saseru*, which is the causative form of *suru*. *Tetsudai* is in fact a noun that comes from *tetsudau/tetsudaimasu* ("to help"), the verb the landlady uses in the abrupt command form in fig. 397. Since *tetsudau* ends in the syllable *-u*, its causative form is *tetsudawaseru* ("make [someone] help") and its passive-causative form is *tetsudawaserareru* ("[someone] is made to help"); see fig. 444.

"Can (or can't) make/let ～"

A causative verb can occur in a "can/be able to" form when speaking of whether a person can make/let someone else do a particular thing. This form of a causative verb is made the same way as its passive form: change the final *-ru* to *-rareru* or *-raremasu*. In this case, *motaserareru* means "can make [someone] carry." Context will tell whether the intended meaning is "can make [someone] do the action," or "[someone] is made to [do the action]."

For the "can't" form of either of these expressions, the final *-ru* is changed to *-nai/-masen* (non-past) or *-nakatta/-masen deshita* (past): *motaserarenai* = "can't make [someone] carry" or "can't be made to carry."

447 Nat-chan's brother is going to play at a friend's house, and Nat-chan wants to go along. Her brother says he thinks she'll be bored because it will be all boys. The precocious Nat-chan's response is a double entendre that would never actually come from the mouth of such a little girl.

"Sigh."

Nat-chan: おんな 一人 楽しませられない なんて...
Onna hitori tanoshimaserarenai nante...
girl/woman 1 count can't cause to enjoy (quote)
"Saying you can't amuse/pleasure a lone woman—[how pathetic!]"
"You mean you can't even show one woman a good time? [How pathetic!]" (PL2)

- the causative *tanoshimaseru* ("make [someone] enjoy [him/herself]" or "give [someone] pleasure") comes from *tanoshimu/tanoshimimasu* ("to enjoy") → *tanoshimaserareru* = "can make [someone] enjoy/can give [someone] pleasure" → *tanoshimaserarenai* = "can't make [someone] enjoy/can't give [someone] pleasure."
- *nante* is a quoting form used in informal speech that expresses surprise, embarrassment, or disdain for the described situation, or implies the preceding statement is silly/ridiculous/foolish/trivial; here it carries a belittling tone that suggests the end of her thought is something like, "How pathetic!" or "And you still call yourselves men?"

Wanting to cause (or not)

When a person wants to make or let something happen, the final *-ru* of the causative form is replaced with *-tai*; when a person wants to prevent it from happening, the final *-ru* is replaced with *-takunai*: *matsu* = "wait" and *mataseru* = "make [someone] wait," so *matasetai* = "want to make [someone] wait," and *matasetakunai* = "don't want to make [someone] wait."

☛ If you prefer to work from the polite form, *-tai* replaces the final *-masu* of the causative verb.

| 448 | With the rice harvest finished, the brewhouse workers have arrived to begin brewing this year's saké. At the banquet to welcome them all, Natsuko's father speaks to the brewmaster. |

Saeki:

杜氏、	あまり	年寄り	に	無理	を
Tōji,	*amari*	*toshiyori*	*ni*	*muri*	*o*
brewmaster	[not] excessively	aged person	(doer)	overexertion	(obj.)

させたくない	が、	今年	も	よろしく	頼みます。
sasetakunai	*ga,*	*kotoshi*	*mo*	*yoroshiku*	*tanomimasu.*
not want to make [you] do	but	this year	too	favorably	[I] request

"Brewmaster, I don't want to drive a man of your years too hard, but please give us the benefit of your expertise again this year."
(PL3)

• the adverb *amari* usually combines with a negative later in the sentence to mean "not too much/not excessively."

• *muri* is a noun for something that is beyond reason or impossible, and *muri (o) suru* typically means "work excessively/try too hard" or "overexert oneself" (fig. 62). *Sasetakunai* is the negative form of *sasetai* ("want to make [someone] do"), from *saseru* ("make [someone] do," the causative form of *suru*), so *amari muri o sasetakunai* = "don't want to make you overexert yourself excessively."

• *yoroshiku* is the adverb form of *yoroshii*, a more formal equivalent of *ii/yoi*; *yorishiku* implies "[do/handle/treat] in a favorable/agreeable fashion." *Tanomimasu* is the polite form of *tanomu* ("ask a favor"), and is often equivalent to "Please ～." *Yoroshiku tanomimasu* in essence asks the listener for his cooperation and best efforts. (When asking a favor of someone of higher status, the form *yoroshiku onegai shimasu* is used.)

Summary: The causative forms of verbs

For Group 1 verbs, change the final *-u* to *-a* and add *-seru* (PL2) or *-semasu* (PL3); for Group 2 verbs, replace the final *-ru* with *-saseru* (PL2) or *-sasemasu* (PL3). The table shows the plain forms. For passive-causative, change the final *-ru* of the causative form to *-rareru*: e.g., *kosaseru → kosaserareru* ("be made to come"); *kawaseru → kawaserareru* ("be made to buy").

	dictionary form			causative form		
irreg.	来る	*kuru*	come	こさせる	*kosaseru*	make/let come
	する	*suru*	do	させる	*saseru*	make/let do
gr. 2	見る	*miru*	see	見させる	*misaseru*	make/let see
	食べる	*taberu*	eat	食べさせる	*tabesaseru*	make/let eat
group 1 verbs	取る	*toru*	take	取らせる	*toraseru*	make/let take
	買う	*kau*[1]	buy	買わせる	*kawaseru*[1]	make/let buy
	持つ	*motsu*[2]	hold	持たせる	*motaseru*[2]	make/let hold
	呼ぶ	*yobu*	call	呼ばせる	*yobaseru*	make/let call
	飲む	*nomu*	drink	飲ませる	*nomaseru*	make/let drink
	死ぬ	*shinu*	die	死なせる	*shinaseru*	make/let die
	落とす	*otosu*	drop	落とさせる	*otosaseru*	make/let drop
	書く	*kaku*	write	書かせる	*kakaseru*	make/let write
	泳ぐ	*oyogu*	swim	泳がせる	*oyogaseru*	make/let swim

[1] For verbs with a final syllable う *u*, the connecting syllable becomes わ *wa*.

[2] For romaji conversions, in *t* row syllables, *t* = *ch* = *ts*. See Introduction.

Lesson 31

Giving and Receiving

How to say "give" and "receive" in Japanese depends on who gives to whom and on who is talking about it. The choice of words is affected by differences in status among the giver, recipient, speaker, and listener; by which of them are socially close; by which of them are present; and by the direction of the giving in relation to the speaker. A basic introduction can't cover all the permutations, but this lesson will illustrate the various words used and the key principles involved in selecting the right one.

The verbs for "give" can be divided into two groups according to their direction: some are used to talk about giving that moves inward, toward the speaker ("give to me/us" or "give to a person who is relatively close to me"), and others are used to talk about giving that moves outward, away from the speaker ("give to you/him/her/them" or "give to a person who is relatively distant from me").

あげる *ageru*: when the giving is outward bound

When the speaker is the giver, the appropriate word is always one of the "moves outward" verbs, and of those, the one that applies in the largest number of social situations is *ageru/agemasu*. This can be considered the "safe" word to use for "give to you/them" when you're not sure which verb provides the correct level of politeness. Be careful though: it may be "safe" in politeness, but that doesn't mean it can be used as a generic "give" without direction; you still need a different verb for the inward "give to me/us."

449 *Omikuji* are slips of paper sold at shrines and temples that tell a person's fortune. Most begin with one of four basic readings: 大吉 *daikichi* ("great good fortune"), 吉 *kichi* ("good fortune"), 小吉 *shōkichi* ("small good fortune"), or 凶 *kyō* ("bad fortune"). When this young man gets a *daikichi*, his girlfriend quickly snatches it away and hands him her *shōkichi* in its place.

FX: パッ
Pa!
Snatch!

Man: あ!
A!
(interj.)
"Hey!"

Girlfriend: わたし に それ ちょうだいっ!
Watashi   ni   sore   chōdai!
I/me   to   that   [please] give me
"Give that to me!" (PL2)

かわりに わたしの あげる から。
Kawari ni   watashi no   ageru   kara.
in exchange   mine   will give [to you]   because
"I'll give you mine in exchange." (PL2)

- *chōdai* is an informal equivalent of *kudasai*, "(please) give me/let me have."
- *no* shows possession, so *watashi no* before a noun means "my ～"; when *watashi no* stands alone because the item possessed is understood, it means "mine." *O*, to mark this as the direct object, has been omitted.

Besides when the speaker is the giver, *ageru* is the verb of choice when the giver is someone relatively close to the speaker, and the recipient is someone more distant. It could be used, for example, when speaking of the speaker's family member, friend, or colleague giving something to the listener's family member, friend, or colleague. Both social and physical distance are factors in determining the relative closeness of the parties and the direction of giving.

242

© Deluxe Company. *Zusetsu Gendai Yōgo Binran*, Futabasha.

やる *yaru* is also outward bound but less polite

When the giver is the speaker (or someone relatively close) and the recipient is of lower status, such as a child or a pet, the verb *yaru/yarimasu* can be used for "give to you/him/her/them/it." (Although they look and sound the same, context will distinguish the *yaru* that means "give" from the *yaru* that's an informal word for "do.") Among family and close friends, *yaru* can also be used for "give to you/them" when the giver and recipient are social equals, but in all contexts you'll want to be careful not to use it to speak of giving to social superiors.

For all "give" verbs, *ga* or *wa* marks the giver, *ni* marks the recipient, and *o* marks the item given.

450 Sayuri finds Sakata writing a letter. She suspects it's to a guy, and she threatens to tell Sakata's boyfriend, Takashi. When Sakata says she doesn't care because she's going to break up with Takashi anyway, Sayuri figures she shouldn't mind showing her the letter either.

Sayuri: じゃ、くれ。
Ja,   kure.
then   give [to me]
"Then give it here." (PL2)

Sakata: やる　　　　よ!
Yaru   *yo!*
will give [to you]   (emph.)
"Sure, I'll give it to you." (PL2)

- *kure* is a command form of *kureru/kuremasu* ("give [to me]"), one of the inward bound "give" verbs, which is formally introduced in fig. 452.
- in spite of what she says, Sakata looks none too eager to hand over her letter, and in the next frame Sayuri lets her off the hook by saying she doesn't really want to see it.

Give (outbound)

"give"
sashiageru/sashiagemasu
ageru/agemasu
yaru/yarimasu

"gave"
sashiageta/sashiagemashita
ageta/agemashita
yatta/yarimashita

"do not/will not give"
sashiagenai/sashiagemasen
agenai/agemasen
yaranai/yarimasen

"did not give"
sashiagenakatta/
* sashiagemasen deshita*
agenakatta/
* agemasen deshita*
yaranakatta/
* yarimasen deshita*

さしあげる *sashiageru* is also outward bound but more polite

In many cases when the giver is the speaker (or someone relatively close) and the recipient is his social superior, *sashiageru/sashiagemasu* is used for "give to you/him/her/them." People outside your group are generally treated as social superiors in business and other formal settings regardless of their individual rank within their own group or your rank within yours.

451 When Yamamoto comes to Tokyo to persuade Kaji to run for his late father's seat in the Diet (fig. 352), he discovers that Kaji has a mistress. Wary of scandal, he meets her without telling Kaji and offers her a large sum of money to disappear from Kaji's life. The fact that she is outside his social group; her close association with Kaji, who will now be stepping into his father's shoes and become Yamamoto's boss; and the delicate nature of the request he is making, all demand that Yamamoto use a high level of politeness with her.

Yamamoto: ここ　に　小切手　が　あります。
Koko ni kogitte ga arimasu.
here at check (subj.) exists/have
"I have a check here." (PL3)

あなた　に　差しあげる　為　に　持ってきました。
Anata ni sashiageru tame ni motte kimashita.
you   to   give   purpose for   brought
"I brought it to give to you." (PL4)

- structurally, *anata ni sashiageru* ("[I] will give [it] to you") is a complete sentence modifying the noun *tame* ("purpose"), but ～ *tame ni* is usually easiest to think of as "for the purpose of ～" (fig. 235): *anata ni sashiageru tame ni* = "for the purpose of giving it to you."
- *motte* is the *-te* form of *motsu/mochimasu* ("hold/carry") and *kimashita* is the polite past form of *kuru* ("come"), so *motte kimashita* = "carried and came" → "brought."

When the giving is inbound: くれる *kureru* or くださる *kudasaru*

Give (inbound)

"give"
kudasaru/kudasaimasu[1]
kureru/kuremasu

"gave"
kudasatta/kudasaimashita[1]
kureta/kuremashita

"do not/will not give"
kudasaranai/kadasaimasen[1]
kurenai/kuremasen

"did not give"
*kudasaranakatta/
kudasaimasen deshita*[1]
*kurenakatta/
kuremasen deshita*

---

[1] *Kudasaru* follows standard Group 1 verb rules for its PL2 forms, but the *r* is conventionally dropped from the PL3 forms. *Kudasai* ("please give me"; figs. 276, 277, and others) is a command form of this verb.

When the speaker wants to say "give/gave to me," or to say that someone relatively close to him/her was given something by someone more distant—that is, when the giving moves inward, toward the speaker—the verbs to use are *kudasaru/kudasaimasu* if the giver is the recipient's social superior and *kureru/kuremasu* if the giver is the recipient's equal or inferior.

Again, people outside your group are automatically treated as social superiors in business and formal situations. If the listener is from outside the speaker's group while both the giver and recipient are insiders, then *kureru* is used even when the giver is a social superior.

In spite of their inward direction, *kureru* and *kudasaru* are "give" verbs, so *ga* or *wa* marks the giver, *ni* marks the recipient, and *o* marks the item given.

452 When Natsu mends Kikue's doll Momo, Kikue becomes upset because the doll is all she has to remember her real mother by (fig. 180). Natsu decides to ask Kikue to tell her what she remembers about her mother. "She made Momo," Kikue begins.

Natsu:
それから?
Sore kara?
in addition to that
"And what else?"
(PL2)

© Oze Akira, *Natsu no Kura*, Kōdansha.

Kikue:

もも	を	菊江	に	くれた。
Momo	*o*	*Kikue*	*ni*	*kureta.*
(name)	(obj.)	(name)	to	gave [to me]

"She gave Momo to Kikue."
"She gave me Momo." (PL2)

- *sore kara* is literally "from that," implying "after that/in addition to that" or "and then."
- small children often refer to themselves by their own name.
- *kureta* is the plain past form of *kureru/kuremasu*. *Ni* marks Kikue as the recipient, and *o* marks Momo as the thing given.

いただく *itadaku*: A polite "receive"

The verbs for "receive" do not have two directions the way the verbs for "give" do: the subject is the recipient whether he/she is the speaker or anyone else. But the difference in social status between the giver and the recipient is still a factor in the choice of words. When the giver is the superior, then the proper word to use for "receive" is *itadaku/itadakimasu*. In this case, *wa* or *ga* marks the recipient, *ni* or *kara* marks the giver, and *o* marks the item received.

"Sir!"

453 When he entered the hostess club, Michael was told the charge would be a flat, all-inclusive ¥10,000, and he had declined the offer of "special service" for ¥20,000 more (fig. 72), so he is shocked to have the cashier demand ¥120,000 from him on his way out. When he starts to protest, three gangster types suddenly appear.

© Kobayashi Makoto. *What's Michael?*, Kōdansha.

Cashier: 12万円 いただきます。
Jūniman-en   itadakimasu.
¥120,000   will receive
"I will receive ¥120,000."
"That'll be ¥120,000." (PL3)

Michael: え?!
E?!
"Huh?" (PL2–3)

- 万 *man* is the ten-thousands unit in the Japanese number system (see p. 46), so 12万 = 12 x 10,000 or 120,000.

もらう *morau*: A neutral "receive"

When the giver is the recipient's social equal or inferior, *morau/moraimasu* is used for "receive." In fact, except in very formal situations, *morau* can be used more or less universally for "receive," even when the giver is a social superior, without causing offense.

For *morau* as for *itadaku*, *ga* or *wa* marks the recipient, *ni* or *kara* marks the giver, and *o* marks the item received.

454 In Japan, the custom on Valentine's Day is for women to give chocolate to men; the women must then wait until "White Day" in March for the men to reciprocate. Since Tanaka-kun doesn't have a girlfriend, he has planned ahead in case a colleague with a girlfriend shows off the chocolate he got.

Colleague:

これ、	カノジョ	に	もらった	バレンタインチョコ	なんだ。
Kore,	*kanojo*	*ni*	*moratta*	*Barentain choko*	*na n da.*
this	her/girlfriend	from	received	Valentine's chocolate	is-(explan.)

"This is some Valentine's chocolate I got from my girlfriend." (PL2)

Tanaka-kun:

これ、	自分	で	買った	バレンタインチョコ	なんだ。
Kore,	*jibun*	*de*	*katta*	*Barentain choko*	*na n da.*
this	self	by	bought	Valentine's chocolate	is-(explan.)

"This is some Valentine's chocolate I bought myself." (PL2)

Colleague:

度胸	ある	なー。
Dokyō	*aru*	*nā.*
nerve/guts/boldness	have	(emph.)

"You sure have guts." (PL2)

- *kanojo* literally means "she/her," but it's also used as a word for "girlfriend."
- *moratta* is the plain past form of *morau*; *kanojo ni moratta* is a complete sentence ("[I] received it from my girlfriend") modifying *Barentain choko*; the modifier is based on the sentence *Boku wa kore o kanojo ni moratta*, with *wa* marking the recipient, *ni* marking the giver, and *o* marking the item received.
- *jibun de katta* is likewise a complete sentence ("[I] bought [it] myself") modifying *Barentain choko*.

Morau = "take"

Morau is also used in situations where no specific giver is identifiable. In such cases it often corresponds to English "take."

455 On oversized garbage pickup day, Garcia sees what looks like a perfectly good space heater set out for the haulers to take away.

Garcia: **"I sure envy the person who can throw out a heater like this."**

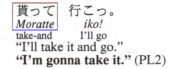

貰って	行こっ。
Moratte	*iko!*
take-and	I'll go

"I'll take it and go."
"I'm gonna take it." (PL2)

- *moratte* is the -*te* form of *morau*, and *iko!* here is a colloquially shortened *ikō*, the "let's/I'll/I think I'll ～") form of *iku* ("go").

Receive

"receive"
itadaku/itadakimasu
morau/moraimasu

"received"
itadaita/itadakimashita
moratta/moraimashita

"do not/will not receive"
itadakanai/itadakimasen
morawanai/moraimasen

"did not receive"
itadakanakatta/
　itadakimasen deshita
morawanakatta/
　moraimasen deshita

-Te ageru = "[do] for you/someone"

The verbs of giving and receiving are also used as helping verbs that follow the -te forms of other verbs, in effect implying "give/receive the action of the verb." The "give" verbs retain their direction in this usage, so a -te form plus *ageru/agemasu* implies that the speaker or someone relatively close to him/her does the action for someone relatively distant: "[do the action] for you/him/her/them."

456 When Toshihiko puts his jacket back on after soccer practice, his student ID is missing from the vest pocket. He wonders where he could have dropped it, but the truth is that Endo swiped it as a pretext to get to know him better. When he gets home, she is waiting near his front gate.

Endō: 拾ってあげた の よ。
Hirotte ageta   *no*   *yo.*
picked up for you   (explan.)   (emph.)
"I picked this up for you."
"I found this for you." (PL2)

- *hirotte* is the -te form of *hirou/hiroimasu* ("pick up [from the ground]").
- *ageta* is the plain past form of *ageru/agemasu*, which after the -te form of a verb implies the action was done for someone.

© Ōshima Tsukasa. *Shoot!,* Kōdansha.

-Te ageru = "[do] to you/someone"

Ageru after the -te form of a verb generally implies that the action is a favor for, or will benefit, the recipient, so "[do the action] for you/him/her/them" is indeed most often the best equivalent in English—as in fig 456. But depending on the particular verb and the situation, the more natural English equivalent may be "[do the action] to you/him/her/them"—e.g., *yonde ageru* (from *yomu*, "read") can be either "read it for you" or "read it to you"; or it may be just a verb + recipient phrase (with neither "for" nor "to")—e.g., *misete ageru* (from *miseru*, "show") is simply "show you."

Machida

457 Machida and a colleague from Gomez Productions drugged Shima and set him up in a compromising position. Now the two men think they can blackmail Shima and Sunlight Records, but Shima and his confidants have figured out their scheme and preserved crucial evidence. Here Sunlight's Yada Hideharu shows them Machida's fingerprints lifted from the glass they used to drug Shima.

Yada:
町田さん、 面白い もの を
Machida-san,   *omoshiroi*   *mono*   *o*
(name-pol.)   interesting   thing   (obj.)
見せてあげましょう。
misete agemashō.
I'll show to you
"Mr. Machida, let me show you something very interesting." (PL3)

- the adjective *omoshiroi* ("interesting") can range in meaning from "funny/amusing/entertaining" at one end to "odd/different/unusual" at the other.
- *misete* is the -te form of *miseru/misemasu* ("show").
- *agemashō* is the polite "let's/I'll ～" form of *ageru/agemasu*. In this case there is a distinct note of irony in the statement, since the action is for the recipients' "benefit" only in the sense that it will set them straight about where they stand.

© Hirokane Kenshi. *Buchō Shima Kōsaku,* Kōdansha.

-Te yaru = "[do] for you/someone"

Like -te ageru, -te yaru/yarimasu is used when an action is done by the speaker or someone close to him for someone more distant. And like the independent verb yaru, the -te yaru form is used when the recipient is of lower status than the giver, such as a child or pet; among family and friends it can also be used informally when the giver and recipient are social equals.

458 The son has reserved a copy of a soon-to-be-released computer game, hoping that his father will agree to buy it for him for Christmas. Father asks, "What if I say no?"

Son: 権利 を 友だち に 3千円 で 売る。
Kenri o tomodachi ni sanzen-en de uru.
rights (obj.) friend to ¥3000 for will sell
"I'll sell my rights to a friend for ¥3000." (PL2)

Father: 買ってやる よ。
Katte yaru yo.
will buy for you (emph.)
"I'll buy it for you." (PL2)

- *de* marks *sanzen-en* ("¥3000") as the amount he will sell for (fig. 175).
- *katte* is the -te form of *kau* ("buy").

-Te yaru = "[do] to you/someone"

Like -te ageru, -te yaru often means "[do the action] to you/him/her/them/it," and the best way to express this in English may be a verb + recipient phrase (without either "for" or "to"), or some other phrasing that implies the action is done for/to the recipient. But an important difference is that -te yaru can often (though by no means always) imply a malicious design—doing the action as a way of harming/taking advantage of/sticking it to the recipient. Even completely benign-sounding verbs can be used this way, so, for example, *tabete yaru* (from *taberu*, "eat") can mean either "I'll eat it for you as a favor" or "I'll eat it as a way of sticking it to you," depending on the context.

When expressing malicious intent in this way, -te yaru is as likely to be used when the recipient of the action is a social superior as with anyone else.

459 Tanaka-kun has been stewing over his boss's repeated remarks that he is no good at anything, has no ability, is no more useful than a cat, and the like. He vows to get his revenge—but chooses a rather roundabout way.

Tanaka-kun: 殺してやる。
Koroshite yaru.
will kill him
"I'll kill him." (PL1–2)

Boss's Wife: これ、 田中さん から の お中元 です。
Kore, Tanaka-san kara no o-chūgen desu.
this (name-hon.) from that is (hon.)-summer gift is
"This is o-chūgen that is from Mr. Tanaka."
"This is a summer gift from Mr. Tanaka." (PL3)

Boss: これ、 ぜんぶ タバコ か?
Kore, zenbu tabako ka?
this/these all cigarettes (?)
"These are all cigarettes?"
"This whole box is cigarettes?" (PL2)

- *koroshite* is the -te form of *korosu/koroshimasu* ("kill"). In a different context, *koroshite yaru* could mean "I'll kill him for you," in which case the direct recipient of the action and the beneficiary of it are separate.
- *o-chūgen* (the honorific *o-* is almost always included) refers to the custom of giving gifts at midsummer to one's boss, important business associates, and other social superiors, as a token of gratitude for favors received. The gifts themselves are also called *o-chūgen*.

Cigarettes

-Te kureru = "[do] for me/someone near me"

When the benefit of an action is given to the speaker or someone relatively close to him/her by someone relatively distant—that is, the giving moves toward the speaker—the *-te* form of the verb is followed by *kureru/kuremasu*; this typically means "[do the action] for me or someone near me."

© Hotta Katsuhiko, *Obatarian*, Take Shobō.

460 When this *obatarian* asks the vendor at a temporary sales booth to break a ¥1000 note for her, the saleswoman explains that she only has enough small change to make change for purchases. Then she points out another place where the lady should be able to get change.

Vendor: あっ、　すぐ　　近く　　の　コンビニエンスストア　で
A!,　　　 *sugu*　 *chikaku*　 *no*　 *konbiniensu sutoa*　 *de*
(interj.) immediately nearby that is convenience store at

やってくれます　よ。
yatte kuremasu　 *yo.*
will do for you (emph.)
"Oh, they'll do it for you at that convenience store right over there." (PL3)

Obat.: えっ?
E!?

- *chikaku* is a noun form of the adjective *chikai* ("close/nearby"); *sugu chikaku* = "immediately nearby"—or, since she is pointing, "right over there."
- *yatte* is the *-te* form of *yaru* ("do"), and *kuremasu* is the polite form of *kureru*.

When the speaker, listener, giver, and recipient are all strangers as they are here, whether to use *-te ageru/yaru* or *-te kureru* is determined by the relative physical locations of the parties involved, or by the fact that a temporary closeness is established between any two people engaged in conversation together. Here, the recipient is the listener (the *obatarian*), who is physically closer to the speaker (the vendor) than to the giver (the convenience store clerk), so the giving moves toward the speaker, and that makes *-te kureru* the appropriate form. From the speaker's perspective, the recipient ("you") is "someone relatively close to me" even though she's a stranger.

-Te kureru = "[do] to me/someone near me"

461 When Natsu tells Kikue she won't try to replace her mother, she'll just be her friend, Kikue decides to test her and throws a ball into the brewhouse. "If you're really my friend, then go get my ball," she says, knowing very well that Natsu is forbidden to enter. Later Zenzō tells Natsu he has heard the full story from Kikue.

With some verbs the best English equivalent of *-te kureru/kuremasu* is "[do the action] to me/someone near me"; or it may be a verb + recipient phrase without either "for" or "to." *-Te kureru* usually implies positive benefit to the recipient, but like *-te yaru* it can also sometimes be used when the action is harmful to him/her.

Zenzō:
なぜ　奈津さん　　が　　蔵　　に　入った　　の　　か　　も
Naze　 *Natsu-san*　 *ga*　 *kura*　 *ni*　 *haitta*　 *no*　 *ka*　 *mo*
why (name-pol.)/you (subj.) brewhouse into entered (explan.) (?) too/also
"'Why was it that you entered the brewhouse?', too,

菊江　　は　教えてくれました。
Kikue　 *wa*　 *oshiete kuremashita.*
(name) as for told me
"as for Kikue, she told me."
"Kikue also told me why you entered the brewhouse." (PL3)

© Oze Akira, *Natsu no Kura*, Kōdansha.

- *haitta* is the plain past form of *hairu/hairimasu* ("enter").
- *oshiete* is the *-te* form of *oshieru/oshiemasu* ("tell/teach"), and *kuremashita* is the polite past form of *kureru/kuremasu*.
- since it begins with *naze* ("why?"), the embedded question ending in *ka* followed by a form of the verb *oshieru* is like "[She] told me why ∼" (fig. 254).

-Te kureru? as a request

Spoken as a question, either *-te kureru?* or its negative form *-te kurenai?* makes a request like "Could/would/won't you [please do the action]?" Such requests feel quite casual, like requests made using just a *-te* form or *-te kure* (see Lesson 19), but they sound somewhat gentler and more polite. For even greater politeness and a more formal feeling, *-te kuremasu?* or *-te kuremasen?* can be used.

462 At a health club, Ōizumi Shōko, wife of Hatsushiba Electric's president, wants Shima to identify Ms. Ōmachi Aiko, a reclusive major shareholder. Although Shima claims he doesn't see her, Ōizumi believes she is present. She asks Shima to go in for a swim in hopes that Ōmachi will say hello when she recognizes him.

© Hirokane Kenshi, *Kachō Shima Kōsaku*, Kōdansha.

Ōizumi: ちょっと、 あなた、 泳いでくれる?
Chotto,   anata,   oyoide kureru?
(interj.)   you   swim for me
"Say, would you mind going in for a swim?" (PL2)

Shima: え? 私 が?
E?   Watashi ga?
huh?/what? I/me   (subj.)
"Huh? Me?" (PL3 implied)

- *chotto* is literally "a little," but it's also used as an interjection for drawing someone's attention, like "say/hey/listen here."
- *oyoide* is the *-te* form of *oyogu* ("swim"); given the speaker's position, the request made by adding *kureru* takes on the force of a gentle command in this case.

-Te kudasaru is even more polite

When the benefit of an action is given to the speaker or someone relatively close to him/her by someone relatively distant and the giver is of superior social status, then *kudasaru/kudasaimasu* is used after the *-te* form instead of *kureru/kuremasu*.

© Maekawa Tsukasa, *Dai-Tōkyō Binbō Seikatsu Manyuaru*, Kōdansha.

463 When Kōsuke tells Sada that he has prepared some tea (fig. 6), Sada calls out to his daughter. Since Kōsuke represents his employer in this case, Sada uses the polite *-te kudasaru* to speak of Kōsuke's action, but since he's speaking to his own daughter, he uses the informal, PL2 form.

Sada: おーい、 お茶 入れてくださった ぞ。
Ōi,   o-cha   irete kudasatta   zo.
(interj.) (hon.)-tea made/poured for us (emph.)
"He-e-ey, they made us some tea!" (PL2)

- *oi* is an abrupt "Hey!" or "Yo!" for getting someone's attention; an elongated *ōi* is used when trying to get the attention of someone relatively far away. At this moment, Sada is closer to Kōsuke than to his daughter in physical position, but social considerations override that closeness: he and his daughter are family, while Kōsuke is an outsider.
- *irete* is the *-te* form of *ireru/iremasu* ("put in," or when speaking of coffee/tea, "make/pour"), and *kudasatta* is the plain past form of *kudasaru*. The particle *o*, to mark *o-cha* as the direct object of *irete kudasatta*, has been omitted.

-Te morau/-te itadaku = "[do] for me/someone near me"

The "receive" verbs can also be used as helping verbs following the *-te* forms of other verbs, and this generally creates a phrase that means the speaker or subject "receives the benefit/favor of the action." In many contexts, *-te morau/moraimasu* is effectively the same as *-te kureru*, implying that someone else "does/did/will do [the action] for me or someone near me." The person doing the beneficial action—equivalent to the giver when *morau* is used as an independent verb—is marked with *ni*.

When the doer is a social superior, someone outside one's circle, or a person otherwise requiring special deference, *-te itadaku/itadakimasu* can be used instead of *-te morau* in the same way.

464 Rumi-chan got a present from her dad and she is showing it off to Nat-chan.

Rumi-chan: パパ に 指輪 買ってもらった の。 ほほほっ
Papa ni yubiwa katte moratta no. Ho ho ho!
father (giver) ring bought for me (explan.) (fem. laugh)
"My dad bought a ring for me. Tee hee hee."
"My dad bought me a ring. Tee hee hee." (PL2)

- *katte* is the *-te* form of *kau* ("buy"), and *moratta* is the plain past form of *morau*. The equivalent form with *-te itadaku* is *katte itadaita no*. Whether "receive" verbs are used independently or as helping verbs, it's important to remember that *ni* marks the source (i.e., giver or doer) rather than the target/destination (i.e., recipient or beneficiary).

-Te morau/-te itadaku = "have someone [do the action]"

In fig. 464, it's impossible to know for sure whether the gift of the ring was the result of Rumi-chan's begging or an unsolicited act of fatherly doting. But in many cases *-te morau/-te itadaku* definitely implies that the speaker or subject personally solicits the action, and in that case the meaning can be like "have someone [do the action]" or "ask/get someone to [do the action]." Such instances may or may not imply "for the benefit of the speaker or subject"; the speaker or subject may merely be the one who calls for the action, and the beneficiary may be the person doing the action or someone else.

465 An American baseball player has come to Japan, hoping to find a spot on a team in the Japanese professional baseball league.

Ballplayer: 日本 の プロ野球 で プレー が したい。
Nihon no puro-yakyū de purē ga shitai.
Japan 's pro baseball in play (obj.) want to do
"I want to play in Japan's pro baseball."
"I want to play pro baseball in Japan." (PL2)

Manager: テスト を 受けてもらう。
Tesuto o ukete morau.
test (obj.) will have you take
"We'll have you take a test." (PL2)

- *purē* is from English "play"; it's used both to speak of an individual play and of playing ball in general—clearly the latter in this case.
- *shitai* is the "want to" form of *suru* ("do"), so *purē ga shitai* is literally "want to do playing" → "want to play." As is often the case with *-tai* forms, *shitai* appears in the *wa-ga* construction here, with *ga* marking the direct object (i.e., the desired thing); *watashi wa* ("as for me") is understood as the topic/subject.
- *ukete* is the *-te* form of *ukeru/ukemasu*, which basically means "receive/obtain," but when speaking of a test means "take/undergo"; *tesuto o ukete morau* = "have [someone] take a test." The equivalent statement using *-te itadaku* would be *tesuto o ukete itadaku/itadakimasu*.

-Te morau/-te itadaku = "have [someone] do to/with me"

Depending on the nature of the verb, the more natural English equivalent for a *-te morau/-te itadaku* form may be "have someone [do the action] to me/with me" (or "to/with someone close to me") instead of "for me": *asobu* = "play," and *asonde morau* = "have [someone] play with me/someone"; *okuru* = "send" and *okutte morau* can mean either "have [someone] send [it] to me/someone" or "have [someone] send [it] for me/someone." In some cases the best English equivalent may require some other way of expressing that the action is done to/with/for the subject. Usually the statement still implies that the recipient of the action benefits from it in some way—even if sometimes you may find the stated benefit rather dubious, as in this example.

466 Nat-chan's kindergarten class is on an excursion to a U-pick strawberry farm. One of the farm workers pauses to ask if they're enjoying the strawberries. When Nat-chan answers "Yes," he remarks:

Mami-chan:
かわいい　だってー!
Kawaii ... *da tte!*
cute ... (quote)
"'Cute,' he said!"
"He called us cute!"
(PL2)

Worker:
こんな　かわいい　コ　に
Konna kawaii ko ni
such cute child (doer)

食べてもらう ... イチゴ　は　幸せだぁ。
tabete morau ... *ichigo wa shiawase dā.*
have [someone] eat [them] ... strawberries as for are happy/fortunate
"As for the strawberries that have such cute girls eat them, they are fortunate."
"The strawberries are blessed to be eaten by such cute little girls." (PL2)

- *konna kawaii ko ni tabete morau* ("[they] have such cute girls eat [them]") is a complete sentence modifying *ichigo* ("strawberries"), which *wa* marks as the topic and subject.
- *shiawase* = "happiness," and *shiawase da* = "is/are happy," but the feeling here is "are fortunate/blessed."
- *da tte* (elongated in glee here) is a colloquial quoting form meaning "[he] says/said ～," or "～, he says/said." The form is used not simply to relay/repeat what was said (*tte* alone would be used for that), but to express surprise at it. Nat-chan, though, isn't impressed: she heard the worker say the same thing to some other girls.

Requests with *-te morau/-te itadaku*

Using a polite "can" or "can't" form of *-te morau* as a question (*-te moraemasu ka?/-te moraemasen ka?*—the *ka* is optional) makes a polite request, with the negative form of the question being more polite. And the polite "can" and "can't" forms of *-te itadaku* can be used in the same way (*-te itadakemasu ka?/-te itadakemasen ka?*) to provide another gradation of politeness when the doer is a social superior, someone outside one's circle, or a person otherwise requiring special deference. The English equivalents are such expressions as "Could/would/won't you [please do the action]?" and "Could I/might I/might I not ask you to [do the action]?" In some cases the feeling can be even more deferential, especially with the negative forms: "I wonder if you might/might not be willing to [do the action]."

Host: さっそく　です　が、　山本さん、
Sassoku desu ga, Yamamoto-san,
immediately is and/but (name-pol.)

金メダル　を　みせていただけません　か?
kin-medaru o misete itadakemasen ka?
gold medal (obj.) won't you please show us (?)
"If I could cut to the chase, Mr. Yamamoto, would you please show us your gold medal?" (PL3–4)

Medalist: ハイハイ。
Hai hai.
"Of course, of course." (PL3)

467 An Olympic gold medalist is being interviewed on a talk show, and the host has just introduced his guest.

- *sassoku* = "directly/immediately/at once," and the expression *sassoku da ga/desu ga* to preface a statement is like "let me get straight to the point."
- *misete* is the *-te* form of *miseru/misemasu* ("show"), and *itadakemasen* is the "can't" form of *itadaku*. The same request using the *-te morau* form is *Kin-medaru o misete moraemasen ka?*

Morau/itadaku after a causative verb

When *morau* or *itadaku* follows the *-te* form of a causative ("make/let ～") verb, a literal translation makes for rather convoluted English: "[I] will receive the favor of being caused to do ～," or "[I] will have [you] allow me to do ～." Such expressions presume the recipient's permission/indulgence, and are essentially just a very polite and humble way of saying "[I] will do ～." *Sasete itadakimasu* in the last frame here is from *saseru*, the causative form of *suru* ("do").

468 Even when he wins a prize, Tanaka-kun must still be described as hapless.

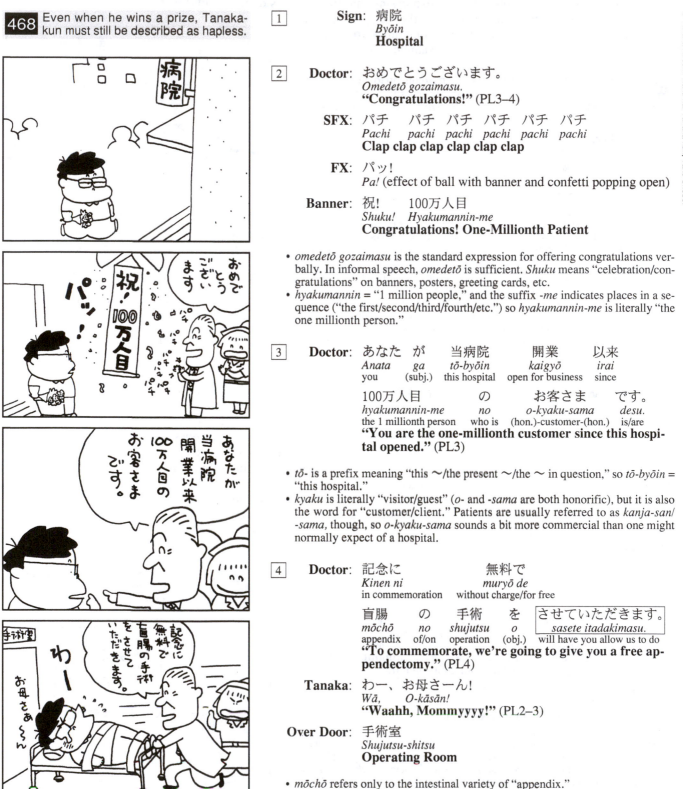

1   **Sign:** 病院
Byōin
Hospital

2   **Doctor:** おめでとうございます。
Omedetō gozaimasu.
"Congratulations!" (PL3–4)

    SFX: パチ　　パチ　パチ　パチ　パチ　パチ
Pachi   pachi pachi pachi pachi pachi
Clap clap clap clap clap clap

    FX: パッ!
Pa! (effect of ball with banner and confetti popping open)

  Banner: 祝!　　　100万人目
Shuku!   Hyakumannin-me
Congratulations! One-Millionth Patient

• *omedetō gozaimasu* is the standard expression for offering congratulations verbally. In informal speech, *omedetō* is sufficient. *Shuku* means "celebration/congratulations" on banners, posters, greeting cards, etc.
• *hyakumannin* = "1 million people," and the suffix *-me* indicates places in a sequence ("the first/second/third/fourth/etc.") so *hyakumannin-me* is literally "the one millionth person."

3   **Doctor:** あなた　が　　　当病院　　　　開業　　　以来
Anata   ga   tō-byōin   kaigyō   irai
you   (subj.)   this hospital   open for business   since

100万人目　　　　　　の　　　お客さま　　です。
hyakumannin-me   no   o-kyaku-sama   desu.
the 1 millionth person   who is   (hon.)-customer-(hon.)   is/are
"You are the one-millionth customer since this hospital opened." (PL3)

• *tō-* is a prefix meaning "this ～/the present ～/the ～ in question," so *tō-byōin* = "this hospital."
• *kyaku* is literally "visitor/guest" (*o-* and *-sama* are both honorific), but it is also the word for "customer/client." Patients are usually referred to as *kanja-san/-sama*, though, so *o-kyaku-sama* sounds a bit more commercial than one might normally expect of a hospital.

4   **Doctor:** 記念に　　　　　　　無料で
Kinen ni   muryō de
in commemoration   without charge/for free

盲腸　　の　　手術　　を　　させていただきます。
mōchō   no   shujutsu   o   sasete itadakimasu.
appendix   of/on   operation   (obj.)   will have you allow us to do
"To commemorate, we're going to give you a free appendectomy." (PL4)

  Tanaka: わー、お母さーん!
Wā,   O-kāsān!
"Waahh, Mommyyyy!" (PL2–3)

Over Door: 手術室
Shujutsu-shitsu
Operating Room

• *mōchō* refers only to the intestinal variety of "appendix."

Politely asking permission

In Lesson 24 you learned that *-te (mo) ii desu ka?* asks for permission to do the action. Following a causative + *-te morau/itadaku* combination with *-te (mo) ii desu ka* makes a very polite request for permission to do the action. In fig. 468, a doctor not quite so determined to give the free operation might have asked *Shujutsu o sasete itadaite ii deshō ka?* ("May I perhaps have you allow me to perform an operation?" → "May I perform an operation?").

469 A first-time customer comes into the bar Lemon Hart carrying a guitar case.

© Furuya Mitsutoshi. *Bar Remon Hāto*. Futabasha.

Customer:
あの、　ここ　　へ
Ano,　　koko　　e
umm　　here　　to

置かせてもらって	いい	です	か?
okasete moratte	*ii*	*desu*	*ka?*

if [I] have you allow me to set   is good/fine   (pol.)   (?)
"Um, may I have you allow me to set this here?"
"Um, would it be all right if I set this here?"
(PL4)

- *okasete* is the *-te* form of *okaseru/okasemasu* ("make/let [someone] set down"), from *oku/okimasu* ("set/place/leave").
- *moratte* is the *-te* form of *morau*.

Summary: Verbs of giving and receiving

Here's a summary of the giving and receiving verbs. As a general rule, the first word given is the one to use, but in certain situations the second one in parentheses may be acceptable or even preferred. When one of these verbs follows the *-te* form of another verb, it implies that that action is given/received—i.e., done by one person for or to another. Only plain forms are given here; for the polite forms, including past and negative, see the margins of pp. 243–45.

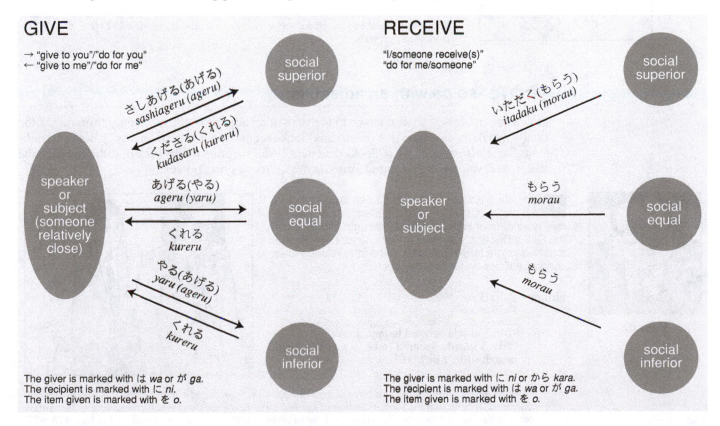

GIVE

→ "give to you"/"do for you"
← "give to me"/"do for me"

さしあげる(あげる) *sashiageru (ageru)*
くださる(くれる) *kudasaru (kureru)*
あげる(やる) *ageru (yaru)*
くれる *kureru*
やる(あげる) *yaru (ageru)*
くれる *kureru*

speaker or subject (someone relatively close)

social superior
social equal
social inferior

The giver is marked with は *wa* or が *ga*.
The recipient is marked with に *ni*.
The item given is marked with を *o*.

RECEIVE

"I/someone receive(s)"
"do for me/someone"

いただく(もらう) *itadaku (morau)*
もらう *morau*
もらう *morau*

speaker or subject

social superior
social equal
social inferior

The giver is marked with に *ni* or から *kara*.
The recipient is marked with は *wa* or が *ga*.
The item given is marked with を *o*.

Lesson 32

Appearances and Hearsay

Japanese has a number of different ways to express conclusions or statements based on appearances or hearsay and often involving an element of uncertainty. *Darō* and *deshō*, introduced in Lesson 26, can be used for that purpose. This lesson introduces several others, beginning with the suffix -*sō da/desu*.

The pre-*masu* stem of a verb plus -*sō da* or -*sō desu* makes an expression for "looks/sounds/feels/seems like [the action will occur]." It expresses a conclusion or guess based on something the speaker has directly observed or experienced with his own senses—most typically visual observation, though not limited to that. In PL2 speech, *da* is often omitted, and the same is true for *desu* in relatively informal PL3 speech. Both *da* and *desu* can change to their past, negative, and negative-past forms.

470 Each year Kōsuke earns free rent in December by applying fresh paper to all of the shoji screens at the Buddhist temple his landlady belongs to. It generally takes him about three days, and on those days his landlady has a hot meal waiting for him when he gets home.

Landlady: あんた、　まだ　終わんない　の　かい?
Anta,　　mada　　owannai　　no　　kai?
you　　　still　　not end/finish　(explan.)　(?)
"You're still not finished?" (PL2)

Kōsuke: 明日　　あたり　で　終わりそーです。
Ashita　atari　　de　　owarisō desu.
tomorrow　around　(scope)　looks like will finish
"It looks like I'll finish tomorrow." (PL3)

• *owannai* is a contraction of *owaranai*, the negative form of *owaru/owarimasu* ("[something] ends/finishes/is finished"). *Owarisō desu* (normally written 終わりそうです) is from the same verb.

-そうだ -*sō da* with an adjective

-*Sō da* (or -*sō desu*) can also attach to the stem of an adjective (the dictionary form minus the final -*i*), making an expression that means "looks/seems like it is [that quality]": *oishii* = "delicious," and *oishisō da/desu* = "looks delicious." An exception to this pattern is the form for the adjective *ii/yoi*, which becomes *yosasō da/desu* ("looks good/fine/okay").

Fukuda

471 Fukuda Keizō's career had been languishing in a minor post at Hatsushiba Electric, but now the new president of Hatsushiba has brought him back as the Sales Division's second-in-command. Here Shima and Nakazawa leave Fukuda's office after offering their congratulations on his first day back.

Shima: 福田さん　嬉しそうでした　ね。
Fukuda-san　ureshisō deshita　ne.
(name-pol.)　looked/seemed happy　(colloq.)
"Mr. Fukuda seemed happy, didn't he?"
"Mr. Fukuda seemed to be in a really good mood, didn't he?" (PL3)

• *ureshisō deshita* is the polite past form of *ureshisō da/desu*, from the adjective *ureshii* ("is happy/pleased/delighted"). Note that the long -*ii* ending of the adjective becomes short when connecting to this suffix because the last -*i* drops out. Retaining the long -*ii* gives a different meaning, introduced in figs. 475–477.

When modifying verbs: -そうに -sō ni

When modifying a verb, -sō da/desu becomes -sō ni ～. The combination typically implies "do ～ with the described appearance/in the described manner" or "do ～ as if [as described]": *oishisō ni taberu* = "eat with a delicious appearance" → "eat as if [the food] is truly tasty/eat with relish." An exception is the verb *naru* ("become"): -sō ni naru/natta after a verb implies "almost [does/did the action]": e.g., *ochiru* = "fall," and *ochisō ni naru* = "almost fall."

The -sō da/desu/ni suffix can be added to certain adjectival nouns, as seen here. It cannot attach to ordinary nouns.

OL1: えーっ! 遭難 した の?
Ē! Sōnan shita no?
what? mishap did/had (explan.-?)
"What? You got lost [in the woods]?" (PL2)

OL2: もう少し で 新聞ざた じゃなーい!
Mō sukoshi de shinbun-zata ja nāi!
a little more in newspaper fuss/spread is not-(rhet.)
"You almost got into the papers!" (PL2)

OL3: 残念そうに 言わないで よ。
Zannensō ni iwanaide yo.
in disappointed manner please don't say (emph.)
"Don't say that as if [you're] disappointed."
"You don't have to sound so disappointed." (PL2)

- *sōnan*, written with kanji meaning "meet difficulty/misfortune/calamity," most typically refers to mishaps at sea or in the mountains/wilderness of the kind that bring out search-and-rescue teams, so in this context *sōnan shita* = "got lost in the woods."
- *mō sukoshi de* ("almost/in just a little more") often prefaces a desirable goal or result that someone barely missed attaining.
- *zannen* is an adjectival noun meaning "disappointment," so *zannen da/desu* is often like the English adjective "(be) disappointed." *Zannensō ni* is literally "with an appearance/sound of disappointment" or "disappointedly."

472 OL3 and some others got lost in the woods while hiking, and spent a cold night wearing garbage bags for warmth before discovering they were in fact only a short distance away from someone's home.

CHATTER CHATTER

When modifying nouns: -そうな -sō na

When modifying a noun, -sō da/desu becomes -sō na ～, making an expression that means "[a/the] ～ that looks/sounds/feels/seems like [the quality or action described]."

In the example here, -sō na is attached to the pre-*masu* stem of a passive verb rather than an ordinary verb. Whether at the end of a sentence or as a modifier, forms of -sō da/desu can also attach to "can/be able to" verbs, causative verbs, and passive-causative verbs—though which of these forms, if any, make sense will depend on the particular verb.

Important note: For this meaning, -sō da/desu, -sō ni, and -sō na can never directly follow a form of *da/desu*; they can attach only to an adjective stem or to the pre-*masu* stem of whatever form of the verb is being used (ordinary, passive, causative, etc.)—not to any full form of the verb or adjective. These are crucial differences from the hearsay expressions introduced in figs. 475–77.

473 Michael's owner has decided today is bath day for all of her cats, and, not surprisingly, none of them is the least bit happy about it.

Reiko: 殺されそうな 声 出す んじゃなーい!!
Korosaresō na koe dasu n ja nāi!!
will be killed-(sounds like) voice put out/make don't
"Don't make a voice that sounds like you will be killed."
"Stop screaming bloody murder!" (PL2)

SPRAY

RGYAA! RGYAA!

- *korosaresō na* is from *korosareru*, the passive form of *korosu* ("kill").
- *koe* = "voice," and *koe (o) dasu/dashimasu* (lit. "put out/emit [one's] voice") can mean to speak out loud or simply to make a sound with one's voice.
- the negative explanatory extension *n ja nai* is being used as a prohibition/negative command, "Don't ～" (fig. 411).

Negatives with *-sō da/desu*

Nai can be followed by *-sō da/desu*, as well as *-sō ni* or *-sō na*, but it takes a special form like the one mentioned at fig. 471 for *ii/yoi: nai → nasasō da/desu/ni/na*. For the independent *nai* (negative of *aru*), *nasasō da/desu/ni/na* implies "appears not to exist/have" or "seems unlikely to exist/have." For a noun + *ja nai* ("is/are not"), including adjectival nouns, ~ *ja nasasō da/desu/ni/na* implies "appears not to be/seems unlikely to be [the stated item/quality]." For negative adjectives, *-kunasasō da/desu/ni/na* implies "appears not to be/seems unlikely to be [the described quality]."

Negative verbs usually are not followed by *-sō da/desu* forms. Instead, the pre-*masu* form of the verb is followed by *-sō ni nai* or *-sō ja nai*.

474 The man in fig. 333 takes it as a personal challenge to ask for something that the amazingly well-supplied Lemon Hart does not have. He figures a bar with so many choices of hard liquor is likely to be weak on other drinks, so he suggests they order a beer. When his companion immediately names one of the national brands, he responds:

Man: バカ、 この 店 に なさそうな ビール だ よ。
Baka, kono mise ni nasasō na biiru da yo.
idiot/silly this shop/bar at seems unlikely to exist beer is (emph.)
"No, silly, [I meant] a brand that this place seems unlikely to have." (PL2)

Woman: そういう の 好き。 私 ドキドキ しちゃう。
Sō iu no suki. Watashi doki-doki shichau.
that kind of thing [I] like I thump-thump do-(involuntary)
"I like that kind of thing. It makes my heart race."
"I love it! This is so exciting!" (PL2)

- *mise* can refer to any kind of store or eating/drinking establishment.
- *nasasō na* (from *nai*, "not exist/have") modifies *biiru* ("beer") → "beer they seem unlikely to have"; *ni* marks the place of existence/non-existence.
- *doki-doki* represents the effect of a racing/pounding heart, and *shichau* is a contraction of *shite shimau*, from *suru* ("do"); *doki-doki suru* can describe either pleasant excitement or nervousness/terror. The *-te shimau* form in this case implies the action is involuntary/spontaneous.

Compare:

Owarisō da = "It looks like [they] will finish/it will be finished." (observation)
Owaru sō da = "I'm told [they] will finish/it will be finished." (hearsay)

そうだ *sō da* for indicating hearsay

When *sō da* (or *sō desu*) follows a complete PL2 verb instead of attaching to its pre-*masu* stem, it implies that the speaker is conveying hearsay information—something he/she has been told by someone else or has learned from a secondary source. When the source is explicitly stated or otherwise known, *sō da/desu* can be equivalent to "So-and-so says/tells me that ~"; when it's not, it can be like "Apparently ~" or "It seems/I hear/they say/I'm told/I understand that ~."

475 Tanaka-kun is at home in bed with a fever, and his boss has to figure out how to cover for some rush work he was scheduled to do today.

OL: 田中さん カゼ で 休む そうです。
Tanaka-san kaze de yasumu sō desu.
(name-pol.) cold (reason) will be absent (hearsay)
"Mr. Tanaka said he'll be staying home today with a cold." (PL3)

Boss: 困った なー。
Komatta nā.
became troubled/inconvenienced (colloq.)
"Hmm, we've got a problem." (PL2)

- *wa*, to mark *Tanaka-san* as the topic, has been omitted.
- *de* marks *kaze* ("a cold") as the cause/reason for the action.
- *yasumu* is the full dictionary form of the verb for "rest/take the day off [from school/work]," so *Yasumu sō da/desu* means "[He/someone] said he will take the day off." Compare this with *Yasumisō da/desu*, which in the right context would mean "[It] looks like [he/someone] will take the day off."
- *komatta* is the past form of *komaru/komarimasu* ("become distressed/troubled/inconvenienced").

Hearsay with an adjective, *nai/-nai*, or *-tai*

Similarly, when *sō da/desu* follows the full dictionary form of an adjective instead of just its stem, it indicates hearsay information: "So-and-so says it is [as described]" or "Apparently/I hear/they say/I'm told/I understand it is [as described]": *Samui sō da* = "She says/I hear it is cold." This *sō da/desu* can follow the adjective's plain past, negative, and negative-past forms as well: *Samukatta sō da* = "She says/I hear it was cold"; *Samukunai sō da* = "She says/I hear it isn't cold"; *Samukunakatta sō da* = "She says/I hear it wasn't cold." It can also follow the *-nai* (plain negative) and *-tai* ("want to") forms of verbs in the same way, since both of these forms act as adjectives: *ikanai* ("not go") → *Ikanai sō da* ("She says/I hear that she won't go"); *ikitai* ("want to go") → *Ikitai sō da* ("She says/I hear she wants to go").

476 As the Japanese pro baseball season progresses and the Hiroshima Carp franchise continues to do better than expected, the manager of the Carp gets a message from the Tokyo Giants' front office.

Assistant: 巨人 の 小正力 オーナー が
Kyojin no Koshōriki ōnā ga
Giants of (name) owner (subj.)

内々で 会いたい そうです、 監督。
nainai de aitai sō desu, Kantoku.
secretly/privately wants to meet (hearsay) manager
"Owner Koshōriki of the Giants says he wants a private meeting with you, Manager." (PL3)

Manager: 巨人の?
Kyojin no?
"The Giants?" (PL2)

• *aitai* is the "want to" form of *au/aimasu* ("see/meet with"). *Aitai sō da/desu* = "[He] says he wants to meet [you]."

Compare:

Omoshirosō da = "It looks interesting." (observation)
Omoshiroi sō da = "I'm told it is interesting/She said it is interesting." (hearsay)

Yosasō da = "It looks fine." (observation)
Ii sō da/yoi sō da = "I'm told it is fine/He said it is fine." (hearsay)

Hearsay with a noun-type sentence

The previous two examples have in effect shown complete verb- and adjective-type sentences followed by *sō da/desu*. The equivalent for noun-type sentences is a noun + *da* + *sō da/desu*. The bolded *da*—it can also be *datta* (past), *ja nai* (negative), and *ja nakatta* (negative-past), but cannot be *darō* (guesswork)—is crucial for indicating hearsay; without *da* or one of its other forms in this position, the sentence either makes an observation based on appearances (for certain adjectival nouns; fig. 472), or makes no sense at all (any other noun).

The sentence preceding *sō da/desu*—whether verb, adjective, or noun type—must end in a PL2 form; the politeness level of the sentence as a whole is determined by the choice of *sō da* (PL2) or *sō desu* (PL3). The hearsay expression *sō da/desu* cannot follow any kind of sentence ending in *darō*; it does not have a *na* or *ni* form and cannot directly modify nouns or verbs.

477 Natsuko has come home for a visit from her advertising job in Tokyo. She can't get the straight story from anyone else, so she asks the brewmaster how much longer the doctors give her brother to live.

Brewmaster:
長く もって 1年 だ そうだ。
Nagaku motte ichinen da sō da.
long if holds up one year is (hearsay)
"If he holds up long, they say one year."
"They're saying one year at most." (PL2)

• *nagaku* is the adverb form of the adjective *nagai* ("long"), and *motte* is the *-te* form of *motsu/mochimasu* ("hold/carry"), which can be used in the sense of "hold up/hold out/last/survive."

らしい *rashii* after a verb

Rashii indicates that the speaker is making a statement based on what he has heard or read, or sometimes what he has seen/felt firsthand; it implies a more confident and reliable guess or conclusion than the verb/adjective stem + *-sō da/desu* pattern (figs. 470–74). *Rashii* after a full PL2 verb means "Apparently/it seems/it looks like [the described action did/does/will occur]." Except for the fact that it normally can't stand alone as a sentence, the word acts as an adjective, so its polite form is *rashii desu*, past is *rashikatta (desu)*, negative is *rashikunai (desu)*, and negative-past is *rashikunakatta (desu)*.

"Let's meet at Luna in Shinjuku at 6:00."

478 When he gets home from the public bath, Kōsuke finds the note at left written by his girlfriend Hiroko. He turns right back around and closes the door behind him.

Kōsuke: カノジョ が ┃来た らしい。┃
(thinking) *Kanojo ga* ┃*kita rashii.*┃
she (subj.) came it appears
"My girlfriend apparently dropped by." (PL2)

隣 の 学生 に 定期券 を 借りて 行こう。
Tonari no gakusei ni teiken o karite ikō.
neighbor (mod.) student from pass (obj.) borrow-and I'll go
"I think I'll borrow a pass from the neighbor student and go."
"I can borrow my neighbor's train pass to go." (PL2)

SFX: バタン
Batan (sound of door closing)

- *kita* is the plain past form of *kuru*, so *kita rashii* = "apparently came/appears to have come."
- *karite* is the *-te* form of *kariru/karimasu* ("borrow"), and *ikō* is the "let's/I'll/I think I'll ～" form of *iku* ("go"). The *-te iku* form here expresses not only the sequence of events ("borrow and then go"), but a little about how he will go/what he has to do in order to go (see figs. 381–382).

Rashii as hearsay

Statements made with *rashii* typically contain some element of guesswork, but the form can be used even when the element of uncertainty is slight or non-existent. In such cases *rashii* is basically the same as the full verb/adjective + *sō da/desu* pattern that indicates direct hearsay (figs. 475–77): "I understand ～/I'm told ～/So-and-so said ～." The speaker below, for example, sounds like he has heard authoritative information.

479 The company is going through a major reorganization, and some of the employees are talking about it.

A: 第二部門 は 関連会社 として ┃独立する らしい┃ ね。
Dai-ni bumon wa kanren-gaisha to shite ┃*dokuritsu suru rashii*┃ *ne.*
Division Two as for affiliated co. as will go independent it appears (colq.)
"I understand Division Two is being spun off as an independent affiliate." (PL2)

B: へー、 いい な。
Hē, ii na.
(interj.) good/fine (colloq.)
"Really? The lucky stiffs." (PL2)

OLs: 広く なる わね。 / うれしい。
Hiroku naru wa ne. / Ureshii.
spacious will become (fem.-colloq.) / be happy/delighted
"This place will become more spacious." / "I'm delighted."
"We'll have more space." / "That'll be nice." (PL2)

- *kanren-gaisha* is literally "related/affiliated company" (*-gaisha* is from *kaisha*, "company"; the *k* changes to *g* in combinations).
- *dokuritsu* = "independence," and *dokuritsu suru* = "go/become independent."
- *hē* is an interjection showing interest/mild surprise, like "Really?/Oh?/Hmm."
- *ii na* (or *ii nā*) can be used to express envy: "I'm envious/you lucky stiff."
- *hiroku* is the adverb form of the adjective *hiroi* ("spacious"), so *hiroku naru* = "(will) become spacious" (fig. 78).

Rashii after an adjective, *nai/-nai*, and *-tai*

Rashii after the dictionary form of an adjective means, "Apparently/it seems/it looks like/I hear it is [as described]": *Takai rashii* ("Apparently/I hear it is expensive"). The word can follow the adjective's plain past, negative, and negative-past forms as well: *Takakatta rashii* = "Apparently/I hear it was expensive"; *Takakunai rashii* = "Apparently/I hear it isn't expensive"; *Takakunakatta rashii* = "Apparently/I hear it wasn't expensive." It can also follow the *-nai* (plain negative) and *-tai* ("want to") forms of verbs in the same way, since both of these forms act as adjectives: *ikanai* ("not go") → *Ikanai rashii* ("Apparently/I hear that he won't go"); *ikitai* ("want to go") → *Ikitai rashii* ("Apparently/I hear he wants to go").

480 As these men wait in line at the taxi stand, one of them sneezes.

A: 花粉症　です　か?
Kafun-shō desu ka?
hay fever is (?)
"Hay fever?" (PL3)

B: ええ、今年　は　ひどい　らしいです　ね。
Ē, kotoshi wa hidoi rashii desu ne.
yes this year as for is terrible (hearsay-pol.) (colloq.)
"Yes, I understand [the pollen] is particularly bad this year." (PL3)

- *kafun* = "pollen" and *-shō* is a suffix used for a wide variety of health symptoms/conditions/syndromes, so *kafunshō* = "hay fever/pollinosis."
- the topic marker *wa* in this case sets off *kotoshi* ("this year") as a contrast, so *kotoshi wa hidoi* implies "this year as opposed to others, [the pollen] is terrible" → "the pollen is particularly bad this year."

KERCHOO!

Rashii after a noun

For verb- and adjective-type statements (figs. 478–80), *rashii* in effect follows complete PL2 sentences (including single word sentences). The complete PL2 sentence rule holds for noun-type statements as well—with one crucial exception: for sentences ending with a noun + *da* (but not with a noun + *datta*, *ja nai*, or *ja nakatta*), *rashii* replaces *da* instead of following it: *Koko wa byōin da* ("This place is a hospital") → *Koko wa byōin rashii* ("This place appears to be a hospital"; the *da* is dropped).

A noun + *rashii* phrase has the same basic meanings already described for *rashii*—"Apparently/it seems/it looks like/I hear it is [the stated item]." But it also has an additional special meaning. In certain contexts, a noun + *rashii* implies "is so like/so characteristic of [the stated thing/person]."

481 Even after being drafted and sent to the battlefront, Zenzō's letters are filled with his concerns and ideas about processing rice and brewing saké. Natsu mentions this to Shizu. Shizu responds:

Shizu:

旦那さま　　らしいです　ね。
Danna-sama rashii desu ne.
master/husband-(hon.) is like-(pol.) (colloq.)
"That is so like him, isn't it?" (PL3)

もう　あと　ふた月　で　生まれる　と　言う　のに。
Mō ato futa-tsuki de umareru to iu no ni
now more two months (scope) will be born (quote) say even though
"Even though [the baby] will be born now in just two more months."
"[To be dwelling on such things] when the baby's only two months away." (PL3)

- in another context, *Danna-sama rashii desu* could mean "It seems to be the master" or "I understand it's your husband," but here there is no guesswork or hearsay involved; she is saying it's just like Zenzō to stay so focused on rice and saké even at the battlefront and even when his first child is due in two months.

Rashii after other noun-type sentences

Apart from the above exception for non-past noun-type sentences, *rashii* is added to the end of a complete PL2 sentence, so you get noun + *datta rashii* (past), noun + *ja nai rashii* (negative), and noun + *ja nakatta rashii* (negative-past): *Koko wa byōin datta* ("This place was a hospital") → *Koko wa byōin datta rashii* ("This place was apparently a hospital"; *datta* remains in place). As with the hearsay expression *sō da*, *rashii* cannot follow any kind of sentence ending in *darō*.

482 Kaji and Ōmori have come back to the rugby field at their alma mater, where they plan to meet Ōmori's reporter colleague, Higashino, who was on the same rugby team ten years after Kaji and Ōmori. As they wait, Ōmori reflects on Kaji's and his own contributions to the team, then remarks on what he has heard about Higashino's exploits.

Ōmori: そして 10年後 の 後輩 に なる が、
Soshite jū-nen ato no kōhai ni naru ga,
and 10 yrs later of junior (result) becomes but

東野 記者 は 名フォワード だった らしい。
Higashino kisha wa mei-fōwādo datta rashii.
(name) reporter as for excellent forward was it seems/I hear

"And moving on to a junior who came ten years later, reporter Higashino was apparently an excellent forward."

"And he came ten years after us, but reporter Higashino was apparently a real standout at forward." (PL2)

- *kōhai* refers to a person with more junior standing within a given group by virtue of having joined the group later; it's the junior counterpart to *senpai* (fig. 318).
- *naru* = "become(s)" and *ni* marks the end result, so ～ *ni naru* as a phrase typically means "become(s) ～"; this can be used as an expression for "the focus of this discussion becomes/changes to ～."
- the prefix *mei-* means "excellent/masterful/famous."

Rashii as a modifier

Since *rashii* acts as an adjective, a noun + *rashii* phrase can directly modify another noun: *kodomo* ("child") → *kodomo rashii* ("like a child/childish") → *Kodomo rashii koto o iu* ("[He/she] says a childish thing"). It's often easiest to think of the modifier *X rashii* as equivalent to "X-like": *X rashii* ～ = "an X-like ～." This can simply imply "characteristic of X," as with *kodomo rashii*, but it often also implies "befitting X/just like X should be": *otoko rashii hito* = "a man-like person" → "a masculine/manly/virile man" or "a real man"; *onna rashii hito* = "a woman-like person" → "a feminine/womanly/demure woman" or "a real woman." (Because *rashii* implies "befitting," *onna rashii hito* cannot normally refer to "a womanish man.")

By the same token, the word's -*ku* form, *rashiku*, can be used to modify a verb or adjective. *X rashiku* typically means "in an X-like manner"—implying "in a manner characteristic of X/ befitting X." But when modifying the verb *naru* ("become"), as in the example here, it usually means "become(s) X-like" (see fig. 78).

483 Upon returning to her advertising job in Tokyo after her brother's funeral, Natsuko submits new copy for the assignment that had her struggling for inspiration before (fig. 417). Her supervisor Harada gives it a passing grade, and commends her for learning to suppress her personal views about the product.

Harada: プロ らしく なってきた な、 佐伯くん。
Puro rashiku natte kita na, Saeki-kun.
pro -like are becoming (colloq.) (name-fam.)

"You have started to become pro-like, haven't you, Miss Saeki?"

"Now you're starting to work like a real professional, Miss Saeki." (PL2)

- *natte* is the -*te* form of *naru* ("become"), and *kita* is the plain past form of *kuru* ("come"); *natte kuru* = "start to become" and *natte kita* = "has/have started to become" or "is/are becoming" (fig. 380).

みたいだ *mitai da*

Mitai da (or *mitai desu*) is another expression that's added to the end of a complete PL2 sentence, and it means "that's the way it appears/seems/sounds/feels." It generally implies first-hand observation and/or more direct knowledge than *rashii* does, and therefore, even greater reliability. (This *mitai* has nothing to do with the "want to" form of *miru*.)

After a verb (or the sentence it completes), *mitai da/desu* means "It looks like [someone] does/did/is doing/will do the action" or "It looks like the action occurs/occurred/is occurring/will occur."

484 As Kōsuke labors at the task of repapering the temple's shoji screens (fig. 470), the priest comes by to see how things are going.

Priest: コースケ! まだ だいぶ 残ってる みたいだ な。
Kōsuke! Mada daibu nokotteru mitai da na.
(name) still quite a bit remains/is left looks like (colloq.)
"Kōsuke! It looks like still a lot remains."
"Kōsuke! It looks like you've still got quite a bit left to do." (PL2)

Kōsuke: はあ...
Hā...
"Yes..." (PL3)

- *daibu* is an adverb like "considerably" or "quite a lot."
- *nokotteru* is a contraction of *nokotte iru* ("remains/is left"), from *nokoru/nokori-masu* ("be left over").
- *hā* is a relatively formal-sounding equivalent of *hai* ("yes") that typically feels rather tentative or uncertain/noncommittal.

Mitai da with an adjective

Mitai da (or *mitai desu*) after the plain form of an adjective typically means "looks like [it] is [as described]" or "appears/seems to be [the described quality]." *Mitai da/desu* can also follow the plain past form of an adjective, in which case it means "looks like [it] was [as described]" or "appears/seems to have been [the described quality]."

485 The mom-and-pop sushi shop owners were telling their son they absolutely cannot keep the stray kitten he brought home, when customers walk in and start treating the kitten as if it's the shop mascot.

Mom: しよう が ない わねえ。 お客さん の 評判 も
Shiyō ga nai wa nē. O-kyaku-san no hyōban mo
way of doing (subj.) not exist (fem.-colq.) (hon.)-customers s' estimation also
いい みたいだ し、飼ってみる こと に しましょう か?
ii mitai da shi, katte miru koto ni shimashō ka?
is good it appears and/so try keeping thing to let's make [it] (?)
"I suppose there's no help for it. The customers' estimation [of the kitten] appears to be good, so shall we decide to try keeping it?"
"What can I say? It seems to be popular with the customers, so shall we perhaps try keeping it?" (PL3)

Son: やったあ!!
Yattā!!
"All right!" (PL2)

- *shiyō ga nai* is literally "there is no way to do/nothing one can do" → "it can't be helped/what can one do?"
- *hyōban* = "public estimation/popularity," so *hyōban ga ii* = "estimation/popularity is good" → "is popular." Using *mo* instead of *ga* implies "popularity among the customers" is an additional factor—i.e., after the son's imploring—in deciding to keep the kitten.
- *katte* is the *-te* form of *kau/kaimasu*, which when written with this kanji means "keep/raise [a pet/domestic animals]"; the *-te miru* form of a verb implies "try [the action]" or "try doing [the action] and see" (figs. 369–70).
- ～ *koto ni shimashō* is the "let's/I'll ～" form of ～ *koto ni suru* (lit. "make it the thing" → "decide to do"; fig. 275), so it means "let's decide to ～"; in a question this becomes "Shall we decide to ～?" or just "Shall we ～?"

Mitai da after a noun

Like *rashii*, *mitai da/desu* is best thought of as attaching to the end of a complete PL2 sentence, and this includes noun-type sentences ending in the past *datta*, the negative *ja nai*, and the negative-past *ja nakatta* forms. But when the noun-type sentence ends with *da*, the *da* drops out and *mitai da/desu* connects directly to the final noun. The typical meanings are, "looks like [it] is [the stated item]," "appears/seems to be [the stated item]," or sometimes simply "is like [the stated item]."

Mitai da/desu cannot follow any kind of sentence that ends in *darō*. Except for the fact that it can't normally stand alone, *mitai da/desu* functions as an adjectival noun, so *da/desu* sometimes changes to *na* or *ni* (see facing page). *Da/desu* can also be omitted after *mitai* in any situation where it can be omitted after an ordinary noun, such as before the sentence particle *ne* in this example.

486 After one OL catches her coworker sneaking a peek at a special photograph (fig. 112), others nearby come to look.

OL1: いい 　人 みたい ね。
Ii 　*hito* *mitai* *ne*.
good/nice 　person 　looks like 　(colloq.)
"He looks like a nice person." (PL2)

OL2: や、 　優しそう。
Ya- 　*yasashisō*.
(stammer) 　looks/seems kind
"He looks kind."
"He has a kind face." (PL2)

OL3: えへへっ
Ehehe!
(embarrassed giggle)

- a straightforward statement without any element of guesswork would be *Ii hito da ne* ("He is a nice person"). The *da* after *hito* must be dropped when *mitai (da/desu)* is added to express the "looks like" meaning. Omitting *da* after *mitai* can be considered somewhat feminine; male speakers are more likely to keep the *da* and say *Ii hito mitai da ne* (the *da* after *hito* still disappears).
- *yasashisō* is from the adjective *yasashii* ("is kind/sweet/gentle"); since the final -*i* of the adjective has been dropped before -*sō*, the word expresses a guess/conclusion based on appearance (fig. 471).

Compare:

taberu mitai = "looks like she will eat"
tabete mitai = "want to try eating" (from the -*te* form of *taberu* plus the -*tai* form of *miru*)

nomu mitai = "looks like he will drink"
nonde mitai = "want to try drinking" (from the -*te* form of *nomu* plus the -*tai* form of *miru*)

Mitai da with *nai/-nai*

Mitai da/desu follows the plain negative form of a verb in the same way as it follows an adjective: *nai* ("not exist") → *Nai mitai* ("[It] looks like [it] doesn't exist/isn't here" or "[It] appears/seems not to exist/be present"); *ikanai* ("not go") → *Ikanai mitai* ("[It] appears/seems/looks like [someone] won't go" or "[It] doesn't appear/seem/look like [someone] will go"); *omoshirokunai* ("not interesting") → *Omoshirokunai mitai* ("[It] appears/seems/looks uninteresting" or "[It] doesn't appear/seem/look interesting); *neko ja nai* ("is not a cat") → *Neko ja nai mitai* ("[It] appears/seems not to be a cat" or "It doesn't appear/seem to be a cat").

487 The boy's pet frog isn't his usual self. "Maybe he has a cold," Kariage-kun says, and brings a thermometer.

Kariage-kun: 熱 　は ない みたいだ な。
Netsu 　*wa* 　*nai* *mitai da* 　*na*.
fever 　as for 　not exist/have 　it appears 　(colloq.)
"As for a fever, it doesn't exist, it appears."
"He doesn't seem to have a fever." (PL2)

In the next panel, the frog himself is shown thinking, "I'm cold-blooded, you idiot."

When modifying nouns: みたいな *mitai na*

Mitai da/desu acts as an adjectival noun, so its form for modifying another noun is *mitai na* ～. Since *mitai da/desu* must always be preceded by something else, it's in fact the entire phrase or sentence ending in *mitai na* that is the modifier. The most common use of *mitai na* is to express a resemblance: when X is a noun, *X mitai na* ～ implies "an X-like/X-ish ～," or "a ～ that looks/sounds/feels/seems/acts like X."

488 Natsuko knows that even though Old Man Miyakawa has stopped growing rice, he was always considered the expert. Here she shows him for the first time the 1350 grains of Tatsunishiki that her brother had managed to track down at an agricultural experiment station just before he died. She wants Miyakawa to teach her how to grow the rice.

Miyakawa: 龍錦?
Tatsunishiki?
"Tatsunishiki?" (PL2)

Natsuko: 兄 の 形見 みたいな もの です。
Ani no katami mitai na mono desu.
older bro. of keepsake/legacy -like thing is
"They're something like a keepsake of my brother."
"You could say those are my brother's legacy to me." (PL3)

- *katami* typically refers to something that is kept to remember a person by after his or her death: "keepsake/memento/remembrance." She could say *Ani no katami desu* ("They're a keepsake of my brother"), but since rice seeds don't fit the typical notion of *katami*, she says they are merely "like" a *katami*.
- *mono* = "thing," so ～ *mitai na mono* = "a thing that's like ～" → "something like a ～."

When modifying verbs: みたいに *mitai ni*

When modifying a verb or adjective, *mitai da/desu* becomes *mitai ni* ～. Again, it's in fact the entire phrase or sentence ending in *mitai ni* that is the modifier, and the most common use of *mitai ni* is to express a resemblance: using the phrase to modify a verb implies "[do the action] like X/in an X-like manner"; using the phrase to modify an adjective implies "[something] is of the described quality, just like X."

489 Two OLs gazing out the window of their office building see a bird fly by. (There are two different kinds of *mitai* in this example.)

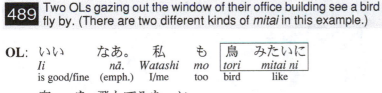

OL: いい なあ。 私 も 鳥 みたいに
Ii nā. Watashi mo tori mitai ni
is good/fine (emph.) I/me too bird like

空 を 飛んでみたーい。
sora o tonde mitāi.
sky (obj.) want to try flying
"I'm so envious. I, too, want to try flying through the sky like a bird."
"Birds are so lucky. I sure wish I could fly like them." (PL2)

- *ii nā* is an expression of envy like "I'm so envious" or "You're/they're so lucky." You can think of *ii* ("is good/nice") as meaning "It is so nice [for you/them/someone]" or "[You/they] have it so good."
- *mitai ni* after a noun means "like ～," so *tori mitai ni* = "like a bird"; this expression modifies the rest of the sentence.
- *tonde mitai* (the long vowel simply expresses the strength of her desire) is the *-te* form of *tobu* ("fly") plus the "want to" form of *miru*. Since a verb's *-te miru* form means "try to do/try doing [the action]," *tonde mitai* = "want to try flying."
- *o* marks *sora* ("sky") as where she'd like to fly; *tobu* can also mean "jump," so *sora o* is included with *tobu* any time the meaning might be ambiguous, and often even when it's not. In most cases the entire expression *sora o tobu* is equivalent to just "fly."

ようだ *yō da*

Yō da/desu can be considered a more formal equivalent of *mitai da/desu*—though both can be used in both PL2 and PL3 speech. The two forms are essentially the same in meaning and in most aspects of their usage. *Yō da* follows a complete PL2 sentence, connecting to the various plain forms of verbs and adjectives, including the negative forms; it never follows a sentence ending in *darō*. (There is again an exception for noun-type sentences, which is illustrated in the next example.)

490 Matsuda arrives at his grade school class reunion about half an hour before the festivities are officially scheduled to begin. He looks for his friend Yamazaki Gō but does not see him.

Matsuda:
まだ 来てない ようだ な。
Mada kitenai yō da na.
still/yet has not come it appears (emph.)
"It appears that he has not yet come."
"He doesn't appear to be here yet."
(PL2)

- *mada* ("still") followed by a negative means "not yet."
- *kitenai* ("has not come/is not here") is a contraction of *kite inai*, negative of *kite iru* ("has come/is here"), from *kuru* ("come"). Since Matsuda is drawing his own conclusions based on his own limited observation of those in attendance, he adds *yō da* ("it appears that ～").

のようだ *no yō da after nouns*

The pattern of *yō da/desu* attaching to the end of a complete PL2 sentence includes noun-type sentences ending in the past *datta*, negative *ja nai*, and negative-past *ja nakatta* forms. But once again, noun-type sentences ending in *da* present an exception: this time, *da* is replaced by *no* (or *na* for adjectival nouns) before *yō da/desu*: *Neko da* ("It's a cat") → *Neko no yō da* ("It appears to be a cat"). The typical meanings are, "looks like [it] is [the stated item]," "appears/seems to be [the stated item]," or sometimes simply "is like [the stated item]." Structurally, *no* makes the preceding noun into a modifier for *yō*, which is essentially an adjectival noun meaning "appearance."

491 The police are going over the scene of a crime. When the chief detective arrives, one of his assistants gives him a report.

- *dōyara* often appears together with *rashii/mitai da/yō da* to reinforce the meaning of "apparently."
- *-garami* is a noun suffix that implies "involving/related to [the stated item/matter]."
- *koroshi* is the pre-*masu* form of *korosu/koroshimasu* ("kill/murder"); the pre-*masu* form is here being used as a noun. A more categorical statement would be *Fudōsan-garami no koroshi da* ("It is a murder over real estate interests"); replacing *da* with *no* and adding *yō da/desu* expresses an element of uncertainty/guesswork.

Assistant:
死亡 推定 時刻 は 14時30分。
Shibō suitei jikoku wa jūyoji sanjuppun.
death estimated time as for 1430 hours/2:30 PM
"The estimated time of death is 2:30 PM." (PL3 implied)

どうやら 不動産 がらみの 殺し の よう です ね。
Dōyara fudōsan -garami no koroshi no yō desu ne.
apparently real estate -related murder (mod.) appearance is (colloq.)
"It appears to be a murder over real estate interests." (PL3)

Detective: うむ。
Umu.
"Uh-huh." (PL2)

When modifying nouns: ような *yō na*

When modifying a noun, *(no) yō da/desu* becomes *(no) yō na* ～. Since *(no) yō da/yō na* cannot stand alone, it's in fact the entire phrase or sentence ending in *(no) yō na* that is the modifier. Like *mitai na*, one of the most common uses of X *(no) yō na* ～ is to express a resemblance. Where X is a noun, X *no yō na* ～ implies "an X-like/X-ish ～," or "a ～ that looks/sounds/feels/seems/acts like X": *onna* = "woman," and *koe* = "voice," so *onna no yō na koe* = "a womanish voice" (this would be said of a man). Where X is a verb, the pattern more typically expresses a kind/type: *doki-doki suru* = "heart pounds" (fig. 474) and *eiga* = "movie," so *doki-doki suru yō na eiga* = "a heart-pounding-type movie" → "a movie that makes your heart pound."

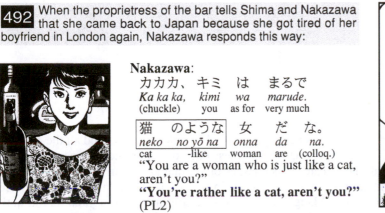

492 When the proprietress of the bar tells Shima and Nakazawa that she came back to Japan because she got tired of her boyfriend in London again, Nakazawa responds this way:

Nakazawa:

カカカ、	キミ	は	まるで
Ka ka ka,	*kimi*	*wa*	*marude.*
(chuckle)	you	as for	very much

猫 のような	女	だ	な。
neko no yō na	*onna*	*da*	*na.*
cat -like	woman	are	(colloq.)

"You are a woman who is just like a cat, aren't you?"
"You're rather like a cat, aren't you?" (PL2)

- *ka ka ka* is a gentle, back-of-the-throat sort of chuckle.
- *marude* is used to emphasize likeness in a comparison, and is often followed by forms that mean "is like," such as *mitai da/desu* or *yō da/desu*. The emphatic meaning ranges from "just/exactly like" to "much/almost/practically/rather like."

She retorts that she prefers to simply think of herself as a free spirit.

When modifying verbs: ように *yō ni*

When modifying a verb or adjective, *(no) yō da/desu* becomes *(no) yō ni* ～. Again, it's in fact the entire phrase or sentence ending in *(no) yō ni* that is the modifier. Where X is a noun, using X *no yō ni* to modify a verb implies "[do the action] like X/in an X-like manner"; using the same phrase to modify an adjective implies "[something] is of the described quality, just like X."

If X is a non-past verb and the phrase modifies the verb Y, X *yō ni* Y can imply "do Y so that X occurs/doesn't occur/can occur/etc.": *mieru* = "be visible" (fig. 424) and *oku* = "set" → *mieru yō ni oku* = "set [it] so that [it] is visible." (X *mitai ni* Y does not have this meaning.) There are some other special uses of *yō ni* that you will want to be on the lookout for as well.

Father:

カニさん のように	横	に	歩いて
Kani-san no yō ni	*yoko*	*ni*	*aruite*
crab-(pol.) like	side	to	walk-(manner)

斜面	を	登る。
shamen	*o*	*noboru.*
hill/slope	(obj.)	climb

"You climb the slope by walking sideways like a crab." (PL2)

SFX: ザッ ザッ
Za! za!
Crunch crunch (ski edges crunching into snow)

- when adults speak to small children, they often add *-san* to the names of animals.
- *yoko* = "side," and *yoko ni* = "to/toward the side" → "sideways."
- *aruite* is from *aruku/arukimasu* ("walk"); the *-te* form is being used to indicate manner.
- the polite form of *noboru* ("climb") is *noborimasu*.

493 On Shin-chan's very first trip to the ski slopes (fig. 65), his father demonstrates how to climb uphill on skis.

Appendixes

Appendix A: Useful resources

This book is designed to stand on its own, providing all the helps you need in order to grasp the grammar points and follow the manga panels used to illustrate them. The book is also comprehensive in presenting, at a basic level, all the key building blocks of the language. But *Japanese the Manga Way* does not pretend to be a complete, full-service course in Japanese. It offers a concise introduction—or if you're already taking classes or studied before, a review—after which you'll need to turn to other books and learning aids to fully master the language. Bookstores stock a wide variety of materials to choose from, and you can find an increasingly broad range of language learning sites on the Internet as well.

This appendix lists a few suggestions to get you started, with an emphasis on print resources. To find the latest web-based offerings, simply type words like "hiragana," "katakana," "kanji," or "learn Japanese" into your favorite search engine and explore the links that come up. If a web address given below fails to work, try searching on the title given for the resource. See item 6 for a note about displaying and typing Japanese on your computer.

1. Mangajin

The now defunct *Mangajin* magazine provided a variety of manga in each issue in a format that helped readers through that awkward stage where they know a little bit of Japanese, but not quite enough yet to read manga on their own. Fortunately, as of this writing, the majority of the seventy issues published remain available from mangajin.com, either by subscription or on a single-copy basis (to order in Japan, follow the link to the Japanese site). It's worth getting hold of at least an issue or two for extra reading material almost as soon as you begin this book—though various aspects of the explanations may remain difficult to grasp until you've finished at least the first half. By the time you're through with this book, you should be able to understand all the notes the magazine provides. For your reference, Appendix B indicates which issues of the magazine carried episodes of each manga title used in this book. (Disclaimer: I worked for Mangajin as an outside contractor throughout its run in the 1990s, but receive no benefit from sales of back issues.)

2. Learning to read and write

With the help of the romaji transcriptions provided in the lessons and in supplemental readings like *Mangajin*, you really can learn to read Japanese script just by picking it up as you go. But if that's your only method, it's going to be a long time before you can do without the crutch of romaji. At some point, the sooner the better, you'll want to make a more focused effort to learn to read kana and kanji—and to write them, since learning to write reinforces your reading skills. Here are some books and websites that can help you on your way:

Rowley, Michael. *Kanji Pict-o-Graphix: Over 1,000 Japanese Kanji and Kana Mnemonics*. Berkeley: Stone Bridge Press, 1992.

Rowley, Michael. *Kana Pict-o-Graphix: Mnemonics for Japanese Hiragana and Katakana*. Berkeley: Stone Bridge Press, 1995.

Hadamitzky, Wolfgang, and Mark Spahn. *Kanji & Kana: A Handbook of the Japanese Writing System*. Rev. ed. Rutland: Charles E. Tuttle, 1997.

Hadamitzky, Wolfgang, and Mark Spahn. *Guide to Writing Kanji & Kana: A Self-Study Workbook for Learning Japanese Characters*. 2 vols. Rutland: Charles E. Tuttle, 2003–4.

Hiragana Practice: www.mala.bc.ca/~furutak/Hiragana.htm

Katakana Practice: www.umich.edu/~umichjlp/Katakana pro/

Java Kanji Flashcards 500: www.nuthatch.com/java/kanji
cards/

3. Reading manga in the original

Eventually, of course, you'll want to try reading original manga on your own. One way to get some of the help you need is to choose a manga you can get in both English and Japanese and use the English translation as a crib. Be fore-warned that the translation of any given balloon may be very loose, conveying the general sense or feeling of what's being said rather than the precise words spoken. That is as it should be, since the publishers of these manga are concerned with readability rather than with teaching Japanese. You may need to consult a dictionary to confirm what the individual Japanese words really mean. Also, English editions may offer only excerpts of the original editions, or differ from them in other ways that the publishers/editors deemed appropriate.

If you're in Japan, the Kodansha Bilingual Comics series published by Kodansha International offers an equivalent option. The series reprints manga with English inside the panels and the original Japanese dialog in the margins. You may be able to order these through certain online vendors.

4. Dictionaries and other references

When you start reading original manga, whether with the aid of translations or entirely on your own, you will need dictionaries to help you. Traditionally this meant paper dictionaries, but there are now an increasing number of electronic and web-based options as well; these often offer search modes that are not available in their paper predecessors (you'll need Japanese text support enabled on your computer to use most of them—see item 6). When examining both paper and electronic products, determine whether they are truly targeted at native English speakers (like the dictionaries listed here), or are intended for Japanese learners of English. Most dictionaries available are the latter, and although they are fine for students of Japanese at a more advanced level, they are difficult for relative beginners to use.

General dictionaries

Merriam-Webster's Japanese–English Learner's Dictionary. Springfield: Merriam-Webster, 1993.

The Japan Foundation, ed. *Basic Japanese–English Dictionary: An Easy-to-Use Dictionary for Beginners*. Oxford: Oxford University Press, 1989.

Kodansha's Furigana Japanese Dictionary: Japanese–English English–Japanese. Tokyo: Kodansha International, 1999. (Also available in separate J–E and E–J editions.)

Bunt, Jonathan, and Gillian Hall, eds. *The Oxford Starter Japanese Dictionary*. Oxford: Oxford University Press,

2000. (A combined J–E and E–J dictionary. Does not use romaji.)

Jim Breen's WWWJDIC Japanese-English Dictionary Server: www.csse.monash.edu.au/~jwb/wwwjdic.html (A bi-directional dictionary that can be searched with romaji. A number of other dictionary resources on the web are based on this dictionary, but provide different interfaces.)

Kanji dictionaries

Halpern, Jack, ed. *The Kodansha Kanji Learner's Dictionary*. New ed. Tokyo: Kodansha International, 2001.

Kodansha's Essential Kanji Dictionary: A Compact Character Dictionary for Students and Professionals. Tokyo: Kodansha International, 2002.

OCJS Online Kanji Dictionary: www.yamasa.org/ocjs/kanjijiten/english. (Can search for kanji by reading, meaning, total stroke count, or radical. Some levels available only to subscribers.)

Other

Chino, Naoko. *All About Particles*. Power Japanese. Tokyo: Kodansha International, 1991.

Lange, Roland A. *501 Japanese Verbs*. 2nd ed. New York: Barrons, 1998.

Jim Breen's Japanese Page: www.csse.monash.edu.au/~jwb/japanese.html. (Information about the WWWJDIC dictionary listed above as well as links to many other Japanese resources.)

5. When you're ready for more advanced dictionaries

Before you invest in one of the more comprehensive dictionaries targeted at Japanese learners of English, you can get an idea of how much use they will be to you by visiting some online sites. But you'll first have to learn how to input kana on your computer to use the Japanese–English lookup (see item 6). At this writing, the following two sites remain free of charge:

dictionary.goo.ne.jp/

Enter your search term in the search field and click the red dictionary button for English–Japanese and the blue dictionary button for Japanese–English. For the latter, the term must be entered in kana, kanji, or a combination of the two, not in romaji. If you enter a term entirely in kana, the search results will include all terms in the dictionary beginning with the syllables you entered.

www.alc.co.jp/

This site automatically determines whether your search is E–J or J–E, so you can simply hit the carriage return after you have entered your search term. For J–E searches, you must use kana, kanji, or a combination, not romaji (which will be seen as English and result in an E–J search). What you enter must exactly match how the term is recorded in the database, so entering an all-kana term will work only if that is how that particular term appears in the dictionary; it will not bring up all words that begin with the same syllables, as the goo dictionary will. This sometimes means repeating a search with and without kanji or with different kanji, which is something of a chore. But the rewards can be great when you find the term you're looking for because you'll often be shown not just one or two but dozens or even hundreds of examples of how the word is used.

6. Using Japanese on your computer

Current Windows and Macintosh operating systems have multilingual support built in, so you do not need to purchase a separate Japanese operating system to view and input Japanese text. If your web browser is up to date, properly coded Japanese web pages should display correctly without your having to install anything new or change any settings. (You may occasionally have to select a different Japanese "text encoding" or "character set" on the View menu of your browser if a particular page does not display correctly.)

If the function you want to use on the web page accepts English or romaji input, you can use it without enabling Japanese input or learning how to type kana and kanji (e.g., Jim Breen's dictionary server mentioned in item 4, or the English-to-Japanese function of the goo dictionary mentioned in item 5). But most online Japanese-to-English reference tools require you to input your search term in Japanese, so to use them you must activate your keyboard for Japanese and learn how to switch between English and Japanese mode. Once you have done that, whenever you're in Japanese mode, you'll be able to type in romaji and have the computer convert the words you typed into kanji and kana.

Computer operating systems change too rapidly to offer detailed instructions here, so the best place for you to start is by searching the Help system on your computer. You may need to search not only on "Japanese," but on terms like "other languages," "East-Asian languages," "multilingual support," and so forth. The links on Jim Breen's Japanese Page (item 4, "Other") may provide helpful information. Look for instructions on how to activate Japanese input, and also on how to go about the input (i.e., get your romaji to change into kanji/kana). Because Japanese has so many words that sound alike and therefore look exactly the same when written in romaji, the input process involves an extra step that you're not accustomed to when typing English: you often have to tell the computer which of several homonyms you want to type or, in the case of a dictionary, look up.

Older English operating systems do not have multilingual support built in. If you're using Mac OS9, a separate Japanese Language Kit included on the installation CD must be custom installed (before OS9, the JLK was a separate

purchase). If you're using Windows 95/98/Me/NT4.0, you'll need to download and install the Microsoft Global IME with Language Pack available at www.microsoft.com/windows/ie/downloads/recommended/ime/install.asp. Check your Help system or the links on Jim Breen's Japanese Page for further information.

If you're using OS X on a Macintosh but need Japanese support for a Classic application (e.g., someone has given you an older version of a CD-ROM reference), you can activate Japanese for the Classic environment by running the Language Kits Installer in Applications (OS9) > Apple Extras > Language Kits.

7. About manga

For those interested in finding out more about the manga phenomenon in Japan in general, the following books are an excellent place to start:

Schodt, Frederik L. *Dreamland Japan: Writings on Modern Manga.* Berkeley: Stone Bridge Press, 1996.

Schodt, Frederik L. *Manga! Manga!: The World of Japanese Comics.* Tokyo: Kodansha International, 1983.

Appendix B: The manga titles used in this book

Brief descriptions are provided here for the manga titles used in illustrating this book, arranged alphabetically by artist name. Figure numbers are included so you can easily find all the examples taken from a particular title.

Virtually all Japanese manga are first published in magazines or newspapers. Many titles are subsequently compiled in *tankōbon* (trade paperback—or occasionally hardcover) editions; the more popular titles are often issued again as pocket-sized *bunkobon* paperbacks, and remain in print indefinitely in one or both book formats. The volume figures in each entry below indicate how many volumes of that title had appeared in *tankōbon* compilations at the time this book went to press. For ongoing series, you can find up-to-date information on the Internet or at your local Japanese bookstore.

In Japan, books that are no longer in print can often be found at second-hand bookstores. Even outside of Japan, it's worth checking your local second-hand bookstores for manga; if you live in a larger city, especially near a university or college, you may be surprised at what you find. Searching online for specific titles is another option, but beginners will need help from a more fluent friend.

Many of the titles used to illustrate this book appeared in *Mangajin*. For those who would like to seek out back issues of the magazine in libraries or at mangajin.com to read more of a specific title, the *Mangajin* numbers at the end of each entry indicate which issue(s) carried the manga. For four-frame manga, a given issue usually contains several strips, but in some cases may have only one or two. For longer stories, a single episode may span several issues: the first and last issues are indicated with a dash between them. (The magazine also carried many manga not found in this book, including additional titles by Akizuki Risu, Hirokane Kenshi, Maekawa Tsukasa, and Oze Akira.)

秋月りす、OL進化論 and 奥さま進化論
Akizuki Risu, *OL Shinkaron*, and *Okusama Shinkaron*
Kōdansha
OLS: Figs. 10, 84, 91, 101, 112, 128, 137, 165, 171, 204, 208, 210, 215, 225, 234, 235, 251, 253, 257, 258, 289, 299, 315, 329, 334, 339, 341, 344, 354, 368, 374, 396, 398, 458, 472, 479, 486, 489
OS: Figs. 348, 409

OL (pronounced *ōeru*) is a Japanese acronym for the English "office lady" and refers to young female workers who handle most secretarial/menial tasks around the office. *Okusama* is a polite term for referring to another person's wife or to housewives in general. *Shinka* means "evolution" and *-ron* is a suffix meaning "theory/doctrine/opinion/view," so

the titles of these two four-frame series can be translated as "Evolutionary View of the Office Lady" and "Evolutionary View of the Housewife."

OL Shinkaron focuses on life in and out of the office from the stereotypical OL's point of view, revealing much about a stage of life that a huge segment of Japanese women pass through between graduating from high school or college and getting married. *Okusama Shinkaron* focuses mainly on the wives of young salarymen—which is to say the life-stage that usually follows a woman's stint as an OL.

The *Okusama* strip ran for only a short time (1 volume), but *OL Shinkaron* continues to appear (21 volumes). Several volumes of the latter have been published by Kodansha International in a bilingual edition under the title *Survival in the Office: The Evolution of Japanese Working Women*.
Mangajin: 4, 5, 10, 11, 15, 20, 23, 26, 27, 29, 30, 31, 33, 34, 36, 37, 38, 40, 41, 42, 43, 47, 51, 54, 56.

デラックスカンパニー、図説現代用語便覧
Deluxe Company, *Zusetsu Gendai Yōgo Binran*
Futabasha
Figs. 44, 49, 134, 144, 148, 184, 243, 268, 280, 322, 326, 363, 413, 430, 444, 449

Offering its own English cover title, *A Visual Glossary of Modern Terms*, this four-frame gag strip ranges across all aspects of contemporary life in sections titled "Health," "Gambling," "Environment," "Unexplained Mysteries," "Work," "New Year's," "Fads," "Style," "High Tech," "Cults," and so forth. The strips were created jointly by the staff of a small graphic design house. The language in the panels is usually quite dense and more suitable to advanced students.

1 volume.
Mangajin: 32, 33, 34, 36, 41, 42, 51, 57, 58.

古谷三敏、BARレモンハート
Furuya Mitsutoshi, *Bar Remon Hāto*
Futabasha
Figs. 2, 7, 13, 27, 37, 54, 55, 61, 67, 69, 70, 106, 110, 115, 149, 154, 172, 179, 249, 265, 266, 284, 302, 303, 304, 314, 333, 469, 474, 490

This long-running series takes place mostly in a bar named after a Jamaican rum called "Lemon Hart" (*Remon Hāto* is the Japanese rendering of this name) and centers on the conversations of its bartender and the patrons who come there to unwind. The creator of the series owns a real bar that caters to connoisseurs of fine spirits by offering a huge selection of brands from all over the world, so it's no coincidence that the fictitious bar has a similar selection, or that the stories almost always feature informative tidbits about various alcoholic beverages and how they are best enjoyed. This information is embedded in humorous stories about events in the day-to-day lives of the regular patrons or of others who happen to drop in.

20 volumes.
Mangajin: 25.

弘兼憲史、課長島耕作 and 部長島耕作
Hirokane Kenshi, *Kachō Shima Kōsaku*, and *Buchō Shima Kōsaku*
Kōdansha
Kachō: Figs. 17, 30, 32, 41, 43, 66, 77, 79, 86, 111, 160, 168, 174, 176, 178, 202, 216, 230, 245, 269, 285, 287, 288, 296, 340, 382, 387, 418, 428, 462, 471
Buchō: Figs. 25, 40, 78, 118, 126, 159, 197, 320, 323, 331, 364, 389, 391, 392, 393, 408, 421, 431, 457, 492

Kachō means "section head/chief," and *buchō* means "division head/chief," so the only difference between these two titles is the rank of the title character, Shima Kōsaku. When the *Kachō* series ended (17 volumes), the *Buchō* series followed (13 volumes), and this then gave way to *Torishimari-yaku Shima Kōsaku* ("Director Shima Kōsaku"; 6 volumes). Together, these titles present a continuing corporate epic centering on the eponymous hero who works for the giant consumer electronics and appliance maker Hatsushiba Electric Company—loosely modeled on the real-life Matsushita conglomerate (best known by the Panasonic brand name outside Japan). Following Shima through countless corporate crises, management intrigues, and romantic entanglements, the story provides an entertaining window on Japanese corporate culture and the lives of its hardworking salarymen. Warning: includes sexual content and nudity.

Several volumes of *Buchō Shima Kōsaku* have appeared in the Kodansha Bilingual Comics series as *Division Chief Kōsaku Shima*.
Mangajin: 28–29.

弘兼憲史、加治隆介の議
Hirokane Kenshi, *Kaji Ryūsuke no Gi*
Kōdansha
Figs. 3, 14, 35, 46, 59, 63, 85, 105, 117, 132, 156, 162, 209, 228, 252, 259, 272, 277, 279, 306, 311, 312, 321, 328, 337, 350, 352, 353, 366, 369, 377, 395, 403, 410, 414, 420, 423, 426, 437, 451, 482

Gi refers to a discussion or debate, and following a person's name and the possessive *no* it implies that person's position/argument/stand in the discussion/debate, so this title can be translated "Kaji Ryūsuke's Stand." Although he initially resists the idea, elite salaryman Kaji agrees to run for his father's seat in the Japanese House of Representatives after

his father's death in an auto accident. But since he is running for national office, he insists he will campaign on national and international issues, thinking only of what is best for the country as a whole, rather than on the traditional list of pork-barrel promises to his local constituency. His election begins a maverick journey through the corridors of Japanese power. Created by the same artist as Shima Kōsaku, Kaji is almost a dead ringer for Shima—some of the other characters are close look-alikes as well—in a series that does for the world of Japanese politics what the Shima Kōsaku series does for Japanese corporate culture. Warning: includes sexual content and nudity.

20 volumes.
Mangajin: 59–61.

堀田かつひこ、オバタリアン
Hotta Katsuhiko, *Obatarian*
Take Shobō
Figs. 16, 133, 187, 188, 195, 244, 438, 460

The artist coined the title of this four-frame gag series by combining *obasan* (lit. "aunt," but also used as a generic word for "middle-aged woman") with *Batarian*, the Japanese title of the film *Return of the Living Dead*. *Obatarian* has now entered the dictionary as a colloquial/slang term for the kind of middle-aged women caricatured in the strip: loud and pushy, selfish, shameless, often tactless and rude, insensitive, vulgar, etc.

11 volumes.
Mangajin: 4, 5, 6, 7, 10, 11, 14, 15, 18, 19, 20, 23, 25, 26, 27, 30, 35, 38, 39, 40, 50, 51, 54, 59.

いがらしみきお、ぼのぼの
Igarashi Mikio, *Bonobono*
Take Shobō
Figs. 42, 147, 155, 161, 290, 399

This is a four-frame strip (often expanded to eight frames—which is to say a full page in the standard Japanese format) centering on its eponymous hero, the young sea otter Bonobono, his father, and an entire community of wildlife friends and family. Bonobono himself is a relentlessly inquisitive child, constantly asking questions of those around him or pondering imponderables on his own. The manga is popular among both children and adults, and for the latter group it can perhaps be described as a thinking person's comic strip, with "gags" that are often more philosophical or Zen-like than humorous—though there is plenty of humor as well.

25 volumes, plus a number of children's books based on the same characters.
Mangajin: 16.

いまぜき伸、オジャマします

Imazeki Shin, *Ojama Shimasu*
Take Shobō
Figs. 8, 53, 64, 114, 151, 153, 305

Ojama shimasu is a polite phrase that visitors use when entering someone else's room or home, literally meaning "I will intrude" but having more the feeling of "Please pardon my intrusion"; so the title of this four-frame strip can be translated as "Pardon the Intrusion." There's no easy way to describe the humor of this strip except to say that it is very offbeat. Most of the characters are human, but many of the gags also feature one or more sheep, dog(s), an aardvark, or occasionally some other animal(s), either alongside the human characters or by themselves. Although some of the strips offer pure sight gags and others make relatively spare use of very simple language, many also depend on subtle aspects of usage that will remain opaque to beginners. This is not to say that beginners should shy away; just be prepared to remain mystified some of the time.

4 volumes.
Mangajin: 10, 11, 13, 16, 18, 19, 20, 12, 34, 37.

いしいひさいち、いしいひさいち選集

Ishii Hisaichi, *Ishii Hisaichi Senshū*
Futabasha
Figs. 68, 76, 93, 158, 185, 191, 325, 349, 427, 465, 467, 476, 480

Senshū means "selected works," so the title given here translates as "Selected Works of Ishii Hisaichi"; the books also bear the English title *Doughnuts Books* on the cover. This is a collection of four-frame gag strips that have appeared under a wide variety of titles in a similarly wide variety of magazines and newspapers over more than three decades. Current events and contemporary life make up the most prominent themes, but mixed among these are also a substantial number of strips featuring samurai and ninja from pre-modern Japan.

The strip is written in *Kansai-ben*, the traditional dialect of the Kyoto/Osaka/Kobe region (with some variation even among these three cities), rather than the standard Tokyo Japanese that is now spoken nationwide. The basic structure of the language is the same, and in many cases the only difference from standard Japanese is in how the speaker would accent his words (which of course does not show up on the printed page). In other instances, though, different forms replace key grammatical elements, and because of this difference in the language used, these strips are not generally recommended for beginners; they are suitable for more advanced students who are ready to broaden their exposure to include common dialect elements that are often heard mixed in with standard Japanese.

37 volumes.
Mangajin: 30, 31, 33, 38, 39, 44, 58, 59, 63, 64.

小林まこと、ホワッツ マイケル

Kobayashi Makoto, *What's Michael?*
Kōdansha
Figs. 11, 22, 47, 57, 72, 81, 94, 97, 99, 121, 131, 150, 163, 193, 214, 217, 218, 219, 220, 226, 232, 238, 240, 247, 255, 261, 262, 271, 292, 298, 310, 347, 355, 359, 361, 365, 370, 372, 386, 390, 400, 406, 411, 415, 425, 432, 443, 453, 473, 485, 491

The "hero" of this series is Michael the cat, who appears in different episodes as just himself, as one of five cats belonging to a young single woman, as the pet of a married couple or of a tough-as-nails gangster, and so forth. In still other episodes, Michael belongs to a world of cats, or cats and dogs, in which the animals dress and act like humans. Don't expect narrative consistency from one episode to the next. This is a relatively good series for beginning readers because of the often spare dialogue and vivid visuals that make much of the humor self-explanatory.

9 volumes. Also 9 volumes have appeared in English from Black Horse Comics.
Mangajin: 1, 2, 3, 5, 8, 9, 11, 13, 14, 17, 20, 24, 33, 40, 45, 57, 68.

前川つかさ、大東京ビンボー生活マニュアル

Maekawa Tsukasa, *Dai-Tōkyō Binbō Seikatsu Manyuaru*
Kōdansha
Figs. 6, 15, 19, 24, 50, 51, 52, 73, 74, 80, 82, 87, 100, 102, 109, 116, 119, 120, 124, 135, 138, 140, 146, 173, 186, 190, 194, 198, 206, 222, 224, 231, 237, 239, 256, 274, 275, 276, 278, 301, 317, 327, 330, 371, 375, 378, 381, 388, 397, 422, 424, 446, 463, 470, 478, 484

The title of this series can be translated "Manual for Cheap Living in Greater Tokyo." The episodes follow the life of Kōsuke, a young college grad who chooses to live a simple, no-frills life instead of joining the corporate rat-race. Having no regular job, he's always willing to lend a hand, and he usually gets something out of the deal in return. It's a life-style that goes against the grain of Japanese society in many ways, but everyone seems to like him and respect his independence. Although *binbō seikatsu* is literally "poverty" + "life" → "life of poverty," Kōsuke's life is one remarkably rich in warm friendships and life's simple pleasures.

5 volumes.
Mangajin: 3, 4, 5, 6, 7, 8, 10, 11, 12, 14, 15, 16, 19, 22, 26, 27, 34, 35, 42, 44, 51, 65.

南ひろこ、なっちゃんはね!?
Minami Hiroko, *Nat-chan wa ne!?*
Take Shobō
Figs. 205, 260, 332, 358, 419, 447, 464, 466

The title of this four-frame gag strip literally means "As for Nat-chan..." Nat-chan is a cute, innocent-looking girl of kindergarten age who often talks and behaves more like she's a grown woman—typically leading to the embarrassment or chagrin of her family, playmates, neighbors, kindergarten teacher, and others.

2 volumes.

野中のばら、愛がほしい
Nonaka Nobara, *Ai ga Hoshii*
Futabasha
Fig. 192, 236, 440

This is another four-frame gag strip focusing on the lives of OLs, similar to the strips created by Akizuki Risu, above. *Ai ga hoshii* literally means "love is wanted," so the title might be translated as "Wanting to be Loved" or "I Want to be Loved."

The examples in this book were taken directly from *Manga Land* magazine, and the strips have not yet been compiled in book form.

Mangajin: 49, 57.

大橋ツヨシ、かいしゃいんのメロディー
Ōhashi Tsuyoshi, *Kaisha-in no Merodii*
Take Shobō
Figs. 28, 48, 75, 113, 129, 136, 142, 170, 297, 346, 434

Kaishain literally means "company member/employee," but is generally limited to white-collar workers. *Merodii* is from English "melody," so the title can be translated as "The Salaryman's Melody." This four-frame gag strip centers on life at the office for salaryman Uzuratani and three of his colleagues, together with their boss, Section Head Izumiya.

7 volumes.

大島司、シュート!
Ōshima Tsukasa, *Shūto!*
Kōdansha
Figs. 26, 33, 92, 98, 104, 127, 139, 181, 203, 263, 286, 293, 295, 405, 407, 416, 442, 456

The title is the Japanese rendering of English "Shoot!" This long-running series centers on three entering students at Kakegawa High School who go out for the soccer team. As ninth graders the previous year (Japanese high school starts at tenth grade), Toshihiko, Kazuhiro, and Kenji were star players on their junior high team, leading the squad to the final four in the annual nationwide tournament. But Kakegawa's best players from last year are returning, so competition for starting positions is stiff. The three must also overcome personal obstacles, such as a disapproving father who wants his son to give up soccer and get serious about studying for college entrance exams now that he's in high school.

33 volumes in the original *Shoot!* series; an additional 32 volumes in three sequels.

Mangajin: 39.

尾瀬あきら、夏子の酒 and 奈津の蔵
Oze Akira, *Natsuko no Sake*, and *Natsu no Kura*
Kōdansha
NS: Figs. 4, 12, 23, 29, 31, 34, 36, 56, 60, 62, 108, 123, 125, 145, 157, 164, 166, 169, 182, 189, 196, 213, 248, 250, 254, 267, 283, 300, 307, 318, 324, 336, 345, 360, 376, 380, 394, 402, 404, 417, 433, 436, 439, 448, 477, 483, 488
NK: Figs. 58, 71, 122, 143, 152, 180, 199, 207, 211, 212, 227, 233, 309, 342, 343, 379, 429, 452, 461, 481

At the beginning of *Natsuko no Sake* ("Natsuko's Saké") 22-year-old Saeki Natsuko of the title is just beginning to hit her stride as a budding copywriter after two years at an ad agency in Tokyo. But when her brother dies, she decides to return to the family saké business and carry on his dream of brewing saké with an old strain of rice known as Tatsunishiki, which fell out of cultivation when it proved unsuited to modern chemical farming methods. Her brother had heard from an elderly brewer at a gathering of brewmasters that nothing could compare to the saké made from this rice. The story follows Natsuko's efforts, in the face of considerable opposition from local farmers, to first grow enough seed from the small sample of Tatsunishiki rice her brother had been able to obtain just before his death, and then to grow a sufficient crop for actually making saké—all using labor-intensive organic methods. The story runs to twelve volumes in book form, at times going into considerable detail about the saké-making process and the complex set of traditions surrounding it. It also provides a rare view of rural life in contemporary Japan.

Natsu no Kura ("Natsu's Brewery") is a prequel to *Natsuko no Sake*, telling the story of Natsuko's grandmother, Natsu, who married into the Saeki family in 1928 as the wife of second son Zenzō. Until his brother's death two years before, Zenzō had been in Tokyo, studying to become an electrical engineer, never expecting to have any part in the family enterprise; now he applies himself diligently to learning the business, struggling against antiquated ways of thinking and working to modernize operations—most notably by campaigning to bring electricity to the village. Meanwhile, Natsu discovers she has a better nose for saké than her husband, but faces longstanding taboos against women having any part in the saké brewing enterprise; and she must also struggle to gain acceptance from her mother-in-law and the young daughter left behind by her husband's brother. When her husband is drafted during the war, it falls largely to her to somehow keep the brewery running. The story runs to four volumes in book form, and provides a window on the dynamics of the traditional Japanese extended family as well as on saké-making in an earlier era.

佐藤竹右衛門、 竹右衛門家のひとびと
Satō Take'emon, *Take'emon-ke no Hitobito*
Futabasha
Figs. 95, 107

The title translates literally as "The People/Members of the Take'emon Family." This four-frame gag strip often features a cat or dog (or both) acting like a normal human character, and covers a wide range of topics: work, leisure, social trends, annual observances, and so forth.

1 volume.
Mangajin: 33, 36, 40, 51, 59.

竹内章、 ガルシア君
Takeuchi Akira, *Garushia-kun*
Futabasha
Figs. 223, 316, 319, 338, 351, 445, 455

Also bearing the title *Sr. Garcia* on the cover, this four-frame gag strip centers on the foreign laborer named in the title, who has come to Japan to find work and send money home to his family in Colombia. Garcia gets a job with a flower shop and quickly earns the respect of his employer for his hard work ethic. His unfamiliarity with Japanese customs and the language are the basis for many of the gags, but the strip also pokes fun at the insular attitudes many Japanese have toward foreigners.

2 volumes.
Mangajin: 29, 30, 40, 44, 53, 60.

タナカヒロシ、 泣くな! 田中くん
Tanaka Hiroshi, *Naku na! Tanaka-kun*
Take Shobō
Figs. 18, 83, 141, 201, 229, 241, 270, 281, 308, 383, 454, 459, 468, 475

The cover bears the English title *Don't Cry, Tanaka-kun*, which is a literal translation of the Japanese. This four-frame gag strip features the hapless salaryman Tanaka Motoi, age 24. Having graduated from a fourth-rate university and landed a job in an architectural office only by clerical error, Tanaka-kun's principal talents seem to be for goofing off and screwing up—both at work and with women. And on those rare occasions when he manages not to bungle things himself, he can always count on pure bad luck to do the honors. Still, somehow, he keeps a stiff upper lip and never says die.

1 volume.
Mangajin: 1, 2, 6, 8, 10-14, 17, 19, 22, 23, 24, 25, 27, 28, 29, 34, 42, 46, 51.

丹沢恵、あしたもゲンキ!
Tanzawa Megumi, *Ashita mo genki!*
Take Shobō
Fig. 167

Ashita means "tomorrow," and *genki* means "full of energy/in good spirits," so the title of this four-frame manga could be translated as "Peppy Again Tomorrow." The series focuses on an office at a public works design company, and most particularly on 25-year-old Miyata Yun. Her duties include both drafting and accounting, and she's also the designated gofer; but even after seven years at the firm, she still gets lost on errands, and anything else she "helps" with takes twice as long to get done. In spite of her ineptness, though, she's always a ray of sunshine, and her office family seems willingly resigned to covering for her constant miscues.

5 volumes.

内田春菊、幻想の普通少女
Uchida Shungicu, *Maboroshi no Futsū Shōjo*
Futabasha
Figs. 1, 38, 246, 282, 313, 356, 367, 373, 385, 435, 450

Maboroshi means "phantom" or "illusion," *futsū* means "ordinary," and *shōjo* means "girl," so the title translates as "The Illusory Ordinary Girl." This manga explores changing gender roles in Japanese society through a story centering on two high school girls who represent opposite ends of the spectrum: Sakata strives to become an "ordinary/normal" girl in the traditional mold—i.e., suppressing her own desires and identity in selfless, all-forbearing deference to her boyfriend. Yamashita Sayuri, raised by a single, working mother, has no use for such old-fashioned norms and seeks to be her own person—tough, resourceful, and independent, on an equal footing with her boyfriend. Warning: includes sexual content and nudity.

3 volumes.
Mangajin: 37–38.

植田まさし、フリテンくん

Ueda Masashi, *Furiten-kun*
Take Shobō
Figs. 9, 45

The title character of this four-frame gag manga is a salaryman, but relatively few of the strips take place in the office. The series focuses mostly on sports, gambling, and other leisure activities from a male perspective.

19 volumes in the original series, plus a number of volumes in a variety of sequels.
Mangajin: 22, 24, 26, 28, 35, 36, 37, 38, 40, 52, 64.

植田まさし、かりあげクン

Ueda Masashi, *Kariage-kun*
Futabasha
Figs. 21, 88, 89, 96, 175, 200, 357, 487

Kariageru is a verb that refers to cutting/trimming the hair on the sides and back of the head very short, and *kariage* is a noun for that kind of haircut—which the young salaryman at the center of this four-frame strip has. The gags range widely over all aspects of daily life, and many of them hinge on the title character's excessive cleverness and resourcefulness.

38 volumes in the original series, plus a number of volumes in a variety of sequels.
Mangajin: 60.

臼井儀人、クレヨンしんちゃん

Usui Yoshito, *Kureyon Shin-chan*
Futabasha
Figs. 5, 20, 39, 65, 90, 103, 130, 177, 183, 242, 264, 273, 291, 294, 335, 362, 384, 401, 412, 441, 493

Kureyon is from English "crayon," and Shin-chan is the diminutive name of Nohara Shinnosuke, the 5-year-old terror of this manga series. The stories draw their humor by turns from Shin-chan's innocence and precociousness. He is forever taking things too literally, misunderstanding instructions, speaking up when he should remain silent, getting into things he shouldn't, imitating grown-ups inappropriately, and so forth, resulting in no end of exasperation and embarrassment for his parents and other adults around him.

Dozens of volumes have appeared in book form, and the series has spawned an entire industry of spinoffs. English translations are being published by ComicsOne under the title *Crayon Shinchan.*
Mangajin: 23, 24, 36, 41, 43, 45, 52, 58, 68.

Appendix C: Bibliography of grammatical references

Alfonso, Anthony. *Japanese Language Patterns.* 2 vols. Tokyo: Sophia University, 1971.

Bleiler, Everett F. *Essential Japanese Grammar.* New York: Dover Publications, 1963.

Chino, Naoko. *All About Particles.* Power Japanese. Tokyo: Kodansha International, 1991.

Drohan, Francis G. *Handbook of Japanese Usage: An Authoritative Reference Work for Students, Teachers, and Translators of Japanese.* Rutland: Charles E. Tuttle, 1992.

Fukuda, Hiroko. *T-Shirt Japanese versus Necktie Japanese: Two Levels of Politeness.* Power Japanese. Tokyo: Kodansha International, 1995.

Gurūpu Jamashii. *Kyōshi to gakushūsha no tame no Nihongo bunkei jiten.* Tokyo: Kuroshio Shuppan, 1998.

Hirose, Masayoshi and others. *Effective Japanese Usage Guide: A Concise Explanation of Frequently Confused Words and Phrases.* Tokyo: Kodansha, 1994.

Jorden, Eleanor Harz, and Mari Noda. *Japanese: The Spoken Language.* 3 vols. New Haven: Yale University Press, 1987–90.

Lampkin, Rita L. *Japanese Verbs and Essentials of Grammar: A Practical Guide to the Mastery of Japanese.* Lincolnwood: Passport Books, 1995.

Makino, Seiichi, and Michio Tsutsui. *A Dictionary of Basic Japanese Grammar.* Tokyo: Japan Times, 1986.

———. *A Dictionary of Intermediate Japanese Grammar.* Tokyo: Japan Times, 1995.

Martin, Samuel E. *A Reference Grammar of Japanese: A Complete Guide to the Grammar and Syntax of the Japanese Language.* Rutland: Charles E. Tuttle, 1988.

Matsumura, Akira, ed. *Nihon bunpō daijiten.* Tokyo: Meiji Shoin, 1971.

Maynard, Senko K. *An Introduction to Japanese Grammar and Communication Strategies.* Tokyo: Japan Times, 1990.

McClain, Yoko M. *Handbook of Modern Japanese Grammar.* Tokyo: Hokuseido Press, 1981.

McGloin, Naomi Hanaoka. *A Student's Guide to Japanese Grammar.* Tokyo: Taishukan Publishing Company, 1989.

Miura, Akira. *Japanese Words and Their Uses.* Rutland: Charles E. Tuttle, 1983.

Mizutani, Osamu, and Nobuko Mizutani. *An Introduction to Modern Japanese*. Tokyo: Japan Times, 1977.

Morita, Yoshiyuki. *Kiso nihongo jiten (A Dictionary of Basic Japanese)*. Tokyo: Kadokawa, 1989.

Niyekawa, Agnes M. *Minimum Essential Politeness: A Guide to the Japanese Honorific Language*. Tokyo: Kodansha International, 1991.

Rubin, Jay. *Gone Fishin': New Angles on Perennial Problems*. Power Japanese. Tokyo: Kodansha International, 1992.

Seward, Jack. *Learning Basic Japanese: A Guide to Spoken and Written Japanese for Self-Study and Classroom Use*. Tokyo: Yohan Publications, 1990.

Young, John, and Kimiko Nakajima-Okano. *Learn Japanese: New College Text*. 4 vols. Honolulu: University of Hawaii Press, 1984–85.

Appendix D: Selective glossary

Adjectival noun. A descriptive noun that often translates into English as an adjective. Requires *na* when modifying another noun, and *da*/*desu* as the main noun at the end of the sentence. Sometimes called *na*-adjective.

Adjective. A word that describes or characterizes a noun. For Japanese, further restricted to words ending in -*i* that have the meaning of the verb "to be" built in, and that have a variety of form changes (past, -*te* form, etc.).

Adverb. A word that describes when, where, how, how much, or in some other way qualifies or limits an action (verb), characterization (adjective or adverb), or the sentence as a whole.

Connecting word. A word that joins two simple sentences into a single complex sentence. Or a word that comes at the beginning of a sentence to refer back to the previous sentence.

Direct object. The part of the sentence that states what or whom the action of the verb most directly affects or acts upon.

Interjection. A short, often exclamatory word that stands apart from a sentence's basic structure, or stands entirely alone. Expresses feeling, draws attention, responds to a question or command, etc.

Intonation. The changing tone or pitch of a speaker's voice, such as at the end of a question.

Modifier. A word, phrase, or complete sentence that describes, characterizes, or limits another word. Always comes before the word it modifies.

Noun. A word that names a person, place, thing, or idea.

Particle. A *phrase particle* "marks" the function of the word it follows, identifying it as the topic, subject, direct object, time phrase, place phrase, etc. A *sentence particle* comes at the very end of a sentence and shows how the speaker feels about what he/she has just said.

Pronoun. A word used in place of a noun; a *personal pronoun* is a word used in place of a person's name.

Relative time word. A word that expresses time in relation to when the speaker is speaking, like English "now/a while ago/later," "today/yesterday/tomorrow."

Sentence adjective or noun. An adjective or noun + *da*/*desu* phrase serving as the equivalent of the main verb at the end of the sentence.

Subject. The part of the sentence that states who does the action or what is being described or identified.

Topic. The part of the sentence that states what the sentence is about.

Verb. An action word.

Index

- Small roman numerals refer to pages in the introduction; all other numbers refer to figures. Bold type indicates the most important reference(s) under an entry or subentry.
- References to figures include all surrounding material (the entire page if there is only one figure on the page). Italic type directs you to the surrounding explanatory material rather than to the figure itself.
- A figure number followed by *f* refers to the facing page.
- Verb type is shown in brackets following the head word: [G1], [G2], [irreg.]. Adjectival nouns are followed by "(na)," or "(na/ni)" if they appear in their adverb form. An adjective listed with its -*ku* form indicates both forms appear.
- Entries do not necessarily list every instance of the headword. The aim was simply to provide enough references for students to compare a few additional examples of the same word in a variety of contexts. Many words appearing only once or having no useful comparisons have been omitted.

About the author

Born in Ohio but raised in Japan, Wayne P. Lammers grew up speaking both Japanese and English. He has taught Japanese language and literature formally at the undergraduate and graduate level, and he served as translation editor for *Mangajin*, a magazine for students of Japanese featuring manga as language texts, during its seven-year run. More recently he has been pursuing commercial and literary translation alongside his work on *Japanese the Manga Way*. Translations by Wayne P. Lammers include:

Strangers, by Yamada Taichi. New York: Vertical, Inc., 2003.

Evening Clouds, by Shōno Junzō. Berkeley: Stone Bridge Press, 2000.

Taken Captive: A Japanese POW's Story, by Ōoka Shōhei. John Wiley, 1996.

Still Life and Other Stories. by Shōno Junzō. Berkeley: Stone Bridge Press, 1992.

The Tale of Matsura: Fujiwara Teika's Experiment in Fiction. Michigan Monograph Series in Japanese Studies 9. Ann Arbor: University of Michigan Center for Japanese Studies, 1992.

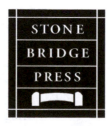

Berkeley, California • sbp@stonebridge.com~• www.stonebridge.com

All Stone Bridge Press titles are available at booksellers worldwide and online.

CPSIA information can be obtained
at www.ICGtesting.com
Printed in the USA
JSHW050458240623
43594JS00001B/1

9 781880 656907